Bureaucracy, Work and Violence

BUREAUCRACY, WORK AND VIOLENCE

The Reich Ministry of Labour in Nazi Germany, 1933–1945

Edited by
ALEXANDER NÜTZENADEL

Translated by Alex Skinner

berghahn
NEW YORK · OXFORD
www.berghahnbooks.com

Published in 2020 by
Berghahn Books
www.berghahnbooks.com

English-language edition
© 2020, 2025 Berghahn Books
First paperback edition published in 2025

German-language edition
© 2017 Wallstein Verlag, Göttingen

Originally published in German as
Das Reichsarbeitsministerium im Nationalsozialismus. Verwaltung – Politik – Verbrechen

The translation of this work was funded
by the Federal Ministry of Labour and Social Affairs.

All rights reserved. Except for the quotation of short passages for the purposes of criticism and review, no part of this book may be reproduced in any form or by any means, electronic or mechanical, including photocopying, recording, or any information storage and retrieval system now known or to be invented, without written permission of the publisher.

Library of Congress Cataloging-in-Publication Data

Names: Nützenadel, Alexander, editor. | Germany. Unabhängige Historikerkommission zur Geschichte des Reichsarbeitsministeriums 1933–1945.
Title: Bureaucracy, Work and Violence: The Reich Ministry of Labour in Nazi Germany, 1933–1945 / edited by Alexander Nützenadel; translated by Alex Skinner.
Other titles: Reichsarbeitsministerium im Nationalsozialismus. English.
Description: First edition. | New York: Berghahn Books, 2020. | Includes bibliographical references and index.
Identifiers: LCCN 2020005044 (print) | LCCN 2020005045 (ebook) | ISBN 9781789204582 (hardback) | ISBN 9781789204599 (ebook)
Subjects: LCSH: Germany. Reichsarbeitsministerium. | National socialism and labor. | Labor policy—Germany. | Germany—Social policy. | Germany—Politics and government—1933–1945.
Classification: LCC HD8455 .R4513 2020 (print) | LCC HD8455 (ebook) | DDC 331.12/042094309043—dc23
LC record available at https://lccn.loc.gov/2020005044
LC ebook record available at https://lccn.loc.gov/2020005045

British Library Cataloguing in Publication Data
A catalogue record for this book is available from the British Library.

EU GPSR Authorized Representative
LOGOS EUROPE, 9 rue Nicolas Poussin, 17000, LA ROCHELLE, France
Email: Contact@logoseurope.eu

ISBN 978-1-78920-458-2 hardback
ISBN 978-1-83695-066-0 paperback
ISBN 978-1-83695-211-4 epub
ISBN 978-1-78920-459-9 web pdf

https://doi.org/10.3167/9781789204582

Contents

List of Figures and Tables   vii

Preface   ix

List of Abbreviations   xii

Introduction   1
     Alexander Nützenadel

PART I.   **ADMINISTRATIVE STRUCTURE, PERSONNEL AND INSTITUTIONAL CONFLICTS**

Chapter 1   The Reich Ministry of Labour, 1919–1945: Organization, Leading Personnel and Political Room for Manoeuvre   23
     Ulrike Schulz

Chapter 2   Mid-Level Civil Servants' Education, Professional Life and Career Structure   82
     Lisa-Maria Röhling

Chapter 3   The Reich Ministry of Labour and the German Labour Front: Permanent Conflict and Informal Cooperation   113
     Rüdiger Hachtmann

PART II.   **POLICY FIELDS**

Chapter 4   The Housing Policies of the Reich Ministry of Labour   147
     Karl Christian Führer

Chapter 5   Pension Insurance Policy: The Impact of Labour Deployment and Discrimination   181
     Alexander Klimo

Chapter 6	Labour Law in the Nazi State: The Labour Trustees and the Criminalization of Breaches of Employment Contract *Sören Eden*	208
Chapter 7	The Labour Administration and the Organization of the War Economy *Henry Marx*	239

PART III. EXPANSION, WAR AND CRIMES

Chapter 8	Social Policy: External Propaganda and Imperial Ambitions *Kiran Klaus Patel and Sandrine Kott*	269
Chapter 9	Labour Administration and Manpower Recruitment in Occupied Europe: Belgium and the General Government *Elizabeth Harvey*	298
Chapter 10	The General Plenipotentiary for Labour Deployment and the Reich Ministry of Labour *Swantje Greve*	332
Chapter 11	Holocaust and Labour Administration: Jewish Labour Deployment in the Ghettos of the Occupied Eastern Territories *Michael Wildt*	363

PART IV. THE MINISTRY AFTER 1945

Chapter 12	A Vanishing Act: The Reich Ministry of Labour and the Nuremberg Trials, 1945–1949 *Kim Christian Priemel*	397
Chapter 13	New Beginning and Continuities: The Top Personnel of the Central German Labour Authorities, 1945–1960 *Martin Münzel*	425

Appendix I	Designations of Office	475
Appendix II	Biographies	476
Index		496

FIGURES AND TABLES

Figures

1.1.	Average age of top-level staff at the Reich Ministry of Labour (starting at ministerial counsellor level), 1919–1945	33
1.2.	Religious affiliation of top-level staff at the Reich Ministry of Labour (starting at ministerial counsellor level), 1919–1945 (in per cent)	33
1.3.	Main subjects of university study among top-level staff at the Reich Ministry of Labour (starting at ministerial counsellor level), 1919–1945 (in per cent)	33
1.4.	Organizational structure of the Reich Ministry of Labour, 1929	36
1.5.	Staffing trends at the Reich Ministry of Labour, 1919–1943	37
1.6.	Nazi Party membership among government counsellors and senior government counsellors at the Reich Ministry of Labour, 1933–1945 (in per cent)	46
1.7.	Nazi Party membership among top-level staff at the Reich Ministry of Labour (starting at ministerial counsellor level), 1933–1945 (in per cent)	47
7.1.	Structure of the labour administration and its integration into the Four-Year Plan Authority, 1936–1939	243
10.1.	Organizational and communicative structure of the occupation regime in Ukrainian territory under military and civilian administration, autumn 1941	342
10.2.	Changed communicative structures of the occupation regime in Ukrainian territory under military and civilian administration, spring 1943	352

Figures and Tables

13.1.	Structure of the Central Office for Labour, 1947	428
13.2.	Structure of the Federal Ministry of Labour, 1955	429
13.3.	Institutional background of senior personnel at the Central Office for Labour, the Administration for Labour and the Federal Ministry of Labour, 1946–1960 (in per cent)	432
13.4.	Number of civil servants, white-collar workers and blue-collar workers at the Administration for Labour and Federal Ministry of Labour, 1948–1960	434
13.5.	Average age of senior personnel at the Central Office for Labour, the Administration for Labour and the Federal Ministry of Labour, 1946–1960 (in per cent)	435
13.6.	Religious affiliation of senior personnel at the Central Office for Labour, the Administration for Labour and the Federal Ministry of Labour, 1946–1960 (in per cent)	435
13.7.	Former Nazi Party, SA and SS members as a share of senior personnel at the Central Office for Labour, the Administration for Labour and the Federal Ministry of Labour, 1946–1960 (in per cent)	445
13.8.	Date of entry into and post held in the Nazi Party among senior personnel at the Central Office for Labour, the Administration for Labour and the Federal Ministry of Labour, 1946–1960 (in per cent)	445
13.9.	Structure of the Ministry of Labour and Vocational Training, spring 1956	456

Tables

2.1.	Civil servants and white-collar workers by pay grade on 21 March 1929	87
2.2.	Overview of civil servants' pay grades after reforms, 1920 and 1927	88

Preface

This volume presents the results of the research carried out by the Independent Commission of Historians Investigating the History of the Reich Ministry of Labour in the National Socialist Period. The commission was convened in April 2013 by the Federal Ministry of Labour and Social Affairs (Bundesministerium für Arbeit und Soziales), to analyse the history of the ministry during the 'Third Reich' on the basis of a comprehensive study of the existing archival sources. The present volume is supplemented by five research monographs dedicated to the development of the bureaucratic apparatus of the ministry and to specific fields of labour and social policy in the Nazi period.[1] The main findings of this project were also presented to a broad public in 2019 in an exhibition held at the Stiftung Topographie des Terrors in Berlin.[2]

The commission's research was guided by three major principles. First, the project aims to go beyond a classical institutional history and explore the politics and policies of the Reich Ministry of Labour (Reichsarbeitsministerium). The objective is to write a modern administrative history that analyses state institutions and bureaucratic practices within their particular historical environment. This volume brings together perspectives from political, cultural and social history and explores the interplay between institutional structures, administrative decision-making and bureaucratic knowledge under the conditions of totalitarian dictatorship.

Second, the project is not limited to the period between 1933 and 1945, but analyses the development of the Ministry of Labour within the overarching trends and continuities of German history. While most recent projects on state institutions in the Nazi period have concentrated on the continuities in personnel and policy after 1945, we also examine the transition from the Weimar Republic to Nazism in order to understand the role played by the 'Third Reich' in the development of the German welfare state in the twentieth century. This requires a nuanced approach that eschews a focus on individual personalities and instead considers German welfare and administrative experts and officials as a social group, analysing them within their specific institutional context. Third, the project aims to analyse the Ministry of Labour beyond a purely German perspective. We thus explore the transnational and comparative aspects of Nazi social policy, casting light on the imperial ambitions of the 'Third Reich' in Europe. This applies not just to the phenomenon of forced labour but also to the use of labour and social policy as an instrument for cementing German hegemony within Europe over the long term.

This volume is the product of a collaborative venture, which was enriched by input from a wide range of individuals in addition to the authors. The student assistants of our project made a significant contribution, particularly when it came to accessing and trawling through the extensive archival sources and acquiring literature. Our thanks go to Celeste Copes, Alexander Dietz, Johan Moosleitner, Julian Nindl, Viktoria Peymann, Lisa-Maria Röhling, Hannes Schrader, Daniel Stienen and Mischa Weber for their energetic assistance during various phases of the project.

We also benefited greatly from the expert advice and support of Matthias Meissner (Federal Archive [Bundesarchiv] Berlin-Lichterfelde), Dieter G. Maier and Stefan Pabst (SEAD-BA – Sammlung der Bundesagentur für Arbeit zur Entwicklung der Arbeitsverwaltung in Deutschland [Collection of the Federal Employment Agency on the Development of the Labour Administration in Germany]) and Andreas Grindau (Federal Ministry for Economic Affairs and Energy [Bundesministerium für Wirtschaft und Energie]).

Many external scholars supported the project in an advisory capacity. We would particularly like to thank Johannes Bähr, Karl Christian Führer, Ute Frevert, Neil Gregor, Ulrich Herbert, Hans Günter Hockerts, Jürgen Kocka, Stefan Kühl, Daniela Liebscher, Karsten Linne, Stefanie Middendorf, Jörg Raab, Sabine Rudischhauser (†), Carola Sachse, Wolfgang Schieder, Christine Schoenmakers, Wolfgang Seibel and Winfried Süss.

We owe a debt of gratitude to Andreas Mix, Martin Münzel, Kim Christian Priemel and Paul Rehfeld for their contribution to the preliminary study conducted at the Chair in Social and Economic History, Humboldt University of Berlin.

Our thanks also to Aurélie Denoyer, Andrej Doronin, Nicola D'Elia, Ralf Futselaar, Ákos Kárbin, Iryna Kashtalian, Vlad Pașca, Charel Roemer, Christine Strotmann and Radka Šustrová, who laid the ground for research in non-German archives.

We are also grateful to Frau Jutta Mühlenberg for her meticulous copy-editing of the original German volume, and to Hajo Gevers at Wallstein Verlag for supervising the book series of which the German volume forms part. We would like to express our gratitude to Alex Skinner for the translation and to Stephen Grynwasser for the English copy-editing.

Last but not least, our thanks go to Annette Schicke at the Federal Ministry of Labour and Social Affairs, who supported the project from the outset with great commitment and competence. She played a major role in the positive and productive collaboration between the ministry, the commission of historians and the research group.

—Rüdiger Hachtmann (Potsdam), Elizabeth Harvey (Nottingham), Sandrine Kott (Geneva), Alexander Nützenadel (Berlin), Kiran Klaus Patel (Munich) and Michael Wildt (Berlin)

Notes

1. A. Klimo, *Im Dienste des Arbeitseinsatzes. Rentenversicherungspolitik im 'Dritten Reich'*, Göttingen: Wallstein, 2018; Swantje Greve, *Das 'System Sauckel'. Der Generalbevollmächtigte für den Arbeitseinsatz und die Arbeitskräftepolitik in der besetzten Ukraine 1942–1945*, Göttingen: Wallstein, 2019; H. Marx, *Die Verwaltung des Ausnahmezustands. Wissensgenerierung und Arbeitskräftelenkung im Nationalsozialismus*, Göttingen: Wallstein, 2019; S. Eden, *Die Verwaltung einer Utopie. Die Treuhänder der Arbeit zwischen Betriebs- und Volksgemeinschaft 1933–1945*, Göttingen: Wallstein, 2020 (forthcoming); the study on the organization of the Ministry of Labour will be published by Rüdiger Hachtmann in 2022.

2. Stiftung Topographie des Terrors (ed.), *Das Reichsarbeitsministerium 1933–1945. Beamte im Dienst des Nationalsozialismus/The Reich Ministry of Labour 1933–1945. Civil Servants of the Nazi State*, Katalog zur gleichnamigen Ausstellung/Exhibition catalogue, Berlin: Stiftung Topographie des Terrors, 2019.

Abbreviations

ADGB	Allgemeiner Deutscher Gewerkschaftsbund (General German Trades Union Confederation)
AdsD	Archiv der sozialen Demokratie (Archive of Social Democracy)
AN	Archives Nationales, Paris (National Archives, Paris)
AOG	Gesetz zur Ordnung der nationalen Arbeit (Law on the Organization of National Labour)
AVAVG	Gesetz über Arbeitsvermittlung und Arbeitslosenversicherung (Law on Job Placement and Unemployment Insurance)
AWI	Arbeitswissenschaftliches Institut der DAF (DAF Labour Science Institute)
BABl.	*Bundesarbeitsblatt* (Federal Labour Gazette)
BArch	Bundesarchiv (Federal Archive)
BBG	Berufsbeamtengesetz (Gesetz zur Wiederherstellung des Berufsbeamtentums, the Civil Service Law or Law for the Restoration of the Professional Civil Service)
BdS	Befehlshaber der Sicherheitspolizei (Commander of the Security Police)
BGBl.	*Bundesgesetzblatt* (Federal Law Gazette)
BLHA	Brandenburgisches Landeshauptarchiv (Brandenburg Main State Archive)
BMA	Bundesministerium für Arbeit (Federal Ministry of Labour)
BMWi	Bundesministerium für Wirtschaft (Federal Ministry of Economic Affairs)

Abbreviations

BStU	Bundesbeauftragte(r) für die Unterlagen des Staatssicherheitsdienstes der ehemaligen DDR (Federal Commissioner for the Records of the State Security Service of the former GDR)
CDAVO	Central'nyi deržavnyj archiv vyščych orhaniv vlady i upravlinnja Ukraïny (Central State Archive of the Supreme State Organs and Administrations of Ukraine)
CDU	Christlich Demokratische Union Deutschlands (Christian Democratic Union of Germany)
CLS	Columbia Law School
CSU	Christlich-Soziale Union in Bayern (Christian Social Union in Bavaria)
DAF	Deutsche Arbeitsfront (German Labour Front)
DAKhO	Deržavnyj archiv Charkivs'koï oblasti (State Archive of Kharkov Oblast)
DDR	Deutsche Demokratische Republik (GDR or German Democratic Republic)
DNVP	Deutschnationale Volkspartei (German National People's Party)
DP	Deutsche Partei (German Party)
DVAS	Deutsche Verwaltung für Arbeit und Sozialfürsorge (German Administration for Labour and Social Welfare)
DVP	Deutsche Volkspartei (German People's Party)
DWK	Deutsche Wirtschaftskommission (German Economic Commission)
FDGB	Freier Deutscher Gewerkschaftsbund (Free Federation of German Trades Unions)
FDP	Freie Demokratische Partei (Free Democratic Party)
GBA	Generalbevollmächtigter für den Arbeitseinsatz (General Plenipotentiary for Labour Deployment)
GBW	Generalbevollmächtigter für die Wirtschaft (General Plenipotentiary for the Economy)
GDR	German Democratic Republic (East Germany)
Gestapo	Geheime Staatspolizei (Secret State Police)
GLAK	Generallandesarchiv Karlsruhe (General Land Archive Karlsruhe)

Abbreviations

HStA	Hauptstaatsarchiv (Main State Archive)
HVAS	Hauptverwaltung für Arbeit und Sozialfürsorge (Main Administration for Labour and Social Welfare)
ILO	International Labour Organization
ILOA	International Labour Organization Archives, Geneva
IMT	Internationales Militärtribunal (International Military Tribunal)
ITS	International Tracing Service
JFKL	John F. Kennedy Presidential Library
KPD	Kommunistische Partei Deutschlands (Communist Party of Germany)
LArch	Landesarchiv (Land Archive)
LDP	Liberal-Demokratische Partei (Liberal Democratic Party)
LHASA	Landeshauptarchiv Sachsen-Anhalt (Main Land Archive of Saxony-Anhalt)
LoC	Library of Congress
MfS	Ministerium für Staatssicherheit (Ministry of State Security)
NLA	Niedersächsisches Landesarchiv (Land Archive of Lower Saxony)
NMT	Nuernberg Military Tribunals
NRW	Nordrhein-Westfalen (North Rhine-Westphalia)
NSBO	NS-Betriebszellenorganisation (National Socialist factory cell organization)
NSDAP	Nationalsozialistische Deutsche Arbeiterpartei (National Socialist German Workers' Party; the Nazi Party)
NSV	Nationalsozialistische Volkswohlfahrt (National Socialist People's Welfare Association)
OCCWC	Office of Chief of Council for War Crimes
OKW	Oberkommando der Wehrmacht (Wehrmacht Supreme Command)
PA	Personalakte (personal files)
PAAA	Politisches Archiv des Auswärtigen Amtes Berlin (Foreign Office Political Archive, Berlin)
PAS	Privatarchiv Stothfang (Stothfang Private Archive)

Abbreviations

PG	Parteigenosse ([Nazi] party comrade)
RABl.	*Reichsarbeitsblatt* (Reich Labour Gazette)
RAM	Reichsarbeitsministerium (Reich Ministry of Labour)
RGBl	*Reichsgesetzblatt* (Reich Law Gazette)
RJM	Reichsjustizministerium (Reich Ministry of Justice)
RM	Reichsmark
RMWi	Reichsminister für Wirtschaft (Reich Minister of Economic Affairs)
RVA	Reichsversicherungsamt (Reich Insurance Office)
SBZ	Sowjetische Besatzungszone (Soviet Occupation Zone)
SD	Sicherheitsdienst der SS (SS Security Service)
SEAD-BA	Sammlung der Bundesagentur für Arbeit zur Entwicklung der Arbeitsverwaltung in Deutschland (Collection of the Federal Employment Agency on the Development of the Labour Administration in Germany)
SED	Sozialistische Einheitspartei Deutschlands (Socialist Unity Party of Germany)
Sipo	Sicherheitspolizei (Security Police)
SMAD	Sowjetische Militäradministration in Deutschland (Soviet Military Administration in Germany)
SPD	Sozialdemokratische Partei Deutschlands (Social Democratic Party of Germany)
SS	Schutzstaffel (Protection Squadron)
StA	Staatsarchiv (State Archive)
StA N	Staatsarchiv Nürnberg (State Archive, Nuremberg)
TDRC	Thomas J. Dodd Research Center
ThHStAW	Thüringisches Hauptstaatsarchiv Weimar (Thuringian Main State Archive, Weimar)
USHMM	United States Holocaust Memorial Museum
VfA	Verwaltung für Arbeit des Vereinigten Wirtschaftsgebiets (Administration for Labour of the United Economic Area)
WiRüAmt	Wehrwirtschafts- und Rüstungsamt des Oberkommandos der Wehrmacht (War Economy and Armament Office of the Wehrmacht Supreme Command)

Abbreviations

ZfA	Zentralamt für Arbeit (Central Office for Labour)
ZRBG	Gesetz zur Zahlbarmachung von Renten aus Beschäftigungen in einem Ghetto (Law Regarding the Conditions for Making Pensions Payable on the Basis of Employment in a Ghetto)
ZVAS	Zentralverwaltung für Arbeit und Sozialfürsorge (Central Administration for Labour and Social Welfare)

Introduction

Alexander Nützenadel

As one senior official at the Reich Ministry of Labour wrote in 1940, the Nazi regime had reorganized the ministerial administration after 1933 not primarily for objective reasons but in the spirit of the 'national socialist worldview'. The latter, he explained, had defined labour and social policy as the 'most important branch of general policy', making a stand-alone ministry with far-reaching powers indispensable.[1]

Labour and social policy did in fact play an outstanding role in the ideology of the Nazi Party. Its claim to be a 'workers' party' was more than just symbolism: from the perspective of the new regime, the creation of the 'Volksgemeinschaft' (the community of the folk, as an ethnonational ideal) required deep intervention in the social order. Leading Nazi ideologues, such as Robert Ley, pushed for the rapid and radical restructuring of the German welfare state, assailing it as a product of the Weimar Republic. Following the Nazi seizure of power, the new regime launched numerous initiatives in this field. In 1934, the Law on the Organization of National Labour (Gesetz zur Ordnung der nationalen Arbeit) abolished freedom of association and collective bargaining. Henceforth, employment contracts and wages were regulated by the labour trustees ('Treuhänder der Arbeit') appointed in May 1933, which were subordinate to the Reich Labour Ministry. Institutions such as the German Labour Front (Deutsche Arbeitsfront or DAF), the National Socialist People's Welfare Association (Nationalsozialistische Volkswohlfahrt or NSV) and the National Socialist factory cell organizations (NS-Betriebszellenorganisationen or NSBO) left no room for doubt about the new rulers' aspirations to reshape this entire field of policy.

Through the expansion of its formal competences, the Reich Labour Ministry was strengthened significantly after 1933. Few Reich authorities possessed such a wide range of responsibilities. The ministry was not only in charge of labour and social policy but also held authority in adjacent fields, such as housing and settlement, labour law and regulation as well as family and health policy. Last but not least, a large number of Reich agencies were subordinate to the ministry, enabling it to intervene directly in the local sphere.

The present volume thus investigates one of the most important governmental institutions in the 'Third Reich', which has nevertheless received very little scholarly attention. We will address the following questions. What role did the Reich Labour Ministry play within the Nazi power structure? Was it the central planning authority for the '*völkisch* [folkish, meaning ethnonationalist] welfare state' or was it one of many administrative bodies with essentially secondary powers? How did the ministry manage to assert itself vis-à-vis the numerous new bodies created by the party in the field of labour and social policy? How deeply was the ministry integrated into the dictatorship's apparatus of power? To what degree were staff members involved in the criminal practices of the Nazi system? What continuities on the level of personnel and institutions might we identify in the years before 1933 and after 1945?

As well as illuminating the specific role of the Reich Ministry of Labour, however, the present book also seeks to answer fundamental questions of crucial importance to the study of Nazism. In particular, we are keen to explore the responsibilities held and roles played by the classical ministerial administration and its staff within the Nazi regime's power structure.[2] The image of the bureaucracy within Nazism was long moulded by two interpretations. The first is the ideal-typical distinction, going back to Max Weber, between 'legal' and 'charismatic' power.[3] The second is Ernst Fraenkel's interpretation of Nazism as a 'dual state', in which elements of the normative state (*Normenstaat*) and prerogative state (*Massnahmenstaat*) existed alongside one another.[4] Both interpretations tended to present the classical administration as a remnant of the old system, one that was increasingly eclipsed by genuinely Nazi power structures.

There is a considerable need for research on these topics. While many studies have been produced on social and labour policy under National Socialism,[5] little research has been conducted on the role of the Reich Ministry of Labour in this field.[6] Comprehensive, archive-based research has not yet been carried out either on the structure of the ministry and the evolution of its personnel, or on its various fields of activity. The absence of scholarly research is not primarily due to a dearth of sources, given the large body of archival materials on the Reich Labour Ministry. Instead, the lack of interest in this institution goes back to a specific interpretation of the 'Third Reich', which ascribed negligible significance to the ministerial bureaucracy. This already affected the early research on Nazism, which focused heavily on Hitler's role. As is widely recognized, Hitler himself had little interest in administrative processes. Within his worldview, 'administering' was vastly inferior to 'leading' as it contributed little to the exercise of political power. Hitler paid little attention to the everyday business of government. From 1935 onwards, meetings of the Cabinet were an irregular occurrence and only a few ministers had direct access to the Führer. This lack of 'immediate access' was considered a gauge of the political importance of particular politicians and the institutions they represented. Reich Labour Minister Seldte occupied a lowly position within this hierarchy: from 1938 at the latest, he no longer had access to Hitler and did not attend official occasions arranged at the Führer's behest.[7]

Even the studies of the institutions and structures of Nazism first undertaken in the 1960s continued to leave the ministerial bureaucracy out of account. Most of the research on the civil service brought out how the administrative elites supported Hitler's 'seizure of power'.[8] Few researchers, however, grappled with the specific role of the state bureaucracy within the Nazi power system because they failed to recognize it as a relevant factor. For example, as early as 1969, in his influential book *Der Staat Hitlers*, Martin Broszat referred to the 'loss of prestige and dwindling significance of the state bureaucracy'.[9] This process, he asserted, had already begun when the Nazis took power and had accelerated again as the state prepared for war from 1936. Broszat argued that the gradual disempowerment of the civil service was partly bound up with the unfulfilled expectations of many Nazi leaders (particularly Hitler and Bormann), who had hoped to form a new elite out of it, one that would implement Nazi ideology efficiently and radically. The 'stymying of the civil service and the traditional administration' through the establishment of new special administrations under the direct control of the party or Hitler, Broszat asserted, was a conscious strategy intended to solve this problem: 'In terms of their form, the old government ministries and their subordinate administrations remained untouched. But the real decisions were made without them; the old ministerial bureaucracy was increasingly bypassed and politically paralysed'.[10]

This picture was reinforced by the interpretation of Nazism as a 'polycratic system of rule'. The polycratic model shifted scholars' attention away from Hitler towards the institutions of the Nazi state. Moreover, they attributed the true dynamism of 'cumulative radicalization' (Hans Mommsen) to the new special administrations and party organizations. As a result of the 'party's unrestrained intrusion into the administration', according to Peter Hüttenberger, 'despite putting up resistance' the 'civil service gradually disintegrated politically'.[11]

This perspective, however, has not gone unchallenged. By 1978, Jane Caplan had already pointed out that the attempt to identify the classical state administration as part of the 'normative state' was an element in an exculpatory strategy – one through which leading ministerial officials sought to exonerate themselves after 1945.[12] Rather than a general loss of significance, Caplan perceived a contradictory development: the ministries had come under pressure from the Nazi regime's new institutions, yet they had been granted additional powers from the Weimar era onwards.

Caplan's insights, gleaned from examination of the Reich Ministry of the Interior, apply even more to the Reich Labour Ministry. During the period of the presidential cabinets at the latest, the strengthening of the executive as a technocratic authority had made the bureaucracy significantly more important, while the economic depression left it with new and onerous responsibilities. After the Nazi takeover, numerous new laws and measures were implemented in order to deal with the challenges of the economic crisis. This intensified the pressure to take action within the agencies of the labour and social administration, engendering a permanent process of 'adaptive reproduction'.[13]

The present volume regards the Reich Ministry of Labour not as a passive institution but as one of many political actors seeking to assert themselves within the Nazi state's complex and increasingly confusing power structures. This throws up the question of what strategies the different branches of the ministerial apparatus used to preserve their institutional power. Our assumption is that precisely because access to Hitler – and thus to the centre of political power – was limited, the ministerial bureaucracy increasingly focused on its core classical competencies: the performance of policy-related administrative tasks through efficient action in conformity, as far as possible, with the regulations. Against the background of vigorous Nazi policymaking, officials' expert knowledge was of great significance: policies could only be implemented administratively with their support. Until the end of the Nazi period, administrative action was geared towards specific rules and routines. These could be bypassed or adapted situationally but not rendered entirely inoperative. Though Nazism destroyed the liberal legal system, core areas of administrative law thus remained intact.

Hence, the following analyses go beyond the ministerial leadership's political action within the Nazi apparatus of power. This is because we can acquire an adequate grasp of the Reich Ministry of Labour's authority and modus operandi only by exploring officials' everyday administrative practices. A praxeological approach of this kind entails a number of implications. First, it means taking the bureaucracy seriously as a key factor within the Nazi regime. But rather than assuming that it played a static part within the power hierarchies of the 'Third Reich', we must view its role as the outcome of processes of social and political negotiation within a dynamic framework of competing forces. Second, a bureaucratic apparatus cannot be analysed as a monolithic entity. It is a complex organization in which actors proceed in light of varying interests and pursue a variety of strategies. Rather than restricting itself to the description of formal structures, an approach of this kind, drawing on theories of organization, requires a micro-historical analysis of internal processes of communication, informal hierarchies, personal networks and everyday routines.[14]

Anatomy of a Ministry

What kind of body was the Reich Labour Ministry? Its genesis alone gave it a special status. Not one of the classical ministries, it was relatively young and specialized in character, its origins lying in the First World War and the regime's extensive wartime interventions in the labour market. One important impetus for the establishment of a discrete ministry on the Reich level derived from the system of welfare for war veterans, which required a tremendous administrative effort; the central coordination of the Public Aid Offices (Versorgungsämter) was one of the most difficult tasks of the postwar period. The dynamic development of the labour and social administration, however, was not solely a consequence of the First World War but was also due to the dynamic evolution of the welfare state in the Weimar Republic, which created new fields of social policy, relating in particular to labour and wages, housing and social provision. Hence, during this period no other ministry saw a greater increase in personnel and financial resources, but also in regulatory powers of a legal and administrative nature.

This trend was reinforced rather than interrupted by the Great Depression and the Nazi 'seizure of power'. In the course of the centralization of social policy and the extension of Reich jurisdiction over it, the ministry became significantly more important on the formal level. The autonomy of social insurance agencies, as it had existed since the nineteenth century, was superseded by the 'leader principle' (*Führerprinzip*), with most insurers and welfare corporations being made directly subordinate to the ministry. In 1935, meanwhile, Prussian powers over social policy were transferred to the ministry. The year 1939 brought probably the most important change, when the Reich Institution for Job Placement and Unemployment Insurance (Reichsanstalt für Arbeitsvermittlung und Arbeitslosenversicherung) was integrated into the ministry and its president Friedrich Syrup appointed second state secretary. On the eve of the Second World War, the Reich Ministry of Labour reached what was at that point its greatest extent, encompassing sixteen departments. Its responsibilities ranged from labour market and wages policy through social housing, urban planning and resettlement to family policy. They also took in occupational safety and health, plant security, labour law, social welfare and the entire field of social insurance and health policy. Finally, the ministry was responsible for the working conditions inspectorates, the labour and social welfare tribunals, the Reich Insurance Office (Reichsversicherungsamt or RVA) and the cooperatives.

We can get a true sense of the specific role played by the Reich Labour Ministry within National Socialism only by considering the political and institutional legacy of the First World War and the Weimar Republic. In her chapter, Ulrike Schulz shows how, since its establishment, the ministry was confronted with an unceasing flow of new tasks and organizational challenges, so that it had to strive constantly to achieve institutional stability. This might explain the strikingly high degree of continuity among senior staff at the ministry from its foundation until the end of the Second World War. As a rule, state secretaries and department heads occupied their posts for lengthy periods, while there were generally few changes of personnel despite the numerous Cabinet changes that marked the Weimar period. Moreover, neither in an institutional sense nor with respect to staffing did the year 1933 represent a profound break with the past. The Nazi leadership only briefly considered dissolving the ministry and merging it with the Reich Ministry of the Economy (Reichswirtschaftsministerium). They soon backed away from this idea, mainly because of the far more pressing tasks confronting them. It was in large part the 'crisis management' (Ulrike Schulz) it had practised so extensively in the late Weimar era that made the ministry indispensable to the Nazi regime after 1933.

Examination of the ministry's personnel structure makes it clear that very few changes were made at the leadership level and that – at least until 1938 – professional aptitude was more important in the appointment and promotion of officials than Nazi convictions. As in other authorities, however, Jewish employees had already been dismissed by 1933, women were ousted from leading positions and many members of trade unions, the Communist Party of Germany (Kommunistische Partei Deutschlands or KPD) and the Social Democratic Party of Germany (Sozialdemokratische Partei Deutschlands or SPD) were dismissed from the ministry's administration and its subordinate agencies. Nonetheless, the ideal of the professionally qualified and administratively trained official was deeply rooted in ministerial culture. This went not just for the leadership level but for the entire apparatus, including much of the mid-level civil service, as demonstrated by Lisa-Maria Röhling's chapter on recruitment practices in the public aid authorities (Versorgungsbehörden). With respect to education as well, the practice-oriented, professional qualification continued to play a prominent role, while initially ideological elements were adopted in an essentially superficial way. It was not until the passing of the Civil Service

Law (Beamtengesetz) of 1937 that this changed, as membership of, and loyalty to, the Nazi Party became the central criteria of appointment and promotion. In the Reich Ministry of Labour, the recruitment of new personnel within the framework of the war economy provided an opportunity to appoint 'old party fighters' and ideologically reliable individuals, a trend reinforced when hard-line Nazi Wilhelm Börger became head of personnel in 1938. As Schulz's analysis of ministry staff reveals, the number of Nazi Party members – who made up well below 20 per cent until 1938 – now increased by leaps and bounds. At the same time, the proportion of leading officials trained in law declined markedly, evidence that Nazism helped erode the lawyers' monopoly within the ministerial administration.

The growth in the Reich Labour Ministry's staff and responsibilities shows that Nazism, contrary to its antibureaucratic posture, was not hostile to administration, but in fact set in motion a massive wave of bureaucratization. As Rüdiger Hachtmann shows with reference to the DAF, this applied both to the classical authorities and to the numerous party and special administrations.

As is well known, administrative and political turf wars led to grave personal conflicts between DAF Reich Leader Robert Ley and Labour Minister Franz Seldte, but also enveloped other functionaries in both institutions. However, as Hachtmann explains, these clashes do not necessarily indicate substantive divergences; often, they were more a matter of habit and were moulded by personal rivalries. Ley not only laid claim to powers over business and wages policy but also pressed for the state's housing and settlement building programmes as a whole to be incorporated into his domain, something he finally achieved in 1942. The impression that Ley rapidly gained the upper hand within this conflict came about in significant part as a result of his aggressive style and the effective propaganda disseminated by the DAF, which seemed organizationally superior to the Reich Ministry of Labour. Franz Seldte, by way of contrast, was considered uncharismatic and lacking in experience in social policy. Many observers believed Hitler appointed the long-standing head of the Stahlhelm paramilitary organization to his Cabinet – rather than Friedrich Syrup, who possessed relevant expertise – as a tactical, coalition-building manoeuvre, one that inspired complaints both from established social policy experts and Nazi leaders. Goebbels, for example, saw this as a 'blemish' that must be 'erased' as soon as possible.[15] That Seldte remained in charge of the ministry until the end of the regime may seem surprising in light of these profound antagonisms, but is fully consonant with Hitler's political strategy. In any event, Seldte's entire period in office was characterized by serious conflicts with other Nazi politicians active in the field of social policy; in 1935 he offered to resign, only to be turned down by Hitler.

Scholars long interpreted the profound conflicts and Seldte's rather cautious manner as evidence that 'under his weak, impotent leadership' the Labour Ministry 'was unable to cope within a highly competitive environment'. According to Willi Boelcke, for example, Seldte 'had virtually no expertise and as a minister he showed no particular ambition, but he had excellent staff whom he trusted and shielded from the party's attacks and opposition'.[16] This assessment also indicates that what looked like weakness from the outside ultimately proved a relative strength. Seldte clearly succeeded in riding out conflicts and thus protecting the ministry from external attack. In this way he gained the loyalty of his colleagues, who were permitted to act with a considerable degree of freedom.[17] Ultimately, Ley's continual attacks on the ministry were probably beneficial to Seldte: the head of the DAF was a controversial figure within the Nazi leadership and his sweeping political ambitions triggered countervailing forces. Seldte's long stint at the head of the ministry, moreover, represented a form of continuity with the Weimar period, when it was also headed by the same individual, namely Heinrich Brauns, for an exceptionally long period.

We should not, however, overlook the fact that the Labour Ministry's responsibilities were constantly altered, while the boundaries between the ministry and the new party and special administrations often became blurred. This applied not just to the DAF but also to the Reich Labour Service (Reichsarbeitsdienst or RAD), led by Konstantin Hierl until 1945. The latter had been appointed state secretary in the Reich Ministry of Labour in March 1933 and was granted the title 'Reich labour leader' (*Reichsarbeitsführer*). In order to obtain as independent a post as possible, in 1934 Hierl switched from the Labour to the Interior Ministry.[18] Even more importantly, the Four-Year-Plan Authority (Vierjahresplanbehörde) under Hermann Göring, established in 1936, secured its ability to shape labour and wages policy by appointing Friedrich Syrup, president of the Reich Institution for Job Placement and Unemployment Insurance, and Werner Mansfeld, head of the relevant department in the Labour Ministry, as plenipotentiaries. Finally, in the shape of Fritz Sauckel, appointed general plenipotentiary for labour deployment (Generalbevollmächtigter für den Arbeitseinsatz or GBA) in March 1942, a new power centre emerged during the war that enjoyed direct access to the departments of the Labour Ministry.

On the one hand, these overlapping powers weakened the autonomy of the Reich Ministry of Labour. On the other, they resulted in its indirect strengthening, because its administrative units were constantly allocated new responsibilities. In fact, the chapters in the present volume show that at the administrative level the relations between the ministry and the new authorities were far smoother and more efficient than has been assumed. This finding is consonant with recent research on the Nazi power system that underlines the functional shift in state structures. From this perspective, rather than being dysfunctional, the rivalries between different agencies and their overlapping powers were an expression of a 'hybrid' organizational type, one that transcended the strict division between classical bureaucracy and non-state institutions. In this context, personal networks, informal decision-making procedures and new communicative forums played an important role.[19] Here Rüdiger Hachtmann perceives nothing less than the beginnings of a 'new statehood'; for him, this explains the radical efficiency of the Nazi regime but also paved the way for the genesis of modern institutions.[20]

The Ministry in Action: Spheres of Political Action and Conflicts

More than other state agencies, the Reich Ministry of Labour was characterized by constant interaction with subordinate authorities and associations. Many social and labour policies could in fact only be implemented through close coordination with the relevant administrative units at the level of the Länder and municipalities. The outsourcing of administrative tasks to subordinate agencies and organizations was already a characteristic of the ministry during the Weimar Republic and became a pronounced feature of its development during the Nazi period. According to Ulrike Schulz, what contemporaries perceived as 'bad design' turned out to be an organizational advantage, enhancing the enforceability of laws and administrative directives and facilitating communication between the ministry, as central authority, and the executive administrative bodies.

The specific interactions between the Reich Ministry of Labour and its subordinate institutions, then, are of crucial significance to its historical investigation. The present volume sheds light on these interactions by examining the core aspects of labour and social policy. Taking pensions policy as his example, Alexander Klimo asks what impact Nazi labour market policy had on insurance systems and, in particular, the practice of pension provision. This also enables him to refute the idea, commonly held by historians, that social insurance largely remained untouched under the Nazis. At the same time, two examples reveal how complex the interactions between the ministry and social insurance agencies were. The differing interests and logics of action often led to conflicts. While, for example, the ministry pushed for the provision of pensions to be adapted to the requirements of the labour market, the insurance agencies adopted a restrictive approach to the approval of disability pensions in order to minimize their financial burdens. And yet, until the end of the regime, officials continued to take their lead from legal norms and bureaucratic procedures. This proved a considerable problem when the state stripped Jews and others subject to racial persecution of their rights to future pension payments, as this required the comprehensive modification of the laws governing social welfare.

The Ministry of Labour also had to make far-reaching modifications when it came to public housing schemes in order to support the war economy, as Karl Christian Führer shows. It proved impossible to implement either the liberalization of the housing market to which the Ministry of Labour aspired or the ambitious public building and settlement programmes propagated chiefly by the DAF. In 1941, with Ley's appointment as Reich commissioner for social housing (Reichskommissar für den sozialen Wohnungsbau), the ministry lost political responsibility for the building of public housing, though this came to a standstill during the war due to the lack of financial resources.[21]

In order to regulate labour markets, new institutions gained tremendous importance. Sören Eden examines the 'labour trustees', who exercised a significant influence on labour and wages laws during the Nazi period. As bodies subordinate to the Labour Ministry, the trustees discharged important tasks involved in the reconfiguration of the labour market, as Eden shows with reference to breaches of employment contracts. In light of this example, Eden demonstrates that the organization of labour law was not – as has generally been assumed – dictated at the ministerial level but in fact resulted from a process of negotiation involving all levels of authority, one in which a broad range of actors were involved in a variety of ways, ranging from the individual employee through the courts to the general plenipotentiary for labour deployment. Due to their status as 'hinge' between the workplace and the Reich Labour Ministry, the labour trustees played an important role through the criminalization of breaches of employment contracts.

Taking the labour administration as an example, Henry Marx probes the interactions between the ministerial level and the local labour offices, which faced tremendous challenges from 1936 onwards. The gradual transformation of the Reich Institution for Job Placement and Unemployment Insurance into an agency responsible not primarily for the placing of workers but for job creation and the regulation of employment required the expansion and centralization of administrative authority. The Reich Institution was incorporated into the ministry in 1939 chiefly in an attempt to solve these increasingly complex problems of coordination and communication. Though this could not eliminate the labour shortage, the labour administration helped maintain the production of armaments until the end of the war.

The Expanded Ministry: Social Order, Occupation and Violence

Despite its radical, nationalistic self-image and its pursuit of autarky, the Nazi state was not a hermetically sealed economic and sociopolitical system. In reality it drew ideologically on, and overlapped politically with, other authoritarian movements and regimes of the interwar period. This was especially true of fascist Italy, whose corporative employment and welfare regime made it a role model for right-wing circles under the late Weimar Republic.[22] International social policies continued to find a reception in Germany after 1933 as well, as Kiran Klaus Patel and Sandrine Kott demonstrate in their contribution. In the summer of 1933, for example, Seldte travelled to Milan to learn about the fascist state's job creation measures. The Labour Ministry thus closely followed international developments. And while Germany left both the League of Nations and the International Labour Organization in 1933, German social policy makers remained active on the international level – whether through welfare agreements or, for example, within the framework of the binational treaties governing the recruitment of foreign workers, which Germany had concluded with a number of states before the war began. Finally, the ministry also played an important role in propaganda, aimed at foreign countries, which exalted the alleged achievements of the Nazi system. This propaganda campaign benefited from the widespread interest in new instruments of labour market organization and social policy, an interest that had surged everywhere in the wake of the world economic crisis. On the international stage too the Labour Ministry competed with its domestic political adversaries – particularly the DAF and the RAD, which tried to monopolize external propaganda.[23]

Propaganda glorifying German labour and social policy was, however, simultaneously an aspect of visions of imperial domination that imagined the long-term reordering of Europe under German leadership.[24] This is evident in the attempts, beginning in 1940, to develop a 'brown' International as an alternative to the International Labour Organization. There is plenty of evidence to suggest that this was more than just propaganda. In fact, the Nazi state was making long-term plans to establish a *völkisch* social order in Europe. Just what this social order ought to entail was, however, far from clear. Divergent economic development and race-based hierarchies, as evident in the contrast between the eastern European territories, which the Nazis planned to 'Germanize' completely, and the occupied countries of western and northern Europe, are likely to have played a key role here.

Comparative analysis of the forced labour regime in the occupied territories provides us with a powerful tool for reconstructing the different models of social order in 'Hitler's imperium'.[25] As Elizabeth Harvey explains, the specific form taken by labour policy depended on a range of different factors. These included experiences of the First World War, whether a functioning system for arranging employment already existed or had to be developed and the local elites' and authorities' willingness to collaborate. Local administrative conditions were also of crucial importance. Had a given territory been annexed and earmarked for integration into the Reich? Was it an occupation zone with a civil administration or was it under military occupation? The economic structure also played an important role because eastern European regions chiefly served as a reservoir of labour, raw materials and foodstuffs that could be ruthlessly exploited, whereas in industrially developed regions – such as Belgium, France, the Netherlands or northern Italy – the Nazi regime proceeded in a more measured way to avoid disrupting local production of industrial goods and armaments. Finally, a comparison between Belgium and the General Government (Generalgouvernement) – two territories featuring particularly high numbers of forced labourers – demonstrates that the 'racial divide' between east and west did much to determine the degree of violence involved in the recruitment of forced labour until the end of the 'Third Reich'.

But what role did the Reich Ministry of Labour play in Nazi forced labour policies? Swantje Greve shows that the appointment of the GBA did not signify a major rupture in the organization of forced labour policy. Fritz Sauckel used the established structures of the ministry, its departments and their staff in order to actively shape the deployment of forced labourers. His involvement was not limited to administrative processes within the Berlin headquarters but extended to local recruitment. In the wake of the Wehrmacht, almost everywhere officials seconded from Reich, Land and municipal authorities were dispatched to the occupied territories. Most of them were promoted and gained far greater responsibilities than in their previous posts in the Reich. These officials made a major contribution to ensuring that the labour force was 'successfully' mobilized to benefit the war economy of the 'Third Reich'. This applied not just to the recruitment of the more than twelve million forced labourers transported into the Reich territory but also to the ever more strictly enforced obligation to work in the occupied territories.

With reference to the Wartheland Reichsgau (Reich District), the General Government and Lithuania, furthermore, Michael Wildt shows how deeply the labour administration was involved in the organization of the ghettos and, indirectly, the Holocaust as well.[26] Officials not only registered and recorded workers but also decided who in the Jewish ghettos was categorized as 'fit for work' – as a rule, the latter equated to a death sentence, as those working in the offices concerned were generally aware.

In certain cases, labour administration staff sought to spare Jewish ghetto residents this fate. This shows that they had options. 'It was a personal decision whether to become an accomplice or do everything possible to save human lives' (Michael Wildt).

Continuities

There is no lack of evidence of the labour administration's involvement in the criminal practice of forced labour and the murder of the Jewish population. As Kim Christian Priemel elaborates, the long-standing scholarly and cultural failure to come to terms with its responsibility is partly bound up with the successful defence strategy adopted during the Nuremberg trials, in which Seldte and his colleagues managed to play down their own role in forced labour policy. They pointed out that the Labour Ministry was in charge of policy only until 1942 within the framework of the voluntary recruitment of workers. The brutal forced labour policy pursued from the spring of 1942 onwards, meanwhile, had come under the sole remit of GBA Fritz Sauckel, who had been aided chiefly by the Wehrmacht and the firms involved. In Nuremberg, leading ministry officials such as Hubert Hildebrandt, Wilhelm Kimmich, Walter Letsch, Walter Stothfang and Max Timm benefited from their ability, as witnesses and experts, to make extensive statements – including attempts to exonerate themselves. Furthermore, in the shape of Fritz Sauckel and Albert Speer, two of the main protagonists in the war economy had already been sentenced, while Seldte died in April 1947, escaping potential criminal charges. Because the Allies were pressing for the war crimes trials to be wound up as rapidly as possible, in the end the leading officials at the Labour Ministry were spared prosecution. Most of them were soon able to find their feet again professionally in West Germany and return to their middle-class lives. These top officials' successful exoneration strategy, however, has also moulded the historical assessment of the Reich Labour Ministry. It was perceived as an authority that – definitively stripped of its powers during the war – carried out merely minor administrative activities and bore no responsibility for the Nazi state's criminal practices.

Martin Münzel's chapter brings out the complexities of staffing continuities after 1945. Initially, in all four Allied occupation zones, former Nazis were almost entirely removed from leading positions in the labour and welfare administration. The upper levels of the relevant authorities in East Germany were also systematically denazified, the vast majority of newly appointed officials and other staff being loyal members of the Socialist Unity Party of Germany (Sozialistische Einheitspartei Deutschlands or SED). The permanent removal of former Nazis from senior administrative posts was carried out more consistently in East Germany than in the western occupation zones and West Germany, with the latter showing a precocious tendency to reappoint qualified officials despite their Nazi past. Often, during the era of the bizonal administration, the lack of trained administrative personnel was already cited as the rationale for returning former senior staff to responsible roles despite their political baggage. The ongoing effects of the exculpatory strategy pursued in Nuremberg are evident in the case of Walter Stothfang. Despite having been a close colleague of Sauckel, following a number of occupational stopovers he was employed in the ministry once again. As in other cases, personal networks from the pre-1945 period played an important role in Stothfang's rehabilitation: individuals were frequently issued with denazification certificates ('Persilscheine'), which had a mitigating effect in the context of the denazification trials. Due to Adenauer's policy of reintegration, beginning in the early 1950s all Federal authorities had to reserve at least 20 per cent of their permanent posts for officials, dismissed after 1945, who had not been categorized, within the framework of the denazification trials, as 'major offenders' (Hauptschuldige) or the 'encumbered' (Belastete, including activists, militants and profiteers). Most Nazi bureaucrats found employment once again in the ministries of West Germany; in some cases this involved the reactivation of old networks.

As Münzel shows, in 1953 former Nazi Party members occupied 57 per cent of senior roles in the state bureaucracy, increasing to more than 70 per cent by 1960. Hence, at the most senior levels, the Federal Ministry of Labour and Social Affairs was among the 'Federal ministries employing the highest proportion of former Nazi Party members' (Martin Münzel). During this period, the Federal Labour Office (Bundesanstalt für Arbeit) and its subordinate labour offices also employed many former party members, sometimes in senior roles. Formal party membership, however, does not tell us the whole story when it comes to political continuities. More significant is the fact that the ministerial elites clearly consisted of a largely homogeneous group of welfare specialists, administrative experts and officials, a group characterized by shared professional socialization and political experiences, both extending from the Weimar Republic through the Nazi era and into the postwar period.

Alexander Nützenadel, Dr. phil., Professor of social and economic history at Humboldt University of Berlin, and spokesperson for the Independent Commission of Historians Investigating the History of the Reich Ministry of Labour in the National Socialist Period. Publications include: with Marc Buggeln and Martin Daunton (eds), *The Political Economy of Public*

Finances. Taxation, State Spending and Debt since the 1970s (Cambridge University Press, 2017); *Stunde der Ökonomen. Wissenschaft, Expertenkultur und Politik in der Bundesrepublik 1949–1974* (Vandenhoeck & Ruprecht, 2005); with Wolfgang Schieder (eds), *Zeitgeschichte als Problem. Nationale Traditionen und Perspektiven der Forschung in Europa* (Vandenhoeck & Ruprecht, 2004); *Landwirtschaft, Staat und Autarkie. Agrarpolitik im faschistischen Italien 1922–1943* (de Gruyter, 1997).

Notes

1. M. Zschucke, *Das Reichsarbeitsministerium*, Berlin: Junker und Dünnhaupt, 1940, 5 f.
2. On the recent debate, see W. Gruner and A. Nolzen (eds), *'Bürokratien'. Initiative und Effizienz*, Berlin: Assoziation A, 2001; C. Kuller, '"Kämpfende Verwaltung". Bürokratie im NS-Staat', in D. Süss and W. Süss (eds), *Das 'Dritte Reich'. Eine Einführung*, Munich: Pantheon, 2008, 227–45; S. Reichardt and W. Seibel (eds), *Der prekäre Staat. Herrschen und Verwalten im Nationalsozialismus*, Frankfurt am Main: Campus, 2011.
3. M. Weber, *Wirtschaft und Gesellschaft*, Tübingen: Mohr, 1922; see also S. Breuer, *Max Webers Herrschaftssoziologie*, Frankfurt am Main: Campus, 1991; M.R. Lepsius, 'Das Modell der charismatischen Herrschaft und seine Anwendbarkeit auf den "Führerstaat" Adolf Hitlers', in Lepsius, *Demokratie in Deutschland. Soziologisch-historische Konstellationsanalysen. Ausgewählte Aufsätze*, Göttingen: Vandenhoeck & Ruprecht, 1993, 95–118; U. Gerhardt, 'Charismatische Herrschaft und Massenmord im Nationalsozialismus. Eine soziologische These zum Thema der freiwilligen Verbrechen an Juden', *Geschichte und Gesellschaft* 24(4) (1998), 503–38.
4. E. Fraenkel, *The Dual State. A Contribution to the Theory of Dictatorship*, translated from the German by E.A. Shils in collaboration with E. Lowenstein and K. Knorr, New York: Oxford University Press, 1941, reprinted New York: Octagon Books, 1969; see also H. Buchstein and G. Göhler (eds), *Vom Sozialismus zum Pluralismus. Beiträge zu Werk und Leben Ernst Fraenkels*, Baden-Baden: Nomos, 2000.
5. See W. Buchholz, *Die nationalsozialistische Gemeinschaft 'Kraft durch Freude'. Freizeitgestaltung und Arbeiterschaft im Dritten Reich*, Ph.D. dissertation, Munich: University of Munich, 1976; T.W. Mason, *Sozialpolitik im Dritten Reich. Arbeiterklasse und Volksgemeinschaft*, Opladen: Westdeutscher Verlag, 1978; M.-L. Recker, *Nationalsozialistische Sozialpolitik im Zweiten Weltkrieg*, Munich: Oldenbourg, 1985; M.H. Geyer, *Die Reichsknappschaft. Versicherungsreformen und Sozialpolitik im Bergbau*, Munich: Beck, 1987; W. Spohn, *Betriebsgemeinschaft und Volksgemeinschaft. Die rechtliche und institutionelle Regelung der Arbeitsbeziehungen im NS-Staat*, Berlin: Quorum, 1987; M. Frese, *Betriebspolitik im 'Dritten Reich'. Deutsche Arbeitsfront, Unternehmer und Staatsbürokratie in der westdeutschen Grossindustrie 1933–1939*, Paderborn: Schöningh, 1991; E. Hansen, *Wohlfahrtspolitik im NS-Staat. Motivation, Konflikte und Machtstrukturen im 'Sozialismus der Tat' des Dritten Reiches*, Augsburg: Maro, 1991; C. Sachsse and F. Tennstedt, *Der Wohlfahrtsstaat im Nationalsozialismus*, Stuttgart: Kohlhammer, 1992; W. Ayass, *'Asoziale' im Nationalsozialismus*, Stuttgart: Klett-Cotta, 1995; T. Harlander, *Zwischen Heimstätte und Wohnmaschine. Wohnungsbau und Wohnungspolitik in der Zeit des Nationalsozialismus*, Basel: Birkhäuser, 1995; H.G. Hockerts (ed.), *Drei Wege deutscher Sozialstaatlichkeit. NS-Diktatur, Bundesrepublik und DDR im Vergleich*, Munich: Oldenbourg, 1998; D.P. Silverman, *Hitler's Economy. Nazi Work Creation Programs, 1933–1936*, Cambridge, MA: Harvard University Press, 1998; W. Süss, *Der Volkskörper im Krieg. Gesundheitspolitik, Gesundheitsverhältnisse und Krankenmord im nationalsozialistischen Deutschland 1939–1945*, Munich: Oldenbourg, 2003; M. Becker, *Arbeitsvertrag und Arbeitsverhältnis*

während der Weimarer Republik und in der Zeit des Nationalsozialismus, Frankfurt am Main: Klostermann, 2005; D. Humann, 'Arbeitsschlacht'. Arbeitsbeschaffung und Propaganda in der NS-Zeit 1933–1939, Göttingen: Wallstein, 2011.
  6. But see H.-W. Schmuhl, Arbeitsmarktpolitik und Arbeitsverwaltung in Deutschland 1871–2002. Zwischen Fürsorge, Hoheit und Markt, Nuremberg: Institut für Arbeitsmarkt- und Berufsforschung, 2003; D.G. Maier, Anfänge und Brüche der Arbeitsverwaltung bis 1952. Zugleich ein kaum bekanntes Kapitel der deutsch-jüdischen Geschichte, Brühl: Fachhochschule des Bundes für Öffentliche Verwaltung, 2004; D.G. Maier: Geschichte der Arbeitsmarktpolitik und Arbeitsverwaltung in Deutschland. Ausgewählte Texte 1877–1952, Brühl: Fachhochschule des Bundes für Öffentliche Verwaltung, 2008; K. Linne, 'Von der Arbeitsvermittlung zum "Arbeitseinsatz". Zum Wandel der Arbeitsverwaltung 1933–1945', in M. Buggeln and M. Wildt (eds), Arbeit im Nationalsozialismus, Munich: De Gruyter Oldenbourg, 2014, 53–73.
  7. See the chapter by Ulrike Schulz in this volume.
  8. See H. Mommsen, Beamtentum im Dritten Reich. Mit ausgewählten Quellen zur nationalsozialistischen Beamtenpolitik, Stuttgart: Deutsche Verlags-Anstalt, 1966; D. Rebentisch and K. Teppe (eds), Verwaltung contra Menschenführung im Staat Hitlers. Studien zum politisch administrativen System, Göttingen: Vandenhoeck & Ruprecht, 1986; D. Rebentisch, Führerstaat und Verwaltung im Zweiten Weltkrieg. Verfassungsentwicklung und Verwaltungspolitik 1939–1945, Stuttgart: Steiner, 1989; with a strong focus on administrative history, see also H. Hattenhauer, Geschichte des deutschen Beamtentums, Cologne: Heymanns, 1993; S. Mühl-Benninghaus, Das Beamtentum in der NS-Diktatur bis zum Ausbruch des Zweiten Weltkrieges. Zu Entstehung, Inhalt und Durchführung der einschlägigen Beamtengesetze, Düsseldorf: Droste, 1996.
  9. M. Broszat, Der Staat Hitlers. Grundlegung und Entwicklung seiner inneren Verfassung, 10th ed., Munich: Deutscher Taschenbuch-Verlag, 1983, 323.
  10. Ibid., 324 f.
  11. P. Hüttenberger, 'Nationalsozialistische Polykratie', Geschichte und Gesellschaft 2(4) (1976), 417–42, here 430; on the polycracy debate, see H.-U. Thamer, 'Monokratie – Polykratie. Historiographischer Überblick über eine kontroverse Debatte', in G. Otto and J. Houwink ten Cate (eds), Das organisierte Chaos. 'Ämterdarwinismus' und 'Gesinnungsethik'. Determinanten nationalsozialistischer Besatzungsherrschaft, Berlin: Metropol, 1999, 21–34.
  12. J. Caplan, 'Bureaucracy, Politics and the National Socialist State', in P.D. Stachura (ed.), The Shaping of the Nazi State, London: Croom Helm, 1978, 234–56; see also J. Caplan, Government without Administration. State and Civil Service in Weimar and Nazi Germany, Oxford: Clarendon, 1988.
  13. Caplan, 'Bureaucracy', 251.
  14. See the contributions in Reichardt and Seibel (eds), Der prekäre Staat.
  15. Die Tagebücher von Joseph Goebbels. Sämtliche Fragmente, series editor E. Fröhlich, Part I: Aufzeichnungen 1924–1945, vol. 2/III: Oktober 1932–März 1934, ed. A. Hermann, Munich: Saur, 2006, 120 (entry, 30 January 1933).
  16. W.A. Boelcke, 'Arbeit und Soziales', in K.G.A. Jeserich, H. Pohl and G.-C. von Unruh (eds), Deutsche Verwaltungsgeschichte, vol. 4: Das Reich als Republik und in der Zeit des Nationalsozialismus, Stuttgart: Deutsche Verlags-Anstalt, 1985, 793–807, here 795.
  17. See the chapter by Ulrike Schulz in this volume.
  18. K.K. Patel, 'Soldaten der Arbeit'. Arbeitsdienste in Deutschland und den USA, 1933, Göttingen: Vandenhoeck & Ruprecht, 2003, 74–123.
  19. S. Reichardt and W. Seibel, 'Radikalität und Stabilität: Herrschen und Verwalten im Nationalsozialismus', in Reichardt and Seibel (eds), Der prekäre Staat, 7–27, here 11.
  20. R. Hachtmann, '"Systemverfall" oder "Neue Staatlichkeit"? Thesen zur Binnenstruktur des NS-Regimes', in F. Bösch and M. Sabrow (eds), ZeitRäume. Potsdamer Almanach 2011, Göttingen: Wallstein, 2012, 89–100.

21. Ultimately, Ley was made Reich housing commissioner (Reichswohnungskommissar) in October 1942, a post that enhanced his powers; see also R. Smelser, *Robert Ley. Hitler's Labor Front Leader*, Oxford: Berg, 1989.

22. W. Schieder, 'Das italienische Experiment. Der Faschismus als Vorbild in der Krise der Weimarer Republik', *Historische Zeitschrift* 262(1) (1996), 73–125; S. Reichardt and A. Nolzen (eds), *Faschismus in Italien und Deutschland. Studien zu Transfer und Vergleich*, Göttingen: Wallstein, 2005; D. Liebscher, *Freude und Arbeit. Zur internationalen Freizeit- und Sozialpolitik des faschistischen Italien und des NS-Regimes*, Cologne: SH-Verlag, 2009.

23. K. Linne, 'Die Deutsche Arbeitsfront und die internationale Freizeit- und Sozialpolitik 1935 bis 1945', 1999. *Zeitschrift für Sozialgeschichte des 20. und 21. Jahrhunderts* 10(1) (1995), 65–81.

24. See also K.-H. Roth, 'Die Sozialpolitik des "europäischen Grossraum" im Spannungsfeld von Okkupation und Kollaboration (1938–1945)', in W. Röhr (ed.), *Okkupation und Kollaboration (1938–1945). Beiträge zu Konzepten und Praxis der Kollaboration in der deutschen Okkupationspolitik*, Berlin: Hüthig, 1994, 461–565.

25. M. Mazower, *Hitler's Empire. Nazi Rule in Occupied Europe*, London: Allen Lane, 2008.

26. See also J. Hensel and S. Lehnstaedt (eds), *Arbeit in den nationalsozialistischen Ghettos*, Osnabrück: Fibre, 2013.

Bibliography

Ayass, W. *'Asoziale' im Nationalsozialismus*. Stuttgart: Klett-Cotta, 1995.

Becker, M. *Arbeitsvertrag und Arbeitsverhältnis während der Weimarer Republik und in der Zeit des Nationalsozialismus*. Frankfurt am Main: Klostermann, 2005.

Boelcke, W.A. 'Arbeit und Soziales', in K.G.A. Jeserich, H. Pohl and G.-C. von Unruh (eds), *Deutsche Verwaltungsgeschichte*, vol. 4: *Das Reich als Republik und in der Zeit des Nationalsozialismus* (Stuttgart: Deutsche Verlags-Anstalt, 1985), 793–807.

Breuer, S. *Max Webers Herrschaftssoziologie*. Frankfurt am Main: Campus, 1991.

Broszat, M. *Der Staat Hitlers. Grundlegung und Entwicklung seiner inneren Verfassung*, 10th ed. Munich: Deutscher Taschenbuch-Verlag, 1983.

Buchholz, W. *Die nationalsozialistische Gemeinschaft 'Kraft durch Freude'. Freizeitgestaltung und Arbeiterschaft im Dritten Reich*, Ph.D. dissertation. Munich: University of Munich, 1976.

Buchstein, H., and G. Göhler (eds). *Vom Sozialismus zum Pluralismus. Beiträge zu Werk und Leben Ernst Fraenkels*. Baden-Baden: Nomos, 2000.

Caplan, J. 'Bureaucracy, Politics and the National Socialist State', in P.D. Stachura (ed.), *The Shaping of the Nazi State* (London: Croom Helm, 1978), 234–56.

Caplan, J. *Government without Administration. State and Civil Service in Weimar and Nazi Germany*. Oxford: Clarendon, 1988.

Fraenkel, E. *Der Doppelstaat*, retranslated from the English by M. Schöps in collaboration with the author (1974), ed. Alexander von Brünneck, 3rd ed. Hamburg: Europäische Verlagsanstalt, 2012.

Fraenkel, E. *The Dual State. A Contribution to the Theory of Dictatorship*, translated from the German by E.A. Shils in collaboration with E. Lowenstein and K. Knorr. New York: Oxford University Press, 1941; Reprinted New York: Octagon Books, 1969.

Frese, M. *Betriebspolitik im 'Dritten Reich'. Deutsche Arbeitsfront, Unternehmer und Staatsbürokratie in der westdeutschen Grossindustrie 1933–1939*. Paderborn: Schöningh, 1991.

Gerhardt, U. 'Charismatische Herrschaft und Massenmord im Nationalsozialismus. Eine soziologische These zum Thema der freiwilligen Verbrechen an Juden'. *Geschichte und Gesellschaft* 24(4) (1998), 503–38.

Geyer, M.H. *Die Reichsknappschaft. Versicherungsreformen und Sozialpolitik im Bergbau*. Munich: Beck, 1987.

Gruner, W., and A. Nolzen (eds). *'Bürokratien'. Initiative und Effizienz*. Berlin: Assoziation A, 2001.

Hachtmann, R. '"Systemverfall" oder "Neue Staatlichkeit"? Thesen zur Binnenstruktur des NS-Regimes', in F. Bösch and M. Sabrow (eds), *ZeitRäume. Potsdamer Almanach 2011* (Göttingen: Wallstein, 2012), 89–100.

Hansen, E. *Wohlfahrtspolitik im NS-Staat. Motivation, Konflikte und Machtstrukturen im 'Sozialismus der Tat' des Dritten Reiches*. Augsburg: Maro, 1991.

Harlander, T. *Zwischen Heimstätte und Wohnmaschine. Wohnungsbau und Wohnungspolitik in der Zeit des Nationalsozialismus*. Basel: Birkhäuser, 1995.

Hattenhauer, H. *Geschichte des deutschen Beamtentums*. Cologne: Heymanns, 1993.

Hensel, J., and S. Lehnstaedt (eds). *Arbeit in den nationalsozialistischen Ghettos*. Osnabrück: Fibre, 2013.

Hockerts, H.G. (ed.). *Drei Wege deutscher Sozialstaatlichkeit. NS-Diktatur, Bundesrepublik und DDR im Vergleich*. Munich: Oldenbourg, 1998.

Humann, D. *'Arbeitsschlacht'. Arbeitsbeschaffung und Propaganda in der NS-Zeit 1933–1939*. Göttingen: Wallstein, 2011.

Hüttenberger, P. 'Nationalsozialistische Polykratie'. *Geschichte und Gesellschaft* 2(4) (1976), 417–42.

Kuller, C. '"Kämpfende Verwaltung". Bürokratie im NS-Staat', in D. Süss and W. Süss (eds), *Das 'Dritte Reich'. Eine Einführung* (Munich: Pantheon, 2008), 227–45.

Lepsius, M.R. 'Das Modell der charismatischen Herrschaft und seine Anwendbarkeit auf den "Führerstaat" Adolf Hitlers', in Lepsius, *Demokratie in Deutschland. Soziologisch-historische Konstellationsanalysen. Ausgewählte Aufsätze* (Göttingen: Vandenhoeck & Ruprecht, 1993), 95–118.

Liebscher, D. *Freude und Arbeit. Zur internationalen Freizeit- und Sozialpolitik des faschistischen Italien und des NS-Regimes*. Cologne: SH-Verlag, 2009.

Linne, K. 'Die Deutsche Arbeitsfront und die internationale Freizeit- und Sozialpolitik 1935 bis 1945'. 1999. *Zeitschrift für Sozialgeschichte des 20. und 21. Jahrhunderts* 10(1) (1995), 65–81.

Linne, K. 'Von der Arbeitsvermittlung zum "Arbeitseinsatz". Zum Wandel der Arbeitsverwaltung 1933–1945', in M. Buggeln and M. Wildt (eds), *Arbeit im Nationalsozialismus* (Munich: De Gruyter Oldenbourg, 2014), 53–73.

Maier, D.G. *Anfänge und Brüche der Arbeitsverwaltung bis 1952. Zugleich ein kaum bekanntes Kapitel der deutsch-jüdischen Geschichte*. Brühl: Fachhochschule des Bundes für Öffentliche Verwaltung, 2004.

Maier, D.G. *Geschichte der Arbeitsmarktpolitik und Arbeitsverwaltung in Deutschland. Ausgewählte Texte 1877–1952*. Brühl: Fachhochschule des Bundes für Öffentliche Verwaltung, 2008.

Mason, T.W. *Sozialpolitik im Dritten Reich. Arbeiterklasse und Volksgemeinschaft*. Opladen: Westdeutscher Verlag, 1978.

Mazower, M. *Hitler's Empire. Nazi Rule in Occupied Europe*. London: Allen Lane, 2008.

Mommsen, H. *Beamtentum im Dritten Reich. Mit ausgewählten Quellen zur nationalsozialistischen Beamtenpolitik*. Stuttgart: Deutsche Verlags-Anstalt, 1966.

Mühl-Benninghaus, S. *Das Beamtentum in der NS-Diktatur bis zum Ausbruch des Zweiten Weltkrieges. Zu Entstehung, Inhalt und Durchführung der einschlägigen Beamtengesetze*. Düsseldorf: Droste, 1996.

Patel, K.K. *'Soldaten der Arbeit'. Arbeitsdienste in Deutschland und den USA, 1933–1945*. Göttingen: Vandenhoeck & Ruprecht, 2003.

Rebentisch, D. *Führerstaat und Verwaltung im Zweiten Weltkrieg. Verfassungsentwicklung und Verwaltungspolitik 1939–1945*. Stuttgart: Steiner, 1989.

Rebentisch, D., and K. Teppe (eds). *Verwaltung contra Menschenführung im Staat Hitlers. Studien zum politisch administrativen System*. Göttingen: Vandenhoeck & Ruprecht, 1986.
Recker, M.-L. *Nationalsozialistische Sozialpolitik im Zweiten Weltkrieg*. Munich: Oldenbourg, 1985.
Reichardt, S., and A. Nolzen (eds). *Faschismus in Italien und Deutschland. Studien zu Transfer und Vergleich*. Göttingen: Wallstein, 2005.
Reichardt, S., and W. Seibel (eds). *Der prekäre Staat. Herrschen und Verwalten im Nationalsozialismus*. Frankfurt am Main: Campus, 2011.
Reichardt, S., and W. Seibel. 'Radikalität und Stabilität: Herrschen und Verwalten im Nationalsozialismus', in Reichardt and Seibel (eds), *Der prekäre Staat. Herrschen und Verwalten im Nationalsozialismus* (Frankfurt am Main: Campus, 2011), 7–27.
Roth, K.-H. 'Die Sozialpolitik des "europäischen Grossraum" im Spannungsfeld von Okkupation und Kollaboration (1938–1945)', in W. Röhr (ed.), *Okkupation und Kollaboration (1938–1945). Beiträge zu Konzepten und Praxis der Kollaboration in der deutschen Okkupationspolitik* (Berlin: Hüthig, 1994), 461–565.
Sachsse, C., and F. Tennstedt. *Der Wohlfahrtsstaat im Nationalsozialismus*. Stuttgart: Kohlhammer, 1992.
Schieder, W. 'Das italienische Experiment. Der Faschismus als Vorbild in der Krise der Weimarer Republik'. *Historische Zeitschrift* 262(1) (1996), 73–125.
Schmuhl, H.-W. *Arbeitsmarktpolitik und Arbeitsverwaltung in Deutschland 1871–2002. Zwischen Fürsorge, Hoheit und Markt*. Nuremberg: Institut für Arbeitsmarkt- und Berufsforschung, 2003.
Silverman, D.P. *Hitler's Economy. Nazi Work Creation Programs, 1933–1936*. Cambridge, MA: Harvard University Press, 1998.
Smelser, R. *Robert Ley. Hitler's Labor Front Leader*. Oxford: Berg, 1989.
Spohn, W. *Betriebsgemeinschaft und Volksgemeinschaft. Die rechtliche und institutionelle Regelung der Arbeitsbeziehungen im NS-Staat*. Berlin: Quorum, 1987.
Süss, W. *Der Volkskörper im Krieg. Gesundheitspolitik, Gesundheitsverhältnisse und Krankenmord im nationalsozialistischen Deutschland 1939–1945*. Munich: Oldenbourg, 2003.
Die Tagebücher von Joseph Goebbels. Sämtliche Fragmente, ed. E. Fröhlich, 9 vols. Munich: Saur, 2000–2009.
Thamer, H.-U. 'Monokratie – Polykratie. Historiographischer Überblick über eine kontroverse Debatte', in G. Otto and J. Houwink ten Cate (eds), *Das organisierte Chaos. 'Ämterdarwinismus' und 'Gesinnungsethik'. Determinanten nationalsozialistischer Besatzungsherrschaft* (Berlin: Metropol, 1999), 21–34.
Weber, M. *Wirtschaft und Gesellschaft*. Tübingen: Mohr, 1922.
Zschucke, M. *Das Reichsarbeitsministerium*. Berlin: Junker und Dünnhaupt, 1940.

PART I
ADMINISTRATIVE STRUCTURE, PERSONNEL AND INSTITUTIONAL CONFLICTS

Chapter 1

THE REICH MINISTRY OF LABOUR, 1919–1945
Organization, Leading Personnel and Political Room for Manoeuvre

Ulrike Schulz

There is certainly no escaping the bureaucratic organization. It makes no difference whether we place the substrate and the necessities of our lives, those aspects that require organization, in the hands of the state and its subdivisions, or whether we surrender them to those who lay claim to them as organizers or private firms and exploit them for monetary and other purposes. No matter what, it is the same machinery, the same immense structure that results, in whose bleak, innumerable chambers our soul dies, as in catacombs of its being. It makes no difference who creates it, to whom it belongs – the cage is built; it is now our fate.

— Alfred Weber, 'Der Beamte'

When Alfred Weber published these lines in 1910, he still hoped to warn his readers about the imperceptibly growing bureaucratic machine that was, he believed, taking over every sphere of life. He wanted to cast light on what he perceived as the ever-deepening antagonism between the free and dynamic professional (*Berufs-Menschen*) and the impersonal, 'bureaucratic' (*beamtlich*) hegemony of 'machines' (*Apparate*). He imputed to these 'machines' an inherent metaphysical dynamic that was supposedly reordering society but was, in reality, subjugating it.[1] Alfred Weber's older and incomparably more famous brother, Max Weber, also ascribed tremendous sociopolitical significance to the ever-enlarging 'bureaucracies', which he observed and analysed in the world around him. He too saw in this development a tendency to curtail the freedom of the individual. But unlike his brother, Max Weber believed this form of rule by cadres of administrative staff (*Verwaltungsstäben*), as he called them, was 'legal' because they acted in accordance with rational and objective principles. These principles included the separation of office and individual; a commitment to neutrality; the gearing of administrative processes towards rational perspectives; standardized training and professionalization.[2] For Max Weber, the task of the administrative cadres was to enforce these principles and thus to ensure that individuals could neither be advantaged nor disadvantaged due to bias. He bequeathed to posterity a perspective on administration as a democratic institution.

The two visions presented by Alfred and Max Weber regarding the genesis of modern administration have retained their potency to this day – the former espousing the negative semantics of an all-conquering bureaucratic machine, the latter the positive semantics of an efficient organization, based on a division of labour, in which the supra-individual dimensions of the polity are steered in accordance with rational procedures.[3] These contemporary analyses were prefigured above all by the seemingly inexorable growth of large companies since the turn of the century and by the agencies of public administration. While Alfred Weber held that it was irrelevant who was driving the bureaucratization of society, Max Weber set out an ideal-typical analysis of the principles he thought constitutive of this process. The principles themselves apply, according to Max Weber, regardless of whether they hold sway in a company, a hospital or a political association. And it makes very little difference what form these principles take in a given organization. Certainly, an insurance office has a different task within the polity than a hospital. But both form part of an administrative system, featuring a division of labour, within an overarching societal framework.

Particularly for Max Weber, the generalizing perspective – transcending specific organizations and their characteristics – was a challenge posed by his era. What he sought to provide was a general schema of a system rather than a sociology of 'public administration' as such. Nonetheless, he might well have produced such a sociology had he not died in 1920. His early death deprived the pioneer of organizational sociology of the opportunity to observe, over an extended period, the Reich ministries – organizations of a democratic orientation whose structure reflected the principles of the division of powers – after the First World War and the November Revolution. On 21 March 1919, these ministries were established as a major element in the executive of the Weimar National Assembly (Nationalversammlung).[4] By decree, the National Assembly provided itself with a government consisting of a Reich chancellor (Reichskanzler) and a so-called Reich Ministry, the latter consisting of a number of specialized ministers and ministers without portfolio. For the first time, this included a Labour Ministry as one of the supreme Reich authorities.

Given his prior studies, within this organization of ministers, the Reich Labour Ministry, its sociopolitical implications and organizational setup would surely have captured Max Weber's attention. First, because here the interests of the two major camps in the labour struggle (*Arbeitskampf*) came up against one another. For the organized labour movement, that is, the SPD and the trades unions, but also for social reformers and national liberals, the ministry was a major step towards a future in which the working class would enjoy dignified living conditions and participate fully in the body politic. Members of the conservative-bourgeois camp, conversely, regarded state social policy as economically unproductive. The German National People's Party (Deutschnationale Volkspartei or DNVP) and most of the business community thus regarded the ministry as an expensive, crisis-prone and biased workers' interest group at the beck and call of the trades unions.[5] Second, from an organizational perspective, the Reich Labour Ministry, impelled by social deprivation in the aftermath of the First World War, brought together such a wide and complex range of responsibilities that, when it was set up, its staff often found themselves entering uncharted territory. Predecessor organizations on the Reich level were either absent or failed to reflect the new challenges faced by a modern mass administration.

A history of the Reich Labour Ministry that examines both dimensions of the organization's work – the policy fields it administered, some of which were highly contested, and its organizational characteristics – affords new and perhaps even surprising insights into the work of governance and state social and labour policy in the period between 1919 and 1945. In such a history one must inevitably pay special attention to the role of the ministry and its staff under Nazism. Ultimately, the fields of labour and social affairs were of tremendous importance to Nazi ideology (the key word here being Volksgemeinschaft), but also to the German policy of occupation after 1939 (the crucial term in this case being forced labour). Accordingly, from 1933 onwards, various Nazi party officeholders and the Hitler regime paid great political attention to the Reich Labour Ministry. To understand the ministry's significance within Nazism, it is vital to systematically analyse its internal organization. Only in this way can one fully grasp the ministry's role, powers, responsibilities and impact. It is also crucial to ask what criteria one might deploy, today, to evaluate the work of its staff, while also contemplating the kinds of issues they found themselves confronted with in their own era.

In what follows I flesh out three aspects of the history of the Reich Ministry of Labour. The first is that this history cannot begin with Hitler's 'seizure of power' in 1933. Any examination limiting itself to the years between 1933 and 1945 would neglect the period of just fourteen years from the ministry's establishment in 1919, through its development to its stabilization during the 'utopian-democratic' and crisis-hit years of the Weimar Republic.[6] Yet these years are crucial to understanding the organizational prerequisites and policy foci of the Reich Labour Ministry, part of Hitler's regime from 1 February 1933. Second, in this context it is essential to consider the roles and responsibilities of the politicians, political civil servants and permanent staff in the ministry within specific constellations of actors. Otherwise, one risks a foreshortened view that reduces this organization's complex functional mechanisms to the decisions made by the minister or leading officials. What impact did Franz Seldte,[7] as sole Reich labour minister between 1933 and 1945, make in his role? Why, for example, was he considered a 'weak' minister? Third and finally, it is crucial to identify the external influences affecting the ministry between 1933 and 1945. Among those bodies to which the Reich Labour Ministry was relevant for various reasons were Nazi Party organizations such as the German Labour Front, but also the other ministries. How might one describe their influence on the Reich Labour Ministry?

The Establishment and Development of the Reich Labour Ministry in the Weimar Republic, 1919–1933

The Reich Labour Office (Reichsarbeitsamt) was founded on 4 October 1918, just under six months before the establishment of the ministries. It took over responsibility for the social policies previously dealt with by the Reich Economic Office (Reichswirtschaftsamt), which had come into being precisely one year earlier, in October 1917, and had itself been allocated certain areas of responsibility previously under the remit of the Reich Office of the Interior (Reichsamt des Innern). The latter had been the leading institution of domestic policy in the German Empire until 1917. Under the direct control of the imperial chancellor (Reichskanzler), it brought together all important fields of domestic policy under one roof, from coinage to workers' accident insurance.[8] During the First World War, this agency found itself overwhelmed by this wide range of duties. It thus seemed essential to achieve a more fine-grained division of labour and redistribute its responsibilities.

Before the end of October 1918, nine expert counsellors (*vortragende Räte*) and about twenty department heads (*Referenten*), a total of fifty-six established civil servants (*planmässige Beamte*) and thirty-seven white-collar employees (*Angestellte*) began to restructure the Reich Labour Office.[9] Most of them came from the Reich Office of the Interior and the Reich Economic Office, though some had served in the Prussian Domestic

Administration (Innenverwaltung). Gustav Bauer, an SPD politician and trades union official, was appointed head of this agency, and was made state secretary to this end.[10] At the point of transition, the Reich Labour Office was responsible for welfare provision for blue- and white-collar workers, labour market regulation, job placement, unemployment benefit and workers' insurance. The new Reich Labour Office also subsumed the Reich Insurance Company (Reichsversicherungsanstalt), which provided workers' disability insurance and had existed since 1884, and the White-Collar Workers' Insurance (Angestelltenversicherung), a public corporation and supervisory authority founded in 1911, as a second strand of statutory old-age insurance.[11]

The orderly development of the organization, however, lasted for just a few days. The Reich Labour Office had barely seen the light of day when it found itself at the epicentre of the November Revolution of 1918. Over a period of a few months, the organized labour movement managed for the first time to force the elites of the German Empire to respond to their political demands. The momentum engendered by the First World War and the Communist Revolution of 1917 in Russia enabled the working class to establish itself henceforth as a political force in its own right. This set in motion a rebalancing of political forces that was to mould the development of the entire twentieth century.[12] Key demands put forward by the workers' and soldiers' councils, which had now been formed in Germany on the model of the Russian Revolution, were addressed directly to the nominally responsible Reich Labour Office. The first priority was gaining recognition for the trades unions as the legitimate representatives of the workers. This role as political representative was associated with far-reaching demands for workers' rights, including worker participation, free collective bargaining and company-related social policies of benefit to workers.[13] Before they had time to catch their breath, the officials in the new Reich Labour Office found themselves participating in the first, fraught negotiations between employees' and employers' representatives and were witness to hitherto unthinkable accords, as in the case of the Stinnes-Legien Agreement (Stinnes-Legien-Abkommen).[14] Also of enduring significance to the future of the Reich Labour Office and, from March 1919, the Reich Labour Ministry were those demands delegated to the constituent National Assembly during the negotiations between the transitional government and the workers' and soldiers' councils, demands that were enshrined in the Weimar constitution in August 1919. These ranged from a comprehensive labour code through a central employment agency to state-subsidized housing and unemployment insurance. The workers' representatives thus sought to remedy the failures of the previous twenty years as rapidly as possible.

This left very little time to think systematically about the Labour Office's organizational setup. Looking back, the staff of the new agency must have found it breathtaking how rapidly it grew, month on month, from the last few weeks of 1918 onwards.[15] Certainly, in the fields taken over from the Reich Economic Office, there were preliminary plans as well as sometimes long-established organizational structures. But even here there were few fields of responsibility with respect to which officials could straightforwardly build on the state of affairs as at 1914. The top priority and political dictate of the moment was to develop the body of legislation concerning labour law, worker protection and company-related social policy, in such a way as to improve the working and living conditions of workers and their families and thus also – in the spirit of *raison d'état* – to help prevent their further political radicalization during this febrile period. In this context, the Works Councils Act (Betriebsrätegesetz) of 4 February 1920 was just one example of the legislative texts in the offing, but it was unquestionably the most significant initiative at the time.[16] Another priority was to reorganize job placement and determine how to standardize the structures of the various agencies, which were organized quite differently in the different states. One issue with considerable explosive potential, both socially and politically, was how best to organize and calculate the financial resources for a system of unemployment insurance that was yet to be elaborated.[17] At the time, however, the government had little choice but to begin providing unemployed workers with financial support without delay. It concurrently revamped the system of pension insurance for blue- and white-collar workers, the first priority here being to make the requisite changes to the law, then to bring prospective entitlements into line with it.

These tasks alone brought officials at the Reich Labour Office up against the limits of their capacities. Yet now they had to take on additional, in some cases entirely new responsibilities in rapid succession. It was the tremendous hardship suffered by the general population from the end of the war until the hyperinflation of 1923 that set the pace for these developments. Responsibility for housing and settlement had already been conferred on the Labour Office in December 1918. This was an area that had previously been regarded neither as a social policy priority nor as an administrative task for the central agencies of the state. Both urban and rural house-building and housing provision, the regulation of land, including the reallocation of arable land, the regulation of rent and protection of tenants had been the sole province of the Länder and the municipalities until 1914.[18] In view of the acute housing shortage resulting from a construction business that had stagnated during the war and the hundreds of thousands of soldiers pouring back from the front, the regulation of housing became a major priority and was incorporated into the Weimar constitution. Henceforth, the Reich Labour Office took on responsibility for coordinating the relevant legislative work.

Before the end of February 1919, the transitional government and the National Assembly had already conferred yet another area of responsibility on the Reich Labour Office. Its remit now included the provisioning of war victims and their dependants. The Labour Office thus took over the army's welfare infrastructure, previously organized on a military basis, with a mandate to transform it into a form of civilian aid, while ensuring this was reflected in legislation. Between October 1919 and June 1923, the ministry then took over completely the system of military and medical welfare provision and also had to wind up the military authorities responsible for regulating pensions.[19] Until well into 1924, the associated responsibilities previously held by the Ministry of War (Kriegsministerium), the Reich Colonial Ministry (Reichskolonialministerium), the Ministry for Economic Demobilization (Ministerium für wirtschaftliche Demobilmachung) and the Länder were transferred to what was known, from March 1919 onwards, as the Reich Ministry of Labour. These extended from unemployment benefits for officers to the central oversight of explosives and munitions factories.[20]

In a sense, the Reich Labour Ministry's takeover of social services on 5 October 1919 marked its re-foundation. Its staff grew exponentially, overnight, to a total of 572 civil servants and 3,818 white-collar personnel.[21] When it came to legislation, the system of public aid touched on sociopolitical issues as fundamental as those involved in labour law. For example, until 1918 the eligibility for benefits enjoyed by disabled veterans and their surviving dependants was still calculated according to rank and thus essentially in line with their social status. In light of the millions of individuals who returned home from war with serious impairments, this state of affairs no longer reflected social realities. Social services, which were known as Reich Public Aid (Reichsversorgung), were another important and very extensive sphere of responsibility held by the Reich Labour Ministry, and one that shaped it at least as much. Hence, both fields, labour law and public aid, were constitutive of the establishment and development of the Reich Labour Ministry during the Weimar Republic. Apart from anything else, both fields set the course in significant ways for the organizational development of the ministry as a whole, as becomes clear from examination of the next few years.

How did the ministry achieve stability given its constantly expanding responsibilities? Initially, in line with its main fields of activity, it was divided into four sections (*Abteilungen*): I Workers' Issues (Arbeiterfragen), II Workers' Insurance (Arbeiterversicherung), III Housing and Settlement (Wohnungs- und Siedlungswesen) and IV Aid for Disabled Ex-Servicemen and their Surviving Dependants (Versorgung der Kriegsbeschädigten und

-hinterbliebenen, that is, Reichsversorgung). In 1921, the first three sections moved into the building at 35 Scharnhorststrasse, home to the Reich Ministry of Labour until 1934. Section IV remained in the building of the Kaiser Wilhelm Akademie at 32/43 Luisenstrasse until 1923, when it too was integrated into the main ministry premises.

All four sections began their work by taking stock of the concrete issues requiring their attention, both in terms of policy substance and how best to organize them. Initially, all incoming mail, that is, all enquiries, letters and petitions, were lumped together in an as yet entirely unsystematic way according to various topics. Running to no less than eighteen pages, the first schedule of responsibilities, of July 1919, encompassed ten sections, which were assembled amid the chaos.[22] It was only during the course of 1920 that the relevant section heads arranged the various fields of activity into clusters, allocating sections to deal with them while also allocating departments to these sections. Over the next few years the sections were often relocated and subdivided in new ways in an attempt to stake out the various spheres of responsibility. These now overlapped with the policy concerns of other Reich ministries, inducing rivalries. For example, the Reich Ministry of Labour was embroiled in protracted disputes with the Reich Ministry of the Interior over whether the Reich Health Office (Reichsgesundheitsamt or RGA) and the Poor Relief Service (Armenfürsorge) should continue to come under its remit or whether they should be transferred to the Labour Ministry.[23] There were other responsibilities that, rather than sparking disputes, triggered regular contact and cooperation. For example, the Reich Labour Ministry collaborated with the Reich Ministry of the Economy (Reichswirtschaftsministerium) with respect to the supervision of working conditions (*Gewerbeaufsicht*) and the Ministry of Justice with regard to laws on rent. Very slowly, over the decade until 1929, a stable structure crystallized featuring five sections: Central Administration and Reich Public Aid (Zentrale Verwaltung und Reichsversorgung; Main Section I), Social Insurance in All Fields (Sozialversicherung in allen Bereichen; Main Section II), Labour Law and Wages Policy (Arbeitsrecht und Lohnpolitik; Main Section III), Housing and Settlement (Wohnungs- und Siedlungswesen; Main Section IV) and Job Placement and Administration (Arbeitsvermittlung und -verwaltung; Main Section V).

The ministry was characterized by great stability on the level of personnel, particularly when it came to the appointment of its two leading figures, namely the minister and state secretary. Following Gustav Bauer's intermezzo as the first official Reich labour minister, beginning in February 1919, in July of the same year he handed over the reins to Alexander Schlicke, long-standing president of the German Metal Workers' Union (Metallarbeiterverband) and another SPD politician.[24] The latter steered the ministry's fate for just over a year until Heinrich Brauns[25] was appointed Reich labour minister in June 1920. Brauns was to hold this office for eight years almost to the day, until June 1928. This lengthy period in office was almost improbable given the political crises of the Weimar Republic; Brauns was confirmed in his post as labour minister as a succession of fourteen governments took office. Brauns, a member of the Centre Party (Zentrumspartei), developed into virtually the ideal candidate for this ministry, one accepted across party lines. He was an established expert on social policy and brought with him a certain focus on labour law as a result of his earlier activities as a chaplain in the People's Association for Catholic Germany (Volksverein für das katholische Deutschland) and trades union official.[26] Expertise alone would probably not have secured his position in the precarious political setting of the Reich Labour Ministry during this period. But he earned a reputation as mediator between political camps, above all due to the active and even offensive role he played in parliamentary debates, the budget committee and the broader public sphere. He managed to present the ministry's work to the rest of the world in a convincing way. In the spirit of the Catholic social teaching he espoused, the basic principle of his politics was the need for balance. While he openly sought to support the workers in their demands for recognition and participation, he kept his mind open to the employers' argument that social policy must be geared towards the economically feasible.[27] This engagement brought him respect and criticism in equal measure, but his achievements as mediator between the two sides of the labour struggle were undisputed. They even made an impression within the context of international negotiations. For example, in 1927 Albert Thomas, at the time director of the International Labour Office, wrote to the minister: 'You left me in no doubt about your unerring ability to integrate the associations of employers and employees into the construction of social policy as its two crucial mainstays, thus inextricably linking economy, social policy and concept of state (*Staatsgedanken*)'.[28]

A group of senior and top-level officials worked under Heinrich Brauns. Like their minister, they clearly demonstrated outstanding commitment and identified personally with the ministry's endeavours. This was epitomized by Hermann Geib,[29] nominally the only state secretary in the Reich Labour Ministry. Geib managed to surpass Heinrich Brauns's impressive period in office and held his post until 1932 – twelve years without interruption. Moreover, he complemented the minister's expertise as a renowned expert in social services and war victim support. Geib, a doctor of law, had a classic administrative career behind him. Beginning in 1915, he headed the Reich Office for War Victims (Reichsstelle für Kriegsopfer) in Berlin, a position that is likely to have been pivotal, in addition to his excellent qualifications, to his appointment to the Reich Ministry of Labour.

In the shape of Heinrich Brauns and Hermann Geib, for a lengthy period the two most senior positions in the ministry were occupied by individuals who provided precisely the sort of stability necessary to get, and keep, the organization on track. First, the working relationship between the two was distinguished by an exceptional degree of trust. Second, they enjoyed the requisite support from the senior staff who assisted them.[30] Under these two, in parallel to the senior staff, a stable group of officials took shape who also helped ensure great continuity in strategically important areas. It is true that the prescribed career of the civil servant kept fluctuations to a minimum in any case. Nonetheless, the section heads' (very) long periods of service were mainly due to the turbulent circumstances prevailing when the ministry was established during the November Revolution of 1918, which engendered loyalty and cohesion. The staffing and recruitment policy pursued by Heinrich Brauns and State Secretary Hermann Geib further reinforced this tendency.

For the period of the Weimar Republic until 1933, the group of top officials in the Reich Labour Ministry comprised a total of around forty individuals. From the time of the salaries reform in 1920 onwards, this group included all positions with the rank of a minister, state secretary, section head (*Ministerialdirigent*), ministerial director (*Ministerialdirektor*) and ministerial counsellor (*Ministerialrat*). This group contained few individuals from the ambit of the SPD, the trades unions, workers' associations or social reformers. The same went for the Centre Party and the Christian trades unions. Under Heinrich Brauns, the number of staff who were members of the Centre Party increased slightly, but overall they were no more dominant than those from the socialist camp.[31] Instead, over the entire period of the Weimar Republic, a homogeneous group of officials with a classical training and career occupied the ministry's top positions.

One special feature for the time – and in comparison with other Reich ministries – were the six women among the senior officials, some of whom even managed to obtain the top-level position of ministerial counsellor by 1933; their appointment was closely bound up with the ministry's responsibilities for social policy, in which women had played a steadily growing role since the turn of the century. Even within the Reich Labour Ministry the women's appointment and education were exceptional in every way, whereas the biographical characteristics of their male colleagues were very similar.[32]

Qualitative analysis of the average of fourteen ministerial counsellors in the Weimar Republic who occupied the post of section head for at least three years reveals a uniform picture. The overwhelming majority came from a single age cohort, were born between 1877 and 1887 (8), were Protestant (8), had a degree in jurisprudence (11) and had gone on to obtain a doctorate in the same field (8). Most of these individuals had joined the ministry between 1919 and 1921 (10) and remained in post for ten years on average, and no less than twenty-one years in the case of the most senior roles.

Figure 1.1. Average age of top-level staff at the Reich Ministry of Labour (starting at ministerial counsellor level), 1919–1945

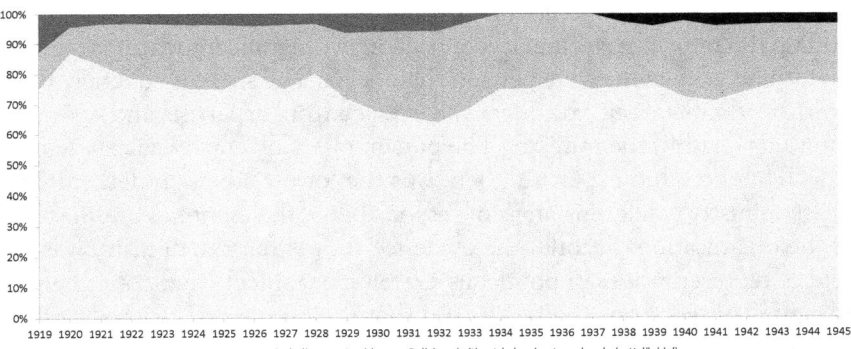

Figure 1.2. Religious affiliation of top-level staff at the Reich Ministry of Labour (starting at ministerial counsellor level), 1919–1945 (in per cent)

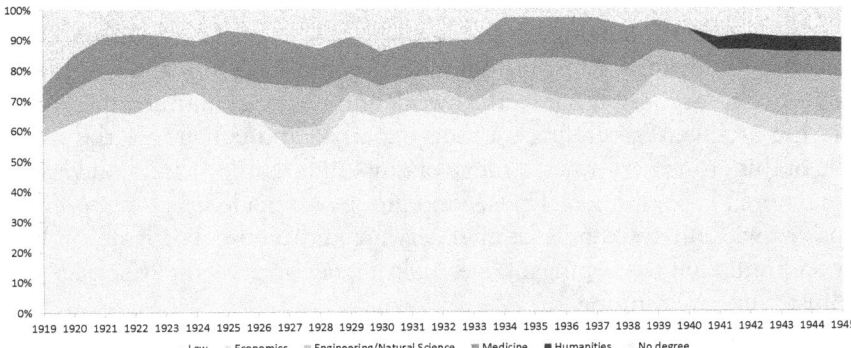

Figure 1.3. Main subjects of university study among top-level staff at the Reich Ministry of Labour (starting at ministerial counsellor level), 1919–1945 (in per cent)

Overall, these characteristics of the ministerial counsellors continued to pertain and had changed only slightly by 1939, as the following data reveal. Between 1919 and 1933, this group of staff comprised forty-five to fifty individuals. From 1933 onwards, their number showed no significant growth; only from 1939 was there an increase to an average of fifty-six individuals.

These trends in senior staff remained significant when it came to the next rung down the hierarchy, namely the (senior) government counsellors (*[Ober-]Regierungsräte*), though with a number of structural qualifications. This was a larger group, comprising, on average, around sixty individuals between 1919 and 1933. Moreover, the ministry's different fields of activity meant that the jurists, who also dominated this level of the hierarchy at more than 50 per cent, found themselves mingling with individuals with a different professional background: physicians, (civil) engineers, and social and political scientists. Experts from a variety of disciplinary, professional, regional and political backgrounds thus came together in the Reich Labour Ministry, lending the organization as a whole a genuinely cosmopolitan character.

As for the ministry's senior officials, whom I have examined up to and including the rank of government counsellor, two significant features emerge. First, these were eminent experts in their fields. The sources generally leave us in no doubt about the high value placed on expertise and specialist knowledge within the ministry. The pursuit of an 'objective', fact-based approach anchored in expertise, then, was the lowest common denominator of the ministry's different areas of responsibility, the *esprit de corps* fostered by the organization. Second, the evidence shows that the ministry was devoid of representatives of politically extreme or radical views, of either left or right. This confirms the impression that during the first few years of the ministry's existence and under the Weimar Republic its top officials were bound by the Weberian principles of neutrality and professionalism.

Our picture would be incomplete, however, if I failed to mention the two remaining groups of workers at the ministry. The first consisted of mid-level officials, making up the largest share of staff at 100 to 150 individuals on average. Most of them ran the ministry's so-called technical institutions, responsible for clerical work and financial matters, the library and the archive. Depending on their expertise and education, the members of this group performed a range of quite different jobs and had varying educational backgrounds. The second group was made up of white-collar workers without the status of civil servant and blue-collar staff, both of whom were vital to keeping a large-scale agency such as the Reich Labour Ministry up and running.

However, in considering the ministry's formal structure, the constant development of its personnel and their biographical characteristics, it is important not to lose sight of the fact that, over the course of the Weimar Republic, the Reich Labour Ministry's numerous fields of activity turned it into a kind of 'superministry'. Ministerial Counsellor Georg Hartrodt's attempt, dating from 1929, to provide an at-a-glance overview of the ministry's fields of activity, highlights another characteristic crucial to the organization's development: its subordinate bodies.[33] Both in the Weimar Republic and under the Nazis, the Reich Labour Ministry was a top-level Reich agency featuring an administrative apparatus that was both highly specific and vast. It is crucial to take account of this large-scale administrative machinery in order to understand the ministry's structure and modus operandi. To omit this factor and focus solely on the central decision-making level would be to disregard much of the ministry's practical administrative activities.[34]

Figure 1.4 only gives us a hint of this, but the fields of social insurance, Reich public aid and job placement each entailed a distinct chain of command. These administrative branches were coordinated, supervised and regulated by the Reich Insurance Company, the main public aid offices (Hauptversorgungsämter) and the Reich Institution for Job Placement and Unemployment Insurance (from 1927 onwards) as subordinate agencies of the ministry. They formed the interface between the ministry's Berlin headquarters, the Land-level administration and the chains of command within the municipalities.[35] Until 1933, the chains of communication and command, in other words the oversight and supervision practised by the ministry vis-à-vis these three administrative levels, were subject to a highly uneven degree of regulation. The Reich Insurance Company and the Reich Institution for Job Placement and Unemployment Insurance were autonomous organizations under public law that were merely supervised by the ministry. Both could act with a fairly high degree of independence, whereas, right from the start, the main public aid offices were directly answerable to the Berlin headquarters. Moving one step further down the ladder, each of these three branches of the administrative apparatus in turn spawned a variety of agencies and offices on the level of the Länder (intermediate level) and municipalities (lowest level).

In seeking to provide a complete picture of the Reich Labour Ministry's subordinate agencies, I have yet to mention the most important bodies. While these did not develop chains of command of their own, they stood ready to represent the ministry in its various spheres of action or, alternatively, required its supervision. They included the Reich Provisioning Court (Reichsversorgungsgericht), an autonomous body with the power to make legal rulings, the permanent arbitrators (Schlichter), responsible for dealing with pay disputes, and the Reich Insurance Company for White-Collar Workers (Reichsversicherungsanstalt für Angestellte), which administered insurance as an autonomous body. Housing and Settlement (Main Section IV) had no subordinate agencies but instead had to

Ulrike Schulz

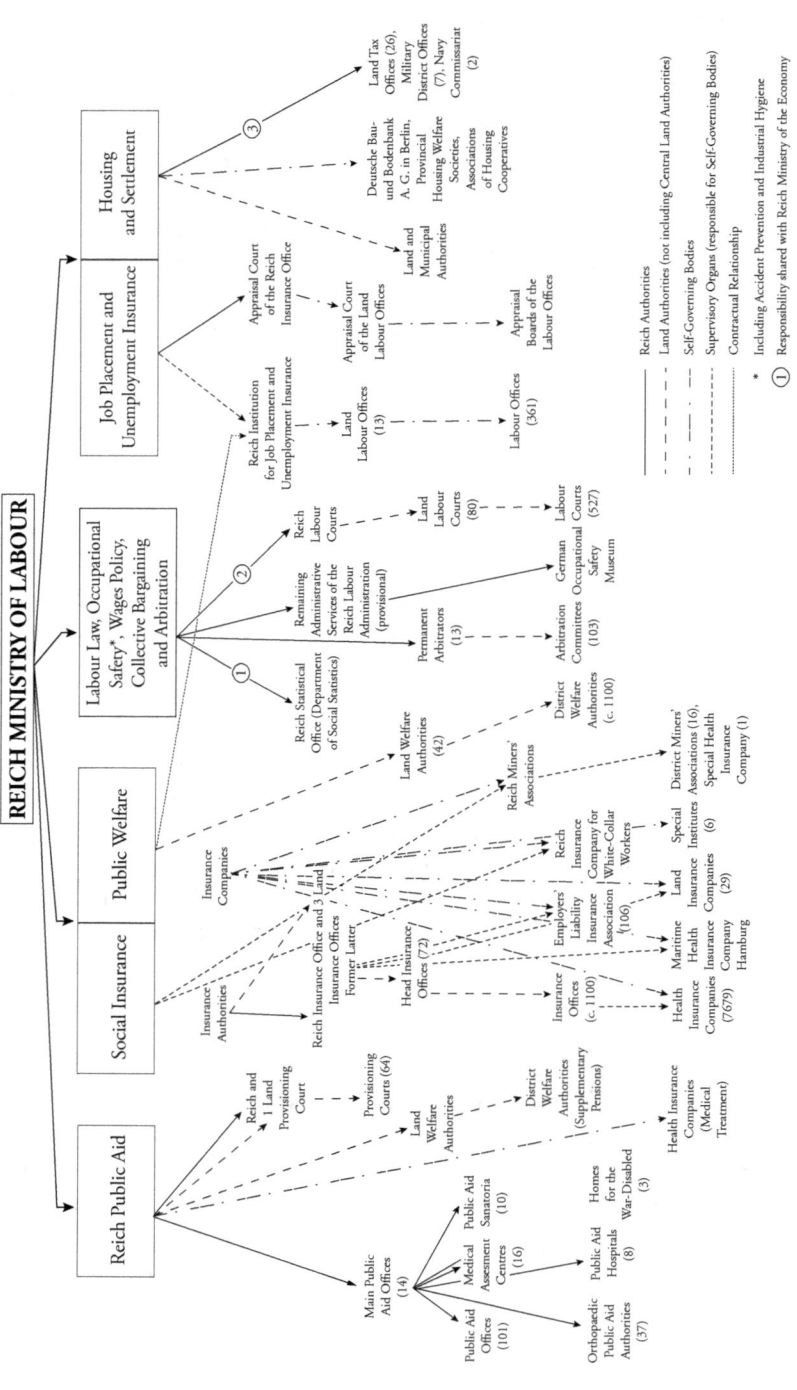

Figure 1.4. Organizational structure of the Reich Ministry of Labour, 1929

Source: Georg Harrodt, *Die Ausstellung. Die Arbeitsgebiete des Reichsarbeitsministeriums*, Berlin: Reichsdruckerei, 1929, 14.

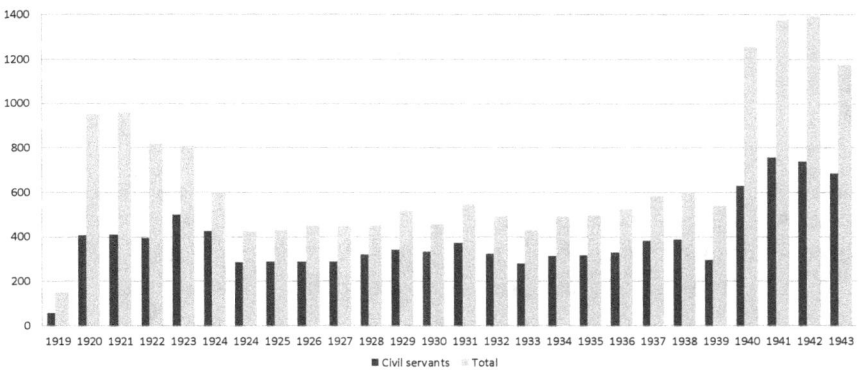

Figure 1.5. Staffing trends at the Reich Ministry of Labour, 1919–1943

negotiate with the Land and municipal authorities (Land ministries and rent offices [Mietämter]).[36]

This polymorphous subordinate realm of the ministry was crucial to its overall functioning for three reasons. First, it served to divide up the tasks within the organization. Here the Berlin headquarters sought to outsource, to an ever-increasing degree, as many as possible of its specific administrative tasks and technical institutions – involving anything from financial transactions in relation to the payment of pensions to the bed occupancy rate in sanatoriums – to the subordinate agencies. The ministerial headquarters, by way of contrast, tried to focus on the fundamental issues involved in the state's labour and social policy and on framework legislation in the other policy fields. For the entire period until 1945 and with respect to the various chains of command, however, this succeeded only partially: a great deal of friction and conflict arose, both within the ministry and with the other ministries, that could only be resolved centrally. Second, the subordinate realm concentrated and centralized administrative tasks for the ministry itself. Conversely, it was only via communication with the subordinate agencies that the ministry received the information necessary, on the level of Reich politics, to determine its own position and formulate its legislation accordingly. Importantly, it was through these channels that ministerial officials could most rapidly discover which regulations were or were not having the desired effect in practice. Third, the subordinate sphere extended the reach of the ministry and the Reich government into the Länder – because the relevant chains of command within the welfare and labour administration were not absorbed into the administrative tiers of the Länder and municipalities. They had been constructed in parallel and enjoyed an autonomous existence. As a result, between 1919 and 1945 they were already regarded by contemporaries and administrative experts as a 'special administration', one that attracted criticism for this very reason and for its alleged duplication of work.[37] Yet this structure within the social welfare administration, criticized as a 'faulty construct', turned out to be a tremendous organizational boon for the ministry. In the event of conflict, the ministry could deploy this subordinate sphere to enforce its legislation and administrative instructions down to the local level and, if necessary, in the face of political opposition from Land governments. All three functions of the subordinate realm – internal division of labour, information transmission and processing and policy implementation – were of key importance to the Berlin headquarters and provided the organization as a whole with stability.

After a decade-long process, the Reich Labour Ministry had become a fairly established organization by 1929. Well-practised routines had taken hold when it came to contact with other actors and with respect to the ministry's core tasks: in the legislative process when interacting with the Reichstag and the Land parliaments, when drawing up the budget, in those committees relevant to the ministry and so on. An extensive network encompassing a great variety of organizations and individuals had grown up around the ministry and worked together with the section and department heads, sometimes on a regular basis. This chiefly meant professional associations and lobbying organizations, ranging from the health insurance companies (*Krankenkassen*) through medical societies to tenants' associations. Also relevant in this context were credit institutions such as the Bau- und Bodenbank, a body close to the state that processed the financial transactions associated with house-building. These service providers were tremendously important to the ministry, sparing it the need to function as a source of funding for specific interest groups but also enabling it to keep an eye on the recipients of financial support. This network also included scientific institutes, which frequently produced expert reports for the ministry, such as the Rheumatism Research Institute (Rheumaforschungsinstitut) in Bad Elstar, which was involved in the approval of maintenance claims. Other bodies operating within this framework were the Reich Statistical Office (Statistisches Reichsamt), which collected data on the development of social and labour policy in cooperation with the ministry, and the Institute for Cyclical Analysis (Institut für Konjunkturforschung). Finally, the ministry cooperated with certain firms on a regular basis, such as prosthesis manufacturers and the suppliers of its office buildings.

Diplomatic links were also up and running on the international level, some of which the ministry itself maintained in consultation with the Foreign Office (Auswärtiges Amt). During the Weimar Republic, ministry staff had made intensive efforts to help normalize Germany's relations with other countries. The German government ratified the most important social policy agreements concluded on the international level, such as those mediated by the International Labour Organization. Ministry employees were more than capable of representing German interests within the framework of these negotiations.[38] Even more relevant to the ministry's everyday working processes in this context were international treaties. Particularly in regions where cross-border labour relations were par for the course, the German state supported those of its citizens employed abroad. For example, it quickly took steps to harmonize its social insurance regulations in cooperation with Austria and Alsace-Lorraine.[39]

But the ministry's regular monitoring of international developments in social and labour policy was by no means restricted to these border regions. In fact, this was one of its core tasks, pursued on a permanent basis by an entire department since 1919. The ministry concerned itself with all geostrategically important countries and all those relevant to social and labour policy, from the United States to the Soviet Union. Every main section thus appointed social policy officers dedicated to particular countries, where they regularly spent two to three years.

Internally too, by the late 1920s the Reich Labour Ministry had achieved a high degree of standardization and professionalization.[40] To some extent the ministry trained its staff itself. There had been a considerable need for this, particularly in the subordinate agencies. Ministry staff also taught at the Berlin Administrative Academy (Berliner Verwaltungsakademie), which had integrated the topic of social and labour policy into its curriculum. In addition to training, by 1922 at the latest the ministry had produced formalized instructions to guide its day-to-day business on all levels. This applied above all to communication with external actors, such as parliamentarians and other ministries, and responding to enquiries from the public. But internally, too, the rules were now tightened up. For example, ministry staff were permitted to publish texts under their own names in newspapers and academic journals only with the minister's approval (with the exception of the ministry's own organs of publication). In other words, a clear distinction was made between the ministry's self-presentation and that of its staff. Probably the most important principle here was to keep discussion of the ministry's organization to a minimum and, ideally, avoid discussing its internal modus operandi entirely. The main goal in this context was to shield the ministry from the demands of, and potential exploitation by, third parties as it went about its work. It sought, for example, to avoid having to discuss its work on legislative texts in public before it had determined its own position.

Internal communication benefited from the ministry's acquisition, in 1925, of a new automatic telephone system. Previously its officials' only option had been to register their calls the day before at a central telephone exchange or communicate with each other through letters and messengers. And in 1925 their working hours were standardized, that is, reduced from 51 to 48.5 hours a week. The ministry's offices were crowded and it had established a system to supply itself with foodstuffs and items of everyday need. For example, clothing firm representatives regularly visited the building during working hours to tout their wares. For ministerial counsellors in particular, this opportunity to purchase goods was important because they did not enjoy reduced or regular working hours. Top officials worked an average of fourteen hours a day. The personnel files include a fair number of cases in which their excessive workload led to staff being diagnosed as suffering from hazardous levels of exhaustion. One reason for this was that senior officials in the ministry in particular, in addition to their allotted work in the office, frequently had to be present at conferences, in committees and in the Reichstag. They functioned as members of parliamentary committees, gave talks at the conferences of professional associations, learned a foreign language or made trips to subordinate offices.

Last but not least, officials' parliamentary and legislative work had become routinized. The ministerial counsellors, whose key task was to represent the ministry to external actors, participated in expert panels (*Fachgruppen*) and committees. Meeting in the corridors of the Reichstag or holding informal meetings in the vicinity of Wilhelmstrasse, they undertook tasks such as clarifying in advance the prospects for new amendments to a particular law. By the second half of the 1920s there no longer seemed to be any serious doubt that labour and social policy was a task for the state. Within its sphere of responsibility, the Reich Labour Ministry had become established as the government's legitimate representative.

The world economic crisis burst upon this relatively stable situation in October 1929. In the wink of an eye, much of what the state had only just accomplished faced new and fundamental challenges. Over the next few years, until the power shift in 1933, ministry staff too came under enormous public pressure. They found themselves pulled between the necessity for a frugal budget and the general public's growing deprivation. Since 1920, the Reich Labour Ministry had always had the largest budget of any ministry. Pension payments, subsidies for new housing and the Reich Public Aid (Reichsversorgung) accounted for the largest shares of expenditure. Up to 1933, the Budget Office (Haushaltsabteilung) found itself having to meet the needs of the various departments and the subordinate bodies with an ever-decreasing budget. At the same time, however, year on year those eligible for benefits had an ever-greater need for support. Budget cuts made themselves felt in every area of the ministry's work, but took on particularly dramatic form when it came to unemployment insurance and pension insurance.[41] Due to the rampant unemployment, the ministry had to abandon the target rates, which had only been fixed in 1927, and the original definition of unemployment. At the same time, its income estimates were no longer correct. It was the question of how they might be changed that caused the collapse of the last grand coalition of the Weimar Republic in March 1930. The assets of the Reich Institution for Job Placement and Unemployment Insurance melted away with alarming rapidity. It was only a matter of time before emergency subsidies were required to plug the holes in its budget. The same went for the Reich Insurance Company, benefit rates for war victims and financial support for house-building. Cuts to social services were an explicit part of the emergency decrees issued by the presidential governments. Despite the drastic spending cuts, at the same time the extra expenditure made available increased significantly as an ever-growing number of individuals made requests for support. As a result, to take just one example, between 1929 and 1932 the share of the extraordinary budget made up of extra spending doubled from 767 million to 1.5 billion Reichsmarks.[42]

Alongside the Reich Labour Ministry, now other ministries, committees and extra-parliamentary panels of experts tried to come up with compensatory non-cash forms of support. The most important of the proposed measures that the government went on to implement were job creation programmes, flanked by relief works, reduced working hours, the introduction of a voluntary labour service and a number of other steps.[43] During this period the ministry lost its sole responsibility for these matters. Its officials, moreover, sometimes had to implement recommendations that clashed explicitly with their own preferred solutions. They were, for example, highly sceptical about a compulsory labour service for the unemployed, querying who, exactly, was going to pay for such a service.[44]

Nonetheless, the ministry retained its capacity for effective action. One of the most important levers available to it was to stipulate, and if necessary redefine, who was entitled to receive support. It expanded, for example, the sphere of short-time work quite rapidly by means of ordinances between 1931 and 1932. By extending companies' ability to introduce short-time work and simultaneously raising state benefits for short-time workers, the ministry managed, to a degree, to curb the rapid increase in the number of those registering as unemployed. Above all, over the short term these measures relieved some of the pressure on the public coffers.[45] The ministry responded to this situation of financial crisis in similar fashion in many areas of activity. It thus redefined groups of beneficiaries and those entitled to benefits, rearranged budget items or, as in the case of unemployment insurance, removed certain groups entirely from the total of those entitled to unemployment benefit. The ministry made active use of such measures: within the organization's logic, these were the levers it could apply to counteract public pressure, to some extent, over the short term. This form of crisis management adumbrated the situation that was to become the Reich Labour Ministry officials' new normality after January 1933. It was the new 'government by decree' that made these adaptations possible in the first place: the Reichstag now exercised negligible control over such changes.[46]

The substantial structural growth in the ministry's policymaking power stood in sharp contrast to public perceptions, which threw the organization, sometimes quite forcefully, onto the defensive. It was deluged with criticisms from every quarter. On the one hand, the ministry came under pressure to rescind the severe benefits cuts, chiefly from the organizations and interest groups representing workers and benefits recipients. On the other, reductions in support payments had not gone far enough for industrial lobbying groups and the business community. To take one example, the ministry promulgated the 6th Emergency Decree (Notverordnung) of 1931, which reduced the wages and salaries of blue- and white-collar workers across the board by 10 per cent.[47] In addition, workers and their representatives regarded the compulsory arbitration, introduced first in the iron and steel industry and subsequently in other sectors as well, as a case of profound state intervention carried out solely in the interests of employers.[48] Such measures finally put paid to the vision of a state deploying labour law to reconcile the two camps in the labour struggle, a vision Heinrich Brauns, along with pioneering thinkers such as Hugo Sinzheimer and Ernst Fraenkel, had regarded as crucial to pacifying and democratizing society.

When it came to the ministry's work, these processes and decisions threw up a complex range of issues and power-political ambiguities that were near-impossible to manage in the febrile climate of the time. The fragile political and economic situation was starkly apparent, and it constantly required the state to make savings, leaving no scope for the active formulation of labour and social policy. Those who held the office of labour minister during these years also saw a drastic diminution in their room for manoeuvre. Heinrich Brauns had had to leave as a result of tactical, party-political factors when the new government was formed in June 1928. Over the next four years he was replaced by two highly experienced politicians and trades union officials. From June 1928 until April 1930, the ministry was headed by Rudolf Wissell of the SPD; Adam Stegerwald of the Centre Party then took over until June 1932. Both were heavily involved in the work of government and in the Cabinet's crisis management. On the senior level of the ministry itself, it will likely have been State Secretary Hermann Geib and his close colleagues who did most to sustain everyday operations. Not long after the departure of Adam Stegerwald, however, the long-standing state secretary too handed in his resignation for personal reasons. A vacuum now emerged at the top of the ministry, one initially filled by high-ranking ministry staff. Hugo Schäffer, previously president of the RVA, was then appointed Reich minister of labour, remaining in office for exactly 180 days, from June to December 1932. His successor, Friedrich Syrup, managed to outdo him by remaining in post for just fifty days. Both interim ministers were supported by State Secretary Andreas Grieser, head of Main Section II.

The removal of Syrup and Grieser was set in motion, without their knowledge, on 28 January 1933, at a secret meeting between Adolf Hitler, Franz von Papen and Hermann Göring.[49] There they offered Franz Seldte, then leader of the 'Steel Helmet' League of Frontline Soldiers (Stahlhelm, Bund der Deutschen Frontsoldaten e. V.), the post of Reich labour minister, which he accepted.

Role and Function of the Reich Labour Ministry under the Nazi Regime, 1933–1945

Franz Seldte did not become a minister and part of Hitler's new government as the latter's personal candidate. He was in fact a member of the circle around incumbent Reich President Hindenburg. As leader of the 'Steel Helmets' and co-initiator of the Harzburg Front (Harzburger Front) he was valuable to Hitler: he could function as an exponent of a broad-based, right-wing conservative alliance during the critical phase of the 'seizure of power' and thus foster a sense of trust in the new Reich government. Moreover, in propaganda terms it probably suited the Nazi leadership rather well that Franz Seldte was a severely disabled war veteran, an injury sustained in 1916 having left him with kidney disease and cost him his left arm.

Despite or perhaps precisely because of his impairments, as co-founder of the Steel Helmets he represented the interests of the soldiers and war victims of the First World War, earning him a great deal of respect both among simple recruits and in the highest military and political circles.[50] Seldte's popularity and associated credibility was especially valuable to Hitler because veterans in particular – the war-disabled but even more the healthy, able-bodied soldiers – were an extremely important group for him, which the regime courted accordingly. In terms of symbolic politics, appointing Franz Seldte head of the leading 'social' ministry appears to have been a smart move by the Nazi Party.

In administrative circles and among career politicians, conversely, he was regarded as a novice and the reaction to his appointment at home and abroad was often derisive.[51] Seldte had previously run the family firm in Magdeburg, which manufactured aromatic essences and essential oils. While he may have possessed organizational experience, he had little concrete expertise in social and labour policy. And yet Franz Seldte retained the post of Reich labour minister for the entire period of Nazi rule. During his time in office, but above all after 1945, he was labelled the 'weak' minister. Recent studies have shown that when interrogated as a prisoner of war, Seldte himself reinforced this seemingly unfavourable assessment, allowing him to exonerate himself along with high-ranking ministry staff. Neither Seldte nor the officials close to him were charged during the Nuremberg war crimes trials.[52] Does this amount to a narrative of exoneration that still retains its potency? And what does the 'weak minister' label tell us about Seldte's policy-related and political leadership skills? Does historical analysis of the Reich Labour Ministry confirm this assessment or is there a case for a more nuanced evaluation?

It is apparent from the history of the Reich Labour Ministry during the Weimar Republic that the Hitler regime had at its disposal a multi-layered and competent organization staffed by qualified personnel. Only in the very early days following the Nazi takeover did the ministry face threats to its existence; its responsibilities – and above all its expenditure – were up for negotiation. Apparently, Franz Seldte and Alfred Hugenberg, briefly the minister for economy, agriculture and food, had specifically agreed that the Labour Ministry would be integrated into the Ministry of the Economy without further ado. When Hugenberg was ejected from office before the end of summer 1933, however, these plans were dropped.[53] The ministry remained as it was, with just a few adjustments being made to the senior staff. There was certainly no shakeup on the basis of the Law for the Restoration of the Professional Civil Service (Gesetz zur Wiederherstellung des Berufsbeamtentums or Berufsbeamtengesetz) from April 1933 onwards.[54] But for those affected by this discriminatory law, which specifically targeted the civil service, it caused a severe rupture in their employment history and their professional and personal self-image as well as economic problems. Furthermore, the pensioning-off of these officials was a substantial loss for the organization because some of them were experienced and long-serving members of staff. One of those to leave was State Secretary Andreas Grieser. He was considered vulnerable as a social policy specialist under the Weimar Republic and likely pre-empted his demotion or transfer by taking voluntary retirement. He was replaced by Johannes Krohn,[55] previously head (Abteilungsleiter) of Main Section II (Social Insurance). Beginning in 1919, Krohn's career within the ministry had taken him from the post of government counsellor (*Regierungsrat*) to that of ministerial director (*Ministerialdirektor*). Still nominally the only state secretary in the ministry, he was more than familiar with its internal processes and required no lengthy settling-in period.

All women in senior positions had been ousted by the end of 1933. It was not the legal mechanism of the Law for the Restoration of the Professional Civil Service that removed them. In this case the ministries quickly bowed to the political pressure brought to bear by the German Labour Front through the so-called Double Earner Campaign (*Doppelverdiener-Kampagne*) against women. In October, the Reich minister of the interior, who was responsible for civil service issues, sent out an internal letter in which he recommended appointing male candidates on a preferential basis.[56] In most cases, female officials in top-level roles were transferred to subordinate authorities – as long as they were not Jewish. Both in the ministry itself and at the senior level of the subordinate authorities, those members of staff, whether male or female, who now faced discrimination as Jews were pensioned off before the end of 1933. They included leading experts such as Oscar Weigert.[57] He had worked in the ministry since 1919 and is today considered a pioneer and founder of the unemployment insurance established in 1927. The vacant posts that resulted were filled internally, so very few staff from outside were appointed to leading positions within the ministry following the Nazi takeover in 1933.[58]

Two changes of personnel after January 1933, however, were significant as both newcomers were directly appointed as section heads. Hans Engel took charge of Main Section II (Social Insurance), thus replacing Johannes Krohn. Engel came from the Ministry of Food and Agriculture (Ministerium für Ernährung und Landwirtschaft), where he had been a ministerial counsellor since 1929. The new head of Main Section III (Labour Law and Wages Policy), meanwhile, was Werner Mansfeld, previously at the University of Münster before taking up his new post in Berlin.[59] Both had completed the education required for their positions and were specialists in their fields. They had not been employed because of long-standing party membership. Mansfeld had only just joined the Nazi Party before being appointed in May 1933; Engel did so only in 1936. Most of the remaining section heads and ministerial counsellors remained in post. The ministry's subordinate authorities must be examined on a case-by-case basis in this regard. For example, many members of the SPD, KPD and trades union representatives worked at the Reich Institution for Job Placement and Unemployment Insurance. Here, the assessments made necessary by the 'Civil Service Law' resulted in the dismissal of 3,160 blue- and white-collar workers by 1935.[60] For the period between 1933 and 1945, the data on the biographical characteristics of personnel, right up to the rank of ministerial counsellor, again show the homogeneous distribution that might be predicted on the basis of the formalized civil service career path, in much the same way as in the Weimar Republic. There was no radical restructuring of the ministry; education and specialist knowledge retained their tremendous importance, and there were no significant changes in the religious composition of the civil service.[61]

Nonetheless, the data show that from 1938–1939 onwards, Nazi rule did have concrete effects on the composition of staff in the ministry and its staffing policies. This was because a large number of new staff had been appointed at the Berlin headquarters during this period to deal with the impending war-related tasks. It was by this point at the latest that Nazi civil service policies made their presence felt in the ministry's appointment practices. In concrete terms, this meant that since the beginning of 1936 it was not just the personnel officer (*Personalreferat*) and state secretary who made decisions about appointments. Proposed candidates also required the approval of the 'Führer's representative' (*Stellvertreter des Führers*) in the Party Chancellery (Parteikanzlei).[62] At this point in time, membership of the Nazi Party, though not vital to obtaining a leading position within the ministerial administration, had certainly become politic, as had an ideologically sound curriculum vitae as a National Socialist. Yet when it came to appointments, senior officials at the Reich Labour Ministry continued to play a major role. Within the ministry this meant that it was only from 1938 onwards that a significantly larger number of party members were appointed. This was because, first, the ideological requirement of Nazi Party membership had previously not been crucial to obtaining a post. Second, the Nazi Party allowed people to join again from mid 1937. Only then could a given member of staff expect membership of the party to boost his career.

Among the ministerial counsellors, conversely, a surprisingly uniform picture emerges up to 1939. Just a handful of them had opted to join the party.[63] This is consonant with the non-partisanship that had taken hold among ministry staff under the Weimar Republic. But it is likely that Hermann Rettig, head of the Personnel Department (Personalabteilung), who was highly regarded within the ministry, also played a significant role in this allocation of posts. He worked at the ministry between 1919 and

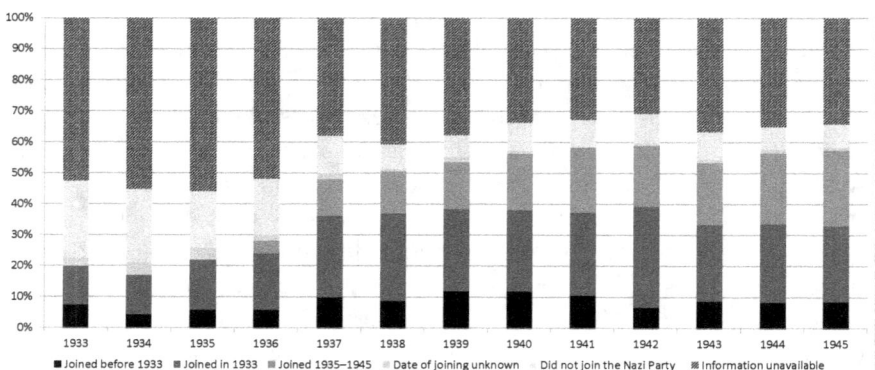

Figure 1.6. Nazi Party membership among government counsellors and senior government counsellors at the Reich Ministry of Labour, 1933–1945 (in per cent)

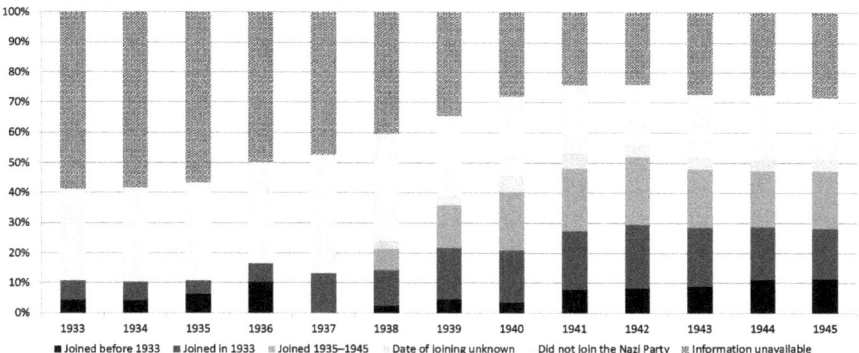

Figure 1.7. Nazi Party membership among top-level staff at the Reich Ministry of Labour (starting at ministerial counsellor level), 1933–1945 (in per cent)

1938 and remained in post until the latter year. In consultation with State Secretary Krohn, he maintained the tried and tested approach to recruitment. This meant that the appointment of staff, as well as reflecting the formally prescribed career path, was chiefly geared towards the necessary educational qualifications. In fact, as Nazi Party functionaries saw it, over the years there developed a pronounced 'disparity' between party members and non-members. In 1938, the Reich Chancellery received a furious complaint about the proposed appointment to the post of ministerial counsellor of an individual who was not a member of the Nazi Party:

> The staffing situation in the Reich Labour Ministry has long been a source of grave concern to me. How far from satisfactory this situation is can be seen in the simple fact that – as I have been informed – of the thirty-eight ministerial counsellors working in the ministry just five are party members. . . . Further, the Reich Labour Ministry has taken advantage only in a highly unsatisfactory manner of the opportunity to purge its corps of civil servants of non-Aryans and those married to Jews [*jüdisch-versippt*] within the framework of the Civil Service Law.[64]

This picture reflected the realities on the ground. To make matters worse, some of the most senior members of staff, such as Friedrich Syrup and Johannes Krohn, had to be pressed to take up membership of the Nazi Party several times, before finally giving in to the pressure in 1937 and 1938 respectively. The ministry also yielded to the political pressure that had built up by pensioning off Hermann Rettig in 1938 and replacing him with 'old fighter' and Nazi hardliner Wilhelm Börger.[65] From that point forward, Börger ensured the promotion or appointment of party members to senior posts.

Minister Franz Seldte, meanwhile, as these examples show, backed the internal staffing decisions made by Rettig and Krohn prior to 1938–1939. It would, however, be presumptuous to conclude that he did so for political reasons, let alone to regard this as a form of latent resistance. In fact,

Seldte's policy was most likely based on his pragmatic – and realistic – assessment that ministry officials' expertise was vital if it was to carry out its substantive policy work. Nonetheless, the sources show that in the event of conflict Franz Seldte and his top officials consistently backed their colleagues – even against high-ranking representatives of the Nazi Party.[66] This is illustrated by the cases of ministerial counsellors Heinrich Goldschmidt and Bernhard Lehfeld, who were not dismissed despite being so-called 'half-Jews' (*Halbjuden*).[67] Seldte also tended to shield 'Aryan' officials who were found wanting by the Nazi Party. For example, the minister took up the cudgels on behalf of Ministerial Counsellor Oskar Karstedt,[68] who was attacked by the party soon after it took power in 1933. Karstedt had to defend himself against the 'accusation' that he was himself a Jew. In addition, it had not escaped the notice of a number of Nazi Party functionaries that Karstedt received 'Jewish' physicians at the Reich Labour Ministry. Up to 1938, the evidence shows that his office at the ministry was a port of call for 'Jewish' physicians seeking to reverse bans on practising their profession.[69]

In Karstedt's case but also in other instances, Minister Seldte acted to support his colleagues. Throughout his tenure as minister he never enforced a hard party line and he generally gave his state secretaries, section heads and department heads free rein, and not just when it came to staffing issues. He delegated substantive tasks directly to his subordinates. At Cabinet meetings with Hitler, it was usually State Secretary Krohn who spoke for the ministry, in Seldte's presence. By the same token, his colleagues among the senior staff seem to have been loyal to him.[70] In any event, there is no evidence that they tried to circumvent the minister or make him look bad. During his period in office there would have been plenty of opportunities to do so, because Franz Seldte was quite simply not as present as the responsibilities of his office required. He had to make lengthy official trips to receptions and conferences. Due to his disabilities, however, time and again he required medical treatment or had to retreat to a health spa, often for long periods.

Yet these observations do not automatically mean that the minister was a weak leader within the ministry itself. To perform the duties of Reich minister, a specific education was desirable, and most of those who held the post had acquired one. But it was not a prerequisite. Until October 1933, Seldte, like all ministers who had previously served under the Weimar Republic (heading the ministries of Labour, the Foreign Office, Finance, the Interior, Justice, Post, the Armed Forces [Reichswehr], Transport and Economy), was a public employee (*öffentlicher Angestellte*) rather than a civil servant. He was, fundamentally, beholden solely to the constitution rather than being subordinate to any other organ.[71] From October 1933 onwards, perfectly embodying the spirit of the Führer's State (*Führerstaat*), ministers gave an oath of office in which they pledged their personal fealty to Adolf Hitler and now found themselves in an unambiguously subordinate relationship.[72] Nonetheless, Martin Broszat is correct to state that within the practice of governance ministers suffered no loss of importance as a result. Quite the opposite: the ministries took on greater responsibility and enjoyed greater independence within the government in order – through the division of responsibilities among themselves – to spare Hitler the need to concern himself with the business of government.[73] Ministers' overriding task as members of Hitler's regime was to support – through the provision of advice – the political decision-making process when it came to matters within their remit. They were then responsible for implementing the decisions made by Hitler and his cadre of advisers in accordance with the relevant laws or, if necessary, had to draw up new ones. It is often difficult to determine – even through a historical retrospective – how they secured this role within their particular ministry or what personal influence and individual creative drive they brought to bear internally. Many arrangements were made informally in this context. What can be stated generally about Seldte is that the minister, along with his colleagues, managed to safeguard his ministry's long-standing responsibilities until the final years of the war, adapting them to the political and later wartime realities. Franz Seldte took a great deal of advice from his state secretaries and section heads and was quite ready to delegate tasks that exceeded his own capabilities, a leadership style that guaranteed the continuity of the ministry's substantive policymaking and the survival of the institution itself.

It would, however, be a serious misunderstanding to assume a straightforward match between Seldte's persona as a leader on the one hand and his position and status within the Nazi regime on the other, or to equate them simplistically with those of other ministers. The political influence exercised by the various ministers on Hitler's thinking and the authority to which they could lay claim within the political decision-making process depended on a number of factors that were by no means solely down to their individual strengths or weaknesses.

In assessing Seldte's room for manoeuvre as Reich labour minister within the Nazi regime, the relevant factors relate to both the (power-) political and institutional changes that occurred over the course of the Nazi period: 1. The ministries' structurally altered position within the Nazi state system; 2. Personal proximity to Hitler, his advisers and the associated personal networks; 3. The Reich Labour Ministry's and its subordinate authorities' relationship with the Nazi Party organizations charged with complementing their work; 4. The significance of the ministry's core tasks; and 5. The significance of the ministry's core tasks to Nazi occupation and the war economy. In what follows, I describe these five factors with reference to examples.

1. The ministries' altered position within the Nazi state system. Following Hitler's assumption of power, the so-called Enabling Law (Ermächtigungsgesetz) and the Law to Secure the Unity of Party and State (Gesetz zur Sicherung der Einheit von Staat und Partei) established the ministries' legal and power-political position.[74] The 'Enabling Law' represented a clear break with the constitution and political conditions of the Weimar Republic.[75] It granted Hitler unlimited power to promulgate laws for the coming four years while failing to allow for parliamentary control or constitutional review. This enabled him to change the constitution, which continued to apply on a formal level, or suspend parts of it.[76] Among the consequences of the 'Enabling Law' that made an immediate impact was change in the formal and informal aspects of the legislative process. The collective consultation process involving parliament, experts, interest groups and the ministerial administration was suspended. Henceforth, whatever Adolf Hitler expressed as his political will, the relevant ministries had to implement, because the Reich chancellor alone enjoyed legislative authority and the right to enforce laws. The ministries, meanwhile, conceived, took advice on and drew up the draft laws, decrees (*Erlasse*) and ordinances (*Verordnungen*) within their areas of responsibility. The collective processes of coordination were also diminished in another sense: draft laws were no longer circulated among all departments, allowing them to express their views. Instead, ministries were only involved if the new law fell within their remit. Hitler set great store by having legislative texts presented to him solely in the form of skeleton laws. He had no wish to involve himself in substantive details. Instead he left it to the ministries responsible to clarify and disseminate these details through the subsequent implementing regulations. On the face of it, this simplified the process of consultation but it also made it more autocratic.[77] Once the ministries had completed the draft of a new law, the procedure concluded in obligatory evaluation by the Reich Chancellery and the Ministry of the Interior.[78] After approval by these two institutions, the document was issued, presented to Hitler for signing and published in the *Reich Law Gazette (Reichsgesetzblatt)*.[79]

The 'Enabling Law', then, not only 'liberated' the ministries from parliamentary control and the need to ensure conformity with the constitution, but, as executive organs, gave them de facto legislative powers – to the extent that Hitler did not lay sole claim to them. The ministries thus gained tremendous formal and practical room for manoeuvre. This new legal reality within the state's constitution applied across the board from 1 August 1933 when Hitler, following Hindenburg's resignation, formally became the Reich's sole head of state.⁸⁰ Just a few months later, in February 1934, the Imperial Council (Reichsrat), as the body representing the previous Land governments, was finally disbanded, having already lost much of its political importance as a result of the 'coordination' (*Gleichschaltung*) of the Länder in April 1933. This 'coordination' also spelt the end of the Prussian State Ministry (Staatsministerium) and its administrative apparatus. Over the course of 1934, the ministries (Labour, Finance, Interior, Justice and Economy) fully absorbed the tasks performed by these institutions into their own structures. From March 1935 onwards, this takeover also found linguistic expression: henceforth, the Reich labour minister was officially called the 'Reich and Prussian labour minister' (Der Reichs- und Preussische Arbeitsminister). At Hitler's behest, however, this title was abbreviated again to 'Reich labour minister' in 1938.⁸¹

Ultimately, as a result of this reorientation of the legislative process, in addition to Hitler himself, his closest advisers and confidants, but above all the Reich ministers, exercised a major influence on political decisions and the legislation to which they gave rise: 'The Reich government is now no longer the Cabinet in the traditional sense, in which all decisions were reached through a majority vote, but instead a Council of the Führer (Führerrat), which advises and supports the Führer and Reich chancellor with respect to the decision he has to make'.⁸² If a law, decree or ordinance had been agreed within these internal circles, the relevant draft also went through a process of consultation in which only a few external experts and interest groups – having already been 'coordinated' – now took part. Overall, this dramatic curtailment of the consultation process may have accelerated the formulation of laws, decrees and ordinances within the Führer's State. Yet at the same time it created an increased need for later coordination and re-negotiation, the outcome of which had in turn to be presented to Hitler for approval. Even a Führer's order (*Führerbefehl*) could not simply eliminate the necessary process of consultation, particularly if it touched on financial issues.

2. Access to Hitler and his networks. Hitler, however, in no way wished to be involved in the process of consultation and negotiation that went on between the ministries. They had to clear up any disputes among themselves.⁸³ Should consensus prove elusive, he generally left it to his state secretary in the Reich Chancellery, Hans Heinrich Lammers, to sort things out. Lammers, meanwhile, had to present political questions to Hitler once again if they were of a fundamental nature. As time wore on, Hitler responded to this decision-making cycle with irritation. One of the consequences was that he largely ceased to allow ministers who were not members of his immediate 'Führer's Council' to present their concerns

in person. This even applied to long-standing 'comrades-in-arms' such as Reich Minister of the Interior Wilhelm Frick. By the time the Nazi state was gearing up for impending war in 1939, and then during the war itself, such ministers no longer had access to Hitler.[84] For Franz Seldte, from around 1938 onwards it was no longer possible to talk to Hitler in person. Furthermore, examination of Hitler's itinerary shows that he no longer came into contact with Seldte at official or semi-official events.[85] Like most of his colleagues in the other civilian ministries, henceforth Seldte's only option was to assure himself of Hitler's approval indirectly via his cadres of advisers, his entourage or the Reich Chancellery, an inner circle that changed over the course of time. Yet a qualifying remark is necessary here: very little research has so far been carried out on Seldte's personal networks or those of his closest colleagues in the ministry. The latter, after all, had in most cases been involved in the political operation on Wilhelmstrasse for well over a decade, so they are likely to have maintained relationships with other long-standing officials and decision-makers, while personal sympathies and informal collegial get-togethers will no doubt have played a role as well.[86]

3. The relationship between the Reich Labour Ministry and Nazi Party agencies. To summarize, the ministries acquired tremendous power within Hitler's state because they had gained the authority to initiate legislation and were endowed with executive allocative functions. The ministerial administration was not only responsible for translating the policy precepts formulated by Hitler and his 'Führer's Council' into legislation. It also had to put Nazi policy ideas into practice within the subordinate administrations it supervised and that were subject to its directives. However, the ministries' new power was already reined in again on the formal level by the Law to Secure the *Unity* of Party and State of 1 December 1933.[87] This law declared the Nazi Party the sole state party and established the interleaving of state and party. The state administration was charged with providing the Nazi Party with administrative and legal assistance and accommodating the state party's pre-eminent status.[88] This dualism between the state administration and the party authorities now gave rise to a quite specific dynamic for the organization of the administrative system. On the level of legislation, cooperation between the two still proceeded in concrete forms. For the ministerial administration, this cooperation meant that the 'Führer's representative' and the Party Chancellery had to be involved in all the legislative work done by the ministries. For the most part, the ministries continued to dominate proceedings as the party mustered up very few specialists who might have reviewed the laws, decrees and ordinances submitted over the course of the twelve years of Nazi rule. When it came to practical implementation, there was broad room for manoeuvre regard-

ing how the Nazi Party's leadership role, always emphasized on the level of symbolic politics, was to be ensured within legally framed administrative processes.[89] Between the Nazi Party, its organizations and associations (*Gliederungen und Verbände*) as well as the state administrative authorities, there thus arose – sometimes intense – rivalries over the powers and resources of the state administration. This applied in particular to the filling of posts within the internal administration of the Land governments, cities and municipalities. In some cases, personnel, such as mayors, had already been extensively replaced in 1933. But bitter rivalries over resources and power also developed between the party and the ministries on both the Reich and Land level.

As the organ responsible for labour and social policy, the Reich Labour Ministry was particularly affected by this. The Nazi Party, with its programmatic, claimed commitment to equality and community and its alleged affinity for the workers as a national 'socialist' movement, had made it a signature aspiration to improve the living conditions of all those admitted into the 'Volksgemeinschaft'.[90] An interventionist social and labour market policy seemed like an apt means of achieving this. For Hitler, a little more than a decade after the controversial foundation of the Reich Labour Ministry, it was a self-evident step to deploy state social and labour policy to legitimize his own politics and secure his power. In line with this, he and his advisers attached great significance and paid much attention to this policy field, particularly in the first four years of Nazi rule, that is, the phase during which the Nazis took power and consolidated their hegemony. It thus seems merely logical that, particularly before 1936, a whole range of figures and party organizations promoted their vision of Nazi social and labour policy, seeking to make themselves heard on everything from labour market measures to housing and settlement.

The DAF outdid them all. Since its foundation in May 1933 until the end of the war, its leader, Robert Ley, sought to compete with Seldte and his ministerial colleagues.[91] Ley laid claim to powers in every one of the ministry's areas of responsibility. He probably also saw himself as Hitler's real Reich labour minister. As time went by, he increasingly focused on redirecting the financial resources administered by the ministry to the DAF. Astonishingly, and despite his tremendous power-political position within Hitler's circle of advisers, Robert Ley managed to exercise virtually no influence on the ministry. He failed to get his way with respect to legislation, the ministry's established administrative duties or allotted budget items. Franz Seldte, then, together with his senior staff, succeeded in fending off Ley's encroachment on the ministry's organizational structures while also seeking to cooperate with the DAF and find an accommodation with it when it came to substantive policymaking.

Yet Ley and the DAF exercised an indirect and powerful influence on the ministry by keeping it under constant political pressure. Ley put his concerns to Hitler at regular intervals, complaining about Seldte or specific members of staff time and again. He gave speeches and published articles criticizing the ministry's policies. He commissioned the Labour Science Institute (Arbeitswissenschaftliches Institut or AWI), which was affiliated with the DAF, to produce position papers and used them to attack the ministry's legislation, whether with respect to wages policy or housing. Barely any of the ministry's areas of responsibility escaped his attention as he sought to boost his profile and promote the DAF's agenda. The ministry had to counter his accusations and digest his proposals and, not least, translate them into a compromise in order to avoid creating the impression – which was exactly what Ley intended – that the ministry was hostile to Nazi policy aspirations or was consciously seeking to oppose the DAF. The DAF's activities thus tied up a great deal of the ministry's time and energy. Together with Hitler's guiding precepts in the field of labour and social policy, this pressure will no doubt have played a role in ensuring that the ministry quickly adapted the core regulations for which it was responsible to the Hitler regime's antisemitic, racial and militaristic worldview.

4. The Reich Labour Ministry's core tasks. These adaptations were soon apparent in several legislative packages drawn up or reworked by the ministry before the end of 1933. Of these, the Law on the Organization of National Labour (Gesetz zur Ordnung der nationalen Arbeit, or AOG), adopted on 20 January 1934, had the most far-reaching consequences.[92] The immediate and fundamental reform of labour law to bring it into line with Nazi ideas – in addition to the fight against unemployment – was the Hitler regime's social policy priority. The AOG deprived workers of their collective rights to workplace participation. On the model of the Führer state, it one-sidedly advantaged employers, who were in turn kept in check by a strong state, which dictated its guidelines on working conditions and pay to them. Finally, it enabled employers and the state to profoundly curtail workers' individual rights, previously enshrined in the employment contract, if this promised to aid the Nazi 'Works Community' (Betriebsgemeinschaft).[93]

As described retrospectively by the head of Section III, Werner Mansfeld, the ministry had been caught completely off-guard by the smashing of the trades unions and thus came under tremendous pressure to act in early May 1933. What the evidence shows is that Section III immediately entered into consultations with the Reich Ministry of the Economy and with Robert Ley of the newly established DAF in order to modify the associated legal framework. The first law formulated as a result was the 'Trustee Act' (Treuhändergesetz) of 19 May 1933.[94] In future, instead of state arbitrators, so-called 'labour trustees' (Treuhänder der Arbeit) were to determine pay policies and make sure workers were upholding the 'labour peace' (*Arbeitsfrieden*). In the shape of these 'labour trustees', the ministry created a new subordinate authority, partly in order to fill the vacuum created by the dissolution of the trades unions. The first draft of the AOG was then finalized on 8 December 1933, the Cabinet passing it without much discussion despite its exceptional importance.[95] With unusual clarity, looking back Werner Mansfeld acknowledged his responsibility as the main author of this law, both morally and in terms of content. At the same time, he described the political imperatives that the ministry had to consider and the pressure imposed by Robert Ley at the negotiating table:

> When judging [the AOG] in the present day, however, one should not overlook the fact that certain basic principles had been fixed in immutable form and decreed explicitly by the then state leadership, such as putting the Führer principle (Führerprinzip) into practice in firms and ensuring that those involved [i.e. the unions and employers' associations] played no part in laying down working conditions. . . . In every consultation on a future employment regime, of which he [Robert Ley] aspired to be in overall control, though he was thwarted in this thanks to my opposition, Dr Ley – supported by the Party Chancellery – demanded a strict military order.[96]

Just how closely, right from the start, the Reich Labour Ministry was involved in Nazi policy and in what ways it facilitated such policy, given its responsibilities, and converted it into concrete action is apparent in the development of labour regulations. As in the Weimar Republic, but within a quite different political framework, the ministry continued to be the recipient of political directives. At the same time, one can discern the organization's specific interest in finding solutions – with the newly established DAF breathing down its neck – in order to assert its control over its own areas of responsibility and avoid having to cede its traditional tasks. Without further ado, ministry staff thus made the adaptations required by the political leadership's priorities, a process that extended into the use of language: 'As in the Nazi state system, in the firm, too, the principle of authoritarian leadership holds sway but also that of the Führer's unqualified and strict responsibility'.[97] The authoritarian reworking of labour law and the comprehensive state control of wages policy through the labour trustees, then, was the latest manifestation of the brutality and terror meted out to the organized labour movement and its political leaders – including the disbandment of the trades unions and the banning of the KPD and SPD.

Less prominent, but hardly less dramatic in its effects on those concerned, was the new body of laws on pension insurance. The key pieces of legislation here were the 'Rehabilitation Law' (Sanierungsgesetz) of 7 December 1933 and the so-called 'Development Law' (Aufbaugesetz) of 5 July 1934.[98] The effect of both was to cut pensions and increase contributions. The payment of pensions was linked far more than ever before with individuals' productivity and capacity for work and was no longer solely derived from the acquired entitlement to future payments based on the payment of contributions. Hence, in the context of the Nazi propagation of a Volksgemeinschaft and an achievement-based community (*Leistungsgemeinschaft*), these two laws fundamentally changed the character of the insurance system developed over previous decades.[99] In addition, insurees' right of complaint was curtailed in their wake. Overall, the evidence shows that the ministry introduced authoritarian measures with striking rapidity in the field of pension insurance as well. In contrast to labour law, however, in this field these steps were triggered not by the new political situation but by the financial crisis afflicting social insurance as a result of the global economic depression. For the measures devised by the ministry had been subject to intense discussion even before the Nazi takeover and were probably ready to hand as an off-the-shelf solution. The adaptations the ministry made in light of the Nazi regime's job creation plans, however, imposed a new framework and made such a rigid savings policy at the expense of the insured possible in the first place. The officials involved at the ministry were well aware of this. Upon publication of the 'Development Law', State Secretary Johannes Krohn, who had long worked in Main Section II, stated that such a regulation could only have been sanctioned 'by a purely authoritarian regime, never in a parliament'.[100]

For the Hitler regime, the labour administration and labour market policy were the most important of all the Reich Labour Ministry's areas of responsibility until 1936.[101] With the help of a major propaganda campaign, Hitler had tied his chancellorship to his promise to lower unemployment appreciably. A great deal has been written about the concrete measures pursued in the 'labour battle' (*Arbeitsschlacht*), to cite the martial jargon deployed by the Nazis, about the job creation programmes, the introduction of the RAD and state investment in those economic sectors that could help boost the country's military forces.[102] However, the Reich Labour Ministry and the Reich Institution for Job Placement and Unemployment Insurance were not the key players with respect to all these policies. While the ministry had already lost some of its authority over this policy field when the Weimar Republic came to an end, this tendency was now reinforced. A growing number of Nazi Party functionaries and party organizations began to encroach on the field of 'labour deployment' (*Arbeitseinsatz*). This trend gathered pace as the Nazi state geared up for impending war and intensified further during the war itself and as the Reich expanded through conquest. Once again, however, it is necessary to qualify this picture by noting that these policy takeovers related chiefly to the highest level of political decision-making. The ministry and the Reich Institution for Job Placement and Unemployment Insurance always remained directly involved in turning policies into administrative practice – giving them substantial scope for their own regulations. And here too, up to 1939 the staff of the Reich Institution and the ministry developed and proposed a succession of measures that put tremendous pressure on employees. Particularly worth noting here is the introduction of the labour book (*Arbeitsbuch*) in 1935 and the compulsory labour order (*Dienstverpflichtung*) in 1938. While the former served to collate information on employees, the latter could be used to force them to take a job. Both were the prerequisites or levers that enabled the state to 'steer' the workers and 'adapt' them – to quote the euphemistic term the authorities used – to the needs of the armaments industry. Within Nazism and with respect to the war economy, henceforth one of the ministry's core tasks was to obtain information on the workforce, and – building on this basis – to coordinate the registering and control of workers.

The few examples selected here from the Reich Labour Ministry's core areas of responsibility cast light on phenomena that are significant to its overall institutional embedding. The ministry's task was not just to issue laws and ordinances but, above all, to work out how best to put them into practice. Both dimensions must be integrated into the analysis and evaluation of the ministry's self-directed coordination [Gleichschaltung] and adaptation, which seemingly occurred so smoothly.[103] Nonetheless, looking back across time, it remains extraordinarily difficult to assess civil servants' political views in light of their action. It is also problematic to ascertain individual officials' precise degree of responsibility for these administrative processes, as they were explicitly not at their discretion. While it is true that the civil service was not a coercive organization like the police or the army, it too featured strict hierarchies and formalized, non-personalized structures of communication and instruction with which officials had to comply.[104] At the same time, the staff of the Reich Ministry of Labour – like those of other ministries – were confronted very early on and in an all-encompassing way with changes intended to embed the Nazi regime's hegemony in every sphere of life and work. The 'Hitler salute' (*der Deutsche Gruss* or German greeting) had been introduced as the official form of greeting in the ministry by July 1933. A circular issued by the Ministry of the Interior informed Labour Ministry staff that they were expected to make the salute not just within the institution but even 'when not on duty'.[105] There was, no doubt, some scope for individuals to avoid doing so, within a particular office or section, but it may be assumed that such room for manoeuvre diminished over time.

To prevent possible deviations from the official political line, in its civil service policy the Nazi regime pursued a diffuse combination of propaganda, intimidation and incentives that touched on fundamental aspects of civil servants' status. This found reflection in the Reich Ministry of Labour. In July 1933, officials were explicitly ordered to put up political posters in the ministry's offices – a visible and telling break with the Weimar Republic, in which civil servants were permitted to engage in political activity in private but not at work. They were now explicitly enjoined to view themselves as politically active 'national comrades' (*Volksgenossen*) and to present their role in these terms to the outside world. All civil servants in the ministry were given time off work to vote in elections and plebiscites or participate in Nazi Party conferences and party-ordained physical exercises. Participation remained voluntary – yet every civil servant was required to play a 'political vanguard role', so one's loyalty to the state was constantly at issue. It was far from insignificant, particularly among officials with some way to go along the career ladder, that their individual efforts on the political front were associated with recognition and institutional support, such as special paid leave. As clearly defined and privileged servants of the state, the new realities required of civil servants, more than other occupational groups, that they regularly inform their employer about their private affairs. Henceforth, the Nazi Party subjected them to political evaluation. They had to prove they were 'Aryan' and, if married, that their spouse was 'Aryan' too, and that they had never been members of any 'Marxist' parties. Members of ministry staff who attempted to avoid making such statements could expect measures, sometimes of a draconian nature, to be taken against them. Anyone wishing to leave the Nazi Party from 1936 onwards was threatened with dismissal from the ministry.[106] When the Civil Service Law was implemented, ancillary staff (*Hilfskräfte*) without the status of civil servant who had made inaccurate statements about previous party membership or their 'Aryan' descent were summarily dismissed from December 1933 onwards.[107]

Furthermore, ministerial officials were regularly confronted with administrative tasks that served to implement specific aspects of Nazi ideology and facilitate the political leadership's access to individuals or specific groups of people. A significant portion of the Berlin headquarters' core duties consisted in collating, analysing and making available information about its entire field of responsibility. It produced statistical data on job placement and economic cycles, sectoral economic trends and labour protection. But officials also collected and aggregated personal data about insurees, those entitled to benefits and the sick. This information now became relevant to the agencies tasked with implementing Nazi policies of discrimination and persecution. For example, in January 1935 the ministry was instructed to help improve access to medical records detailing the examinations undertaken to determine 'the physical and mental fitness and, even more importantly, the hereditary characteristics (*Erbanlagen*)' of party candidates and those applying for posts in the various Nazi organizations.[108] Officials could scarcely refuse to hand over these and other files, making them accomplices to the Nazi state's racist and antisemitic policies.

In sum, given its core functions, the Reich Ministry of Labour played an important role in advancing the projects pursued by the Nazi state. It is clear that between 1933 and 1945, Seldte's ministry in no way became less relevant or less politically present. The Nazis were aware that they were reliant on the existing administrative structures and the ministry's expertise if they wished to use labour and social policy to achieve their goals. The significance of the ministry's various areas of responsibility, meanwhile, varied over the course of time, and each requires analysis on a case-by-case basis. Moreover, the conditions under which all the ministry's sections worked depended on shifts in the Hitler regime's ideological and political priorities. This became especially evident when the state stepped up the production of arms from 1936 onwards, when Hitler launched his aggressive policy of expansion in early 1938, and during the war.

5. The Reich Ministry of Labour under the conditions of Nazi expansionism and the war economy, 1938–1945. The Four-Year Plan, which began in 1936, was a significant turning point with respect to the labour administration and wages policy.[109] Hermann Göring, Hitler's commissioner for the Four-Year Plan, established an office within his Four-Year Plan Authority (Vierjahresplanbehörde) specifically dedicated to labour deployment,[110] which was answerable to Friedrich Syrup and Werner Mansfeld at the Reich Ministry of Labour. Externally, the new office's task was to mitigate the lack – felt since 1936 – of skilled workers in industries important to the war effort.[111] When it came to the internal organization of those parts of the Reich Labour Ministry concerned with labour deployment, meanwhile, the Four-Year Plan Authority now began to coordinate the intensified programme of arms production and preparation for war. This institutional change also applied to other ministries, but especially the Ministry of the Economy. The ministries were not only allocated new duties but also saw a shift in the chain of command. Henceforth, Göring was authorized to tap the relevant ministries' resources and, in case of doubt, was authorized to issue the ministers with instructions, a right he exercised in many instances. For the most part, this 'takeover' occurred with very little fuss and was barely questioned, at least within the Reich Ministry of Labour, because the leading officials there retained the initiative with respect to their areas of specialization. Nonetheless, this shift of powers was the first

indication of one of the Hitler regime's most striking characteristics, which made a particular impact on the Reich Labour Ministry, with its diverse responsibilities, namely the burgeoning commissarial system. Time and again Hitler appointed various commissioners (*Kommissare*) or plenipotentiaries (*Sonderbevollmächtigten*), who were supposed to carry out a specific and temporary task more quickly, more flexibly and 'more unbureaucratically', sometimes with and sometimes without their own agency and organizational substructure.[112] For the ministries, this growth in new agencies and offices working within their fields of responsibility not only meant a source of competition over jurisdiction and resources. Far more seriously, an increasing number of party agencies and offices sprang up that did not feel beholden to the ministries' formal, legalistic procedures – and that frequently departed from them. Over time, the ministries found themselves confronted ever more often with situations in which they were neither listened to nor consulted. This not only meant a loss of political power. Above all there was a lack of central, substantive coordination of the work that was now being done in parallel. The Reich Chancellery was unable to perform this coordinating role over the long term because increasingly, but during the war at the latest, it too became less important to Hitler's decisions.

Significant in this connection – within the Reich Labour Ministry's field of responsibility – is the appointment of Gauleiter (Gau leader, head of a Nazi Party district) Fritz Sauckel as GBA in March 1942 and that of Robert Ley as Reich housing commissioner (Reichswohnungskommissar) in October 1942.[113] The appointment of two more plenipotentiaries profoundly affected the Reich Labour Ministry's image. It gave the institution a reputation – disseminated above all by Albert Speer – as a 'rump ministry headed by a weak minister'.[114] There was, however, no connection between the two appointments on the level of substantive content or anything else; they were markedly different. To put it in a nutshell, Robert Ley generated numerous problems for the ministry, while the appointment of Fritz Sauckel relieved it of a major problem.

That Robert Ley tended to fight for authority only to immediately 'launch into a new battle for new powers' is confirmed by his work as Reich housing commissioner.[115] He had no interest in policymaking and behaved erratically and often with no discernible plan. He appointed his own staff but ceased to trust them at the first opportunity.[116] Closer inspection, moreover, reveals that the while ministry staff now had to comply with his instructions, they generally maintained their routines. Overall, then, his activities made little impact, not least because house-building came to a standstill during the war, construction materials were needed for war-related tasks and Ley's visions of the building of social housing in the middle of an aerial war inevitably seemed unrealistic and bizarre. It might be argued that as

Reich housing commissioner Ley epitomized the ham-fisted party functionary bringing chaos to the state's administrative structures. Rather than solving problems 'unbureaucratically', he simply created more.

The situation in the labour administration was quite different. Since the launch of the Four-Year Plan of 1936, labour deployment had already been regarded as important to the war effort; it was soon to become decisive to it.[117] Even before the outbreak of the Second World War, a range of quite different actors on the senior leadership level had attempted to gain acceptance for their particular ideas about labour deployment. From 1938, for example, in addition to the Wehrmacht authorities, newly appointed Reich defence commissioners (Reichsverteidigungskommissare) registered their demands.[118] When the war broke out, they were joined by Hitler's new appointees – Gauleiters, military commanders, Reich protectors and other new office-holders in the occupied territories. All of them were granted various powers over and rights of access to the labour force. The Reich Labour Ministry and its labour administration, therefore, while responsible for such matters across the board, increasingly lost actual power because there was no central, overarching coordination of labour deployment in the Reich or the occupied territories. Yet in the exceptional circumstances of war, and given the immense territorial expansion that occurred, such coordination was a prerequisite for an efficient labour administration.

Ultimately, it was only the creation of the GBA in March 1942 that solved the ministry's enforcement problems. In contrast to Ley, Sauckel and his planning staff did not undermine the ministry's regulatory function, expertise or organization. Instead, within the labour administration's chain of command they availed themselves, without further ado, of the ministry's sections and its resources, if necessary in opposition to Labour Minister Seldte, who had to make concessions. Sauckel brooked no interference when it came to staffing decisions, established a new Main Section VI (Europe Office for Labour Deployment; Europaamt für den Arbeitseinsatz) and a number of departments (*Referate*), issuing directives as he saw fit. This may have been detrimental to Seldte's reputation and the esteem in which he was held, yet it eased the burden on the ministry significantly because it allowed those of its sections concerned with labour deployment to get on with their work. This enhanced the efficiency of the measures implemented within the Reich Deployment programme (Reichseinsatz) and accelerated the recruitment of foreign and forced labourers – with fatal consequences for millions of people throughout Europe.

Sauckel as an individual became crucially important in this context. He took charge of diplomacy at the highest level on the ministry's behalf and kept the party functionaries and Gauleiters in the 'Old Reich' and occupied territories in check, for which he possessed the necessary authority and powers. He had direct access to Hitler and could also give competitors in the field of labour recruitment, such as Speer, a run for their money. In this sense, the GBA reflected the 'elasticity', 'flexibility' and 'catastrophic efficiency' of a system of administrative organization in which the existing administrative bodies developed a form of cooperation with intelligent and determined party functionaries, which explains the comparatively long duration and efficiency of the Nazi state, particularly during the war.[119] From late 1938 onwards, Seldte, his state secretaries (Engel, Krohn and Syrup) and senior staff generally lacked the formal position or power-political strength to implement decisions at the highest level. This was clearly linked with the shift in Hitler's policies, away from domestic and international stabilization towards radical expansionism.

The new political climate took on palpable form for the Reich Labour Ministry following the annexation of Austria in March 1938. For the relevant officials at the ministry, the so-called 'Anschluss' triggered the first 'takeover' in the wake of the Nazi policy of expansion. For the organization of the ministry and for its officials, this was to be an experience that adumbrated the shape of things to come: not only was the state playing the role of occupier for the first time, but the ministry's powers and political freedom of movement underwent dramatic curtailment. After German troops had marched into Vienna, Hitler declared the Austrian state part of the German Reich territory, which meant that the German administrative system was to be established there. For ministry officials it was beyond question that the administrative authorities in the 'Eastern March' (Ostmark) – from the labour trustees to the system of insurance for white-collar workers – must precisely reflect their German equivalents. Heterogeneous administrative structures would severely hamper their ability to cope with the tasks at hand.[120] However, the relevant officials had barely taken the first steps in this direction when they found themselves facing massive opposition from party functionaries among the staff of Josef Bürckel, Reich commissioner for the reunification of Austria with the German Reich (Reichskommissar für die Wiedervereinigung Österreichs mit dem Deutschen Reich). With Hitler's backing, Bürckel and a number of Gauleiters wished to use the foreign policy success of the 'Anschluss' to enhance their scope for action vis-à-vis the Reich administration. The plan was for the Gaus to unite all mid-level administrative powers under the leadership of the Gauleiters. The central Reich administration in Berlin would thus have to cede its responsibilities and budgetary authority in the Länder. Bürckel deliberately demanded from the ministries powers of such a far-reaching nature that they had no choice but to protest. He deftly used the resulting conflict to his own ends. These clashes took up time and created a vacuum in the ministries' substantive policy work as no decision had yet been made on how to divide up the administrative districts in Austria. In the absence of these districts, the ministries were unable to set up their subordinate agencies. In the meantime, Bürckel and his local staff preempted important decisions. They filled key positions with their cronies and deliberately locked the ministerial section heads and state secretaries out of the decision-making process. This strategy had a significant impact on the Reich Labour Ministry with its large and complex administrative substructure. For example, the decision to dissolve the Federal Ministry for Social Administration (Bundesministerium für Soziale Verwaltung) in Vienna – that is, the Reich Labour Ministry's counterpart within the Austrian system – was taken with no involvement of the latter.[121] Ultimately, Bürckel established the new administrative districts himself, transferring the disbanded institution's responsibilities to other ministries.

Hitler's new course now became relevant on the level of symbolic politics as well. In June 1938, Reich Labour Minister Franz Seldte came under open attack when a new labour trustee was appointed for Austria. During a visit to Vienna, he had been asked to back the candidate proposed by Bürckel, namely Alfred Proksch, who had been one of the Führer's schoolmates. Once his appointment had been processed through the official channels in the usual way, Seldte had his state secretary inform the candidate that he could present himself to Seldte in Berlin. Rather than making the trip to Berlin, however, Proksch immediately occupied the office of the previous trustee in Vienna, terminated his telephone connection and lease agreement and decreed the 'relocation of his agency'.[122] The Reich Labour Ministry had to confirm Proksch's appointment shortly afterwards. Events like this were unprecedented provocations with respect to ministries' normal working practices. But it was extremely difficult for the ministry to take a stand against them because they came from the government itself. Bürckel was able to get away with these political intrigues because Hitler gave him free rein to push the ministerial administration out of the Land-level administrative apparatus, an objective that became particularly apparent in the regulations on the administrative organization of the newly occupied territories of the Sudetenland, the Reich Protectorate of Bohemia and Moravia (Reichsprotektorat Böhmen und Mähren) and in the occupation of Poland. With the exception of finance, the postal service and the Reich Railways (Reichsbahn), the ministries were largely ousted from the political decision-making process – in favour of the Gau administration in the Reich Gaus and by a wide variety of authorities in the occupied territories (Reich protectors, military or civilian commissioners and the SS [Schutzstaffel, literally 'Protection Squadron']).

For the Reich Labour Ministry and all other affected ministries, this affront signified a clear diminution in their powers of enforcement. They were in principle excluded from political decision-making at the highest level of leadership. Though Adolf Hitler had decreed the formal annexation of a given territory and its alignment with Reich law, only at an intermediate structural level did the Reich Labour Ministry construct its welfare administration on the model of the Reich. In all other cases, depending on an occupied territory's legal status and the requirements of 'Volkstumspolitik' (folkdom policy, where folkdom refers to the shared personality of an entire ethno-nation), bespoke divisions covering the ministry's responsibilities were integrated into a given occupation administration. Often, this administration was no longer directly subordinate to the ministry, limiting the Berlin headquarters' influence on decisions at the local level. The Reich Labour Ministry was present in the occupied territories as a regulatory authority but was now barely visible as an independent actor on the political stage.

During the war and in the various war zones, this was partly because the ministry, as a civilian authority, had no authority over police, security and military agencies. The extent to which its headquarters in Berlin was nonetheless able to influence decisions depended on the specific status of its subordinate authorities within a given occupation administration. Of course, the ministry still had its policy expertise, legislative powers and, above all, financial, staffing and infrastructural resources. So it still had to be consulted and involved in many decisions and processes. Informal links and forms of cooperation are also likely to have played an important role. For example, the Reich Labour Ministry was involved to a significant degree in coordinating and acquiring information about the various Länder, produced statistics on welfare and social affairs and carried out cost-benefit analyses relevant to the execution of various tasks in the occupied territories. Moreover, the Berlin headquarters coordinated the dispatch of its own personnel and, importantly, made available financial resources for wages policies or other social policy instruments in the occupied territories. The specific tasks taken on by the headquarters in these cases, meanwhile, were highly dependent on the political and administrative structures established in a given occupied territory. It is, for example, virtually impossible to compare conditions in occupied Belgium with those in the Protectorate of Bohemia and Moravia. While there was very little scope for the ministry's representatives in Belgium to intervene in the organization of its administrative apparatus, officials in the German labour administration autonomously steered elements of the labour administration in the Protectorate.[123]

Due to the significant growth of wartime administrative tasks, then, the ministry neither 'shrank' nor was it 'gutted' by other authorities. On the contrary, its areas of responsibility increased between 1936 and 1943 –

from the expanded system of trustees to labour deployment. Its staff also grew significantly during this period. This growth made itself felt chiefly on the intermediate and lower levels, that is, in the regional, district and municipal administrative authorities. As the war raged and as a result of the organizational steps taken to simplify the state administration, these authorities increasingly took on the concrete tasks of administration. How did the Reich Labour Ministry's labour and social administration cope with its duties as the war progressed? Here too the overall picture was anything but uniform. In addition to the transfer of resources, mentioned above, from the headquarters to other authorities and offices, the mid-level authorities were of crucial importance during the war and occupation. Only on this level was the Reich Labour Ministry present 'locally' in a concrete way, and it was chiefly here that its officials could become embroiled in the Nazis' mass crimes and the Holocaust.

Finally, what does all this mean when it comes to Franz Seldte's position in the ministry and the ministry's role within Nazism? Mainly because of his physical afflictions, Seldte offered Hitler his resignation on several occasions. Hitler refused every time and confirmed him in office. In order to hang onto him, the Reich Chancellery even provided him with a regular bonus.[124] This indicates that Hitler regarded Seldte as a de facto useful minister. Plainly, until the end of 1945, the advantages of having Seldte at the head of the ministry outweighed the disadvantages, not least his ability to keep the organization on course while simultaneously hedging in Robert Ley and the DAF. The lack of direct access to Hitler can scarcely be seen as persuasive evidence of a lack of appreciation since virtually all ministers were in the same boat in this regard. Leaving an incompetent and weak minister in post as an act of 'mercy' would have run counter to the vision of the Führer's state long cultivated by Hitler, one in which the strongest prevailed in a 'natural way'.[125] But the importance of the Reich Labour Ministry itself also contradicts such an interpretation. It is probably significant that in the first few years of the Nazi regime, until 1938, labour and social policy was regarded as too important to its legitimacy, and to ensuring the loyalty of the population, to put it at risk in any way through personally or ideologically motivated power struggles. Together with his senior officials, Seldte ensured the necessary stability. Precisely how he managed this is very difficult to determine through the sources produced within the ministry. In any case, the senior officials loyally assisted him, which must in itself be regarded as a leadership quality. When the wartime situation and occupation caused profound shifts in the entire fabric of political operations in Berlin, those ministries not directly relevant to the war suffered a general loss of importance within Hitler's regime. To sum up, then, in seeking to grasp and describe Seldte's position within the Nazi state, the notion that he was a weak minister requires significant qualification. Further research on his professional networks and those of his senior officials could be particularly valuable to evaluating his effectiveness more precisely. The notion of the 'weak' minister is consonant with the picture painted by contemporaries, ranging from Albert Speer to senior officials such as Werner Mansfeld, as an element in their strategy of exoneration shortly after 1945. This idea was reinforced when Seldte himself constructed the same narrative to avert charges against him and his officials. Ultimately, the fact that this notion has persisted to this day is also due to the fact that the supposedly technical matters typical of the social and labour administration have so far been seen as less important than seemingly more politically charged topics such as policy on armaments or occupation.

Closing Remarks

Any attempt to sum up the role and activities of the Reich Labour Ministry between 1919 and 1945 must inevitably make generalizations and some audacious chronological leaps. The responsibilities entrusted to the ministry over the years were too complex, heterogeneous and technical to make specific statements that go beyond particular phases (foundation, consolidation, Nazi seizure of power, military build-up, war-related tasks). Nonetheless, in what follows, I attempt to condense and highlight a number of general observations, thus providing a basis for future discussions on the significance of the Reich Labour Ministry until 1945, while at the same time formulating overarching research questions on the ministerial administration within Nazism.

Founded in exceptional political circumstances, in an astonishingly short period of time the ministry managed to put down roots in the Weimar Republic. It became indispensable amid the historical realities of post-First World War Germany. Despite all the debates on the pros and cons of state social policy, it supported millions of people, helping supplement individual incomes during a time of political and economic crisis. The ministry's political success, then, lay in the relevance of the topics with which it was concerned. Issues of labour and social policy, in all their complexity, represented a core pillar of public debate and politics in the Weimar Republic. In fact, to a large degree they legitimized the first German democracy – as well as Hitler's dictatorship. As a result, in spite of all the opposition to and debate over this ministry, it proved indispensable after the First World War. Curbing unemployment, providing support for war victims and invalids, assessing and paying pensions, providing housing – no government, whether of a democratic or authoritarian nature, could afford to ignore these imperatives.

The ministry owed its rapid establishment to committed and qualified staff, who spent much of their professional life within the organization. In line with this, it was distinguished by a strikingly high degree of continuity on the level of both personnel and structure. What emerged as a result was a kind of nonpartisan corporate identity, which contributed to its organizational stability, particularly in the context of the world economic crisis and the Nazi seizure of power. The fact that the ministerial officials had managed, within a short period of time, to construct a functional structure for the ministry's many areas of responsibility made at least parts of the organization unassailable. A key aspect here was the delegation of its core tasks to subordinate bodies, making it more difficult for external actors to encroach on it. The Nazis, who made great efforts to centralize the administrative system, could not simply 'take over' the Reich Ministry of Labour, nor, despite frequently proclaiming their will to do so, could they straightforwardly alter its internal chains of command. The risk of causing serious disruption to the processes occurring within this many-tiered organization was simply too great. If the Nazis wished to keep their promises with respect to labour and social policy and thus retain the backing of the general population, they were reliant upon the expertise of the Reich Labour Ministry and its agencies. This explains, among other things, why Franz Seldte remained in office until the end of the war. In Seldte, Hitler had a minister who ensured the necessary degree of constancy. Hitler himself did not, and had no wish to, involve himself in the ministry's day-to-day operations or in the reality of concrete administrative processes.

It was the self-image and external perception of ministerial officials as objective experts that undergirded the ministry's high degree of continuity in terms of staff and institutionally. Many of them were unquestionably specialists in their particular field. And it was in this high regard for such specialist knowledge that the ministry's *esprit de corps* was rooted. But one may also interpret officials' references to 'objective' and 'technical' themes – communicated in an administrative language pervaded by legal formulae – as an attempt to cope with the political challenges of the fragile Weimar Republic and fend off attacks on the ministry. Ministry officials also benefited from this crisis management after 1933. However, this implicit or explicit emphasis on 'objectivity' should not be viewed as merely a technocratic variant of the political radicalism described by Ulrich Herbert with reference to the 'generation of objectivity' (*Sachlichkeit*). It was in fact more a facet of ministerial officials' self-image.[126] Looking back from the present day, it is scarcely possible to determine to what extent this self-image was underpinned by strategic considerations or was the authentic stance of individual members of staff. Certainly, the sources leave one with the impression that many members of the ministry's staff had no wish to become the henchmen of a radical regime. Oskar Karstedt's engagement is a case in point. As yet, the personnel files of the Reich Chancellery, Presidential Chancellery (Präsidialkanzlei) and Party Chancellery have failed to turn up further examples of any form of resistance to implementing Nazi policies. Next to nothing is known about ministry officials' stance on political events when not on duty, though it is surely out of the question to impute support for Nazi ideology to them on a collective basis. When it comes to the historical evaluation of the ministry's moral and material responsibility as an organization within Nazism, what this means is that generalizing statements are essentially impossible. Instead, the imperative must be to investigate the individual acts and attitudes of specific officials in key positions.

This throws up the question of whether there was individual room for manoeuvre within the narrowly defined and highly formalized professional structures of the organization, and in what respect individual officials or groups of officials acted to expedite or slow, if not obstruct, the implementation of Nazi ideas and plans. After the Second World War, within both the public sphere and among historical researchers, an image took hold of a 'closed cast' of politically (arch-)conservative, antidemocratic ministerial officials inclined towards state authoritarianism, both in the Weimar Republic and under the Nazis.[127] When it comes to the actions of officials under Nazism, two evaluations are bound up with this. On the one hand, some have claimed that the ministerial administration exercised a moderating influence, that some officials sought to counter the worst excesses of the Nazi regime. Others have suggested that civil servants degenerated into Hitler's compliant dupes, zealously implementing his ideas and enhancing the regime's effectiveness.[128] While there is evidence to back both assessments within the Reich Labour Ministry, it is inadequate to apply either of these assessments pars pro toto to the ministry, let alone the entire ministerial administration – and simply leave it at that. As examination of the Reich Labour Ministry and the conduct of its sections and staff shows, how easy or difficult it was to maintain control over specific administrative realms in the face, for example, of intervention by party agencies largely depended on specific circumstances, whether in terms of personnel or policy area, and on the actors involved. When it came to Robert Ley's demands for more powers as Reich housing commissioner, the leadership and the relevant section of the Reich Labour Ministry managed to fend off his encroachment over a long span of time. Conversely, Fritz Sauckel's takeover, as a figure at the highest level of diplomacy within Hitler's inner circle, solved serious problems hampering the ministry's capacity for enforcement within the labour administration. When studying the ministerial administration, therefore, researchers should seek to demonstrate the validity of concepts such as 'overzealous obedience' or 'bureaucratic moderation' in light of such specific constellations of actors rather than simply adopting them as sweeping, decontextualized categories. As indicated above, within the Reich Labour Ministry's area of responsibility alone, only to a limited extent do such categories allow us to grasp the specific conditions in the fields of housing or labour administration, for example. The same goes for our efforts to characterize the Reich Labour Ministry as a whole. Before concluding that the ministry was a remnant of bourgeois-liberal ideas under the Nazi state, one would have to compare all its areas of responsibility and relate them to one another. The adaptations made within the field of labour law, for example, generally point to autocratic attitudes and support for a strong, interventionist state among ministry staff. It remains to be established whether such views also held sway when it came to support for war victims.

However, this overarching perspective should not obscure one key function of the officials in the ministries, including those employed at the Reich Labour Ministry. Often quite unnoticed by those engaged in 'grand politics', they pursued their work on detailed issues within the context of everyday practice and put political precepts into practice. This was not a 'pure' or 'neutral' form of implementation but rather a process in which officials' daily work and attempts to solve specific problems fed back into 'grand politics'. In line with this, it would be quite wrong to refer to an unpolitical 'bureaucracy' or officials with a purely implementing role who concealed their 'ideological orientation'.[129] On the contrary, it is crucial not to underestimate the significance of the role played by the administrative system in setting standards and institutionalizing regulations on social and labour policy. The labour book is an example. In order to determine, precisely and systematically, this contribution to standard-setting and administrative practice, it is vital to analyse the organization of the administrative apparatus and to engage with the logic of administrative processes. Otherwise it will be impossible to discover the concrete administrative techniques that might reveal how much explicit or implicit say officials actually had.

In sum, most of the evidence points to a deft institutional strategy of adaptation, with the help of which the ministry and its staff secured its powers over the various thematic fields and discharged its new institutional role of executive responsibility. In this sense, it is possible to confirm the presence of the ideal-typical criteria formulated by Max Weber, namely a rationally-acting administrative apparatus focused on formalized procedures. The history of the Reich Labour Ministry within the Weimar Republic and under the Nazis, however, also provides plenty of scope to flesh out empirically and differentiate these ideal-typical observations and link them with a historical dynamic not witnessed by the Webers. This involves disrupted routines, many technical inadequacies, failed processes of coordination, failures of modernization and conflictual gridlock within the administrative work itself. Also part of this picture is the often tremendous, virtually unmanageable pressure piled on the ministry by lobbying organizations and interest groups within the Weimar Republic, and the dualism, of such intense power-political dynamism, between the state and party authorities under Nazism. The picture, derived from Max Weber's studies, of an efficient administrative machine adhering to objective principles can certainly be found in historical actors' self-descriptions. Yet it would be misleading and anachronistic to deploy the contemporary belief in the possibility of an 'objective' and 'rational' administration as an analytical approach to present-day historical research, or to believe that this model represents the historical reality. Here a process of historicization is necessary in order to obtain a more nuanced grasp of the significance of the administrative apparatus to political action and the historical structures of governance in both the Weimar Republic and the Nazi state.

Ulrike Schulz, Dr. phil., research fellow in the Department of Social Sciences and Public Affairs, University of the Armed Forces, Munich; research associate (2014–2018) for the project being undertaken by the Independent Commission of Historians Investigating the History of the Reich Ministry of Labour in the National Socialist Period. Publications include: 'The First Takeover. The Implementation of Social Policy Measures in Austria by the Reich Labour Ministry after the Anschluss', in S. Kott and K.K. Patel (eds), *Nazism across Borders. The Social Policies of the Third Reich and their Global Appeal* (Oxford University Press, 2018), 53–79; with Thomas Welskopp, 'Wieviel kapitalistisches Unternehmen steckte in den Betrieben des real existierenden Sozialismus? Konzeptionelle Überlegungen und ein Fallbeispiel', *Jahrbuch für Wirtschaftsgeschichte* 58(2) (2017), 317–30; *Simson, 1856–1993. Vom unwahrscheinlichen Überleben eines Unternehmens* (Wallstein, 2013).

Notes

1. A. Weber, 'Der Beamte', *Die Neue Rundschau* 21(4) (1910), 1321–39, here 1328.
2. M. Weber, *Wirtschaft und Gesellschaft*, Tübingen: Mohr, 1972, 125–28; H.-U. Derlien, D. Böhme and M. Heindl, *Bürokratietheorie. Einführung in eine Theorie der Verwaltung*, Wiesbaden: Verlag für Sozialwissenschaften, 2011, 19–66.
3. P. Becker, 'Bürokratie, Version: 1.0', in *Docupedia-Zeitgeschichte*, 30 August 2016, retrieved 27 September 2018 from http://docupedia.de/zg/Becker_buerokratie_v1_de_2016.
4. Decree, Concerning the Establishment and Designation of the Supreme Reich Authorities, 21 March 1919, *RGBl*. 1919, 327–28.
5. See especially the Reichstag debates (*Verhandlungen des Reichstags*, vol. 310/311,

1917) on the establishment of a Reich Labour Office and, on the general context, R. vom Bruch (ed.), *Weder Kommunismus noch Kapitalismus. Bürgerliche Sozialreform in Deutschland vom Vormärz bis zur Ära Adenauer*, Munich: Beck, 1985.

6. See T.B. Müller and A. Tooze, 'Demokratie nach dem Ersten Weltkrieg', in Müller and Tooze (eds), *Normalität und Fragilität: Demokratie nach dem Ersten Weltkrieg*, Hamburg: Hamburger Edition, 2015, 9–36.

7. For detailed information on Franz Seldte, see Biographical Appendix.

8. Memorandum on the development of the Reich Office of the Interior and its subdivision, in *Verhandlungen des Reichstags* (1914/18), vol. 321, no. 1025, attachment II, 8–12.

9. H. Geib, 'Zur Organisationsgeschichte des Reichsarbeitsministeriums', *RABl.* II (1928), 196.

10. PA Gustav Bauer, 1918–1926, Bundesarchiv (BArch), R 3901/100039; and P. Mayer, 'G. Bauer', in Historische Kommission bei der Bayerischen Akademie der Wissenschaften (ed.), *Neue Deutsche Biographie*, vol. 1, Berlin, 1953, 638.

11. G.A. Ritter, *Soziale Frage und Sozialpolitik in Deutschland seit Beginn des 19. Jahrhunderts*, Opladen: Leske + Budrich, 1998, 27–69.

12. See E. Hobsbawm, *The Age of Extremes. A History of the World, 1914–1991*, New York: Pantheon Books, 1994.

13. H.A. Winkler, *Von der Revolution zur Stabilisierung. Arbeiter und Arbeiterbewegung in der Weimarer Republik, 1918 bis 1924*, Berlin: Dietz, 1984; K. Tenfelde and U. Borsdorf (eds), *Geschichte der deutschen Gewerkschaften von den Anfängen bis 1945*, Cologne: Bund, 1987; T. Welskopp, *Das Banner der Brüderlichkeit. Die deutsche Sozialdemokratie vom Vormärz bis zum Sozialistengesetz*, Bonn: Dietz, 2000.

14. K.C. Führer et al. (eds), *Revolution und Arbeiterbewegung in Deutschland 1918–1920*, Essen: Klartext, 2013; G.A. Ritter, *Arbeiter, Arbeiterbewegung und soziale Ideen in Deutschland. Beiträge zur Geschichte des 19. und 20. Jahrhunderts*, Munich: Beck, 1998; G.D. Feldman, *Army, Industry and Labor in Germany. 1914–1918*, Princeton, NJ: Princeton University Press, 1966.

15. G. Hartrodt, 'Rückblick auf die organisatorischen Reformarbeiten im Geschäftsbereich des Reichsarbeitsministeriums', *RABl.* II (1929), 179.

16. *RGBl.* I 1920, 147–85.

17. K.C. Führer, *Arbeitslosigkeit und die Entstehung der Arbeitslosenversicherung in Deutschland. 1902–1927*, Berlin: Colloquium, 1990.

18. See the chapter by Karl Christian Führer in this volume; and L. Niethammer, 'Ein langer Marsch durch die Institutionen. Zur Vorgeschichte des preussischen Wohnungsgesetzes 1918', in Niethammer (ed.), *Wohnen im Wandel: Beiträge zur Geschichte des Alltags in der bürgerlichen Gesellschaft*, Wuppertal: Hammer, 1979, 363–84.

19. Transfer of Social Services to the Reich Ministry of Labour, 30 October 1919, BArch, R 3901/6875, fol. 177–79.

20. Reich Ministry of Labour, Re. Plan of Distribution for the Departments taken over from the Ministry for Economic Demobilization and the War Office (Kriegsamt), May 1919, BArch, R 43 I/916, fol. 5; Heinrich Brauns, Re. Transfer of Central Oversight of Explosives and Munitions Factories, 28 May 1924, Bayerisches Hauptstaatsarchiv, MA/103597.

21. Geib, 'Organisationsgeschichte'.

22. Reich Ministry of Labour, Schedule of Responsibilities 1919, 1 July 1919, BArch, R 43 I/916, fol. 6–23.

23. The Reich Ministry of the Interior got its way in both cases; see Reichsgesundheitsamt (ed.), *Das Reichsgesundheitsamt 1876–1926. Festschrift aus Anlass seines 50jährigen Bestehens*, Berlin: Springer, 1926, 22; C. Sachsse and F. Tennstedt, *Geschichte der Armenfürsorge in Deutschland*, vol. 2: *Fürsorge und Wohlfahrtspflege 1871–1929*, Stuttgart: Kohlhammer, 1988, 108–72; A.C. Hüntelmann, *Hygiene im Namen des Staates. Das Reichsgesundheitsamt 1876–1933*, Göttingen: Wallstein, 2008, 135–43.

24. PA Alexander Schlicke, 1919–1920, BArch, R 3901/100802.
25. For detailed information on Heinrich Brauns, see Biographical Appendix.
26. PA Dr Heinrich Brauns, 1920–June 1933, BArch, R 3901/100094.
27. H. Brauns, 'Entwicklung der Sozialpolitik', *RABl.* II (1928), 194–96.
28. H. Mockenhaupt, *Weg und Wirken des geistlichen Sozialpolitikers Heinrich Brauns 1868–1939*, Munich: Schöningh, 1977, 156.
29. For detailed information on Hermann Geib, see Biographical Appendix.
30. Geib, Re. Correspondence A–Z, BArch, N 2091, vol. 1–2.
31. The caveat, however, is that the personnel files and other sources contain only scattered indications of party membership. The only option here is to identify the general trends; see the database of the research project on the history of the Reich Ministry of Labour.
32. For detailed information on Dorothea Hirschfeld, see Biographical Appendix.
33. G. Hartrodt, *Die Ausstellung. Die Arbeitsgebiete des Reichsarbeitsministeriums*, Berlin: Reichsdruckerei, 1929, 14.
34. Ibid., 15; W. Berg, '§ 8 Arbeits- und Sozialverwaltung', in K.G. Jeserich, H. Pohl and G.-C. Unruh (eds), *Deutsche Verwaltungsgeschichte*, vol. 4: *Das Reich als Republik und im Nationalsozialismus*, Stuttgart: Deutsche Verlags-Anstalt, 1985, 231–41.
35. The organizational development of the labour administration followed a very specific course between 1919 and 1945, which, moreover, underwent frequent alteration; see the chapter by Henry Marx in this volume.
36. On the organization of Housing and Settlement, see also the chapter by Karl Christian Führer in this volume.
37. For an incisive example of the debate, see Vollweiler, 'Das Problem der Verfahrensvereinfachung in der Sozialverwaltung', *Reichsverwaltungsblatt* 62(19) (1941), 300–306.
38. See the chapter by Kiran Klaus Patel and Sandrine Kott in this volume.
39. A. Klimo, 'An Unhappy Return: German Pension Insurance Policy in Alsace', in S. Kott and K.K. Patel (eds), *Nazism across Borders. The Social Policies of the Third Reich and their Global Appeal*, Oxford: Oxford University Press, 2018, 81–104.
40. The following remarks on working regulations and on staff members' everyday reality are based on the news bulletins and circular decrees issued by the Reich Ministry of Labour within its sphere of responsibility from 1920 to 1929.
41. On the ministry, see above all F. Syrup, *Hundert Jahre staatliche Sozialpolitik 1839–1939. Aus dem Nachlass von Friedrich Syrup*, general ed. J. Scheuble, ed. O. Neuloh, Stuttgart: Kohlhammer, 1957, 233–386; L. Preller, *Sozialpolitik in der Weimarer Republik*, Kronsberg/Ts.: Athenäum, 1978, 433–98.
42. Reich Budgets 1929–1932, Berlin 1929–1932.
43. Reich Institution for Job Placement and Unemployment Insurance, Proposals and Measures to Combat Unemployment, 1931, Geheimes Staatsarchiv Preussischer Kulturbesitz, I. HA Rep. 77, MdI, Dept. I General Dept, sec. 19, heading 923, no. 16, vol. 1; C. Berringer, *Sozialpolitik in der Weltwirtschaftskrise. Die Arbeitslosenversicherungspolitik in Deutschland und Grossbritannien im Vergleich*, Berlin: Duncker & Humblot, 1999; G. Golla, *Nationalsozialistische Arbeitsbeschaffung in Theorie und Praxis*, Aachen: Shaker, 2008.
44. Geib, Re. Speech of Introduction to the Meeting on Compulsory Labour Service, 17 January 1931, BArch, N 2091/8, fol. 42–48.
45. M. Zschucke, 'Die Verordnung über die Kurzarbeiter', *RABl.* II (1934), 425–28.
46. M. Broszat, *Der Staat Hitlers. Grundlegung und Entwicklung seiner inneren Verfassung*, reprint of 6th ed., Munich: Deutscher Taschenbuch-Verlag, 2000, 24–33.
47. Geib, Re. Address on Consequences of the New Emergency Decree, 12 January 1931, BArch, N 2091/8, fol. 133–37.
48. J. Bähr, *Staatliche Schlichtung in der Weimarer Republik. Tarifpolitik, Korporatismus und industrieller Konflikt zwischen Inflation und Deflation 1919–1932*, Berlin: Colloquium, 1989;

W. Plumpe, *Betriebliche Mitbestimmung in der Weimarer Republik. Fallstudien zum Ruhrbergbau und zur chemischen Industrie*, Munich: Oldenbourg, 1999, 37–67, 407–40; M. Becker, *Arbeitsvertrag und Arbeitsverhältnis während der Weimarer Republik und in der Zeit des Nationalsozialismus*, Frankfurt am Main: Klostermann, 2005.

49. R. Sturm, *Zerstörung der Demokratie 1930–1933. Weimarer Republik*, Bonn: Bundeszentrale für politische Bildung, 2011.

50. See the still authoritative study of the Steel Helmets by V.R. Berghahn, *Der Stahlhelm. Bund der Frontsoldaten 1918–1935*, Düsseldorf: Droste, 1966.

51. Defamatory Article on Franz Seldte, 14 March 1933, BArch, R 3901/2832, fol. 39.

52. Rüdiger Hachtmann's entry on Franz Seldte in *Neue Deutsche Biographie* thus requires correction: R. Hachtmann, 'Seldte, Franz', in Historische Kommission bei der Bayerischen Akademie der Wissenschaften (ed.), *Neue Deutsche Biographie*, vol. 24, Berlin: Duncker & Humblot, 2010, 215–16. See the Master's dissertation by Celeste Copes, produced within the framework of the research project on the history of the Reich Labour Ministry: C. Copes, '. . . *one of the less harmful personalities of Hitler's government'. Der ehemalige NS-Reichsarbeitsminister Franz Seldte in seiner Darstellung und in der Fremdwahrnehmung der Alliierten anhand der Akten der Nürnberger Prozesse 1945–1946*, Master's dissertation, Berlin, Humboldt-Universität zu Berlin, 2017; and the chapter by Kim Christian Priemel in this volume.

53. Hugenberg to Seldte, Re. RAM, 17 April 1933, in *Akten der Reichskanzlei. Regierung Hitler 1933–1938*, vol. 1: *Die Regierung Hitler, Teil I: 1933/34*, ed. K.-H. Minuth, series editors K. Repgen and H. Booms, Boppard am Rhein: Boldt, 1983, 340–42.

54. 'Gesetz zur Wiederherstellung des Berufsbeamtentums vom 7. April 1933', *RGBl*. I 1933, 175–77.

55. For detailed information on Johannes Krohn, see Biographical Appendix.

56. Reich Minister of the Interior to Reich Ministry of Labour, Re. Removal of Female Civil Servants, Teachers and White-Collar Workers, 5 October 1933, BArch, R 3901/20796, fol. 164.

57. For detailed information on Oscar Weigert, see Biographical Appendix.

58. Ministerial Office (Ministeramt), Submissions to Reich Minister of Labour Seldte, 1932–1937, BArch, R 3901/20006.

59. S. Felz, *Recht zwischen Wissenschaft und Politik. Die Rechts- und Staatswissenschaftliche Fakultät der Universität Münster 1902–1952*, Münster: Aschendorff, 2016, 372–83.

60. H. Mommsen, *Beamtentum im Dritten Reich. Mit ausgewählten Quellen zur nationalsozialistischen Beamtenpolitik*, Stuttgart: Deutsche Verlags-Anstalt, 1966, 55; S. Mühl-Benninghaus, *Das Beamtentum in der NS-Diktatur bis zum Ausbruch des Zweiten Weltkrieges: zu Entstehung, Inhalt und Durchführung der einschlägigen Beamtengesetze*, Düsseldorf: Droste, 1996, 80; D.P. Silverman, *Hitler's Economy. Nazi Work Creation Programs, 1933–1936*, Cambridge, MA: Harvard University Press, 1998, 15 f.

61. See Figure 1.5 detailing the development of the Reich Labour Ministry's staff.

62. This practice was affirmed in the 'German Civil Service Law' of 26 January 1937 and reinforced by further regulations; see Mommsen, *Beamtentum im Dritten Reich*, 62–91; Broszat, *Der Staat Hitlers*, 301–21.

63. These findings, however, apply only to the ministry, not to its subordinate agencies. For further analysis of the ministry's staff under Nazism and on membership of the Nazi Party, see the chapter by Martin Münzel in this volume.

64. Führer's representative to Lammers, 1 February 1938, BArch, R 43 II/1138b, fol. 25.

65. For detailed information on Wilhelm Börger, see Biographical Appendix.

66. On the support given in problematic cases, see, for example, BArch, R 43 II/1138b.

67. Goldschmidt remained at the Reich Labour Ministry until 1945, while Lehfeld died in 1941 in unexplained circumstances; see the database of the research project on the history of the Reich Ministry of Labour.

68. For detailed information on Oskar Karstedt, see Biographical Appendix.

69. On the disciplinary complaint (*Disziplinarbeschwerde*) procedure, see Reich Governor (Reichsstatthalter) of Braunschweig and Anhalt to Hans Heinrich Lammers, Re. Complaint against Oskar Karstedt, 12 August 1933, BArch, R 43 II/1138b, fol. 8–9; F. Goldschmidt, *Meine Arbeit bei der Vertretung der Interessen der jüdischen Ärzte in Deutschland seit dem Juli 1933*, Bremen: Universität Bremen, 1979, 5, 22.

70. The sources up to 1945 contain no reliable evidence that the minister suffered from a lack of recognition among his colleagues. The post-1945 sources, meanwhile, may reflect individual strategies of self-exoneration; see the chapter by Kim Christian Priemel in this volume.

71. 'Gesetz über die Rechtsverhältnisse des Reichskanzlers und der Reichsminister (Reichsministergesetz) vom 27.3.1930', *RGBl.* I 1930, 96–100.

72. 'Gesetz über den Eid der Reichsminister und der Mitglieder der Landesregierungen vom 17.10.1933', *RGBl.* I 1933, 741.

73. Broszat, *Der Staat Hitlers*, 353–55.

74. 'Ermächtigungsgesetz vom 24. März 1933', *RGBl.* I 1933, 141; 'Gesetz zur Sicherung der Einheit von Staat und Partei vom 1. Dezember 1933', *RGBl.* I 1933, 1016.

75. C. Möllers, 'Ernst Rudolf Hubers letzte Fussnote. Die normative Ordnung des Nationalsozialismus und die Grenzen der Kulturgeschichte', *Zeitschrift für Ideengeschichte* 11(2) (2016), 47–64.

76. After four years, this authority was renewed for another four years. The possibility of reforming the constitution was discussed again and again, but Hitler himself balked at this. See O. Meissner and G. Kaisenberg, *Staats- und Verwaltungsrecht im Dritten Reich*, Berlin: Verlag für Sozialpolitik, Wirtschaft und Statistik, 1935, 8–16; D. Rebentisch, *Führerstaat und Verwaltung im Zweiten Weltkrieg. Verfassungsentwicklung und Verwaltungspolitik 1939–1945*, Stuttgart: Steiner, 1989, 395–404; C. Kuller, '"Kämpfende Verwaltung". Bürokratie im NS-Staat', in D. Süss and W. Süss (eds), *Das 'Dritte Reich'. Eine Einführung*, Munich: Pantheon, 2008, 227–45, here 230 f.

77. Lammers, Re. Procedure for the Notification of Laws, 16 October 1934, BArch, R 3901/20003, fol. 10.

78. The Reich Ministry of the Interior evaluated laws in place of the Reich president, who had now been eliminated from the process. See Lammers, Re. Draft Reich Minister, 22 January 1934, BArch, R 3901/20003, fol. 16.

79. During the Second World War, however, in an increasing number of cases important and politically sensitive laws and Führer's decrees were not published. See M. Moll (ed.), '*Führer-Erlasse' 1939–1945. Edition sämtlicher überlieferter, nicht im Reichsgesetzblatt abgedruckter, von Hitler während des Zweiten Weltkrieges schriftlich erteilter Direktiven aus den Bereichen Staat, Partei, Wirtschaft, Besatzungspolitik und Militärverwaltung*, Stuttgart: Steiner, 1997.

80. Meissner and Kaisenberg, *Staats- und Verwaltungsrecht*, 12.

81. Franz Seldte to Supreme Reich authorities, Re. Transfer of Prussian Responsibilities to the RAM, 18 March 1935, BArch, R 2/18378.

82. Richard Wienstein, Speech at the Verwaltungsakademie Bonn, 15 December 1936, in Broszat, *Der Staat Hitlers*, 353.

83. Broszat, *Der Staat Hitlers*, 301–303; Rebentisch, *Führerstaat*, 371–94.

84. In any case, this finding applies to Franz Seldte. By February 1938, in addition to Seldte, only in exceptional cases did the heads of the ministries of Finance, Justice, Agriculture, Post, Transport, Economy and Education have regular access to Hitler at the end of Cabinet meetings. My thanks to the long-standing editor of the Reich Chancellery's files, Hartmut Weber, for this information; see Broszat, *Der Staat Hitlers*, 380 f.

85. H. Sandner, *Hitler – Das Itinerar. Aufenthaltsorte und Reisen von 1889 bis 1945*, vols I–IV, Berlin: Berlin Story Verlag, 2016.

86. These are, for example, vividly described by Arnold Brecht for the Weimar period.

See A. Brecht, *Mit der Kraft des Geistes. Lebenserinnerungen 1927–1967*, Stuttgart: Deutsche Verlags-Anstalt, 1967.
87. *RGBl.* I 1933, 1016. See F.L. Neumann, *Behemoth. The Structure and Practice of National Socialism*. London: Gollancz, 1942, 69–72.
88. *Nachrichtenblatt des Reichsarbeitsministeriums* (News Bulletin of the Reich Ministry of Labour) 17 (3 January 1936), 2–3.
89. Broszat, *Der Staat Hitlers*, 244–73.
90. T.W. Mason, *Sozialpolitik im Dritten Reich. Arbeiterklasse und Volksgemeinschaft*, Opladen: Westdeutscher Verlag, 1978; M. Schneider, *Unterm Hakenkreuz: Arbeiter und Arbeiterbewegung 1933 bis 1939*, Bonn: Dietz, 1999; F. Bajohr and M. Wildt (eds), *Volksgemeinschaft. Neue Forschungen zur Gesellschaft des Nationalsozialismus*, Frankfurt am Main: Fischer, 2009; D. Schmiechen-Ackermann (ed.), '*Volksgemeinschaft'. Mythos, wirkungsmächtige soziale Verheissung oder soziale Realität im 'Dritten Reich'? Zwischenbilanz einer kontroversen Debatte*, Paderborn: Schöningh, 2012.
91. On the DAF's organization and duties and its competitive relationship with the ministry, see the chapter by Rüdiger Hachtmann in this volume.
92. *RGBl.* I 1934, 45–56.
93. T.W. Mason, 'Zur Entstehung des Gesetzes zur Ordnung der nationalen Arbeit vom 20. Januar 1934. Ein Versuch über das Verhältnis "archaischer" und "moderner" Momente in der neuesten deutschen Geschichte', in H. Mommsen, D. Petzina and B. Weisbrod (eds), *Industrielles System und politische Entwicklung in der Weimarer Republik*, Düsseldorf: Droste, 1977, 322–51; A. Kranig, *Lockung und Zwang. Zur Arbeitsverfassung im Dritten Reich*, Stuttgart: Deutsche Verlags-Anstalt, 1983; R. Hachtmann, *Industriearbeit im 'Dritten Reich'. Untersuchungen zu den Lohn- und Arbeitsbedingungen in Deutschland 1933–1945*, Göttingen: Vandenhoeck & Ruprecht, 1989.
94. *RGBl.* I 1933, 285; on the labour trustees and the role of the Reich Labour Ministry, see the chapter by Sören Eden in this volume, on which I base the following analysis.
95. Reich Chancellery, Re. No. 284, Ministerial Meeting of 12 January 1933, in *Akten der Reichskanzlei*, vol. 1, part 1, 1070–72.
96. Werner Mansfeld, Re. Curriculum Vitae and Political Activity, 1947, federal commissioner for the records of the State Security Service (Staatssicherheitsdienst) of the former GDR, MfS BV Halle, Ast 7473, fol. 23.
97. K. Andres, 'Das Gesetz zur Ordnung der nationalen Arbeit vom 20. Januar 1934', *RABl.* II (1934), 37.
98. K. Teppe, 'Zur Sozialpolitik des Dritten Reiches am Beispiel der Sozialversicherung', *Archiv für Sozialgeschichte* 17 (1977), 195–250; E. Reidegeld, *Staatliche Sozialpolitik in Deutschland*, vol. 2: *Sozialpolitik in Demokratie und Diktatur 1919–1945*, Wiesbaden: Verlag für Sozialwissenschaften, 2006, 447–54; and the chapter by Alexander Klimo in this volume, on which I base the following remarks.
99. M. Stolleis, 'Historische Grundlagen. Sozialpolitik in Deutschland bis 1945', in Bundesministerium für Arbeit und Sozialordnung and Bundesarchiv (eds), *Geschichte der Sozialpolitik in Deutschland seit 1945*, vol. 1: *Grundlagen der Sozialpolitik*, Baden-Baden: Nomos, 2001, 199–332, here 208–10, 223 f.
100. Statement by Johannes Krohn, 2 December 1933, quoted in Teppe, 'Sozialpolitik', 217.
101. See the chapter by Henry Marx in this volume, on which I base the following analysis.
102. For a good introduction to the various aspects of these themes, see the recent works by M. Buggeln and M. Wildt (eds), *Arbeit im Nationalsozialismus*, Munich: De Gruyter Oldenbourg, 2014; D. Humann, '*Arbeitsschlacht'. Arbeitsbeschaffung und Propaganda in der NS-Zeit 1933–1939*, Göttingen: Wallstein, 2011; Silverman, *Hitler's Economy*; H.-W. Schmuhl, *Arbeitsmarktpolitik und Arbeitsverwaltung in Deutschland 1871–2002. Zwischen*

Fürsorge, Hoheit und Markt, Nuremberg: Institut für Arbeitsmarkt- und Berufsforschung, 2003; K.K. Patel, '*Soldaten der Arbeit*'. *Arbeitsdienste in Deutschland und den USA, 1933–1945*, Göttingen: Vandenhoeck & Ruprecht, 2003.

103. See Broszat, *Der Staat Hitlers*.

104. S. Kühl, *Ganz normale Organisationen. Zur Soziologie des Holocaust*, Berlin: Suhrkamp, 2014, 22–25.

105. Circular Decree issued by the Reich Ministry of Labour, 19 July 1933, fol. 42. The following remarks are based on the news bulletins and circular decrees issued by the ministry concerning its sphere of responsibility 1933–1939.

106. News Bulletin of the Reich and Prussian Ministry of Labour, 21 March 1936, fol. 17.

107. Circular Decrees issued by the Reich Ministry of Labour, 19 December 1933, fol. 73.

108. Circular Decrees issued by the Reich Ministry of Labour, 16 January 1935, fol. 3.

109. D. Petzina, *Autarkiepolitik im Dritten Reich. Der nationalsozialistische Vierjahresplan*, Stuttgart: Deutsche Verlags-Anstalt, 1968; and A.J. Tooze, *The Wages of Destruction. The Making and Breaking of the Nazi Economy*, London: Penguin, 2007, 203–43.

110. 'Hermann Göring, betr. Entwurf und Begründung der Kabinettsvorlage eines Zweiten Gesetzes zur Durchführung des Vierjahresplans über die Regelung des Arbeitseinsatzes, 22.10.1936', in *Akten der Reichskanzlei. Regierung Hitler 1933–1945*, vol. 3: *1936*, ed. F. Hartmannsgruber, series editors H.G. Hockerts and F.P. Kahlenberg, Munich: de Gruyter, 2002, 567–75.

111. Flügge, 'Arbeitseinsatz im Vierjahresplan', *RABl*. II (1936), 471–73.

112. R. Hachtmann and W. Süss (eds), *Hitlers Kommissare. Sondergewalten in der nationalsozialistischen Diktatur*, Göttingen: Wallstein, 2006.

113. On the GBA, see the chapter by Swantje Greve in this volume. Robert Ley had been appointed 'Reich commissioner for social housing' by 1940. This appointment, however, which essentially a matter of political symbolism, made just one section of the Reich Ministry of Labour available to him, and his authority over it was limited. To Ley's great disappointment, he received just a small office in the premises of the Reich Ministry of Labour and had no policymaking power; there were major limitations on his authority to issue instructions, and he administered none of the ministry's finances. Hence, there seems to be little justification for thinking in terms of an autonomous special authority by the end of 1942. On Ley's role as housing commissioner, see the chapters by Karl Christian Führer and Rüdiger Hachtmann in this volume; and M.-L. Recker, 'Der Reichskommissar für den sozialen Wohnungsbau. Zu Aufbau, Stellung und Arbeitsweise einer führerunmittelbaren Sonderbehörde', in D. Rebentisch and K. Teppe (eds), *Verwaltung contra Menschenführung im Staat Hitlers. Studien zum politisch administrativen System*, Göttingen: Vandenhoeck & Ruprecht, 1986, 333–50.

114. Rebentisch, *Führerstaat*, 390.

115. Ibid., 336.

116. Leo Killy, Re. Conflict of Authority Reich housing Commissioner, 22 September 1941, BArch, R 43 II/1009, fol. 151–56.

117. On labour deployment during the Second World War, see U. Herbert, *Hitler's Foreign Workers. Enforced Foreign Labor in Germany under the Third Reich*, trans. W. Templer, Cambridge: Cambridge University Press, 1997; U. Herbert (ed.), *Europa und der 'Reichseinsatz'. Ausländische Zivilarbeiter, Kriegsgefangene und KZ-Häftlinge in Deutschland 1938–1945*, Essen: Klartext, 1991; for further reading and on the specific role of the Reich Ministry of Labour, see also the chapters by Elizabeth Harvey, Henry Marx and Michael Wildt in this volume.

118. Main Section I, Defence Economy (Wehrwirtschaft), Reich Defence Commissioners (Reichsverteidigungskommissare), 1938–1941, BArch, R 3901/20536.

119. U. Herbert, *Werner Best. Radikalismus, Weltanschauung und Vernunft*, Berlin: Arenhövel, 1997; S. Reichardt and W. Seibel, 'Radikalität und Stabilität. Herrschen und Verwalten im Nationalsozialismus', in S. Reichardt and W. Seibel (eds), *Der prekäre Staat. Herrschen und Verwalten im Nationalsozialismus*, Frankfurt am Main: Campus, 2011, 7–27; and R. Hachtmann, 'Elastisch, dynamisch und von katastrophaler Effizienz. Zur Struktur der Neuen Staatlichkeit des Nationalsozialismus', in S. Reichardt and W. Seibel, *Der prekäre Staat*, 29–74.

120. On what follows, see Reich Chancellery to Wilhelm Frick, Re. Law on Austria and Saar-Palatinate (Österreich- und Saarpfalzgesetz), 6 August 1938, BArch, R 43 II/1353a and 1357; and U. Schulz, 'The First Takeover. The Implementation of Social Policy Measures in Austria by the Reich Labour Ministry after the Anschluss', in Kott and Patel, *Nazism across Borders*, 53–79.

121. Franz Seldte, Development of the Administration in the Eastern March, 27 April 1939, BArch, R 3901/1771, fol. 31–33.

122. Hans Engel, Note: Trustee Proksch, 2 June 1938, BArch, R 3901/1770, fol. 194.

123. Case-by-case contextualization, therefore, is vital when it comes to the organizational structures of the labour administration and social policy within the occupied territories' administrative systems; see K. Bertrams and S. Rudischhauser, 'Blurred Legacy: Nazi Social Policies in Belgium', in Kott and Patel, *Nazism across Borders*, 389–418; H. Marx, 'The German Labour Administration in the "Protectorate Bohemia and Moravia"', in J. Rákosník and R. Šustrová (eds), *War Employment and Social Policies in the Protectorate Bohemia and Moravia*, Prague: Univerzita Karlova, 2018, 34–54..

124. My thanks to Celeste Copes for pointing this out.

125. Joseph Goebbels, quoted in Rebentisch, *Führerstaat*, 345.

126. Herbert, *Werner Best*.

127. The writings of Franz Neumann, still a widely used resource among historians, were especially influential. Neumann provided an in-depth analysis of the Reich Ministry of the Economy and the Reich Ministry of the Interior in particular; see Neumann, *Behemoth*, 300–304, quotation on 301.

128. Broszat, *Der Staat Hitlers*, 426 f.; Mommsen, *Beamtentum im Dritten Reich*, 15; Rebentisch, *Führerstaat*, 543; Kuller, '"Kämpfende Verwaltung"', 243.

129. Kuller, '"Kämpfende Verwaltung"', 243.

Bibliography

Akten der Reichskanzlei. Regierung Hitler 1933–1945, vol. 3: *1936*, ed. F. Hartmannsgruber, series editors H.G. Hockerts and F.P. Kahlenberg. Munich: de Gruyter, 2002.

Akten der Reichskanzlei. Regierung Hitler 1933–1938, vol. 1: *Die Regierung Hitler*, part I: 1933/34, ed. K.-H. Minuth, series editors K. Repgen and H. Booms. Boppard am Rhein: Boldt, 1983.

Andres, K. 'Das Gesetz zur Ordnung der nationalen Arbeit vom 20. Januar 1934'. *Reichsarbeitsblatt* II (1934), 37.

Bähr, J. *Staatliche Schlichtung in der Weimarer Republik. Tarifpolitik, Korporatismus und industrieller Konflikt zwischen Inflation und Deflation 1919–1932*. Berlin: Colloquium, 1989.

Bajohr, F., and M. Wildt (eds). *Volksgemeinschaft. Neue Forschungen zur Gesellschaft des Nationalsozialismus*. Frankfurt am Main: Fischer, 2009.

Becker, M. *Arbeitsvertrag und Arbeitsverhältnis während der Weimarer Republik und in der Zeit des Nationalsozialismus*. Frankfurt am Main: Klostermann, 2005.

Becker, P. 'Bürokratie, Version: 1.0', in *Docupedia-Zeitgeschichte*, 30 August 2016. Retrieved 27 September 2018 from http://docupedia.de/zg/Becker_buerokratie_v1_de_2016.

Berg, W. '§ 8 Arbeits- und Sozialverwaltung', in K.G. Jeserich, H. Pohl and G.-C. Unruh (eds), *Deutsche Verwaltungsgeschichte*, vol. 4: *Das Reich als Republik und im Nationalsozialismus* (Stuttgart: Deutsche Verlags-Anstalt, 1985), 231–41.

Berghahn, V.R. *Der Stahlhelm. Bund der Frontsoldaten 1918–1935*. Düsseldorf: Droste, 1966.

Berringer, C. *Sozialpolitik in der Weltwirtschaftskrise. Die Arbeitslosenversicherungspolitik in Deutschland und Grossbritannien im Vergleich*. Berlin: Duncker & Humblot, 1999.

Bertrams, K., and S. Rudischhauser. 'Blurred Legacy: Nazi Social Policies in Belgium', in S. Kott and K.K. Patel (eds), *Nazism across Borders. The Social Policies of the Third Reich and their Global Appeal* (Oxford: Oxford University Press, 2018), 389–418.

Brauns, H. 'Entwicklung der Sozialpolitik'. *Reichsarbeitsblatt* II (1928), 194–96.

Brecht, A. *Mit der Kraft des Geistes. Lebenserinnerungen 1927–1967*. Stuttgart: Deutsche Verlags-Anstalt, 1967.

Broszat, M. *Der Staat Hitlers. Grundlegung und Entwicklung seiner inneren Verfassung*, reprint of 6th ed. Munich: Deutscher Taschenbuch-Verlag, 2000.

Bruch, R. von (ed.). *Weder Kommunismus noch Kapitalismus. Bürgerliche Sozialreform in Deutschland vom Vormärz bis zur Ära Adenauer*. Munich: Beck, 1985.

Buggeln, M., and M. Wildt (eds). *Arbeit im Nationalsozialismus*. Munich: De Gruyter Oldenbourg, 2014.

Copes, C. '. . . one of the less harmful personalities of Hitler's government'. *Der ehemalige NS-Reichsarbeitsminister Franz Seldte in seiner Darstellung und in der Fremdwahrnehmung der Alliierten anhand der Akten der Nürnberger Prozesse 1945–1946*, MA thesis. Berlin: Humboldt-Universität zu Berlin, 2017.

Derlien, H.-U., D. Böhme and M. Heindl (eds). *Bürokratietheorie. Einführung in eine Theorie der Verwaltung*. Wiesbaden: Verlag für Sozialwissenschaften, 2011.

Feldman, G.D. *Army, Industry and Labor in Germany. 1914–1918*. Princeton, NJ: Princeton University Press, 1966.

Felz, S. *Recht zwischen Wissenschaft und Politik. Die Rechts- und Staatswissenschaftliche Fakultät der Universität Münster 1902–1952*. Münster: Aschendorff, 2016.

Flügge. 'Arbeitseinsatz im Vierjahresplan'. *Reichsarbeitsblatt* II (1936), 471–73.

Führer, K.C. *Arbeitslosigkeit und die Entstehung der Arbeitslosenversicherung in Deutschland. 1902–1927*. Berlin: Colloquium, 1990.

Führer, K.C., et al. (eds). *Revolution und Arbeiterbewegung in Deutschland 1918–1920*. Essen: Klartext, 2013.

Geib, H. 'Zur Organisationsgeschichte des Reichsarbeitsministeriums'. *Reichsarbeitsblatt* II (1928), 196.

Goldschmidt, F. *Meine Arbeit bei der Vertretung der Interessen der jüdischen Ärzte in Deutschland seit dem Juli 1933*. Bremen: Universität Bremen, 1979.

Golla, G. *Nationalsozialistische Arbeitsbeschaffung in Theorie und Praxis*. Aachen: Shaker, 2008.

Grebing, H. 'Brauns, Heinrich', in Historische Kommission bei der Bayerischen Akademie der Wissenschaften (ed.), *Neue Deutsche Biographie*, vol. 2 (Berlin: Duncker & Humblot, 1955), 334.

Hachtmann, R. 'Elastisch, dynamisch und von katastrophaler Effizienz. Zur Struktur der Neuen Staatlichkeit des Nationalsozialismus', in S. Reichardt and W. Seibel (eds), *Der prekäre Staat. Herrschen und Verwalten im Nationalsozialismus* (Frankfurt am Main: Campus, 2011), 29–74.

Hachtmann, R. *Industriearbeit im 'Dritten Reich'. Untersuchungen zu den Lohn- und Arbeitsbedingungen in Deutschland 1933–1945*. Göttingen: Vandenhoeck & Ruprecht, 1989.

Hachtmann, R. 'Seldte, Franz', in Historische Kommission bei der Bayerischen Akademie der Wissenschaften (ed.), *Neue Deutsche Biographie*, vol. 24 (Berlin: Duncker & Humblot, 2010), 215–16.

Hachtmann, R., and W. Süss (eds). *Hitlers Kommissare. Sondergewalten in der nationalsozialistischen Diktatur*. Göttingen: Wallstein, 2006.
Hartrodt, G. *Die Ausstellung. Die Arbeitsgebiete des Reichsarbeitsministeriums*. Berlin: Reichsdruckerei, 1929.
Hartrodt, G. 'Rückblick auf die organisatorischen Reformarbeiten im Geschäftsbereich des Reichsarbeitsministeriums'. *Reichsarbeitsblatt* II (1929), 179.
Herbert, U. *Europa und der 'Reichseinsatz'. Ausländische Zivilarbeiter, Kriegsgefangene und KZ-Häftlinge in Deutschland 1938–1945*. Essen: Klartext, 1991.
Herbert, U. *Hitler's Foreign Workers. Enforced Foreign Labor in Germany under the Third Reich*, trans. W. Templer. Cambridge: Cambridge University Press, 1997.
Herbert, U. *Werner Best. Radikalismus, Weltanschauung und Vernunft*. Berlin: Arenhövel, 1997.
Hobsbawm, E. *The Age of Extremes. A History of the World, 1914–1991*. New York: Pantheon Books, 1994.
Humann, D. *'Arbeitsschlacht'. Arbeitsbeschaffung und Propaganda in der NS-Zeit 1933–1939*. Göttingen: Wallstein, 2011.
Hüntelmann, A.C. *Hygiene im Namen des Staates. Das Reichsgesundheitsamt 1876–1933*. Göttingen: Wallstein, 2008.
Klimo, A. 'An Unhappy Return: German Pension Insurance Policy in Alsace', in S. Kott and K.K. Patel (eds), *Nazism across Borders. The Social Policies of the Third Reich and their Global Appeal* (Oxford: Oxford University Press, 2018), 81–104.
Kranig, A. *Lockung und Zwang. Zur Arbeitsverfassung im Dritten Reich*. Stuttgart: Deutsche Verlags-Anstalt, 1983.
Kühl, S. *Ganz normale Organisationen. Zur Soziologie des Holocaust*. Berlin: Suhrkamp, 2014.
Kuller, C. '"Kämpfende Verwaltung". Bürokratie im NS-Staat', in D. Süss and W. Süss (eds), *Das 'Dritte Reich'. Eine Einführung* (Munich: Pantheon, 2008), 227–45.
Lembeck, E. *Die Partizipation von Frauen an der öffentlichen Verwaltung in der Weimarer Republik 1918–1933*, Ph.D. dissertation. Hanover: University of Hanover, 1991.
Marx, H. 'The German Labour Administration in the "Protectorate Bohemia and Moravia"', in J. Rákosník and R. Šustrová (eds), *War Employment and Social Policies in the Protectorate Bohemia and Moravia* (Prague: Univerzita Karlova, 2018), 34–54.
Mason, T.W. *Sozialpolitik im Dritten Reich. Arbeiterklasse und Volksgemeinschaft*. Opladen: Westdeutscher Verlag, 1978.
Mason, T.W. 'Zur Entstehung des Gesetzes zur Ordnung der nationalen Arbeit vom 20. Januar 1934. Ein Versuch über das Verhältnis "archaischer" und "moderner" Momente in der neuesten deutschen Geschichte', in H. Mommsen, D. Petzina and B. Weisbrod (eds), *Industrielles System und politische Entwicklung in der Weimarer Republik* (Düsseldorf: Droste, 1977), 322–51.
Mayer, P. 'G. Bauer', in Historische Kommission bei der Bayerischen Akademie der Wissenschaften (ed.), *Neue Deutsche Biographie*, vol. 1 (Berlin, 1953), 638.
Meissner, O., and G. Kaisenberg. *Staats- und Verwaltungsrecht im Dritten Reich*. Berlin: Verlag für Sozialpolitik, Wirtschaft und Statistik, 1935.
Mockenhaupt, H. 'Heinrich Brauns (1868–1939)', in R. Morsey (ed.), *Zeitgeschichte in Lebensbildern. Aus dem deutschen Katholizismus des 20. Jahrhunderts* (Mainz: Matthias-Grünewald-Verlag, 1973), 148–59.
Mockenhaupt, H. *Weg und Wirken des geistlichen Sozialpolitikers Heinrich Brauns 1868–1939*. Munich: Schöningh, 1977.
Moll, M. (ed.). *'Führer-Erlasse' 1939–1945. Edition sämtlicher überlieferter, nicht im Reichsgesetzblatt abgedruckter, von Hitler während des Zweiten Weltkrieges schriftlich erteilter Direktiven aus den Bereichen Staat, Partei, Wirtschaft, Besatzungspolitik und Militärverwaltung*. Stuttgart: Steiner, 1997.

Möllers, C. 'Ernst Rudolf Hubers letzte Fussnote. Die normative Ordnung des Nationalsozialismus und die Grenzen der Kulturgeschichte'. *Zeitschrift für Ideengeschichte* 11(2) (2016), 47–64.

Mommsen, H. *Beamtentum im Dritten Reich. Mit ausgewählten Quellen zur nationalsozialistischen Beamtenpolitik*. Stuttgart: Deutsche Verlags-Anstalt, 1966.

Mühl-Benninghaus, S. *Das Beamtentum in der NS-Diktatur bis zum Ausbruch des Zweiten Weltkrieges: zu Entstehung, Inhalt und Durchführung der einschlägigen Beamtengesetze*. Düsseldorf: Droste, 1996.

Müller, T.B., and A. Tooze. 'Demokratie nach dem Ersten Weltkrieg', in T.B. Müller and A. Tooze (eds), *Normalität und Fragilität: Demokratie nach dem Ersten Weltkrieg* (Hamburg: Hamburger Edition, 2015), 9–36.

Neumann, F.L. *Behemoth. Struktur und Praxis des Nationalsozialismus 1933–1944*, ed. Gert Schäfer. Frankfurt am Main: Fischer, 1993 (1st ed. 1942/44).

Neumann, F.L. *Behemoth. The Structure and Practice of National Socialism*. London: Gollancz, 1942.

Niethammer, L. 'Ein langer Marsch durch die Institutionen. Zur Vorgeschichte des preussischen Wohnungsgesetzes 1918', in L. Niethammer (ed.), *Wohnen im Wandel: Beiträge zur Geschichte des Alltags in der bürgerlichen Gesellschaft* (Wuppertal: Hammer, 1979), 363–84.

Patel, K.K. *'Soldaten der Arbeit'. Arbeitsdienste in Deutschland und den USA, 1933–1945*. Göttingen: Vandenhoeck & Ruprecht, 2003.

Petzina, D. *Autarkiepolitik im Dritten Reich. Der nationalsozialistische Vierjahresplan*. Stuttgart: Deutsche Verlags-Anstalt, 1968.

Plumpe, W. *Betriebliche Mitbestimmung in der Weimarer Republik. Fallstudien zum Ruhrbergbau und zur chemischen Industrie*. Munich: Oldenbourg, 1999.

Preller, L. *Sozialpolitik in der Weimarer Republik*. Kronsberg/Ts.: Athenäum, 1978.

Rebentisch, D. *Führerstaat und Verwaltung im Zweiten Weltkrieg. Verfassungsentwicklung und Verwaltungspolitik 1939–1945*. Stuttgart: Steiner, 1989.

Recker, M.-L. 'Der Reichskommissar für den sozialen Wohnungsbau. Zu Aufbau, Stellung und Arbeitsweise einer führerunmittelbaren Sonderbehörde', in D. Rebentisch and K. Teppe (eds), *Verwaltung contra Menschenführung im Staat Hitlers. Studien zum politisch-administrativen System* (Göttingen: Vandenhoeck & Ruprecht, 1986), 333–50.

Reichardt, S., and W. Seibel. 'Radikalität und Stabilität. Herrschen und Verwalten im Nationalsozialismus', in S. Reichardt and W. Seibel (eds), *Der prekäre Staat. Herrschen und Verwalten im Nationalsozialismus* (Frankfurt am Main: Campus, 2011), 7–27.

Reichsgesundheitsamt (ed.). *Das Reichsgesundheitsamt 1876–1926. Festschrift aus Anlass seines 50jährigen Bestehens*. Berlin: Springer, 1926.

Reichshandbuch der deutschen Gesellschaft, vol. 1: A–K. Berlin: Deutscher Wirtschaftsverlag, 1930.

Reidegeld, E. *Staatliche Sozialpolitik in Deutschland*, vol. 2: Sozialpolitik in Demokratie und Diktatur 1919–1945. Wiesbaden: Verlag für Sozialwissenschaften, 2006.

Ritter, G.A. *Arbeiter, Arbeiterbewegung und soziale Ideen in Deutschland. Beiträge zur Geschichte des 19. und 20. Jahrhunderts*. Munich: Beck, 1998.

Ritter, G.A. *Soziale Frage und Sozialpolitik in Deutschland seit Beginn des 19. Jahrhunderts*. Opladen: Leske + Budrich, 1998.

Röder, W., and H. Strauss (eds). *Biographisches Handbuch der deutschsprachigen Emigration nach 1933*. Munich et al.: Saur, 1980–1999.

Rohrbeck, W., and M. Sauerborn (eds). *Beiträge zur Sozialversicherung. Festgabe für Johannes Krohn zum 70. Geburtstag*. Berlin: Duncker & Humblot, 1954

Sachsse, C., and F. Tennstedt. *Geschichte der Armenfürsorge in Deutschland*, vol. 2: Fürsorge und Wohlfahrtspflege 1871–1929. Stuttgart: Kohlhammer, 1988.

Sandner, H. *Hitler – Das Itinerar. Aufenthaltsorte und Reisen von 1889 bis 1945*, 4 vols. Berlin: Berlin Story Verlag, 2016.

Schmiechen-Ackermann, D. (ed.). *'Volksgemeinschaft'. Mythos, wirkungsmächtige soziale Verheissung oder soziale Realität im 'Dritten Reich'? Zwischenbilanz einer kontroversen Debatte.* Paderborn: Schöningh, 2012.

Schmuhl, H.-W. *Arbeitsmarktpolitik und Arbeitsverwaltung in Deutschland 1871–2002. Zwischen Fürsorge, Hoheit und Markt.* Nuremberg: Institut für Arbeitsmarkt- und Berufsforschung, 2003.

Schneider, M. *Unterm Hakenkreuz. Arbeiter und Arbeiterbewegung 1933 bis 1939.* Bonn: Dietz, 1999.

Schulz, U. 'The First Takeover. The Implementation of Social Policy Measures in Austria by the Reich Labour Ministry after the Anschluss', in S. Kott and K.K. Patel (eds), *Nazism across Borders. The Social Policies of the Third Reich and their Global Appeal* (Oxford: Oxford University Press, 2018), 53–79.

Silverman, D.P. *Hitler's Economy. Nazi Work Creation Programs, 1933–1936.* Cambridge, MA: Harvard University Press, 1998.

Stolleis, M. 'Historische Grundlagen. Sozialpolitik in Deutschland bis 1945', in Bundesministerium für Arbeit und Sozialordnung and Bundesarchiv (eds), *Geschichte der Sozialpolitik in Deutschland seit 1945*, vol. 1: *Grundlagen der Sozialpolitik* (Baden-Baden: Nomos, 2001), 199–332.

Sturm, R. *Zerstörung der Demokratie 1930–1933. Weimarer Republik.* Bonn: Bundeszentrale für politische Bildung, 2011.

Syrup, F. *Hundert Jahre staatliche Sozialpolitik 1839–1939. Aus dem Nachlass von Friedrich Syrup*, general ed. J. Scheuble, ed. O. Neuloh. Stuttgart: Kohlhammer, 1957.

Tenfelde, K., and U. Borsdorf (eds). *Geschichte der deutschen Gewerkschaften von den Anfängen bis 1945.* Cologne: Bund, 1987.

Tennstedt, F. 'Krohn, Johannes', in Historische Kommission bei der Bayerischen Akademie der Wissenschaften (ed.), *Neue Deutsche Biographie*, vol. 13 (Berlin: Duncker & Humblot, 1982), 69.

Teppe, K. 'Zur Sozialpolitik des Dritten Reiches am Beispiel der Sozialversicherung'. *Archiv für Sozialgeschichte* 17 (1977), 195–250.

Tooze, A.J. *The Wages of Destruction. The Making and Breaking of the Nazi Economy.* London: Penguin, 2007.

Verein Aktives Museum e. V. (ed.). *Vor die Tür gesetzt. Im Nationalsozialismus verfolgte Berliner Stadtverordnete und Magistratsmitglieder 1933–1945.* Berlin: self-published, 2006.

Vollweiler. 'Das Problem der Verfahrensvereinfachung in der Sozialverwaltung'. *Reichsverwaltungsblatt* 62(19) (1941), 300–306.

Weber, A. 'Der Beamte'. *Die neue Rundschau* 21(4) (1910), 1321–39.

Weber, M. *Wirtschaft und Gesellschaft.* Tübingen: Mohr, 1972.

Welskopp, T. *Das Banner der Brüderlichkeit. Die deutsche Sozialdemokratie vom Vormärz bis zum Sozialistengesetz.* Bonn: Dietz, 2000.

Winkler, H.A. *Von der Revolution zur Stabilisierung. Arbeiter und Arbeiterbewegung in der Weimarer Republik, 1918 bis 1924.* Berlin: Dietz, 1984.

Zschucke, M. 'Die Verordnung über die Kurzarbeiter'. *Reichsarbeitsblatt* II (1934), 425–28.

Chapter 2

MID-LEVEL CIVIL SERVANTS' EDUCATION, PROFESSIONAL LIFE AND CAREER STRUCTURE

Lisa-Maria Röhling

In 1928, in the monthly journal *Das Beamtenjahrbuch* (Officials' Yearbook), the specialized press discussed the content of a possible administrative reform that was, among other things, intended to modify the education of mid-level civil servants (I use the terms 'civil servant' and 'official' synonymously in what follows). Rather than honing their skills exclusively in the context of administrative practice within a public authority, from now on they would receive theoretical instruction as well.

> In practice, when it comes to his education, to this day the mid-level civil servant is almost entirely dependent on the cases that happen to arise in the office during his period of training. Systematic and theoretical training, to which the existing regulations ascribe a secondary status, mostly plays a wholly marginal role in practice. . . . Even the education of mid-level civil servants must not be limited solely to knowledge of laws and regulations.[1]

This was a strikingly open approach, given that every decision on the content of education and the imparting of specialist theoretical knowledge would shape the thinking and action of an entire generation of administrative officials.[2] To state that the work done by civil servants – a group of such vital importance to every kind of state – depended on their education may seem to be stating the obvious. Yet the significance of this education cannot be overstated. More than any other form of professional training, civil servants' education meant more than just the imparting of specialist knowledge. It established an interpretive authority over the future of the state, because the latter's functioning, alongside political and economic aspects, depended (and still depends) on its administrative system. Because the thematic foci of the programme of education laid on for trainee civil servants influenced their work routine and expertise, the execution and structuring of this education ultimately did much to shape how the general public interpreted the administrative system. Particularly in the Weimar Republic and under Nazism, social, economic and, not least, political developments all played a role in shaping civil servants' educational trajectory.

The training of mid-level civil servants and their opportunities for promotion had an especially powerful impact on a public authority's functionality. This group already made up the largest contingent of civil servants in the German Empire and its members came into direct contact with the general population, especially in the regional authorities. Almost continuously, from the German Empire through the Weimar Republic until the end of Nazi rule, two-thirds of the entire civil service were mid-level officials. They occupied the desks in the government bodies that processed, on a day-to-day basis, a variety of requests from members of the general public, which the senior civil servants merely signed and finalized.

Within the ambit of the Reich Ministry of Labour (Reichsarbeitsministerium), the public aid authorities were among the subordinate agencies mostly staffed by mid-level officials and – going by the total number of employees – made up the largest share of all the ministry's organs. Into the early years of the Nazi regime, the number of staff was in the high three-figure range, its only rival in this regard being the labour administration. In terms both of their size and the composition of their civil servants, then, the public aid authorities present themselves as an obvious case study for elucidating officials' education.

As yet, historians have paid merely superficial attention to the education of mid-level civil servants and to the public aid agencies. Yet it is quite possible to reconstruct the education of mid-level officials working for the Reich Ministry of Labour by examining its subordinate agencies. In what follows, then, I focus on three key questions. What did beginning one's professional career at the Reich Labour Ministry's public aid agencies involve? What was the nature of the administrative practice that provided the framework for the training of novice mid-level officials, and what opportunities for advancement did they have? Finally, how did the Nazi 'seizure of power' impact on civil servants' education and career structure?

The Public Aid Authorities under the Reich Ministry of Labour

In common with many of the agencies subordinate to the Reich ministries, the public aid system was administered by numerous regional bodies whose staff consisted chiefly of mid-level officials. Like the Reich Labour Ministry itself, the public aid administration came into existence between 1918 and 1919. Within the framework of the restructuring carried out after the First World War, many formerly military pensions agencies, along with welfare institutions run by the Reich Ministry of the Economy and the Reich Ministry of the Interior, together with the civil servants working in them, were incorporated into the remit of the Reich Ministry of Labour. The public aid administration, then, was among those bodies particularly affected by the consequences of the First World War. The administrative apparatus of Reich public aid consisted of main public aid offices and public aid offices. While the former, as supervisory bodies in the provinces, emerged from the offices of the former General Command (Generalkommando), the latter, as local agencies, were accessible to the general population.[3] As time went by, their responsibilities were constantly expanded, necessitating an ever-greater number of mid-level officials to carry out everyday operations. The public aid authorities were the central administrative organs organizing public aid, though other organs, such as the provisioning courts and healthcare institutions (medical assessment centres and hospitals), were also affiliated with the Reich Ministry of Labour.[4]

Regardless of its multiple predecessor authorities, the structure of Reich public aid in the Weimar Republic was a novelty. This influenced working processes within its agencies and meant that the first priority was to establish a working routine. These bodies' administrative tasks encompassed the processing and granting of benefits and pensions and covering the costs of medical treatment for disabled ex-servicemen and their dependants.[5] Those entitled to such aid, with whom civil servants dealt on a daily basis, derived this right from injuries sustained in the course of active military service, if these injuries had health-related or economic consequences for the injured or their families.[6] In concrete terms, what this meant was that – in the context of everyday administrative practice – mid-level officials were entrusted with a wide range of tasks: assessing pensions applications, creating a new file, corresponding with those entitled to aid, granting and calculating pensions and arranging medical or orthopaedic care. The amount of the pension depended on an individual's circumstances at the time of application as well as on his occupation before the war. But the amount paid out was also linked with civil servants' earnings. Because these welfare recipients had once served the Reich, their pensions were aligned with the earnings of current civil servants.[7] A detailed form requested information on marital status, employment history and professional background, with officials providing support in some cases. The extent of an individual's war disablement was ascertained externally by the medical assessment centres, which provided officials with a precise list of factors that enabled them to calculate pension payments or other forms of material aid.

The year 1927 may be described as the zenith of Reich public aid: never before had so many individuals received financial or medical support as in this financial year. The relevant budget items amounted to just under 1.5 billion Reichsmarks.[8] Despite the tremendous squeeze on the Reich budget and the fact that many agencies had been closed in the preceding years to cut costs and simplify administrative processes, the administrative apparatus of Reich public aid largely remained in place. But the financial strains had a deleterious effect on the prospects for individuals hoping to make a start on the career ladder. Nonetheless, in 1927, 55 per cent of the total ministerial staff with civil service status was still employed in the public aid agencies, a total of 7,600 officials.[9]

Ruptures and Continuities: The Politics of the Civil Service in the German Empire and Weimar Republic

The roots of the notion of the official as servant of the state and as representative of a permanent civil service lie in the German Empire. Max Weber defined the bureaucratic administrative system as the only institution capable of meeting the needs of the state because, as he asserted, it acted on the basis of continuities, rules, clear-cut spheres of responsibility and a strict chain of command within the framework of a bureaucratic hierarchy.[10] No one was simply 'employed' as a civil servant. This was a status that was conferred as a distinction and those embarking on a career as a civil servant were pursuing a vocation. Gaining a permanent post or being appointed to a particular office, however, was not something that could be taken for granted. Civil servants ought to 'see a track stretching in front of them, in other words have the opportunity for promotion according to length of service, or performance, or both, and be subject to a strict, consistent chain of command or supervision'.[11] The prescribed professional trajectory and a fixed salary, permanent employment status and the loyalty pledged in the oath of office all reflected the state's role as provider during and after the civil servant's working life. The route into a Reich agency was always linked with the particular occupational path one had entered upon, whose regulations determined entry requirements as well as one's salary and promotion prospects.

Officials on the mid-level career path already made up almost two-thirds of the civil service at the turn of the century and thus constituted its core. This state of affairs persisted, as did the fundamental requirements for appointment and the training guidelines. Immediately after the First World War and in 1930, in fact, three-quarters of civil servants were mid-level officials.[12] Not just their educational background but also their ongoing training were thus key themes in the internal governmental debate on the civil service and administrative structures.

On a number of levels, the turning point of 1918 represented a major challenge for the civil service. As a new form of state emerged, the Kaiser released every member of the civil service from his oath of loyalty. But there were very few changes of staff with the status of civil servant, with most officials remaining in post.[13] When sworn in to office, the new civil servant pledged his loyalty to the Weimar constitution, thus becoming an organ and functionary of the state, which endowed him with the role of intermediary between state and people.[14] Through this oath of loyalty, he gained a permanent civil service post and was dependent on the state for his salary and pension – in contrast to the classic service sector employee. In the early Weimar Republic, most contemporaries thus saw civil servants as representatives of a nurturing state, one playing a role similar to that of the territorial princes (*Landesfürsten*) prior to the November Revolution of 1918.[15] The work done by civil servants for the people as a whole was closely bound up with their highly regulated employment status and clearly defined social status, with most officials regarding the professional civil service chiefly as a means of obtaining secure employment and guaranteeing their old-age pension and dependants' benefits.[16] Most civil servants found themselves in a difficult position in the Weimar Republic because they did not see themselves as servants of the people, as the ideals of a republic would imply. They regarded their oath of loyalty to the constitution, which they thought would be merely temporary, as superfluous or as incompatible with their previous pledge of loyalty to the Kaiser.[17]

This conceptual model was partly anchored in the ongoing tripartite division of the civil service. It had always been subdivided into junior, mid-level and senior sections. In the German Empire there was a particularly strict division between the senior and mid-level group of officials, which was justified in light of their very different entry requirements. Only senior officials enjoyed the right to issue instructions and sign documents, which frequently obstructed the smooth operation of the administrative apparatus. Again and again, the strict division of professional trajectories sparked debate within the civil service: neither mid-level officials, aspiring to cross over to the senior track, nor senior officials observing these ambitions with tremendous scepticism, were satisfied with the status quo. Over the decades, mid-level officials' potential for advancement into the senior realm, the differing entry requirements and the two groups' supposedly very different workplace skills repeatedly led to heated discussions.[18] Most mid-level civil servants considered themselves every bit as capable as their senior colleagues and thus strove to obtain greater autonomy and enhanced authority over administrative processes; this, they argued, would

Table 2.1. Civil servants and white-collar workers by pay grade on 21 March 1929

Territorial authorities	Fixed salaries		A1–A2c X and above		A2d–A4c VII–IX		A4d–A9 IV–VI		A10–A12 I–III		Total
	Number	%	Number	%	Number	%	Number	%	Number	%	Number
Reich (or military personnel)	323	0.3	8,305	6.7	41,741	34.0	61,192	49.8	11,240	9.2	122,901
Länder	468	0.1	52,945	13.9	115,482	30.2	133,615	35.0	79,654	20.8	382,164
Local authorities	811	0.3	25,716	9.2	130,532	46.9	102,314	36.7	19,155	6.9	278,528
Ämter (administrative units)	6	0.1	274	3.9	2,232	31.5	3,243	45.8	1,323	18.7	7,078
District associations	1	0.0	857	3.2	5,745	21.6	12,629	47.5	7,383	27.7	26,615
Provincial associations	49	0.2	1,299	5.1	3,200	12.6	11,736	46.3	9,071	35.8	25,355
Associations of local authorities tog.	56	0.1	2,430	4.1	11,177	18.9	27,608	46.8	17,777	30.1	59,048
Hanseatic cities	104	0.3	2,888	7.2	11,317	28.1	12,591	31.2	13,384	33.2	40,284
Total Civil servants	1,762	0.2	83,955	11.9	289,345	40.9	234,673	33.2	97,213	13.8	706,948
White-collar workers	—	—	8,329	4.7	20,904	11.9	102,647	58.3	44,097	25.1	175,977
Total	1,762	0.2	92,284	10.5	310,249	35.1	337,320	38.2	141,310	16.0	882,925

Note: The Arabic numerals A1–A12 relate to the civil service pay brackets, the Roman to the groups in the white-collar workers' collective wage agreement.
Source: Hans Völter, *Die deutsche Beamtenbesoldung*, Leipzig: Duncker & Humblot, 1932, 94.

not only be good for them but would also speed up the workings of the administrative apparatus and reduce the strain on it.[19] Even in the 1920s, however, senior officials still insisted that it was out of the question for promotions to be made dependent on exams. Instead they must be based on officials' capacity to 'prove themselves on the job'.[20]

When it comes to officials' career advancement, we should not underestimate the role of remuneration. The various pay grades structured officials' career paths. The first 'Salary Law' (Besoldungsgesetz) of the Weimar Republic, of 30 April 1920, reduced the previous 180 salary brackets to twenty, and more closely aligned the different levels of pay to prevent an excessive financial gap.[21] The mid-level civil service was subdivided into a lower and upper grade, though these two groups were not as sharply delineated from one another as was the mid-level civil service as a whole from its senior counterpart. Through the legislation on salaries of 16 December 1927, the number of salary groups grew once again to fifty-eight.[22] As a consequence, a total of 74.1 per cent of civil servants worked in the mid-level part of the administrative system, of whom 40.9 per cent were in the upper grade and 33.2 per cent the lower grade.[23]

Upper-grade mid-level officials, to whom pay grades A2d to A4c (previously pay grades VII–IX) applied, comprised senior secretaries (*Obersekretäre*), senior inspectors (*Oberinspektoren*), administrative officials (*Verwaltungsamtmänner*) and senior ministerial officials (*Ministerialamtmänner*). Lower-grade mid-level officials, meanwhile, who were in pay grades A4d to A9 (previ ously pay grades IV–VI), included administrative assistants (*Kanzleiassistenten*), ministerial administrative assistants (*Ministerialkanzleiassistenten*), secretaries (*Sekretäre*), ministerial secretaries (*Ministerialkanzleisekretäre*) and certified secretaries (*sondergeprüfte Sekretäre*).[24]

It was only as a result of the 'German Civil Service Law' of 26 January 1937 that the legislation on salaries underwent fundamental change, profoundly restructuring the career of civil servant and the apparatus of the civil service in accordance with Nazi ideology.[25]

Table 2.2. Overview of civil servants' pay grades after reforms, 1920 and 1927

Civil servants	Reform 1920	Reform 1927
Senior civil servants	X and above	A1 to A2c
Upper-grade mid-level civil servants	VII to IX	A2d to A4c
Mid-level civil servants	IV to VI	A4d to A9
Junior civil servants	I to III	A10 to A12

Source: Hans Völter, *Die deutsche Beamtenbesoldung*. Leipzig: Duncker & Humblot, 1932, 94.

The Mid-Level Civil Service Career in the Public Aid Authorities

If we wish to understand the civil servants' career path, we need to examine their entry requirements, the everyday reality of the agencies in which they worked and their promotion prospects. The responsibilities of the public aid authorities fluctuated substantially in the first few years of their existence because certain spheres of activity were only gradually allocated to them, generating an ever-broadening range of duties.[26]

Throughout the Reich civil service, entry as a mid-level official usually began with a period of probation in a public agency and with the so-called period of candidacy (*Anwartschaft*), in the course of which it was possible for an individual to be admitted to the career of mid-level civil servant. In order to attain a post in a Reich agency, the first step was to gain one of the places on the official, always crowded list of applicants. The so-called *Anwärter* or candidates were selected from this list. Here a distinction was made between two groups: civilian candidates (*Zivilanwärter*), who got onto the list of candidates as a result of a regular application, and the so-called military and public aid candidates (*Militär- und Versorgungsanwärter*), who were entitled to a civil servant certificate (*Beamtenschein*) that gave them priority access to the candidates' list.

If they were to have any chance of success, the civilian candidates had to first show evidence of a primary school education or the *Primareife*, that is, evidence of education beyond the statutory minimum, or provide an *Einjährigenzeugnis* (which was equivalent to the *mittlere Reife*; see below). In a small number of cases the candidate sat a qualifying exam. While the state did not standardize entry requirements for the mid-level civil service, the tendency to regard the secondary school leaving certificate (*mittlere Reife*) as a requirement had already become common practice under the German Empire.[27] Nonetheless, skilled craftsmen or other individuals previously employed in occupations requiring formal training were admitted to the civil service in exceptional cases.

Candidates typically began their so-called preparatory or probationary service (*Vorbereitungs- oder Probedienst*) between the ages of seventeen and twenty-five.[28] Depending on the particular career path to which an individual aspired, the institution involved or the individual's capabilities, the probationary service could last between two and five years, as the candidate had to pass a final examination to complete this stage.[29] This preparatory service began with a trial period, after which the candidate was given the official title of 'civil service candidate' (*Beamtenanwärter*) or 'probationary candidate' (*Anwärter im Probedienst*). The candidates were mostly paid in accordance with the Expenses Regulations (*Diätenordnung*), their wages amounting to between roughly 70 and 90 per cent of the pay grade in which they were initially to be placed.[30]

Generally speaking, the preparatory service took place in a public authority, with candidates being trained by older officials. The priority was for them to acquire specialist knowledge and master administrative operations.[31] Finally, when they had passed the first examination, the so-called *Diätarprüfung*, the candidates were slotted into the staffing schedule of a given agency, marking the beginning of their official career. As candidates in a subordinate organ of a Reich ministry, they might be assigned to the ministerial headquarters if required.[32]

In the public aid authorities, examinations were carried out under the guidance of the main public aid offices, which also set the exam questions and established the examination boards. Typically, exams consisted of three tasks, namely the description of a simple situation relating to support for disabled ex-servicemen and their dependants, questions about the duties and structure of the public aid authorities, and finally questions on internal operations, including finances. In the so-called *Inspektorenprüfung*, candidates faced questions on pensions law (*Versorgungsrecht*), the administrative system, constitutional and administrative law, social welfare and medical care.[33] In concrete terms, this meant that examinees, for example, had to explain the process of granting approval for medical treatment.[34]

The military and public aid candidates gained a place on the official list of candidates on a preferential basis with the help of a civil service certificate or various forms of public aid certificate. This applied to former members of the armed forces, who were entitled to a certificate affirming their right to be employed as a civil servant (*Zivilversorgungsschein*), holders of a civilian service certificate (*Zivildienstschein*) on the basis of the Wehrmacht Public Aid Law (Wehrmachtsversorgungsgesetz), holders of a police public aid certificate (*Polizeiversorgungsschein*) and holders of a civil service certificate on the basis of the Reich War Victims Compensation Law (Reichsversorgungsgesetz), most of them severely disabled in the latter case.[35] Conferring the status of candidate on these severely disabled individuals was regarded as a state benefit, as many former career officers lacked the appropriate educational background for a civilian candidacy or were ill-suited to other lines of work due to their disability.[36] The civil service certificate, then, was a form of support both for the war-disabled and for former career soldiers.

The guidelines of 26 July 1922 on the appointment of those in possession of a public aid certificate stipulated that a particular number of places on the list of candidates must be set aside for them. On a variable basis according to pay grade, between 50 and 75 per cent of posts in the mid-level civil service had to be occupied exclusively by those holding a public aid certificate.³⁷ The career of civil servant, then, was not just a service to the state but in this case also a service provided by the state for its citizens. Most public aid candidates, meanwhile, had significantly less school education than civilian candidates due to their previous military career. Contemporaries explained this in light, for example, of the education received in the Reichsmarine (navy), which was often claimed to be deficient and inadequate. Acquisition of a civil service certificate or public aid certificate, then, was not linked to an agency-specific educational background or a particular kind of expertise.³⁸

In 1927, for example, the mid-level civil service was subdivided as follows. Fifty per cent of assistants were public aid and civilian candidates, while 30 per cent of secretaries were former assistants. Thirty per cent of senior secretaries were *Aufstiegsbeamte* (that is, individuals who had entered a public agency as blue- or white-collar workers, later becoming civil servants on the basis of in-house training), 50 per cent were public aid candidates who had passed the second final exam and 20 per cent were civilian candidates who had achieved the *Unterprimareife* (certificate for the eighth class of a Mittelschule, a kind of vocational high school).³⁹

There was, however, no guarantee that the candidates would gain a permanent post in a public agency, which became more difficult during the years of financial crisis, particularly for civilian candidates, because unoccupied permanent posts were filled by public aid candidates and so-called non-active service officials (*Wartestandbeamte*) on a preferential basis. The latter, having been granted 'temporary retirement', received a salary in any case in the form of a temporary allowance, while the state aimed to 'provide for' the severely disabled as well as possible during the economic crisis.⁴⁰ This was already evident in the list of candidates; from 1929 onwards, regulations stipulated that two-thirds of them had to be public aid candidates.⁴¹ As a result, in the final years of the Weimar Republic significantly fewer young school leavers, whose school-leaving certificates had qualified them for a civilian candidacy, managed to take up a post in a public agency. Instead, older holders of public aid and civil service certificates as well as non-active service officials were selected to begin a civil service career, most of them either inexperienced or older administrative officials.

Civil service candidates (*Beamtenanwärter*) were made familiar with the everyday activities of a given agency through a purely practical form of training. In the Reich public aid authorities, it was not just typical administrative tasks that stood centre stage for trainees, but also their interaction with public aid recipients and the need to acquaint oneself with a copious and constantly changing body of laws relating to social services.

In light of the increased workload in the public aid agencies, in 1927 the Reich Ministry of Labour felt compelled to take action to reduce the burden on its largest subordinate organ. Despite the gravity of the situation, the ministry declined to create more civil service posts for new recruits, let alone to draw on the contingent of junior officials who had sat exams qualifying them for the mid-level civil service or the non-active service officials.[42] The public aid authorities expressed discontent with this attitude, having come out strongly in favour of appointing new civil service candidates to relieve the pressure, 'as the constant overburdening of the available officials is not sustainable and can now only be borne at the cost of officials' health'.[43] In addition, this fraught situation frequently inspired a general critique of the training of mid-level civil servants and sparked efforts to restructure it of the kind cited at the start of this chapter. Officials' extreme workload represented the greatest problem when it came to the provision of training: 'This training [was] not pleasant for the agencies and was often disruptive because the candidates were perceived as a burden for an entire year, in other words during the training period, only to be of very limited use to the performance of difficult office work later, before completing their exams, because of their restricted signing rights'.[44]

One of the public aid agencies' key tasks was to deal with benefits recipients, particularly given that the fate of the war-disabled and their dependants was a matter of broad public concern. Guidelines were thus developed specifically for such interaction in order to keep the number of complaints as low as possible. The 'Guidelines for the Provision of Services as a Whole' (*Richtschnur für den gesamten Dienstverkehr*) defined officials' overriding goal as follows: 'Constant concern for the well-being of those seeking public aid and an unstintingly helpful attitude even with respect to the most minor matters'.[45] These guidelines, however, not only helped provide well-structured instructions and a theoretical foundation preparing civil service candidates for their everyday practical activities. They also called for a flexible approach to quotidian administrative work. We may interpret this point in particular as a response to contemporary accusations that the average civil servant tended to be slow and over-bureaucratized, leading to the inefficient execution of administrative processes.[46]

Particularly during the years of economic crisis, officials were repeatedly exposed to threats of extreme violence from those receiving or seeking benefits who felt misunderstood or mistreated, and there were many cases of damage to property in public aid offices.[47] This made it all the more important to induct the civil service candidates as precisely as possible into their administrative duties in order to keep potential conflicts to a minimum. Above all, officials were to handle the typical bone of contention between the agencies and those claiming benefits, namely the appeal or objection, with great care and only after scrutinizing the facts of a given case very carefully should they pass it on to the main public aid offices for reassessment or to the provisioning courts for a decision.[48] The same went for cases of pension renewal, which was carried out ten years after the First World War to check whether individuals were now entitled to a lower level of pension or any at all.[49] Striking a balance between an accommodating, understanding approach to claimants and an uncompromising one in cases where appeals were rejected was one of the public aid officials' core tasks and constantly influenced their public image.

The complex body of laws underpinning Reich public aid represented a major challenge to officials and risked slowing down administrative processes. The first steps taken to counter this problem involved handouts designed to simplify procedures and a drive to eliminate obstructive administrative regulations. In 1932, the *Handbuch der Reichsversorgung* (Handbook of Reich Public Aid) was published. This collated the entire body of relevant laws for the first time and included handouts relating to all administrative processes and the legal foundations of public aid.[50] This volume was revised annually, with new information then being pasted into the current edition in an attempt to keep up with the constant changes in laws and spheres of activity. Hence, when it came to training as well, it was essentially impossible to lay down a substantive standard: even experienced civil servants struggled to ensure the smooth running of their institution's processes.

However hard the public aid agencies strove to simplify administrative processes, the changes they made rapidly lost their efficacy as a growing number of individuals claimed public aid for the first time or requested additional benefits. In 1928, one official stated that the 'volume of work at the public aid offices [has] become so enormous that orderly procedures can no longer be guaranteed. The entire administrative process has gradually developed in such a way that it has become impossible to ensure its orderly execution'.[51] Under these working conditions, both morale and workflow suffered, as did the training of those officials who had shown initiative and were thus earmarked for promotion. Finally, in 1932 many (main) public aid offices were closed due to the world economic crisis, while the number of civil servants was cut. Furthermore, the government's emergency decrees soon reduced salaries, putting a strain on those officials still working in these agencies.[52]

For mid-level officials, for the first time there were limited opportunities to advance into pay grade VII (A4c from 1927), that is, the upper-grade mid-level civil service, because this required them to pass a qualifying exam.[53] They automatically moved through all the lower pay grades within the framework of a normal career. Beginning in 1927, passage into other pay grades, such as pay grade A4d, also involved a supplementary exam. Gaining permission to sit this exam for promotion required backing from one's institution, which entailed the enclosure of a detailed recommendation describing and rating the official's abilities.[54]

Because far fewer promotion exams than usual were held between 1925 and 1929, the state allowed some officials to sit such exams who had already failed to pass on a number of occasions or had not yet had the opportunity to sit one. The main goal here was to prevent the over-ageing of the civil service and ensure there were sufficient potential candidates for promotion. As a result of the state's precarious finances, more than 1,200 mid-level civil servants had been unable to sit exams, because it was seen as too expensive to appoint them to a permanent post and promote them into a higher pay grade. Older officials were given preference when it came to these exams so they could advance their careers. At the same time, this meant that younger and less well-educated officials tended to be transferred to other agencies, quite simply because this was a cheaper option than promoting them.[55]

Civil Service Policy in the First Few Years of Nazi Rule, 1933–1937

The advent of the Nazi regime under Adolf Hitler not only transformed the political power structure in Germany but also the structure of government bodies and the bureaucracy. The 'Civil Service Law' of 7 April 1933 represented a major turning point for administrative practices in the public authorities, not least because it instigated a sharp break with the Weimar Republic.[56] Section 2 resulted in the dismissal of all civil servants who had gained their status after 9 November 1918 and had supposedly lacked the prescribed qualifications. This chiefly affected so-called 'party membership book, revolutionary or November officials'.[57] At the same time, with a small number of exceptions, § 3 resulted in the dismissal of all 'non-Aryan' officials, while § 4 removed those 'whose unstinting efforts on behalf of the National Socialist state could not be guaranteed'. As a result of the Third Implementing Decree of 6 May 1933, membership of the Communist Party was now viewed as a form of 'national untrustworthiness'.[58] Within the Reich Labour Ministry's subordinate agencies, §§ 2 and 4 of the 'Civil Service Law' triggered the dismissal of many individuals in the face of dogged resistance from the ministry itself.[59] This mainly affected the labour and public aid offices, in which the number of former social democrats and trades unionists was particularly high.[60] It did not, however, automatically result in the wholesale transformation of the civil service to bring it into line with Nazi ideology. Instead, what we can discern here is an effort to accommodate the Nazi Party's demands while simultaneously maintaining the traditional career structure and career guidelines as far as possible.[61]

It was not just changes in the law but also the 'National Socialist worldview' that endowed the civil service with a new role: 'As a cornerstone of the Reich, the profession of civil servant warrants the respect of the people [Volk]. The more he inspires trust through his efforts, the more [respect] he will be granted'.[62] Chiefly in specialist circles, the government official was to receive a new designation. Within the structure of the Nazi state, it was profoundly important that the civil servant no longer be viewed as an 'agent of the authorities' but instead as a 'representative of the Führer and both executive organ and mediator of the Führer's will as anchored in the people's trust'.[63] He was supposed to be more just and understanding than the party officials in the Weimar Republic had been, because people would judge both government and state in light of his actions. Appropriate and fair action were to be the premises of all administrative activity.[64] In this case, the requirements of officials in contact with citizens match those emphasized in the Weimar Republic precisely. Inspired by the concept of the Führer, however, officials were now supposed to find fresh motivation and break with the civil service policies of the 1920s. The new emphasis on the 'people's will', of course, ultimately meant carrying out the will of the Nazi Party.[65]

Mid-level civil servants played a special role in this new state structure. 'The upper-grade mid-level civil servant working in the general administration is, in the end, the fully independent mainstay, irreplaceable by any other type of civil servant, of the system of finance and accounting that is of such fundamental importance to the functioning of the state.'[66] This statement was hugely significant to the Reich Labour Ministry's subordinate agencies in particular because the ministry was supposed to fill its mid-level posts almost exclusively with officials working in them.[67] Within the new state form and within the context of Nazi ideology, civil servants and the administrative system were now judged in light of their efforts on behalf of the People's State (*Volksstaat*). In this role, the civil servant's task was to create optimum living conditions for the German people, supporting them as much as possible by ensuring an efficient bureaucracy.[68] The new regime certainly influenced the provision of financial support for approximately 809,000 disabled ex-servicemen and almost 650,000 widows, orphans and parents, whose cases were processed by one hundred public aid offices in 1933.[69] Nonetheless, the state's influence on legislation and government agencies' ideological orientation did not diminish the significance of the civil service itself. The regime's interventions in the affairs of the civil service and administrative system, then, should not be seen merely as a powerful instrument of repression, because even the Nazi state was dependent on a smoothly functioning civil service. This is surely also the reason why the state made absolutely no effort to force through the root-and-branch restructuring of the civil service.

As with many other Reich agencies, the Nazi seizure of power brought about numerous changes in the process of gaining a civil service post in the public aid authorities. Reflecting the priorities of the new regime, debates on administrative matters began to centre on the selection of 'up-and-coming civil servants', the idea being to prepare them to give their all for the state.[70] Beginning in 1935, not only did the Reich budget include funding for civil servants' training for the first time after the 'seizure of power', but the regime urgently requested new civil service candidates as well. It thus took active steps to counter the ongoing effects of the emergency decrees issued between 1930 and 1932 in an attempt to cope with the financial crisis.[71] Meanwhile, as had happened when a new form of state emerged in 1918, the actual educational and career guidelines for the mid-level civil service initially remained unchanged.

Beginning in 1933, however, in addition to appropriate qualifications, an active commitment to the nation state and the ability to prove one's 'Aryan' descent became significant to the recruitment of candidates.[72] The relevant officials must 'make a point of ensuring that applicants have fully absorbed the notion of the Volksgemeinschaft and ... have put it into practice'.[73] These demands made by the state leadership found reflection in an interplay between ascent within the party and bureaucratic routine: while 81.4 per cent of individuals who had joined the Nazi Party between January and May 1933 were civil servants, at the same time there were few well-educated party members who could straightforwardly begin a career in the civil service solely on the basis of their party membership.[74] By 1930, around 8.3 per cent of all German civil servants were already members of the Nazi Party – a large portion of them mid-level and junior officials.[75] Opposition to the Nazi Party and its policies, then, was relatively low within the civil service.

With the exception of these minimal changes imposed by the state, however, there was no fundamental restructuring of training in the Reich Ministry of Labour or any other Reich agency. This had nothing to do with a lack of engagement on the part of the various Reich authorities, but with their general restructuring in 1935, which placed the topic of civil servants' training on the backburner. The fundamental characteristics of the civil service, the traditional career path and the regulations governing entry exams were to be provisionally retained.[76] The rules relating to appointments and training thus remained almost the same in structural terms, as a result of which the administrative agencies tended to make autonomous decisions on the appointment of candidates – because in general staffing policy remained in their hands.[77] Certainly, when it came to the appointment of civil servants, they paid attention to candidates' 'political reliability',[78] but initially this did not make Nazi Party membership a sine qua non.

The evidence requires us to qualify the assumption that, when it comes to entry into a standard civil service career, after the Nazi 'seizure of power', posts were preferentially filled by 'old fighters' and party members, regardless of their expertise and education. It is true that Nazi Party members sometimes found it easier to obtain a post in a government body, but this occurred as a result of a change in the Reich War Victims Compensation Law. Through the Law on the Provision of Public Aid to Fighters for the National Uprising (Gesetz über die Versorgung der Kämpfer für die nationale Erhebung) of 27 February 1934, members of the Nazi Party and Steel Helmets, along with their associated organizations, were guaranteed public aid. They and their dependants were able to apply for public aid payments (Versorgungsgebührnisse) due to the effects on their health of physical injuries they had sustained while members of these groupings prior to 13 November 1933 as a result of the 'battle' with their political adversaries.[79] This meant that these party members also had a right to a public aid certificate, permitting them to obtain a preferential place on the lists of applicants for the civil service as public aid candidates. In addition, the requirements for sitting the civil service entry exams could be eased for 'old fighters'.[80]

Furthermore, a circular issued by the Reich Ministry of the Interior of 16 July 1935 endowed officials responsible for recruitment with the authority to ensure that 'designated National Socialists' made up a larger share of lower-grade and junior mid-level civil servants: posts within these levels that had not been filled by 1936 should be given to 'old fighters' on a preferential basis, before being offered to public aid candidates.[81] How many individuals began their civil service career as a result of the circular, however, is not clear. There had after all been long lists of applicants since 1933.

The next change occurred as a result of another circular issued by the Reich Ministry of the Interior of 1 November 1935, which made membership of the Hitler Youth (Hitlerjugend) a condition for becoming a civil service candidate for all those who had reached the age of sixteen after 31 December 1935. As a consequence of prerequisites of this kind, an ideologically conditioned civil service gradually took shape.[82] In a 1935 submission sent by the Reich Ministry of Labour to the main public aid offices, Ministerial Counsellor Schroeder clarified how the training of junior mid-level officials was to be organized within the framework of the public aid authorities. The candidates were to be made familiar with the administrative processes and statutory regulations 'as rapidly and thoroughly as possible' so that they could contribute to the work of administration as soon as possible. To this end, Schroeder considered it necessary, indeed vital, not to rely solely on practical forms of training. Instead, the candidates must be prepared for service with the help of lectures and through practical instruction supervised by senior and experienced officials.[83] Officials working at the public aid authorities, meanwhile, continued to find themselves the subject of public attention, placing their daily work under close scrutiny. 'The public aid officials are fully aware of their duty to war victims. The more deeply they are rooted in the People, the better they will be able to fulfil the responsibility with which they have been invested.'[84] A large number of new public aid laws, though they did not revolutionize the everyday reality of the public bodies, did lead to many shifts in practice. Disabled ex-servicemen and those in receipt of public aid had already been a special focus of Nazi propaganda since the 1920s. When the Nazis took power, the Reich authorities viewed it as their supreme objective to mitigate all hardships suffered by this group. This entailed, for example, helping them hold on to their own homes.[85] These minimal forms of relief, however, must be viewed in relation to the entire population of the German Reich. Within the overall construct of the 'Volksgemeinschaft', the concerns and needs of disabled ex-servicemen were no more than a small fragment, and administrative officials' efforts to meet their needs were correspondingly limited.

It was not until 1937, in the shape of the 'German Civil Service Law'[86] of 26 January, that the first efforts were made to shorten the period of training and reduce the school education required for entry.[87] These greatly diminished requirements went hand in hand with the curtailment of preparatory service.[88] The most marked change, however, related to applicants' required characteristics, though initially these were not enshrined in law: they had to be healthy 'Aryan' Reich citizens committed to the Nazi state and also had to be persons of good standing. All were required to have attended the Volksschule (primary school), but there was no requirement for a more advanced leavers' certificate. Civilian candidates also had to provide evidence of party membership. They were then admitted to the probationary service, which continued to last for six months.[89] The most enduring party political intervention in civil servants' education was the requirement for Nazi Party membership in order to sit the exam necessary to conclude preparatory service or achieve promotion. In order to ensure adherence to these guidelines, the Reich Ministry of Labour had the right to send a ministerial official to supervise all exams if it deemed it necessary.[90]

Furthermore, the 'German Civil Service Law' laid down highly detailed requirements for appointments, and strengthened the state's power of intervention. Preference was to be given to candidates from families with lots of children and those in possession of a leaving certificate from a recognized, full-fledged secondary school (Mittelschule) or who had completed an appropriate extension course at a Volksschule.[91] This law, however, also bolstered the party's and superordinate ministries' right of intervention. It specified that 'the candidate for a civil service post must be a member of the party or one of its organizations. A civil servant thoroughly steeped in the National Socialist spirit will be a true servant of the German People; he will have the capacity for absorption into the Volksgemeinschaft, will consider himself a friend [Kamerad] and will at all times provide his national comrades with help and advice'.[92] Finally, further steps were taken to ensure that the seriously disabled could gain employment in government bodies. Chiefly due to the intervention of Reich Labour Minister Franz Seldte, the authorities not only recruited seriously disabled individuals to train as civil servants on a preferential basis but consciously exceeded the legally prescribed minimum number of such candidates.[93]

These rigorous selection criteria, however, should not be seen as atypical acts or as examples of Nazi authoritarianism as such. Even prior to the Nazi 'seizure of power', selection criteria were determined by the state. The Nazi regime merely exercised an existing right to ensure the selection of ideologically sound candidates. Conversely, the ministries only briefly discussed making real changes in civil servants' career structure, such as linking their appointment with a stint of labour service (Arbeitsdienst).[94]

The structures of everyday administrative practice in public agencies barely changed, while the goals set for civil servants were no different from those pursued in preceding years, namely to speed up administrative procedures and boost efficiency. Here too, however, as with the reorientation of the civil service as a whole, emphatic efforts were made to establish distance from the Weimar Republic. For example, the new regime was determined to ensure that 'public aid [was] apportioned fairly' among all 'national comrades', thus eliminating the allegedly unequal allocations of previous years. The 'injustices' afflicting public aid, however, were more a matter of ideology than social reality. 'It is incompatible with the dignity and standing of the fighters who put their lives and health on the line to defend the Fatherland when national comrades are unjustly granted public aid.'[95] This ideological shift led to the statutory restructuring of the category of public aid recipient. All those who, at the time of their injury, were members of a 'party hostile to the state or its ancillary or front organizations' or who had been injured within the context of such membership, were barred from receiving public aid.[96] But while the state was modifying the right to such benefits, otherwise normality reigned in the public aid agencies, as in many other local authorities. The notion of the Volksgemeinschaft, together with its exclusionary and inclusionary components, influenced the granting of public aid payments, but the administrative process involved barely changed.

Promotions and Further Training

The further education of mid-level civil servants and the bolstering of their expertise were already key concerns of the civil service associations in the German Empire. Immediately after the founding of the Weimar Republic, then, the first administrative academies in Germany were founded. This was also an attempt to underline administrative officials' commitment and the qualitative value of their work.[97] Their teachers included officials from the various ministries. From the outset, as well as seeking to optimize the mid-level civil service, the academies played a major role in enabling officials to advance to the senior level.

Nonetheless, in the early days of the Weimar Republic, senior civil servants and their associations strongly resisted their mid-level counterparts' efforts to advance, fearing that promoting them in this way would ultimately cause the two levels to merge. The key argument for preventing such structural fusion was the supposed lack of relevant qualifications among mid-level officials.[98] In the case of the public aid candidates and non-active service officials, it must be said, these arguments turned out to be entirely valid. Many of the former already demonstrated a conspicuous lack of educational prerequisites during their training, while most of the latter had been given their status in the first place due to their poor educational record and were thus recruited exclusively into the mid-level civil service.[99] In the administrative academies, mid-level officials had the opportunity to sit a diploma exam in a subject area of their choice, through a six-semester course of study for example.[100] The topics included political science, economics, law and a number of other disciplines, and students of these subjects could opt to take courses enhancing their knowledge of social security and pensions legislation.

In light of the increasing complexity of administrative processes, the educational background of the civilian candidates came in for particular criticism: their deficiencies were creating an ever-greater discrepancy between the demands of the job and their ability to do it. Further education at the administrative academy, therefore, was often viewed as an essential means of moulding the mid-level civil service into a productive unity. Public aid officials, moreover, were taking on special importance for the organizers of the administrative academies, who increased the range of courses specifically for this group in 1929.[101] This theoretical input provided a useful supplement to practical training in a given agency. Non-active service officials could also benefit from such further education. Having often gained this status due to average or deficient educational accomplishments, they had the opportunity to learn theory, plug the glaring gaps in their mastery of everyday office life, improve their performance and, after years without practical professional experience, work efficiently with an updated stock of knowledge.

These efforts by aspiring mid-level civil servants to advance their career and optimize their skills went hand in hand with a comprehensive programme of further education, solving a problem that had long afflicted their training.[102] Despite this, a number of Reich ministers were implacably opposed to any move to give administrative academy graduates preferential treatment. They did not consider their qualifications proof of their suitability and were in any case determined to retain full control over the promotion of civil servants. This was partly due to the problems involved in funding such promotions, given that a senior civil servant was of course significantly better paid than a mid-level one.

The new regime that took power in 1933 also failed to solve the problem of how to sequence civil servants' career advancement. At this point in time, many proven civil servants were waiting to obtain the permanent post that they saw as their due. But it was officials close to the Nazi Party who were the first to benefit from the new political reality. In 1934, the Reich minister of labour decided that 'proven fighters for the national uprising' were to be promoted on a preferential basis. This applied to all those civil servants who had joined the party before 1 September 1930, whose status as 'fighter' had been confirmed by the Gau, and who also possessed impeccable qualifications.[103] In order to simplify administrative procedures and accelerate promotions, then, during this period Nazi Party members with civil servant status were given preferential treatment.

In the Nazi state, promotion both within the mid-level civil service and into the senior level was also linked with further education at the administrative academies. Their potential was recognized at an early stage. By 1933, Hans Heinrich Lammers, head of the Reich Chancellery, had become president of the Reich Association of Administrative Academies (Reichsverband der Verwaltungsakademien). Furthermore, funding for the academies was included in the Reich budget, to the tune of fifty thousand Reichsmarks in both 1937 and 1938.[104]

The courses taken in the administrative academies, however, no longer served chiefly to enhance civil servants' skills but instead focused on inculcating them with Nazism: up to seventy-two hours of lectures rooted in Nazi ideology and exalting the nation were provided in the administrative academies, turning them into a carefully calculated blend of 'knowledge schools' (Wissensschulen) on the one hand and 'martial and character-building schools' (Kampf- und Charakterschulen) on the other.[105] When it came to the sequencing of promotion, then, expertise played second fiddle to officials' ideological reliability. Until 1936, an increasing number of students attended the administrative academies[106] and the promotion of further education courses was enshrined in the 'German Civil Service Law' of 1937. 'In-service further education is intended to ensure that upon completing their course civil servants are equal to the ever-increasing demands of their work.'[107] Education and further training, then, were closely intertwined.

However, even the Nazi leadership faced the problem that the diplomas acquired in the administrative academies were not recognized by individual government bodies. As late as 1941, Lammers complained to the Reich minister of the interior that, despite a number of relevant decrees, officials' further education was not being factored in when appointments were made, while those who had participated in such courses were at an explicit disadvantage in the subordinate agencies. With their newly acquired theoretical knowledge, Lammers argued, they must at least be given the chance to demonstrate their practical abilities.[108] Not just candidates for the mid-level civil service, then, but also those mid-level civil servants eager to advance to the senior level had to demonstrate not so much expertise and a good education as a positive attitude towards the Nazi state. Every form of promotion, whether to a higher pay grade within the mid-level civil service or to the senior level, much like permission to sit exams, was earmarked for 'active members of the Nazi movement'.[109] This also went for promotion or appointment to the Reich Ministry of Labour itself. Professional merit receded into the background; in many cases, officials were 'promoted on a preferential basis . . . for rendering outstanding services to the national uprising'.[110] This approach received powerful backing from leading ministerial figures through the issuance of seventeen decrees, directives and orders.[111]

If we consider the example of clerk (*Bürobeamte*) Bernhard Traulsen, however, we find that professional expertise was not disregarded entirely, particularly in the early years of the Nazi state. In 1933, Traulsen (b. 1893) was recommended for promotion to the Reich Labour Ministry's Record Office (Registraturdienst). Prior to the First World War, he had worked as a clerical assistant (*Bürogehilfe*) in the District (military) Command of Flensburg, in other words one of the predecessors of the public aid offices, and until 1919 was an employee of the armed forces. On 1 April 1920 he took up a post as *Diätar* (an official employed on a temporary basis) for the Reich Ministry of Labour within the public aid system, was then made assistant (*Assistent*) and finally, in 1924, was promoted to the post of administrative secretary (*Verwaltungssekretär*). A particular aptitude with respect to Reich public aid and the fields of administrative and economic affairs is noted in his personnel file.[112] Nonetheless, with all his abilities, Traulsen had to meet a requirement imposed equally on all civil servants, one central to becoming the ideal Nazi official: 'professional proficiency' in combination with the 'strength of [one's] militant character'.[113]

Future Prospects: Military Build-Up and War

It was not until the Nazi state began to gear up for war and initiated a massive military build-up that a problem reappeared with which the authorities had already had to struggle in the crisis-hit early 1930s, one that brought administrative processes to a standstill and created tensions among civil servants. It also affected civil service candidates' training. As the state adapted itself to the war economy, from 1937 onwards numerous officials were delegated to other agencies, which were designated 'important to the war'.[114] The public aid agencies, which were not directly involved in the military build-up and made no other crucial contributions to the state's preparations for war, were hit particularly hard by this. It was above all the 'capable and dependable officials of the upper-grade mid-level civil service [who were] ceded to the ministry, the Supreme Auditing Office (Rechnungshof), the Wehrmacht and the labour trustees',[115] while those who were unable to demonstrate these attributes remained in place. The number of staff members diminished drastically and the remaining officials were overworked, so that the civil service candidates, who required observation and guidance, were perceived as a tremendous burden. Not only did officials work long hours, but efficiency declined because it was chiefly the less educated and/or older officials who remained in the 'less important' agencies. Numerous public aid offices reported to the ministry an ever-worsening mood among officials and a negative working atmosphere.[116] Those civil servants appointed since 1936, meanwhile, were said to be of little use because they lacked 'years of practical experience in the public aid system'.[117] At the same time, there were more and more complaints about the so-called 'replacement of civil servants' (*Beamtenersatz*) because new appointees and the civil service candidates could 'only [be regarded] as adequate on paper but not in practice, particularly in the public aid sections'. In many public aid offices, due to the transfer of officials to agencies of importance to the war, posts that became available could only be filled inadequately or not at all; some officials were responsible for almost eleven thousand public aid files.[118] Through the new public aid legislation from 1938 onwards, 90 per cent of posts in the mid-level civil service were occupied by public aid candidates.[119] We cannot rule out the possibility that many officials dismissed in the wake of the 'Civil Service Law' managed to re-enter public agencies as the state sought to offset the lack of civil servants.[120]

When it came to civil service candidates, once again it was the civilian candidates and thus, for the most part, the better educated ones who found their route into the public agencies obstructed. Even if there was a sufficient number of candidates to establish a new cohort of trainees, the beginning of the war brought another setback. In 1940, of applicants for public aid posts, thirty-one candidates were admitted – of whom one resigned, twenty-one were called up for military service at the start of their preparatory service, and two more were enlisted during that phase.[121] The lists of applicants do not indicate that the newly vacant civil service posts were filled by female candidates, which suggests that young women found their way into public bodies at best as white-collar employees.

Training suffered severely under the new conditions: as a result of the lack of staff, the supervision of candidates was regarded as a tremendous disruption to everyday institutional life. In 1940, the authorities were still seeking to remedy this situation by providing a form of preparatory instruction for candidates in study groups, which entailed the teaching of theory in regional divisions. But this plan was not a success.[122] As a result of the shrinking civil service staff, both practical and theoretical training suffered major shortcomings that could not be offset by shared training days of this kind.[123] Similarly, the system of further education largely came to a standstill. Due to bottlenecks in the agencies and the growing expenditure on war-related tasks, in 1942 state and municipal further education courses were temporarily suspended.[124]

Ultimately, the lack of staff led to a lack of instructors. The agencies contained ever fewer officials with the abilities or capacity to induct candidates into administrative practice. During the war, these institutions increasingly regarded the education of mid-level civil servants and the structured continuation of their career paths as a matter of marginal importance, so that administrative officials focused on achieving efficiency and ensuring the orderly fulfilment of their responsibilities.

The assignment of mid-level civil servants from the public aid agencies to numerous other Reich agencies demonstrated the professional competence and importance of this group of officials, even under Nazism. This even applied to those less qualified officials who had remained in the agencies. Their importance was anchored in the fact that the administrative system, particularly as the state apparatus was mobilized to meet the needs of the Four-Year Plan, had expanded and been compelled to cope with an unprecedented range of tasks, an endeavour further complicated by a 'bewildering number of laws'.[125] It was largely down to the mid-level civil servants to deal with this situation and thus sustain everyday administrative operations.

Conclusion

The training of mid-level civil servants in the public aid authorities involved a practical education that was generally carried out in parallel with and on the basis of everyday administrative operations. Particularly in these agencies, such operations were characterized by constant adaptations to the law, new instructions and processes of restructuring. What was demanded of candidates in public agencies was an orientation towards practice and a flexibility that would allow them to organize the agencies' work efficiently. These officials had a huge amount of work to get through, so a firm grasp of legislation relating to Reich public aid and an ability to deal with the workload were important. There were two key requirements here: specialist knowledge about the core aspects of Reich public aid and an ability to interact confidently and proficiently with public aid recipients.

Practical administrative knowledge could be enhanced within the framework of further education courses, thus enabling even mid-level officials to aspire to a career in the senior civil service. Such courses also helped ensure a more flexible and efficient workflow, providing those with backgrounds in quite different fields of work with solid training and better integrating them into a given agency. Practice-oriented in-service training, supplemented by courses in administrative academies, was essentially an outgrowth of mid-level civil servants' efforts to obtain greater rights and authority within their institutions. The everyday work of these officials was essential to the functioning of the administrative system.

Initially, the Nazi 'seizure of power' did not result in structural changes in training, but eventually alterations were made to the admission requirements and the demands made of trainees: candidates' expertise played second fiddle to their political and ideological reliability. This is evident in the appointments made within the administrative system and in admission to exams; from 1937 onwards, both were linked with membership of the Nazi Party, in much the same way as promotions and appointments to the Reich Ministry of Labour. Furthermore, the practical training was to be shorter; preparing candidates for everyday administrative life, then, increasingly faded into the background.

However, the state made absolutely no attempt to reform the administrative system when it came to training, which continued to be practice-oriented and thus dependent on the guidance provided in a particular agency. Candidates could still only acquire a systematic theoretical education outside of the training they received in the public bodies, namely in the administrative academies. These began to foreground Nazi ideology, which increasingly supplanted education in specialized subjects.

The evidence does not show the Nazi state forcing through an entirely new form of training for civil servants. At first sight this seems astonishing given the central role mid-level civil servants played in the functioning of the state. Certainly, particularly from 1937 onwards, we can discern a strong link between appointments and membership of the Nazi Party and

Nazi ideology. But as we have seen, there was no educational revolution and thus no sharp break with the Weimar Republic. The Nazi regime was dependent on the embedded structures of the civil service.

The state's influence on training and on officials' career trajectory within the public aid authorities of the Weimar Republic and then under Nazism is an exemplary case. The associated shift away from a focus on a practice-oriented form of specialist knowledge, acquired in the agency itself, towards an emphasis on officials' ideological reliability, shows unambiguously how the mid-level civil service was shaped by its education and thus how its future action was generated. There was, however, neither any simplification of administrative processes nor any fundamental reorganization of the civil service. The structure of the civil service, officials' training and their key role within the state persisted as the Weimar Republic gave way to the Nazi regime.

Lisa-Maria Röhling, MA, bachelor's degree in English and American studies and history; master's in history at Humboldt University of Berlin. Student assistant on the project being undertaken by the Independent Commission of Historians Investigating the History of the Reich Ministry of Labour in the National Socialist Period (2014–2016); editor at the *Weser-Kurier* newspaper in Bremen since September 2016.

Notes

1. Haussmann, 'Beamtenausbildung und -fortbildung als Teil der Verwaltungsreform', *Beamtenjahrbuch* 15(1) (1928), 54.
2. J.A. Luttenberger, *Verwaltung für den Sozialstaat – Sozialstaat durch Verwaltung? Die Arbeits- und Sozialverwaltung als politisches Problemlösungsinstrument in der Weimarer Republik*, Berlin: LIT, 2013, 290.
3. See G. Hartrodt, *Das Reichsarbeitsministerium, seine Entstehung, sein Aufgabenkreis und seine Organisation und der Behördenorganismus auf dem Arbeitsgebiet des Reichsarbeitsministeriums*, n.p. [c. 1926], 13.
4. Ibid., 11, 16.
5. See Karstedt, 'Aufwand und Kosten des Versorgungswesens im Jahre 1927', *RABl.* II (1927), 175.
6. See Reichsarbeitsministerium (ed.), *Handbuch der Reichsversorgung*, Berlin: Reichsdruckerei, 1932, 1.
7. See Reichsarbeitsministerium, *Deutsche Sozialpolitik 1918–1928. Erinnerungsschrift des Reichsarbeitsministeriums*, Berlin: Mittler, 1928, 225.
8. See Karstedt, 'Aufwand', 175.
9. Ibid.; and Reichsministerium des Innern, *Reichshaushaltsplan für das Rechnungsjahr 1927*, Berlin, 1927.
10. Quoted in H. Fenske, *Bürokratie in Deutschland. Vom späten Kaiserreich bis zur Gegenwart*, Berlin: Colloquium, 1985, 7.
11. Ibid., 8.

12. Ibid., 10; Luttenberger, *Verwaltung für den Sozialstaat*, 289; and B. Wunder, *Geschichte der Bürokratie in Deutschland*, Frankfurt am Main: Suhrkamp, 1986, 113.
13. Even by 1930, two-thirds of civil servants had already been employed in this role since the time of the German Empire. See Wunder, *Geschichte der Bürokratie*, 109.
14. See F. Winters, 'Das Beamtenbildungsproblem in seiner Bedeutung für Volk, Staat und Beamtenschaft', *Beamtenjahrbuch* 15(10) (1928), 516.
15. See H. Potthoff, 'Was heisst Berufsbeamtentum?', *Der Beamte* 1(2) (1929), 108.
16. See Winters, 'Das Beamtenbildungsproblem'; and Potthoff, 'Was heisst Berufsbeamtentum'.
17. See H. Hattenhauer, *Geschichte des deutschen Beamtentums*, Cologne: Heymanns, 1993, 331; Luttenberger, *Verwaltung für den Sozialstaat*, 198; J. Grotkopp, *Beamtentum und Staatsformwechsel. Die Auswirkungen der Staatsformwechsel von 1918, 1933 und 1945 auf das Beamtenrecht und die personelle Zusammensetzung der deutschen Beamtenschaft*, Frankfurt am Main: Lang, 1992, 82.
18. See Luttenberger, *Verwaltung für den Sozialstaat*, 291.
19. See Memorandum by the Association of Prussian State Administrative Officials for the Simplification of the Administrative System (Verband der staatlichen Verwaltungsamtmänner Preussens zur Vereinfachung der Verwaltung), 18 December 1928, Bundesarchiv (BArch), R 8082/89, fol. 34.
20. Guidelines on the Regulation of the Administrative Career Path of Civil Servants Employed by the Reich, Länder and Municipalities, 28 January 1922, BArch, R 1501/102431, fol. 157.
21. Salary Law, 30 April 1920, *RGBl.* I 1920, 805–16.
22. See H. Völter, *Die deutsche Beamtenbesoldung*, Leipzig: Duncker & Humblot, 1932, 23.
23. Ibid., 93.
24. Ibid., 92. The official titles cited here relate to those offices of relevance to this study and do not reflect the entire Reich civil service.
25. *RGBl.* I 1937, 39–70.
26. Hecker, Concerning Volume of Work in the Fields within the Ambit of the Main Public Aid Office, Berlin, 28 May 1927, BArch, R 3901/9461, n.p.
27. Excerpt from the draft produced by the supreme Reich authorities, the Prussian central authorities, the Land governments and the offices subordinate to the Reich Ministry of the Interior, 1920, BArch, R 3901/102430, n.p.; and Luttenberger, *Verwaltung für den Sozialstaat*, 305.
28. Guidelines on the Regulations to be issued by the Ministries on the Educational Background, Qualifications and Examination of the Officials of the Mid-Level Administrative and Judicial Service, 1922, BArch, R 1501/102431, fol. 68.
29. Günther, 'Das Wesen des Anwärters und der Anwartschaft', *Beamtenjahrbuch* 20(9) (1933), 434.
30. See W. Isberner, *Jahrbuch für Beamte im Versorgungs- und Fürsorgewesen*, Berlin: Gerstmann, 1921, 85.
31. See Luttenberger, *Verwaltung für den Sozialstaat*, 309.
32. Professional Association of Senior Civil Servants (Berufsverein der höheren Beamten), Excerpt from *Nachrichten des Berufsvereins der höheren Verwaltungsbeamten* (November 1922), 11/12, 83, BArch, R 8081/42, n.p.
33. Reichsarbeitsministerium, *Handbuch der Reichsversorgung*, 1724a.
34. Examination Question on the Public Aid System, n.d., BArch, R 3901/6599, n.p.
35. Reichsarbeitsministerium, *Handbuch der Reichsversorgung*, 1597.
36. See Günther, 'Das Wesen', 434–50.
37. Employment Principles (Principles Underpinning the Employment of Those Holding a Certificate Affirming their Right to be Employed as a Civil Servant [Versorgungsschein]), 16 July 1923, *RGBl.* 1923, 651–82, here 653 (§ 8).

38. Circular issued by the Reich labour minister on the official use of the Public Aid Offices, 3 July 1931, BArch, R 3901/20502, fol. 71.
39. See Herberger, Civil Service Careers, 14 October 1928, BArch, R 8082/89, fol. 65–66.
40. Foerster, Announcement on the Replacement of Civil Servants in 'Excerpt from *Reichsministerialblatt* no. 49, 17 November 1928', 13 November 1928, BArch, R 3901/20499, fol. 29; cf. Schulte-Holthausen, 'Anstellungsgrundsätze', *Reichsversorgungsblatt* 5 (1930), 28.
41. Max Schroeder to Member of the Reichstag Director E. Rossmann, 8 July 1930, BArch, R 3901/20502, n.p.
42. Note by Senior Government Counsellor Schroeder and Senior Government Inspector (Regierungsoberinspektor) Hussmann, 30 August 1927, BArch, R 3901/20501, n.p.
43. League of Civil Servants Working in Fields within the Remit of the Reich Ministry of Labour (Bund der Beamten im Bereich des Reichsarbeitsministeriums), Concerning Up-and-Coming Staff in the Public Aid Offices, 29 July 1927, BArch, R 3901/20501, fol. 101.
44. Head of Public Aid Office III Berlin to the Director of the Main Public Aid Office Brandenburg-Pommern, Concerning Civil Servant Matters, 3 December 1937, BArch, R 3901/20584, fol. 161.
45. Guidelines on the Interaction between the Public Aid Offices and Public Aid Recipients, in *Reichsversorgungsblatt* 14 (1928), 64.
46. Ibid.
47. Main Public Aid Office Lower Saxony-Nordmark to the Reich Ministry of Labour, Concerning the Need to Protect Civil Servants, 30 September 1929, BArch, R 3901/6573, n.p.
48. Schott, Complaint made by the Leadership of the League of Frontline Soldiers (Frontkriegerbund e. V.) in Munich about the Handling of Claims for Public Aid, 8 April 1927, BArch, R 3901/9461, n.p.
49. Many of these cases can be found in the file BArch, R 3901/9537.
50. Reichsarbeitsministerium, *Handbuch der Reichsversorgung*.
51. Reschke, Concerning the Public Aid Offices' Excessive Workload, 3 April 1928, BArch, R 3901/9361, n.p.
52. See Völter, *Die deutsche Beamtenbesoldung*, 17.
53. Guidelines for the Career of Civil Servant, 28 January 1922, BArch, R 1501/102431, fol. 43–44.
54. Letter from Reich minister of finance, 31 December 1927, BArch, R 3901/6608, n.p.; and Letter from Griessmeyer, 16 June 1928, BArch, R 3901/6609, n.p.
55. Schroeder, Note on the Issue of Examinations 1930, 23 July 1930, BArch, R 3901/6611, n.p.
56. *RGBl.* I 1933, 175–77.
57. See Grotkopp, *Beamtentum und Staatsformwechsel*, 111.
58. *RGBl.* I 1933, 245–52, here 247.
59. See H. Mommsen, *Beamtentum im Dritten Reich. Mit ausgewählten Quellen zur nationalsozialistischen Beamtenpolitik*, Stuttgart: Deutsche Verlags-Anstalt, 1966, 47, 72.
60. Ibid., 47.
61. Ibid., 69.
62. F. Triebel, 'Das Problem des Beamtennachwuchses', *Der deutsche Reichsverwaltungsbeamte/Der Deutsche Verwaltungsbeamte* 1 (1940/41), 2.
63. L. Reck, '"Der Wert der Beamtenarbeit"', *Der deutsche Reichsverwaltungsbeamte/Der Deutsche Verwaltungsbeamte* 3 (1935), 65.
64. Ibid.
65. 'Zwei Jahre Nationalsozialistische Beamtenpolitik', *Der deutsche Reichsverwaltungsbeamte/Der Deutsche Verwaltungsbeamte* 6 (1938), 172.

66. The Prussian Minister of Finance, Concerning Guidelines on Admission and Education for the Upper-Grade Mid-Level Civil Service, of the General Administrative System in Particular, 7 December 1937, BArch, R 3901/11930, n.p.

67. Reich Ministry of Labour, Career Guidelines for Mid-Level Civil Servants, 22 July 1937, BArch, R 3901/11925, n.p.

68. See J. Weidemann, *Führertum in der Verwaltung*, ed. Dr Lammers, Berlin: Spaeth & Linde, 1936, 9.

69. See Foerster, 'Die Zahl der versorgungsberechtigten Kriegsbeschädigten und Kriegshinterbliebenen und die Zahl der versorgungsberechtigten ehemaligen Angehörigen der neuen Wehrmacht und ihre Hinterbliebenen im Mai 1933', *RABl.* II(24) (1933), 335–37.

70. See 'Zwei Jahre Nationalsozialistische Beamtenpolitik', *Der deutsche Reichsverwaltungsbeamte/Der Deutsche Verwaltungsbeamte* 6 (1938), 172.

71. Reichsministerium des Innern, *Reichshaushaltsplan für das Rechnungsjahr 1935*, Berlin, 1935, VII. 'Ordentlicher Haushalt', ch. 11, section 5, 58.

72. 'Gesetz zur Änderung von Vorschriften auf dem Gebiete des allgemeinen Beamten-, des Besoldungs- und des Versorgungsrechts vom 30. Juni 1933', *RGBl.* I (1933), 433–47, here 434.

73. Reich Minister of the Interior, Concerning the Appointment of Civilian Candidates to the Mid-Level Civil Service, 8 February 1934, BArch, R 3901/20502, n.p.; see also Concerning the Instruction of Civil Servants and White- and Blue-Collar Workers in National Socialism, 30 November 1933, BArch, R 3901/20514, fol. 304 f.

74. See Wunder, *Geschichte der Bürokratie*, 140.

75. See Grotkopp, *Beamtentum und Staatsformwechsel*, 111.

76. See Wunder, *Geschichte der Bürokratie*, 141.

77. Ibid.; and Training New Recruits for Ministerial Office Service and the Record Office, 27 April 1935, BArch, R 3901/20499, fol. 97.

78. Seel, 'Beamtenrecht. Grundlinien des Beamtenrechts', *Beamtenjahrbuch* 21(1) (1934), 5.

79. *RGBl.* I 1934, 133–34; and 'Gesetz über die Versorgung der Kämpfer für die nationale Erhebung vom 27. Februar 1934', *Reichsversorgungsblatt* 3 (1934), 15–18.

80. Wunder, *Geschichte der Bürokratie*, 140; and Mommsen, *Beamtentum im Dritten Reich*, 70.

81. See 'Stellen vorbehalten für Nationalsozialisten', *Der deutsche Reichsverwaltungsbeamte/Der Deutsche Verwaltungsbeamte* 16 (1935), 497.

82. See Grotkopp, *Beamtentum und Staatsformwechsel*, 135; Mommsen, *Beamtentum im Dritten Reich*, 36.

83. Schroeder, Concerning Civil Service Candidates, 16 January 1935, BArch, R 3901/20502, fol. 148–49.

84. Feige, 'Der Versorgungsbeamte – Vertrauensmann der Kriegsopfer', *Der deutsche Reichsverwaltungsbeamte/Der Deutsche Verwaltungsbeamte* 9 (1934), 154.

85. L. Münz, 'Die Sozialpolitische Gesetzgebung seit dem 30. Januar 1933', *RABl.* II (1933), 329–35, here 330.

86. *RGBl.* I 1937, 39–70.

87. Prussian Finance Minister, Concerning Regulations on Admission and Education for Upper-Grade Mid-Level Civil Servants, Particularly those Working in General Administration, 7 December 1937, BArch, R 3901/11930, fol. 4, 9.

88. See *Die Laufbahnen der deutschen Beamten. Ein Nachschlagewerk für Behörden; ein Ratgeber für Zivil und Versorgungsanwärter*, vol. 3: *Textabdruck der Laufbahnbestimmungen sämtlicher Fachrichtungen, Verordnung der Reichsregierung über die Vorbildung und die Laufbahnen der deutschen Beamten vom 28.2.1939*, Berlin: Beamtenpresse, 1940, §§ 20–24, 20 f.

89. M. Eggerdinger, 'Ausbildung der Anwärter des einfachen Dienstes', *Der deutsche Reichsverwaltungsbeamte/Der Deutsche Verwaltungsbeamte* 17 (1939), 560.

90. Gies, Concerning Regulations on Education and Exams, 19 April 1939, BArch, R 3901/11930, n.p.

91. See *Die Laufbahnen der deutschen Beamten*, 6 f., 20.

92. Training New Recruits for Ministerial Office Service and the Record Office, 27 April 1935, BArch, R 3901/20499, fol. 97.

93. F. Seldte, 'Betrifft: Arbeitsbeschaffung für Kriegsbeschädigte', *Reichsversorgungblatt* 4 (1936), 32.

94. See Max Schroeder to the Reich League of Those Entitled to a Civil Service Post (Reichsbund der Zivildienstberechtigten e. V.), Dissolution of Public Aid Offices, 31 December 1931, BArch, R 3901/20502, fol. 128–29.

95. '5. Gesetz zur Änderung des Gesetzes über das Verfahren in Versorgungssachen, 4. Juli 1934', *Reichsversorgungsblatt* 6 (1934), 53.

96. Reichsarbeitsministerium (ed.), *Handbuch der Reichsversorgung*, Berlin: Reichsdruckerei, 1934, n.p.

97. Luttenberger, *Verwaltung für den Sozialstaat*, 325.

98. Concerning the Work of Senior Civil Servants for the Governments, 3 July 1931, BArch, R 8082/89, fol. 46.

99. Record of the Meeting with the Heads of the Main Public Aid Offices at the Reich Ministry of Labour, 6 January 1928, BArch, R 3901/9361, n.p.

100. Administrative Academy to Reich Ministry of Labour, 15 June 1929, BArch, R 3901/6598, n.p.

101. See Fenske, *Bürokratie in Deutschland*, 19.

102. Ibid.

103. See 'Aus dem Bereich des Reichsarbeitsministeriums, Beförderung bevorzugter Kämpfer um die nationale Bewegung', *Der deutsche Reichsverwaltungsbeamte/Der Deutsche Verwaltungsbeamte* 7 (1934), 110.

104. See Weidemann, *Führertum in der Verwaltung*, 42; State Secretary and Head of the Reich Chancellery, Concerning Financial Support for the Reich Association of Administrative Academies (Reichsverband Deutscher Verwaltungs-Akademien), 21 January 1937, BArch, R 43 II/947, n.p.

105. Müssigbrodt, 'Die Verwaltungs-Akademie als Kampfschule des deutschen Beamten', *Beamtenjahrbuch* 23(1) (1936), 50–53, here 52.

106. See Sigrun Mühl-Benninghaus, *Das Beamtentum in der NS-Diktatur bis zum Ausbruch des Zweiten Weltkrieges: zu Entstehung, Inhalt und Durchführung der einschlägigen Beamtengesetze*, Düsseldorf: Droste, 1996, 131.

107. *Die Laufbahnen der deutschen Beamten*, § 38, 24.

108. Reich Association of Administrative Academies to the Reich Minister of the Interior, 20 June 1941, BArch, R 43 II/947, n.p.

109. Reich Ministry of Labour, Compilation to the Main Public Aid Offices. Sequence of Promotion for Mid-Level Civil Servants, March 1935, BArch, R 3901/20555, fol. 107.

110. Reich Ministry of Labour to the Heads of the Main Public Aid Offices, Concerning Appointments to the Reich Ministry of Labour, 12 January 1935, BArch, R 3901/20499, fol. 62.

111. See Grotkopp, *Beamtentum und Staatsformwechsel*, 135 f.

112. Evaluation of Administrative Secretary Bernhard Traulsen by the Hamburg Public Aid Office, 9 June 1933, BArch, R 3901/20499, fol. 51.

113. Müssigbrodt, 'Die Verwaltungs-Akademie'.

114. See Head of the Brandenburg-Pomerania Main Public Aid Office to the Reich Minister of Labour, Concerning List of Names of Mid-Level Civil Servants, n.d., BArch, R 3901/20499, fol. 135–36.

115. See Head of the Westphalia Public Aid Office to the Reich Minister of Labour, Workload and Allocation of Staff, 2 August 1938, BArch, R 3901/20499, fol. 170 f.

116. Head of Berlin Public Aid Office I to the Head of Brandenburg-Pomerania Main Public Aid Office, Concerning Civil Service Affairs, 16 November 1937, BArch, R 3901/20584, fol. 157.
117. Reich Public Aid Factory Cell to the Head Officials of the Münster Public Aid Offices, 30 June 1938, BArch, R 3901/20499, fol. 424.
118. Soest Public Aid Office to the Westphalia Main Public Aid Office, Concerning Workload of the Public Aid Offices, 14 June 1938, BArch, R 3901/20499, fol. 208–9.
119. Concerning Regulations on Education and Exams, 19 April 1939, BArch, R 3901/11930, n.p.; see also Welfare and Provision Law for the Former Members of the Wehrmacht and their Dependents – Wehrmacht Welfare and Provision Law (WFVG) (Fürsorge- und Vorsorgesetz für die Angehörigen der Wehrmacht und ihre Hinterbliebenen – Wehrmachtfürsorge und -versorgungsgesetz [WFVG]), *RGBl.* I (1938), 1080–124, here 1087 f. (§ 40).
120. See Mommsen, *Beamtentum im Dritten Reich*, 58 f.
121. Haberkorn, Concerning Experiences with the Regulations on Education and Exams, 17 October 1940, BArch, R 3901/11930, n.p.
122. Ibid.
123. Danzig-West Prussia Main Public Aid Office, Concerning Regulations on Education and Exams of 12 January 1940, 25 October 1940, BArch, R 3901/11930, n.p.
124. Reich Minister of the Interior to the Supreme Reich Authorities, Concerning Staffing Cuts, 20 January 1942, BArch, R 43 II/947, fol. 77.
125. Prussian Minister of Finance, Concerning Regulations on Admission and Education for Upper-Grade Mid-Level Civil Servants, Particularly those Working in General Administration, 7 December 1937, BArch, R 3901/11930, fol. 2.

Bibliography

Eggerdinger, M. 'Ausbildung der Anwärter des einfachen Dienstes'. *Der deutsche Reichsverwaltungsbeamte/Der Deutsche Verwaltungsbeamte* (17) (1939), 560.
Feige. 'Der Versorgungsbeamte – Vertrauensmann der Kriegsopfer'. *Der deutsche Reichsverwaltungsbeamte/Der Deutsche Verwaltungsbeamte* (9) (1934), 154.
Fenske, H. *Bürokratie in Deutschland. Vom späten Kaiserreich bis zur Gegenwart*. Berlin: Colloquium, 1985.
Foerster. 'Die Zahl der versorgungsberechtigten Kriegsbeschädigten und Kriegshinterbliebenen und die Zahl der versorgungsberechtigten ehemaligen Angehörigen der neuen Wehrmacht und ihre Hinterbliebenen im Mai 1933'. *Reichsarbeitsblatt* II(24) (1933), 335–37.
Grotkopp, J. *Beamtentum und Staatsformwechsel. Die Auswirkungen der Staatsformwechsel von 1918, 1933 und 1945 auf das Beamtenrecht und die personelle Zusammensetzung der deutschen Beamtenschaft*. Frankfurt am Main: Lang, 1992.
Günther. '"Das Wesen des Anwärters und der Anwartschaft"'. *Beamtenjahrbuch* 20(9) (1933), 434.
Hartrodt, G. *Das Reichsarbeitsministerium, seine Entstehung, sein Aufgabenkreis und seine Organisation und der Behördenorganismus auf dem Arbeitsgebiet des Reichsarbeitsministeriums*. N.p. [c. 1926].
Hattenhauer, H. *Geschichte des deutschen Beamtentums*. Cologne: Heymanns, 1993.
Haussmann. 'Beamtenausbildung und -fortbildung als Teil der Verwaltungsreform'. *Beamtenjahrbuch* 15(1) (1928), 54.
Isberner, W. *Jahrbuch für Beamte im Versorgungs- und Fürsorgewesen*. Berlin: Gerstmann, 1921.

Karstedt. 'Aufwand und Kosten des Versorgungswesens im Jahre 1927'. *Reichsarbeitsblatt* II (1927), 175.
Die Laufbahnen der deutschen Beamten. Ein Nachschlagewerk für Behörden; ein Ratgeber für Zivil und Versorgungsanwärter, vol. 3: *Textabdruck der Laufbahnbestimmungen sämtlicher Fachrichtungen, Verordnung der Reichsregierung über die Vorbildung und die Laufbahnen der deutschen Beamten vom 28.2.1939*. Berlin: Beamtenpresse, 1940.
Luttenberger, J.A. *Verwaltung für den Sozialstaat – Sozialstaat durch Verwaltung? Die Arbeits- und Sozialverwaltung als politisches Problemlösungsinstrument in der Weimarer Republik*. Berlin: LIT, 2013.
Mommsen, H. *Beamtentum im Dritten Reich. Mit ausgewählten Quellen zur nationalsozialistischen Beamtenpolitik*. Stuttgart: Deutsche Verlags-Anstalt, 1966.
Mühl-Benninghaus, S. *Das Beamtentum in der NS-Diktatur bis zum Ausbruch des Zweiten Weltkrieges: zu Entstehung, Inhalt und Durchführung der einschlägigen Beamtengesetze*. Düsseldorf: Droste, 1996.
Münz, L. 'Die Sozialpolitische Gesetzgebung seit dem 30. Januar 1933'. *Reichsarbeitsblatt* II (1933), 329–35.
Müssigbrodt. 'Die Verwaltungs-Akademie als Kampfschule des deutschen Beamten'. *Beamtenjahrbuch* 23(1) (1936), 50–53.
Potthoff, H. 'Was heisst Berufsbeamtentum?' *Der Beamte* 1(2) (1929), 108.
Reck, L. '"Der Wert der Beamtenarbeit"'. *Der deutsche Reichsverwaltungsbeamte/Der Deutsche Verwaltungsbeamte* (3) (1935), 65.
Reichsarbeitsministerium (ed.). *Handbuch der Reichsversorgung (HdR)*. Berlin: Reichsdruckerei, 1932–1939.
Reichsarbeitsministerium (ed.). *Deutsche Sozialpolitik 1918–1928. Erinnerungsschrift des Reichsarbeitsministeriums*. Berlin: Mittler, 1928.
Reichsministerium des Innern. *Reichshaushaltsplan für das Rechnungsjahr 1927*. Berlin, 1927.
Reichsministerium des Innern. *Reichshaushaltsplan für das Rechnungsjahr 1935*. Berlin, 1935.
Schulte-Holthausen. 'Anstellungsgrundsätze'. *Reichsversorgungsblatt* (5) (1930), 28.
Seel. 'Beamtenrecht. Grundlinien des Beamtenrechts'. *Beamtenjahrbuch* 21(1) (1934), 5.
Seldte, F. 'Betrifft: Arbeitsbeschaffung für Kriegsbeschädigte'. *Reichsversorgungblatt* (4) (1936), 32.
Triebel, F. 'Das Problem des Beamtennachwuchses'. *Der deutsche Reichsverwaltungsbeamte/ Der Deutsche Verwaltungsbeamte* (1) (1940/41), 2.
Völter, H. *Die deutsche Beamtenbesoldung*. Leipzig: Duncker & Humblot, 1932.
Weidemann, J. *Führertum in der Verwaltung*, ed. Dr Lammers. Berlin: Spaeth & Linde, 1936.
Winters, F. 'Das Beamtenbildungsproblem in seiner Bedeutung für Volk, Staat und Beamtenschaft'. *Beamtenjahrbuch* 15(10) (1928), 516.
Wunder, B. *Geschichte der Bürokratie in Deutschland*. Frankfurt am Main: Suhrkamp, 1986.

Chapter 3

THE REICH MINISTRY OF LABOUR AND THE GERMAN LABOUR FRONT
Permanent Conflict and Informal Cooperation

Rüdiger Hachtmann

In mid 1938, conflict flared up between the state secretary in the Reich Labour Ministry, Johannes Krohn, and Rudolf Schmeer,[1] then deputy head of the DAF, with Krohn challenging Schmeer to a duel. What had happened? The 33-year-old Schmeer and other top DAF functionaries (many of them even younger than him) had enraged Krohn by delivering a calculated flow of little jabs. The 49-year-old Krohn, socialized in late Wilhelmine Germany and imbued with notions of honour rooted in that estates-based social order, had been an official at the Ministry of Labour since 1920. 'Literally bristling with outrage', he had earlier described Schmeer as a 'traitor'.[2] Schmeer himself was a noted yob and ruffian who became active in far-right organizations in 1920 at the age of fourteen or fifteen. In 1923, at just sixteen years of age, he joined the Nazi Party for the first time and had been one of Robert Ley's[3] closest lieutenants ever since. When Hitler charged his close confidant Ley with the task of establishing a new, paternalistic Nazi organization for workers in early May 1933, Schmeer followed him to the Reich capital. He was twenty-eight years old when he was formally appointed Ley's 'deputy' in October 1933.

During the Nazi movement's 'years of struggle' (*Kampfzeit*) prior to 1933, in Aachen and the surrounding area, Schmeer had been preceded by his reputation as the 'biggest lout and ruffian' as well as a 'first-class brute'.[4] According to Walter Kiehl, Ley's press secretary, who stylized Ley and his closest colleagues as heroes of the Nazi movement in a 1938 pamphlet, Schmeer was 'one of Dr Ley's most valuable colleagues'; in the late 1920s and early 1930s, he had 'frequently led from the front' when it came to 'chasing' members of the SPD or the Catholic Centre Party 'through pubs, restaurants and along streets', while he and his comrades engaged their foes in 'bloody battles'.[5]

Enraged by Schmeer's constant provocations, what the distinguished ministerial official Krohn, son of an accounting counsellor (*Rechnungsrat*) and exemplar of Prussian punctiliousness, had failed to remember when he challenged the leading DAF functionary to an 'honourable duel' was that Hitler had banned the practice shortly before (in 1937).[6] Because the DAF subsequently refused to tone down its aggressive approach to the Ministry of Labour, Krohn stood down voluntarily from his post as state secretary towards the end of 1938. Continuing his career in a political field in which the DAF was not active, from October 1941 until 1945 he was the Reich commissioner for the administration of enemy property (Reichskommissar für die Behandlung feindlichen Vermögens). Krohn thus became a key actor in the Nazi regime's policy of expropriation in the occupied territories.

This illustrates three things above all. First, conflicts between the DAF and the Reich Ministry of Labour were not necessarily down to political differences. They were often essentially matters of habitus and a response to the over-casual conduct and aggressive politicking of many DAF functionaries. Ley and his entourage, furthermore, were distinguished by typical antibureaucratic sentiments. Second, Krohn's proposed duel reveals that the differences between the leading protagonists of the DAF and the Labour Ministry were in large part a matter of generation. Schmeer, thirty-three years old in 1938, was almost two decades younger than Krohn. Of Robert Ley's three closest confidants, Schmeer was not even the youngest. The lawyer Heinrich Simon, who joined the Nazi Party for the first time at the same age as Schmeer, was just twenty-two when Ley made him his personal adjutant in 1932. Otto Marrenbach, originally a commercial clerk and member of the Nazi Party since 1928 – another multifunctional official and important chiefly as executive director of the DAF – was the oldest, aged thirty-nine in 1938. Even Marrenbach, though 'more restrained' than Schmeer, was like the latter retrospectively proud of the 'terrific fights' in which he had been involved in the late 1920s.[7] Third and finally, this episode highlights the fact that the DAF was the Labour Ministry's main political antagonist. This mass-membership Nazi organization, equipped with a vast apparatus of personnel, muscled its way into many spheres of society that had previously been the exclusive demesne of the Labour Ministry and laid claim to powers that had been its uncontested preserve until 1933 and beyond.

What does this episode *not* show? It tells us nothing about the causes of the conflict beyond its habitual and situational aspects. Was it underpinned by fundamental conceptual antagonisms over key issues in labour and social policy? Was it more a case of superficial wrangling over power and influence? The above episode, moreover, suggests that the relationship between the Labour Ministry and the DAF was generally characterized by conflict. The many forms of what was often amicable cooperation tend to fade into the background in light of such incidents. To pre-empt the following analysis a little, we can in fact discern a form of 'rivalry-based cooperation'[8] between the two camps – which was not untypical of the multifaceted relationships between the key political actors of the Nazi period.

This chapter is divided into two parts along general lines. In the first, I use the opportunity provided by a (brief) presentation of the history of the DAF to bring out the difficulties the Reich Ministry of Labour had with this elusive organizational colossus. In the second part, I describe some of the social fields common to both the Labour Ministry and the DAF and outline the rivalry-based cooperation between the two.

The DAF's Responsibilities and Self-Image

The DAF was founded at a grandiose congress held on 10 May 1933 and attended by Hitler, Goebbels and other prominent Nazis as well as Reich Labour Minister Franz Seldte. It was an expression of the 'Cabinet of national unity' appointed by Reich President Paul von Hindenburg and its cast-iron determination to make it impossible for autonomous trades unions to even begin to get off the ground. The very name of the new organization indicated the regime's objectives.[9] The goal was not to develop a 'workers' front' but rather a 'labour front'. The Nazi regime and its leading protagonists had no interest in the individual 'worker', and in no way did they want a substantial body representing the interests of blue- and white-collar workers within and across firms. Instead, the regime's focus was on the labour performed by the workers, whom it reduced to the status of 'members of the retinue' (*Gefolgschaftsmitglieder*), as part of a racially conceived German 'Volkskörper' (the body of the folk, in an ethnic national sense). 'Labour' mattered as an economic factor. By the same token, the mobilization of labour occurred not for its own sake but with a specific goal in mind. The second part of this organization's name was 'front', implicitly marking both objective and means, namely the 'militarization of labour' in accordance with the regime's bellicist mindset. In other words, the nation must strain every sinew to build up its military forces, wage war and bolster the war economy. This found its terminological focus in the Volksgemeinschaft, which was in turn inspired, tellingly, by the (idealized) 'community of the front' (*Frontgemeinschaft*) that emerged during the First

World War.[10] All of this occurred with the consent of the Nazi movement's right-wing conservative allies, not least with the key protagonists of the Reich Ministry of Labour, now headed by Seldte, former leader of the Steel Helmets (Stahlhelm – Bund der Frontsoldaten).

As the main speakers at its founding congress on 10 May 1933, Hitler and Ley left their listeners in no doubt about the goals to be pursued by the DAF. Both railed against the supposed 'class struggle' waged by the trades unions and workers' parties, and thus made it abundantly clear that the wages policy characteristic of the Weimar democracy, based on negotiations and contracts, was to come to an end. Ley fleshed out the tasks to be executed by the DAF through slogans such as 'education [to inculcate a] will to work', 'awakening work discipline', 'cultivating vocational pride', 'ennobling the concept of "work"' and 'education [to establish a] Volksgemeinschaft'.[11] Such phrases did little to conceal the consequences for the workers. The goal was to bring about the social and organizational atomization of the 'retinue members', in order to render autonomous social structures of communication, independent of Nazism, impossible. Further, the intention was to achieve the enduring individual and collective disenfranchisement of the workforce,[12] robbing workers of their political voice across the board. The DAF pursued these objectives from the outset. Repressing, intimidating and stripping workers of their rights, however, were not in themselves enough to permanently immobilize them, let alone to turn them into active 'national comrades' of a staunchly Nazi persuasion. So the DAF, via its largest suborganization, Strength through Joy (Kraft durch Freude, or KdF), and a vast network of DAF-run firms, also strove to provide concrete material incentives and nonmaterial 'services'.[13] Through initiatives such as the so-called Reich Vocational Contest (Reichsberufswettkampf), meanwhile, it gave young workers in particular hope of ascending the social ladder.

Reich-wide campaigns aggressively pursued by a DAF outfit called 'Beauty of Work' (Schönheit der Arbeit) and large-scale annual events such as the Reich Vocational Contest and the 'Companies' Performance Battle' (Leistungskampf der Betriebe), which were omnipresent for weeks in the German media, were always in part major – often deftly orchestrated – spectacles. For the Labour Ministry, this and the mass Nazi organization's ubiquitous media presence in general represented a problem, because the two were in competition with one another in numerous fields. Both sought to mobilize 'labour' as a key factor in the economy in order to advance the interests of the Nazi dictatorship, and both tried to create a Volksgemeinschaft and an achievement-based community (*Leistungsgemeinschaft*) overarching all social classes and strata. In contrast to the workers' associations of the Weimar Republic or even the later Federal Republic, the DAF did not restrict itself merely to predictable forms of intervention in specific social policy fields. Just as the powers, for example, of the SS soon began to overlap and merge with those of the interior ministries of the Reich and the states, in a comparable way the DAF de facto arrogated powers to itself that had been the sole preserve of the Reich Ministry of Labour until 1933. That the Berlin-based ministry and the DAF were very different types of organization in structural terms did nothing to change the fact that in many fields both were engaged in an extremely intense and often personal competitive battle.

In its clashes with the rather restrained Labour Ministry, the DAF's media presence provided it with 'atmospheric' advantages. For this reason alone, the latter organization managed to become a tremendously powerful player in the sphere of labour and social policy, even without having to formally contest the ministry's powers. The kind of trump cards held by the DAF as a result of its vast apparatus of press and propaganda become apparent if we consider just the sheer scale of the print media under its control. In 1937 alone, a total of 389 paper factories, printing works and bookbinderies were engaged in the printing and production of newspapers, magazines, pamphlets and so on at the behest of the DAF[14] – not including the five large, modern printing works run by the organization, which were among the largest in the sector. In contrast to the DAF, the Labour Ministry largely failed to use the media to advance its agenda – a grave disadvantage amid the polycratic struggle for power and influence.

However, the polemics unleashed so often upon the Reich Ministry of Labour by key DAF protagonists should not blind us to the fact that the two camps were not so very far apart in most of their fundamental tendencies. Given the objectives laid down by Hitler and Ley, particularly to do away with 'class struggle' and the autonomy of trades unions while educating the German workforce to embrace a 'will to work' and 'work discipline', it is no surprise that the DAF leadership welcomed, with outright enthusiasm, the Law on the Organization of National Labour (Gesetz zur Ordnung der nationalen Arbeit, or AOG) of 20 January 1934, namely the law that laid the foundations for the labour regime of the 'Third Reich'. That this law (contrary to the view widely held by researchers) was not a defeat for the DAF is evident in the fact that, in addition to senior officials in the Reich Labour Ministry (particularly Werner Mansfeld), significant figures in the DAF also played a major role in formulating it, particularly Rudolf Schmeer and Wolfgang Pohl.[15] In early 1935, the latter, one of Ley's confidants and one of his few good friends as well as a senior ministerial official both in the Reich Ministry of Labour and in the Reich Ministry of the Economy, was made head of the Labour Science Institute, the DAF's 'brain trust', which cooked up the strategies then pursued by the organization as a whole. Ley himself was involved in drawing up the AOG.

Retrospectively (and probably exaggerating), he explained that he had 'immediately taken the reins' in drafting the law.[16] Only in one respect were Ley and his comrades dissatisfied: what they actually wanted was a 'Basic Law of Labour' (Grundgesetz der Arbeit) focused on a small number of key elements. Here, however, they were as yet unable to get their way vis-à-vis a ministerial bureaucracy captive to traditional legal concepts.

The AOG circumscribed the DAF's activities chiefly in a 'negative' sense. Meanwhile, in a decree of 24 October 1934, Hitler formulated the Labour Front's responsibilities in a 'positive' sense. To quote this decree on the 'Nature and Objectives of the German Labour Front', the 'goal of the German Labour Front [is] the formation of a true German Volksgemeinschaft (community of the people) and Leistungsgemeinschaft (community of achievement)'. Its task was to 'ensure that each individual is able to take up his place in the economic life of the nation in the mental and physical condition that enables him to perform at his best and thus provide the greatest benefit to the Volksgemeinschaft'.[17] For the DAF, this woolly yet far-reaching wording made the decree into a kind of 'enabling law' – a lever that made it possible to question the powers and ultimately the very existence of the Reich Ministry of Labour.

Unsurprisingly, then, the key protagonists of the Labour Ministry were greatly alarmed by the 'Führer' decree. Mansfeld tried to play down its importance by remarking that it had not been 'announced in the Reich Law Gazette but merely in the daily press'. It should, he asserted, only be regarded as a stimulus for future legislation.[18] Krohn, the key figure in the Berlin ministry alongside Mansfeld until his resignation, believed that its roots lay in a 'gap in the structure of our law on the organization of national labour'. He wished to 'fill' this 'gap' through more precise legal provisions and thus render Hitler's decree obsolete.[19] But this is not what happened. Much to their chagrin, Mansfeld, Krohn and other ministerial officials soon discovered that this decree had the status of 'national law', which meant that it superseded all previous laws and decrees.

An Overwhelming Opponent: The Organization of the Labour Front

The DAF's organizational structure is also hard to nail down. In contrast to the Reich Ministry of Labour with its relatively firmly established institutional structure – despite all the internal organizational changes – the Labour Front, as Hitler had demanded in 1933, was a 'changeling'.[20] Hitler required that the new mass association be organized with flexibility in mind, in order to rule out any 'regression' to trades union-like structures and ensure its ability to adapt with agility to changing circumstances. This precept continued to apply even during the war. In 1941, Ley thus declared that 'the entire German Labour Front' is 'one great testing ground'[21] and that the regime was determined to maintain the organization's 'elasticity' from 'top to bottom' in future.[22] As a result, the DAF never attained a 'final' form even by 1945. The four phases in the development of its organizational structure outlined in what follows are based on the problems that each entailed for the Labour Ministry.

The first phase, until 1936–1937, marks the period of the DAF's internal consolidation. During this phase, its initially strong regional branches, the so-called Gauwaltungen, as well as divisions based on different economic sectors, the so-called Reich works communities (*Reichsbetriebsgemeinschaften*), lost influence. Instead, the central offices, based in Berlin, developed into the key power centre. The Reich works communities degenerated into subaltern units and, consistently enough, were renamed 'special offices' (*Fachämter*) in 1937.

The heads of the central offices, the Reich works communities and Gauwaltungen had to demonstrate both political and professional accomplishments to attain their posts. More than 90 per cent of senior DAF functionaries were 'old fighters', that is, they had joined the Nazi Party prior to 1932, three-quarters of them (76 per cent) before the Reichstag election of 14 September 1930. As if this was not enough, every sixth top official had joined the Nazis before the Beer Hall Putsch, almost half (45 per cent) by mid 1928, at a time when the Nazi Party by no means seemed assured of success. Just 2 per cent of senior DAF functionaries had joined the Nazi Party between 1 August 1932 and 30 January 1933, and 7 per cent afterwards. The contrast with the Reich Labour Ministry could scarcely have been greater. In 1933, just 10 per cent of all senior officials in the latter were members of the Nazi Party, including 'March victims' (*Märzgefallene*, an ironic allusion to the revolution of 1848). Among top DAF functionaries, long-standing membership of the Nazi Party was in fact by no means incompatible with higher education and professional qualifications, above all from 1936–1937 onwards. Among the heads of the central offices in particular, the most powerful group of officials within the mass Nazi organization, there were numerous academics, one-third of whom (33 per cent) had obtained doctorates. Merely 9 per cent of all heads of the central offices, Reich works communities and Gauwaltungen could be categorized as blue-collar workers,[23] who made up just over half of the total workforce at the time in statistical terms.

In the second phase (1936/37 to 1939/40), the DAF leadership became one of the key political actors in the 'Third Reich'. This phase began in September 1936 with the so-called Four-Year Plan, which ushered in the period of accelerated military build-up. The DAF and its recreational organ, the KdF, subsequently grew into an ever more important role. They were intended to avert the 'danger' of growing real income – a threat to the military build-up – against the background of an increasingly severe lack of labour, by offering services that did not directly increase the general population's purchasing power and, as far as possible, required no foreign currency for imports. On 2 September 1936, with reference to Hitler's aforementioned decree of 24 October 1934, Robert Ley issued a directive to the forty thousand full-time and two million voluntary DAF functionaries,[24] in which he explicitly made the 'aspiration to totality' in many spheres of labour and social policy the guiding principle of 'his' organization. This directive, which bore the title 'Basic Instructions', enduringly bolstered the DAF as it sought – at the expense, notably, of the Labour Ministry – to set itself up as the central institution in this policy field and lay claim to an ever-widening range of powers.

For the DAF's opponents, its 'aspiration to totality' became synonymous with unpredictability and an unchecked desire for power. Many decision-makers within the regime suspected that the Labour Front had 'long since detached itself from the party', and feared that it would like to reduce the 'state to the DAF's executive organ' or at least become 'a new, equal entity, an equal state within the state'.[25] The fact that Krohn scrupulously collated numerous statements of this kind by almost all Reich ministries and Nazi Party organs in a 'reference file', that is, his personal papers, is hardly surprising. It was in fact the Labour Ministry, of all Nazi institutions, that faced the greatest threat from the DAF's aspiration to totality.

Alarmed by the DAF's totalistic aspirations, virtually all Reich ministries and a number of central party authorities sought to rein in Ley's mass organization and make it more politically predictable.[26] A 'Law on the German Labour Front' was, however, never to be passed. The DAF defied all attempts to circumscribe it legally, sociologically (in terms of its internal structures) and typologically. It was not comparable with any of the associations or organizations that had existed hitherto, and it changed constantly. Furthermore, by 1938–1939, Ley and his DAF had become far too powerful for a 'Law on the German Labour Front' to simply be imposed upon them. The Nazi Party's Reich organizational leader (NSDAP-Reichsorganisationsleiter) and head of the DAF also possessed a privilege that, with the exception of Rudolf Heß, no Reich minister enjoyed: he had direct personal access to Hitler at all times and could fend off all the ministries' political interventions with the help of his 'Führer'.

Because it was impossible to constrain the DAF by legal means, in early 1938 certain members of the party's upper echelons began to contemplate the possibility of Ley 'becoming Reich minister of labour on 1 May [1939]'. The hope was that he might then be prepared 'to resign from the DAF'.

These leading figures wished to replace Ley as head of the Labour Front with Josef Bürckel, Gauleiter of the Gau Rhenish-Palatinate, entirely dissolve the Nazi Party's Reich Organizational Leadership (Reichsorganisationsleitung), also headed by Ley, and incorporate it into the staff of the 'deputy Führer'.[27] It would appear that Ley himself was unaware of these plans – which never got beyond the stage of tentative reflections because Ley would have rejected them anyway. As a minister, he would have been one among many; he would have felt demoted. To sit at the top of the most financially powerful mass Nazi organization with the greatest number of members, meanwhile, brought him far more power and influence. The proposal to make Ley a minister, then, also sheds telling light on Seldte and on the position of the ministry itself within the institutional structure of the 'Third Reich'. Leading figures within the regime clearly regarded it as a political chess piece that could be moved around at will. By 1938, Seldte himself had long since lacked any supporters among the Nazi grandees. Neither the minister nor senior officials in his ministry appear even to have been informed about the proposals outlined above.

It was not the start of the war that marked the key turning point for the DAF in terms of its organizational structure but rather the 'lightning victories' (*Blitzsiege*) of spring 1940, particularly France's devastating defeat. The following period, until autumn 1942, represents the third phase in the DAF's organizational history. Among other things, this period saw the Nazi leadership forge plans for the time after the Reich's seemingly impending 'final victory' (*Endsieg*). Over the course of these two years, particularly from mid 1940 until mid 1941, the DAF busied itself with systematically expanding its organizational apparatus in order to be prepared for the 'time after the final victory' and bolster its prospects of claiming more political powers. In parallel, Ley wooed the Nazi public with his megalomaniacal sociopolitical visions for the German 'master race' (*Herrenmenschen*) in the 'thousand-year Reich'. Crucial to the DAF's position vis-à-vis the Ministry of Labour, meanwhile, during this phase, its apparatus of officials remained in place. It was only later, in the spring and above all the autumn of 1942, that the deferral from military service enjoyed by DAF functionaries was increasingly rescinded, even in the case of full-time employees – substantially weakening the organization.[28]

The DAF seemed to scale new heights in May 1942 when Fritz Sauckel, general plenipotentiary for labour deployment, put it in charge of the 'supervision of foreign workers', a new and 'broad field' of a magnitude, after the 'Russia campaign', that could scarcely be predicted. In reality, this authority, which the DAF was unable to make full use of for want of resources, was more of a consolation prize following Ley's unsuccessful attempts to become general plenipotentiary for labour deployment himself. Finally, the third phase saw Ley's appointment as Reich commissioner for social housing on 15 November 1940.[29] Ley's subsequent appointment as Reich housing commissioner on 23 October 1942, meanwhile, already marks the transition to the fourth phase in the DAF's organizational history.

Although the DAF still managed to nominally claim further powers in 1943 and even 1944, from late 1942 onwards the buzz around the largest Nazi mass organization died down. There are a number of reasons for the DAF's rapid loss of importance in the final two years of the war. The four most important are as follows. (1) An increasing number of German workers had to head to the front. As a consequence, the DAF, which allowed only 'German national comrades' into its ranks, was deprived of its social base. (2) In view of the Wehrmacht's desperate need for soldiers, the DAF's corpus of staff was depleted to such an extent that it threatened its ability to function. (3) The concentrated aerial attacks triggered the collapse of the communicative and transport infrastructure. Subaltern branches thus frequently received no instructions for lengthy periods of time. Furthermore, ever larger parts of the Berlin headquarters were evacuated to the remote provinces, which were supposedly safe from bombing. (4) In the final year of the war, the focus shifted to the very survival of the Nazi regime. There was ever less room for power-political battles with one eye on the future or the usual jealousies among Nazi officeholders. Parts of the DAF apparatus successively merged with other governmental institutions. The DAF had long since ceased to exist as an independent organization when the Allies formally banned it on 10 October 1945.

The spheres of activity in which the Labour Ministry and the DAF became simultaneous rivals and parties to cooperation are numerous. We know, for example, that in 1940–1941 the DAF put forward plans for a comprehensive welfare system (*Sozialwerk*) that would have revolutionized every aspect of social insurance (including white-collar workers' and disability insurance) had it seen the light of day. While the Reich Ministry of Labour, in agreement with the other powerholders of the Nazi regime, had dropped the principle of self-administration and the juridification of welfare entitlements, otherwise, in contrast to the DAF, it essentially held to the structure of the social insurance system established in the late nineteenth century.[30] Another topic I am unable to go into here is the DAF's foreign policy and international initiatives, which began in 1936, reached their apogee between 1940 and 1943 and were summed up in the claim that, in competition with the Reich Ministry of Labour, the Labour Front wished to develop a 'European welfare ministry'.[31] Other fields in which the DAF's claims to authority and activities touched on the interests of the Labour Ministry (among other institutions) were vocational education and the Reich Vocational Contest, carried out annually in collaboration with the Hitler Youth, and (indirectly) the 'Companies' Performance Battle'.

From Demobilization to Mobilization: The Gainful Employment of Women

Another field in which the powers and practices of the Labour Ministry and the DAF overlapped heavily with one another was the wage-dependent gainful employment of women. The DAF became active in this field immediately after its foundation in mid May 1933. It was one of the driving forces behind the so-called Double Earner Campaign, and between 1933 and 1935 it was one of the most active supporters of the dismissal of female industrial and white-collar workers.[32] The Berlin headquarters of the DAF Social Welfare Office (Sozialamt) established a bespoke department to handle the 'double earner issue'.[33] The DAF and Seldte's ministry were of one mind when it came to this campaign. Both built on older traditions, above all the demobilization campaigns pursued by the trades unions in 1919–1920 and a 'crisis management strategy' initiated by the Catholic Centre Party in 1930, both at the expense of female workers.[34]

In the mid 1930s, both the DAF and the Labour Ministry underwent a paradigm shift in their policy on female industrial workers. Against the background of the rapidly worsening labour shortage, the employment of women, now even in the armaments industry, seemed essential. Nonetheless, neither camp dropped gender-specific role attributions, according to which the place of women was really in the kitchen and with the children. In order to square this circle, the DAF propagated part-time employment and half-day shifts for women looking to return to industrial work or take up such jobs for the first time. It was quite successful in this and found a receptive audience among the top management of many firms, who hoped it would alleviate the labour shortage. Just how successful the efforts to mobilize female part-time labour were from 1938 onwards is apparent in the aggregate data of the official working hours statistics. Throughout the Reich, as the female activity rate increased, the weekly working hours of unskilled female workers fell from 46.8 hours in March 1939 to 39.0 hours in March 1944 in the intermediate goods industry, from 46.8 hours to 39.3 hours in the consumer goods industry over the same period, and on a similar scale among the – few – skilled female workers as well. Among men, by way of contrast, in both economic sectors weekly working hours increased substantially over the same period, regardless of skill level.[35]

In its women-related policy as a whole, the DAF sought to reconcile the premises of eugenics with a pragmatism informed by the needs of armaments policy. In addition to the campaigns that attempted to mobilize mothers – against the background of 'biopolitics' – for 'eugenically tolerable' part-time work, this included a policy calling on 'works leaders' (Betriebsführer) to treat female blue- and white-collar workers generously in social policy terms. The Labour Ministry never questioned and in fact shared the biopolitical and pragmatic armaments-focused premises that always remained the guiding light of the DAF's policies towards women. This is evident in the 'Maternity Protection Law' (Mutterschutzgesetz) of 17 May 1942, which included, among other things – though only for German women – a prohibition on work hazardous to health and on overtime, Sunday and night work for pregnant women while allowing for the extension of this maternity protection far beyond its previous sphere of application.[36] The Labour Ministry had taken the lead in laying the ground for this law since mid 1940. The DAF had earlier called for such regulations to resolve the contradiction between the 'labour battle' and 'birth battle' and had managed to embed similar provisions in the regulations of numerous firms via its (female) 'company supervisors' (Betriebsfrauenwalterinnen). The criticisms aired by the DAF did not entail a fundamental challenge to the Maternity Protection Law of 1942. Rather, they boiled down to the assertion that its provisions failed to go far enough and that from a biopolitical perspective the German Volkskörper, the body of the nation, had still not been given sufficient protection.[37]

'A Castle for Every German': The DAF's Social Housing

This is not the place to go into detail about the DAF's activities in the field of housing policy, culminating in Robert Ley's ascent to the post of Reich commissioner for social housing in late 1940 and, in an entirely different context, Reich housing commissioner two years later, along with his takeover of the corresponding section of the Reich Ministry of Labour.[38] But because the two camps tussled with particular intensity over this field, I will highlight three crucial aspects.

First, the catchphrase 'social housing' (Sozialer Wohnungsbau), consciously disseminated by DAF propaganda, was a polemical term aimed at the Reich Labour Ministry. It was intended to flag up the extensive powers the DAF sought to claim. In early 1938, the DAF's Reich Homestead Office (Reichsheimstättenamt) introduced this term in place of the traditional 'people's housing' (Volkswohnungsbau) or 'workers' housing' (Arbeiterstättenwohnungsbau) as a rhetorical stick with which to beat the Labour Ministry within public political discourse.[39] The great advantage of the new buzzword was that it was not precisely defined. While the Reich Labour Ministry initially continued to refer to 'workers' dwellings' (*Arbeiterwohnstättenbau*) and 'regulated housing' (*gesteuerter Wohnungsbau*),[40] then reluctantly adopted the term 'social housing', though it defined it narrowly, Ley and the DAF used it as the 'central vehicle'[41] to enhance their power across the board as they strove to legitimize their political authority over 'Greater German' housing as a whole.

The catchphrase 'social housing' – omnipresent in the German public sphere thanks to the DAF propaganda machine – paved the way for Ley's appointment as Reich commissioner for social housing on 15 November 1940. At this point in time, following the crushing military defeat of France and the occupation of large parts of Europe by the Wehrmacht, most contemporaries believed that a Nazi 'final victory' was close at hand, and the dictatorship's political and state institutions were busy marking out their future territory vis-à-vis their rivals. In 1939, a DAF status report proclaimed that the 'dwellings' created by social housing, featuring running water and hygienic bathrooms, were to provide 'every German with a castle',[42] a phrase in which we can discern the bellicist character of the DAF's house-building plans as well as their racial exclusivity. The Labour Front and Labour Ministry were of one mind on this topic, even if they otherwise disagreed vehemently on issues of size, facilities and so on. By 21 September 1933, in a document entitled 'Guidelines for New Residential Estates', the Reich labour minister had already summed up the racist and eugenic principles underpinning his ministry's housing policy, stating that supposedly 'inferior settlers, namely those suffering from hereditary mental and physical defects, whose sick and asocial progeny merely burden the community as whole and diminish the strength of the people (Volkskraft)', were to be ruled out as potential residents from the outset. Those selected must be 'racially valuable and hereditarily healthy families of settlers'. They must be able to prove their 'Aryan' descent, extending back at least as far as their great-grandparents.[43]

Ley's appointment towards the end of 1940 as Reich commissioner for social housing was in part an indirect result of the transfer to the DAF of the housing associations (*Wohnungsgenossenschaften*) formerly owned by the trades unions in 1933. In significant part because of its prodigious stock of residential property and its construction business, also stolen from the trades unions, Hermann Göring – whom Hitler had appointed commissioner for the Four-Year Plan at the beginning of September 1936 – put the DAF in charge of the 'Settlement Programme (Siedlungswerk) of the Four-Year Plan'. The title 'Settlement Programme' was ultimately misleading. In reality, its primary goal was to erect multi-storey blocks of rented flats for the workforce to be employed in the new industrial plants.[44] While Göring had to reverse his decision to assign this task to the DAF after

Ley's rivals successfully intervened, it had still made the DAF – and this is the second key point – a serious political actor on the housing policy stages of the 'Third Reich'.[45] In late 1938 and early 1939, it built on this position by transforming what had been the trades unions' housing associations into powerful, regionally organized New Home societies (*Neue Heimat-Gesellschaften*). These large-scale housing associations, along with the DAF's construction firms, which were also expanding, lent powerful additional weight to all the DAF's housing policy ambitions. From 1937 to 1938 alone, the stock of residential buildings run by the DAF's housing societies grew by a substantial 17.6 per cent. This was more than 10 per cent of all new home construction in the Reich. These bodies owned around seventy-two thousand residential units by the end of 1938 and just over eighty-three thousand by the beginning of 1941; a further twenty-four thousand homes were under construction.

Third, Ley and his colleagues provided no in-depth statements on how their long-term megalomaniacal house-building programmes were to be financed. In 1941, the Labour Science Institute (AWI) even failed to rule out a temporary generous state subsidy for the planned social housing because otherwise it would be impossible to overcome the extreme housing shortage and, above all, to achieve the Nazi regime's biopolitical objectives.[46] Defying the assumptions of some contemporaries, however, the DAF leadership decisively rejected the idea of doing away with a private property-based housing industry. This they regarded as 'Bolshevism'. In the final year of the war, with respect to the 'people's housing', which had been subject to speculation regarding its nationalization until 1933, Ley was still declaring that he was not only against any nationalized housing but was even opposed to the burgeoning subsidies for public housing.[47] What this lays bare is that even the housing policy competition between the Labour Ministry and the DAF was not underpinned by any fundamental political-ideological disagreement. Instead it was chiefly the result of power-political rivalries, a 'play' in which each performed a specific role. The DAF was to integrate the workers throughout the Reich into the 'Volksgemeinschaft and achievement-based community' envisaged by the Nazi regime – and thus pursued a welfarist populism greatly reinforced in the media, without bothering itself with the problem of how to finance grandiose building programmes. By way of contrast, the ministry, which struggled to cast off its tradition of economic liberalism – a pronounced element in its character since the late 1920s, particularly when it came to housing policy – focused its attention on concrete problems, particularly the financing of the housing programmes about which Ley and other members of the DAF leadership liked to boast.

Uncontroversial: The DAF Legal Advisory Service (Rechtsberatung)

Yet another field of activity entrusted to the DAF at an early stage, through the AOG of 20 January 1934, was the (monopolistic) provision of legal advice both to workers (with the exception of rural labourers, civil servants and Nazi Party employees) and employers. In mid 1937, this agency employed 1,270 legal advisers throughout the Reich in 367 offices,[48] which were subdivided into departments for workers, employers and social insurance law (also allocated to the DAF with its advisory monopoly).[49] By autumn 1939, the number of legal advice offices, including those in Austria and the Sudetenland, had grown to 478. In addition, surgeries were held once a week in 1,765 other locations (in 1939).[50]

The activities of the legal advice offices established by the DAF were basically uncontroversial from the Labour Ministry's perspective. The key reason for this was that – in contrast to the former legal advisers, who had worked for the trades unions or been aligned with employers – the legal representatives supplied by the DAF did not attempt to advance the interests of the worker or employer presenting their complaint. Instead (to quote the unambiguous words of Otto Marrenbach, DAF executive director and a close confidant of Ley), they were to be 'completely independent of the party concerned' and were always to 'take into account and acknowledge the views of the opposing party'. As 'the Führer's political soldiers', Marrenbach went on, in the course of their 'practical front-line work' the DAF legal advisers were meant to correct 'false notions' regarding 'claims entailed in the employment contract', that is, supposedly overblown demands put forward chiefly by workers, and 'in any event' to try to 'settle [conflicts] amicably' by 'means of compromise'.[51] As a result of this privileging of the Nazi 'community principle', between 1936 and 1942 alone the number of legal protection issues that DAF legal advisers recognized as disputes in the first place, rather than dismissing them out of hand, fell from more than eighty-four thousand to fewer than nineteen thousand, that is, less than a quarter (22 per cent).[52]

Regardless of this, the DAF legal advisory service functioned like a filter between those seeking justice and the labour courts. It is true that the latter had become less significant: when the labour trustees were installed, there were no more legal disputes between 'unions and management' as this structure had ceased to exist and the AOG, along with other decrees on changing jobs, wage ceilings and so on, significantly diminished individual labour law. This meant there was vastly less prospect of workers seeking legal protection achieving justice from the labour courts. But due to the activities of the DAF's legal advisory service, focused as it was on achieving an accommodation informed by the notion of the Volksgemeinschaft,[53] the number of disputes considered by labour courts fell even further. By 1938, the last 'year of peace', this number shrank by just under two-thirds over 1931, from more than 440,000 to just over 150,000. In 1940, just 82,000 disputes made it to a labour court. Even fewer such disputes were considered by higher authorities.

The DAF's legal advisory service, designed to uphold the principle of 'community', was soon functioning to the satisfaction of all Nazi power-holders.[54] Significantly, the Reich labour minister – whose ministry played a substantial role in formulating the AOG and was thus partly responsible for putting the DAF in charge of the provision of legal advice – explicitly supported the establishment of a DAF service of this kind committed to the 'Volksgemeinschaft and the achievement-based community'. The labour minister agreed with the Reich minister of the economy and the other ministers that the new 'legal advisory service' represented 'one of the heaviest blows to the principle of class struggle'.[55] It is difficult to imagine a greater compliment to the DAF. The approach taken by the Labour Front's legal advisers tallied perfectly with the expectations of Seldte and his colleagues. Once their activities had bedded down, Werner Mansfeld – the leading labour law specialist in the Labour Ministry who, together with Wolfgang Pohl and Rudolf Schmeer of the DAF, had taken the lead in formulating the AOG – was full of praise for the Labour Front's 'often nothing less than exemplary provision of legal advice on social welfare'.[56]

Cooperation Despite Competition: The DAF and the Working Conditions Inspectorate (Gewerbeaufsicht)

For a long time the DAF's cooperation with the working conditions inspectors (*Gewerbeaufsichtsbeamten*) subordinate to the Labour Ministry was also amicable. Local DAF offices or local officials from the Beauty of Work organization often carried out company inspections jointly with the Working Conditions Inspectorate, though admittedly it was stricken by staff shortages.[57] Alternatively, they kept each other informed about the results of such inspections. In a general sense, the working conditions inspectors felt supported by Beauty of Work, not least by its campaigns to improve such conditions.[58] The DAF Office for Women (Frauenamt) and the Working Conditions Inspectorate were also pursuing the same objective. Both were keen to ensure that the employment of women as industrial labourers, which was increasing rapidly due to the intensified military build-up since 1935, did not occur at the expense of the regime's pro-natal and eugenic objectives and that the relevant labour protection regulations were upheld.⁵⁹ Furthermore, since before the war, the cooperation with the accident representatives (*Unfallvertrauensmänner*) appointed by the DAF since late August 1935 and, since the beginning of the war, with the DAF light duty assistants (*Revierdiensthelfer*), particularly the female ones, had been fairly close.⁶⁰ This close cooperative relationship was further cemented by joint working conferences and lecture evenings along with other 'comradely events'.⁶¹

Symptomatic of the good relationship between the two camps was the fact that leading representatives of the DAF explicitly refrained from denouncing the Working Conditions Inspectorate – in marked contrast to other agencies subordinate to the Labour Ministry – as a cumbersome bureaucratic apparatus. On the contrary, the DAF praised it as a corrective to what it regarded as a sometimes selfish business community. The Inspectorate for its part stated with satisfaction that while it was true that 'some businessmen . . . have attempted to play the two agencies off against one another', they had discovered that 'the activities of the trades unions' had 'in no way been continued' in the DAF's sociopolitical engagement, as the Inspectorate summed things up with reference to 1937–1938.⁶²

In the final year of the war, however, the DAF unilaterally terminated its cooperation with the Working Conditions Inspectorate – with a head-on attack on the agency. At this point in time, because most of its staff had been called up for military service, but also because of the aerial attacks and destruction, the Inspectorate had long been incapable of carrying out its normal inspections. In a letter of 26 August 1944 to State Secretary Werner Naumann at the Reich Ministry for Public Enlightenment and Propaganda (Reichsministerium für Volksaufklärung und Propaganda) – which, following Goebbels's appointment as Reich commissioner for total warfare (Reichsbevollmächtigter für den totalen Kriegseinsatz) two days before, had received comprehensive powers in the field of labour and social policy as well – Otto Marrenbach, executive director of the DAF and Ley's deputy, expressed his wish to simply dissolve the Inspectorate without further ado. Its activities, he averred, could be 'straightforwardly integrated into the work of the voluntary DAF accident prevention officers (Unfallschutzwalter)'.⁶³ The idea of dissolving the Inspectorate, however, ultimately failed to get anywhere.

Rivalry and Cooperation

The four fields of DAF activity outlined here show that, when it came to their objectives and ideas concerning labour and social policy, it would be misleading to think in terms of fundamental political differences, let alone antagonism, between the Labour Front and Labour Ministry. File memos and correspondence from the archival holdings of the Reich Labour Ministry and certain other ministries tend to magnify the bones of contention, but these were mostly underpinned by differing political emphases. In fact, with respect to the dictatorship's general objectives – summed up here through the buzzwords of racism, biopolitics and bellicism – the DAF and the other institutions generally worked in concert. The reasons for the temporary upsurges in conflict lay on other levels, with four aspects being particularly significant.

First, the Labour Ministry was simply worried about its power and influence. It felt marginalized by the DAF, a mass Nazi organization with a huge staff and vast propaganda apparatus. From 1936–1937 onwards, the ministry found itself thrown onto the strategic defensive vis-à-vis its rival in power-political terms. Until 1943, the Labour Front was a constantly growing colossus; driven by the mission of anchoring Nazism as an ideology and mentality throughout as much of the German population as possible, it sought to incorporate ever more of the very fields of action and powers that the ministry and its leading protagonists claimed as their own.

Second, while the spheres of action allocated to the two institutions entailed the same basic objectives, the DAF and the ministry acted in line with differing logics when it came to their internal structure. The ministry retained a classical administrative system (though one which, as many of the chapters in the present volume show, increasingly adapted itself to the hegemonic practices prescribed and 'modelled' by the Nazi regime). In a range of ways, by contrast, in its organizational structure and development, recruitment of personnel and political practices, the DAF featured elements of a 'charismatic administrative staff' – corresponding to Max Weber's ideal type.[64] This gave rise to different forms of action. When it came to matters of substance, moreover, the two camps tended to have rather different priorities within the same political fields. Their objectives and practices differed in the manner of a division of labour.

Third, the Labour Ministry continued to administer and regulate 'bureaucratically' in accordance with standardized, routinized procedures, much like most other ministries and Land or municipal authorities. This mitigated the frictions generated by the (seemingly) erratic and unpredictable politics pursued by leading Nazi protagonists on the Reich level, that is, the newly installed Reich ministers (Speer, Göring, Darré, Rust, Rosenberg and so on), the special commissioners 'with direct access to the Führer' and party organizations such as the SS, the DAF and so on. The leadership of the latter, in contrast, pursued Nazi-inspired 'national educational' (*volkspädagogisch*) objectives – which mostly meant socially integrative ones. In this sense, more than other mass Nazi organizations, it embodied the 'Volksgemeinschaft' of German 'national comrades' and saw itself as their 'trustee', 'custodian' or even 'guarantor'. A core aspect of this was the integration of much of the German workforce into the Nazi system.

Fourth and finally, despite all the agreement on fundamental political and ideological matters, the conflicts that raged behind the scenes and the constant disputes between high-ranking DAF functionaries and the top level of the ministerial bureaucracy were rooted in major differences of habitus and generation. The DAF leadership corps of around 170 top functionaries was of a middle-class complexion, while its predominantly academically educated senior Central Office staff, around a third of whom had obtained doctoral degrees, might best be described as bourgeois – and had been socialized during the Nazi movement's 'time of struggle' between 1925 and 1932. The high-ranking actors in the ministry, on the other hand, mostly had a classical career in the ministerial bureaucracy behind them or comparable professional trajectories (in employers' associations for example). Only just over 10 per cent of civil servants with the rank of ministerial councillor or above even joined the Nazi Party – and most of them did so only after 1933. The leading DAF functionaries, by way of contrast, retained their belligerent, actionist, seemingly thuggish habitus, forged during the 'time of struggle', even after 1933. This was entirely alien to their rivals in the Labour Ministry, who were accustomed to transpersonal routines, rigid hierarchies and well-worn official channels; they had developed a cultured, demure habitus that entailed avoiding unforeseen events as far as possible. The antibureaucratic sentiments characteristic of Ley and his entourage – expressed in Ley's motto 'people before files'[65] – further aggravated the personal antagonisms. The kind of 'leadership' (*Menschenführung*) propagated by the DAF as an antibureaucratic principle[66] ran starkly counter to the conception of the sober 'official' or 'bureaucrat' focused on the matter at hand, that is, the ministerial ideal.

This sociocultural and habitual clash was imbued with a strong generational charge. While the leading ministerial officials (with the rank of ministerial counsellor or above) were on average a little above fifty years of age in 1933, and were thus fairly mature, not only were the three senior officials on whom Ley directly depended extremely young, so was the entire leadership corps of DAF functionaries. Most of the leading DAF officials (54 per cent) were born after the turn of the century and were thirty-two years old or younger at the time of the 'seizure of power'.[67] At the same time, the 'fascist youth movement', to which most of the leading DAF cadres had belonged, paradoxically consisted of particularly 'old fighters'. Early membership of the Nazi Party, however, by no means equated with an absence of professional qualifications.

Why, though, did the DAF and the Labour Ministry – despite all their rivalries and despite serious generational and habitual antagonisms – cooperate very successfully in many fields of activity? The answer is simple. When it came to their fundamental objectives, the two camps were of one mind, despite a division of labour that ascribed to the DAF the role of socially paternalistic Nazi visionary. Through projects such as KdF mass tourism and the Prora holiday resort, the promise of generous pensions within the framework of the DAF 'Sozialwerk', the KdF car from the Volkswagen plant or attractive factory buildings embodying the 'beauty of work', the DAF sought to bewitch the public and broad swathes of the workforce. The Labour Front left it to the Reich Ministry of Labour to play the pragmatic part. This was the role of the 'realist' or 'policy expert' that grounded the visions expounded by Ley and others or rejected them as overly 'utopian'. Regardless of this, in true ministerial tradition – and with no 'sprinkling' of democracy – the ministry remained committed to the 'German path' that began in the late nineteenth century with regard to social, health and labour (law) policy.

In addition to the rapidly changing external and internal circumstances, it was in large part the aggressive and actionist Labour Front that forced on the ministry an unprecedented determination to adapt and change. 'Competition is good for business' – this motto applies not just to the economy but also to politics, and more strongly in the 'Third Reich' than in other political systems. During the Nazi period, ambition, rivalries and permanent competition between officeholders over power and authority stimulated (self-)mobilization to a previously unimaginable degree, prompting the actors involved to strain every sinew to achieve their desired outcomes and unleashing a meteoric momentum that culminated in the Second World War, with all its disasters and Nazi crimes against humanity. Depending on political and military circumstances, the plethora of institutions that arose from 1933 onwards could be linked and modified through special commissioners or other coordinating entities. Despite all the frictional losses, this engendered an ultimately elastic power system that was finally wrestled to the ground by superior opponents after six years of war. Established Reich administrative organs such as the Labour Ministry and the embedded routine of the traditional bureaucratic apparatus became key anchors of the regime's stability, breaking the ideological precepts and often erratic ideas of the 'Führer' and other leading Nazi protagonists down into bite-size chunks, so to speak.

Despite the competition and rivalry, the actors involved cooperated and, at times, even maintained close personal relationships. Below the level of the most senior officials, intensive informal forms of cooperation developed between protagonists at the Labour Ministry and the DAF that were not visible from outside; a number of notable figures came to enjoy relationships that can only be described as amicable. In the mid 1980s, in an interview with the then director of the Institute of Contemporary History (Institut für Zeitgeschichte) in Munich, Martin Broszat, Theodor Hupfauer[68] provided details of such sometimes personally close cooperation. Hupfauer headed the important DAF agency 'Social Self-Responsibility' (Soziale Selbstverantwortung). From 1936 onwards, moreover, he functioned as commissioner for the overall execution of the Companies' Performance Battle (Beauftragter für die Gesamtdurchführung des Leistungskampfs der Betriebe). Beginning in 1943, Hupfauer played a lead role in the Ministry for Armaments and War Production (Ministerium für Rüstung und Kriegsproduktion) and was one of Albert Speer's closest colleagues. It is significant that, despite his senior roles in the Labour Front, Hupfauer was not a member of Ley's inner circle, the so-called Waldbröl clique (named after Ley's long-term place of residence), which had formed around Schmeer, Marrenbach, Simon and a number of others. All of them hailed from Ley's home region and formed a cohesive and exclusive group vis-à-vis other leading functionaries – among other things through their use of Cologne dialect, which the others did not speak and struggled to understand.

Non-membership of the Waldbröl clique predestined Hupfauer and a number of other leading DAF functionaries to build informal communicative structures with the Labour Ministry over a long period of time, until 1943–1945. Despite all the frictions 'at the top', these ensured amicable and – from the perspective of the Nazi dictatorship – productive cooperation between the DAF and the Labour Ministry. In the notes, unfortunately consisting of just a few keywords, that Broszat committed to paper concerning the interview, Hupfauer stated that he himself, Wolfgang Pohl, head of the Labour Science Institute (the DAF's 'brain trust'), and his deputy Theodor Bühler met regularly over a number of years with leading representatives of the Reich Labour Ministry. In conversation with Broszat, Hupfauer mentioned Werner Mansfeld and Johannes Krohn as participants in such meetings from the ministry. In a relaxed, cordial atmosphere, he stated, both camps had discussed all pending issues in detail and considered how to damp down the rivalries between the Labour Ministry and the DAF. Neither in the Labour Front nor the Labour Ministry, according to Hupfauer, 'did anyone know that all of us were constantly sitting down together'[69] – and given the Labour Ministry's conflicts with Ley and his closest circle of confidants, they were no doubt keen to keep their get-togethers under wraps.

Likewise, the lower levels of the DAF and of the ministry, after initial frictions, often cooperated well, as illustrated by the reports of the Working

Conditions Inspectorate. This cooperation, which proceeded amicably in many fields, was, however, repeatedly breached by DAF functionaries who felt the need to make their names by stoking controversy or sensed opportunities to expand their power.

Though counterfactual questions are in a sense meaningless simply because the structures of the Nazi dictatorship would not have permitted it to survive for long, it is hard not to wonder what sort of political constellations might have emerged had the regime managed to achieve stability, at least for a time. Theodor Hupfauer provides us with an indirect answer if we consider him both as an individual and in terms of his career. It is important in this context that, even after he stopped working for the DAF in 1944, Hupfauer maintained a close personal relationship with Robert Ley. It was probably Ley who introduced Hupfauer to the 'Führer'. Hitler, meanwhile, named Hupfauer successor to Seldte as Reich labour minister in his 'testament' of 29 April 1945. In terms of 'real history', this testament is irrelevant. But Hupfauer's appointment as Reich labour minister tells us quite a bit about the key protagonists' perspectives on the relationship between the ministry and the DAF. The Reich Labour Ministry and its subordinate authorities were to be reduced to the mere execution of administrative tasks. The Labour Front, on the other hand, was to become an 'educational organization'. At least partially overarching the ministry's agencies, its task would have been to prepare the 'works leaders' and above all the 'followers' to realize the 'Volksgemeinschaft', while readying them to supervise and rule over a racially segregated Nazi Europe.

Conclusion

When it came to their internal organization and the habitus of their leading protagonists, the Labour Ministry and the DAF were very different institutions. After 1933, the ministry continued to function as a Reich body with a classical approach to administration. Making certain parts of it subordinate to the general plenipotentiary for labour deployment (Sauckel) and the Reich housing commissioner (Ley) did nothing to fundamentally change this. The task of the Labour Ministry and of the other established Reich ministries was to ground the political visions and racist utopias propagated by leading Nazis by breaking them down into viable steps. In the fields within its remit, until 1939 Seldte's ministry contributed with bureaucratic pragmatism to the authoritarian pacification of Nazi society and helped bolster the production of armaments, subsequently making a substantial contribution to the smooth functioning of the war economy. It could do so because the key actors in the ministry generally shared the

Nazi leaders' basic political and ideological beliefs. In addition to the desire to turn Germany into a world power, prevent an organized labour movement from ever arising again and eliminate democracy once and for all, these included the racist and eugenic ideology that guided the regime's actions until the end.

In sharp contrast to the Labour Ministry as an established Reich body, the DAF was a large-scale organization of an entirely new type. This mass Nazi association not only had nothing in common with the Labour Ministry in terms of its structure but also differed fundamentally from all workers' organizations prior to 1933 and after 1945. As a Nazi body whose task was in a sense educational, it was supposed to persuade the great mass of the German working class – particularly the initially resistant, crippled and disoriented core of the industrial workforce – to embrace the Nazi Volksgemeinschaft and achievement-based community. Repression alone could not achieve this. The Labour Front thus developed into a mass organization espousing a form of social paternalism and strictly geared towards the Führer principle, a body that, together with its subunit the KdF, strove to achieve the broadest possible resonance in society. It became a 'service provider within the framework of the Volksgemeinschaft', one that offered its members many positive material incentives as well as a wide range of recreational and educational services and opportunities for upward social mobility.

In order to achieve the socially integrative goals it had been set, the DAF's leading protagonists soon cultivated a near-unbridled populism. The organization's welfarist promises were consciously undergirded by the often aggressive rhetoric unleashed by Ley and his entourage. Until just before the war, this went hand in hand with diatribes assailing individual, supposedly antisocial businessmen and traditional sections of the state administration such as the Labour Ministry. These were lambasted for being captive to 'old thinking' and the categories of 'class struggle' typical of the Weimar Republic. Verbal invective and social populism left many members of the Nazi public and many of the officials who came under attack, notably in the Labour Ministry, with the impression of a fundamental opposition between the two camps. The sense of two worlds colliding was reinforced by fundamental differences of habitus. When Hitler was appointed Reich chancellor, many leading DAF functionaries had not yet reached the age of thirty, and for the most part had joined the Nazi Party before 1930 and, often, as early as 1922–1923. Senior ministerial officials, by contrast, had mostly reached a mature age, often looking back over long careers in the civil service or employers' organizations. If they joined the Nazi Party at all, they were generally among the 'March victims' or 'May bugs' (*Maikäfer*) who joined only when the Nazi dictatorship had taken root.

Yet the appearance of a fundamental opposition between the two sides is deceptive. If we look more closely, we find that both camps largely pursued the same goals when it came to matters of substance. The fields of activity discussed here could be supplemented by other examples, all of which reveal that for the most part differences were due to the clash of habitus, contrasting organizational structures and the resulting differences of emphasis in everyday practice. These were given an extra charge by the aggressive demeanour and often yobbish manner of the DAF leaders, socialized as they were during the ferocious 'system time' before 1933. In reality, regardless of all the power-political rivalries, from the mid 1930s onwards the two sides generally worked together amicably within quotidian contexts. Symptomatically, leading and pragmatically inclined DAF functionaries and senior ministerial officials developed friendly forms of informal coordination and cooperation long before the start of the war. From the mid 1930s, despite all the frictions on the leadership level, the Labour Ministry and the Labour Front became well-oiled cogs within the machinery of the Nazi power system, playing a significant part in ensuring that it continued to function until the last few months of the war.

Rüdiger Hachtmann, Dr. phil., senior fellow at the Centre for Contemporary History, Potsdam, adjunct professor at the Technische Universität, Berlin and member of the Independent Commission of Historians Investigating the History of the Reich Ministry of Labour in the National Socialist Period. Publications include *Das Wirtschaftsimperium der Deutschen Arbeitsfront* (Wallstein, 2012); *Wissenschaftsmanagement im 'Dritten Reich'. Geschichte der Generalverwaltung der Kaiser-Wilhelm-Gesellschaft*, 2 vols (Wallstein, 2007); *Berlin 1848. Politik- und Gesellschaftsgeschichte der Revolution* (Dietz, 1997).

Notes

1. For detailed information on Rudolf Schmeer, see Biographical Appendix.
2. See, including the quotations, T. Harlander, *Zwischen Heimstätte und Wohnmaschine. Wohnungsbau und Wohnungspolitik in der Zeit des Nationalsozialismus*, Basel: Birkhäuser, 1995, 139.
3. For detailed information on Robert Ley, see Biographical Appendix.
4. *Deutschland-Berichte der Sozialdemokratischen Partei Deutschlands (Sopade) 1934–1940, Vierter Jahrgang: 1937*, ed. K. Behnken, Salzhausen: Nettelbeck, 1980, 521.
5. See, including the quotations, W. Kiehl, *Mann an der Fahne. Kameraden erzählen von Dr. Ley*, Munich: Eher, 1938, 60 f.
6. See H. Kater, 'Die Ehrauffassung der SS. Nationalsozialismus und das Duell. Himmler als Burschenschaftler: Das Duell R. Strunk gegen Horst Krutschinna', *Einst und Jetzt* 38 (1993), 265–70.
7. Kiehl, *Mann an der Fahne*, 45–47.

8. On this concept, which denotes an important structural element in the Nazi power system, see R. Hachtmann, 'Die Deutsche Arbeitsfront und die NS-Gemeinschaft "Kraft durch Freude" – "volksgemeinschaftliche" Dienstleister?', in D. Schmiechen-Ackermann (ed.), *Volksgemeinschaft*. *Mythos, wirkungsmächtige soziale Verheißung oder soziale Realität im 'Dritten Reich'? Zwischenbilanz einer kontroversen Debatte*, Paderborn: Schöningh, 2012, 111–31, here 114 f.; and R. Hachtmann, 'Elastisch, dynamisch und von katastrophaler Effizienz – Anmerkungen zur Neuen Staatlichkeit des Nationalsozialismus', in S. Reichardt and W. Seibel (eds), *Der prekäre Staat. Herrschen und Verwalten im Nationalsozialismus*, Frankfurt am Main: Campus, 2011, 29–73, esp. 49, 56 f., 67.

9. For an overview of the DAF's history, see R. Smelser, *Robert Ley. Hitler's Labor Front Leader*, Oxford: Berg, 1989, 121–280; R. Hachtmann, 'Einleitung', in Hachtmann (ed.), *Ein Koloss auf tönernen Füßen. Das Gutachten des Wirtschaftsprüfers Karl Eicke über die Deutsche Arbeitsfront vom 31. Juli 1936*, Munich: Oldenbourg, 2006, 7–94.

10. On the language, see R. Hachtmann, 'Vom "Geist der Volksgemeinschaft durchpulst" – Arbeit, Arbeiter und die Sprachpolitik der Nationalsozialisten', *Zeitgeschichte-Online*, January 2010, retrieved 26 September 2018 from http://www.zeitgeschichte-online.de/thema/vom-geist-der-volksgemeinschaft-durchpulst; R. Hachtmann, 'Arbeit und Arbeitsfront: Ideologie und Praxis', in M. Buggeln and M. Wildt (eds), *Arbeit im Nationalsozialismus*, Munich: De Gruyter Oldenbourg, 2014, 83–106, esp. 89–91, 95–98.

11. Speech by Robert Ley, 10 May 1933, quoted in W. Müller, *Das soziale Leben im neuen Deutschland unter besonderer Berücksichtigung der Deutschen Arbeitsfront*, Berlin: Mittler, 1938, 67.

12. The 'councils of confidence' (Vertrauensräte) installed by the AOG in 1934 had none of the rights previously enjoyed by the works councils (Betriebsräte); they were mere instruments of the 'works leaders' (Betriebsführer) for the maintenance of industrial peace. For an overview, see A. Kranig, *Lockung und Zwang. Zur Arbeitsverfassung im Dritten Reich*, Stuttgart: Deutsche Verlags-Anstalt, 1983, esp. 41–43.

13. On the DAF-run enterprises (Volkswagen, the People's Welfare organization [Volksfürsorge], several of the largest publishing houses, housing and construction companies, among others), whose turnover approached that of the firm IG Farbenindustrie and that (from 1940) employed far more blue- and white-collar workers than, for example, Siemens, see R. Hachtmann, *Das Wirtschaftsimperium der Deutschen Arbeitsfront*, Göttingen: Wallstein, 2012. On 'Strength through Joy', see W. Buchholz, *Die nationalsozialistische Gemeinschaft 'Kraft durch Freude'. Freizeitgestaltung und Arbeiterschaft im Dritten Reich*, Ph.D. dissertation, Munich: University of Munich, 1976; S. Baranowski, *Strength through Joy. Consumerism and Mass Tourism in the Third Reich*, Cambridge: Cambridge University Press, 2004; R. Hachtmann, *Tourismus-Geschichte*, Göttingen: UTB, 2007, 120–39; R. Hachtmann, '"Bäuche wegmassieren" und "überflüssiges Fett in unserem Volke beseitigen" – der kommunale Breitensport der NS-Gemeinschaft "Kraft durch Freude"', in F. Becker and R. Schäfer (eds), *Sport und Nationalsozialismus*, Göttingen: Wallstein, 2016, 27–65.

14. Amt für die wirtschaftlichen Unternehmungen der DAF, *Die wirtschaftlichen Unternehmungen der Deutschen Arbeitsfront im Jahre 1939*, Berlin: self-published, 1940, 103.

15. For detailed information on Wolfgang Pohl, see Biographical Appendix.

16. Quoted in H.-J. Reichhardt, *Die Deutsche Arbeitsfront. Ein Beitrag zur Geschichte des nationalsozialistischen Deutschlands und zur Struktur des totalitären Herrschaftssystems*, Ph.D. dissertation, Berlin: Freie Universität Berlin, 1956, 85.

17. Quoted in T. Blanke et al. (eds), *Kollektives Arbeitsrecht. Quellentexte zur Geschichte des Arbeitsrechts in Deutschland*, vol. 2: *1933 bis zur Gegenwart*, Reinbek bei Hamburg: Rowohlt, 1975, 67 f.

18. Mansfeld to Krohn, 5 September 1936, Bundesarchiv (BArch), R 3901/20644, fol. 165.

19. Note by Krohn on a meeting with Wilhelm Keppler, the Führer's representative on economic issues (Beauftragter des Führers für Wirtschaftsfragen), 31 October 1934, BArch, R 3901/20644, fol. 8–9.

20. Hitler as quoted by Ley; quoted in *Der Parteitag der Arbeit vom 6. bis 13. September 1937. Offizieller Bericht über den Verlauf des Reichsparteitages mit sämtlichen Kongreßreden*, Munich: Eher, 1937, 265. The full text of the speech also appears in the *Völkischer Beobachter*, 12 September 1937.

21. R. Ley, *Haltet den Sieg und beutet ihn aus*, Berlin: Verlag der Deutschen Arbeitsfront, 1941 (n.p., pamphlet).

22. To quote G. Weise, 'Heeresbericht von der Deutschen Arbeitsfront', *Völkischer Beobachter*, 30 April 1938.

23. Figures based on my own research, mainly informed by personnel files in the former Berlin Document Center. For more detail on this, see my forthcoming comprehensive overview of the DAF. On education and occupation, see R. Hachtmann, 'Kleinbürgerlicher Schmerbauch und breite bürgerliche Brust – zur sozialen Zusammensetzung der Führungselite der Deutschen Arbeitsfront', in U. Bitzegeio, A. Kruke and M. Woyke (eds), *Solidargemeinschaft und Erinnerungskultur im 20. Jahrhundert. Beiträge zu Gewerkschaften, Nationalsozialismus und Geschichtspolitik*, Bonn: Dietz, 2009, 233–57. On the Reich Labour Ministry's ministerial bureaucracy, see the chapter by Ulrike Schulz in this volume.

24. Verbatim in *Deutsche Arbeitskorrespondenz* (DAK-'Sondernachrichten'), 3 September 1936, no. 205, n.p., and *Amtliches Nachrichtenblatt von DAF und KDF* 2 (1936), 146–50.

25. Excerpts from the tentatively submitted 'Statements on the Legislation Submitted by Pg. Reichsleiter [Party Comrade Reich Leader] Dr Ley Concerning the Duties and Objectives of the German Labour Front', as attachment to: Staff of the Deputy Führer to State Secretary Krohn in the Reich Ministry of Labour, 3 May 1938, BArch, R 3901/20646, fol. 3–35, and BArch, R 43 II/592, fol. 90–122.

26. For an (incomplete) overview of the initiatives intended to bring about a DAF law, mainly in 1937–1938, see W. Spohn, *Betriebsgemeinschaft und Volksgemeinschaft. Die rechtliche und institutionelle Regelung der Arbeitsbeziehungen im NS-Staat*, Berlin: Quorum, 1987, 139, 176–85; Smelser, *Robert Ley*, 236, 245, 254–56; M. Schneider, *Unterm Hakenkreuz. Arbeiter und Arbeiterbewegung 1933 bis 1939*, Bonn: Dietz, 1999, 188–90.

27. Communication from SS-Hauptsturmführer Grosche based on 'a reliable source' (probably Heß) to the deputy head of Office VI of the SS Reich Security Main Office, Walter Schellenberg (1900–1952), in Note by Schellenberg, 21 April 1939, Institut für Zeitgeschichte, Munich (IfZ), MA 433, fol. 2728144. See also Note by Schellenberg, 11 August 1938, ibid., fol. 2728149.

28. For an (initial, incomplete) overview of the history of the DAF from 1939, see R. Hachtmann, 'Die Deutsche Arbeitsfront im Zweiten Weltkrieg', in D. Eichholtz (ed.), *Krieg und Wirtschaft. Studien zur deutschen Wirtschaftsgeschichte 1939–1945*, Berlin: Metropol, 1999, 69–108; Smelser, *Robert Ley*, 259–80; M. Schneider, *In der Kriegsgesellschaft. Arbeiter und Arbeiterbewegung 1939 bis 1945*, Bonn: J.H.W. Dietz Nachf., 2014, esp. 333–64.

29. See the section '"A Castle for Every German": The DAF's Social Housing' within this chapter and the chapters by Ulrike Schulz and Karl Christian Führer in this volume.

30. See M.-L. Recker, *Nationalsozialistische Sozialpolitik im Zweiten Weltkrieg*, Munich: Oldenbourg, 1985, 82–154; and the chapter by Alexander Klimo in this volume.

31. In addition to the chapter by Klaus Kiran Patel and Sandrine Kott in this volume, see esp. K.-H. Roth, 'Die Sozialpolitik des "europäischen Großraum" im Spannungsfeld von Okkupation und Kollaboration (1938–1945)', in W. Röhr (ed.), *Okkupation und Kollaboration (1938–1945). Beiträge zu Konzepten und Praxis der Kollaboration in der deutschen Okkupationspolitik*, Berlin: Hüthig, 1994, 461–565, quotation 559.

32. On the denunciation of female 'double earners' by the DAF and National Socialist

factory cell organizations (NS-Betriebszellenorganisationen, or NSBO), see, for example, D. Humann, 'Arbeitsschlacht'. *Arbeitsbeschaffung und Propaganda in der NS-Zeit 1933–1939*, Göttingen: Wallstein, 2011, esp. 172 f.; S. Schumann, *Die Frau aus dem Erwerbsleben wieder herausnehmen. NS-Propaganda und Arbeitsmarktpolitik in Sachsen 1933–1939*, Dresden: Hannah-Arendt-Institut für Totalitarismusforschung, 2000, 32–35. In 1933–1934, DAF periodicals published a large number of articles such as 'Muttertum und industrielle Frauenerwerbstätigkeit', *Informationsdienst der DAF* (InDie) A, 9 May 1934, no. 105, fol. 1–2.

33. See the Eicke Report, named for its author Karl Eicke, in Hachtmann, *Ein Koloss auf tönernen Füßen*, 97–242, here 135.

34. For an overview, see L. Preller, *Sozialpolitik in der Weimarer Republik*, unaltered reprint of the 1948 edition, Düsseldorf: Droste, 1978, 120 f., 436 f., 444.

35. See R. Hachtmann, 'Industriearbeiterinnen in der deutschen Kriegswirtschaft 1936–1944/45', *Geschichte und Gesellschaft* 19(3) (1993), 332–66, here 338 f., 364 (table 3).

36. RGBl. I 1942, 321–24. See also C. Sachse, 'Das nationalsozialistische Mutterschutzgesetz. Eine Strategie zur Rationalisierung des weiblichen Arbeitsvermögens im Zweiten Weltkrieg', in D. Reese et al. (eds), *Rationale Beziehungen? Geschlechterverhältnisse im Produktionsprozeß*, Frankfurt am Main: Suhrkamp, 1993, 189–221.

37. See, for example, Ley to Bormann, 20 August 1942, BArch, NS 5 I/338.

38. See esp. M.-L. Recker, 'Der Reichskommissar für den sozialen Wohnungsbau. Zu Aufbau, Stellung und Arbeitsweise einer führerunmittelbaren Sonderbehörde', in D. Rebentisch and K. Teppe (eds), *Verwaltung contra Menschenführung im Staat Hitlers. Studien zum politisch administrativen System*, Göttingen: Vandenhoeck & Ruprecht, 1986, 333–50; see also Recker, *Nationalsozialistische Sozialpolitik*, 128–54.

39. See Reichsheimstättenamt der DAF (ed.), 'Richtlinien zur Heimstättensiedlung', in *Siedlung. Planungsheft der DAF*, Berlin: Verlag der Deutschen Arbeitsfront GmbH, 1938, 9. On this and what follows, see Hachtmann, *Wirtschaftsimperium*, esp. 444–53, 648–55 (tables). On the history, from 1934 onwards, of the DAF's Reich Homestead Office, long an agency with very little influence, see the chapter by Karl Christian Führer in this volume.

40. See Harlander, *Zwischen Heimstätte und Wohnmaschine*, 96 f., 212 f., 216 f.

41. Ibid., 212.

42. Amt für die wirtschaftlichen Unternehmungen der DAF, *Die wirtschaftlichen Unternehmungen*, 57.

43. Reich Labour Ministry guidelines quoted in R.J. Jaud, *Der Landkreis Aachen in der NS-Zeit. Politik, Wirtschaft und Gesellschaft in einem katholischen Grenzgebiet 1929–1944*, Frankfurt am Main: Lang, 1997, 495. For a detailed account of the selection of residents, see K.C. Führer, 'Das NS-Regime und die "Idealform des deutschen Wohnungsbaues". Ein Beitrag zur nationalsozialistischen Gesellschaftspolitik', *Vierteljahrschrift für Sozial- und Wirtschaftsgeschichte* 89(2) (2002), 141–66, here 161–63. For a general account of housing in the 'Third Reich', see Führer, *Mieter, Hausbesitzer, Staat und Wohnungsmarkt. Wohnungsmangel und Wohnungszwangswirtschaft in Deutschland 1914–1960*, Stuttgart: Steiner, 1995.

44. See DAF position paper, 'The Settlement Programme of the Four-Year Plan', n.d. [1937], BArch, R 41/915, fol. 97–104; and U. Haerendel, *Kommunale Wohnungspolitik im Dritten Reich. Siedlungsideologie, Kleinhausbau und 'Wohnraumarisierung' am Beispiel München*, Munich: Oldenbourg, 1999, 142–44.

45. For more detail, see Hachtmann, *Wirtschaftsimperium*, 442 f. For an in-depth treatment of what follows, see ibid., 437–40, 444–46.

46. For a discussion of the ideas explored by the DAF's Labour Science Institute, which expressly wished to avoid pre-empting political decisions, put its faith chiefly in company housing (*Werkswohnungsbau*) and wanted to build on the previous forms of state housing subsidies, see 'Die Wohnungsfrage', *Jahrbuch des AWI* (1939), part I, 347–87, here esp. 383–87; and (in the form of reflections of a general nature) 'Kapital und Zins in der Wohnungswirtschaft', *Jahrbuch des AWI* (1940), part II, 1020–23.

47. See R. Ley, 'Wohnungsbau in Deutschland', *Wohnungsbau in Deutschland* 4 (1944), 49–53, here 50. This was no mere lip service. For a detailed account, see Hachtmann, *Wirtschaftsimperium*, 573–80.

48. 'Arbeitsfriede durch Rechtshilfe', *Berliner Tageblatt*, 26 August 1937.

49. See § 17 of the Law Concerning the Authority to Receive Timely Claims Arising from Pensions, Disability, White-Collar, Accident and Miners' Insurance (Gesetz betr. Die Befugnis zur fristgerechten Entgegennahme von Anträgen aus der Renten-, Invaliden-, Angestellten-, Unfall- und Knappschaftsversicherung), 23 December 1936, *RGBl.* I 1936, 1128. For an in-depth treatment, see the book by Alexander Klimo, *Im Dienste des Arbeitseinsatzes. Rentenversicherungspolitik im 'Dritten Reich'*, Göttingen: Wallstein, 2018.

50. Data in O. Marrenbach, *Fundamente des Sieges. Die Gesamtarbeit der Deutschen Arbeitsfront*, Berlin: Verlag der Deutschen Arbeitsfront, 1940, 188. See also S. Rücker, *Rechtsberatung. Das Rechtsberatungswesen von 1919 bis 1945 und die Entstehung des Rechtsberatungsmissbrauchsgesetzes von 1935*, Tübingen: Mohr Siebeck, 2007, 298.

51. Marrenbach *Fundamente des Sieges*, 186, 191, 194. Leading DAF functionaries regularly made statements of this kind.

52. This and the following data taken from R. Hachtmann, 'Die rechtliche Regelung der Arbeitsbeziehungen im Dritten Reich', in D. Gosewinkel (ed.), *Wirtschaftskontrolle und Recht in der nationalsozialistischen Diktatur*, Frankfurt am Main: Klostermann, 2005, 135–56, here 144 f. (table). For details of the DAF's legal advisory service, see also Rücker, *Rechtsberatung*, esp. 285–87, 294–312.

53. For an in-depth treatment, see Rücker, *Rechtsberatung*, 304–12.

54. Employers' representatives were also full of praise. See, for example, Pietzsch, president of the Reich Chamber of Commerce (Reichswirtschaftskammer, de facto a lobbying organization for the business community), at the constitutive meeting of the Socioeconomic Committee of the Reichsgruppe Industrie, 18 October 1935 (minutes), 13, BArch, R 12 I/266.

55. Reich Ministry of the Economy, Schmitt, and Reich Ministry of Labour, Seldte, to the state secretary at the Reich Chancellery, Lammers, re. passage of the AOG bill by the Reich government, 8 December 1933, BArch, R 43 II/547, fol. 37 f.

56. Mansfeld, re. German Labour Front, 24 November 1936, BArch, R 3101/10321, fol. 8, 10 f. See also T. von Freyberg and T. Siegel, *Industrielle Rationalisierung unter dem Nationalsozialismus*, Frankfurt am Main: Campus, 1991, 73.

57. See C. Friemert, *Produktionsästhetik im Faschismus. Das Amt 'Schönheit der Arbeit'*, Munich: Damnitz, 1980, 153; also M. Karl, *Die Fabrikinspektoren in Preußen. Das Personal der Gewerbeaufsicht 1854–1945*, Opladen: Westdeutscher Verlag, 1993, 300 (table 15).

58. See, for example, *Jahresberichte der Gewerbeaufsichtsbeamten für 1933/34*, 1 (Preußen), 6; *Jahresberichte der Gewerbeaufsichtsbeamten für 1935/36*, 1 (Preußen), 9, 320; *Jahresberichte der Gewerbeaufsichtsbeamten für 1937/38*, 1 (Preußen), 18 f.; see also Ordinance issued by Ley, no. 24/34, 8 October 1934, BArch, NS 5 I/256; and Edict issued by the Reich Ministry of Labour, 19 July 1935, for example in Hauptstaatsarchiv (HStA) Munich, StK 6754. The edict was also published in the daily press.

59. See *Jahresberichte der Gewerbeaufsichtsbeamten für 1935/36*, 1 (Preußen), 353, 4 (Württemberg), 72; and, for the war years, the minutes of a meeting between the two camps on 16 February 1943, attachment to DAF Gauwaltung of Brandenburg, Dept. Social Self-Administration to the Neuruppin Working Conditions Inspectorate, 23 February 1943, Brandenburgisches Landeshauptarchiv (BLHA), Pr.Br., Rep. 43 (Neuruppin Working Conditions Inspectorate), no. 8.

60. See *Jahresberichte der Gewerbeaufsichtsbeamten für 1937/38*, 44–46; see also, for example, M. Höfler-Waag, *Die Arbeits- und Leistungsmedizin im Nationalsozialismus von 1939–1945*, Husum: Matthiesen, 1994, 116, 120.

61. See *Jahresberichte der Gewerbeaufsichtsbeamten für 1937/38*, 19; and, for example, *Der Führerorden*, newsletter of the Social Department of the DAF Gauwaltung Bayerische Ostmark, 13 August 1937, BArch, NS 5 I/143; see also M. Frese, *Betriebspolitik im 'Dritten Reich'. Deutsche Arbeitsfront, Unternehmer und Staatsbürokratie in der westdeutschen Großindustrie 1933–1939*, Paderborn: Schöningh, 1991, 87 f.

62. *Jahresberichte der Gewerbeaufsichtsbeamten für 1937/38*, 19.

63. BArch, NS 5 I/341. On the increasingly close cooperation during the war until this point and on the personal unions between the two sides, see for example Memorandum on the Meeting of Leading Working Conditions Inspectorate Officials on 18 May 1943 in Munich, esp. 21 (attachment to Circular issued by the Reich Ministry of Labour, 8 July 1943, BLHA, Pr.Br., Rep. 43, no. 8).

64. See esp. Hachtmann, 'Einleitung', 48 f.; Hachtmann, 'Elastisch', 35–51.

65. R. Ley, *Soldaten der Arbeit*, Berlin: Eher, 1938, 9. This became a standard phrase for Ley and other top DAF functionaries.

66. On the term, see D. Rebentisch and K. Teppe, 'Einleitung', in Rebentisch and Teppe, *Verwaltung contra Menschenführung im Staat Hitlers*, 7–32, here esp. 23–32.

67. See note 23. On the age and Nazi Party membership of the top officials in the Reich Labour Ministry, see the chapter by Ulrike Schulz in this volume.

68. For detailed information on Theodor Hupfauer, see Biographical Appendix.

69. Notes on two conversations between Broszat and Hupfauer (1906–1993) on 23 January and 14 February 1985, 6, Archiv der Stiftung für Sozialgeschichte des 20. Jahrhunderts, Bremen, DAF holdings, 6.2 Biographies, File Hi-Kosiol.

Bibliography

Amt für die wirtschaftlichen Unternehmungen der DAF. *Die wirtschaftlichen Unternehmungen der Deutschen Arbeitsfront im Jahre 1939*. Berlin: self-published, 1940.

Baranowski, S. *Strength through Joy. Consumerism and Mass Tourism in the Third Reich*. Cambridge: Cambridge University Press, 2004.

Blanke, T., et al. (eds). *Kollektives Arbeitsrecht. Quellentexte zur Geschichte des Arbeitsrechts in Deutschland*, vol. 2: *1933 bis zur Gegenwart*. Reinbek bei Hamburg: Rowohlt, 1975.

Buchholz, W. *Die nationalsozialistische Gemeinschaft 'Kraft durch Freude'. Freizeitgestaltung und Arbeiterschaft im Dritten Reich*, Ph.D. dissertation. Munich: University of Munich, 1976.

Degener, H.A.L. (ed.). *Degeners Wer ist's?*, 10th ed. Berlin: Degener, 1935.

Das deutsche Führerlexikon. Berlin: Stollberg, 1934.

Deutschland-Berichte der Sozialdemokratischen Partei Deutschlands (Sopade) 1934–1940, Vierter Jahrgang: 1937, ed. K. Behnken. Salzhausen: Nettelbeck, 1980.

Eichholtz, D. *Geschichte der deutschen Kriegswirtschaft 1939–1945*, 5 vols. Munich: Saur, 2003.

Frese, M. *Betriebspolitik im 'Dritten Reich'. Deutsche Arbeitsfront, Unternehmer und Staatsbürokratie in der westdeutschen Großindustrie 1933–1939*. Paderborn: Schöningh, 1991.

Freyberg, T. v., and T. Siegel. *Industrielle Rationalisierung unter dem Nationalsozialismus*. Frankfurt am Main: Campus, 1991.

Friemert, C. *Produktionsästhetik im Faschismus. Das Amt 'Schönheit der Arbeit'*. Munich: Damnitz, 1980.

Führer, K.C. *Mieter, Hausbesitzer, Staat und Wohnungsmarkt. Wohnungsmangel und Wohnungszwangswirtschaft in Deutschland 1914–1960*. Stuttgart: Steiner, 1995.

Führer, K.C. 'Das NS-Regime und die "Idealform des deutschen Wohnungsbaues". Ein Beitrag zur nationalsozialistischen Gesellschaftspolitik'. *Vierteljahrsschrift für Sozial- und Wirtschaftsgeschichte* 89(2) (2002), 141–66.

Hachtmann, R. '"Bäuche wegmassieren" und "überflüssiges Fett in unserem Volke beseitigen" – der kommunale Breitensport der NS-Gemeinschaft "Kraft durch Freude"', in F. Becker and R. Schäfer (eds), *Sport und Nationalsozialismus* (Göttingen: Wallstein, 2016), 27–65.

Hachtmann, R. 'Arbeit und Arbeitsfront: Ideologie und Praxis', in M. Buggeln and M. Wildt (eds), *Arbeit im Nationalsozialismus* (Munich: De Gruyter Oldenbourg, 2014), 83–106.

Hachtmann, R. 'Die Deutsche Arbeitsfront im Zweiten Weltkrieg', in D. Eichholtz (ed.), *Krieg und Wirtschaft. Studien zur deutschen Wirtschaftsgeschichte 1939–1945* (Berlin: Metropol, 1999), 69–108.

Hachtmann, R. 'Die Deutsche Arbeitsfront und die NS-Gemeinschaft "Kraft durch Freude" – "volksgemeinschaftliche" Dienstleister?', in D. Schmiechen-Ackermann (ed.), *'Volksgemeinschaft'. Mythos, wirkungsmächtige soziale Verheißung oder soziale Realität im 'Dritten Reich'? Zwischenbilanz einer kontroversen Debatte* (Paderborn: Schöningh, 2012), 111–31.

Hachtmann, R. 'Einleitung', in Hachtmann (ed.), *Ein Koloss auf tönernen Füßen. Das Gutachten des Wirtschaftsprüfers Karl Eicke über die Deutsche Arbeitsfront vom 31. Juli 1936* (Munich: Oldenbourg, 2006), 7–94.

Hachtmann, R. 'Elastisch, dynamisch und von katastrophaler Effizienz – Anmerkungen zur Neuen Staatlichkeit des Nationalsozialismus', in S. Reichardt and W. Seibel (eds), *Der prekäre Staat. Herrschen und Verwalten im Nationalsozialismus* (Frankfurt am Main: Campus, 2011), 29–73.

Hachtmann, R. 'Industriearbeiterinnen in der deutschen Kriegswirtschaft 1936–1944/45'. *Geschichte und Gesellschaft* 19(3) (1993), 332–66.

Hachtmann, R. 'Kleinbürgerlicher Schmerbauch und breite bürgerliche Brust – zur sozialen Zusammensetzung der Führungselite der Deutschen Arbeitsfront', in U. Bitzegeio, A. Kruke and M. Woyke (eds), *Solidargemeinschaft und Erinnerungskultur im 20. Jahrhundert. Beiträge zu Gewerkschaften, Nationalsozialismus und Geschichtspolitik* (Bonn: Dietz, 2009), 233–57.

Hachtmann, R. 'Die rechtliche Regelung der Arbeitsbeziehungen im Dritten Reich', in D. Gosewinkel (ed.), *Wirtschaftskontrolle und Recht in der nationalsozialistischen Diktatur* (Frankfurt am Main: Klostermann, 2005), 135–56.

Hachtmann, R. *Tourismus-Geschichte*. Göttingen: UTB, 2007.

Hachtmann, R. 'Vom "Geist der Volksgemeinschaft durchpulst" – Arbeit, Arbeiter und die Sprachpolitik der Nationalsozialisten'. *Zeitgeschichte-Online*, January 2010. Retrieved 26 September 2018 from http://www.zeitgeschichte-online.de/thema/vom-geist-der-volksgemeinschaft-durchpulst.

Hachtmann, R. *Das Wirtschaftsimperium der Deutschen Arbeitsfront*. Göttingen: Wallstein, 2012.

Haerendel, U. *Kommunale Wohnungspolitik im Dritten Reich. Siedlungsideologie, Kleinhausbau und 'Wohnraumarisierung' am Beispiel München*. Munich: Oldenbourg, 1999.

Harlander, T. *Zwischen Heimstätte und Wohnmaschine. Wohnungsbau und Wohnungspolitik in der Zeit des Nationalsozialismus*. Basel: Birkhäuser, 1995.

Höfler-Waag, M. *Die Arbeits- und Leistungsmedizin im Nationalsozialismus von 1939–1945*. Husum: Matthiesen, 1994.

Humann, D. *'Arbeitsschlacht'. Arbeitsbeschaffung und Propaganda in der NS-Zeit 1933–1939*. Göttingen: Wallstein, 2011.

Jaud, R.J. *Der Landkreis Aachen in der NS-Zeit. Politik, Wirtschaft und Gesellschaft in einem katholischen Grenzgebiet 1929–1944*. Frankfurt am Main: Lang, 1997.

Karl, M. *Die Fabrikinspektoren in Preußen. Das Personal der Gewerbeaufsicht 1854–1945*. Opladen: Westdeutscher Verlag, 1993.

Kater, H. 'Die Ehrauffassung der SS. Nationalsozialismus und das Duell. Himmler als Burschenschaftler: Das Duell R. Strunk gegen Horst Krutschinna'. *Einst und Jetzt* 38 (1993), 265–70.

Kiehl, W. *Mann an der Fahne. Kameraden erzählen von Dr. Ley*. Munich: Eher, 1938.

Klimo, A. *Im Dienste des Arbeitseinsatzes. Rentenversicherungspolitik im 'Dritten Reich'*. Göttingen: Wallstein, 2018.

Kranig, A. *Lockung und Zwang. Zur Arbeitsverfassung im Dritten Reich*. Stuttgart: Deutsche Verlags-Anstalt, 1983.

Ley, R. *Haltet den Sieg und beutet ihn aus*. Berlin: Verlag der Deutschen Arbeitsfront, 1941.

Ley, R. *Soldaten der Arbeit*. Berlin: Eher, 1938.

Ley, R. 'Wohnungsbau in Deutschland'. *Wohnungsbau in Deutschland* 4 (1944), 49–53.

Lilla, J. *Statisten in Uniform. Die Mitglieder des Reichstags 1933-1945. Ein biographisches Handbuch*. Düsseldorf: Droste, 2004.

Marrenbach, O. *Fundamente des Sieges. Die Gesamtarbeit der Deutschen Arbeitsfront*. Berlin: Verlag der Deutschen Arbeitsfront, 1940.

Müller, W. *Das soziale Leben im neuen Deutschland unter besonderer Berücksichtigung der Deutschen Arbeitsfront*. Berlin: Mittler, 1938.

Der Parteitag der Arbeit vom 6. bis 13. September 1937. Offizieller Bericht über den Verlauf des Reichsparteitages mit sämtlichen Kongreßreden. Munich: Eher, 1937.

Preller, L. *Sozialpolitik in der Weimarer Republik*, reprint. Düsseldorf: Droste, 1978.

Rebentisch, D., and K. Teppe. 'Einleitung', in Rebentisch and Teppe (eds), *Verwaltung contra Menschenführung im Staat Hitlers. Studien zum politisch administrativen System* (Göttingen: Vandenhoeck & Ruprecht, 1986), 7–32.

Recker, M.-L. *Nationalsozialistische Sozialpolitik im Zweiten Weltkrieg*. Munich: Oldenbourg, 1985.

Recker, M.-L. 'Der Reichskommissar für den sozialen Wohnungsbau. Zu Aufbau, Stellung und Arbeitsweise einer führerunmittelbaren Sonderbehörde', in D. Rebentisch and K. Teppe (eds), *Verwaltung contra Menschenführung im Staat Hitlers. Studien zum politisch administrativen System* (Göttingen: Vandenhoeck & Ruprecht, 1986), 333–50.

Reichhardt, H.-J. *Die Deutsche Arbeitsfront. Ein Beitrag zur Geschichte des nationalsozialistischen Deutschlands und zur Struktur des totalitären Herrschaftssystems*, Ph.D. dissertation. Berlin: Freie Universität Berlin, 1956.

Reichsheimstättenamt der DAF (ed.). *Siedlung. Planungsheft der DAF*. Berlin: Verlag der Deutschen Arbeitsfront GmbH, 1938.

Roth, K.-H. *Intelligenz und Sozialpolitik im 'Dritten Reich'. Eine methodisch-historische Studie am Beispiel des Arbeitswissenschaftlichen Instituts der Deutschen Arbeitsfront*. Munich: Saur, 1993.

Roth, K.-H. 'Die Sozialpolitik des "europäischen Großraum" im Spannungsfeld von Okkupation und Kollaboration (1938–1945)', in W. Röhr (ed.), *Okkupation und Kollaboration (1938–1945). Beiträge zu Konzepten und Praxis der Kollaboration in der deutschen Okkupationspolitik* (Berlin: Hüthig, 1994), 461–565.

Rücker, S. *Rechtsberatung. Das Rechtsberatungswesen von 1919 bis 1945 und die Entstehung des Rechtsberatungsmissbrauchsgesetzes von 1935*. Tübingen: Mohr Siebeck, 2007.

Sachse, C. 'Das nationalsozialistische Mutterschutzgesetz. Eine Strategie zur Rationalisierung des weiblichen Arbeitsvermögens im Zweiten Weltkrieg', in D. Reese et al. (eds), *Rationale Beziehungen? Geschlechterverhältnisse im Produktionsprozeß* (Frankfurt am Main: Suhrkamp, 1993), 189–221.

Schneider, M. *In der Kriegsgesellschaft. Arbeiter und Arbeiterbewegung 1939 bis 1945*. Bonn: J.H.W. Dietz Nachf., 2014.

Schneider, M. *Unterm Hakenkreuz. Arbeiter und Arbeiterbewegung 1933 bis 1939*. Bonn: Dietz, 1999.

Schumann, S. *Die Frau aus dem Erwerbsleben wieder herausnehmen. NS-Propaganda und Arbeitsmarktpolitik in Sachsen 1933–1939*. Dresden: Hannah-Arendt-Institut für Totalitarismusforschung, 2000.

Smelser, R. *Robert Ley. Hitler's Labor Front Leader*. Oxford: Berg, 1989.

Spohn, W. *Betriebsgemeinschaft und Volksgemeinschaft. Die rechtliche und institutionelle Regelung der Arbeitsbeziehungen im NS-Staat*. Berlin: Quorum, 1987.

Weise, G. 'Heeresbericht von der Deutschen Arbeitsfront'. *Völkischer Beobachter*, 30 April 1938.

Wer leitet? Die Männer der Wirtschaft und der einschlägigen Verwaltung 1940. Berlin: Hoppenstedt, 1940 and 1941/42.

Part II
POLICY FIELDS

Chapter 4

THE HOUSING POLICIES OF THE REICH MINISTRY OF LABOUR

Karl Christian Führer

The Reich chancellor and 'Führer', who as a rule liked to make speeches swathed in nebulous rhetoric about the big questions of world politics, was on this occasion unusually down to earth and specific. In a radio address broadcast throughout the Reich on 12 March 1936, Adolf Hitler informed his listeners that, as it built up the Wehrmacht, the German Reich was currently paying three thousand Reichsmarks for every single '30-cm grenade'. Meanwhile, for 4,500 Reichsmarks 'a worker's home' could be built. Given the ratio between these figures, Hitler went on, there was no question as to how he wished to secure his posthumous reputation as a politician among the German people: 'If I stack up a million such grenades in a great heap, that's no monument at all. But if I have a million such houses, in which the same number of German workers can live, then I've built my own memorial'.[1] Robert Ley, head of the German Labour Front and one of the few top-level Nazi dignitaries to enjoy personal access to Hitler at all times, publicly aired an even more breathtaking figure just a few months later. In 'the next few years' alone, he proclaimed, the 'Third Reich' would construct five million new homes, because 'creating healthy living conditions' was a particularly urgent social priority.[2] In his announcement, Ley referred explicitly to the 'Führer's settlement programme', before going on to explain that the DAF would be centrally involved in implementing it as planning and executive agency.[3]

Tellingly, the Labour Ministry made no public comment either on Hitler's speech or the declarations of Robert Ley, although it was responsible for German housing policy and had its own Main Section IV (Hauptabteilung IV) for 'Housing and Settlement'. In reality, the officials in Main Section IV must have been dismayed in both cases. In 1936, both Hitler and the head of the DAF were, with much aplomb, publicly propagating a housing and housebuilding policy officially rejected by the 'Third Reich'. From 1933, the Reich Ministry of Labour and the Reich government had repeatedly underlined that the construction of new houses and flats must not be publicly subsidized if at all possible. 'The task of providing housing will be left largely in the hands of the private sector', to quote the articulation of this credo by one of the Berlin ministry's leading housing policy experts.[4]

The 'Führer', by way of contrast, promised that from now on the Reich would cover the costs of every new 'worker's home'. Ley too, who wanted the DAF to take over the provision of housing, made no reference to 'private initiative' or the private financing of new homes. Yet even the Labour Ministry saw an urgent need to build more homes in National Socialist Germany. Just one day before Hitler's appearance in Karlsruhe, in an internal letter to the Finance Ministry, Labour Minister Franz Seldte had described the situation of the housing markets in gloomy terms. In the towns and cities of Germany, the lack of housing had reached such a magnitude 'that if it gets any worse we will be faced with the gravest of domestic political, health-related and population policy risks'.[5]

A public programmatic disagreement of the kind that opened up in 1936 between the Labour Ministry on the one hand, and Hitler and Ley, as the leading exponents of Nazi rule, on the other, was an extremely rare event in the 'Third Reich'. At the same time, the question of how to step up the construction of housing touched on vital interests of the dictatorial system. If we wish to understand the position of the Labour Ministry in Nazi Germany, its concepts, plans, accomplishments and problems, housing policy is clearly of special significance. The following outline of the ministry's activities in this field during the years of the dictatorship, however, requires a fairly detailed introductory retrospective on the Weimar Republic, because after 1933 the ministry pursued an approach to housing policy that it had already begun in the last few years of democracy. It is only against this background that we can discern just how much its housing and settlement strategy was influenced by a specific concept of *Ordnungspolitik*, that is, the notion that when it came to constructing dwellings for tenants, the state should provide a framework for economic activity but leave it essentially in private hands.

Rekindling Private Initiative: The Housing Policy of the Reich Ministry of Labour after 1930

Among the cultural achievements of the Weimar Republic that still dominate the historical remembrance of this period, public housing is of great importance. When the years of high inflation came to an end in 1924, in many German towns and cities ample financial support in the shape of low- or even zero-interest public loans resulted in the construction of large blocks of flats and large-scale residential complexes, built, owned and let by cooperatives and public enterprises. These so-called *Siedlungen* (housing estates) were striking architectural additions to the urban scene that systematically realized multiple ideas on social hygiene and housing reform that had previously tended to be mere hypotheticals aired by well-meaning experts.

What is less well-known is that this modern housing policy, conceived and sustained mainly by the local authorities, was already terminated during the Weimar Republic. As early as 1929–1930, the number of new projects dwindled. Furthermore, commenting on the estates that had only just been completed, key actors in German housing policy now criticized them as questionable achievements. On this view, the new flats were too expensive and did not help those who really needed new dwellings. To make matters worse, they were also financed on shaky economic foundations. Officials at the Reich Ministry of Labour were among the leading exponents of this reinterpretation. The ministry also used its influence to push through new regulations to foster the construction of dwellings for tenants that tied the hands of the Länder and local authorities in an entirely new way.

Originally the ministry, established in 1918–1919, exercised negligible influence in this field of public policy. All the crucial decisions relating to the construction of new housing were made by the various Länder and – to an even greater degree – the local authorities. The Reich had the authority to impose a regulatory framework but made no use of this right. Prior to 1929–1930, therefore, the most important step taken by the ministry with respect to the construction of new housing was to secure financial support for the Länder. In the spring of 1924, the ministry reserved 10 per cent of all proceeds from the newly introduced 'house rent tax' (*Hauszinssteuer*) to support the building of new homes. This statutory share became the leading source of credit for new housing during the stable years of the Weimar Republic. The Reich Ministry of Labour itself, however, exercised no influence on the allocation of funds (and when it came to their calculation, many Land governments went well beyond the 10 per cent statutory share).[6]

In 1927, the ministry also failed in its attempt – by modifying older laws – to acquire the right at least to issue its own guarantees (*Bürgschaften*) for building loans due to the resistance of the Länder. Such guarantees, to quote the Interior Ministry of Württemberg, would enable the Reich to implement 'far-reaching measures in housing and settlement policy' without consulting the other public authorities.[7] Particularly when it came to funding construction, however, the Württemberg ministry contended, centralism had to be strenuously avoided, because housebuilding must seek to respond to local needs and take account of regional traditions. The Prussian government even feared the 'gradual erosion of the Land administration', were the Reich Labour Ministry to gain greater powers over construction policy.[8] In this respect, then, the ministry remained a have-not.

It was only the start of the world economic crisis in 1929, which hit Germany very hard and ushered in the semi-authoritarian system of the 'presidential cabinets', that reshuffled the cards in this game over money, influence and power. With backing from the Reich president, the Berlin government was now able, to a large degree, to shut out not only the Reichstag but also the Länder and local authorities from the political decision-making process. This made it possible to enforce even prescriptions and programmes subject to a great deal of political controversy, and this is exactly what happened in the field of construction policy in 1930–1931.

First, the Reich Labour Ministry ensured that public subsidies could now be deployed only for the 'cheapest of homes' intended 'for the lowest ranks of the population'.[9] Through this regulation, which was issued in spring 1931 by emergency decree and also applied to the Länder and local authorities, the Reich government was reacting to a problem that had undeniably plagued the building of 'reform housing' (*Reformwohnungsbau*, that is, progressive, modern housing) since 1924: the homes built in the new housing estates were too expensive for the vast majority of the population and particularly for those families in desperate need of accommodation. The Reich Labour Ministry thought it was wrong for such a 'socially exclusive' product to receive state subsidies. Otto Wölz, ministerial counsellor in Main Section IV, declared that to use public money to create homes for 'economically better-off families' would be to 'misdirect' it.[10] Ultimately, the housing policy experts at the ministry were trying to uphold the principle of social policy subsidiarity. Believing that state funding for housing must directly and 'genuinely' help 'those groups of the less well-off most in need of social welfare', for these experts public support for housing essentially entailed keeping rents as low as possible. What this meant in practice was that now subsidies went only to the construction of very small homes that were fitted out as simply as possible.[11]

In retrospect, the Labour Ministry was also disturbed by the financing methods the local authorities and Länder had been using for publicly supported housing. Not only had their loans covered the greater part of building costs, but a large share of these loans was derived from other loans. Since 1924, many local authorities had run up a great deal of debt to fund 'reform housing'. The house rent tax, then, was used creatively. On the one hand, much of it flowed into the general budget and, on the other, as prospective income over the ensuing years, it funded loans for buildings that could not have been paid for solely with the limited portion earmarked for construction. The Reich Labour Ministry regarded this debt-fuelled economy as a social 'evil' that was disruptive to the 'orderly progress of the general administration of public funds'.[12] As a result, new regulations were introduced that not only prohibited these forms of deficit spending but also placed tight restrictions on the amount of public support per home. The goal here was not just to relieve the strain on government budgets. The ministry also hoped that investors in new housing, now facing serious financial challenges themselves, would adopt a more frugal approach.[13]

Second, the Labour Ministry integrated these regulations on the construction of the cheapest possible 'small homes' into a new housing policy programme that was to be rolled out over several years. Again by emergency decree, in December 1930 the Reich government imposed a time limit of five years not only on the public financing of construction but also on current laws regulating the amount of rent in flats in old residential buildings and protection against eviction for tenants. The government was determined that the end of the accounting and budgetary year of 1935–1936 (that is, 1 April 1936) would mark the end of all housing subsidies in Germany. On the same date, moreover, both the 'Reich Rent Law' (Reichsmietengesetz) and the 'Eviction Protection Law' (Kündigungsschutzgesetz) would cease to apply. These had enabled the state to limit landlords' freedom of action and protect the tenants of flats in old buildings against a tenancy termination notice.[14]

With this plan, the Brüning Cabinet adopted an unambiguous stance with respect to *Ordnungspolitik*. In the housing markets, the government's avowed goal was essentially to return to the conditions that had pertained in Germany prior to 1914.[15] If we exclude the building regulations established locally, the German Empire featured only a negligible degree of state intervention, both in housing construction and in the relationship between landlords and tenants. Public financial support for housing existed only in a highly rudimentary form. Rents followed the laws of supply and demand and freedom of contract applied virtually without restriction when it came to rented dwellings. It was not until the final phase of the First World War that the state began to intervene in this free market on behalf of tenants, in order to achieve social peace on the 'home front', whose various segments were threatening to fall out over steep rent rises. In the early Weimar Republic, these beginnings led to the emergence of a complex 'state-controlled housing market', which comprehensively disempowered all landlords and functioned like a rent freeze. Under these conditions, very few private investors continued to build new rental flats, so the Länder and municipalities took over, not least because, due to the house rent tax introduced in 1924, they had their own source of capital, the revenue from which they could use to this end.

Coordinating the termination both of state support for housing construction and the two interventionist laws, the Reich government prospectively declared an end to this comprehensive public control of housing, whose individual parts were systematically and closely interlinked, in the winter of 1930–1931. It made just one exception. The special protection for tenants even against a timely termination notice from their landlord was not to disappear entirely in 1936. Instead it would continue in an unspecified manner through a yet to be formulated 'social law on rented housing' ('soziales Mietrecht'). Otherwise, though, the Cabinet's goal, and thus that of the Reich Ministry of Labour as well, was to strip itself, as well as the Länder and municipalities, of their powers over housing policy. The literature thus refers to a 'conservative turn' and a 'radical change' in this field of German domestic policy.[16]

Yet such assessments are misleading. At the highest political level, three representatives of the Catholic Centre Party were responsible for the housing policy decisions of the winter of 1930–1931: Reich Chancellor Heinrich Brüning, Reich Labour Minister Adam Stegerwald and long-serving Prussian Minister for Social Welfare Heinrich Hirtsiefer. Jointly, they conceived of the plan outlined above and agreed, in person, to the date when the 'controlled housing market' was to be terminated. As Stegerwald stated, this deadline in particular was the 'expression of a political decision'. For the three Centre Party politicians, the new regulations intended to limit public construction subsidies to small homes, and the announcement that the rent law and the eviction protection law would be strictly time-limited, were inextricably linked. The two laws, as they saw it, could only be revoked when there was no longer an acute shortage of housing: balanced housing markets would eliminate the need for more state intervention and secure a smooth transition to a deregulated housing market because they would banish the risk of general rent increases. Since it was affordable small homes above all that were lacking, the state should concentrate its efforts on eliminating this shortage. At the same time, they were convinced, the announcement that in the foreseeable future Germany would once again have a 'free' housing market was indispensable 'to ensure that private capital can operate as smoothly and securely as possible with respect to housebuilding'.[17]

The decisions made by Brüning, Stegerwald and Hirtsiefer did not amount to a new policy concept. On the contrary, like all bourgeois political parties, the Centre Party had always viewed the 'state-controlled housing market' as a stopgap measure intended to mitigate the social consequences of the severe lack of housing reported by most German towns and cities by 1916–1917. The goal was to swiftly terminate state intervention when conditions had once again 'normalized'.[18] What was new in 1930–1931 was merely the consistency with which the Labour Ministry and the Reich government sought to deploy the reformed public financing of housing to facilitate the abolition of the 'controlled housing market'.

The emergency decree of December 1930 and the regulations on the construction of small homes, then, articulated a stringent political programme that the Centre Party had in principle been pursuing since the early years of the Weimar Republic. This policy was straightforwardly derived from the fundamental ideological views held by the Centre Party as well as by the Christian trades unions. They opposed state socialist structures, put their faith in a free market tamed by moderate legal forms of intervention (hence the pledge to create a 'social law on rented housing') and, as a matter of principle, wished to grant government aid only in cases of genuine need. With the help of emergency decrees, the Labour Ministry in particular pursued this course energetically within the system of 'presidential cabinets'. This reveals how strongly the ministry had been infused by the specific conceptual framework of bourgeois Catholic social teaching between 1920 and 1928, under Heinrich Brauns. Under Adam Stegerwald, whose background also lay in the Catholic trades union movement, this orientation was reinforced.[19]

However, from the outset, the Labour Ministry's internally consistent plan to return to a housing market governed by liberal principles and do away entirely with the 'controlled housing market' in the spring of 1936 suffered from one tremendous shortcoming. The Brüning government impeded the implementation of the plan that it itself had drawn up by restricting the construction of new homes, which was supposed to increase the supply of small and inexpensive flats and houses and thus create a well-balanced housing market by 1936. Responsibility for this discrepancy did not lie with the Reich Ministry of Labour. In fact, it recognized the problem very clearly but, despite its warnings and alternative proposals, failed to gain support for its views. Instead it was the Finance Ministry that dominated on this issue, demanding an extremely strict focus on savings and balanced government budgets. As a result, all the revenue from the house rent tax was redirected to the general budget in two stages over the course of 1931–1932. At the same time, the Reich government banned the municipalities, across the board, from taking out new loans. The era of cheap building loans from the Länder and municipalities thus came to an abrupt end.[20]

The Nazi Party was one of the many critics of this paradoxical policy. In autumn 1930, its party organ, the Völkischer Beobachter, referred to 'amateurism', opining that the 'goal of a responsible state policy' must be to 'create the primary precondition for improving our social conditions by strongly supporting the construction of new housing'.[21] This statement repays our attention when we consider the years after 1933. Particularly in the Labour Ministry, the relevant civil servants may have listened. However, after 1930 the Reich did little to fill the financial void left by the new regulations on the house rent tax. Certainly, in the winter of 1930–1931, the Labour Ministry was allowed to spend a total of 100 million Reichsmarks to support the construction of additional small homes, which the ministry would have liked to see at the centre of state building policy. These funds, which covered the construction of around twenty-six thousand flats, had been used up within a few months. But there were no more subsidies of this kind. Instead, the ministry received another 100 million Reichsmarks just once more to provide indirect support for small and affordable rented dwellings. In this way, the Reich government aimed to secure private loans for such homes through guarantees. However, the money was not to be used for government building loans. The government thus sought to underline once again its political determination to liberalize the housing market, while first reacquainting private investors with the idea of putting their money into the construction of dwellings for rent.

In the midst of the epoch-making economic crisis from 1930 onwards, however, this decision quickly proved to have been a mistake. In line with the admonitory forecasts produced by Main Section IV, potential investors considered Germany's economic and social prospects far too uncertain to build homes for low-income families, who were already viewed within the housing market as unreliable tenants. As a result, in the spring of 1933, almost 90 per cent of this second tranche of 100 million Reichsmarks was still to be used. But the Labour Ministry's repeated calls for the building of small homes to be subsidized once again directly, through government loans, went unheeded due to the joint veto of the Reich Finance Ministry and its Prussian counterpart.[22]

The fiscal policymakers' miserliness is astonishing in as much as the Reich Labour Ministry, along with virtually every housing policy expert, discovered a new form of housing in 1931 that seemed perfectly suited to the period of severe economic crisis. I am referring to the 'small suburban housing estate' (*vorstädtische Kleinsiedlung*). The idea of this scheme was to make the unemployed and their families home owners on the periphery of the cities, rendering them 'crisis-proof' by providing them with very simple houses but the largest possible gardens, in which they could grow their own food and – as property owners – immunize them politically against the promises of communism. The housing policy experts of Main Section IV quickly became resolute advocates of this concept, which was fed by a long tradition of bourgeois fears concerning supposedly 'rootless' urban industrial workers, but which also attained a great deal of popularity in left-wing circles during the crisis. By 1932, the leading civil servant (Abteilungsdirigent) Karl Durst had decreed that the small housing estate was the best form of state-backed small home construction and must therefore be strongly supported.[23]

Political practice, however, did not keep pace with these enthusiastic avowals. It is true that, in 1931–1932, a total of seventy-three million Reichsmarks from the Reich budget were made available specifically to fund small suburban housing estates. In contrast to the rules relating to normal small homes, these funds could also be used as loans. But the authorities only managed to 'settle' just under thirty thousand unemployed individuals with the available sum. Given that there were more than six million officially registered jobless, this result was anything but impressive. Half-resignedly and half-accusingly, in May 1932, in an internal letter to the Reich Chancellery, the Labour Ministry stated that it was an entirely open question how the construction of new housing in Germany was to be financed in the foreseeable future.[24] Due to the economic slump, the number of homes built in 1932 was 50 per cent lower than as recently as 1929. This letter, then, identified a grave political problem, one that placed a question mark over the Labour Ministry's reform plan as a whole, if it wished to honour its pledge to deregulate the housing market only if the demand for, and the supply of, flats for tenants had achieved a state of equilibrium.

In addition, the ministry and its plan came under even more pressure as a result of an almost absurd political manoeuvre by Reich Chancellor Heinrich Brüning. In December 1931, almost exactly a year after the first emergency decree, issued by the presidential cabinet, had stipulated that the 'controlled housing market' must end in 1936, the chancellor issued a new decree shortening this deadline to less than one and a half years. The comprehensive protection against eviction for tenants and the 'Reich Rent Law', as the core of the state's control of the housing market, were to cease to apply on 1 April 1933. With this provision, Brüning was courting the support of the Reich Party of the German Middle Class (Reichspartei des deutschen Mittelstandes or Wirtschaftspartei [WP]), which saw itself as representing the interests of landlords and land owners. Like the Länder and municipalities, the Labour Ministry considered the new deadline far too tight, but true to the principle of collective Cabinet responsibility, defended it once again as a 'political decision'.[25]

This new date, however, proved meaningless. During the few weeks, in the winter of 1932–1933, when the office of Reich chancellor was occupied by Kurt von Schleicher, Brüning's arbitrary decision was overturned. Since there was still no agreement on what was to happen to landlords' right to terminate tenancies, the short-term chancellor, partly at the behest of the

Labour Ministry, removed all deadlines relating not just to protection from eviction but also to the 'Reich Rent Law'.[26] Once again, the question of how and when the government would achieve the balanced housing market that was supposed to facilitate the end of the state control of housing was an entirely open one.

In housing policy terms, then, the Reich Ministry of Labour found itself in a highly contradictory position when the Nazi Party took power a few weeks later. Certainly, from 1930 onwards the ministry clearly stood at the centre of German construction policy, which had, for the most part, previously been decided autonomously by the Länder and municipalities. A key component of this centralization was the detailed plan setting out how to abolish the 'controlled housing market'. By 1933, however, this plan was already looking rather tattered. Heinrich Brüning's drastic shortening of the initial deadline had already damaged this project's credibility. To make things worse, after von Schleicher's rescinding of Brüning's emergency decree, the lack of an explicitly identified final date diminished the pressure on the relevant political actors to actively combat the housing shortage.

Furthermore, the Berlin ministry simply lacked the finances and authority to concentrate housebuilding unambiguously on genuinely affordable small homes. Yet there was an urgent need to increase the number of such homes, if rents were to remain stable once the housing market was deregulated.

Moreover, due to the severe economic crisis, the idea had taken hold that these small dwellings, if at all possible, ought to take the form not of normal rented flats but of houses in small suburban estates. Because this represented a very special ownership-creating measure requiring both personal input from the unemployed settler (specifically, a substantial contribution to clearing the ground and erecting the house) and an unusually vast amount of land because of the requisite large gardens, the business of facilitating construction became even more complex than it already was in the middle of a severe economic depression. By 1933, then, the work being done in Main Section IV was surely among the most difficult tasks of the Reich Ministry of Labour.

New Rationales for an Unchanged Policy: The First Years of the 'Third Reich'

In late August 1933, the *Reichsarbeitsblatt* carried the first article in which a member of staff of the Berlin ministry addressed the political changes that had overtaken Germany since 30 January of that year. Senior Governmental Counsellor Ludwig Münz took stock of social policy legislation since Hitler's assumption of office, and he used a surprising metaphor to convey the Nazi Party's political actions. The 'National Socialist revolution [has] swept over Germany', the ministerial official wrote, like a 'storm surge'.[27]

Yet the senior government counsellor cannot have had the field of housing policy in mind as he looked back with such surprising scepticism over the 'first stage of the revolution' that, according to the Nazis' declarations, Germany had just completed. Tellingly, Münz made only marginal mention of this policy sphere, while the question of how to foster new housing was entirely absent from his article. There were, in fact, no grounds for complaint about interventions by the governing Nazi Party in this respect. In the first few years of the dictatorship, the housing policy of the 'Third Reich' followed exactly the same course as prior to 1933.

The Labour Ministry's remit also remained unaffected. Certainly, in March 1934, on Hitler's orders, responsibility for the development of small housing estates passed to a specially appointed Reich commissioner for settlement (Reichskommissar für das Siedlungswesen), who was assigned to the Reich Ministry of the Economy and simultaneously acquired the housing experts previously working at the Labour Ministry. Through this bureaucratic reform, the Nazi regime supposedly wished to underline the character of the small housing estate as an 'economic measure', while also speeding up decisions in this field. In reality, however, the primary goal was to find a worthy post for Gottfried Feder, an 'old [Nazi Party] fighter' who had risen to the position of state secretary in the Reich Ministry of the Economy following Hitler's assumption of power. This institution, however, was desperate to 'dispose' of him, as he was both out of his depth and hyperactive. Feder, a self-appointed expert on issues of job creation, town planning and housing, had already made his public mark before 1933 as an irrepressible fantasist, a reputation he soon bore out as the new Reich commissioner, by hatching utopian plans to build around one thousand new and perfectly planned towns across Germany.[28] By December 1934, he had been 'dispatched' once and for all, that is, shunted off to a professorship, while the old Main Section IV in the Labour Ministry was re-established.[29]

Feder's housing policy reign was an inconsequential episode. Even in 1934, while seemingly stripped of its authority over housing policy, the Labour Ministry had continued to have a say over it. Tellingly, unlike other Reich commissioners, at no point did Feder, with his small staff, enjoy the status of 'independent, supreme Reich authority'. Every decision he made, he had to coordinate not just with the minister of the economy but also with Labour Minister Seldte.[30]

It is also crucial to note the strong *esprit de corps* among the officials under Feder's authority. On 17 May 1934, the sixteen members of staff involved, at their own explicit request, were given a small collective ceremonial send-off at the Labour Ministry, an event not originally envisaged by that institution. In the in-house newsletter, Section Director Karl Durst wrote that for him and his colleagues the administrative reform meant 'parting with the members of the ministry, with whom they feel connected as a result of long-standing cooperation and, in some cases, the closest of personal relationships, and to whom it is hard for them to say good-bye'. They were, however, keen to remain 'in close contact'.[31] When their new boss introduced himself, State Secretary Johannes Krohn emphasized that the section 'embodies ... good old civil service tradition in the best sense'. Feder should 'take [this] into account as he makes use of these officials in future', which the Nazi ideologue naturally promised to do.[32]

More than three months later, Feder's deputy, another Nazi Party man, declared to the Reich commissioner's subordinates that it was 'absolutely crucial that administrative practice is not only technically reconfigured but also pervaded by a new spirit'. This was, in all likelihood, an admission that the officials continued to regard themselves as part of the Labour Ministry. On the same occasion, the deputy warned of an 'urgent need' for the officials to 'begin their practical work', leaving us with the impression that the redeployed staff may have used inactivity to thwart the intentions of their two Nazi superiors.[33] By the same token, Feder's dismissal just three months later appears to suggest a victory for the 'civil service tradition'.

At the start of the 'Third Reich', then, the dominant concept in housing policy continued to be the shift away from the generous culture of subsidies dating from the mid 1920s. As the *Reichsarbeitsblatt* reported in 1934, the Labour Ministry was seeking, as rapidly as possible, to organize the housing market in such a way that private investors would be responsible, as they had been before 1914, for the building of new rented dwellings, a task they would undertake 'free of the direct involvement of the authorities'.[34] It did not take the Labour Ministry long to come up with new Nazi-friendly rationales for this policy, which had already been formulated before 1933. The forgoing of subsidies, it now stated, was consonant with 'National Socialism's programmatic insistence that while the state may guide the economy, it must not engage in economic activity itself'.[35] At present, the ministry contended, it was still necessary to support housebuilding with public means. But these financial stimuli and subsidies must be eliminated step by step in order to 'lay the ground for the gradual transition to private sector financing'.[36]

'Ensuring the provision of homes truly suited to the less well-off sections of the population, in terms of size and amount of rent' remained one of the ministry's key objectives.[37] Anyone applying for state funding, therefore, had to present plans tailored to 'the most modest aspirations within current demand'[38] and undertake to push construction costs down 'to the lowest possible level at all times'.[39]

With even less ambiguity than prior to 1933, the ministry now defined the publicly subsidized small home as a 'settlement site' (*Siedlungsstelle*) within a small suburban housing estate. It was chiefly outside the cities, therefore, that construction was to take place. What both the ministry and the regime now wanted, rather than large blocks of rented flats, were 'settler'-owned, single-family houses with ample gardens. After the Nazis took power, the small estate, as a special form of housing, received an even greater ideological charge, as part of an envisioned social utopia, than it had already had in the late years of the Weimar Republic. The Berlin ministry's housing policy experts made a major contribution to this 'ideologically' grandiloquent discourse, readily adopting the core vocabulary emanating from the *völkisch*, nationalistic milieu and the Nazi Party. By 1933, Senior Governmental Counsellor Georg Heilmann was already declaring that the small housing estate was a means of achieving a crucial goal of 'state policy', namely the 'de-proletarianization of the German worker', who must 'be brought back into a direct relationship with the state in an internal sense'.[40] Ministerial Counsellor Wilhelm Gisbertz wrote in 1935 that, as a resident of the small housing estate, 'the worker [will] become the custodian of a piece of sacred German soil' and thus be delivered from the 'deracination' of industrial workers, one of the 'gravest failures of an earlier era'.[41] Ernst Knoll, head of Main Section IV since 1936, put forward similar ideological arguments. The resident of the small housing estate, he contended, would leave behind the 'unnaturalness of city life' and the 'abstract thought [*Kopfdenken*] of intellectualism'.[42]

Knoll also managed, without a hitch, to justify the demand for personal work, which the resident of the small housing estate along with his family, unlike the tenant of a normal rented home, had to satisfy, in Nazi jargon. Due above all to this prerequisite, he claimed, the small housing estate was consonant with the Nazi 'notion of performance' (*Leistung*) and the Nazi-specific conception of social policy, namely that support must be given to the 'worthy' and strong rather than the weak.

> In the case of the small housing estate, a man is given the opportunity, on a not insignificant scale, to make his own decisions and choices, to work for himself and to see the advantages accruing from his accomplishments as his own success. We need people like this, and we must support them. Just as, in a future war, every man at the front almost has to wage war alone, within the nation as a whole we need people who can make decisions independently, who are determined to take on responsibility and proceed at their own risk . . .[43]

Robert Ley himself could scarcely have made a more ideologically pure comment.

The small housing estate programme, and the Labour Ministry's heavy involvement in it, was one of the crucial factors in the housing policy harmony that prevailed in Germany in the first few years of the 'Third Reich'. It is true that, before 1933, a number of Nazis had made public statements expressing grave doubts about the special form of dwelling involved. In 1932, for example, Hjalmar Schacht, former president of the Reichsbank turned apologist for Hitler, referred disparagingly to the homesteads on the small housing estates as 'a kind of allotment plus primitive dwelling'.[44] The same year, Nazi municipal politician Karl Fiehler in Munich referred to the *Kleinsiedlung* as a 'wooden shack' plus garden, which might well provide the unemployed with 'some distraction from their destitution' but would neither secure their livelihood nor create healthy living conditions.[45]

From January 1933, however, such criticisms ceased. The newly established German Labour Front, which believed that all social policy measures, and thus also housing, should come under its remit, backed the idea of the small housing scheme with notable enthusiasm. Wilhelm Ludowici, head of the DAF's Reich Homestead Office, which had been established before 1933 was over, had expressed his support for the Reich Labour Ministry's housing policy even before the Nazi takeover. The ministry's strategy of funding and building only the smallest and most affordable of homes from now on deserved 'complete support' because, he asserted, it reflected the social reality of crisis-ridden Germany. A housing policy on any other basis would be rooted in 'self-delusion'. The ministry's plan to 'leave the building sector once again to the private businessman' also met with Ludowici's explicit approval.[46]

Because Adolf Hitler, in his new role as Reich chancellor, also fundamentally rejected a 'policy of subsidization', opining that 'instead the goal must be to reawaken the individual's faith in his own pursuits', in the field of housing policy the Nazi Party, the DAF and the Reich Ministry of Labour initially called, in concert and without conflict, for the building of the largest possible number of small suburban housing estates.[47] These three institutions also acted collectively to alter the programme's social policy orientation. They quickly regarded the provision of homes for the unemployed as a mistake, because, prior to January 1933, as one of the officials at the Berlin ministry put it retrospectively, some 'downright antisocial elements' had benefited from public funds.[48] The small housing estate thus became the 'estate for those in full employment' (*Vollbeschäftigtensiedlung*), which must above all benefit the low-earning 'reliable worker' (*Stammarbeiter*) and his family. Finally, in 1935, the Labour Ministry, in perfect alignment with the Nazi Party, decreed that homes in such estates would be provided only to 'Aryan national comrades' who were 'nationally and politically reliable, racially valuable, healthy and hereditarily sound'.[49] At least in the case of the small housing estates, therefore, government housing policy functioned precisely in accordance with the selective principles espoused by Nazi welfare strategists. Ernst Knoll praised this decision as pointing the way forward. Thanks to the 'strict selection' of the residents of small estates, he averred, state construction policy now guaranteed the preferential reproduction of the 'best hereditary stock'.[50]

All these declarations and decisions help us evaluate the above-cited sceptical metaphor for the Nazi 'revolution' deployed by the *Reichsarbeitsblatt* as late as August 1933. The discomfort articulated in the comparison with a 'storm surge' referred to procedural issues, to the Nazis' tendency to allocate to the party and the organizations it controlled direct governmental and administrative authority. However, Labour Ministry officials had no problem with provisions of a *völkisch*, nationalistic or racist character, enacted 'according to the rules'. Indeed, they themselves issued regulations of this kind. For example, in July 1933 the ministry standardized the rules governing the 'coordination' (*Gleichschaltung*) of the public housing associations, rules that had previously taken a wide variety of forms at Land level.[51] The Berlin ministerial officials thus legitimized and regulated not just the dismissal of Social Democrats and Communists but also of Jews in a field that was in no way part of the civil service. Similar antisemitic decisions by the ministry had earlier made it impossible for Jewish physicians and dentists to continue to invoice the health insurance companies to cover the treatment of public health patients (*Kassenpatienten*). The ministry also formulated an 'Aryan paragraph' for functionaries in the voluntary institutions of social insurance and the system of public aid for war veterans, imitating the Nazi civil service law.[52]

Conflicts flared up only if the ministry believed its authority was under threat. The ministry thus regarded the DAF, which conducted itself with such self-confidence and virtually defied political definition, with tremendous distrust. As early as October 1934, after local subdivisions of the DAF's Reich Homestead Office had, on numerous occasions, attempted to make independent decisions regarding the selection of 'suitable' settlers, Franz Seldte protested to the Reich Chancellery. The ministry could only 'work successfully' to develop the small housing estates if the DAF and all its subdivisions were kept in their place.[53] Reich Commissioner Gottfried Feder spoke in even plainer terms in a complaint about the work of his deputy Wilhelm Ludowici. Far from having represented him and relieved the pressure on him in his new post, the DAF man had devoted his energies exclusively to positioning the Homestead Office and its many subdivisions 'as an adversary and competitor to the offices of state'. For 'reasons of state authority', Feder demanded, this tendency should immediately be nipped in the bud.[54]

Feder himself did not reap the rewards of this protest. Only after his forced resignation did Hitler bolster the Labour Ministry in its struggle against the DAF. The ministry was permitted to officially declare that the DAF offices discharged no state functions and enjoyed no rights of decision. Their primary task, the ministry underlined, was to promote the small housing estate through propaganda and, when it came to the implementation of specific projects, potentially to assist in an advisory role at the request of the authorities.[55] Also, the ministry had already managed to expand its authority over construction policy. A law issued in March 1934, which imposed uniform regulations governing the oversight and recognition of public housing associations across the Reich for the first time, tasked Main Section IV with the supervision of all supraregional enterprises of this kind. That is, it now oversaw the operations of the major construction firms, which had passed to the DAF in spring 1933 following the breakup of the free trades unions.[56] Finally, in July 1934, the ministry secured for itself 'very extensive powers' over regional development plans, though previously it was in no way involved in the related decisions. The Länder and municipalities subsequently required approval from the Main Section in Berlin if they wished to instigate major new construction projects by sanctioning new development areas.[57]

As a 'precarious state'[58] governed by ad hoc decisions, however, Nazi Germany was to feature no lasting solutions and no inviolable conventions when it came to administrative matters. By 1936, the Labour Ministry once again had to defend its housing policy pre-eminence against the DAF, which was still aggressively seeking to expand its authority. In this second conflict, however, the ministry was thrown on the defensive. There were two reasons for this. First, the ministry's track record in fostering and regulating the construction of new housing was open to legitimate criticism. Second, the DAF now developed its own housing plan, which it presented, ever more self-confidently, as genuinely 'National Socialist' in nature. It clashed with the Labour Ministry's desire to largely liberalize the housing market, triggering a policy turf war, which the DAF pursued in public. Behind the scenes, the Labour Ministry defended itself with the traditional tools of Cabinet politics – and was defeated. From 1940, the official housing policy of the 'Third Reich' was largely determined by the DAF, because Adolf Hitler had come down on its side.

Success and Failure: An Initial Assessment of Housing Policy from 1933 to 1939

At first glance, the development of housing construction in Germany after 1933 looks like a success story. By 1936, the number of homes built, at around 330,000, was twice as high as in the final year of the Weimar

Republic. In 1937, with 340,000 new homes, the country chalked up a result that even slightly surpassed the previous record year of 1929.[59] In propaganda terms, the regime, of course, made much of this boom. However, if we take into account the political goals formulated by the Labour Ministry itself, then despite these figures what we find is a twofold failure. The housing market did not attain the kind of equilibrium that was regarded as the prerequisite for the abolition of the 'Reich Rent Law' and the ending of comprehensive protection from eviction. Nor was construction concentrated as clearly on cheap small homes and on suburban areas as Main Section IV had wanted. In this sense, the ministry's attempt to govern the market centrally, before going on to liberalize it, failed in several ways at once.

The housing market defied ministerial plans and interventions both in terms of the demand for and supply of newly built homes. As a result of the economic upturn after 1933 and the optimism that Hitler and the Nazi Party aroused in many Germans, during the first few years of Nazi rule the interest in housing grew far more rapidly and dynamically than the supply. In particular, the persistently high number of marriages drove up demand, especially for affordable small homes, of which there had already been far too few in the Weimar Republic. The Labour Ministry kept a watchful eye on this development. By the spring of 1935, within the Cabinet Franz Seldte was warning about a 'worsening housing shortage', which threatened to thwart 'all the Reich government's efforts to improve the living conditions and thus also the sturdiness of the German *Volk*'.[60] We have already seen Seldte's second urgent missive, of 1936, on the same topic. The same year, Section Head Ernst Knoll publicly declared that there was now a lack of housing 'of a magnitude that has never been seen before in Germany'. This problem was 'at the limits of the tolerable, at the limits, in terms of public health (*Volksgesundheit*) and of politics, of what is tolerable'.[61]

This shortfall was also grave in the sense that the new homes were far too expensive for most of the young married couples pressing to enter the housing market. Despite all the Berlin ministry's efforts to deploy public funding for housebuilding in a targeted way in order to strengthen the lower market segment, as in the past the truly affordable small homes did not make up the majority of newly built dwellings. According to the wishes and plans of the ministry, well over 50 per cent of them were supposed to be homes of up to three rooms (including the kitchen). De facto, however, between 1933 and 1939 these only made up 37 per cent. Even the Weimar Republic had achieved a better outcome in this respect. After 1933, then, Germany's stock of small homes failed to expand, though this was one of the main objectives of official construction policy.[62]

This failed attempt to govern the new housing market was largely due to the failure of the ambitious plans to foster small housing estates, which the Reich Ministry of Labour and the DAF continued to espouse, with one voice, until 1936–1937. It rapidly became evident that, in practice, this supposedly 'ideal form' of housing could, for many reasons, be no more than a niche product. The 'settlement' of workers on a truly large scale failed, for example, due to the overly complex approval procedure; the problem of finding parcels of land that were affordable, close to a city, sufficiently large and also arable; the disappointment felt by many prospective settlers about the primitive nature of the dwellings on offer; and the widespread reservations that many people felt about submitting themselves and every member of their family to political and 'racial' assessment, extending into the most intimate sphere of life, merely because they wished to get a roof over their head. In addition, 'reliable workers' in full-time employment, who were the preferred recipients of such homes, were hard put to contribute the kind of labour required. In principle, it was possible to contribute money instead. Lower-income families, however, lacked the necessary funds to make such payments. Only bourgeois households possessed the amount of capital required, and they typically aspired to own the kind of home not found on such estates. Of total construction output between 1933 and 1939, therefore, less than 10 per cent involved the building of such settlements. As Gottfried Feder, downgraded to the status of academic observer of construction policy, critically remarked, these small estates made up a 'vanishingly small' share of all occupied dwellings in Germany.[63]

Certainly, the Labour Ministry recognized the problem, and it even tried to respond. In the summer of 1935, it created a new funding programme for the construction of small homes, which was intended to supplement the continuing subsidization of small suburban estates. The Reich now made loans available for 'people's homes' (*Volkswohnungen*) as well, which were rented out in the normal way. As with all publicly funded dwellings since 1930, the 'people's homes' too were subject to a culture of extreme frugality. As defined by Main Section IV, these were the 'cheapest rented homes ... which are extremely limited with respect to their size and facilities', and were intended for 'workers on the lowest of incomes'.[64]

The construction of 'people's homes' took off more rapidly than the small housing estate programme, which was only ever implemented at a snail's pace. However, restrictive cost regulations and the meagre budget of, initially, just thirty-five million Reichsmarks, which, moreover, came from a public construction budget that had already been approved, limited the efficacy of this new support measure. In the construction years after 1935, therefore, the 'people's home' remained as marginal a phenomenon within the German housing sector as the small-scale suburban estate.[65] Moreover, due to the strict limitations on its size and always very basic facilities, it attracted a great deal of criticism. For example, Ernst von Stuckrad, new head of the DAF's Reich Homestead Office, scorned the Labour Ministry's new funding approach as a 'determined leap back into the nineteenth century'.[66] The Ministry of Propaganda, meanwhile, expressed grave concern behind the scenes: 'The most unpleasant of consequences' were bound to ensue 'if the term "people" [*Volk*], which has taken on an entirely new resonance in National Socialist Germany, is enduringly linked with the most primitive and makeshift of homes'.[67]

The third funding programme for fostering housing in Nazi Germany also proved rather ineffective in social terms. This was the system of Reich guarantees for private building loans, which the dictatorship had inherited from the Weimar Republic. Certainly, thanks to the economic upturn from 1935, this system functioned markedly better than at the peak of the economic crisis, that is, the available money could in fact now be deployed. Indeed, until 1939 the guarantee budget was increased on several occasions. However, this indirect form of public financial assistance engendered the construction of far more single-family detached houses than flats for tenants. The especially affordable small homes, which the Reich Ministry of Labour wished to support above all else, were conspicuous by their absence. Overall, then, during the Nazi era politicians focusing on construction policy faced the same problem with which they had struggled during the years of the Weimar Republic: the supply of newly built dwellings and the most pressing demand for new housing were out of sync, because the majority of new homes were clearly priced in the upper segment of the housing market. As prior to 1933, even the indirect relief provided by the flats that became available in old buildings when their tenants moved out made little difference.[68]

The Reich guarantees made an even more dubious impact if we consider the loans subsequently secured by the public purse. In reality, of course, through this programme the Labour Ministry wanted to lay the ground for a return to private sector financing of housing, free of any dependence on the state. The loan loss guarantee was intended to help reawaken private investors' interest in investing their money in residential property. In public, Main Section IV always gave the impression that this objective had been achieved by 1935 at the latest. In reality, however, it was a quite different set of investors that had their junior mortgages secured by the state. The vast majority of Reich guarantees covered loans taken out by the administration responsible for compulsory old-age insurance for white- and blue-collar workers, by publicly owned local savings banks (*Sparkassen*) and other financial institutions under public law, that is, these investments were made by institutions that were themselves part of the state or were directly influenced by it. Private investors, meanwhile, availed themselves of the Reich guarantees only to a marginal degree.[69]

In this sense, we might almost refer to these guarantees as a propagandistic *mise en scène*. To demonstrate the withdrawal of the public purse from the ongoing subsidization of housebuilding, the Labour Ministry tied up large sums in its budget in order to secure quasi-public loans, while at the same time the means to directly subsidize genuinely affordable small homes were notoriously meagre.

Relief could have been provided if the Nazi state had made available significantly more money, on appreciably more favourable terms, to fund reduced-cost small homes. This, however, did not happen. Of total direct investment in housebuilding in Germany between 1933 and 1939, a mere 11.7 per cent came from the public budget, compared with a share of 49.5 per cent in the construction boom years of the Weimar Republic from 1924.[70] It is true that the Labour Ministry continued to do all it could to attain a larger housing construction budget, always arguing that only a temporary intensification of public subsidies could achieve the desired transition to a liberalized housing market. Yet it failed to chalk up any significant successes, despite the earlier reassurances, quoted above, from the Nazi Party that it was in favour of 'strong support for housebuilding'. The additional funds the Berlin ministry managed to extract from the Reich Ministry of Finance, through arduous battles, barely offset the increase in building costs. To a large extent, this was because, when it came to funds intended as interest subsidies, the Finance Ministry pursued a highly restrictive course. Finance officials repeatedly referred their colleagues in the Labour Ministry to their self-proclaimed housing policy credo, namely that in principle it was not the state's task to invest funds in the building of new homes. Even the Labour Ministry's warnings, expressed in ever more dramatic terms, about the political and social problems engendered by the worsening lack of housing, proved ineffective.

If the Nazi regime stubbornly ignored the housing policy-related complaints and demands emanating from the relevant ministry, it was after the state and party leadership had coolly weighed up their interests. Ultimately, the Nazi regime had absolutely no interest in a major expansion of housing construction. It made no difference whether this involved the investment of public funds or construction projects financed on a purely private basis. What the 'Third Reich' wanted above all was to be the one doing the building. From 1933, the state used the capacities of the German construction industry (which were less extensive under the conditions of Nazi autarky than in the Weimar Republic) to advance its own interests on a far larger scale than had ever happened before, namely to bolster the Reich's military build-up or to demonstrate the power of the 'Third Reich' by erecting massive public buildings. In 1932, the amount of investment in industrial buildings, housing and public construction projects lay at quite similar levels, respectively at six, seven and nine hundred million Reichsmarks. A very different picture pertained in 1935. One billion Reichsmarks went to commercial buildings and 1.1 billion to housebuilding. State contractors, however, now accounted for 4.4 billion Reichsmarks, despite the fact that the major job creation measures had largely been completed by this point. Two-thirds of the total construction volume, then, consisted of state projects.[71]

In order to achieve this pre-eminent position in the construction market and secure it for the future, the Nazi state claimed the right to steer the entire capital market according to its own needs. In addition, during the last few years before the war, all key construction materials and the sectoral labour force were already 'rationed', that is, deployed mainly for state purposes. Housebuilding in particular suffered from state control of the banking system. With a ban on the issue of new mortgage bonds, which was eased intermittently only for brief periods, the regime deliberately kept the mortgage banks on a tight financial leash, despite their constant protests, because it was determined that the mortgage bond, as a well-established, secure capital investment, should present the Reich bonds with as little competition as possible. In the absence of new mortgage bonds, however, the mortgage banks lost their function as accumulators of capital for property loans.[72]

An open and unbiased discussion of this policy and its negative impacts on housing construction would have meant addressing, on a very fundamental level, the 'peace-time war economy' that the Nazi regime constructed so methodically and perfected at great cost. Under Adolf Hitler, a debate of this kind was impossible. The Reich Labour Ministry respected this taboo. Hence, the staff of Main Section IV, choosing their words carefully, restricted themselves to publicly remarking that housebuilding could only really take off again if the Reich ceased to lay claim so exclusively to the funds available on the capital market.[73]

Given the circumstances, the ministry thus accepted its insufficient ability to shape housing policy and the role that had de facto been allotted to it, which was chiefly to ensure, through its warnings and demands, that the public funding of new homes at least did not decline further. However, in programmatic terms, Main Section IV continued to champion the cause of market deregulation. As late as 1938–1939, on several occasions the officials working there affirmed their support for the principle that, when it came to housing, 'private initiative' always ought to enjoy primacy over state action and public money.[74]

During the last few years before the Second World War, we must conclude that these statements were just a grand political delusion. The state took absolutely no practical steps during this period to lay the ground for the end of the 'controlled housing market'. Quite the opposite. In the spring of 1936, shortly before 1 April, which the Labour Ministry had once envisaged as a historical turning point, it decreed a substantial tightening of the 'Reich Rent Law', because 'with respect to the policy of stable wages, it is crucially important to maintain the current price range when it comes to rent levels'. The ministry, therefore, revoked almost all the easing measures that had previously constrained the system of state rent control for flats in old buildings since the late 1920s.[75] After this backwards shift at the latest, the ministry no longer pursued a consistent housing policy, given the sharp clash between the institution's practices and purported conceptual framework.

The Conflict between the Reich Ministry of Labour and the DAF

Under a totalitarian dictatorship that permitted no open clash of opinions, the contradictory nature of the ministry's policies would probably have had few consequences for that institution if not for the existence of the DAF. The Labour Front, however, was constantly on the lookout for opportunities to expand and become even more influential. So it triggered the open conflict, which I touched on briefly above, between the ministry and the DAF over the 'right' housing policy for the 'Third Reich'.

Of course, this dispute was also in part a trial of strength, in which two bureaucratic apparatuses of different kinds vied with one another. Yet there was more to this conflict than quarrels rooted in organizational egos. From 1936 to 1937, in an attempt to ensure victory over the Reich Ministry of Labour, the DAF increasingly sought to put forward a political rationale for its aspiration to control housing policy.

The Labour Front's point of departure here consisted mainly in population policy arguments. If the Reich exclusively funded small homes, it contended, it was building dwellings that were unattractive for larger families and would thus fail to help increase the German birth rate. This criticism, long a traditional feature of debates on the public financing of housing construction, was initially couched in very moderate terms. In 1938–1939, however, the tone became ever shriller. 'Tiny homes bring death, not life, to the people', thundered Robert Ley himself in a public speech in autumn 1938. Ley explicitly demanded that housebuilding policy should be formulated by the Nazi Party, and for him, of course, this meant the DAF.[76] The Labour Ministry responded to this attack, in its usual way, with the purely pragmatic argument that the low level of financial solvency of most tenants, and particularly of young couples, should be accepted as a basic reality. It was, the ministry contended, therefore also simply an indisputable fact that truly affordable homes could only be achieved by limiting their size and facilities.[77]

The DAF, however, insisted on its position. In the last few years before the war, it put forward the same population-related arguments to criticize, ever more vehemently, not just the social policy principle of subsidiarity, towards which the Labour Ministry geared its housing policy, but also its belief in the need to strictly limit public financing. In political terms, the DAF had the necessary backing for this stance. The speeches by Hitler and Ley, quoted at the start of this chapter, must have seemed like an invitation to step up the conflict with the Labour Ministry. Housebuilding, as one representative of the DAF's Homestead Office wrote as early as 1937, should 'not be seen as a private investment carried out to earn interest'. Instead, the Reich must develop a '100 per cent cohesive form of financing' for the construction of rented homes and forget all 'the auxiliary measures such as state guarantees, interim financing, and other contrivances'.[78] In 1939, the DAF's Labour Science Institute explicitly reinforced this position. The Reich must undertake to 'fully' finance an annual total of around three hundred thousand new homes. This would be the 'most clear-cut form' of building subsidy.[79] One year later, the Institute, which served the DAF as a kind of think tank, demanded in even plainer terms that housing construction in Germany be freed 'from its entanglement with private interests and private money'. The 'notion of housebuilding as an interest-bearing investment' should be regarded as fundamentally alien to the Nazi way of thinking. In future, the children that would undoubtedly be produced in large numbers in spacious and healthy but nonetheless affordable homes were to be considered the 'return' on the capital invested.[80]

There was no common ground between these demands and the Labour Ministry's conception of housing policy. The latter institution, however, responded cautiously to this challenge. The officials of Main Section IV left it to their colleagues in the Reich Ministry of Finance to highlight the incalculable financial consequences of the DAF's ideas, which were premised on a housing policy Shangri-La featuring inexhaustible state funding.[81] They themselves, meanwhile, tended to argue in formal, bureaucratic terms. For example, the Labour Ministry insisted on the principle that a Nazi Party institution could not and must not seek to play the 'sole dominant leadership role with respect to housing policy', thus ignoring the authority of a Reich ministry.[82] Above all else, what the ministerial officials showed here was how little, after seven years of Nazi rule, they had understood the basic principle of the 'Third Reich', namely that the Nazi Party always decided unilaterally what responsibilities to arrogate to itself and its institutions. Furthermore, the ministry had, as yet, obviously failed to identify the Nazis' characteristic tendency to respond to crisis by taking refuge in utopianism.

From 1939–1940 onwards, housing in Germany was unquestionably beset by profound crisis. When the war began, civilian housebuilding was terminated in its entirety. In 1940, the Reich regime reversed this decision but the number of completed new homes nonetheless fell massively. The longer the war went on, the bleaker the prospect of large-scale construction programmes, simply because of the acute shortage of manpower and materials.[83] Tellingly, Robert Ley ascended the housing policy career ladder with particular rapidity during this period. Hitler first appointed the DAF leader Reich commissioner for social housing in November 1940 and then, in October 1942, he was made Reich housing commissioner and was thus responsible for state construction policy in its entirety. He took charge of all the staff of what had been Main Section IV. Without exception, therefore, the ministry had lost its powers in this policy field.

Of necessity, then, the ministerial officials switched for the second time to one of the special Nazi authorities. Gottfried Feder had spread himself far too thin when he held the office in 1934, and in any case only had limited room for manoeuvre. Ley, together with the experts of the DAF Homestead Office, in contrast, wasted no time in restructuring official construction policy in accordance with DAF principles in 1942. Since the Reich housing commissioner was explicitly identified as the 'supreme Reich authority', DAF leaders were free to make their own decisions. Hence, in future the Reich was only to support the construction of dwellings of at least four rooms, rather than the small homes promoted hitherto. Each home was to be no less than sixty-two square metres in size. Previously, according to the rules of the Reich Labour Ministry, public funding for homes of more than sixty square metres had been prohibited. Thanks to interest-free state loans, the DAF promised that the homes resulting from this new 'social housing' would nonetheless be highly affordable. However, crucially important details, particularly with respect to financing, remained open. This was possible because, until 1945, only a small number of showcase projects were realized, which could easily be generously funded. So Ley's plans and policy, which treated housebuilding solely as an instrument of state population policy and explicitly sought to shut private investors out of the construction of dwellings for rent, were never really tested. The circumstances after 1949, meanwhile, when large numbers of new buildings were again being put up in Germany, were radically different in every respect.[84]

After 1942, then, the staff of Main Section IV served ideologues and dreamers. We do not know what the transplanted officials thought of their new superiors. Publicly, as we might imagine, they now criticized the policy for which they had previously fought so doggedly. For example, in 1943, Joachim Fischer-Dieskau[85] praised Robert Ley's pre-eminence in housing policy as a victory for the 'dynamic forces of the authoritarian concept of the state' over the 'intellectual concept and power of the liberalist and capitalist legacy'. Now, Germany would be poised to pursue a 'total housing policy'.[86] Surprisingly, however, at least occasionally the DAF leaders also tried to show respect for the staff formerly of the Labour Ministry. For example, in 1944 Robert Ley publicly declared himself fundamentally opposed to the state subsidization of housebuilding, 'quite regardless of what form it takes'. After the preceding conflict, this was a very surprising statement.[87] Perhaps someone from the old Main Section IV had cunningly slipped this sentence, which clashed with DAF policy as pursued so far, into this article, published under the name of the Reich housing commissioner. Otherwise, this can only have been an attempt to sugar the pill for ministerial officials who had been subject to a 'hostile takeover' by the DAF. In any case, this verbal reference, in 1944, to an older housing policy concept, had no practical consequences.

Conclusion and Outlook

When it came to its plan, drawn up in 1930, to liberalize the German housing market, the Reich Labour Ministry thus failed miserably during the Nazi era. First, the housing market resolutely refused to equilibrate as envisaged. Second, the Nazi regime pursued very different objectives to the ministry. The policy of uncompromising rearmament, which was already introduced in 1933, necessitated a massive state construction programme in order to render the Reich's armed forces and industry 'ready for war' (*Wehrbarmachung*) and strict control of the capital market. It also required rent levels to remain as stable as possible (which could best be achieved through direct state control) in order to ensure that wages too remained broadly stable. However, the Labour Ministry clung to the political goals it had set itself in the late Weimar Republic for an astonishingly long time. From 1936 at the latest, however, it took practical steps to expand the 'controlled housing market'. The Nazi 'peacetime war economy' could only continue to function with the help of such ancillary measures. In conceptual terms, however, even during this period the ministry continued to invoke the ideal of housing organized and financed chiefly by the private sector.

On the other hand, the staff of Main Section IV had no problem with the basic politically and 'racially' selective principles of Nazi social policy, incorporating them, on a one-to-one basis, into the state programme of subsidies for small suburban housing estates. In this sense at least, then, the ministry's housing policy experts' later subordination to the ideologues of the DAF was not particularly surprising. Evidently, however, even in the final years of the Second World War, the Labour Ministry and the DAF continued their battle, which had begun in 1936 and was informed by their differing views on the basic principles of public housing policy, although by this time the DAF was finally the decisive power within this political field in the 'Third Reich'.

Finally, we must also ask whether there are connecting links between the plans and practices of the old Reich Labour Ministry and the policies pursued by the West German Ministry of Housing (Ministerium für Wohnungsbau) established in 1949. In the absence of studies devoted to the topic and given the highly complex nature of this political field, it is far from easy to answer this question. In-depth research is required on staffing continuities as well.[88] At least in one respect, however, it seems likely that there is one clear tradition linking the two institutions and their policies. After 1960, the Bonn ministry tried once again to deregulate the German housing market. The 'Lücke Plan', named after then Housing Minister Paul Lücke, resembled the plan of 1930. Once again, a specific date was identified (1 January 1966) by which the housing market was supposed to be sufficiently equilibrated to render further governmental control unnecessary. Once again, until then construction was to take place with the help of state funding. Subsequently, new homes were supposed to be built in accordance with purely 'economic criteria' and left to the private sector.

The parallels do not stop there, however. This liberalization plan (which was elaborated in far more detail and featured markedly more social cushioning than the 1930 version) also failed, despite the fact that the Nazi regime, with its particular needs determined by the war economy, lay far in the past. First, the elaborate plan was not implemented as originally intended. The CDU and CSU, as the most important ruling parties, soon got cold feet when it became clear that rents, particularly in the cities, were showing a marked upward tendency as the housing market was gradually liberalized. Second, in spring 1970 the freshly installed government under Willy Brandt and Walter Scheel, also concerned about rising rents, adopted a new version of state rent control in the shape of the 'local reference rent' (ortsübliche Vergleichsmiete). At the same time, the SPD-FDP coalition greatly boosted publicly subsidized housing once again. Essentially, this outcome too can be explained mainly in light of the unforeseen intensification in the demand for housing, which the ministerial officials had not anticipated, having only ever envisaged the future as an enhanced version of the present.[89]

At its core, the specific regulatory framework of the West German housing market, which came into being in 1970, still exists today. The durability of homes, it would appear, induces a matching durability of housing policy problems and tasks, as well as state responses. But whether, and if so how, the housing market can and should regulate itself 'free of direct governmental involvement', is a question as open in present-day Germany as it was in the years after 1930.

Karl Christian Führer, Dr. phil., professor of German history at the University of Hamburg and visiting professor at Humboldt University of Berlin (2016) at the invitation of the Independent Commission of Historians Investigating the History of the Reich Ministry of Labour in the National Socialist Period. Publications include *Die Stadt, der Markt und das Geld. Immobilienspekulation in der Bundesrepublik 1960–1985* (De Gruyter Oldenbourg, 2016); 'Das NS-Regime und die "Idealform des deutschen Wohnungsbaues". Ein Beitrag zur nationalsozialistischen Gesellschaftspolitik', *Vierteljahrschrift für Sozial- und Wirtschaftsgeschichte* 89 (2002), 141–66; *Mieter, Hausbesitzer, Staat und Wohnungsmarkt. Wohnungsmangel und Wohnungszwangswirtschaft in Deutschland 1914–1960* (Steiner, 1995).

Notes

1. Quoted in 'Granaten oder Häuser?', *Die Deutsche Wohnwirtschaft* 43 (1936), 196–99, here 196. With this speech in Karlsruhe, Hitler fired the starting gun on the Nazi Party's 'election campaign' for the entirely unfree Reichstag election of 29 March 1936.
2. R. Ley, 'Fünf Millionen Wohnungen', *Die Deutsche Wohnwirtschaft* 43 (1936), 648–49.
3. R. Ley, 'Das Siedlungsprogramm des Führers', *Bauen, Siedeln, Wohnen* 16 (1936), 329–30.
4. J. Fischer-Dieskau, 'Staatsgedanke und Wohnungswesen', *Soziale Praxis* 44 (1935), col. 306–12, here col. 310.
5. Reich Ministry of Labour to Reich Ministry of Finance, 11 March 1936, Bundesarchiv (BArch), R 2/18927.
6. On the complex details, see, for example, K.C. Führer, *Mieter, Hausbesitzer, Staat und Wohnungsmarkt. Wohnungsmangel und Wohnungszwangswirtschaft in Deutschland 1914–1960*, Stuttgart: Steiner, 1995, 155–64. In brief, through this tax, in the case of all rented flats built before 1914, the authorities siphoned off the share of the rent that was no longer used to pay off pre-war mortgages devalued by inflation. That is, while the tenants paid the tax, it derived de facto from the almost complete dispossession of the private investors who had financed German housing construction before 1914.
7. Württemberg Ministry of the Interior to Württemberg Ministry of the Economy, 4 June 1927, Hauptstaatsarchiv (HStA) Stuttgart, E 130b 2731.
8. Prussian Ministry of Finance to Prussian Minister President, 10 December 1927, Geheimes Staatsarchiv Preussischer Kulturbesitz, Rep. 84a 5827.
9. O. Wölz, 'Reichsgrundsätze für den Kleinwohnungsbau', *RABl.* II (1931), 24–30, 49–53, here 51.

10. O. Wölz, 'Das zusätzliche Wohnungsbauprogramm des Reichs 1930 als Glied der Reichswohnungspolitik', *Die Wohnung* 5 (1930–31), 249–52, here 251.

11. F. Schmidt, 'Erfahrungen bei Durchführung des zusätzlichen Wohnungsbauprogramms des Reichs für das Jahr 1930', *RABl.* II (1931), 197–201 and 221–25, here 225.

12. Wölz, 'Reichsgrundsätze', 25.

13. Ibid., 25–30.

14. For a detailed account, see Führer, *Mieter*.

15. O. Wölz, 'Die Verordnung des Reichspräsidenten zur Sicherung von Wirtschaft und Finanzen vom 1. Dezember 1930', *Deutsches Wohnungs-Archiv* 6 (1931), col. 1–5, here col. 1 f.

16. T. Harlander, K. Hater and F. Meiers, *Siedeln in der Not. Umbruch und Siedlungsbau am Ende der Weimarer Republik*, Hamburg: Christians, 1988, 12.

17. Memorandum on the Meeting between the Reich Ministry of Labour and the Land Representatives, 7 November 1930, BArch, R 3901/10980. See also the speech by Heinrich Hirtsiefer in *Die Zukunft der Wohnungswirtschaft. Bericht über die 12. Hauptversammlung der Kommunalen Vereinigung für Wohnungswesen in Frankfurt a. M. am 5. und 6. Juni 1930*, Berlin: n.p., 1930, 5 f.

18. See, for example, H. Mockenhaupt, *Priesterliche Existenz und sozialpolitisches Engagement von Heinrich Brauns*, Ph.D. dissertation, Saarbrücken: University of Saarbrücken, 1976, 244; H. Hirtsiefer, *Die Wohnungswirtschaft in Preussen*, Eberswalde: Müller, 1929, 544–48.

19. For a detailed summary of Stegerwald's policies as a minister, see B. Forster, *Adam Stegerwald (1874–1945). Christlich-nationaler Gewerkschafter, Zentrumspolitiker, Mitbegründer der Unionsparteien*, Düsseldorf: Droste, 2003, 475–576.

20. For a summary, see, for example, Deutscher Baugewerksbund, *Jahrbuch 1931*, ed. Vorstand des Deutschen Baugewerksbundes, Berlin: Deutscher Baugewerksbund, 1932, 37–42.

21. 'Zielloser Dilettantismus', *Völkischer Beobachter*, 20 October 1930.

22. Memorandum by the Reich Ministry of Labour on the Reich's Next Tasks in the Field of Housing and Settlement, 11 September 1933, BArch, R 3901/20678.

23. See, for example, K. Durst, 'Zeitfragen der Bau- und Wohnungswirtschaft', *Siedlung und Wirtschaft* 14 (1932), 93–97, here 94 f.

24. Reich Ministry of Labour to the State Secretary at the Reich Chancellery, 12 May 1932, BArch, R 43 I/2353.

25. Note on the Meeting at the Reich Ministry of Labour, 24 September 1931, HStA Stuttgart, E 151 f. I lfd. no. 42 file number 600.

26. See Führer, *Mieter*, 84.

27. L. Münz, 'Die sozialpolitische Gesetzgebung seit dem 30. Januar 1933', *RABl.* II (1933), 329–35, here 329.

28. Feder became known during the crisis years from 1929 through his plan to create a parallel currency in Germany ('Feder-Geld' or 'Feder money'), which was supposed to finance job creation projects through a closed monetary circuit. Feder sold this economically naive plan as a form of credit expansion entailing no inflationary risks.

29. J. Fischer-Dieskau, 'Zum Problem der verwaltungsmässigen Verankerung von Wohnungswesen, Städtebau und Raumordnung in den ministeriellen Instanzen des Reichs und der Bundesrepublik Deutschland – Rückblick und Ausblick', in V.-E. Preusker (ed.), *Festschrift für Hermann Wandersleb zur Vollendung des 75. Lebensjahres*, Bonn: Deutscher Bundes-Verlag, 1970, 113–43, here 125–27, quotation 127.

30. Ibid., 125. On Feder's activities as an 'episode', see also U. Haerendel, *Kommunale Wohnungspolitik im Dritten Reich. Siedlungsideologie, Kleinhausbau und 'Wohnraumarisierung' am Beispiel München*, Munich: Oldenbourg, 1999, 139–42, quotation 140.

31. Department Head Durst to the in-house newsletter, 18 May 1934, BArch,

R 3901/20679. The number of employees affected (excluding assistants, etc.) is calculated according to the schedule of responsibilities of Department IV b, February 1934, BArch, R 3901/20679.

32. Memorandum by Department Head Durst on the Transfer of the Section for Housing and Settlement to the Reich Ministry of the Economy, 18 May 1934, BArch, R 3901/20679.

33. Circular by the deputy to the Reich commissioner for settlement (Reichskommissar für das Siedlungswesen), Wilhelm Ludowici, on the course of business, 31 August 1934, BArch, R 3901/20679. On Ludowici as an individual, see my later remarks.

34. O. Blechschmidt, 'Reichsbürgschaften für den Kleinwohnungsbau', RABl. II (1934), 85–86, here 86.

35. J. Fischer-Dieskau, 'Kapitalkraft und Kapitaleinsatz bei der Wohnungsbau- und Siedlungsfinanzierung', in Jahrbuch der deutschen Siedlung, prepared with the assistance of Stiftung zur Förderung von Bauforschungen, ed. C.J. Neumann, Berlin: Verlag Siedlung und Wirtschaft, 1937, 14–32, here 16.

36. J. Fischer-Dieskau, 'Grundsätze für Kapitaleinsatz und Finanzierung von Kleinsiedlung und Wohnungsbau', in Deutscher Bauvereins-Kalender 1937, ed. Hauptverband Deutscher Wohnungsunternehmen with the collaboration of the German housing associations, Berlin: n.p., 1936, 99–135, here 101.

37. Memorandum by Department Head Durst on the Transfer of the Section for Housing and Settlement to the Reich Ministry of the Economy, 18 May 1934, BArch, R 3901/20679.

38. W. Gisbertz, 'Die Fortführung der Kleinsiedlung auf neuer Grundlage', RABl. II (1935), 41–43, here 42.

39. H. Bellinger, 'Weiterführung der Kleinsiedlung', RABl. II (1935), 180–84, here 182.

40. G. Heilmann, 'Fortführung der vorstädtischen Kleinsiedlung', RABl. II (1933), 285–86.

41. Gisbertz, 'Die Fortführung', 42.

42. E. Knoll, 'Kleinsiedlung als staatspolitische Aufgabe', in Die Wirtschaft im neuen Deutschland in Einzeldarstellungen: Bauen und Siedeln, Berlin: Der deutsche Volkswirt, 1937 (special supplement to Der deutsche Volkswirt 11[17] [1936–37], 22 January 1937), 24–28, here 28.

43. E. Knoll, 'Arbeitseinsatz – seine Bedeutung für Wohnungsbau und Siedlungswesen', Die Wohnung 11 (1936), 49–55, here 55.

44. H. Schacht, Brennende deutsche Bevölkerungsfragen, Munich: Eher, 1932, 37.

45. K. Fiehler, Nationalsozialistische Gemeindepolitik, 5th ed., Munich: Eher, 1932, 53.

46. W. Ludowici, 'Die Kleinstwohnung', RABl. II (1931), 433–36, here 436 and 433. An editorial comment on this article presents Ludowici not as a National Socialist but as a representative of 'business circles' (ibid., 433), whose views are being imparted solely to provide readers with relevant information. It is unclear how his article made it into the journal, which, of course, even in its 'Non-Official Section', had the character of an official organ of the Reich Ministry of Labour.

47. Akten der Reichskanzlei. Regierung Hitler 1933–1938, vol. 1: Die Regierung Hitler, part I: 1933–34, ed. K.-H. Minuth, series editors K. Repgen and H. Booms, Boppard am Rhein: Boldt, 1983, 745 (Cabinet meeting, 19 September 1933).

48. Bellinger, 'Weiterführung der Kleinsiedlung', 181.

49. Knoll, 'Kleinsiedlung als staatspolitische Aufgabe', 26.

50. Ibid.

51. J. Walk (ed.), Das Sonderrecht für die Juden im NS-Staat. Eine Sammlung der gesetzlichen Massnahmen und Richtlinien – Inhalt und Bedeutung, 2nd ed., Heidelberg: Müller, 1996, 16 and 22.

52. On the 'coordination' of the public housing associations (which Walk does not mention), see W. Meier, 'Die Sicherung der Gemeinnützigkeit im Wohnungswesen durch das Gesetz vom 14. Juli 1933', RABl. II (1933), 286–88; on 'racial affiliation' as a reason for

dismissal, see 287. The law also sweepingly legitimized, with retroactive effect, dismissals that had already been carried out.

53. Reich Ministry of Labour, Franz Seldte, to State Secretary Lammers, 18 October 1934, BArch, R 43 II/1141 c.

54. State Secretary Gottfried Feder to 'deputy Führer', Rudolf Hess, 25 August 1934, BArch, R 43 II/1141 c.

55. Reich Ministry of Labour to the Bavarian Ministry of State for the Economy, 22 December 1934 (copy), HStA Niedersachsen, Hannover, Hann. 180 Hildesheim 3100.

56. See also the chapter by Rüdiger Hachtmann in this volume.

57. For a summary, see J. Fischer-Dieskau, 'Realkredit und Siedlungswerk', *Die Bank* 29 (1936), 957–61, here 959.

58. S. Reichardt and W. Seibel (eds), *Der prekäre Staat. Herrschen und Verwalten im Nationalsozialismus*, Frankfurt am Main: Campus, 2011.

59. G. Schulz, 'Kontinuitäten und Brüche in der Wohnungspolitik von der Weimarer Zeit bis zur Bundesrepublik', in H.J. Teuteberg (ed.), *Stadtwachstum, Industrialisierung, Sozialer Wandel*, Berlin: Duncker & Humblot, 1986, 135–74, here 173 f.

60. Reich Labour Minister Franz Seldte to the Reich Commissioner, 25 March 1935, BArch, R 43 II/1006.

61. Knoll, 'Arbeitseinsatz', 53.

62. K.C. Führer, 'Anspruch und Realität. Das Scheitern der nationalsozialistischen Wohnungsbaupolitik 1933–1945', *Vierteljahrshefte für Zeitgeschichte* 45(2) (1997), 225–56, here 243.

63. G. Feder, *Arbeitsstätte – Wohnstätte*, Berlin: Springer, 1939, 55. For more detail on the small housing estate, see K.C. Führer, 'Das NS-Regime und die "Idealform des deutschen Wohnungsbaues". Ein Beitrag zur nationalsozialistischen Gesellschaftspolitik', *Vierteljahrschrift für Sozial- und Wirtschaftsgeschichte* 89 (2002), 141–66; Haerendel, *Kommunale Wohnungspolitik*, 197–278.

64. Circular by the Reich Ministry of Labour, 27 July 1935, BArch, R 43 II/1006.

65. In 1935 and 1936, 9 per cent of all new homes were 'people's homes'. In 1937 and 1938 this grew to 13.5 per cent. Figures in 'Deutscher Wohnungsbau 1933 bis 1937', *RABl.* II (1939), 227–32, here 228 (for 1935–1936) and calculated on the basis of H. Aichele, 'Finanzierungsfragen im Arbeiterwohnstättenbau', *Zeitschrift für Wohnungswesen* 37 (1939), 196–201, here 197 (for 1937–1938).

66. E. von Stuckrad, 'Heimstätte und Geschosswohnung', *Bauen, Siedeln, Wohnen* 18 (1938), 167–68.

67. Reich Ministry for Public Enlightenment and Propaganda to Reich Ministry of Labour, 17 August 1935, BArch, R 43 II/1006.

68. See, for example, the contemporary critical commentaries, 'Zuwenig billige Wohnungen!', *Die deutsche Volkswirtschaft* 4 (1935), 112–13; A. Düppe, 'Der Wohnungsbau – Tatsachen und Probleme', *Die Deutsche Wohnwirtschaft* 43 (1936), 558–63, here 561; 'Echte Volkswohnungen!', *Der Deutsche Volkswirt* 11 (1936–37), 1747.

69. E. Wildermuth, 'Die Finanzierung des Wohnungsbaues', *Die Bank* 29 (1936), 944–49, here 947.

70. P.-C. Witt, 'Inflation, Wohnungszwangswirtschaft und Hauszinssteuer. Zur Regelung von Wohnungsbau und Wohnungsmarkt in der Weimarer Republik', in L. Niethammer (ed.), *Wohnen im Wandel. Beiträge zur Geschichte des Alltags in der bürgerlichen Gesellschaft*, Wuppertal: Hammer, 1979, 385–407, here 403, 405. For the 'inflation years' from 1919 to 1923 it is impossible to calculate a comparative figure due to the 'galloping' inflation.

71. R. Schwarz, 'Die Spitzenfinanzierung im Wohnungsbau', *Die Bank* 29 (1936), 420–25, here 420. On the persistence of this state of affairs, see the data for the years until 1937 in H. Boberach (ed.), *Meldungen aus dem Reich 1938–1945. Die geheimen Lageberichte des Sicherheitsdienstes der SS*, vol. 2, Herrsching: Pawlak, 1984, 211.

72. See, for example, the contributions by various experts in the 'thematic issue' collectively entitled 'Wiederbelebung des organisierten Realkredits!', *Die Bank* 29 (1936), 935–80.
73. See, for example, H. Bellinger, 'Neuordnung der Kleinsiedlung', *RABl.* II (1936), 237–46, here 238 f.; J. Fischer-Dieskau, 'Probleme der Wohnbau- und Siedlungsfinanzierung', *Die Bank* 31 (1938), 10–16, here 11; H. Bellinger, 'Neue Kleinsiedlungsfinanzierung', *RABl.* II (1939), 5–9, here 9.
74. See, for example, Fischer-Dieskau, 'Probleme der Wohnbau- und Siedlungsfinanzierung', 11 f.; E. Knoll, 'Das Siedlungswerk in Deutschland', in R. Stegemann and F. Schmidt (eds), *Siedlung und Siedlungspolitik in den Ländern Europas*, Berlin: Elsner, 1939, 75–82, here 79 f.; O. Blechschmidt, 'Fünf Jahre Reichsbürgschaften für den Kleinwohnungsbau', *RABl.* II (1939), 300–304, here 300.
75. Circular by the Reich Ministry of Labour, 10 March 1936, BArch, R 3101/16210. On the details, see Führer, *Mieter*, 213 f.
76. R. Ley, 'Was hat die Partei mit Wohnungsfragen zu tun?', *Bauen, Siedeln, Wohnen* 18 (1938), 563–64, here 563.
77. E. Knoll, 'Kritik an den Volkswohnungen', *Siedlung und Wirtschaft* 20 (1938), 573–78, here 578.
78. O. Wetzel, 'Nationalsozialismus und Wohnungsbau', *Bauen, Siedeln, Wohnen* 17 (1937), 351–53, here 352 f.
79. *Jahrbuch des Arbeitswissenschaftlichen Instituts der Deutschen Arbeitsfront 1939*, vol. I, Berlin, n.p., n.d., 385.
80. *Jahrbuch des Arbeitswissenschaftlichen Instituts der Deutschen Arbeitsfront 1940/41*, vol. II, Berlin, n.p., n.d., 1021 f.
81. For more detail, see M.-L. Recker, *Nationalsozialistische Sozialpolitik im Zweiten Weltkrieg*, Munich: Oldenbourg, 1985, 138–41.
82. Quoted in ibid., 131 f.
83. Given the lack of Reich-wide figures, see the data for Berlin until 1941 in *Beilage zu den Kriegs-Mitteilungen des Statistischen Amtes Berlin*, Jan./Feb. 1943, BArch, R 43 II/1007.
84. For a detailed discussion of the desired exclusion of private homebuilders and investors from the construction of rented homes, see Robert Ley to Reich Labour Minister Franz Seldte, 16 March 1940, BArch, NS 6/22.
85. For detailed information on Joachim Fischer-Dieskau, see Biographical Appendix.
86. J. Fischer-Dieskau, 'Von der Förderung des Kleinwohnungsbaus zur totalen Wohnungspolitik', *Deutsches Wohnungs-Archiv* 18 (1943), col. 74–81, here col. 74.
87. R. Ley, 'Grundsätzliches zum künftigen Wohnungsbau', *Der Wohnungsbau in Deutschland* 4 (1944), 49–53, here 50.
88. Though we do know that Joachim Fischer-Dieskau was section head (Abteilungsleiter) in the Bonn ministry until 1957 (before switching to the board of the public 'Deutsche Bau- und Bodenbank'); Führer, *Mieter*, 22. As stated earlier, it remains to be established whether other officials' careers took them from the Reich Ministry of Labour to the Bonn Ministry of Housing.
89. For an overview of the political fate of the 'Lücke Plan', see K.C. Führer, *Die Stadt, der Markt und das Geld. Immobilienspekulation in der Bundesrepublik 1960–1985*, Berlin: De Gruyter Oldenbourg, 2016, 237–63, 315–26.

Bibliography

Aichele, H. 'Finanzierungsfragen im Arbeiterwohnstättenbau'. *Zeitschrift für Wohnungswesen* 37 (1939), 196–201.
Akten der Reichskanzlei. Regierung Hitler 1933–1938, vol. 1: *Die Regierung Hitler*, part I:

1933/34, ed. K.-H. Minuth, series editors K. Repgen and H. Booms. Boppard am Rhein: Boldt, 1983.

Bellinger, H. 'Neue Kleinsiedlungsfinanzierung'. *Reichsarbeitsblatt* II (1939), 5–9.

Bellinger, H. 'Neuordnung der Kleinsiedlung'. *Reichsarbeitsblatt* II (1936), 237–46

Bellinger, H. 'Weiterführung der Kleinsiedlung'. *Reichsarbeitsblatt* II (1935), 180–84.

Blechschmidt, O. 'Fünf Jahre Reichsbürgschaften für den Kleinwohnungsbau'. *Reichsarbeitsblatt* II (1939), 300–304.

Blechschmidt, O. 'Reichsbürgschaften für den Kleinwohnungsbau'. *Reichsarbeitsblatt* II (1934), 85–86.

Boberach, H. (ed.). *Meldungen aus dem Reich 1938–1945. Die geheimen Lageberichte des Sicherheitsdienstes der SS*, 17 vols. Herrsching: Pawlak, 1984.

Degener, H.A.L. (ed.). *Degeners Wer ist's?* 10th ed. Berlin: Degener, 1935.

Deutscher Baugewerkbund. *Jahrbuch 1931*, ed. Vorstand des Deutschen Baugewerkbundes. Berlin: Deutscher Baugewerkbund, 1932.

Düppe, A. 'Der Wohnungsbau – Tatsachen und Probleme'. *Die Deutsche Wohnwirtschaft* 43 (1936), 558–63.

Durst, K. 'Zeitfragen der Bau- und Wohnungswirtschaft'. *Siedlung und Wirtschaft* 14 (1932), 93–97.

Feder, G. *Arbeitsstätte – Wohnstätte*. Berlin: Springer, 1939.

Fiehler, K. *Nationalsozialistische Gemeindepolitik*, 5th ed. Munich: Eher, 1932.

Fischer-Dieskau, J. 'Grundsätze für Kapitaleinsatz und Finanzierung von Kleinsiedlung und Wohnungsbau', in *Deutscher Bauvereins-Kalender 1937*, ed. Hauptverband Deutscher Wohnungsunternehmen with the collaboration of the German housing associations (Berlin: n.p., 1936), 99–135.

Fischer-Dieskau, J. 'Kapitalkraft und Kapitaleinsatz bei der Wohnungsbau- und Siedlungsfinanzierung', in *Jahrbuch der deutschen Siedlung*, prepared with the assistance of Stiftung zur Förderung von Bauforschungen, ed. C.J. Neumann (Berlin: Verlag Siedlung und Wirtschaft, 1937), 14–32.

Fischer-Dieskau, J. 'Probleme der Wohnbau- und Siedlungsfinanzierung'. *Die Bank* 31 (1938), 10–16.

Fischer-Dieskau, J. 'Realkredit und Siedlungswerk'. *Die Bank* 29 (1936), 957–61.

Fischer-Dieskau, J. 'Staatsgedanke und Wohnungswesen'. *Soziale Praxis* 44 (1935), col. 306–12.

Fischer-Dieskau, J. 'Von der Förderung des Kleinwohnungsbaus zur totalen Wohnungspolitik'. *Deutsches Wohnungs-Archiv* 18 (1943), col. 74–81.

Fischer-Dieskau, J. 'Zum Problem der verwaltungsmässigen Verankerung von Wohnungswesen, Städtebau und Raumordnung in den ministeriellen Instanzen des Reichs und der Bundesrepublik Deutschland – Rückblick und Ausblick', in V.-E/ Preusker (ed.), *Festschrift für Hermann Wandersleb zur Vollendung des 75. Lebensjahres* (Bonn: Deutscher Bundes-Verlag, 1970), 113–43.

Forster, B. *Adam Stegerwald (1874–1945). Christlich-nationaler Gewerkschafter, Zentrumspolitiker, Mitbegründer der Unionsparteien*. Düsseldorf: Droste, 2003.

Führer, K.C. 'Anspruch und Realität. Das Scheitern der nationalsozialistischen Wohnungsbaupolitik 1933–1945'. *Vierteljahrshefte für Zeitgeschichte* 45(2) (1997), 225–56.

Führer, K.C. *Mieter, Hausbesitzer, Staat und Wohnungsmarkt. Wohnungsmangel und Wohnungszwangswirtschaft in Deutschland 1914–1960*. Stuttgart: Steiner, 1995.

Führer, K.C. 'Das NS-Regime und die "Idealform des deutschen Wohnungsbaues". Ein Beitrag zur nationalsozialistischen Gesellschaftspolitik'. *Vierteljahrsschrift für Sozial- und Wirtschaftsgeschichte* 89 (2002), 141–66.

Führer, K.C. *Die Stadt, der Markt und das Geld. Immobilienspekulation in der Bundesrepublik 1960–1985*. Berlin: De Gruyter Oldenbourg, 2016.

Gisbertz, W. 'Die Fortführung der Kleinsiedlung auf neuer Grundlage'. *Reichsarbeitsblatt* II (1935), 41–43.
Habel, W. (ed.). *Wer ist wer? Das deutsche Who's Who*, 12th ed. of *Degeners Wer ist's?* Berlin: Arani, 1955.
Haerendel, U. *Kommunale Wohnungspolitik im Dritten Reich. Siedlungsideologie, Kleinhausbau und 'Wohnraumarisierung' am Beispiel München*. Munich: Oldenbourg, 1999.
Harlander, T., K. Hater, and F. Meiers. *Siedeln in der Not. Umbruch und Siedlungsbau am Ende der Weimarer Republik*. Hamburg: Christians, 1988.
Heilmann, G. 'Fortführung der vorstädtischen Kleinsiedlung'. *Reichsarbeitsblatt* II (1933), 285–86.
Hirtsiefer, H. *Die Wohnungswirtschaft in Preussen*. Eberswalde: Müller, 1929.
Jahrbuch des Arbeitswissenschaftlichen Instituts der Deutschen Arbeitsfront 1939, vol. I. Berlin: n.p., n.d.
Jahrbuch des Arbeitswissenschaftlichen Instituts der Deutschen Arbeitsfront 1940/41, vol. II. Berlin: n.p., n.d.
Knoll, E. 'Arbeitseinsatz – seine Bedeutung für Wohnungsbau und Siedlungswesen'. *Die Wohnung* 11 (1936), 49–55.
Knoll, E. 'Kleinsiedlung als staatspolitische Aufgabe', in *Die Wirtschaft im neuen Deutschland in Einzeldarstellungen: Bauen und Siedeln* (Berlin: Der deutsche Volkswirt, 1937), 24–28 (special supplement to *Der deutsche Volkswirt* 11[17] [1936/37], 22 January 1937).
Knoll, E. 'Kritik an den Volkswohnungen'. *Siedlung und Wirtschaft* 20 (1938), 573–78.
Knoll, E. 'Das Siedlungswerk in Deutschland', in R. Stegemann and F. Schmidt (eds), *Siedlung und Siedlungspolitik in den Ländern Europas* (Berlin: Elsner, 1939), 75–82.
Ley, R. 'Fünf Millionen Wohnungen'. *Die Deutsche Wohnwirtschaft* 43 (1936), 648–49.
Ley, R. 'Grundsätzliches zum künftigen Wohnungsbau'. *Der Wohnungsbau in Deutschland* 4 (1944), 49–53.
Ley, R. 'Das Siedlungsprogramm des Führers'. *Bauen, Siedeln, Wohnen* 16 (1936), 329–30.
Ley, R. 'Was hat die Partei mit Wohnungsfragen zu tun?' *Bauen, Siedeln, Wohnen* 18 (1938), 563–64.
Ludowici, W. 'Die Kleinstwohnung'. *Reichsarbeitsblatt* II (1931), 433–36.
Meier, W. 'Die Sicherung der Gemeinnützigkeit im Wohnungswesen durch das Gesetz vom 14. Juli 1933'. *Reichsarbeitsblatt* II (1933), 286–88.
Mockenhaupt, H. *Priesterliche Existenz und sozialpolitisches Engagement von Heinrich Brauns*, Ph.D. dissertation. Saarbrücken: University of Saarbrücken, 1976.
Münz, L. 'Die sozialpolitische Gesetzgebung seit dem 30. Januar 1933'. *Reichsarbeitsblatt* II (1933), 329–35.
Recker, M.-L. *Nationalsozialistische Sozialpolitik im Zweiten Weltkrieg*. Munich: Oldenbourg, 1985.
Reichardt, S., and W. Seibel (eds). *Der prekäre Staat. Herrschen und Verwalten im Nationalsozialismus*. Frankfurt am Main: Campus, 2011.
Schacht, H. *Brennende deutsche Bevölkerungsfragen*. Munich: Eher, 1932.
Schmidt, F. 'Erfahrungen bei Durchführung des zusätzlichen Wohnungsbauprogramms des Reichs für das Jahr 1930'. *Reichsarbeitsblatt* II (1931), 197–201 and 221–25.
Schulz, G. 'Kontinuitäten und Brüche in der Wohnungspolitik von der Weimarer Zeit bis zur Bundesrepublik', in H.J. Teuteberg (ed.), *Stadtwachstum, Industrialisierung, Sozialer Wandel* (Berlin: Duncker & Humblot, 1986), 135–74.
Schulz, G. *Wiederaufbau in Deutschland. Die Wohnungsbaupolitik in den Westzonen und der Bundesrepublik von 1945 bis 1957*. Düsseldorf: Droste, 1994.
Schwarz, R. 'Die Spitzenfinanzierung im Wohnungsbau'. *Die Bank* 29 (1936), 420–25.
Stuckrad, E. von. 'Heimstätte und Geschosswohnung'. *Bauen, Siedeln, Wohnen* 18 (1938), 167–68.

Walk, J. (ed.). *Das Sonderrecht für die Juden im NS-Staat. Eine Sammlung der gesetzlichen Massnahmen und Richtlinien – Inhalt und Bedeutung*, 2nd ed. Heidelberg: Müller, 1996.

Wetzel, O. 'Nationalsozialismus und Wohnungsbau'. *Bauen, Siedeln, Wohnen* 17 (1937), 351–53.

Wildermuth, E. 'Die Finanzierung des Wohnungsbaues'. *Die Bank* 29 (1936), 944–49.

Witt, P.-C. 'Inflation, Wohnungszwangswirtschaft und Hauszinssteuer. Zur Regelung von Wohnungsbau und Wohnungsmarkt in der Weimarer Republik', in L. Niethammer (ed.), *Wohnen im Wandel. Beiträge zur Geschichte des Alltags in der bürgerlichen Gesellschaft* (Wuppertal: Hammer, 1979), 385–407.

Wölz, O. 'Reichsgrundsätze für den Kleinwohnungsbau'. *Reichsarbeitsblatt* II (1931), 24–30 and 49–53.

Wölz, O. 'Die Verordnung des Reichspräsidenten zur Sicherung von Wirtschaft und Finanzen vom 1. Dezember 1930'. *Deutsches Wohnungs-Archiv* 6 (1931), col. 1–5.

Wölz, O. 'Das zusätzliche Wohnungsbauprogramm des Reichs 1930 als Glied der Reichswohnungspolitik'. *Die Wohnung* 5 (1930–31), 249–52.

Die Zukunft der Wohnungswirtschaft. Bericht über die 12. Hauptversammlung der Kommunalen Vereinigung für Wohnungswesen in Frankfurt a. M. am 5. und 6. Juni 1930. Berlin: n.p., 1930.

Chapter 5

PENSION INSURANCE POLICY
The Impact of Labour Deployment and Discrimination

Alexander Klimo

Due to deafness and a mental disorder, on 9 May 1917 the Baden Land Insurance Company granted 35-year-old farmhand Julius Danner a disability pension for an indefinite period. This pension remained unaffected by the great upheavals of the era: the end of the First World War, the founding of the Weimar Republic and the rise of Nazism. In the fifth year of Nazi rule, however, Julius Danner finally felt the consequences of Nazi policy. After more than twenty years, in February 1938, at the height of the labour shortage in pre-war Germany, the Baden Land Insurance Company revoked his pension, as a result of a 'significant improvement in his condition', as attested by a resident physician. The alarmed Danner submitted an appeal to the next higher authority, which, however, sided with the Baden Land Insurance Company. The rationale given is instructive. 'In light of the demand for manpower of all kinds, which has increased significantly and is set to remain at a high level, it is vital that full use be made of an able-bodied agricultural worker.' Danner, however, refused to accept this and turned to the next higher, and final, authority, namely the Reich Insurance Office (Reichsversicherungsamt), headquartered in Berlin. When it too backed the decision, there was no-one left to appeal to. The former pension recipient, seriously affected by illness and, as the court conceded, difficult to place in employment, was left with no choice but to look for a job in order to support himself.[1]

The revocation of a pension due to a medically attested improvement in a person's health was by no means a Nazi invention. The pension insurance introduced in the German Empire was designed to respond to precisely such cases. Because the pension chiefly protected against the risk of an inability to work, the relevant authorities had the option of withdrawing it should an individual's health improve.[2] Thus, disability (hence the name 'Disability and Old-Age Insurance' [Invaliditäts- und Altersversicherung]), as attested by a medical assessment, was by far the most common means of acquiring pension benefits, even under the 'Third Reich'.[3] It was not until the second half of the twentieth century that reaching a particular age, such as sixty-five, became the usual route to obtaining a pension.[4] In Nazi Germany, 'age' was still regarded merely as a subset of disability, and both blue- and white-collar workers' pension insurance chiefly took the form of disability insurance.

When Julius Danner was stripped of his disability pension, the protagonists involved acted within the legal framework that had applied since the time of the German Empire. Yet something had changed during the Nazi era. That the rejection of the appeal could be justified with reference to the massive labour shortage was strongly linked with the policies of the Reich Ministry of Labour. Main Section II, which was responsible for social insurance, pursued a quite specific course, attempting to reactivate a supposedly dormant pool of labour by organizing pension insurance in a particular way. This was inevitably a hard task, because the social insurance system was deeply juridified and its structures had become entrenched over the decades, impeding targeted efforts to instrumentalize pension insurance to the benefit of Nazi 'labour deployment'. The notion of community (*Gemeinschaft*), however, propagated incessantly by the highest levels of the Nazi state, provided a lever that appeared to make this possible. In 1936, State Secretary Johannes Krohn explained:

> Everyone is thus responsible for everyone else within the social insurance system and everyone, that is, the community, guarantees the survival of the individual. Only by putting these principles into effect can the national comrade be trained to become a strong and self-confident character capable of proving himself within the struggle of life. If this means that the social insurance system must make heavy demands of the individual, by the same token it leaves the insured in no doubt about the beneficent consequences of his integration into a community.[5]

The case of Julius Danner demonstrates what these words could mean. Despite his illness, the Nazi 'Volksgemeinschaft' made 'heavy demands' of him, because it was unwilling to forego his labour. His case, then, is testimony to a significant shift in the practice of pension insurance that occurred during the years of Nazi rule. Increasingly, the criteria for accessing pension insurance benefits depended on the conditions created by the Nazi regime: the labour shortage and ultimately the Second World War. Between 1933 and 1945, moreover, pension insurance was made to serve the regime's specific interests and objectives. Here the Reich Labour Ministry played the decisive role because it was responsible for social insurance and stood at the top of the bureaucratic apparatus in charge of pension insurance.

At the same time, historical research has identified a high degree of continuity in the social insurance system. Both insurance law and the institutions of German social insurance, it has been claimed, survived the Nazi era virtually unscathed. Certainly, historians have noted the Nazi-specific discrimination against Jewish insurees.[6] Overall, however, the dominant assessment has been that the structures of the German social insurance system successfully resisted the influence of Nazi measures.[7] We will come to a different conclusion, however, if we consider not just the structures of the social insurance system, which indeed remained essentially untouched, and the laws and decrees published in the *Reichsgesetzblatt* (Reich Law Gazette) and *Reichsarbeitsblatt* (Reich Labour Journal), but also the everyday administrative practices of the ministry and its subordinate agencies. This chapter thus concentrates on two key aspects, first, the aforementioned link between pension insurance and Nazi labour market policy and, second, discrimination against Jewish insurees. In light of these two factors, it demonstrates how the Reich Labour Ministry functioned and acted under the conditions of the dictatorship.

Pension Insurance as an Instrument of Labour Deployment

The term 'labour' (*Arbeit*) underwent a profound semantic shift under the Nazis because they centred it on the community.[8] Their emphasis on the individual's duty, whatever form this took, vis-à-vis the collective endowed the concept of labour with elements informed by the notion of the Volksgemeinschaft, while stripping it of its individual aspects geared towards a person's position within industrial society. For the working population, this reorientation of the concept of labour under the Nazis touched on the core premises of pension insurance and its objectives. The insurance authorities, which dealt with insurees claiming benefits to which their compulsory insurance potentially entitled them on the basis of an inability to work, something that had been perceived as an individual matter, now found themselves exposed to Nazi pressure. This arose, as we have seen, from a new concept of work that denied individuality and propagated a nebulous notion of community. Hence, within the pension insurance system, insurance claims no longer solely affected the ministry, the insurance agencies and the insurees. They also impacted on a core aspect of Nazi ideology, namely the individual's membership of the Volksgemeinschaft.

The charging of the concept of labour with elements focused on the community affected pension insurance at its heart, namely the process of negotiation between insurees and governmental insurance agencies over the recognition of entitlements. The previously private affair of an individual insuree thus became a public matter. An application for a disability pension could be interpreted as an attempt to evade one's obligations to the Volksgemeinschaft. When it came to the recognition of the inability to work, the pension insurance institutes and public insurance agencies had to consider the possible negative consequences for the 'common good' and for 'labour deployment', as in the case of Julius Danner outlined at the beginning of this chapter. Meanwhile, with the decline in unemployment from the mid 1930s onwards, the shortage of skilled labour expanded into a general labour shortage, a development that took on tremendous significance within this context.

In what follows I identify four measures instigated by the Reich Ministry of Labour in an attempt to make pension insurance serve labour deployment. These were specific provisions found in the so-called 'Rehabilitation Law' (Sanierungsgesetz) and the so-called 'Development Law' (Aufbaugesetz) and also inherent in the administrative simplifications initiated immediately before the Second World War. What these measures had in common was the restriction of insurees' rights. This they accomplished by making it easier to revoke a pension; eliminating the insurance institutes' self-administration; revamping the practice of medical examinations; and restricting the legal options available to insurees.

First, through the social insurance legislation of 1933–1934, the ministry combined this process of negotiation to the detriment of insurees with the (urgently necessary) financial rehabilitation of the pension insurance institutes.

The Rehabilitation Law of 7 December 1933 continued the cuts to benefits of the preceding years by failing to revoke the pension reductions implemented through the emergency decrees of 1931 and 1932. It also cut the level of future pensions by 7 per cent.[9] The ministry, moreover, appended a provision to the law stating that 'the revocation of a pension [is] also permissible, without establishing a significant change in the pension recipient's circumstances, if a new assessment determines that the recipient is not disabled (incapable of working)'.[10]

The background to this regulation was a report by Reich Savings Commissioner (Reichssparkommissar) Friedrich Saemisch, who had already been appointed under the Weimar Republic to identify potential savings within the administrative system. He worked on the assumption that a large number of pensions had been awarded illegitimately during the world economic crisis on the basis of an 'expanded concept of disability'.[11] The

Reich Labour Ministry thus concluded that it could reduce the pension burden for the Reich and the insurance institutes by implementing a rigorous system of follow-up examinations.

By publishing the Rehabilitation Law in the *Reichsgesetzblatt,* Hans Engel,[12] head of Main Section II (Social Insurance), intervened in an unusual way. He addressed himself to the insurance institutes via the Reich Insurance Office while also highlighting to them individually, in line with the ministry's official rationale, his assumption that 'pensions are being paid on a significant scale in the absence of the disability (occupational incapacity) required by law'. Taken together, the 'new provisions [are designed to] relieve the three branches of the insurance system of such pensions'.[13]

The decision to place pension recipients under general suspicion of receiving such benefits on a false basis had a tremendous signalling effect for the insurance institutes. While this measure was intended to purge the overall pension system of, as it was put at the time, 'unwarranted pensions', it also entailed the new expectation that more stringent criteria be applied in future when granting disability and occupational incapacity pensions.[14] An internal report produced by the pension insurance institute serving the Reich Railways, for example, expressed the belief that 'with respect to the highly unfavourable financial situation of the disability insurance enshrined in Reich law, the Land insurance institutes . . . have been forced to apply a stricter criterion when approving disability pensions than hitherto'. Furthermore, the 'unwarranted approval of pensions at the expense of the community [must] be eliminated in the new state'.[15]

The insurees were far from impressed by the new practice of follow-up examinations. We can get some measure of this from the proceedings of the regional insurance offices (Oberversicherungsämter), which handled pension insurance disputes. The appeals brought before their tribunals show that the pension insurance institutes did in fact implement Engel's recommendation. As a result of the emergency decrees, in 1933 the number of appeals was far above previous levels, tailing off later in the decade. The authorities assumed that the number of appeals

> would have declined further had the numerous follow-up examinations and pension revocations by the Land insurance company not triggered a slew of appeals. In most cases, however, the evidence shows that these pension revocations were entirely justified. They are accepted less willingly by insurees who have already enjoyed a pension than rejections of initial applications.[16]

The Munich Regional Insurance Office also expected pension applications to be dealt with differently in future:

> It is true that the number of these revocations will drop again in the foreseeable future once the insurance institute has completed its reassessment of all pen-

sions. However, it will have to be assumed that the experience gained through the insurance institute's current reassessment will, in future, lead to the use of a criterion that is stricter from the outset when it comes to the approval of pension applications.[17]

Under administrative law, however, the ministry supervised only the pension insurance institutes serving white-collar workers and the Reich Miners' Guild (Reichsknappschaft). Issuing direct instructions to the institutes, as Engel did in this case, was still unusual at the time. The pension insurance institutes serving blue-collar workers, namely the Land insurance companies, were in fact supervised by a different Reich authority altogether: the Reich Insurance Office.

The Reich Insurance Office, a supreme Reich authority (with a wide-ranging decision-making and supervisory role), was directly subordinate to the Reich labour minister. It was responsible for disseminating the edicts and decrees emanating from the Labour Ministry's Main Section II, in cases where these were to be passed on to all pension insurance institutes or a particular member of this category. The agency was also responsible for coordinating the measures arising from the Rehabilitation Law and for statistical analysis of the follow-up examinations, presented in monthly summaries submitted to the Reich Insurance Office.[18] The ministry was authorized to instruct the Reich Insurance Office through the instrument of administrative supervision (*Dienstaufsicht*). In this way, important decrees and edicts, which were not published in the *Reichsarbeitsblatt* or *Reichsgesetzblatt*, could be passed on to all social insurance institutes and state insurance offices. Formally, meanwhile, the institutes, which were legally supervised by the Reich Insurance Office, were not subject to directives from the two higher Reich agencies; their oversight extended solely to ensuring that the local branches of the administrative system complied with the law. In other words, formally the Reich Labour Ministry could not issue decrees compelling the pension insurance institutes to enforce the revocation of pensions on the basis of the Rehabilitation Law. Nonetheless, this is precisely what they did.

This was due, turning to the second crucial aspect, to the next major piece of legislation dating from the early years of the Nazi regime. The so-called Development Law of 5 July 1934, along with the associated implementing regulations, curtailed the rights of insurees substantially.[19] The elimination of self-administration, the very core of the social insurance system, greatly strengthened the leadership of the pension insurance institutes. Their committees, made up of employers' and employees' representatives, which had exercised a major influence, particularly with respect to staff development, were replaced by so-called advisory boards (*Beiräte*), which played a merely consultative role.[20] The destruction of the pension insurance institutes' structures of self-administration, however, augmented the power of the executive board, while the enhanced supervisory powers also ushered in by the law strengthened the hand of the Reich Ministry of Labour and the Reich Insurance Office as they set about enforcing social insurance regulations.

Main Section II of the Reich Ministry of Labour had two tasks above all: to draw up legislation on social insurance within the ministry, in this case the Rehabilitation Law and Development Law, and to supervise the insurance institutes catering to white-collar workers and miners (bodies directly answerable to the Reich) while also overseeing the Reich Insurance Office, which in turn supervised the pension insurance institutes serving blue-collar workers as well as the public insurance agencies. At the time, supervisory authority existed in two basic forms. The stronger variant ('positive supervision') meant the right of the supervisory body to bring about and enforce a desired legal reality vis-à-vis the agencies under its supervision, while the weaker variant ('negative supervision') merely endowed it with the power to oversee the maintenance of existing legal regulations.[21] The Reich Labour Ministry and the Reich Insurance Office had supervisory powers amounting to 'positive legal supervision',[22] which found expression chiefly in the administrative practices of the pension insurance system. There were no codified administrative regulations detailing the supervisory relationship between the ministry and its subordinate agencies. Instead, this was an open process that sometimes involved fraught negotiations within a given political context.[23] The souped-up supervisory powers alluded to above were to play an important role during the Second World War in particular. Before this, however, the insurance institutes had already responded very negatively to the evolution of the right of supervision, which they criticized sharply at their 1936 conference:

> The Reich Insurance Office's powers of instruction and supervision have been extended so dramatically that the Land insurance institutes' self-administration and self-responsibility have been curtailed very substantially, and not just in financial terms. I believe it is high time for the managing committee, without mincing its words, to raise this entire problem with the relevant authorities. This will not do. For the time being we are still self-governing bodies and must be primarily responsible for decisions as to which tasks we are willing and able to take on within the statutory regulations.[24]

The ministry's strengthened supervisory powers were in fact vital to providing it with enough room for manoeuvre to reinterpret pension insurance as an instrument for the advancement of 'labour deployment'.

Third, the instrumentalization of pension insurance to bolster 'labour deployment' is thrown into sharp relief by another regulation included in the Development Law. From now on, the so-called Medical Review Commission (Vertrauensärztlicher Dienst) within the health insurance system was to work with the pension insurance institutes, a move intended to place assessment practices within the social insurance system on a new basis. Henceforth, specially trained independent medical examiners were to carry out follow-up examinations of the relevant benefits recipients. While the Medical Review Commission continued to make its greatest impact within the health insurance system, organizationally it was affiliated with the pension insurance institutes. Ultimately, during the war it served to provide workers for labour deployment through a rigorous examination practice.[25] Even before the war, however, the Labour Ministry sought to extend the reorganization of the Medical Review Commission in such a way as to bolster 'labour deployment':

> Due to the serious consequences of unwarranted claims of occupational incapacity, not only for the finances of the health insurance companies but especially for labour deployment, in every district the Medical Review Commission must immediately be restructured in such a way as to enable it to carry out, as expeditiously as possible, follow-up examinations of insurees who register as unfit for work.[26]

In order to evade the soon notorious Medical Review Commission, some white-collar workers switched to alternative health insurance companies (*Ersatzkassen*) that did not (yet) work with the new independent medical examiners.[27] While the Medical Review Commission was conceived chiefly with health insurance in mind, the pension insurance institutes frequently used it to carry out medical examinations of those applying for disability benefits. The decisions reached by the regional insurance offices in Munich and Augsburg reveal that about one-third of the examinations of pension applicants were carried out by the Medical Review Commission, one-third by the hospitals and one-third by family and specialist doctors. From 1941 onwards, meanwhile, the share of follow-up examinations carried out by independent medical examiners increased to more than half. The assessment of reduced earning capacity was carried out most strictly by the independent medical examiners, who calculated an average drop of 46 per cent, followed by the hospitals at 48 per cent. The house and specialist doctors issued the mildest assessments: on average, they put reduced earning capacity at 52 per cent. In just under half of cases, the house and specialist doctors certified insurees as disabled, while the independent medical examiners did so in just 36 per cent of the cases they dealt with. In 1944, the last year it is possible to analyse seriously, the figure for all medical professionals fell to just 11 per cent.[28] The standard set within the health insurance system, then, applied with equal force within the context of disability insurance.

The fourth and final cornerstone of the state's efforts to curtail insurees' rights was the simplification of the administrative system, which was applied to the insurance authorities on the eve of the Second World War. Their work was already impeded by the large number of appeals. Yet the option of the appeal represented just the first stage of the complaints procedure. The unqualified right to review at the Reich Insurance Office, as the second and final port of call, increased the insurance authorities' administrative work exponentially, as they had long complained. For several years, the regional insurance offices had been proposing the revocation of insurees' right to review in cases solely concerned with the recognition of disability.[29] In 1939, as it drew up legislation to simplify the administrative system, the Reich government took up these impulses by massively restricting the potential for review.[30] Henceforth, the only cases to be heard before the Reich Insurance Office were those involving fundamental decisions. This is also evident in the decisions reached from 1940 onwards. In the overwhelming majority of appeal cases dealt with by the regional insurance offices of Munich and Augsburg, the legal instrument of review was no longer permitted. From now on, tribunal presidents, at both the Reich Insurance Office and the regional insurance offices, enjoyed the right to make decisions independently. Employees' and employers' representatives were no longer present in the chambers. The administrative simplifications advocated by the Reich Ministry of Labour can in fact be traced back to the concrete experiences of the regional insurance agencies.

The Recruitment of Labour during the War

During the Second World War, the combination of a shortage of labour, more rigorous assessment practices and the state's enhanced ability to revoke pensions met with resistance from insurees. The Land Insurance Company of the Sudetenland, for example, feared a 'decline in the mood of the members of the retinue [Gefolgschaftsmitglieder]' if those drawing a disability pension were to face follow-up examinations. The Reich Insurance Office, however, argued that (even)

> more important than taking account of the [public] mood is the fact that the relevant labour office requires manpower. Particularly in wartime, this aspect is the more politically important one. Given the need to exert ourselves as much as possible, we cannot permit workers to go unused if they are still capable of performing reasonably useful labour. The view presented here has also met with the approval of the Reich labour minister. The follow-up examinations must therefore be initiated as soon as possible.[31]

The communication between the labour offices and the pension insurance institutes concerning the procurement of urgently required workers followed a recurring pattern, though its dimensions – given the current state of our knowledge – remain unclear. For example, following the annexation of Alsace, the South-West Land Labour Office (Landesarbeitsamt Südwest) and the Baden Land Insurance Company began to coordinate the placing of Alsatian workers within the Reich.[32] A similar picture emerges with respect to the Danzig-West Prussia Land Insurance Company.[33] Even those insurees admitted to the pension insurance institutes' convalescent homes could not evade the demands of labour deployment, being required to contribute to war production during their supposed recovery.[34]

The most telling expression of the restructuring of pension insurance to bolster the recruitment of labour was the 'War Law', as it was called in bureaucratic jargon, of 15 January 1941.[35] Section 21 of the law in particular was to have far-reaching consequences, stating: 'A pension granted on account of disability (occupational incapacity) cannot be revoked or suspended on the grounds that the beneficiary has resumed employment during the war'.[36] Put differently, if pension recipients resumed work, their disability or old-age pensions were still to be paid without qualification. The Reich Labour Ministry thus sought to feed individuals already in receipt of a pension into the system of labour deployment. This had huge implications for the insurance institutes. While the law was primarily aimed at old-age pensioners, who were to be reintegrated into the labour process with the help of the resulting financial incentives, it also prohibited the revocation of temporary disability pensions. This hampered the normal cancellation of pensions, for example following the successful completion of a course of treatment or improvement in an individual's health. Depending on how it was interpreted, then, it entailed the risk of spiralling financial burdens for the insurance institutes: their cost calculations assumed the eventual withdrawal of temporary disability pensions.

These few lines of law, authored by the Reich Labour Ministry, ultimately spelt the end of the system of pension insurance introduced fifty years earlier through the Bismarckian social insurance legislation. Originally conceived as insurance against the financial risks of a permanent or temporary inability to work, it seemed preposterous that disability pension recipients, who had claimed this insurance-based benefit through a certified inability to work, could now de facto prove their 'non-disability' in accordance with insurance law in order to be reintegrated into the labour process. The course pursued by the ministry, of ensuring that workers were available for labour deployment as long as possible and, in this case, reactivating the pool of unused labour, reflected the Nazi state's reinterpretation of the function and tasks of pension insurance. Until January 1941, the state had mostly sought to impede *access* to the benefits arising from pension insurance, but the 'War Law' was chiefly aimed at those individuals already drawing a pension.

Much as in the case of the limitation of the right of review, however, the prehistory of the 'War Law' began a few years earlier and, once again, the impulse for the new legislation did not come from the ministry itself. On 14 May 1937, the staff of the deputy Führer wrote to Labour Minister Seldte, highlighting the potential for the labour deployment of individuals already receiving an old-age pension. 'For want of suitable skilled workers, a number of weapons factories have begun to employ workers of sixty-five years and over who are already in receipt of an old-age pension. Because they already drew a pension, however, they refused to sign an employment contract'.[37] In order to draw up the response requested by the ministry, Main Section II, in line with normal administrative practice, turned via the Reich Insurance Office to the pension insurance institutes to obtain their assessment. As the latter concluded that the group of insurees involved was relatively small, the Reich Association of Land Insurance Companies (Reichsverband Deutscher Landesversicherungsanstalten) recommended that there be no follow-up examination for old-age pensioners who resumed employment.[38] From this point forward, the momentum leading to the 'War Law' became unstoppable. Expanding its package of measures relating to labour deployment by adding the option of foregoing a follow-up examination, the ministry laid the foundations for tackling the labour shortage with methods that ran counter to the basic character of the pension insurance system – with far-reaching consequences. The requisite funds, however, were to be covered not by the Reich budget but by the pension insurance institutes.

In fact, the recommendation made by the pension insurance institutes' umbrella organization, namely to refrain from re-examining old-age pensioners reintegrated into the labour process, was not adhered to in practice. In the absence of a legal foundation or direct instruction from the Reich Labour Ministry or Reich Insurance Office, in many cases the insurance institutes continued to initiate the pension withdrawal procedure if they discovered that the recipient of a disability pension had demonstrated his or her fitness for work by taking up employment. In September 1939, in a circular, the Reich Insurance Office was still trying to convince the insurance institutes to forgo triggering the pension withdrawal process in these cases:

> In light of the severe lack of labour at present, the labour offices and the German Labour Front are seeking to return pension recipients to workplaces where they can still perform useful labour, as adapted to or corresponding to their remaining abilities and strengths . . . The Reich Insurance Office thus expects

the pension insurance institutes to refrain from merely using the resumption of such work as an opportunity to subject the pension recipient to a follow-up examination.[39]

This expectation was to be disappointed. After numerous pension insurance institutes had revoked pensions due to resumption of work, the ministry felt compelled to issue a legal regulation in the form of the 'War Law'. Yet even after the law came into force, more pensions were withdrawn. The reason for this was very simple: no official commentary had been provided and the wording of the law was not precise enough to avoid misunderstandings. The tremendous scope for interpretation, which there is no room here to describe in detail, and, above all, the profound contradictions and incoherence of this law, impeded the insurance institutes' efforts to implement it. In November 1941, for example, a member of staff at the DAF's 'Office for Labour Deployment' reported to the ministry:

> Time and again I have received complaints from pension recipients who have been stripped of their pension due to resumption of employment during the war. This procedure has scuppered the efforts of the Gauwaltungen [regional DAF branches] to reintegrate recipients of a disability pension into the war economy. The pension recipients immediately cease working when they realize that they are to lose their pension. They are very angry that resuming work is going to cost them their pension, despite having been explicitly called upon to do so, in the newspapers and elsewhere, with the promise that resuming work would have no deleterious implications for their pension payments.[40]

Exemplary of many cases, the German Labour Front appended the report of a dispute in which a pension recipient had been stripped of his pension after resuming employment. The relevant Land insurance company had interpreted § 21 to mean that the withdrawal of the pension was possible if an individual was no longer classified as unfit for work (which was consonant with the insurance institutes' entrenched, decades-long administrative practice) and, reflecting the ministry's wishes, not because the insuree had resumed employment.

By interpreting things in this way, the insurance institutes remained within the legal framework laid down by the ministry. Yet they acted contrary to the intentions of the 'War Law'. The Reich Insurance Office interpreted § 21 in much the same way as the German Labour Front, which believed it should simply be impossible for a pension to be suspended due to a pension recipient's decision to resume employment: 'Hence, this legal situation has now been explicitly approved, in that the law explicitly prohibits the revocation or suspension of a pension granted due to disability or occupational incapacity on the grounds that the beneficiary has resumed employment during the war'.[41] The ministry's enhanced supervisory powers were to prove particularly fruitful here. It instructed the pension insurance institutes to pay the relevant pensions – by decree rather than through the normal legal process.[42] Finally, the Reich labour minister once again explicitly endorsed the DAF's position in an edict issued to the pension insurance institutes on 25 November 1941.[43]

It was not just blue-collar workers' pension insurance but also that of white-collar workers that was affected by the 'War Law'. In an internal note, the Reich Insurance Company for White-Collar Workers confirmed the view set out by the Reich labour minister. The company declared this the only possible interpretation of § 21 of the 'War Law', 'because the point' of the law was to *'foster labour deployment* during the war, that is, the *taking up or continuation of employment'*.[44] The insurance institutes long opposed this far-reaching interpretation of the law on financial grounds. Given the problems it brought in its wake, this was hardly surprising. The unanticipated requirement to refrain from revoking pensions in future placed an additional financial burden on the insurance institutes, one they had not factored into their cost calculations. As mentioned at the beginning of this chapter, the revocation of a pension due to an improvement in an individual's health was by no means unusual. Through the 'War Law', the Reich Labour Ministry saddled the insurance institutes with the cost of facilitating labour deployment. This, however, once again contrary to the ministry's intentions, had a severe impact on the willingness to work and on peaceful labour relations, in those cases in which older or supposedly disabled workers still received a full pension in addition to their wages. The insurance institutes used this fact to argue against the measures set out in § 21 of the 'War Law'.

The longer the war went on, the more apparent the contradictory nature of these regulations became. Six months after Main Section II had set out the narrow interpretive framework in its November edict, the Association of German Pension Insurance Institutes (Verband Deutscher Rentenversicherungsträger) was already warning about the law's unintended consequences, which had the potential to severely diminish employee morale. The association stated that 'it is undesirable for pensions to go on being paid due to temporary disability, alongside a full wage, once an individual is fully capable of working, while at the same time he is exempted from paying pension insurance contributions'.[45] In October 1942, representatives of the Land insurance companies, the Reich Insurance Company for White-Collar Workers and the German Labour Front met at the Reich Insurance Office to discuss the ongoing effects of the 'War Law'. Due to the length of the war and the financial impact of § 21, the Reich Insurance Company for White-Collar Workers called for its reinterpretation: 'However much we might recognize the need to promote labour deployment, this [reinterpretation] is necessitated above all by the unfavourable psychological impact made by pension recipients who are fully capable of working and are in employment on their workmates, who are not in receipt of a pension, and on their willingness to engage in labour deployment'.[46]

The relevant files include many examples excoriating the demoralizing impact of this legislation on people's willingness to work. The Reich Insurance Office responded, in February 1943, by proposing a new way of dealing with the problem posed by § 21. 'Given the length of the war', the goal was 'to prevent workers from drawing a pension for an unjustifiably long period of time, in those cases in which it is clear from the outset that their status as disabled (occupational incapacity) will be revoked in the foreseeable future'.[47] From now on, it would be possible to withdraw such pensions during the war, while they could be approved for a maximum of one year. As the war dragged on, the Reich Insurance Office began to regard the provisions set out in § 21 as too far-reaching. The edict issued by the Reich Labour Ministry on 25 November 1941, which strictly prohibited the revocation of pensions in order to support labour deployment, was also an important source of the cost-intensive awarding of pensions during the war: 'If it was still assumed at the time that the interpretation of the edict of 25 November 1941 might be accepted in the case of pensions paid due to long-term disability, in practice it has emerged that, as a matter of urgency, it must be permissible to revoke even those pensions awarded on the basis of long-term disability'. Ultimately, from the perspective of the Reich Insurance Office, it could not 'be regarded as justified for an insuree to draw a pension due to disability or occupational capacity, despite fully deploying his labour without detriment to his health'.[48]

It was not just the Reich Insurance Office, however, but also the Wehrmacht Supreme Command (Oberkommando der Wehrmacht or OKW) that demanded a new interpretation of the 'War Law'. On the basis of § 17, soldiers were regarded as having earned their entitlement to a pension if they died while serving in the Wehrmacht (this was significant to survivors' insurance) or if they became disabled or incapable of working. The combination of §§ 17 and 21 thus facilitated the awarding of a pension after the payment of a single compulsory contribution – a pension, moreover, that could not be revoked. The OKW feared a profound decline in morale among soldiers if the ministry failed to come up with a new interpretation of the law.[49]

It was not until April 1944 that the Reich Labour Ministry responded to the persistent complaints from the Reich Insurance Office and the OKW. The Second Implementing Decree on the War Law incorporated the demands of the OKW, permitting soldiers to put in a claim for a disability pension only once they had been discharged from active service.[50] Just how urgent the Reich Insurance Office thought this was is evident in the fact that this regulation also applied to pending cases, which were to be discontinued.[51]

The ministry's policy developed in this contradictory manner because the pension insurance system, which had been repurposed to reactivate a supposedly dormant pool of labour, was not designed for this. The state's increasing use of the pension insurance system to advance labour deployment threw up problems with which a number of actors approached the ministry. The stimuli for the policy described in this chapter came mainly from the everyday administrative practice of the pension insurance institutes and the public insurance authorities, as well as from Nazi Party and army agencies. The 'War Law' was the most obvious attempt by the ministry to instrumentalize pension insurance in order to provide a reservoir of labour. The ministry foisted the associated financial burdens on the insurance institutes even before the necessary measures had been translated into legal form, since these institutes were to provide the funds to incentivize work. Because the law was ambiguous and left broad room for interpretation, it took the ministry's souped-up powers of supervision to enforce the required administrative practices on the local level. Can we say much the same about the treatment of Jews within the pension insurance system?

A 'Tacit Agreement': The Position of Jewish Insurees within the Pension Insurance System

The regional institutes providing blue-collar workers with pension insurance rarely addressed themselves directly to the Reich Ministry of Labour when they wished to inform it about a specific case. This is unsurprising given that these bodies were supervised by the Reich Insurance Office, which was normally in charge of their communication with the ministry. Despite this, in March 1941 the Baden Land Insurance Company approached the Reich Labour Ministry directly in relation to an event unprecedented in the former's fifty-year history.

The deportation of the Baden Jews on 22 October 1940, among the first systematic expulsions of Jews from the German Reich,[52] confronted the Baden Land Insurance Company with a new situation. The sweeping juridification of social insurance engendered an administrative practice capable of responding appropriately, within the framework of pension law, to changes in insurees' circumstances – such as regaining the ability to work, moving abroad or the death of a family member. The deportation of insurees, however, was not among these changes. The Baden Land Insurance Company was thus among the first pension insurance providers in the

Reich that had to adapt its administrative practices to the Nazi regime's criminal policies. The company requested specific instructions from the Reich Labour Ministry as to how it should proceed if Jewish insurees were deported to other countries. In his response, however, Hans Engel merely pointed to a decree, being drawn up by the Reich Ministry of the Interior, 'on property law provisions for Jews', and agreed that 'until further notice, [such] pension payments will continue to be suspended'.[53]

Even after the deportation of the Baden Jews, however, the Reich Labour Ministry issued no instructions to the pension institutes. These, moreover, were often in the dark about whether the deported Jews included pension insurance recipients they had processed.[54] In January 1941, for example, the Reich Insurance Company for White-Collar Workers stated: 'Recently, the pensions of Jewish recipients are often returned from Baden and the Saar-Palatinate with the comment "address unknown". As a rule, these are deported Jews whose assets are being administered by a trustee. In such cases, the pension payments are to be stopped'.[55] The Baden Land Insurance Company also discontinued payments to Jewish pension recipients the moment it discovered they had been deported abroad, making do with the improvised administrative practice of 'freezing' pensions solely on the basis that the Jewish recipients were living abroad. In reality, the Reich Social Insurance Code (Reichsversicherungsordnung) facilitated the revocation of a pension only if the recipient lived abroad 'voluntarily and normally' and clearly had no intention of returning to the Reich. Pension insurance law contained no provisions relating to the deportation of Jewish insurees. The insurance institutes, therefore, could not take their lead from the Reich Social Insurance Code when they stopped pension payments. In any case, the institutes' administrative practices varied. In some cases they stopped pension payments, while in others they continued to pay them into security accounts or transferred the contributions to the health insurance fund serving the camp to which Jewish pension recipients had been sent.[56] The Reich Labour Ministry left it to the institutes to take what measures they considered appropriate.

So far, studies of the sources indicate that pension payments to Jewish insurees were stopped only when they were deported abroad, and not before.[57] This, it should be noted, relates merely to whether the pension insurance institutes instructed the payments to be made. Whether, and if so until when, Jewish insurees had access to the funds themselves has yet to be ascertained.

Due to the lack of legal certainty surrounding discrimination against Jewish insurees, from January 1941 the insurance institutes increasingly turned to the Reich Labour Ministry, requesting that it provide them with clear legal parameters. Yet the ministry continued to leave it to the institutes to adapt their administrative practice to their particular situation, declaring itself content with individual decisions to stop pension payments. When it came to pension insurance, the ministry did not produce a specific corpus of legislation placing Jews in Germany in a materially worse position, one that would have provided the insurance institutes with the guiding framework they desired.[58]

The reasons for this are probably easiest to understand if we consider the categories with which the administrative system generally worked. While historians have tended to underline the pension insurance institutes' antisemitic administrative practices, which propelled the expulsion of Jewish insurees from their pension holdings,[59] we do not have evidence of centrally coordinated or targeted actions intended to strip Jewish insurees living in the Reich of their pensions. Rather than taking the initiative when it came to pension insurance, the insurance institutes anticipated the will of the regime and responded to political developments.

For the ministry and the insurance institutes, until 1940–1941 there was no question of stripping Jewish insurees of their entitlement to pension payments, which they had sometimes built up over decades. In some cases, the Reich Insurance Company for White-Collar Workers was still paying pensions to Jewish insurees in the Protectorate of Bohemia and Moravia (which was considered part of the Reich when it came to social insurance law) in 1942.[60]

The insurance institutes were unsettled by the need to take administrative measures in the absence of a clear legal basis. This, however, had little to do with their concern at extending the crimes of the 'Third Reich' into the field of pension insurance. What threw them was a situation of perceived legal uncertainty that ran counter to the previous juridification of social insurance. The antisemitic administrative practice of the 'precautionary' discontinuation of Jewish insurees' pensions prompted the insurance institutes to request that the Reich Labour Ministry draw up legal regulations. The ministry, which was responsible for the configuration of social insurance law as the supreme authority, only became active in this field when the insurance institutes, lacking a template that might have helped them deal with these issues, approached Main Section II.

On the level of the central state, however, the key instrument used to discontinue pension payments to Jews was devised not in the Reich Ministry of Labour but in the Reich Ministry of the Interior. Through the Eleventh Decree on the Reich Citizen Law (Reichsbürgergesetz) of 25 November 1941, Jews lost German citizenship when they became 'normally resident abroad'.[61] This made it possible for the state to acquire the assets of Jews who had left the Reich. While the decree does not explicitly mention pension insurance, it served the Reich Ministry of Labour and the insurance institutes as a lever for stripping Jewish insurees of their pensions. Before the decree had even been drawn up, the Reich Ministry of the Interior had already asked the Reich labour minister whether it should extend the corresponding paragraph regulating Jews' benefit entitlements to social insurance. The ministry 'responded that there is no need to issue such a provision with respect to social insurance pensions because the pension of a foreigner is suspended if he becomes resident abroad and, in such cases, the social insurance system does not provide for payment of the suspended sums to family members within the Reich'.[62] The Reich Labour Ministry regarded it as sufficient if Jews lost German citizenship, because social insurance law allowed for the revocation of a pension if the 'foreigner' involved (in this case Jewish Germans stripped of their citizenship through deportation) resided permanently outside the Reich.

The ministry passed this interpretation of the Eleventh Decree on the Reich Citizen Law on to the insurance institutes, which froze the pensions of deported Jews on this basis and now – in such cases – had the legal certainty they had longed for.[63] The ministry was thus actively involved in discrimination against Jewish insurees when it produced an interpretation of social insurance law consonant with the destruction of their rights. For the insurance institutes, the Eleventh Decree on the Reich Citizen Law turned what had been a legally deficient administrative practice, namely using the Reich Social Insurance Code to justify depriving Jews deported abroad of their pensions, into a more solid foundation.

The complex laws on pension insurance, however, rapidly threw up doubtful cases. How were the insurance institutes to proceed if their Jewish pension recipients had been deported within the Reich, for example to the ghettos of Theresienstadt (Terezín) or Litzmannstadt (Łódź), which were considered 'inland' in terms of social insurance law? If the deported Jewish pension recipients found themselves within the borders of the Reich, there was still no legal means of stripping them of their pensions. The Reich Insurance Company for White-Collar Workers remarked: 'The Jews deported to the ghetto in Litzmannstadt are not covered by the Eleventh Decree on the Reich Citizen Law because Litzmannstadt is in the Warthegau and is not, therefore, abroad. We have, however, provisionally stopped these pensions too, pending a decision by the Reich Labour Ministry'.[64] Here we can discern the same pattern as in the case of the deported Baden Jews. The discontinuation of Jewish insurees' pensions was only inadequately covered by the existing legal framework, but the insurance institutes ceased paying pensions on a 'precautionary' basis and waited for a decision by the Reich Labour Ministry.

It was clear to the Reich Insurance Company for White-Collar Workers that the suspension of the pensions of Jews within the Reich territory was not covered by the Reich Social Insurance Code. When it came to both pension entitlements acquired before the Eleventh Decree of the Reich Citizen Law came into force and the entitlements of Jews resident within the Reich or areas directly bordering it, it concluded that:

> If social insurance law alone were applied, these pensions would not be suspended. It is true that they could under no circumstances be paid to the pension recipient or to another individual on his behalf, because, according to § 3 of the Eleventh Decree on the Reich Citizen Law, they would be forfeited to the Reich as the Jew's assets and, according to § 7, would have to be reported to the Chief Finance President (Oberfinanzpräsident) in Berlin. Senior Governmental Counsellor Dr Bogs[65] in the Reich Ministry of Labour confirmed this to me by telephone, but explained that, according to the Eleventh Decree and the edict of 20 December 1941, in such cases the intention was not for pensions to be paid to the Reich. Instead the entitlement to the pensions should simply be annulled.[66]

The various regulations relating to discrimination against Jewish insurees now became intertwined. According to the legislation, the Reich Social Insurance Code did not provide for the suspension of pensions in the cases dealt with by the insurance institutes. Pension entitlements acquired before the Eleventh Decree on the Reich Citizen Law came into force were valid under insurance law. It was only when Jewish pension recipients had lost their citizenship as a result of deportation, in line with the Eleventh Decree on the Reich Citizen Law, that the ministry recognized a legal foundation for the decision not to pay pensions to Jewish insurees. The ministry's goal, however, was not for these pensions to be paid to the government but for the insurance institutes to cease paying them altogether.

In response to enquiries, the ministry always endorsed the insurance institutes' revocation of Jews' pensions despite the lack of a legal basis. The insurance institutes were initially content with this, but continued to check with Main Section II as to when the planned decree would appear. One particular document, dated 13 March 1942, vividly illustrates this. Below the heading 'resubmission', next to the dates '7 July 1942', '11 January 1943', '1 January 1944' and '7 July 1944', officials had added the phrase 'negative response' (*Fehlanzeige*) to a copy of an enquiry as to when the ministry was likely to issue the decree.[67] The ministry merely made the general recommendation, not covered by social insurance law, to discontinue pension payments to Jewish insurees, and saw no need to establish the legal certainty requested by various insurance institutes.

The gravest problems in terms of social insurance law arose in cases where the insurance institutes wished to stop paying pensions to Jews who held citizenship of another state and were resident in a country with whom the German Reich had negotiated a reciprocal treaty. This included

France, Italy and the special case of Hungary, which already had a reciprocal agreement with Austria that the German Reich inherited when it annexed the latter. Both signatory countries were regarded as one territory in terms of insurance law, enabling insurees to build up entitlements in the other state. The drafting of reciprocal treaties was one of the tasks of Main Section II, so the ministry cannot have been unaware that these treaties did not divide up insurees according to 'racial criteria'. Even in these cases, the ministry refrained from drawing up guidelines, prompting a clerk at the Reich Insurance Company for White-Collar Workers to make

> enquiries by telephone to Senior Governmental Counsellor Dr Bogs at the Reich Ministry of Labour as to whether pensions are to be paid to foreign Jews living abroad, if they are citizens of a state with which equal treatment for citizens has been agreed through reciprocal accords. He stated that such Jews must indeed be treated like German citizens, because the Jews had not been excepted from the reciprocal agreements, and that pensions must therefore be paid to such Jews in other countries.[68]

However, numerous complaints by lawyers, associations and other representatives of Jews who did not hold German citizenship and lived in a country with which the ministry had negotiated a reciprocal treaty evince the insurance institutes' failure to abide by these international agreements. Working closely with the insurance institutes, the Reich Labour Ministry was aware of the breach of treaty, but continued to take the view that foreign Jews ought to enjoy no privileges not shared by German Jews.[69] In putting forward this 'rationale', the ministry demonstrated that it had no interest in eliminating existing legal uncertainties. What is more, it placed the imperative of discriminating against Jewish insurees above the validity of international treaties it itself had devised.

Much as with the discontinuation of pension payments to Jewish insurees deported within the Reich, the insurance institutes also requested, in vain, a decree that might place the revocation of pensions on a 'more solid legal foundation' with respect to the reciprocal agreements. While the ministry invariably approved the anti-Jewish, 'precautionary' measures implemented by the pension insurance institutes, their repeated requests for a clearer legal framework and more precise instructions regarding local administrative practice went unanswered. The ministry thought it unnecessary to clarify the legal situation. This may seem like a minor issue from a present-day perspective, when we consider the Nazi regime's violence and murder. Yet from an administrative point of view it was of considerable importance to the pension insurance institutes that they be able to pursue discrimination against Jewish insurees on a secure legal basis. A perfidious situation thus arose in which the institutes interpreted the unclear legal situation, which they criticized, to the disadvantage of Jewish insurees. In effect, the Reich Labour Ministry and the institutes had reached a 'tacit agreement' to pursue this discriminatory course.

Conclusion

Like no other institution, the German system of social insurance is emblematic of the continuity of the German welfare state. Even the twelve years of Nazi rule did nothing to fundamentally change this. Nonetheless, we can discern specific measures that bear witness to Nazi influence. In addition to discrimination against Jews and all those not regarded as members of the Volksgemeinschaft, this includes the constant attempts by the Reich Ministry of Labour to instrumentalize pension insurance, as it sought to mitigate the massive labour shortage by incorporating seemingly dormant manpower into the labour deployment programme.

As the ministry set about reinterpreting pension insurance to bolster labour deployment, it came up against a certain amount of resistance from the insurance institutes, chiefly for financial reasons. The established structures of social insurance, the high degree of juridification and the remnants of autonomy and self-administration, which the institutes frequently sought to defend, played a key role in this clash. To enforce its new interpretive paradigm, the ministry depended on the institutes' cooperation, as evident in the developments triggered by the 'War Law'. Their administrative practices reveal that the institutes ignored the ministry's demands if they were disadvantageous to them, until the legal framework, in the form of the 'War Law' and the decree of November 1941, permitted no other interpretation than the ministry's. Here its enhanced supervisory powers played a crucial role.

The institutes, however, were also highly dependent on the ministry, as evident in those of their administrative practices that discriminated against Jewish insurees. The institutes were crying out for the ministry to eliminate the uncertain legal situation regarding the discontinuation of Jewish insurees' pensions. Yet the ministry was strikingly passive on this front. Rather than decreeing in advance, through laws and edicts, that the institutes ought to discontinue the pensions of Jewish insurees on a 'precautionary' basis, it merely gave its assent to this practice. Ministry officials, then, made it very easy for themselves. They conferred responsibility for discriminating against Jewish insurees on the local insurance institutes, which anticipated and implemented the regime's policies and measures, but then waited in vain for subsequent legal confirmation from the ministry.

The collaborative activities of the Reich Labour Ministry, its subordinate agencies and the pension insurance institutes injected Nazi objectives into the pension insurance system and resulted in a social insurance policy tailored to wartime priorities. Whenever it faced resistance, the ministry's enhanced supervisory powers played a crucial role in helping it achieve its aims. Discrimination against Jewish insurees was carried out chiefly by the pension insurance institutes, which were responsible for the administration of pension insurance on the local level. Their pre-emptive antisemitic administrative practices – evidently consonant with the regime's intentions – and their subsequent approval by the Reich Labour Ministry, sufficed to strip Jewish pension recipients of their rights. Under these circumstances, a central body of laws regulating discrimination against Jewish insurees would have been surplus to requirements.

Alexander Klimo, Dr. phil., earned a degree in modern and contemporary history, political science and philosophy from the University of Augsburg. From 2014 to 2018 he worked towards his doctorate at Humboldt University of Berlin, and contributed (thanks to a scholarship) to the project being pursued by the Independent Commission of Historians Investigating the History of the Reich Ministry of Labour in the National Socialist Period, with a study on the pension insurance policy of the Reich Ministry of Labour. Having obtained his Ph.D. in March 2018, since November of that year he has been working as a research assistant at the Department of History, University of Heidelberg. Publications: *Im Dienste des Arbeitseinsatzes. Rentenversicherungspolitik im 'Dritten Reich'* (Wallstein, 2018); 'An Unhappy Return: German Pension Insurance Policy in Alsace', in S. Kott and K.K. Patel (eds), *Nazism across Borders. The Social Policies of the Third Reich and their Global Appeal* (Oxford University Press, 2018), 81–104.

Notes

1. Appeal before the Konstanz Regional Insurance Office (Oberversicherungsamt), Julius Danner versus the Baden Land Insurance Company, Staatsarchiv (StA) Freiburg, D 161/2 Oberversicherungsamt Konstanz, no. 129.
2. On the German Empire, see for example L. Kaschke, 'Eine versöhnende und beruhigende Wirkung? Zur Funktion der Rentenverfahren in der Invaliditäts- und Altersversicherung im Kaiserreich', in S. Fisch and U. Haerendel (eds), *Geschichte und Gegenwart der Rentenversicherung in Deutschland. Beiträge zur Entstehung, Entwicklung und vergleichenden Einordnung der Alterssicherung im Sozialstaat*, Berlin: Duncker & Humblot, 2000, 127–44.
3. *Statistisches Handbuch von Deutschland. 1928–1944*, ed. Länderrat des Amerikanischen Besatzungsgebiets, Munich: Ehrenwirth, 1949, 534.
4. See Deutsche Rentenversicherung Bund (ed.), *Rentenversicherung in Zeitreihen*, 21st ed., Berlin: Deutsche Rentenversicherung Bund, Geschäftsbereich Presse- und Öffentlichkeitsarbeit, Kommunikation, 2015, 62.

5. J. Krohn, 'Unsere Sozialversicherung', *Berliner Morgenpost*, 28 March 1936.
6. P. Kirchberger, 'Die Stellung der Juden in der deutschen Rentenversicherung', in G. Aly et al. (eds), *Sozialpolitik und Judenvernichtung. Gibt es eine Ökonomie der Endlösung?* Berlin: Rotbuch, 1987, 111–32.
7. M.-L. Recker, *Nationalsozialistische Sozialpolitik im Zweiten Weltkrieg*, Munich: Oldenbourg, 1985; L.-C. Schlegel-Voss, *Alter in der 'Volksgemeinschaft'. Zur Lebenslage der älteren Generation im Nationalsozialismus*, Berlin: Duncker & Humblot, 2005.
8. For a general account, see M. Buggeln and M. Wildt (eds), *Arbeit im Nationalsozialismus*, Munich: De Gruyter Oldenbourg, 2014.
9. 'Gesetz über die Erhaltung der Leistungsfähigkeit der Invaliden-, der Angestellten- und der knappschaftlichen Versicherung vom 7.12.1933', *RGBl.* I 1933, 1039–43; see also K. Teppe, 'Zur Sozialpolitik des Dritten Reiches am Beispiel der Sozialversicherung', *Archiv für Sozialgeschichte* 17 (1977), 195–250, here 212.
10. See '§ 18 des Sanierungsgesetzes', *RGBl.* I 1933, 1041.
11. See F. Tennstedt, 'Sozialgeschichte der Sozialversicherung', in M. Blohmke (ed.), *Handbuch der Sozialmedizin*, vol. 3: *Sozialmedizin in der Praxis*, Stuttgart, Enke, 1976, 385–492, here 473.
12. For detailed information on Hans Engel, see Biographical Appendix.
13. Hans Engel, Reich Ministry of Labour, to Reich Insurance Office, re. Revocation of Pensions based on Disability Insurance, White-Collar Workers' Insurance and Miners' Insurance in accordance with the Law of 7 December 1933, 15 February 1934, Generallandesarchiv Karlsruhe (GLAK), 462–4, no. 590.
14. For a general account of the construction of the concept of disability, see G. Eghigian, *Making Security Social. Disability, Insurance, and the Birth of the Social Entitlement State in Germany*, Ann Arbor: University of Michigan Press, 2000.
15. Excerpt from the Minutes of the Meeting with the Senior Railways Physicians of 12–13 January 1934 in Munich, 12 January 1934, Bundesarchiv (BArch), R 5/23161, fol. 31–32.
16. See Annual Report of the Augsburg Regional Insurance Office for 1934, StA Augsburg, Augsburg Regional Insurance Office, annual reports (unlisted source material in the StA Augsburg).
17. Ibid.
18. Reich Insurance Office to All Land Insurance Companies, re. Circular on the Follow-Up Examination of Pension Recipients Below the Age of Sixty, 6 June 1933, GLAK, 462–4, no. 590.
19. 'Gesetz über den Aufbau der Sozialversicherung vom 5.7.1934', *RGBl.* I 1934, 577–80.
20. See Schlegel-Voss, *Alter in der 'Volksgemeinschaft'*, 56–61.
21. See H. Triepel, *Die Reichsaufsicht. Untersuchungen zum Staatsrecht des Deutschen Reiches*, Berlin: Springer, 1917.
22. See W. Jellinek, *Verwaltungsrecht*, Berlin: Springer, 1931.
23. On the position of the Reich Insurance Office in the German Empire, see W. Ayass, 'Wege zur Sozialgerichtsbarkeit: Schiedsgerichte und Reichsversicherungsamt bis 1945', in P. Masuch et al. (ed.), *Grundlagen und Herausforderungen des Sozialstaats. Denkschrift 60 Jahre Bundessozialgericht. Eigenheiten und Zukunft von Sozialpolitik und Sozialrecht*, vol. 1, Berlin: Schmidt, 2014, 271–88.
24. See Minutes of the Proceedings of the Conference of the Reich Association of German Land Insurance Companies in Dresden, 24 June 1936, GLAK, 462 Zugang 1994–38, no. 500, fol. 29.
25. W. Süss, *Der Volkskörper im Krieg. Gesundheitspolitik, Gesundheitsverhältnisse und Krankenmord im nationalsozialistischen Deutschland 1939–1945*, Munich: Oldenbourg, 2003.

26. Hans Engel, Reich Ministry of Labour, to Reich Insurance Office, re. Medical Review Commission, 4 February 1939, BArch, R 89/5265, fol. 183.

27. Recker, *Nationalsozialistische Sozialpolitik*, 277.

28. Provisional analysis of the rulings of the regional insurance offices of Augsburg and Munich on appeals relating to disability insurance. A total of 811 individual cases from the 1935–1944 period have been analysed as at June 2016.

29. See StA Augsburg, Augsburg Regional Insurance Office, annual reports.

30. See 'Verordnung über die Vereinfachung des Verfahrens in der Reichsversicherung und der Arbeitslosenversicherung vom 28.10.1939', *RGBl.* I 1939, 2110.

31. Kreissl, Sudetenland Land Insurance Company, to Franz Seldte, Reich Ministry of Labour, re. Provisional Regulation on the Pensions and Entitlements of Retinue Members of the Former Czechoslovakian State Tobacco Monopoly in the Sudeten German Areas, 2 May 1941, BArch, R 89/7192, fol. 12–17, here 14.

32. Wilhelm Pfisterer, Baden Land Insurance Company, to Wilhelm Heller, Reich Ministry of Labour, re. Alsace-Lorraine Land Insurance Company, 12 August 1940, GLAK, 462 Zugang 1994–38, no. 344, fol. 17–18. See also A. Klimo, 'An Unhappy Return: German Pension Insurance Policy in Alsace', in S. Kott and K.K. Patel (eds), *Nazism across Borders. The Social Policies of the Third Reich and their Global Appeal*, Oxford: Oxford University Press, 2018, 81–104.

33. Supplementary Protocol to the Agreement of 5 February 1941 re. Cooperation between the Danzig-West Prussia Land Labour Office and the Danzig-West Prussia Land Insurance Company with a view to the Standardized Evaluation of the Disability and Fitness for Labour Deployment of an Insuree, 5 February 1941, German Pension Insurance Union (Deutsche Rentenversicherung Bund), Documents of the Reich Insurance Company for White-Collar Workers (DRV RfA-Archiv), File 'no. 34'.

34. Briest, Friedrichsheim-Luisenheim Convalescent Home, to Wilhelm Pfisterer, Baden Land Insurance Company, re. Follow-Up Care for Persons Suffering from Lung Diseases after the Successful Clinical Completion of Treatment; here: Occupational Therapy, 19 September 1942, GLAK, 462 Zugang 1994–38, no. 417.

35. 'Gesetz über weitere Massnahmen in der Reichsversicherung aus Anlass des Krieges vom 15.1.1941', *RGBl.* I 1941, 34–36.

36. Ibid., 35.

37. Staff of the Deputy Führer to Franz Seldte, Reich Ministry of Labour, re. Employment of Pension Recipients, 14 May 1937, BArch, R 89/4922, fol. 11.

38. Reich Association of Land Insurance Companies to Reich Insurance Office, re. Employment of Pension Recipients, 8 July 1937, BArch, R 89/4922, fol. 14.

39. Hugo Schäffer, Reich Insurance Office, to All Insurance Institutes, re. Revocation of Pension in the case of Pension Recipients who have been Returned to the Workforce by a Labour Office as Fit for Deployment on a Limited Basis (beschränkt einsatzfähig), 6 September 1939, DRV RfA-Archiv, File '24a'.

40. German Labour Front to Franz Seldte, Reich Ministry of Labour, re. Revocation of Pension in the case of Resumption of Employment during the War, 12 November 1941, BArch, R 89/7044, fol. 92.

41. H. Dersch, 'Gesetz über weitere Massnahmen in der Reichsversicherung aus Anlass des Krieges', *Zentralblatt für Reichsversicherung und Reichsversorgung* 11/12 (1941), 101–8, here 107.

42. Sonderhoff, Reich Insurance Office, to Upper Bavaria Land Insurance Company, re. Resumption of Pension Payments to Josef Berndl, 16 December 1941, BArch, R 89/7044, fol. 94–96.

43. Hans Engel, Reich Ministry of Labour, to Reich Insurance Office, re. Implementation of the War Law, 25 November 1941, BArch, R 89/7044, fol. 194.

44. Reich Insurance Company for White-Collar Workers to the Department Heads

concerning the Statements of the Regional Insurance Office (OVA), Vienna, 23 June 1942 and of Senior Governmental Counsellor Dr Wallentin of 13 July 1942, 15 July 1942, DRV RfA-Archiv, File '27a' (original emphasis).

45. Liebing, Association of German Pension Insurance Institutes, re. Revocation of Pensions during the War, 11 November 1942, DRV RfA-Archiv, File '27b'.

46. Note on a Meeting at the Reich Insurance Office concerning the Interpretation of §§ 21 and 31 of the War Law of 15 January 1941, 7 October 1942, DRV RfA-Archiv, File '27b'.

47. Peter Schmitt, Reich Insurance Office, to the Pension Insurance Institutes, re. Pensions due to Temporary Disability, 23 February 1943, BArch, R 89/4922, fol. 107.

48. Peter Schmitt, Reich Insurance Office, to Franz Seldte, Reich Ministry of Labour, re. Awarding of Pensions to the War-Disabled, 18 September 1943, BArch, R 89/4922, fol. 175.

49. Frese, OKW, to Franz Seldte, Reich Ministry of Labour, re. Awarding of Pensions in cases of Inability to Work, 5 November 1943, BArch, R 89/4922, fol. 201–2.

50. 'Zweite Durchführungsverordnung zum Gesetz über weitere Massnahmen in der Reichsversicherung aus Anlass des Krieges vom 5.4.1944', *RGBl.* I 1944, 93.

51. Peter Schmitt, Reich Insurance Office, re. Advance Pension Payments to Soldiers prior to Discharge from Active Service, 5 August 1944, BArch, R 89/4922, fol. 230.

52. See A. Gottwaldt and D. Schulle, *'Die Judendeportationen' aus dem Deutschen Reich, 1941–1945. Eine kommentierte Chronologie*, Wiesbaden: Marix, 2005, 37–46.

53. Wilhelm Pfisterer, Baden Land Insurance Company, to Reich Ministry of Labour, re. Payment of Pensions to deported Baden Jews, GLAK, 462 Zugang 1994–38, no. 283, fol. 3–5.

54. Karl Rausch, Baden Land Insurance Company, re. Internal Note, 28 August 1940, GLAK, 462 Zugang 1994–38, no. 283, fol. 1.

55. Reich Insurance Company for White-Collar Workers, re. Internal Note, 27 January 1941, DRV RfA-Archiv, File 'no. 26'.

56. See, for example, Württemberg Chief Finance Administrator's Office (Oberfinanzpräsidium) to Reich Insurance Company for White-Collar Workers, re. Confiscation of Jewish assets, 29 January 1942, DRV RfA-Archiv, File 'no. 168'; Reich Insurance Company for White-Collar Workers to Central Office for Resolving the Jewish Question in Bohemia and Moravia (Zentralamt für die Regelung der Judenfrage in Böhmen und Mähren), re. Jewish Pension Recipients, 10 November 1942, DRV RfA-Archiv, File 'no. 168'.

57. Relevant cases in the following sources: Wilhelm Pfisterer, Baden Land Insurance Company, to Reich Ministry of Labour, re. Payment of Pensions to Deported Baden Jews, GLAK, 462 Zugang 1994–38, no. 283, fol. 3–5; Reich Insurance Company for White-Collar Workers to Central Office for Resolving the Jewish Question in Bohemia and Moravia, re. Jewish Pension Recipients, 10 November 1942, DRV RfA-Archiv, File 'no. 168'; Martin Röttcher, Reich Insurance Office, to Reich Ministry of Labour, re. Pension Payments to Jews, 14 September 1943, BArch, R 89/4981, fol. 86; Württemberg Chief Finance Administrator's Office to Reich Insurance Company for White-Collar Workers, re. Confiscation of Jewish Assets, 29 January 1942, DRV RfA-Archiv, File 'no. 168'. See also the recent contribution by A.C. Mierzejewski, *A History of the German Public Pension System. Continuity amid Change*, Lanham, MD: Lexington Books, 2016, 135–42.

58. Schlegel-Voss, *Alter in der 'Volksgemeinschaft'*, 102; H.-J. Bonz, 'Geplant, aber nicht in Kraft gesetzt. Das Sonderrecht für Juden und Zigeuner in der Sozialversicherung des nationalsozialistischen Deutschland', *Zeitschrift für Sozialreform* 38 (1992), 148–64.

59. Kirchberger, 'Die Stellung der Juden', 111–32.

60. Reich Insurance Company for White-Collar Workers to Central Office for Resolving the Jewish Question in Bohemia and Moravia, re. Jewish Pension Recipients, 10 November 1942, DRV RfA-Archiv, File 'no. 168'.

61. *RGBl.* I 1941, 722–24, here 722.
62. Reich Insurance Company for White-Collar Workers, re. Note, 9 December 1941, DRV RfA-Archiv, File 'no. 168'.
63. Reich Insurance Company for White-Collar Workers, re. Departmental Ordinance, 29 December 1941, DRV RfA-Archiv, File 'no. 168'.
64. Reich Insurance Company for White-Collar Workers to Möller, Alsergrund Finance Office, re. Taxation of Jews, 31 March 1942, DRV RfA-Archiv, File 'no. 167'.
65. For detailed information on Walter Bogs, see Biographical Appendix.
66. Reich Insurance Company for White-Collar Workers, Handwritten Note, 19 January 1942, DRV RfA-Archiv, File 'no. 168'.
67. Payment of Pensions to Jews Abroad, 13 March 1942, DRV RfA-Archiv, File 'no. 168'.
68. Reich Insurance Company for White-Collar Workers, re. Note, 18 December 1941, DRV RfA-Archiv, File 'no. 168'.
69. Reich Insurance Company for White-Collar Workers to Reich Ministry of Labour, re. Payment of Pensions to Jews Abroad, 20 December 1941, DRV RfA-Archiv, File 'no. 168'.

Bibliography

Ayass, W. 'Wege zur Sozialgerichtsbarkeit: Schiedsgerichte und Reichsversicherungsamt bis 1945', in P. Masuch et al. (eds), *Grundlagen und Herausforderungen des Sozialstaats. Denkschrift 60 Jahre Bundessozialgericht. Eigenheiten und Zukunft von Sozialpolitik und Sozialrecht*, vol. 1 (Berlin: Schmidt, 2014), 271–88.

Bonz, H.-J. 'Geplant, aber nicht in Kraft gesetzt. Das Sonderrecht für Juden und Zigeuner in der Sozialversicherung des nationalsozialistischen Deutschland'. *Zeitschrift für Sozialreform* 38 (1992), 148–64.

Buggeln, M., and M. Wildt (eds). *Arbeit im Nationalsozialismus*. Munich: De Gruyter Oldenbourg, 2014.

Dersch, H. 'Gesetz über weitere Massnahmen in der Reichsversicherung aus Anlass des Krieges'. *Zentralblatt für Reichsversicherung und Reichsversorgung* 11/12 (1941), 101–8.

Deutsche Rentenversicherung Bund (ed.). *Rentenversicherung in Zeitreihen*, 21st ed. Berlin: Deutsche Rentenversicherung Bund, Geschäftsbereich Presse- und Öffentlichkeitsarbeit, Kommunikation, 2015.

Eghigian, G. *Making Security Social. Disability, Insurance, and the Birth of the Social Entitlement State in Germany*. Ann Arbor: University of Michigan Press, 2000.

Gottwaldt, A., and D. Schulle. *'Die Judendeportationen' aus dem Deutschen Reich, 1941–1945. Eine kommentierte Chronologie*. Wiesbaden: Marix, 2005.

Horkenbach, C. (ed.). *Das Deutsche Reich von 1918 bis heute. Jahrgang 1933*. Berlin: Verlag für Presse, Wirtschaft und Politik, 1935.

Jellinek, W. *Verwaltungsrecht*. Berlin: Springer, 1931.

Kaschke, L. 'Eine versöhnende und beruhigende Wirkung? Zur Funktion der Rentenverfahren in der Invaliditäts- und Altersversicherung im Kaiserreich', in S. Fisch and U. Haerendel (eds), *Geschichte und Gegenwart der Rentenversicherung in Deutschland. Beiträge zur Entstehung, Entwicklung und vergleichenden Einordnung der Alterssicherung im Sozialstaat* (Berlin: Duncker & Humblot, 2000), 127–44.

Kirchberger, P. 'Die Stellung der Juden in der deutschen Rentenversicherung', in G. Aly et al. (eds), *Sozialpolitik und Judenvernichtung. Gibt es eine Ökonomie der Endlösung?* (Berlin: Rotbuch, 1987), 111–32.

Klimo, A. 'An Unhappy Return: German Pension Insurance Policy in Alsace', in S. Kott and K.K. Patel (eds), *Nazism across Borders. The Social Policies of the Third Reich and their Global Appeal* (Oxford: Oxford University Press, 2018), 81–104.

Krohn, J. 'Unsere Sozialversicherung'. *Berliner Morgenpost*, 28 March 1936.
Leibfried, S., and F. Tennstedt. *Berufsverbote und Sozialpolitik 1933. Die Auswirkungen der nationalsozialistischen Machtergreifung auf die Krankenkassenverwaltung und die Kassenärzte. Analyse, Materialien zu Angriff und Selbsthilfe, Erinnerungen*. Bremen: University of Bremen, Presse- und Informationsamt, 1980.
Mierzejewski, A.C. *A History of the German Public Pension System. Continuity amid Change*. Lanham, MD: Lexington Books, 2016.
Recker, M.-L. *Nationalsozialistische Sozialpolitik im Zweiten Weltkrieg*. Munich: Oldenbourg, 1985.
Schlegel-Voss, L.-C. *Alter in der 'Volksgemeinschaft'. Zur Lebenslage der älteren Generation im Nationalsozialismus*. Berlin: Duncker & Humblot, 2005.
Statistisches Handbuch von Deutschland. 1928–1944, ed. Länderrat des Amerikanischen Besatzungsgebiets. Munich: Ehrenwirth, 1949.
Süss, W. *Der Volkskörper im Krieg. Gesundheitspolitik, Gesundheitsverhältnisse und Krankenmord im nationalsozialistischen Deutschland 1939–1945*. Munich: Oldenbourg, 2003.
Tennstedt, F. 'Sozialgeschichte der Sozialversicherung', in M. Blohmke (ed.), *Handbuch der Sozialmedizin*, vol. 3: *Sozialmedizin in der Praxis* (Stuttgart: Enke, 1976), 385–492.
Teppe, K. 'Zur Sozialpolitik des Dritten Reiches am Beispiel der Sozialversicherung'. *Archiv für Sozialgeschichte* 17 (1977), 195–250.
Triepel, H. *Die Reichsaufsicht. Untersuchungen zum Staatsrecht des Deutschen Reiches*. Berlin: Springer, 1917.
Zacher, H.F. 'Walter Bogs – 90 Jahre alt'. *Zeitschrift für ausländisches und internationales Arbeits- und Sozialrecht* 3 (1989), 69–72.

Chapter 6

Labour Law in the Nazi State
The Labour Trustees and the Criminalization of Breaches of Employment Contract

Sören Eden

On 2 September 1941, Wilfriede Rutschke began a new chapter of her life.[1] The nineteen-year-old bid farewell to her family in provincial Upper Silesia and moved to Berlin. At last she was allowed to lead a life of her own, far from parental advice and family obligations. She took a job as a domestic servant in the home of a Mrs Mazej, where she was not only responsible for looking after her children, of two and six, but also helped out in the cafeteria run by Mrs Mazej. Wilfriede's initial euphoria, however, gradually turned into disappointment and resignation. She was paid poorly and had such a heavy workload that she saw very little of the glittering capital. Most of the time, all she got to eat was a tasteless, watery cabbage soup that failed to satisfy her hunger. When she visited her parents for Christmas 1942 and noticed how poorly her mother was, and what a hard time she was having looking after Wilfriede's siblings, she decided not to return to Berlin. Without handing in her notice and without informing Mrs Mazej, she stayed with her family. To bring in a bit of money and enable her to run the household in the evenings, she looked for a new job in the local area. Before she had a chance to find one, however, a representative of the Reich Labour Trustee (Reichstreuhänder der Arbeit) suddenly appeared at the front door to question her.

Today, what the twenty-year-old had done would be nothing more serious than a breach of employment contract due to her failure to respect the period of notice it stipulated. In the Nazi period, however, this misdemeanour had a far greater significance. Wilfriede Rutschke had failed to respect the core of the Nazi labour system, namely the 'works community' (*Betriebsgemeinschaft*).[2]

In a shift away from the collective approach embodied in collective wage negotiations between trades unions and employers' associations, after 1933 the Nazi state transferred responsibility for the regulation of working conditions to individual firms. 'Works leaders' (*Betriebsführer*) and their 'retinue' or 'followers' (*Gefolgschaften*) were supposed to develop a trusting relationship by showing a fundamental understanding of each other's needs and required actions. Mutual 'loyalty' and 'care' were to be the mainstays of this cooperation. The regime did not deny the conflict between capital and labour, but countered it with the utopian belief that it could be overcome through a form of collaboration, anchored in mutual understanding, within the small social unit of the firm. This collective form of economic action was intended to ensure that both the individual workers' social needs and the employers' economic situation were taken into account. This, Nazi leaders believed, would bring to an end the innumerable labour conflicts of the Weimar Republic and establish the long-awaited 'labour peace'. This vision was underpinned by the promised establishment of a holistic 'Volksgemeinschaft' within this central sphere of society. In this way, the Nazi legislature aimed to end the 'class struggle' and thus take a huge step towards overcoming social division.[3] Alongside the family, then, the 'works community' was a cornerstone of the 'Volksgemeinschaft'. Labour, in any case, meant something different after 1933 than it had done before. In Nazi thought, individual labour was not only subordinate to the interests of a given employee or firm, but to those of the state as a whole. Henceforth, that is, labour was to serve the 'Volksgemeinschaft'.[4] This is why Wilfriede Rutschke's breach of contract was so significant. Cases like hers were interpreted as a violation of the principles of the 'works community' and thus of the 'Volksgemeinschaft' itself.[5]

How, though, did the Nazi state respond to such infringements? Ultimately, the creation of the 'Volksgemeinschaft' was one of the regime's key promises to the German people. But the state was confronted by the problem that in 1933 it had no access to the employment relationship itself. Breaches of contract were dealt with through civil rather than penal law, in line with the liberal legal tradition of the nineteenth and twentieth centuries. The state had withdrawn from the employment relationship and dissolved the binding obligations of the past. It was no longer the contracting parties' birth, occupation or social status that legally determined the employment relationship. This was an agreement between free and equal partners. Who worked, when, where and under what conditions, was now determined exclusively by a particular employer and employee. The state still had its employment legislation, but this merely created the framework within which employment contracts operated. Because such contracts were concluded between individuals who were equal before the law but unequal in other important ways, as a rule labour law established minimum, protective conditions that were meant to offset this asymmetry, at least to some degree.[6]

By 1942–1943, however, the legal reality had changed. In line with the ordinance of 20 July 1942, issued by the general plenipotentiary for labour deployment (GBA) to tackle breaches of employment contract, Wilfriede Rutschke was prosecuted and sentenced to several months in prison. This criminalization of breaches of employment contract exemplifies a shift of paradigm in labour law that occurred between 1933 and 1945, as the employment relationship was relocated from the sphere of private law to that of public law. In other words, it was no longer a matter exclusively between employers and employees, with the state arrogating to itself the right of intervention. It seems important to explain this fundamental turning point. What was the genesis of the general plenipotentiary's ordinance, on which the aforementioned verdict was based?

Taking this question as our starting point, we can gain insights not just into the character of labour relations under the Nazi dictatorship but also into the practices of Nazi rule. Ernst Fraenkel's analysis of the 'dual state' has already shown that even the Nazi dictatorship could not make do without the law as an instrument of state control.[7] Labour law plays a significant role in structuring societies. How, though, was labour law produced and how did it change under the conditions of the Nazi dictatorship? How did the Nazi regime seek to enforce its hegemony with respect to labour law? What role was played here by the Reich Ministry of Labour and its subordinate labour trustees, who were responsible for configuring labour relations? Hypothesizing that the Nazi regime did not simply dictate labour law in a top-down fashion, I explain that it was the temporary outcome of a process of mutual negotiation and adaptation.

Breaches of Employment Contract – Causes and Consequences

Breaches of employment contract were not a new phenomenon in 1933; indeed, they were as old as the institution of the employment contract itself.[8] The reasons for such breaches were many and varied. In most cases, as at present, the root cause was the employee's need for better living and working conditions and higher wages. As a result, it was above all mobile workers, in other words the young, footloose section of the workforce, who breached their employment contract to take up a new post.[9]

Under the Nazis, a number of factors converged that worsened workers' lot and made it easier for them to switch jobs in violation of the law.

Wages, particularly in the first few years of the Nazi state, had barely risen since the world economic crisis of 1929–1932 and, often, left workers on the breadline.[10] There was also a structural problem, namely the system of labour relations itself. The flipside of the concept of the 'works community' was the far-reaching disempowerment of employees.[11] Evidently, on the direct instruction of Adolf Hitler and due to the influence of Robert Ley, and to some extent contrary to the attitudes of Reich Labour Ministry staff, the Nazi regime gave the employment regime an extremely hierarchical structure in 1933–1934.[12] Applying the 'Führer principle' to working life, the Law on the Organization of National Labour (Gesetz zur Ordnung der nationalen Arbeit, shortened to Arbeitsordungsgesetz or AOG), passed on 20 January 1934, authorized 'works leaders' to determine working conditions within their firms.[13] Employers also had the fundamental advantage that they could continue to coordinate their actions within their 'self-governing bodies' and business groups, and could articulate their interests collectively. As a result of the smashing of the trades unions, by contrast, employees largely lost their ability to communicate their needs and interests collectively. At best, the German Labour Front (DAF) could exercise a certain pressure in this regard. This body, however, was neither a genuine representative of employees' interests,[14] nor did it have the requisite decision-making powers. The disempowerment of employees, however, was not due solely to the profound curtailment of collective action. It was also due to their loss of all decision-making rights within and across firms and, not least, to intimidation, given the brutal persecution of leading members of the trades unions and communist and social democratic parties. In 1934, then, employees found themselves in a situation in which their potential to improve their working conditions – beyond the merely advisory trust councils (Vertrauensräte) within firms and the trustees' expert councils (Sachverständigengremien) – lay exclusively on the individual level. The breach of contract was such an individual means of improving one's personal living standards by switching jobs prematurely.

This individualization of modes of negotiation, however, rendered the employee's position highly dependent on his or her value to the firm. While this had certainly applied to collective wage negotiations, it was even more true of individual ones, because in the absence of trades unions it was harder to mitigate the imbalance between employers and employees. Against this background, in the Nazi period the labour market determined wage negotiations to a particularly high degree. Employees often breached their contracts only when the labour market situation seemed favourable enough for them to find a better job elsewhere. Because the AOG made it significantly more difficult for workers to achieve better working conditions, it privileged the breach of contract as a negotiating tool.

Breaches of contract were first perceived as a problem in agriculture. This was no coincidence. Here working conditions were particularly poor in comparison to other parts of the economy, reinforcing workers' desire to find a better job.[15] In addition, a specific feature of this sector was the short-term nature of employment contracts, which often ran, for example, for just one year – with no right of termination. In this way, farmers sought to avoid a situation in which they lacked manpower during the labour-intensive periods of sowing and harvesting. On the normative level, then, employees' mobility was sharply limited because they could end the employment relationship only when their contract had run its course. On the other hand, in one respect the labour market situation was favourable for agricultural workers: the sector had been complaining of a 'lack of people' since 1935. Right at the start of the Nazi era, therefore, several factors converged in this sphere that made breaches of employment contract particularly likely.

Breaches of employment contract must be seen not just as a specific way of assimilating the AOG in an attempt to improve working conditions, but also as a symbol of dissatisfaction with existing labour relations. The methodological distinction often used hitherto between 'exit' and 'voice',[16] that is, workers' potential to terminate an employment relationship on the one hand and to articulate their needs on the other, makes sense as a means of analysing the degree of (un-)freedom characteristic of labour relations. This distinction, however, should not be viewed too dichotomously.[17] Ultimately, the breach of contract itself was an (extremely conflictual) form of communication. Even if it formed no part of employees' intentions, breaching a contract was a particularly powerful way of critiquing labour relations: despite all the risks involved, employees withdrew their consent and articulated their rejection. Both employers and offices of state had to get to grips with this.

So it is not the case that employees had no means of exercising pressure. In comparison to employers, however, it was far harder for them to do so. Breaches of employment contract certainly conveyed a given employee's rejection of his or her working conditions. What this critique entailed, however, whether, for example, it was directed at working hours or wages, could at most be specified in court. Furthermore, this form of protest, while highly potent, was not part of a coordinated programme among workers. And the threshold for breaching a contract was high because it was associated with far from insignificant costs and risks. The leading factor here was the brutal terror of the Nazi regime, which made no exception for the sphere of employment. In addition, such action clashed with many employees' work ethic, prompting them to honour their contracts. Those who failed to serve the stipulated period of notice, meanwhile, were subject to a high degree of social pressure. In view of the widely propagated semantics of labour, which construed it as a service to the 'Volksgemeinschaft', and the stigmatization of breaches of contract, this social factor should not be underestimated. Workmates may have taken a very dim view of such breaches. Ultimately, it was those workers who remained 'loyal to the firm' who had to make up for the unplanned absence of a worker, at least for an interim period.

The premature dissolution of the employment contract, moreover, represented a breach with established law. The institution of the employment contract could only remain stable if the parties involved upheld its provisions. At the start of the Nazi period, those who failed to do so thus faced sanctions under civil law. In practice, however, the consequences were negligible. On the one hand, the legal system offered few incentives for employers to demand compensation, because the sums involved were either meagre or, due to the limits to attachability (*Pfändbarkeit*), very hard to obtain. Hence, an employer was unlikely to put in the time and effort needed to make a complaint. On the other hand, the legal system could scarcely have much deterrent effect on employees. They could assume that they would not be prosecuted or that higher wages in the new job would offset any compensation payments. The Reich Food Corporation (Reichsnährstand, a government agency that regulated food production), for example, stated that the legal situation provided 'no effective remedy'[18] for breaches of employment contract. Such breaches, then, must be understood as a specific adaptation to this legal situation by employees, who identified and exploited its loopholes. But there was one major downside to all of this. Breaches of contract threw the limits of the AOG and the existing system of sanctions into sharp relief.

Employers were painfully aware of breaches of employment contract. First, the loss of a worker meant the unplanned loss of a production factor. Second, breaches of contract made it harder for firms to plan ahead. Third, such breaches resulted in an unstable, fluctuating labour market. Fourth, they undermined solidarity between employers. Often, businesses poached workers from other firms by offering them better wages. This weakened employers' positions within wage negotiations, because they could no longer point to the same working conditions in nearby firms. Fifth, breaches of contract intensified wage pressures, as the prospect of higher wages allowed employers to retain or attract workers.[19]

The Labour Trustees within the System of Labour Relations

Breaches of employment contract also came to the attention of the labour trustees, an agency subordinate to the Reich Ministry of Labour, which was established by law on 19 May 1933 and endowed with its specific remit by the AOG of 20 January 1934.[20] Responsible for one region each, the initially thirteen trustees were conceived as the peacemakers of labour relations. They were tasked with ensuring that within their district the negotiation of working conditions between employees and employers took place in conformity with the rules. They were to intervene if these processes went off the rails and conflicts flared up.[21] It was thus their job to monitor the so-called 'labour peace'. To this end, they were granted a wide range of powers that allowed them to intervene in virtually every sphere of working life, even against the will of a given employer.[22] Among other things, they had the authority to prescribe working conditions on the interfirm level through wage regulations. They could also issue guidelines on work regulations and thus influence concrete working conditions within firms. Furthermore, they were entrusted with settling industrial conflicts on a binding basis. Hence, the (partial) powers previously enjoyed by the parties to collective wage agreements, arbitrators, working conditions inspectorates and labour courts, were merged into one authority. The trustees, then, had a very substantial regulatory potential. The state, according to Johannes Krohn, state secretary in the Reich Ministry of Labour, aimed to use the trustees to ensure its 'absolute leadership'[23] in working life.

The extent to which trustees intervened depended essentially on whether labour relations were developing as intended by the Nazi regime. The fact that the staff of the trustee agencies grew exponentially within just a few years thus mirrors the problems bedevilling the sphere of labour relations. While in 1933–1934 the individual trustee agencies still consisted merely of the officeholder, that is, the labour trustee himself, along with a handful of colleagues, the administrative substructure grew dramatically over the next few years. For example, on 28 July 1938, the Westphalian trustee agency had 111 members of staff.[24] The common historical assessment that the trustees were virtually incapable of acting effectively due to their meagre staff[25] thus requires revision.

Reich Labour Ministry staff were well aware that the new employment regime had yet to be internalized by employees and employers, and that labour conflicts were still bound to occur.[26] The profound disempowerment of employees was a particularly ambivalent phenomenon. It impeded the development of collective communication, let alone any kind of protest movement. Yet this asymmetry of labour relations also harboured considerable potential for conflict. It was vital that this be mitigated by system-stabilizing benefits of a material (wages) and immaterial kind (an affirmative semantics of work). In this sense, the stability of the Nazi regime depended to a significant extent on its labour and social policy, endowing the Reich Labour Ministry and its subordinate labour trustees with a key role.

In this context, the unlawful dissolution of employment contracts seems to point us towards an ambivalent assessment of the system of labour relations as a whole. On the one hand, the AOG appears to have achieved its objective in that employees no longer banded together to engage in cross-firm protests. Labour conflicts were thus markedly less intense than in the Weimar Republic.[27] Yet, as outlined at the start of this chapter, every breach of employment contract signified a grave deficiency in the law, because those responsible damaged one of the mainstays of the AOG, namely the 'works community', based on 'loyalty' and 'care'. Furthermore, breaches of employment contract obviously diminished the efficacy of the employment contract itself, a core institution of labour relations.

The erosion of the validity both of employment contracts and of the 'works community' put pressure on the Reich Labour Ministry and its subordinate trustees to take action, as did the wage pressure emanating from breaches of contract. By 1933, the labour trustees had been tasked with keeping wage levels stable. In August 1935, Nordmark trustee Friedrich Völtzer reported slight increases in wages in agriculture. From the perspective of workers, however, this wage rise was cancelled out by the rapid growth in food prices since 1934. This not only caused great dissatisfaction among many employees but also increased the need for higher wages, heightening tensions between employees and both employers and trustees, both of which were keen to keep wages at current levels.[28] Here and there, workers even went on strike, and Adolf Hitler went so far as to predict 'revolutionary conditions among the people'[29] if prices continued to rise, once again expressing his fear that the Nazi tyranny might be overthrown by a workers' revolution.[30]

Because breaches of employment contract intensified wage pressures and, moreover, damaged the foundations of the system of labour relations, the trustees inevitably perceived such violations as a serious problem. The pressure to act, which must have been intense, was further heightened by the dissatisfaction felt among large sections of the population due to the fall in real wages as a result of price rises. This pressure explains why the trustees emerged as the key drivers of measures to tackle breaches of employment contract.

The Labour Trustees' Scope for Action

The trustees were in fact predestined to take effective action against such breaches. They could issue pay regulations, which might have increased wages in the relevant sectors and diminished the wage gap, thus reducing the incentive to switch jobs. However, in the top-level meeting on pay policy held on 2 May 1935, the Reich ministers in attendance decided that it was crucial to maintain present wage levels across sectors 'as rigidly as possible'[31] in order to bolster rearmament and economic growth. The state secretary in the Labour Ministry conveyed this immediately to the subordinate trustee agencies,[32] thus constraining their room for manoeuvre.

Above all, though, it was Main Section III of the Reich Labour Ministry, responsible for labour law and wages policy, that laid down the framework within which the trustees acted. Werner Mansfeld[33] had been head of this section since 1933. With his Ph.D. in law, he not only had the necessary theoretical expertise in labour law but was also an established expert on the configuration of labour relations in practice. While he did not have a conventional civil service career within the ministry behind him, he was closely familiar with the need to strike a balance between the interests of employees and employers. Prior to 1933, he had been directly involved in the relevant negotiations, among other things as a legal adviser in the Mine Owners' Association (Zechenverband). With the exception of this key post, Main Section III was characterized by a profound continuity of personnel. Ministerial Counsellor Kurt Classen,[34] for example, had passed through the classic civil service career and had been working at the Reich Labour Ministry since 1920. The labour arbitrators had come under his remit during the Weimar era, and after 1933 he headed Division (Referat) 5, which was responsible for the trustees.[35]

The Reich Labour Ministry had supervisory authority over the trustees, enabling it to ensure that they implemented its policies and did not act beyond their powers. To this end, the ministry had the right to issue guidelines and instructions. The former were recommendations that the ministry expected the trustees to comply with. But it was only the instructions, for example in the form of edicts, that were legally binding. The Berlin authority also had powers over staffing and finances. While initially the trustees were still formally appointed by the Reich chancellor at the suggestion of the state ministries, the AOG transferred the right of nomination to the Reich Labour Ministry. In addition, the trustees were paid out of the ministry budget. Last but not least, the Reich Labour Ministry and the trustee administration coordinated their work through daily written and oral contact and at regular meetings. The subordinate agency thus found itself highly dependent on the Reich Labour Ministry with respect to personnel, finances and administrative law. It was 'fully incorporated into the Reich's plans and projects'.[36]

Clearly, this constraining framework was intended to ensure that the labour trustees consistently enforced the political will of the Nazi regime and the Reich Labour Ministry within and across firms. This was not only the outcome of a totalitarian conception of the state,[37] but was also due to the experiences gained in the German Empire and the Weimar Republic. In view of the profound crises afflicting the sphere of labour relations and their politically destabilizing effects, the Reich government wished to assure itself of the greatest possible degree of control over this field. This went not just for the content of labour legislation, but also applied in a social sense. The trustees thus functioned, in part, to secure the Reich Labour Ministry's influence vis-à-vis other actors, such as the German Labour Front.[38]

The trustees, however, were not merely an executive organ of the Labour Ministry. In practice, the two were functionally dependent on one another.[39] The trustees gathered most of the information on the social and economic situation in the various regions because they had 'contact with the people they led and with their needs and living conditions'.[40] They thus enjoyed an informational advantage when it came to the practice of labour law. Out of a wealth of cases, the trustees filtered their observations and passed on their assessments to the ministry. This allowed them to prestructure the ministry's actions, feeding it impulses to which it was bound to react. This was especially important within the Nazi dictatorship, because the violent dissolution of the trades unions had eliminated key purveyors of information.[41]

The trustees, however, were not just the 'eyes and ears'[42] of the Reich Labour Ministry, but also asserted their expertise. They frequently proposed to the ministry normative corrections to labour legislation. If these were made, it was once again the trustees that assessed the success or otherwise of the various laws and passed on their interpretation to other actors. The information and interpretations provided by the trustees served the ministry as an important basis for deciding how to proceed. Ultimately, the coordination between the two authorities was a process that was not just top-down but also bottom-up. Moreover, the trustees' statements served the Reich Labour Ministry as a source of legitimacy in negotiations with other organizations. In some cases, the trustees themselves attended meetings with other ministries. Here, it proved advantageous that many trustees were well networked within their regions. Particularly those who were able to look back over lengthy careers in the Nazi Party had close contacts with the Gau leaders. This made their views even more important.[43]

The trustees could also make an impact by exercising their powers and interpreting labour laws. Norms always open up scope for interpretation, whether because they contradict one another or because there are gaps in them.[44] Filling these gaps was not just the trustees' task, but also a potential means of shaping labour relations as they saw fit. 'The new employment regime will be whatever the trustee manages to make of it',[45] as legal scholar Hermann Dersch recognized. The Reich Labour Ministry was in a poor position to do this practical work because it lacked the logistical capacity and personnel to follow up problems in and across firms. Yet because the system of labour relations was authoritarian in character between 1933 and 1945, the representatives of the state actually had a greater reach than during the Weimar era. It was the labour trustees that compensated for this functional deficiency afflicting the Reich Labour Ministry. Though the power relations between the Berlin authority and the trustees was to the advantage of the former, the trustees' room for manoeuvre should not be underestimated.

When it came to breaches of employment contract, in the early days of Nazi rule some trustees sought to use their powers over wages in order to tackle this problem through positive incentives.[46] A number of trustees responded to certain farmers' tendency to employ agricultural workers only during particularly labour-intensive periods, such as harvest time, by using wage regulations to extend the minimum contract period. In addition, some trustees tried to ameliorate the wage freeze, at least to a degree, by introducing so-called 'loyalty bonuses'.[47] In addition to these positive incentives, however, the Silesian trustee, for example, also incorporated restrictions into his wages regulations. He specified that the 'works leader' was permitted to withhold up to 20 per cent of the cash wage of 'retinue members' between the ages of sixteen and twenty-one, and only had to pay it out when the employment relationship had legally ended.[48]

These measures, however, did not solve the real problem. The financial incentives were too meagre to offset the wage difference between jobs.[49] The extensions to the contract term had a more deterrent than integrative effect, because they restricted employees' ability to take up a new job and thus one of their key means of improving their working conditions, making agricultural jobs even less attractive. Hence, given the hierarchical system of labour relations and the restrictive wage policies of the Reich government, the trustees could do little to put teeth into employment contracts. The fact that the Reich Labour Ministry issued the trustees with contradictory guidelines – emphasizing the need to maintain both the 'labour peace' and the low level of wages – caused them tremendous headaches. With their existing powers, it was virtually impossible to reconcile these imperatives.

The debate on breaches of employment contract in agriculture intensified in 1935. Via the so-called 'farmers' associations' (*Bauernschaften*) and the Reich Food Corporation, to which the associations were subordinate, the often well-networked farmers lobbied the Nazi regime.[50] While they did not participate directly in the regime's legislative process, they could build up pressure through a steady flow of complaints, thus sensitizing state actors to their views. In this way,[51] they managed to persuade not just the

Reich Ministry of Food and Agriculture but also a number of Reich governors (*Reichsstatthalter*) and labour administrations of their views. Their lobbying work was made significantly easier because the interests of farmers and the state overlapped to a degree. Though partly for differing reasons, it was not just employers but also the Reich Labour Ministry and the trustees that were keen to prevent breaches of employment contract. The question, however, was how this could be done.

While the trustees tried to solve this problem through wages policy, the regional farmers' associations (*Landesbauernschaften*) placed ways of restricting employees' freedom of movement at the centre of debate. The Ministry of Food and Agriculture saw the labour book (*Arbeitsbuch*), which the labour offices issued to all those in work, as an apt means of limiting workers' freedom. Originally, this book was meant to serve as a source of information, one that would increase the labour administration's knowledge of the labour market and thus make it easier to steer.[52] Spurred on by the regional farmers' associations, the Ministry of Agriculture demanded that the labour book show whether an employment relationship had ended legally and stipulated that an individual could start a new job only upon presentation of such a book. To the chagrin of the farmers' associations, however, Ministerial Director Hans Engel and Ministerial Counsellor Alexander Wende of the Reich Labour Ministry saw no need to pursue this idea further.[53]

The Reich Food Corporation and the Reich Ministry of Food and Agriculture thus rethought their approach. A conference of the regional farmers' associations in Goslar, on 14 and 15 January 1936, discussed measures that would 'put paid' to breaches of contract 'once and for all'. They expected the government to introduce a criminal code as a matter of the 'utmost urgency'. Such 'harmful conduct must be removed from the sphere of monetary compensation under private law and rendered subject to public prosecution and atonement through the criminal justice system'.[54] The agricultural associations thus demanded the criminalization of breaches of employment contract and a partial shifting of labour relations away from private law into the sphere of public law. As they saw it, the state should have more power to intervene directly in the employment relationship.

Tolerated Self-Empowerment

At Reich level, the ministries of Agriculture and Labour disagreed as to the best means of preventing breaches of employment contract, but on the regional level consensus began to emerge between a number of trustees and regional farmers' associations. At the above-mentioned conference, the latter picked up on an idea with which Leon Daeschner, the Brandenburg trustee, had already gone public in September 1935. In an article that appeared not just in his *Amtliche Mitteilungen* (Official News) but also in the DAF newspaper known as *Der Angriff* (The Attack), he stigmatized employees who breached their contracts as selfish, irresponsible and cowardly. Not content to change jobs 'from one day to the next',[55] they even sent family members to collect their working papers 'because they themselves lack the courage to inform their works leader of this "change"'. Daeschner also invoked solidarity between employees by declaring that ignoring the period of notice was not only a 'breach of loyalty' vis-à-vis the employer but also with respect to 'one's workmates'. In addition to these moral criticisms, he identified the breach of contract as a violation of the law. Here, however, he did not base his argument on the civil law regulations contained in the Civil Code (*Bürgerliches Gesetzbuch*) and Industrial Code (*Gewerbeordnung*). Instead he interpreted the breach of contract as a 'grave violation of the principle of personal allegiance [*Gefolgstreue*] found within present-day social law'. According to §§ 22 and 36 of the AOG, repeated premeditated or persistent contravention of the trustees' ordinances could result in prosecution. The recommended sanctions ranged from a warning to several years in prison.

While Leon Daeschner made do with his threat, it laid the ground for a development that culminated in a paradigm shift in labour law. Through his publication, his interpretation of the AOG entered into and altered the debates on how to prevent breaches of employment contract. For the farmers' associations and the Reich Ministry of Food and Agriculture in particular, Daeschner's interpretation was a key source of stimulus.[56] His proposal met with the approval of both actors and was passed on to the Ministry of Labour.[57]

Shortly afterwards, the trustee for East Prussia, Hans Schreiber, put Daeschner's interpretation into practice. At Schreiber's behest, on 2 April 1936, a milker received a warning from the Social Honour Court[58] in accordance with § 36 of the AOG. He had failed to comply with his period of notice, of which the trustee had reminded him in writing after he had breached his employment contract and failed to return to the firm as instructed. The court interpreted his actions as a violation of the AOG.[59] Breaches of contract, then, though not sanctioned directly, were now subject to indirect punishment.

The interpretation put forward by the East Prussian and Brandenburg trustees was highly questionable. It was unclear whether Hans Schreiber's initiation of proceedings exceeded his powers and whether this incursion into the private autonomy of the labour relationship was legitimate. The Reich Labour Ministry thus responded sceptically to the Social Honour

Court's ruling. Hans Engel had already expressed doubts, following the conference of farmers' associations in Goslar, as to the legitimacy of using §§ 22 and 36 of the AOG as discussed there.[60] Further, the fact that the East Prussian trustee had taken this case to the Social Honour Court is bound to have put the Reich Labour Ministry's nose out of joint. It was evidently only informed about this by the trustee for Central Germany and was thus presented with a *fait accompli*. The East Prussian trustee had not violated any instruction, but had failed to agree his approach to a crucial matter in advance with the Reich Labour Ministry. The latter thus slapped down the trustee, by criticizing him not just directly but also in communication with the Ministry of Agriculture. It expressed doubt that the trustees were authorized to issue ordinances in which they decreed the return of the individual in breach of contract to his or her firm. Furthermore, the ministry stated, this decision entailed a form of compulsory service ruled out by § 888 of the Code of Civil Procedure (*Zivilprozessordnung*).[61]

It is equally worth noting what the Reich Labour Ministry did not criticize. It failed to mention that the East Prussian trustee had summarily reinterpreted § 36 of the AOG. The cited paragraph was not intended to punish breaches of employment contract, but, just like § 22, to safeguard the trustees' ability to get things done.[62] Nor did the ministry complain that the trustee had robbed the employment relationship, to some degree, of its anchorage in private law. It was evidently more important to the Berlin authority that the trustees acted within their legal limits and always coordinated their actions with the ministry. Were they to make a habit of acting without authorization, it would seriously curtail the Reich Labour Ministry's capacity for effective action in the field of labour law. The ministry was less concerned about the substance of the case. Certainly, shortly after the Honour Court ruling, Hans Engel was still expressing 'the gravest of concerns'[63] about a draft law drawn up by the Reich Ministry of Food and Agriculture that boiled down to the direct criminalization of breaches of employment contract. Yet in parallel to this, the Reich Labour Ministry was engaged in negotiations with the ministries of Justice and Economy concerning the incorporation of breach of contract into the Penal Code (*Strafgesetzbuch*).[64] It seems likely that the staff of the Reich Labour Ministry regarded direct criminalization as such a radical break with labour law that it was appropriate to embed it in a larger-scale reform.

These different perspectives on the trustees' conduct point to the presence of quite different understandings of labour law, with individual socialization being an important, though not the only, factor in these contrasting interpretations. For the Reich Ministry of Labour, the law was the primary conduit for enforcing its political objectives, so upholding it was crucially important. If its staff were to avoid squandering their credibility and damaging the law itself, the ministry had to ensure that they stuck to the rules. This explains why the ministry criticized the unauthorized actions of the East Prussian trustee chiefly on the formal level of jurisdiction. Moreover, in view of the high degree of continuity of personnel, beyond the watershed of 1933, many members of Main Section III were still accustomed to viewing issues in labour law through the prism of freedom of contract, free enterprise and freedom of occupation. Criminalization of breaches of employment contract not only had the potential to alienate large sections of the population, but also challenged core principles of labour law. Some of those working in Main Section III must have found it difficult to jettison these principles. This is one of the reasons for the ministry's lukewarm response to the state's incursions into the private autonomy of the employment relationship.

Hans Schreiber, by contrast, had undergone a different form of socialization.[65] Rather than having an administrative career behind him, he had signed up for voluntary service in the First World War at the age of eighteen before going on to work as a farmer, after which he qualified as an apprentice then master boatbuilder. By 1920, he had joined the German Nationalist Protection and Defiance Federation (Deutschvölkischer Schutz- und Trutzbund) and from 1930 pursued a career within the Nazi Party. He worked as local group leader, district leader (Kreisleiter) and Gau speaker (Gauredner) as well as acting as Nazi Party group chairman (Fraktionsführer) for two sessions of the East Prussian Chamber of Agriculture (Landwirtschaftskammer) and of the Provincial Diet (Provinziallandtag). It is likely, then, that for him laws possessed far less authority than they did for ministerial staff. In fact, his interpretation of the AOG suggests that he essentially viewed laws as a framework for action amenable to flexible instrumentalization. What mattered to him was the utility he could glean from the law; he was less interested in upholding a given paragraph's original function. Unlike Hans Schreiber, another labour trustee named Karl Heinrich Wiesel was highly critical of the incipient criminalization of breaches of employment contract. Like most members of the Reich Ministry of Labour, this Ph.D. jurist could look back over a long administrative career. He had entered the Thuringian civil service in October 1921, initially working within the welfare system and later in the Labour Department of the Thuringian Ministry of the Economy, before switching to the Reich Arbitration Service (Schlichtungswesen) and becoming a labour trustee in 1933.[66]

This contrast highlights the tremendous influence of biographies, and socialization within organizations,[67] on the specific ways in which individuals appropriated the law. This merits emphasis because these modes of appropriating existing legal norms changed the law and created new forms of law. It is, for example, almost certainly no coincidence that Schreiber turned to a Social Honour Court in accordance with § 36, rather than an ordinary court on the basis of § 22. He functioned as public prosecutor before the former, while the two lay assessors were appointed on the suggestion of the German Labour Front. There was thus a greater probability that the liberal legal tradition would take a backseat, with the actors involved pushing for a ruling consonant with the new understanding of labour. As a result of the highly controversial interpretation of the AOG at play here, workers who breached their employment contract faced the prospect of new sanctions, while the employment relationship was moved unambiguously into the sphere of public law. This entailed a shift in the boundaries of the sayable and doable. Despite the criticisms expressed by the Reich Ministry of Labour and the grave consequences for labour law and the organization of the trustees themselves, over the course of 1936 an increasing number of trustees embraced this new approach.[68] Though it may be assumed that, in the mid 1930s, this was the exception rather than the rule, a new legal situation was being established that laid the foundation for subsequent developments.

The Criminalization of Breaches of Employment Contract

Attitudes among Reich Labour Ministry staff also evolved rapidly. Until early 1936, they had consistently resisted the vehement demands to limit workers' free movement. On 22 December 1936, however, they introduced a regulation that did just that via the Four-Year-Plan Authority. The Ordinance on the Implementation of the Four-Year Plan through Prevention of the Unlawful Dissolution of the Employment Relationship (Anordnung zur Durchführung des Vierjahresplans über die Verhinderung rechtswidriger Lösungen von Arbeitsverhältnissen) stipulated that employers in the iron and metal industry, the building sector, the brick industry and agriculture could hold on to their employees' labour books until they had served their period of notice.[69] Because a worker could only take up a new post upon presentation of the labour book, Werner Mansfeld hoped to make breach of contract an unattractive option.[70] Two years later, however, Ministerial Counsellor Otto Kalckbrenner publicly conceded that the 'expected effect' had not been 'fully' realized.[71] Evidently, this regulation neither prevented employees from violating their notice periods nor did it stop their employers from inaccurately recording new workers' start date in their labour books.

In addition, the Reich Ministry of Labour was working on a general reform of the laws governing employment contracts, though this was never to be completed,[72] while also seeking to simplify the trustees' sanctioning procedures through negotiations on the reform of the AOG. The ministry not only planned to give trustees the power to impose fines, but also sought to ensure that they could punish violations of all ordinances. Because the various ministries, the DAF and the deputy Führer were unable to agree on other aspects of the discussed reform, however, this project was shelved.

And yet, by now the Reich Ministry of Labour too recognized the need for action. Its change of heart was likely due to the fact that breaches of contract were now being perceived as a problem not just in agriculture, but in other sectors as well, such as mining, which was of fundamental importance to the armaments industry. In 1938, within the Ruhr mining industry alone, 15,667 cases of termination of miners' employment with notice contrasted with 5,182 breaches of contract.[73] We can infer from this that such breaches were not due solely to the social situation and contractual realities within agriculture, but also to the structural factors outlined at the start of this chapter. This is likely to have made Reich Ministry of Labour staff more aware of the problem and even found reflection in the institution's organizational structure. 'Employment-related sanctions' were incorporated into the ministry's business plan for the first time in 1938.[74]

The Labour Ministry now stepped up the pressure. At a meeting held at the Four-Year Plan Authority on 13 January 1938, ministry staff pushed through a major expansion in the trustees' powers. This culminated in the Decree on Wage-Setting (Verordnung über die Lohngestaltung) of 25 June 1938, which was signed by Hermann Göring, but was drawn up by the staff of the Reich Labour Ministry's Main Section III.[75] This regulation empowered the authority now renamed the Reich Labour Trustees to 'oversee wages and working conditions and take all measures necessary to eliminate factors impeding the nation's defensive capacity and remove obstacles to the implementation of the Four-Year Plan resulting from wage trends and other working conditions'.[76]

Historians have chiefly considered this decree from the perspective of the wage freeze, because now the trustees could stipulate a pay scale that not only set minimum wages, but also maximum wages. What the research has overlooked so far is that the decree consisted of a comprehensive clause that expanded the trustees' scope for action significantly. For example, the expression 'all measures' entailed enhanced powers that, while limited to the field of wages and working conditions, allowed for a broad scope of interpretation as to the presence of any 'factors impeding the nation's defensive capacity and . . . obstacles to the implementation of the Four-Year Plan'.

Once again, the East Prussian trustee managed to exploit this loophole. For him, 'all measures' included the prosecution of breaches of employment contract. In October 1938, he felt within his rights to issue an ordinance rendering the premature dissolution of such contracts a punishable offence. Breaches of employment contract thus finally became a matter of public law, a move through which this trustee both tightened up and simplified existing procedures. Subsequently, one trustee after another embraced this interpretation and, for the first time, the Thuringian trustee also made incitement to breach of employment contract on the part of employers a punishable offence.[77] Although the private-law foundations of the employment relationship had already been eroded by the differing interpretations of the AOG and by the regulation on labour books, these ordinances were still highly problematic. This is evident in the fact that, unusually, the Thuringian Reich labour trustee felt the need to publish a lengthy justification of his ordinance. His choice of words unmistakably pointing to the AOG and the wage-setting decree, he explained that while the dissolution of the employment relationship was in fact a matter of civil law, because labour was performed for the 'benefit of nation [*Volk*] and state' and, especially in light of the labour shortage, breaches of employment contract represented a risk to the Four-Year Plan, those who violated their contracts must 'answer to the Volksgemeinschaft'.[78]

Furthermore, on the basis of the wage-setting decree, over the next few years the trustees expanded the definition of breach of employment contract significantly. Employees had discovered loopholes in the legal situation. Many got around the existing regulations by honouring their notice periods but reducing their output or conducting themselves in other antagonistic ways, in order to provoke their employers into dismissing them. The refusal to perform certain activities, deliberate slow working, absence without permission or valid excuse, lateness, and insulting the 'works leader' were thus increasingly considered to constitute a breach of employment contract.[79] Hence, it was no longer just the so-called 'non-fulfilment', but also the 'inadequate fulfilment' of such contracts that was now viewed as a criminal offence.[80]

In 1935, the Reich Ministry of Labour was still non-committal. In the summer of 1936, its comment on a draft law issued by the Ministry of Food and Agriculture, which also boiled down to the criminalization of breaches of contract, was that it raised 'extremely difficult issues of civil law'.[81] Two years later, however, the Labour Ministry was quick to dispel law-based reservations about the trustees' conduct and to institutionalize their interpretation of the wage-setting decree, by working to ensure that the latter could attract broad support. This it did, for example, by elaborating the legal foundation in relevant law journals.[82]

The support of the Reich Labour Ministry was also necessary because many courts failed to process, or rejected, the petitions submitted by the labour trustees. In late July 1939, an analysis by Werner Mansfeld on the basis of the trustees' reports revealed that just 18.52 per cent of their demands for prosecution culminated in a criminal conviction[83] – a disastrous figure, which meant that, to a large degree, in this field the Reich trustees were simply unable to take effective action.

This was linked with the formal lawfulness of the Reich trustees' ordinances and the various actors' differing ideas of law. The Linz prosecutor general, for example, rejected petitions from the Reich trustees on the grounds that their ordinances targeting breaches of employment contract were based on the wage-setting decree 'only in terms of their wording' but not their 'content'. The trustees, he averred, simply lacked the 'requisite legal foundation' for their petitions.[84] The regional court in Eisenach even decided that judgements based on the relevant trustee ordinances were legally impermissible.[85] But it was not just legal arguments that proved decisive here. The gravity of the offence was also evaluated in differing ways. Mr Seitz of the Chief Public Prosecutor's Office (Oberstaatsanwaltschaft) in Hanover, for example, criticized the fact that many petitions related to minor offences and would potentially result in fines of between just ten and thirty Reichsmarks. Hence, he contended, the criminal prosecution of these cases was inadvisable given the 'unrest among the workers'[86] that would result.

For the Reich Labour trustees, this widespread hostility on the part of the public prosecutors and judges had dramatic consequences. Their sudden inability to take effective action diminished employers' faith in them and undermined their authority more generally. When the prosecution of an individual guilty of breach of contract had dragged on for eight weeks, for example, one employer raged:

> I cannot afford to wait for months for your help, not least as it would result in hundreds of workers at the construction sites of the Hermann Göring-Werke ceasing to work. I'll make do without the man involved. Go ahead and drop the case. But let me tell you, it is far from pleasant to have people telling us quite openly that your ordinances, as we have disseminated them, are a mere bluff, and, unfortunately, to be in no position to contradict them or refute their views.[87]

In light of these effects, the Reich labour trustees concerned protested furiously. The Reich Ministry of Labour lost no time contacting the Reich Ministry of Justice. We have no detailed information about the negotiations between the ministries of Labour and Justice, but the latter was evidently quick to show understanding for the former's concerns and exercised its influence over the courts. By July 1939, a clerk at the office of the Reich Labour Trustee for Lower Saxony had concluded that the judicial authorities had 'abandoned their previous attitude . . . when it comes to dealing with breaches of contract'.[88] And in 1940, Werner Mansfeld stated that the courts' practices were 'developing more favourably'[89] than during the previous year. In addition, the Reich labour trustees were granted the authority to impose monetary fines to an unlimited amount,[90] such that they performed a 'judicial function'[91] and were themselves able to sanction less serious breaches of contract.

Not all public prosecutors fell in line, however. Some identified another legal loophole, which they felt enabled them to reject Reich labour trustees' demands for prosecution.[92] They based their assessment on the problem of the so-called concurrence of laws. As a result of the Decree on the Curtailment of Changes of Job (Verordnung zur Beschränkung des Arbeitsplatzwechsels) of 1 September 1939, employees could hand in their notice only with the agreement of the relevant labour office. Ultimately, the fact that labour offices were permitted to file demands for prosecution if an employee failed to gain its consent in such cases meant that, in practice, they too were initiating the criminal prosecution of breaches of employment contract. Because the decree on job changes, as an aspect of Reich law, had a higher status than the Reich trustees' district-level ordinances and, moreover, was of more recent vintage, some public prosecutors regarded their ordinances as 'abrogated'.[93] For the Reich labour trustees, it must have seemed absurd that while the heads of the labour offices could file demands for prosecution, they could not – despite the fact that the labour office heads had been the trustees' representatives since 1939. Furthermore, 'thousands of legally binding rulings' had already been issued.[94] The Labour Ministry thus wasted no time in conveying its concerns to the Ministry of Justice once again. While the lawfulness of the Reich trustees' ordinances contra breaches of employment contract had by now been recognized by a ruling of the Reich Court of Justice of 4 April 1941,[95] the ministries of Justice and Labour quickly reached agreement and issued an implementing regulation 'to clarify the legal situation'.[96] This stipulated that the Reich labour trustees too were permitted to file demands for prosecution on the basis of the decree on changes of job.[97]

The legal foundation for the criminal prosecution of breaches of employment contract thus became irretrievably complex and chaotic. Even before the implementing regulation of October 1941 had been issued, the chief public prosecutor in Celle described the 'variable nature of the requirements for filing a demand for prosecution as well as the justification for such petitions' as 'highly confusing'.[98] The AOG, the decree on wage-setting and the war economy, the various regulations relating to the labour book, the decree on job changes, the associated implementing regulations, the numerous ordinances issued by the Reich labour trustees – together they created the legal foundation for the criminal prosecution of breaches of employment contract. It is only against this confusing backdrop that we can understand why, on 20 July 1942, Main Section III of the Reich Ministry of Labour, in the shape of the general plenipotentiary for labour deployment, issued the 'Ordinance to Combat Breaches of Employment Contract, Labour Piracy and Demands for Disproportionate Remuneration in the Private Sector' (Anordnung gegen Arbeitsvertragsbruch und Abwerbung sowie das Fordern unverhältnismässig hoher Arbeitsentgelte in der privaten Wirtschaft).[99] This applied throughout the Reich and simplified the convoluted legal situation by detailing the nature of these offences and clarifying jurisdiction. Even this ordinance, however, could not combat the causes of breaches of contract. The sanctions it entailed merely addressed the symptoms. Ultimately, then, criminalization was chiefly a matter of symbolic politics. Nonetheless, it did have some very real consequences, as evident in the case of Wilfriede Rutschke described at the start of this chapter. Repeat offenders found guilty of 'absenteeism' ('Krankfeiern') or other forms of breach of contract faced up to six months in prison, a labour rehabilitation camp or concentration camp.

Conclusion

The ordinance issued by the general plenipotentiary, on which the 1943 ruling against Wilfriede Rutschke was based, was the outcome of a process of institutionalization, initiated in 1934, which removed the employment relationship from the sphere of private law and made it a matter of public law. During the period of Nazi rule, who worked, when, how long, where and under what conditions was determined ever less by employers and employees themselves and increasingly by state authorities such as the labour administration and the labour trustees. The employment relationship was thus endowed with a fundamentally different character than under the Weimar Republic. There is no space here to provide a detailed analysis of how labour law changed as an instrument of social control under the conditions of the Nazi dictatorship. But to conclude I would like to highlight three key aspects.

First, the ordinance issued by the general plenipotentiary for labour deployment, of 20 July 1942, did not mark the beginning of the criminal prosecution of breaches of employment contract. Nor was it the result of a purely top-down process. On the contrary, it constituted the (provisional) endpoint of a protracted process of institutionalization in which top-down and bottom-up processes converged, influenced one another and encompassed all levels of authority, from employees who had violated their contracts on the micro-level through the trustees initiating legal action and changes in law on the meso-level to the legitimizing ministries on the Reich level. Certainly, this entailed the transformation of the law through legislative changes. But between 1933 and 1945, the day-to-day appropriation and interpretation of norms and regulations also caused them to change. Hence, it was not just state authorities and courts that participated in what amounted to a negotiated process of evolution but also interest groups such as the DAF, business organizations and farmers' associations. Even the individual worker contributed to changing labour law. In this sense, the ordinance of 1942 was merely the state's response within this negotiated process.

Second, the interpretations of established labour laws differed greatly on the individual level and depended in part on the socialization and biographies of the persons involved. Neither agencies such as the trustees nor the Reich Ministry of Labour can be properly understood as monolithic entities. In particular, we can clearly see different actors' contrasting perceptions and conceptions of the law in individual trustees' very different approaches to breaches of employment contract in the mid 1930s, the ambivalent stance of the Reich Ministry of Labour and the variable attitudes of different public prosecutors and judges.

Third, such an interpretation requires us to strip the concept of 'negotiation' of any liberal-democratic connotations and to deploy it in a purely analytical way. This means laying bare the various options for action and constraints on action. Only then can we discern that this negotiation occurred on an anything but equal footing. The potential to enforce one's interests varied greatly depending on the actors involved and on numerous factors. These included the specific context of action (such as the labour market situation), the powers enjoyed by different actors and their right to be heard. Also significant were the different ways in which actors identified and articulated their interests. Employees possessed no right of decision and they were in no position to reach agreement on what their interests were, let alone promote them collectively. Those employees whose skills were in great demand, however, at least found themselves in a fairly good individual negotiating position. In response, the employers and their associations, the labour trustees, the Reich Ministry of Labour and the other ministries, along with the public prosecutors and judges, agreed to curtail the sphere of private law in favour of the state's right of intervention. This was facilitated by a totalitarian vision of the state, a new semantics of labour and new sources of law such as the 'common good', which were open to virtually any interpretation.[100] There was very little employees could do to counter this. On the contrary, in the absence of allies and bodies representing their interests, they faced a repressive response from the Nazi regime, were they to attempt to make their voice heard collectively.

In cooperation with the Reich Ministry of Labour, the labour trustees proved to be the key actors within this process of negotiation. It is true that their scope for action was circumscribed to a great extent by the ministry's policies, as part of the Nazi government. Nonetheless, they were able to exercise an influence on labour policy that can scarcely be overstated. They did so not just by expanding their powers and interpreting legal loopholes as they saw fit, but also by exploiting both their informational advantage over the ministry and their expertise. Their unilateral, unauthorized appropriation of sanctioning powers illustrates how the trustees' actions changed labour law, generating impulses to which the Reich Labour Ministry in particular, as the relevant authority, had to respond. The trustees thus had the means to enforce their political will. In all their actions, however, they were always bound to the ministry, which, in principle, had the final say, given its power to issue them with instructions.

Crucially, the Reich Labour Ministry not only constrained the trustees' scope for action but also enlarged it. Certainly, the Berlin authority was initially critical of certain trustees' tendency to go on the offensive by interpreting the AOG and the wage-setting ordinance in controversial ways. Yet ultimately the ministry supported them in this, taking crucial steps in two of its core fields of action. First, it tried to create a more solid legal foundation through legislation. Second, through interministerial negotiations and a wave of publications in the relevant legal journals, it sought to create a consensus concerning the trustees' sanctioning powers. Not only did the ministry's word carry greater weight than that of its subordinate authority, but the former had access to the necessary channels of communication with the other ministries. In this sense, the Reich Labour Ministry and the trustees stabilized one another. Despite the initially latent conflict between the two, they balanced out each other's functional deficiencies. Through their interpretation of the existing legal situation, the trustees circumvented the cumbersome legislative process on the Reich level. The Labour Ministry, meanwhile, made up for the trustees' lack of access to other Reich authorities, while also offsetting their lack of legislative powers. Their collaboration ultimately endowed the trustees with an instrument that they deployed in an attempt to forcefully suppress the tensions between the (initially still free) labour market, the wage freeze and the 'labour peace', and thus uphold their own and the ministry's legitimacy.

Sören Eden, first state examination in history and German at the Ludwig Maximilian University of Munich; student assistant (2010–2013) and research assistant (2013–2014) at the Institute of Contemporary History working on the project 'Hitler, Mein Kampf. Eine kritische Edition' ('Hitler, *Mein Kampf*. A Critical Edition'); doctoral student at Humboldt

University of Berlin since March 2014 and, with a study of the labour trustees, contributor (thanks to a scholarship) to the project being pursued by the Independent Commission of Historians Investigating the History of the Reich Ministry of Labour in the National Socialist Period.

Notes

1. The following account is based on the Ruling of the Lichterfelde District Court, re. Criminal Case against the Domestic Servant Wilfriede Rutschke, i.e. 15 April 1943, Landesarchiv (LArch) Berlin, A-Rep. 341-02, no. 17118.

2. T. Möbius, '"Deutsche Arbeit" als ideologisches Leitmotiv interner Unternehmenskommunikation. Das Beispiel Gutehoffnungshütte (GHH) 1925 bis 1933', in F. Axster and N. Lelle (eds), *"Deutsche Arbeit". Kritische Perspektiven auf ein ideologisches Selbstbild*, Göttingen: Wallstein Verlag: 2018, 175–208.

3. See *Die Ordnung der nationalen Arbeit. Kommentar zu dem Gesetz zur Ordnung der nationalen Arbeit und zu dem Gesetz zur Ordnung der Arbeit in öffentlichen Verwaltungen und Betrieben unter Berücksichtigung aller Durchführungsbestimmungen*, ed. W. Mansfeld and W. Pohl, 2nd ed., Berlin: Deutsches Druck- u. Verlags-Haus, 1934, 9 f.

4. M. Buggeln and M. Wildt, 'Arbeit im Nationalsozialismus (Einleitung)', in M. Buggeln and M. Wildt (eds), *Arbeit im Nationalsozialismus*, Munich: De Gruyter Oldenbourg, 2014, ix–xxxvii, here xv.

5. See, for example, 'Treuepflicht auf beiden Seiten', *Der Angriff*, 11 September 1936.

6. See the overview by J. Rückert, 'Vor § 611. Regelungsprobleme und Lösungen seit Rom im Überblick', in M. Schmoeckel, J. Rückert and R. Zimmermann (eds), *Historisch-kritischer Kommentar zum BGB*, vol. III: *Schuldrecht. Besonderer Teil*. 2 vols, §§ 433–853, series eds J. Rückert and F.L. Schäfer, Tübingen: Mohr Siebeck, 2013, vol. I, 700–822.

7. See E. Fraenkel, *Der Doppelstaat*, 3rd ed., Hamburg: Europäische Verlagsanstalt, 2012.

8. See T. Keiser, *Vertragszwang und Vertragsfreiheit im Recht der Arbeit von der Frühen Neuzeit bis in die Moderne*, Frankfurt am Main: Klostermann, 2013.

9. Friedrich Syrup, Reich Institution for Job Placement and Unemployment Insurance, to Reich Ministry of Labour, 19 July 1935, Bundesarchiv (BArch), R 3601/1852, fol. 76.

10. On wages, see R. Hachtmann, *Industriearbeit im 'Dritten Reich'. Untersuchungen zu den Lohn- und Arbeitsbedingungen in Deutschland 1933–1945*, Göttingen: Vandenhoeck & Ruprecht, 1989; T. Siegel, *Leistung und Lohn in der nationalsozialistischen 'Ordnung der Arbeit'*, Opladen: Westdeutscher Verlag, 1989.

11. The Nazi employment regime has been the subject of numerous studies, including A. Kranig, *Lockung und Zwang. Zur Arbeitsverfassung im Dritten Reich*, Stuttgart: Deutsche Verlags-Anstalt, 1983; T.W. Mason, *Sozialpolitik im Dritten Reich. Arbeiterklasse und Volksgemeinschaft*, Opladen: Westdeutscher Verlag, 1978; see also the more recent contribution by M. Becker, *Arbeitsvertrag und Arbeitsverhältnis während der Weimarer Republik und in der Zeit des Nationalsozialismus*, Frankfurt am Main: Klostermann, 2005.

12. See Werner Mansfeld, re. Career and Political Activities, 1947, Federal Commissioner for the Records of the State Security Service of the former German Democratic Republic (Bundesbeauftragter für die Unterlagen des Staatssicherheitsdienstes der ehemaligen DDR), MfS BV Halle, Ast 7473, fol. 13–55; Denazification Commission for Jurists (Entnazifizierungskommission für Juristen) (Department for Personnel and Administration of the Greater Berlin Municipal Authorities [Abteilung für Personal und Verwaltung beim Magistrat von Gross-Berlin]), re. Minutes of the Main Trial of 23 August 1949 in the matter of Werner Mansfeld, 23 August 1949, LArch Berlin, B-Rep. 031-01-02, no. 2198. I will be going into the genesis of the AOG in more depth in my dissertation; see T.W. Mason,

'Zur Entstehung des Gesetzes zur Ordnung der nationalen Arbeit vom 20. Januar 1934. Ein Versuch über das Verhältnis "archaischer" und "moderner" Momente in der neuesten deutschen Geschichte', in H. Mommsen, D. Petzina and B. Weisbrod (eds), *Industrielles System und politische Entwicklung in der Weimarer Republik*, Düsseldorf: Droste, 1977, 322–51.

13. 'Gesetz zur Ordnung der nationalen Arbeit vom 20.1.1934', *RGBl.* I 1934, 45–56.

14. R. Hachtmann, '"Volksgemeinschaftliche Dienstleister"? Anmerkungen zu Selbstverständnis und Funktion der Deutschen Arbeitsfront und der NS-Gemeinschaft "Kraft durch Freude"', in D. Schmiechen-Ackermann (ed.), *'Volksgemeinschaft'. Mythos, wirkungsmächtige soziale Verheissung oder soziale Realität im 'Dritten Reich'? Zwischenbilanz einer kontroversen Debatte*, Paderborn: Schöningh, 2012, 111–31, here 120. See also the chapter by Rüdiger Hachtmann in this volume.

15. Among other things, workers complained about obstacles to starting a family, the frequently disastrous living conditions, and, quite often, farmers' physically abusive behaviour, as well as the long working hours, the arduous nature of the work and the miserable pay. See F. Wiesemann, 'Arbeitskonflikte in der Landwirtschaft während der NS-Zeit in Bayern 1933–1938', *Vierteljahrshefte für Zeitgeschichte* 25(4) (1977), 573–90, esp. 577 f.; see also D. Münkel, *Nationalsozialistische Agrarpolitik und Bauernalltag*, Frankfurt am Main: Campus, 1996, 337–51; G. Corni and H. Gries, *Brot – Butter – Kanonen. Die Ernährungswirtschaft in Deutschland unter der Diktatur Hitlers*, Berlin: Akademie-Verlag, 1997, 280–98, 433–68.

16. See M. Buggeln, 'Unfreie Arbeit im Nationalsozialismus. Begrifflichkeiten und Vergleichsaspekte zu den Arbeitsbedingungen im Deutschen Reich und in den besetzten Gebieten', in Buggeln and Wildt, *Arbeit im Nationalsozialismus*, 231–52; M. Spoerer, *Zwangsarbeit unter dem Hakenkreuz. Ausländische Zivilarbeiter, Kriegsgefangene und Häftlinge im Deutschen Reich und im besetzten Europa 1939–1945*, Stuttgart: Deutsche Verlags-Anstalt, 2001.

17. Albert O. Hirschman himself, on whose early studies Buggeln and Spoerer draw methodologically, later called for a less sharp distinction; see A.O. Hirschman, 'Exit, Voice, and the Fate of the German Democratic Republic. An Essay in Conceptual History', *World Politics* 45(2) (1993), 173–202.

18. Reich Food Corporation to Reich Ministry of Food and Agriculture, 25 July 1935, BArch, R 3601/1852, fol. 129–32. Once the trustees gained the right to impose fines, they too became aware of this problem; see Reich Labour Trustee for Lower Saxony to Reich Ministry of Labour, re. Prosecution of Breaches of Contract and Conduct in Violation of the Employment Contract, 21 February 1940, NLA Hannover, Hann. 275, no. 182, fol. 38–39.

19. Friedrich Syrup, Reich Institution for Job Placement and Unemployment Insurance, to Reich Ministry of Labour, 19 July 1935, BArch, R 3601/1852, fol. 76.

20. 'Gesetz über die Treuhänder der Arbeit vom 19.5.1933', *RGBl.* I 1933, 285; and 'Gesetz zur Ordnung der nationalen Arbeit vom 20 January 1934', *RGBl.* I 1934, 45–56.

21. G. Dudenhöffer, *Der Treuhänder der Arbeit in seinem Einfluss auf die Wirtschaft*, Pirmasens: Neumann, 1936, 19.

22. See 'AOG § 19', *RGBl.* I 1934, 47.

23. 'Die Tagesfrage', *Rheinisch-Westfälische Zeitung*, 1 May 1935.

24. Borchardt, Supreme Auditing Office of the German Reich, to Supreme Auditing Office of the German Reich, 7 August 1939, BArch, R 2301/4830, fol. 262–65. The organizational structure of the trustees is one of the focal points of the dissertation on which I am currently working.

25. See, for example, M. Frese, *Betriebspolitik im 'Dritten Reich'. Deutsche Arbeitsfront, Unternehmer und Staatsbürokratie in der westdeutschen Grossindustrie 1933–1939*, Paderborn: Schöningh, 1991, 231; Hachtmann, *Industriearbeit im 'Dritten Reich'*, 116–21.

26. *Die Ordnung der nationalen Arbeit*, 8.

27. This, however, was due not only to the AOG itself, but also to the terror of the Nazi regime. In addition to the brutality meted out to trades unionists and members of the SPD and KPD, the Gestapo kept firms under surveillance.

28. Reich Ministry of Labour, re. Minutes of the Trustees' Meeting, 14 August 1935, BArch, R 3101/10296, fol. 23–44.

29. Excerpt from the Minutes of the Meeting of Reich Ministers on the Draft of a Law on the Appointment of a Reich Commissioner for Price Control, 5 November 1934, BArch, R 43 II/315a, fol. 31–32.

30. On the so-called 'November Syndrome' see Mason, *Sozialpolitik im Dritten Reich*, 15–41.

31. Minutes of the Top-Level Meeting on Pay Policy, 2 May 1935, BArch, R 43 II/541, fol. 87–90.

32. Johannes Krohn, Reich Ministry of Labour, to the Labour Trustees, 1 July 1935, Bayerisches Hauptstaatsarchiv, Stk 5364, 12038.

33. For detailed information on Werner Mansfeld, see Biographical Appendix.

34. For detailed information on Kurt Classen, see Biographical Appendix.

35. On the personnel of the Reich Ministry of Labour and the education of civil servants, see the chapters by Ulrike Schulz and Lisa-Maria Röhling in this volume.

36. L. Richter, *Treuhänder der Arbeit*, Munich: Heerschild, 1934, 18.

37. Ibid., 61.

38. Johannes Krohn, Reich Ministry of Labour, to Reich Ministry of Finance, 1 September 1937, BArch, R 2/18488, fol. 139–43.

39. Referring to organizations in general, Stefan Kühl terms this influence 'from below' 'underveillance' (*Unterwachung*); S. Kühl, *Organisationen. Eine sehr kurze Einführung*, Wiesbaden: Verlag für Sozialwissenschaften, 2011, 81.

40. Richter, *Treuhänder der Arbeit*, 58.

41. See Hachtmann, *Industriearbeit im 'Dritten Reich'*, 31.

42. Richter, *Treuhänder der Arbeit*, 58.

43. On the significance of networks under Nazi rule, see S. Greve, *Das 'System Sauckel'. Der Generalbevollmächtigte für den Arbeitseinsatz und die Arbeitskräftepolitik in der besetzten Ukraine 1942–1945*, Göttingen: Wallstein, 2019. See also S. Reichardt and W. Seibel, 'Radikalität und Stabilität. Herrschen und Verwalten im Nationalsozialismus', in W. Seibel and S. Reichardt (eds), *Der prekäre Staat. Herrschen und Verwalten im Nationalsozialismus*, Frankfurt am Main: Campus, 2011, 7–27.

44. Generally speaking, the everyday interpretation of such gaps is one of the key factors in gradual institutional change; see B. Rehder, 'Institutioneller Wandel und neue Governance im System der Arbeitsbeziehungen', in I. Dingeldey, A. Holtrup and G. Warsewa (eds), *Wandel der Governance der Erwerbsarbeit*, Wiesbaden: Springer VS, 2015, 23–44; see also W. Steinmetz, *Begegnungen vor Gericht. Eine Sozial- und Kulturgeschichte des englischen Arbeitsrechts (1850–1925)*, Munich: Oldenbourg, 2002, 21.

45. *Das Gesetz zur Ordnung der nationalen Arbeit*, with a commentary by H. Dersch, Berlin: Weidmann, 1934, 125.

46. On wages policy, see my forthcoming dissertation.

47. *RABl.* VI (1936), 131. Loyalty bonuses were monetary or in-kind benefits accruing to employees who had worked in a firm for a specified minimum period.

48. But this was a maximum of thirty-two Reichsmarks for male and twenty-five Reichsmarks for female employees; see 'Lohneinbehaltung gegen Bruch des Arbeitsvertrages', *Schlesische Zeitung*, 18 August 1936.

49. Hans Engel, Reich Ministry of Labour, to Reich Ministry of Food and Agriculture, 30 June 1936, BArch, R 3601/1852, fol. 221–24.

50. Despite the fact that they counted workers among their members; see Corni and Gries, *Brot – Butter – Kanonen*, 250.

51. Complaints were received from Baden, Bavaria, Kurmark, Silesia, Schleswig-Holstein, Thuringia and Westphalia; see the numerous reports in BArch, R 3601/1852.

52. On knowledge as a factor within administrative systems, see H. Marx, *Die Verwaltung*

des Ausnahmezustands. Wissensgenerierung und Arbeitskräftelenkung im Nationalsozialismus, Göttingen: Wallstein Verlag, 2019. See also M.C. Schneider, Wissensproduktion im Staat. Das königlich preussische statistische Bureau 1860–1914, Frankfurt am Main: Campus, 2013.

53. Hans Engel, Reich Ministry of Labour, to Reich Ministry of Food and Agriculture, 2 September 1935, BArch, R 3601/1852, fol. 166.

54. Measures Intended to Prevent Breach of Employment Contract in Agriculture, 17 March 1936, BArch, R 3601/1852, fol. 182–85.

55. The following quotes from 'Gegen Treuebruch von Gefolgschaftsmitgliedern', *Der Angriff*, 7 September 1935.

56. The fact that Daeschner's article made it into the files of the Reich Ministry of Food and Agriculture attests to its reception; BArch, R 3601/1852, fol. 160.

57. Reich Food Corporation to Reich Ministry of Food and Agriculture, 17 March 1936, BArch, R 3601/1852, fol. 182–85.

58. Social honour courts were introduced in 1934 and were intended to replace the labour courts. They too dealt with conflicts within firms, though only violations of so-called 'social honour'.

59. Ruling in the Honour Court Trial of the Milker K. A., 2 April 1936, BArch, R 3601/1852, fol. 223–24.

60. Hans Engel, Reich Ministry of Labour, to Reich Ministry of Food and Agriculture, 30 June 1936, BArch, R 3601/1852, fol. 221–24.

61. Reich Ministry of Labour to the Labour Trustees, 29 June 1936, BArch, R 3601/1852, fol. 227.

62. H. Lippert, *Der Treuhänder der Arbeit, seine Stellung und seine Aufgaben*, Erlangen: Döres, 1935, 27–31.

63. Hans Engel, Reich Ministry of Labour, to Reich Ministry of Food and Agriculture, 30 June 1936, BArch, R 3601/1852, fol. 221–24.

64. See the interim report by Grau, 'Die arbeitsrechtlichen Vorschriften im kommenden Strafrecht', *Deutsches Arbeitsrecht* 5 (1937), 65–72.

65. See *Das deutsche Führerlexikon*, Berlin: Stollberg, 1934, 435.

66. See 'Ernennung der Treuhänder der Arbeit', *Wolffs Telegraphisches Bureau*, 15 June 1933 (late-night edition).

67. Stefan Kühl has brought out the influence of organizations on their members' actions in light of the involvement of the Hamburg Police Battalion 101 in the Holocaust; see S. Kühl, *Ganz normale Organisationen. Zur Soziologie des Holocaust*, Berlin: Suhrkamp, 2014.

68. Schnuhr, 'Vertragsbruch in der Landwirtschaft wird bestraft', *Amtliche Mitteilungen des Treuhänders der Arbeit für das Wirtschaftsgebiet Schlesien* 2(26) (1936), 287.

69. 'Siebte Anordnung zur Durchführung des Vierjahresplanes über die Verhinderung der rechtswidrigen Lösung von Arbeitsverhältnissen', *RABl.* I (1937), 13.

70. Werner Mansfeld, Four-Year-Plan Office, to Neumann, Four-Year-Plan Office, 14 December 1936, BArch, R 3601/1852, fol. 295–98.

71. O. Kalckbrenner, 'Die allgemeinen Anordnungen der Reichstreuhänder der Arbeit auf Grund der Lohngestaltungsverordnung', *Deutsches Arbeitsrecht* 6 (1938), 305–8, quotation on 307.

72. E. Iannone, *Die Kodifizierung des Arbeitsvertragsrechts – ein Jahrhundertprojekt ohne Erfolgsaussicht? Eine Untersuchung vorangegangener Bemühungen um ein Arbeitsvertragsgesetz und Analyse möglicher Erfolgsaussichten des Reformprojekts*, Frankfurt am Main: Lang, 2009, 130–77; K. Linne, 'Das Scheitern des NS-Gesetzes über das Arbeitsverhältnis', *Kritische Justiz* 38 (2005), 260–75.

73. Ruhr Coal Mining District Group (Bezirksgruppe Steinkohlenbergbau Ruhr), re. Departure of Miners in the Ruhr Coal Mining Sector, Montanhistorisches Dokumentationszentrum, Bochum/Bergbau-Archiv, 13, 2225. See also H.-C. Seidel, *Der Ruhrbergbau im Zweiten Weltkrieg. Zechen – Bergarbeiter – Zwangsarbeiter*, Essen: Klartext, 2010, 95.

74. Business Plan of the Reich and Prussian Ministry of Labour, 1 March 1938, BArch, R 40/363.
75. Reich Ministry of Labour to Hermann Göring, Four-Year-Plan Office, re. Wage Freeze and Reich Labour Trustees, 21 January 1938, BArch, R 3901/20644, fol. 244.
76. 'Verordnung über die Lohngestaltung vom 25.6.1938', RGBl. I 1938, 691.
77. In practice, however, employers were virtually never punished, as it was difficult to prove incitement. On these two trustees' ordinances, see Kalckbrenner, 'Die allgemeinen Anordnungen'.
78. 'Anmerkungen zur Anordnung zur Verhinderung von Arbeitsvertragsbrüchen', Amtliche Mitteilungen des Treuhänders der Arbeit für das Wirtschaftsgebiet Thüringen 21 (1938).
79. Wolf, Reich Labour Trustee for Lower Saxony, to Reich Ministry of Labour, 24 July 1939, Niedersächsisches Landesarchiv (NLA) Hannover, Hann. 275, no. 182, fol. 11–12.
80. Wilhelm Kimmich, Reich Ministry of Labour, to all Reich Labour Trustees, re. Combating Breaches of Employment Contract, 15 June 1940, BArch, NS 6/456, fol. 8–10.
81. Hans Engel, Reich Ministry of Labour, to Reich Ministry of Food and Agriculture, 30 June 1936, BArch, R 3601/1852, fol. 221–24.
82. See, for example, Kalckbrenner, 'Die allgemeinen Anordnungen'.
83. Werner Mansfeld, Reich Ministry of Labour, to the Reich Labour Trustees, 27 July 1939, NLA Hannover, Hann. 275, no. 191, fol. 62.
84. Eypeltauer, Prosecutor General in Linz, to Reich Ministry of Justice, 12 March 1941, BArch, R 3001/22781, fol. 62.
85. Werner Mansfeld, Reich Ministry of Labour, to Reich Ministry of Justice, 9 July 1941, BArch, R 3001/22781, fol. 98–99.
86. Reich Labour Trustee for Lower Saxony to Wolf, Reich Labour Trustee for Lower Saxony (letter sent within the authority, sender's name unknown), 12 July 1939, NLA Hannover, Hann. 275, no. 182, fol. 14.
87. Leopold Gamsjäger to Reich Labour Trustee for Upper Danube, 3 March 1941, BArch, R 3001/22781, fol. 62.
88. Wolf, Reich Labour Trustee for Lower Saxony, to Reich Ministry of Labour, 24 July 1939, NLA Hannover, Hann. 275, no. 182, fol. 11–12.
89. Werner Mansfeld, Reich Ministry of Labour, to the Reich Labour Trustees, 21 September 1940, NLA Hannover, Hann. 275, no. 182, fol. 98–99.
90. 'Dritte Durchführungsbestimmungen zum Abschnitt III (Kriegslöhne) der Kriegswirtschaftsverordnung – Ordnungsstrafrecht der Reichstreuhänder der Arbeit – (Dritte KLDV) vom 2.12.1939', RGBl. I 1939, 2370–71.
91. Hillemann, Reich Labour Trustee for Lower Saxony, to Reich Ministry of Labour, re. Reich Labour Trustees' Authority to Impose Fines, 9 September 1940, NLA Hannover, Hann. 275, no. 191, fol. 67.
92. We have evidence of this from courts in Bavaria, Linz and Breslau, where the public prosecutors rejected petitions submitted by Reich labour trustees; see Hertle, Reich Labour Trustee for Bavaria, to Reich Ministry of Labour, 16 April 1941, BArch, R 3001/22781, fol. 89; and Reich Ministry of Justice, re. Note on Jurisdiction, 7 May 1941, BArch, R 3001/22781, fol. 72.
93. Draft of a Fourth Implementing Regulation on the Decree on the Restriction of Job Changes, 26 September 1941, BArch, R 3001/22781, fol. 19.
94. Reich Ministry of Justice, re. Note on Jurisdiction, 7 May 1941, BArch, R 3001/22781, fol. 72.
95. Reich Ministry of Justice, re. Note, 30 April 1941, BArch, R 3001/22781, fol. 71.
96. Werner Mansfeld, Reich Ministry of Labour, to the Reich Labour Trustees, 8 November 1941, NLA Hannover, Hann. 275, no. 183, fol. 12.
97. Draft of a Fourth Implementing Regulation on the Decree on the Restriction of Job Changes, 26 September 1941, BArch, R 3001/22781, fol. 19; see 'Vierte Durchführungsver-

ordnung zur Verordnung über die Beschränkung des Arbeitsplatzwechsels vom 28. Oktober 1941', *RGBl.* I 1941, 664.
98. Prosecutor General in Celle to Freisler, Reich Ministry of Justice, re. Criminal Prosecution of Refusal to Work, 3 June 1941, BArch, R 3001/22781, fol. 89.
99. 'Anordnung gegen Arbeitsvertragsbruch und Abwerbung sowie das Fordern unverhältnismässig hoher Arbeitsentgelte in der privaten Wirtschaft vom 20. Juli 1942', *RABl.* I (1942), 341.
100. See B. Rüthers, *Die unbegrenzte Auslegung. Zum Wandel der Privatrechtsordnung im Nationalsozialismus*, 7th ed., Tübingen: Mohr Siebeck, 2012; M. Stolleis, *Gemeinwohlformeln im nationalsozialistischen Recht*, Berlin: Schweitzer, 1974.

Bibliography

Becker, M. *Arbeitsvertrag und Arbeitsverhältnis während der Weimarer Republik und in der Zeit des Nationalsozialismus*. Frankfurt am Main: Klostermann, 2005.
Buggeln, M. 'Unfreie Arbeit im Nationalsozialismus. Begrifflichkeiten und Vergleichsaspekte zu den Arbeitsbedingungen im Deutschen Reich und in den besetzten Gebieten', in M. Buggeln and M. Wildt (eds), *Arbeit im Nationalsozialismus* (Munich: De Gruyter Oldenbourg, 2014), 231–52.
Buggeln, M., and M. Wildt (eds). *Arbeit im Nationalsozialismus*. Munich: De Gruyter Oldenbourg, 2014.
Corni, G., and H. Gries. *Brot – Butter – Kanonen. Die Ernährungswirtschaft in Deutschland unter der Diktatur Hitlers*. Berlin: Akademie-Verlag, 1997.
Das deutsche Führerlexikon. Berlin: Stollberg, 1934.
Dudenhöffer, G. *Der Treuhänder der Arbeit in seinem Einfluss auf die Wirtschaft*. Pirmasens: Neumann, 1936.
Felz, S. *Recht zwischen Wissenschaft und Politik. Die Rechts- und Staatswissenschaftliche Fakultät der Universität Münster 1902 bis 1952*. Münster: Aschendorff, 2016.
Fraenkel, E. *Der Doppelstaat*, retranslated from English by M. Schöps in collaboration with the author (1974), ed. Alexander von Brünneck, 3rd ed. Hamburg: Europäische Verlagsanstalt, 2012.
Fraenkel, E. *The Dual State. A Contribution to the Theory of Dictatorship*, translated from German by E.A. Shils in collaboration with E. Lowenstein and K. Knorr. New York: Oxford University Press, 1941, reprinted New York: Octagon Books, 1969.
Frese, M. *Betriebspolitik im 'Dritten Reich'. Deutsche Arbeitsfront, Unternehmer und Staatsbürokratie in der westdeutschen Grossindustrie 1933–1939*. Paderborn: Schöningh, 1991.
Das Gesetz zur Ordnung der nationalen Arbeit, with a commentary by H. Dersch. Berlin: Weidmann, 1934.
Grau. 'Die arbeitsrechtlichen Vorschriften im kommenden Strafrecht'. *Deutsches Arbeitsrecht* 5 (1937), 65–72.
Greve, S. *Das 'System Sauckel'. Der Generalbevollmächtigte für den Arbeitseinsatz und die Arbeitskräftepolitik in der besetzten Ukraine 1942–1945*. Göttingen: Wallstein, 2019.
Hachtmann, R. *Industriearbeit im 'Dritten Reich'. Untersuchungen zu den Lohn- und Arbeitsbedingungen in Deutschland 1933–1945*. Göttingen: Vandenhoeck & Ruprecht, 1989.
Hachtmann, R. '"Volksgemeinschaftliche Dienstleister"? Anmerkungen zu Selbstverständnis und Funktion der Deutschen Arbeitsfront und der NS-Gemeinschaft "Kraft durch Freude"', in D. Schmiechen-Ackermann (ed.), *'Volksgemeinschaft'. Mythos, wirkungsmächtige soziale Verheissung oder soziale Realität im 'Dritten Reich'? Zwischenbilanz einer kontroversen Debatte* (Paderborn: Schöningh, 2012), 111–31.

Hirschman, A.O. 'Exit, Voice, and the Fate of the German Democratic Republic. An Essay in Conceptual History'. *World Politics* 45(2) (1993), 173–202.

Iannone, E. *Die Kodifizierung des Arbeitsvertragsrechts – ein Jahrhundertprojekt ohne Erfolgsaussicht? Eine Untersuchung vorangegangener Bemühungen um ein Arbeitsvertragsgesetz und Analyse möglicher Erfolgsaussichten des Reformprojekts*. Frankfurt am Main: Lang, 2009.

Kalckbrenner, O. 'Die allgemeinen Anordnungen der Reichstreuhänder der Arbeit auf Grund der Lohngestaltungsverordnung'. *Deutsches Arbeitsrecht* 6 (1938), 305–8.

Keiser, T. *Vertragszwang und Vertragsfreiheit im Recht der Arbeit von der Frühen Neuzeit bis in die Moderne*. Frankfurt am Main: Klostermann, 2013.

Kranig, A. *Lockung und Zwang. Zur Arbeitsverfassung im Dritten Reich*. Stuttgart: Deutsche Verlags-Anstalt, 1983.

Kühl, S. *Ganz normale Organisationen. Zur Soziologie des Holocaust*. Berlin: Suhrkamp, 2014.

Kühl, S. *Organisationen. Eine sehr kurze Einführung*. Wiesbaden: Verlag für Sozialwissenschaften, 2011.

Linne, K. 'Das Scheitern des NS-Gesetzes über das Arbeitsverhältnis'. *Kritische Justiz* 38 (2005), 260–75.

Lippert, H. *Der Treuhänder der Arbeit, seine Stellung und seine Aufgaben*. Erlangen: Döres, 1935.

Marx, H. *Die Verwaltung des Ausnahmezustands. Wissensgenerierung und Arbeitskräftelenkung im Nationalsozialismus*. Göttingen: Wallstein Verlag, 2019.

Mason, T.W. *Sozialpolitik im Dritten Reich. Arbeiterklasse und Volksgemeinschaft*. Opladen: Westdeutscher Verlag, 1978.

Mason, T.W. 'Zur Entstehung des Gesetzes zur Ordnung der nationalen Arbeit vom 20. Januar 1934. Ein Versuch über das Verhältnis "archaischer" und "moderner" Momente in der neuesten deutschen Geschichte', in H. Mommsen, D. Petzina and B. Weisbrod (eds), *Industrielles System und politische Entwicklung in der Weimarer Republik* (Düsseldorf: Droste, 1977), 322–51.

Möbius, T. '"Deutsche Arbeit" als ideologisches Leitmotiv interner Unternehmenskommunikation. Das Beispiel Gutehoffnungshütte (GHH) 1925 bis 1933', in F. Axster and N. Lelle (eds), *"Deutsche Arbeit". Kritische Perspektiven auf ein ideologisches Selbstbild* (Göttingen: Wallstein Verlag: 2018), 175–208.

Münkel, D. *Nationalsozialistische Agrarpolitik und Bauernalltag*. Frankfurt am Main: Campus, 1996.

Die Ordnung der nationalen Arbeit. Kommentar zu dem Gesetz zur Ordnung der nationalen Arbeit und zu dem Gesetz zur Ordnung der Arbeit in öffentlichen Verwaltungen und Betrieben unter Berücksichtigung aller Durchführungsbestimmungen, ed. W. Mansfeld and W. Pohl, 2nd ed. Berlin: Deutsches Druck- u. Verlags-Haus, 1934.

Rehder, B. 'Institutioneller Wandel und neue Governance im System der Arbeitsbeziehungen', in I. Dingeldey, A. Holtrup and G. Warsewa (eds), *Wandel der Governance der Erwerbsarbeit* (Wiesbaden: Springer VS, 2015), 23–44.

Reichardt, S., and W. Seibel. 'Radikalität und Stabilität. Herrschen und Verwalten im Nationalsozialismus', in W. Seibel and S. Reichardt (eds), *Der prekäre Staat. Herrschen und Verwalten im Nationalsozialismus* (Frankfurt am Main: Campus, 2011), 7–27.

Richter, L. *Treuhänder der Arbeit*. Munich: Heerschild, 1934.

Rückert, J. 'Vor § 611. Regelungsprobleme und Lösungen seit Rom im Überblick', in M. Schmoeckel, J. Rückert and R. Zimmermann (eds), *Historisch-kritischer Kommentar zum BGB*, vol. III: *Schuldrecht. Besonderer Teil*. 2 vols., §§ 433–853, series eds J. Rückert and F.L. Schäfer (Tübingen: Mohr Siebeck, 2013), vol. I, 700–822.

Rüthers, B. *Die unbegrenzte Auslegung. Zum Wandel der Privatrechtsordnung im Nationalsozialismus*, 7th ed. Tübingen: Mohr Siebeck, 2012.

Schneider, M.C. *Wissensproduktion im Staat. Das königlich preussische statistische Bureau 1860–1914*. Frankfurt am Main: Campus, 2013.

Schnuhr. 'Vertragsbruch in der Landwirtschaft wird bestraft'. *Amtliche Mitteilungen des Treuhänders der Arbeit für das Wirtschaftsgebiet Schlesien* 2(26) (1936), 287.

Seidel, H.-C. *Der Ruhrbergbau im Zweiten Weltkrieg. Zechen – Bergarbeiter – Zwangsarbeiter*. Essen: Klartext, 2010.

Siegel, T. *Leistung und Lohn in der nationalsozialistischen 'Ordnung der Arbeit'*. Opladen: Westdeutscher Verlag, 1989.

Spoerer, M. *Zwangsarbeit unter dem Hakenkreuz. Ausländische Zivilarbeiter, Kriegsgefangene und Häftlinge im Deutschen Reich und im besetzten Europa 1939–1945*. Stuttgart: Deutsche Verlags-Anstalt, 2001.

Steinmetz, W. *Begegnungen vor Gericht. Eine Sozial- und Kulturgeschichte des englischen Arbeitsrechts (1850–1925)*. Munich: Oldenbourg, 2002.

Stolleis, M. *Gemeinwohlformeln im nationalsozialistischen Recht*. Berlin: Schweitzer, 1974.

Wiesemann, F. 'Arbeitskonflikte in der Landwirtschaft während der NS-Zeit in Bayern 1933–1938'. *Vierteljahrshefte für Zeitgeschichte* 25(4) (1977), 573–90.

Chapter 7

THE LABOUR ADMINISTRATION AND THE ORGANIZATION OF THE WAR ECONOMY

Henry Marx

We knew our enemies would not leave us in peace forever and, with the utmost diligence, we set about securing ourselves economically [with respect to manpower in the event of war]. Not everyone had to hasten to arms. Many had special orders to carry out. . . . But our organization provided us with the necessary overview. . . . Unfortunately, what the labour offices managed to pull off has not become sufficiently known to the general public.[1]

The labour offices played a key role in laying the ground for, and organizing, the war economy. They were responsible for procuring and distributing workers, of which the German economy suffered a severe lack. The more men the Wehrmacht called up over the course of the Second World War, of course, the fewer workers were available to work in the armaments factories. The labour offices sought to solve this problem by registering the available workers and placing them, against their will if necessary, in firms of importance to rearmament and the war.

To gain an understanding of how the labour offices set about this complex task, in the first part of this chapter I trace the development of the labour administration over several years before the war.[2] During this period, this key part of the administrative system gained a number of rights of intervention. This enabled it to take action to steer the labour market in line with the Nazi regime's priorities and channel skilled workers into economic sectors of relevance to rearmament. The labour administration underwent a profound functional shift as it was gradually transformed from a social insurance provider into an agency with governmental responsibilities. This ultimately impacted on its organizational form. Its headquarters, the Reich Institution for Job Placement and Unemployment Insurance, was disbanded in 1939 as an independent agency and incorporated into the Reich Ministry of Labour as the new Main Section V. This profound change in organizational structure represents an exception in the history of the German labour administration. Apart from a few years during the Second World War, it had always been organized as a subordinate and therefore rather independent agency of the Labour Ministry. So far, historians have not investigated in depth why the regime altered this structure in 1939.[3] In a general sense, the Reich Institution was integrated into the Reich Labour Ministry because the former's tasks had changed. Specifically, though, this reform was bound up with the communication technologies used by the labour administration and the regime's efforts to place the economy on a war footing.

Within the ministry, the Reich Institution morphed into Main Section V and took charge of the management of manpower during the war. Numerous agencies, offices and associations played a part in organizing the war economy, many of which have received more attention than the Reich Ministry of Labour within the extensive research literature.[4] Historians have increasingly explored the topic of labour from 1942 onwards, when Gauleiter and General Plenipotentiary for Labour Deployment Fritz Sauckel took over parts of the Labour Ministry, including Main Section V.[5] Yet the ministry already played a central role during the first three years of the war, within the complex mesh of actors involved in organizing the war economy. In the second part of this chapter, I describe how the Reich Ministry of Labour sought to carry out its duties, thus playing a significant role in the waging of war under the Third Reich.[6]

The Labour Administration before the War

The history of the German state's labour administration began in 1927, with the foundation of the Reich Institution for Job Placement and Unemployment Insurance as a self-governing public corporation (*Körperschaft des öffentlichen Rechts*) supervised by the Reich Labour Ministry. This body became the provider of the newly established unemployment insurance. The roughly eight hundred municipal employment agencies (*Arbeitsnachweise*), which were subordinate to this institution, were disbanded and converted into 361 public labour offices. Thirteen Land labour offices were positioned between the Reich Institution and the labour offices as intermediary authorities. Collectively, these bodies formed a public corporation that, in line with municipal tradition, was self-governing. It had the right to organize its personnel and draw up its own budget, and it administered its internal affairs independently. Supervisory boards at local, regional and

Reich level were made up, in three equal parts, of employers' associations, trades unions and representatives of the public sector. The Reich Institution was subject to the legal oversight of the Labour Ministry.[7] Through its Reich-wide and multipartite administrative structure, the state arrogated to itself an unprecedented degree of influence on the labour market. The linkage of unemployment benefits with job placement, meanwhile, found reflection in the labour offices' organizational structure. Those seeking benefits had to register with the labour office's Insurance Department (Versicherungsabteilung), which recorded their data and passed it on to the Department for Job Placement (Abteilung für Vermittlung). If a given labour office was unable to place an individual in work, he or she was referred to the nearest labour office through a procedure known as 'district equalization' (Bezirksausgleich).

The Nazi Seizure of Power

The Nazi seizure of power did not leave the Reich Institution untouched, with the political purges in particular hitting the labour administration hard. While an average of 2 per cent of the staff of other administrative organs were laid off, the figure was 13 per cent in the Reich Institution.[8] The new rulers also jettisoned the principle of self-administration (Selbstverwaltung), as the right of codetermination enjoyed by key labour market players and administrative personnel was known. Both of these developments changed the structure of the Reich Institution, with the end of codetermination strengthening the leadership level around President Friedrich Syrup,[9] who no longer had to coordinate with the organs of self-administration.[10]

In spite of these incursions, during the years of the Nazi dictatorship the labour administration underwent an unprecedented expansion in its powers and responsibilities. Hitler considered eliminating unemployment crucially important to maintaining his grip on power. Because they were responsible for organizing job creation measures, the labour offices thus grew in significance and, in contemporaries' perception, contributed greatly to reducing unemployment. Certainly, the real impact of the job creation measures on employment was negligible, but the regime's propaganda cast these efforts as a major advance in the 'labour battle' (Arbeitsschlacht).[11] This supposed success benefited the labour offices, both in terms of public perception and their own self-image. Previously, they had felt downgraded to the status of mere 'stamping kiosks' (Stempelbuden). Now, however, they were one of the key players responsible for the 'new' state's success.[12]

The fight against unemployment helped furnish the labour administration with rights of intervention that would have been unthinkable in the Weimar Republic. From 1934 onwards, it could issue prohibitions on in-migration for areas with particularly high unemployment. By revoking the free movement of workers, it could now decide who was permitted to move into the major cities of Berlin, Hamburg and Bremen, declaring them restricted zones.[13] The labour administration also had the power to remove workers formerly employed in agriculture from the cities and feed them back into the agricultural sector. Once again to support agriculture, which struggled to obtain enough workers even during periods of mass unemployment, the labour administration forced companies to dismiss younger workers below the age of twenty-five if a labour office provided them with an older, unemployed family man instead. These younger workers were placed in agricultural enterprises. However, due to the harsh working conditions and poor wages in agriculture, many broke the rules and soon quit their jobs, returning to the cities to look for alternative employment.[14]

Economic developments increased the labour administration's importance to the new regime. Boosted by the Nazis' policy of rearmament, the economy recovered, and unemployment figures plummeted. Key economic sectors such as the metal industry were soon facing a shortage of skilled workers. Germany's rearmament had already been threatened by two serious bottlenecks: a lack of both foreign currency and raw materials. Now there was a dearth of skilled workers as well. The regime responded by rationing the meagre supply of both raw materials and labour. To this end, it set up a new apparatus, the Four-Year Plan Authority, under the leadership of Hermann Göring. Within this structure, Friedrich Syrup, president of the Reich Institution, together with Ministerial Director Werner Mansfeld, head of Main Section III (Labour Law and Wages Policy) in the Reich Ministry of Labour, took charge of the 'Working Committee on Labour Deployment' (Geschäftsgruppe Arbeitseinsatz).[15] From this point forward, the labour administration was involved in the organization of the military build-up and preparations for war, with its responsibilities becoming ever less recognizable as those of a classic social insurance provider. The fight against unemployment receded into the background as well. The Reich Institution's primary goal now was to ensure the success of the military build-up through the management and control of workers.[16]

To help it accomplish these tasks, the labour administration was furnished with an array of instruments allowing it to intervene in the labour market. In 1935, legislation was passed introducing the labour book, which the labour offices issued to every employee liable for social insurance. This document contained information on the worker's education and professional skills as well as his or her current and previous employment. The book was deposited with the employer, while the relevant labour office recorded the information in a card index and thus had easy access to it.

All changes in the information entered into the labour books had to be reported to the labour office. The purpose of these books was to gain an overview of the labour market as a whole.[17] Gradually, the labour administration gained additional means of intervention. In the metals, construction and chemicals sectors, henceforth workers were prohibited from changing jobs or altering their employment contracts without its approval.[18] This helped prevent an outflow of skilled workers from these sectors. Ten years earlier, there had been no state-organized labour administration, yet now freedom of employment contract was abolished in key economic sectors, with the employment relationship being placed under the supervision of this administrative apparatus. As unemployment continued to fall, the shortage of skilled workers worsened, expanding into a general lack of labour. As a result, the labour administration's power grew as its authority was gradually extended to more and more economic sectors. From 1938, through the so-called compulsory labour order (*Dienstverpflichtung*), the labour administration could enlist employees, for a limited period of time and even against their will, to perform labour of 'importance to the state'.[19] When the war began, in every sector, employment contracts could only be dissolved without the labour office's approval if employer and employee submitted a request by mutual agreement. From 1942 onwards, all changes in the employment relationship required the labour office's consent.

Under the Nazis, the Reich Institution gained an unprecedented degree of power and importance. It worked determinedly to achieve the regime's

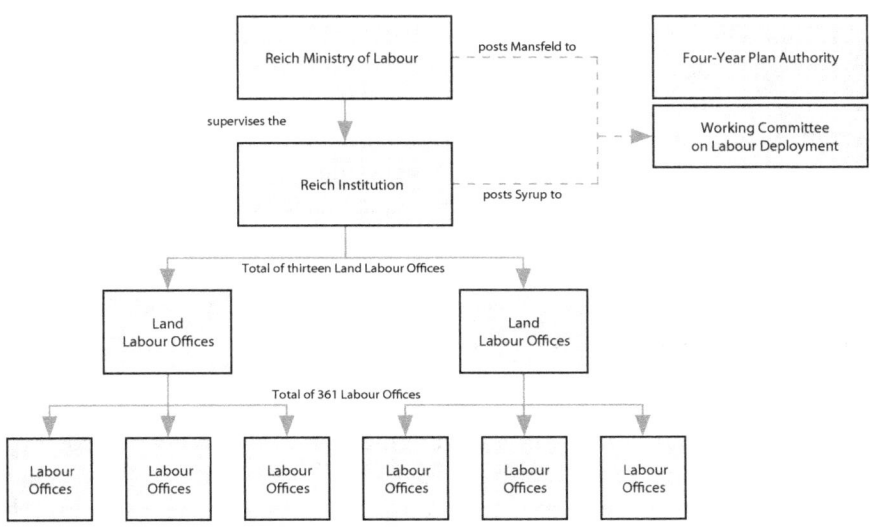

Figure 7.1. Structure of the labour administration and its integration into the Four-Year Plan Authority, 1936–1939

objectives and was also involved in persecuting its opponents.[20] Yet as the preparations for war reached their peak, the Reich Institution was unexpectedly dissolved and incorporated into the Reich Ministry of Labour. Volker Herrmann and Hans-Walter Schmuhl have described this process as the 'external coordination' (*äußere Gleichschaltung*) of the labour administration,[21] implying that the political leadership was seeking to enhance its control over it. There is, however, no evidence at all suggesting that the labour administration put up any form of resistance. There was thus no need for 'external coordination'. Why, then, was the Reich Institution dissolved in late 1938 and incorporated into the Labour Ministry?

The Incorporation of the Reich Institution into the Reich Ministry of Labour

Little is known about when the regime first began planning this administrative reform, the key ideas involved in this development, or how the process of incorporation proceeded in the detail. The process was sparked off by the aforementioned changes in the structure of the labour administration and its tasks in the pre-war years. Four aspects in particular played a crucial role here.

First, some of these changes placed a question mark over the organizational form typical of social insurance, namely the public corporation (*Körperschaft des öffentlichen Rechts*). One of the constituent elements of social insurance, self-administration, had already been abolished by 1933. With full employment from the mid 1930s onwards, meanwhile, the administration of unemployment benefit diminished in importance. When the war began, such benefits even lost their character as a form of insurance based on compulsory contributions, accrued entitlements and a legal right to benefits.[22] The less the structure and responsibilities of the Reich Institution resembled those of a social insurance provider, the less it seemed to merit the description of public corporation.

Second, developments in remuneration policy pointed to the need to shift away from the existing organizational form. In May 1938, the Reich Ministry of Labour proposed a change in the law that would make it easier to give the employees of the Reich Institution and its subordinate agencies the status of civil servant. This was justified on the basis that the staff of the labour administration were increasingly carrying out governmental tasks. Such tasks, it was asserted, could not be left to white-collar workers but must instead be entrusted to civil servants.[23] The Law on Job Placement and Unemployment Insurance (*Gesetz über Arbeitsvermittlung und Arbeitslosenversicherung*) provided only for the presidents and vice-presidents of the Reich Institution, along with the heads of the Land labour offices (Landesarbeitsämter), to become civil servants. Exceptions to this rule required special justification.[24] This regulation changed when the Reich Institution was incorporated into the Labour Ministry. In the labour offices as elsewhere, civil servants could now be appointed according to the provisions of the Reich budget and according to the system of established posts (Planstellen).[25]

The remuneration of President Friedrich Syrup also sparked discussion. The changes in the responsibilities of the Reich Institution prompted Hermann Göring, as commissioner for the Four-Year Plan, to push consistently for Syrup's promotion from 1936 onwards.[26] The Reich Finance Ministry opposed this demand on remuneration policy grounds, fearing that other agencies might press for salary increases for their top personnel too. It appears to have been the Finance Ministry that proposed the closer intermeshing of the Reich Institution and the Labour Ministry. The latter, meanwhile, was the author of a compromise proposal to appoint Syrup second state secretary in the ministry. The Finance Ministry agreed to this, as long as no one else was appointed to the post of president of the Reich Institution.

Third, the argument made within the remuneration policy debate, that the labour administration had taken on governmental tasks, was another important reason for the administrative reform. The Reich Institution's incorporation into the Four-Year Plan Authority, therefore, not only increased its importance, but also placed a question mark over its organizational form. 'In line with the transformation in its character from an insurance provider to an agency with governmental powers', as Ministerial Counsellor Martin Zschucke stated retrospectively in 1940, 'the Reich Institution for Job Placement and Unemployment Insurance was inevitably subsumed into the Reich Labour Ministry's sphere of action'.[27]

Fourth, in addition to these aspects there was another important factor in the Reich Institution's incorporation into the Labour Ministry, which appears to have been the specific trigger for this administrative reform. This comes to light if we turn our attention to the communicative channels of the labour administration and its tasks in the event of war. As mentioned earlier, from 1936 onwards the labour administration was entrusted with steering skilled workers into sectors of relevance to the military build-up. Concurrently, the Reich Institution was planning the labour policies necessary to convert a peacetime to a wartime economy the moment fighting broke out.[28] In contrast to the problems that bedevilled the first few months of the war in the summer of 1914, this time the regime was determined, as far as possible, to prevent unemployment from surging as peace gave way to war.[29] In close coordination with the Wehrmacht administration and the economic administration, the Reich Institution stipulated how many workers they could retain for the economy and how many could be called up by the Wehrmacht, which economic sectors were to be spared the outflow of workers and which would have to make do without a particularly large number of workers.[30] The Reich Institution's plans, however, went far beyond guideline figures and estimated requirements. With painstaking care, it created extensive archives providing details on millions of German workers: whether they were to be called up to fight or deferred from military service, what skills they possessed and how they could best serve the production of armaments.[31] The labour administration meticulously planned the immediate shift from a peacetime to wartime economy,[32] making ready to restructure its own organization within just a few days in order to trigger and control these tectonic shifts in the labour market. The main focus was to be on job placement. The relevant departments, like those concerned with the labour book, were to have their staff augmented on the local, regional and Reich level. All other departments were to reduce their activities and thus their staff in favour of job placement. Labour market statistics were to be simplified and compiled less often. In the Department of Unemployment Benefit (Abteilung Arbeitslosenunterstützung), henceforth a large proportion of its administrative activities, particularly those concerned with evaluating applicants' eligibility for benefits, ceased to apply.[33] The legal framework was, in fact, altered when the war began.[34] Access to unemployment benefits no longer depended on accrued entitlement but solely on medically determined fitness for work. All unemployed individuals fit for action could register at a labour office and receive financial support, delivering them into the clutches of the labour administration. Those unfit for military service were transferred to the welfare agencies, even if they had acquired entitlements to unemployment insurance.[35] The Reich Institution developed its plans for this rapid transition from 1937 onwards, and at regular intervals requested from its subordinate offices so-called 'mobilization calendars' (*Mob.-Kalender*), which had to be constantly updated. These set out the steps to be taken 'in case of mobilization' (*Mob.-Fall*), that is, in the event of war, on the first day and then during the subsequent days and weeks.[36]

These intensive preparations, however, appeared to have been a complete waste of effort when the Reich Postal Authority (Reichspost) pulled the rug from under the planned approach. When it came to the transition to war, the Reich Institution's priority was to facilitate the rapid issuance of its instructions. It was determined not just to hastily restructure its own apparatus but, above all, to exercise control over the workers it had on file, before they unilaterally changed jobs or before Nazi Party or governmental organs, contrary to the understandings reached, seized them for themselves. Only if its orders reached firms and their personnel in the first place could it manage them as it wished. Communication by post seemed too slow for this purpose, so the Reich Institution wanted its orders to be conveyed by telephone or teleprinter. As it turned out, however, the institution had no guaranteed access to the relevant systems.

The use of these two channels of communication by administrative organs and businesses grew rapidly over the course of the 1930s. From the mid 1930s onwards, the Reich Postal Service was unable to expand the telephone system to keep pace with the public administrative bodies' demand for more telephone lines in the offices and private homes of their leading personnel. The existing lines were increasingly overburdened. At peak times, users sometimes had to wait for several hours before the switchboards connected their calls. Several appeals issued by the Reich Postal Service to all branches of the public administration requesting that they cover a greater proportion of their communicative needs through the postal service and keep the use of the telex network and telephones to a minimum went unheeded.[37] The Reich Postal Service thus decided to establish a hierarchy of importance, prioritizing urgent 'state calls' (*Staatsgespräche*) and telegrams during busy periods. Other calls and telex messages had to wait. In the Telephone Regulations (*Fernsprechordnung*), the Reich Postal Service stipulated that only Reich authorities and the state agencies of the Länder were permitted to book urgent state calls and telegrams.[38] This regulation excluded the Reich Institution and the labour offices from these channels of rapid communication, because as public corporations they were considered neither Reich nor state agencies. In the first instance, however, the Reich Institution appears to have been unaware of this.

This problem first came to light as a result of a test run initiated by the Land Labour Office of Bavaria. In the early hours of 11 March 1938, the district labour offices simulated their response to the outbreak of war. Above all, they rehearsed summoning their own personnel, who were not present in their offices during the night, contacting military organs and putting their operations on a war footing. The Land Labour Office evaluated this practice run, its analysis highlighting the heavy use of the telephone system. In addition, a number of labour offices proposed that the homes of office heads be fitted with telephones and that every office acquire a sufficient supply of postage stamps. The president of the Land Labour Office, Karl Durst, forwarded the results of the analysis to the Reich Institution on 19 March.[39] In April, the Reich Institution drew its conclusions from the practice run and passed on the Bavarian report to the other Land labour offices.

The test had demonstrated the importance of telephones. It had, however, taken place at night, in other words during a period when the telephone lines were little used. The Reich Institution rightly doubted that communication would proceed so smoothly should war break out. The risk was that the telephone lines would quickly be overloaded. In May, the Reich Institution asked the Reich Postal Service whether the offices of the labour administration would be straightforwardly entitled to make state calls or whether they were required to submit a special request to do so. Evidently, the relevant staff at the Reich Institution did not consider the possibility that they might not be permitted to make state calls at all. The enquiry was concerned merely with the formalities involved in activating these channels of communication for the labour administration, not with whether it was entitled to use them.

This made the unambiguously negative reply from the Reich Postal Service in June all the more shocking.[40] It triggered a frenzy of activity on the part of the Reich Institution, which further intensified in the course of the 'period of tension' (*Spannungszeit*) during the Sudeten crisis of September. The institution argued against this decision in light of the war-related tasks entrusted to the labour administration, highlighted President Syrup's integration into the Four-Year Plan Authority and mobilized political support. The Reich Labour Ministry, Göring and the general plenipotentiary for the war economy (Generalbevollmächtigter für die Kriegswirtschaft) intervened by expressing their support for the Reich Institution to the Reich Postal Ministry (Reichspostministerium). This conflict dragged on throughout the summer and autumn of 1938, but the Reich Postal Ministry came out on top, its refusal in compliance with the letter of the law:

> The right to book urgent state calls is enjoyed only by the Reich authorities with respect to pure matters of state, while the delivery of state telegrams is the sole preserve of the Reich and state authorities. The Reich Institution for Job Placement and Unemployment Insurance, which is a public corporation, cannot, therefore, be granted the right to book urgent state calls or have state telegrams delivered. In accordance with this, I am regretfully unable to accept your proposals.[41]

It may seem surprising that in a dictatorship such as Nazi Germany, categories drawn from administrative law, relating to whether the Reich Institution was a Reich authority or a public corporation, retained such significance and could thwart the combined will of Hermann Göring and a number of supreme Reich authorities. At first sight, this adherence to the rules seems astonishing given the lawlessness of the Nazi terror. Yet despite the regime's violent despotism, in many respects the German Reich continued to be bound by rules. Legal scholar Ernst Fraenkel analysed this paradox in the 1930s.

> Those who kept their eyes open to the reality of the Hitler dictatorship's administrative and judicial practices were inevitably struck by the frivolous cyni-

cism with which state and party questioned the validity of the legal order when it came to many areas of life, while simultaneously applying its legal provisions with bureaucratic precision in situations they evaluated differently.[42]

In those fields that the regime assessed as political, the traditional legal order was suspended. In all others, the law continued to apply: outside the political sphere, legal certainty was an important commodity, even under Nazism. Otherwise, had state action been wholly unpredictable, the capitalist economic system, based on private property, could not have survived.[43] This applied in particular to the far-reaching and sensitive field of labour policy. It is thus no surprise that with respect to the means of communication to which the Reich Institution laid claim, it was the categories of administrative law that held sway.

The Reich Institution failed to gain access to these means, rendering its plans for the outbreak of war obsolete. The problem was, however, solved in a different, legally sound way. This involved a change in organizational form. The Reich Institution was incorporated into the Reich Ministry of Labour and, henceforth, constituted one of its main sections. This solved the Reich Institution's communication problem. 'As a result of [its] incorporation into the Reich Ministry of Labour, this issue has become irrelevant to the former Central Office of the RA [Reichsanstalt, that is, the Reich Institution].'[44] The same problem was also solved for the subordinate Land labour offices and labour offices, when they were elevated to the status of Reich authorities on 1 April 1939.[45]

There is no known historical evidence to tell us whether the staff of Main Section V obtained such privileged access to the telephone and telex systems in September 1939. But even if it did, the labour administration is likely to have faced technical communication problems. When the war broke out, the authorities' use of the telephone and telex systems increased further. The Postal Service continued to resist the overloading of its switchboards. Through internal missives, agency heads repeatedly warned their staff to moderate their use of the telephone.[46] What is clear, however, is that the chaos in the labour market so widely feared in the event of war did not eventuate. Certainly, Friedrich Syrup, now state secretary in the Reich Labour Ministry, never tired of warning of this risk, but evidently the measures taken by the labour administration had taken effect with sufficient rapidity.[47]

The Reich Ministry of Labour and the Organization of the War Economy

The new Main Section V in the Reich Labour Ministry had a legal and organizational form different from that of the Reich Institution. The institution's budget was now subsumed into that of the Labour Ministry. The system of contributions to unemployment insurance, however, continued to exist. These contributions were paid to the so-called Reich Fund for Labour Deployment (Reichsstock für den Arbeitseinsatz), though here they did not help finance insurance. The Reich Fund made this money available to the Reich as loans, helping fund its expenditure on armaments. The contribution rates were not lowered even when unemployment had diminished. As at the peak of unemployment, insurees continued to pay a contribution rate of 6.5 per cent, regardless of whether, according to the new criteria, they had a right to unemployment benefit or not. The insurance contributions, then, functioned like an indirect tax, with German workers being covertly used to finance the military build-up.

The changed situation with respect to administrative law chiefly affected the former Department I A (Abteilung I A) of the Reich Institution (Staffing and General Administration [Personalangelegenheiten und allgemeine Verwaltung]), which had been responsible for budgetary and personnel issues. All pecuniary aspects of the labour administration now had to be adapted to the Reich budget law. Much the same went for appointments and employment contracts, because members of staff were made Reich civil servants or had the status of (white-collar) employees of the Reich administration. These processes of adaptation required a great deal of work and long preoccupied Division Ia (Abteilung Ia) in Main Section I of the Labour Ministry (which was in charge of general administration, staffing, budgetary matters and economic affairs, among other things). Conversely, for those divisions not concerned with the areas of personnel and budget, the institution's incorporation into the ministry initially made little difference. Certainly, the former staff members of the Reich Institution were incorporated into the ministry, spatially as otherwise, and moved into new offices on Saarlandstrasse in the district of Berlin-Mitte. When it came to their administrative activities, by contrast, for the divisions of Job Placement (Arbeitsvermittlung), Occupational Guidance (Berufsberatung), Labour Book (Arbeitsbuch) and Insurance (Versicherung), among others, the process of incorporation resulted in very few changes. The relevant staff continued to carry out their duties in line with their well-established practices.[48]

It was only with the outbreak of war, nine months later, that the activities of the labour administration changed profoundly. As set out in its detailed plans, it now took charge of managing the labour market. It thus became part of the complex and frequently changing wickerwork of public and private entities organizing Germany's war economy.[49] During the first half of the war, this intricate mesh was geared towards the structures that had evolved under the aegis of the Four-Year Plan Authority. Following a process of state procurement, private firms produced goods of importance to the military build-up, the war and crucial areas of life. The German economy lacked important raw materials and other resources, so firms could not acquire them on the open market. Instead they were allocated by a variety of state authorities in varying combinations.[50] This mesh of public administrative organs had to decide on the right level of production, the required quantities of raw materials and the number of workers to be made available to firms. The Military Economy Department (Wehrwirtschaftsstab; known, from November 1939 onwards, as the War Economy and Armament Office [Wehrwirtschafts- und Rüstungsamt]) of the Wehrmacht Supreme Command (OKW) was in charge of all armaments firms serving the three parts of the Wehrmacht. This body specified the quantity and nature of production for these 'R firms' ('R-Betriebe'; *Rüstungsbetriebe*, namely, armaments firms). It also established a hierarchy of the importance and sequence of production with the help of so-called urgency levels (*Dringlichkeitsstufen*).[51] These levels provided the Wehrmacht administration with a tool that enabled it to repeatedly reorient arms production, adapting it to strategic requirements. Firms not producing for the armed forces, meanwhile, were supervised by the Reich Ministry of the Economy or the general plenipotentiary for the economy. Agricultural enterprises had to deal with the Reich Ministry of Food and Agriculture and the Reich Food Corporation as well.[52] These institutions produced guidelines on the quantities and urgency of goods for production. Taking these guidelines into consideration, other offices made decisions on the amount of resources to be allocated to firms tasked with production. It was then down to the labour administration to decide how many workers these firms ought to receive and to procure them.[53]

Every firm informed its supervisory labour office of its manpower needs. The labour offices worked on the assumption that businesses frequently asked for more than they needed in an attempt to secure as much as possible of the scarce resource of labour. As a result, the firms' requests for resources were not simply accepted at face value. The labour office amended them in light of experience, general guidelines and inspections. Each labour office shared the revised resource requests made by all firms in its district with the relevant Land labour office, which made further modifications. For its region, then, the Land labour office compiled data on manpower requirements according to sector and occupational groups, which it then passed on to the Reich Ministry of Labour. Information from every part of the Reich flowed into the ministry. Main Section V compared the demand for labour with the production guidelines, provided by the Wehrmacht administration or the Reich Ministry of the Economy, depending on jurisdiction. On the basis of these two parameters, the Main

Section calculated the quantity of labour to be redeployed and decided how many workers were to be supplied to produce goods of varying levels of urgency.[54] Because ever fewer workers were available, some had to be removed from certain firms and sent to work in others. The Main Section distributed them to the various Land labour office districts, factoring in their labour market situation, sites of production and the regional demand for labour. If demand within the area covered by a particular Land labour office could not be satisfied, Main Section V used the instrument of so-called 'Reich equalization' (*Reichsausgleich*) to organize the dispatch of workers from one part of the Reich to another. Meanwhile, through 'compulsory labour orders', workers were sent, sometimes against their will, to take up posts outside their home districts. Overall, then, the Reich Labour Ministry guided the distribution of manpower.[55] It was the ministry that formulated the guidelines governing the deployment of workers, with its subordinate organs implementing them and deciding which firms had to relinquish workers.

The Reich Labour Ministry thus played a highly concrete role in the organization of Germany's war economy. The ministry exercised executive responsibilities, implementing the decisions made by other organs by facilitating economic management based on the redeployment of manpower. The Labour Ministry and its subordinate organs of the labour administration, then, had a tremendous influence on the war economy. It was they who determined the number of workers to be allocated. The Reich Labour Ministry, however, did not decide which sectors workers were to be channelled into or what kind of production they would engage in.[56] Hence, despite its influence, the ministry remained an executive rather than a decision-making power. This is probably why historians have paid it little attention so far, though this does not reflect its significance to the war economy. It was other organs that determined the basic *orientation* of the economy or armaments production. What form, though, did the Labour Ministry's administrative practices take as it sought to *steer* the economy?

The armaments sector in particular underwent multiple shifts once the war began. Initially, the focus lay on the production of ammunition and explosives, an emphasis intensified as the German armed forces geared up for the campaign against France.[57] Following the victory over Poland, concurrent preparations got underway for operation 'Sea Lion', the planned invasion of Great Britain. Following the defeat of France, the Nazi regime then cut back on the production of ammunition and set three new priorities, namely equipping mobile troops (*schnelle Truppen*) and producing both submarines and Ju 88 fighter planes.[58] Further priority programmes emerged in the course of preparations for the invasion of the Soviet Union. Within these ever-changing and rival programmes, meanwhile, there were 'special levels' (*Sonderstufen*). The urgent nature of these forms of production gave them priority over all others. In this way, war production as a whole was gradually subdivided into special levels, urgency levels (*Dringlichkeitsstufen*) I, II and III, and a number of other categories. The labour offices were instructed always to focus their initial efforts on covering completely the manpower requirements of the special levels and of urgency level I. Only then were the less important production categories to be supplied.[59]

The frequent reorientation of arms production was due to the ever-changing strategic objectives of warfare. These shifts in production made the armaments firms' job more difficult: long-term business planning was scarcely possible under these circumstances.[60] This uncertainty was exacerbated by the lengthy period required by the state to agree fixed prices for arms with the armaments industry, prices that ideally guaranteed firms a profit and thus provided incentives to invest in their own production facilities.[61] A further impediment was the failure to consistently manage armaments targets. Even the three parts of the Wehrmacht, namely the army, air force and navy, did a poor job of coordinating their arms orders. The War Economy and Armament Office failed to compel them to adopt a unified approach, while many other agencies also sought to exercise an influence on economic policy. In a nutshell, the war economy was not managed consistently,[62] with the result that the special and urgency levels were constantly changed. Armaments firms thus lost contracts or had to begin producing different goods. Manpower and resources were repeatedly redistributed among firms, diminishing the efficiency of war production.

While these shortcomings in the organization of the war economy have often been described in the historical literature, what has generally been overlooked is how rapidly and efficiently the Reich Labour Ministry mastered the redistribution of manpower made necessary by shifts of priority in production. Within a few weeks of the adjustment of the special and urgency levels, the labour administration supplied the newly privileged forms of production with tens of thousands of workers. In November and December 1940 alone, for example, the labour offices respectively redeployed 820,386 and 592,496 (skilled and unskilled) workers through compulsory labour order, allocation and procurement. Around 140,000 of these workers were fed directly into the armaments industry.[63] To this end, the labour offices consciously sought to channel labour market fluctuations to the benefit of the prioritized firms, removed workers from less important businesses and shut down those of no importance to the war economy. These measures had a particularly deleterious effect on the consumer goods industry, which was constantly marginalized in favour of the armaments industry. Yet this enabled the labour administration to provide the war economy with the manpower it needed to produce arms.

The tools deployed by the labour administration to provide an overview of the labour market and channel manpower rapidly became established and proved their worth. A practical example demonstrates how effectively the administration's measures interlocked, while still being insufficient.

Reich Equalization – a Case Study in Manpower Management

In early 1940, during the 'mine war' (*Minenkrieg*) in the North Sea, one of the German navy's 'barrage test commands' (*Sperrversuchskommando*) in Kiel urgently sought three master clockmakers. These skilled workers had become much sought-after during the war as their skills were required for the production of detonators. The barrage test command turned to the Kiel Labour Office, but as it was unable to supply any clockmakers it passed the request on to its superior authority, the Nordmark Land Labour Office. Because no clockmakers were available in its region, its president, Heinrich Peckert, involved Main Section V of the Reich Labour Ministry, thus triggering the process known as 'Reich equalization'.[64] This was intended to ensure that posts were filled should no workers be available on the local or regional level.[65] Following the outbreak of war, the labour reserve vanished almost entirely, which meant that almost all the relevant workers were already employed. In this particular case, appropriate personnel were identified at the Gebrüder Thiel metal goods factory in Ruhla, Thuringia. In March, the Labour Ministry instructed the Central Germany Land Labour Office (Landesarbeitsamt Mitteldeutschland) to furnish the barrage test command with three clockmakers. On 10 April, the Eisenach Labour Office, which was responsible for the town of Ruhla, forwarded the three workers' application documents to the Kiel Labour Office. After consultation with the prospective employer, Kiel requested the three men from the Central Germany Land Labour Office, which in turn instructed the Eisenach Labour Office to subject them to 'compulsory labour orders'. As we saw earlier, this instrument made it possible to suspend the employment contract by order of the labour office and redeploy workers to any post in the Reich, even against their will.[66]

So far, the labour administration had functioned like a well-oiled machine, rapidly scouring the labour market and identifying the required manpower. The actual provision of these employees, however, was significantly more problematic. The firm involved resisted the removal of its workers. Its owner-manager, Reinhold Thiel, was an influential man in Thuringia, the long-standing president of the Central Thuringian Chamber of Commerce (Mittelthüringische Handelskammer) and, since 1936, had worked at the Office of the Nazi Party Gau Economic Adviser (Gauwirtschaftsberater).

In 1938, he was appointed Thuringian state counsellor (*Staatsrat*) and, from 1939, was a permanent member of the influential regional Armament Commission (Rüstungskommission). Through negotiations with the Eisenach Labour Office, Thiel managed to ensure that his firm would be deprived of just one of the three skilled workers.[67] On 20 April, the Eisenach Labour Office informed its counterpart in Kiel of this development and requested that it choose one of the three master clockmakers whose names it had been given. Four weeks later, the barrage command responded by requesting the son of the proprietor, Mr Thiel. The Thuringian side, however, informed their colleagues in Kiel that the Wehrmacht had called up Thiel's son, so he could no longer be subject to a compulsory labour order. The Kiel Labour Office responded immediately, requesting that the second named specialist be dispatched instead. Once again, the Eisenach office had to give a negative response as the man involved had been conscripted into labour service. When the northern Germans then requested the services of the final master clockmaker on 15 June, the business entrepreneur Thiel, the Wehrmacht's Armament Inspectorate (Rüstungsinspektion) and the Eisenach Labour Office agreed in a meeting at the Thuringian Armament Commission that it would be wrong to deprive the firm of its last remaining clockmaker, particularly as he had been tasked with producing goods of the crucial urgency level I.[68]

This incident caused a stir in the labour administration. The Nordmark Land Labour Office complained about its Thuringian counterpart to the ministry, while the Eisenach Labour Office accused its northern equivalent of taking too long to process the application documents.[69] Ministerial staff were surprised that President Peckert had not placed the naval dockyard on the list of establishments whose manpower needs were to be covered within ten days in case of the outbreak of war. They took the view that such prioritization would have long since furnished the barrage command with the requisite skilled workers.[70] Meanwhile, the Nordmark Land Labour Office had turned once again to Main Section V of the Reich Labour Ministry, re-emphasizing the importance of the barrage command, and managed to ensure that its request was passed on to the Saxony Land Labour Office (Landesarbeitsamt Sachsen). Also in mid June, the Saxons informed the Berlin headquarters that they had been unable to find any available master clockmakers in their region. In September, Peckert renewed the request, which the Reich Labour Ministry this time forwarded to the South West Germany Land Labour Office (Landesarbeitsamt Südwestdeutschland).[71] After a difficult search, in early October this office found a clockmaker in the district of Pforzheim. He, however, turned out to be Swiss, which meant that he could not be subjected to compulsory labour in the manner of a Reich German. The clockwork industry in the Black Forest region offered the only remaining hope of finding the relevant manpower. The Rottweil Labour Office thus assessed the potential for removing workers from the local industry. The office established that all master clockmakers were engaged in production of the crucially important special level I or urgency level I. The Gebrüder Junghans firm in Schramberg, however, would be best placed to let go of two clockmakers, as its staff included a particularly high proportion of skilled workers. Before the two employees could take up their work in Kiel, however, Junghans contacted the barrage command. As it turned out, both clockmakers were already working on the production of equipment for use in the 'mine war', which the barrage command involved had in fact ordered from Junghans in July. Removing these workers, then, was not in the navy's interest. The barrage command thus came to an agreement with the firm in Schramberg that the two clockmakers would not be transferred to Kiel until November, when the equipment involved had been completed.[72]

Ultimately, the labour administration failed to supply the navy with the workers it needed. But this was not the result of inefficiency or 'administrative chaos', of too many cooks spoiling the broth. It was impossible to provide master clockmakers because there were not enough of them. The case cited here demonstrates the difficulty of tracking down scarce skilled workers. It also shows that in this instance the labour administration was quite capable of finding the required specialists, even if they were already employed and not registered as looking for work. Every relevant employee it identified, however, was already working on production important to the war, impeding his dispatch to the barrage command in Kiel. In this example, the labour administration failed above all due to the severe lack of skilled workers within the German economy.

The dearth of such workers, in this case as in others, rendered the labour administration's efforts null and void. Alongside the shortage of raw materials and foreign currency, it was in fact the key economic problem afflicting the German Reich. The war stripped the labour market of millions of fit-for-work men, further shrinking the pool of labour from 1939 onwards. While the partial demobilization of certain Wehrmacht troops, upon completion of the campaigns against Poland and France, promised to provide a degree of relief, the situation remained strained. In late summer 1940, the Reich Ministry of Labour felt compelled to dampen expectations in business circles, following the victory over France, that the manpower problem had been solved and that now labour would increasingly be made available to disadvantaged sectors such as the consumer goods industry. The armaments industry continued to report labour shortages, which were exacerbated by preparations for the invasion of the Soviet Union.[73]

The Reich regime could have mitigated this problem, had its key actors resolved to tap the labour potential of larger numbers of German women. Yet the female employment rate was already relatively high in Germany compared with the United States and United Kingdom. Attempts to mobilize female labour were less successful than hoped.[74] Certain elements within the regime also had ideological reservations about stepping up the deployment of women,[75] so Polish and French prisoners of war and forced labourers (*Zivilarbeiter*, literally 'civilian workers') plugged the gaps instead. However, the SS and parts of the Nazi Party in particular were also chary of deploying a greater number of foreigners as forced labourers. Their concerns, of course, were based not on the coercive nature of such labour, but on racist resistance to the presence of 'aliens' (those labelled as *fremdvölkisch*) within the Reich, whom they viewed as a danger to the German population.[76] The regime put its efforts to resolve the labour problem on hold, believing Germany would quickly defeat the Soviet Union. As leading figures in the regime imagined, this victory would remedy the lack of raw materials and other resources in one fell swoop. Due to this certainty of victory, Soviet prisoners of war were not used as forced labourers. In the Nazis' racist worldview, there was no place for Soviet citizens even as forced labourers. By the end of 1941, the Wehrmacht had allowed two of the three million Soviet prisoners of war to starve to death in its detention camps.[77]

The situation changed abruptly with Germany's defeat at the gates of Moscow in December 1941. This forced the German Reich to substitute its 'lightning war' (Blitzkrieg) strategy with a lengthy war of attrition, a shift that required a substantial increase both in war production and conscription – two imperatives that were scarcely reconcilable. The mounting losses suffered by the Wehrmacht exacerbated these problems. In an attempt to satisfy the war economy's new manpower needs, the German leadership now decided to massively expand the labour deployment of foreigners after all. Often with extreme brutality, the labour administration deported millions of civilians from the occupied areas of Europe to perform forced labour in the Reich.[78]

These strategic decisions went hand in hand with the comprehensive reorganization of the war economy. On 8 February 1942, Armaments and Ammunitions Minister Fritz Todt was killed in an accident. The resulting vacancy set in motion a process of restructuring that made Albert Speer Todt's successor and, consequently, the new kingpin of the war economy. In parallel, the regime revamped its labour policy. The office of general plenipotentiary for labour deployment (GBA) was created, with Thuringian Gauleiter Fritz Sauckel being appointed to the post in March 1942. Sauckel put together a small team of individuals with the necessary expertise and political experience. Important parts of the Reich Labour Ministry were made subordinate to this new office, namely Main Section III (Wages) and the aforementioned Main Section V, along with its subordinate agencies. The key innovation was that the GBA, unlike the Reich Labour Ministry, was responsible not just for the German Reich, but for the entire area under German control, including the occupied territories. Previously, the Labour Ministry could make good on its claim to be in charge of social and labour policy in the occupied territories only to a very limited extent. The authority of the Reich organs ended at its borders, while different, sometimes newly established authorities took charge in the occupied territories. This arrangement reinforced Hitler's power, because as Führer and Reich chancellor, he alone held authority over the entire area under German control.[79] In 1942, then, responsibility for German labour policy passed from Reich Labour Minister Franz Seldte to Gauleiter and General Plenipotentiary for Labour Deployment Fritz Sauckel.

Conclusion

In Nazi Germany, the labour administration performed a different function than originally intended when it was established in the Weimar Republic. Its responsibilities changed, shifting from job placement to job creation to the state management of the labour market. To this end, it was granted a range of rights of intervention. Freedom of movement was gradually constrained, and the labour administration ultimately gained control over all workers. The goal here was to facilitate the orderly distribution of the palpably and increasingly scarce manpower to the most important firms in the industrial and agricultural sectors. The large-scale conscription of fit-for-work men into the Wehrmacht seriously impeded this task. Particularly in the second half of the war, therefore, the recruitment of labour became more and more important. During this period, labour administration staff were responsible for the deployment of millions of foreign forced labourers to bolster the German war economy.

Through the systematic procurement and distribution of manpower, the labour administration mitigated one of the key economic problems afflicting the German Reich. It made a major contribution to keeping the war economy up and running and thus to the stability of the regime. The labour administration acted in an efficient and instrumentally rational manner, but chiefly due to the gross labour shortage it was unable to supply firms with enough workers. Shedding light on its administrative conduct is crucial to understanding the German war economy. As the present chapter has sought to do, such an analysis must examine this organization's communicative channels and the constellations of actors within which it proceeded, in addition to its administrative instruments.[80] All three aspects are vital to understanding the labour administration and its administrative action.

Henry Marx, Dr. des., study of history, Romance language and literature and education at Humboldt University of Berlin and Complutense University of Madrid; doctoral student at Humboldt University of Berlin since March 2014 and contributor (thanks to a scholarship) to the project being pursued by the Independent Commission of Historians Investigating the History of the Reich Ministry of Labour in the National Socialist Period, with a study of the history of the German labour administration, 1927–1945. Publications (selection): 'Arbeitsverwaltung im Nationalsozialismus: Disziplinierung und Gewalt', in Stiftung Topografie des Terrors (ed.), *Das Reichsarbeitsministerium 1933–1945. Beamte im Dienst des Nationalsozialismus* (Stiftung Topographie des Terrors, 2019), 278–91; 'Ganz normale Verwaltungen? Methodische Überlegungen zum Verhältnis von Individuum und Organisation am Beispiel des Reichsarbeitsministeriums 1919–1945', with Sören Eden and Ulrike Schulz, *Vierteljahrshefte für Zeitgeschichte* 66(3) (2018), 487–520; 'The German Labour Administration in the "Protectorate Bohemia and Moravia"', in J. Rákosník and R. Šustrová (eds), *War Employment and Social Policies in the Protectorate Bohemia and Moravia* (Univerzita Karlova, 2018), 34–54.

Notes

1. Bernburg Labour Office, re. Record of the Office Roll-Call and Staff Meeting of 23 March 1944, 24 March 1944, Landeshauptarchiv Sachsen-Anhalt (LHASA), DE, Z 140, 2854, fol. 43–46, here fol. 44.

2. In what follows, I use the term 'labour administration' to refer collectively to the Reich Institution for Job Placement and Unemployment Insurance or, as the case may be, Main Section V of the Reich Ministry of Labour and its subordinate Land labour offices and labour offices.

3. The research literature furnishes us with no satisfactory answer to this question. See V. Herrmann, *Vom Arbeitsmarkt zum Arbeitseinsatz. Zur Geschichte der Reichsanstalt für Arbeitslosenvermittlung und Arbeitslosenversicherung 1929–1939*, Frankfurt am Main: Lang, 1993; H.-W. Schmuhl, *Arbeitsmarktpolitik und Arbeitsverwaltung in Deutschland 1871–2002. Zwischen Fürsorge, Hoheit und Markt*, Nuremberg: Institut für Arbeitsmarkt- und Berufsforschung, 2003; D.G. Maier, *Anfänge und Brüche der Arbeitsverwaltung bis 1952. Zugleich ein kaum bekanntes Kapitel der deutsch-jüdischen Geschichte*, Brühl: Fachhochschule des Bundes für Öffentliche Verwaltung, 2004; H. Kahrs, 'Die ordnende Hand der Arbeitsämter. Zur deutschen Arbeitsverwaltung 1933–1939', in G. Aly and W. Gruner (eds), *Arbeitsmarkt und Sondererlass. Menschenverwertung, Rassenpolitik und Arbeitsamt*, Frankfurt am Main: Mabuse, 2009, 9–61.

4. See, for example, A. Tooze, *The Wages of Destruction. The Making and Breaking of the Nazi Economy*, London: Penguin, 2007; L. Herbst, *Der Totale Krieg und die Ordnung*

der Wirtschaft. Die Kriegswirtschaft im Spannungsfeld von Politik, Ideologie und Propaganda 1939–1945, Stuttgart: Deutsche Verlags-Anstalt, 1982; U. Herbert, Hitler's Foreign Workers. Enforced Foreign Labor in Germany under the Third Reich, trans. W. Templer, Cambridge: Cambridge University Press, 1997; M.-L. Recker, Nationalsozialistische Sozialpolitik im Zweiten Weltkrieg, Munich: Oldenbourg, 1985; R.-D. Müller, 'Die Mobilisierung der deutschen Wirtschaft für Hitlers Kriegsführung', in B.R. Kroener, R.-D. Müller and H. Umbreit (eds), Das Deutsche Reich und der Zweite Weltkrieg, vol. 5: Organisation und Mobilisierung des Deutschen Machtbereichs, part-volume 1: Kriegsverwaltung, Wirtschaft und personelle Ressourcen 1939–1941, Stuttgart: Deutsche Verlags-Anstalt, 1988, 349–691; D. Eichholtz, Geschichte der deutschen Kriegswirtschaft 1939–1945, Munich: Saur, 2003; J. Scherner, Die Logik der Industriepolitik im Dritten Reich, Stuttgart: Steiner, 2008.

5. See the chapter by Swantje Greve in this volume.

6. This chapter presents some initial findings of my dissertation project, which encompasses the foundation of the Reich Institution in 1927 and the development of the labour administration until the end of the Second World War in 1945.

7. F. Schröder, Die Reichsanstalt für Arbeitsvermittlung und Arbeitslosenversicherung. Ihr Aufbau und ihre Aufgaben, Berlin: Zentralverband der Angestellten, [1930], 24–48.

8. D.P. Silverman, 'Nazification of the German Bureaucracy Reconsidered: A Case Study', The Journal of Modern History 60(3) (1988), 496–539; Schmuhl, Arbeitsmarktpolitik, 224–27.

9. For detailed information on Friedrich Syrup, see Biographical Appendix.

10. Kahrs, 'Die ordnende Hand', 17 f.

11. See Tooze, Wages of Destruction, 62–66. On these measures' impact and propagandistic staging, see D. Humann, 'Arbeitsschlacht'. Arbeitsbeschaffung und Propaganda in der NS-Zeit 1933–1939, Göttingen: Wallstein, 2011; K.K. Patel, 'Soldaten der Arbeit'. Arbeitsdienste in Deutschland und den USA, 1933–1945, Göttingen: Vandenhoeck & Ruprecht, 2003.

12. Bernburg Labour Office, re. Record of the Office Roll-Call and Staff Meeting of 23 March 1944, 24 March 1944, LHASA, DE, Z 140, 2854, fol. 43–46.

13. 'Gesetz zur Regelung des Arbeitseinsatzes vom 1. Mai 1934', RGBl. I, 381; 'Verordnung über die Verteilung von Arbeitskräften vom 10. August 1934', RGBl. I, 786.

14. 'Jahreslagebericht 1938 des Sicherheitshauptamts', in H. Boberach (ed.), Meldungen aus dem Reich. Die geheimen Lageberichte des Sicherheitsdienstes der SS, vol. 2, Munich: Deutscher Taschenbuch Verlag, 1968, 200. My thanks to Karl Christian Führer for making me aware of this.

15. D. Petzina, Autarkiepolitik im Dritten Reich. Der nationalsozialistische Vierjahresplan, Stuttgart: Deutsche Verlags-Anstalt, 1968, 58–61.

16. Kahrs, 'Die ordnende Hand', 23.

17. Ibid.; G. Aly and K.-H. Roth, Die restlose Erfassung. Volkszählen, Identifizieren, Aussondern im Nationalsozialismus, Frankfurt am Main: Fischer, 2000, 55.

18. Maier, Anfänge und Brüche, 106; W. Sommer (ed.), Die nationalsozialistische Arbeitseinsatz-Gesetzgebung, Berlin: Elsner, 1938.

19. 'Verordnung zur Sicherstellung des Kräftebedarfs für Aufgaben von besonderer staatspolitischer Bedeutung vom 22. Juni 1938', RGBl. I 1938, 652.

20. W. Ayass, 'Asoziale' im Nationalsozialismus, Stuttgart: Klett-Cotta, 1995, 66, 74, 82, 91, 109, 141; D.G. Maier, Arbeitseinsatz und Deportation. Die Mitwirkung der Arbeitsverwaltung bei der nationalsozialistischen Judenverfolgung in den Jahren 1938–1945, Berlin: Ed. Hentrich, 1994.

21. Herrmann, Vom Arbeitsmarkt, 206; Schmuhl, Arbeitsmarktpolitik, 230.

22. See Hermann, Vom Arbeitsmarkt, 294, esp. fn. 34.

23. Reich Ministry of Labour, re. Draft of a Law Intended to Change the Law on Job Placement and Unemployment Insurance (AVAVG), 14 May 1938, Bundesarchiv (BArch), R 43 II/1161b, fol. 13–15.

24. 'AVAVG vom 16. Juli 1927, §§ 34 und 35', RGBl. I 1927, 187–218, here 191.

25. *Verwaltungs-Jahrbuch für die Beamten und Angestellten der Arbeitseinsatzverwaltung 1939/40*, vol. I, Berlin: Elsner, 1939, 37.

26. Dr Johannes Krohn, Reich Ministry of Labour, to Hans Heinrich Lammers, Reich Chancellery, Copy to the Presidential Chancellery of the Führer and Reich Chancellor, re. Draft of the Decree to be Issued by the Führer and Reich Chancellor concerning the Reich Institution for Job Placement and Unemployment Insurance, 20 December 1938, BArch, R 43 II/1161b, fol. 16–17. The following section is based on this source. It also appears in Herrmann, *Vom Arbeitsmarkt*. Herrmann cites this as evidence that the decree, which announced the Reich Institution's incorporation into the ministry, was drawn up in the latter; ibid., 206.

27. M. Zschucke, *Das Reichsarbeitsministerium*, Berlin: Junker und Dünnhaupt, 1940, 39. Friedrich Syrup was simultaneously appointed second state secretary in the Reich Ministry of Labour.

28. Reich Institution for Job Placement and Unemployment Insurance, re. Mobilization Calendar for the Reich Institution for Job Placement and Unemployment Insurance. Mobilization Year 1938/39, BArch, R 3901/20130, fol. 13–21.

29. Schmuhl, *Arbeitsmarktpolitik*, 68.

30. Decree issued by the President of the Reich Institution, 20 July 1937, re: Preparations for the Mobilization of the Personnel of Armaments Firms; Exemption from Military Service, 9 August 1937, Landesarchiv Berlin, A Rep. 242, no. 13, fol. 1.

31. The Labour Book Index (Arbeitsbuchkartei) played a very important role here, but was not the only informational archive on which the labour administration drew. Knowledge played a key role in the labour administration's activities. The question of how the administration generated, stored and processed the required knowledge, and made it available to various offices within and beyond its own structures, is a key theme of my dissertation project; see H. Marx, *Die Verwaltung des Ausnahmezustands. Wissensgenerierung und Arbeitskräftelenkung im Nationalsozialismus*, Göttingen: Wallstein, 2019.

32. The older literature posits that the Nazi regime had failed to mobilize the German economy sufficiently in the first few years of its existence in order to spare the people from social hardship. During the first half of the war, it was asserted, economic conditions in Germany amounted to a 'peace-time economy' in wartime. Alan Milward was the first prominent scholar to articulate this thesis. See A.S. Milward, *The German Economy at War*. London: Athlone Press, 1965, 8f. This notion long dominated research on the economic history of the Nazi era; see, for example, Recker, *Nationalsozialistische Sozialpolitik*, 14. Richard Overy, who had also previously referred to a peace economy, revised this conception in the late 1980s and demonstrated that the roots of the idea of negligible economic demobilization lay in a misinterpretation disseminated by the United States Bombing Survey and Rolf Wagenführ of the Reich Statistical Office; see R.J. Overy, '"Blitzkriegswirtschaft"? Finanzpolitik, Lebensstandard und Arbeitseinsatz in Deutschland 1939–1942', *Vierteljahrshefte für Zeitgeschichte* 36(3) (1988), 379–436, here 379. More than anyone else, Adam Tooze has argued passionately against the notion of a 'Blitzkrieg economy', to cite another term applied to the supposed lack of mobilization in light of social policy imperatives, demonstrating that even before the war the regime had done a great deal to gear the German economy towards its military build-up; see Tooze, *Wages of Destruction*.

33. Reich Institution for Job Placement and Unemployment Insurance to Land Labour Offices, including the Nuremberg Branch and the Austria Branch, re. Mobilization Calendar, August 1938, BArch, R 3901/20130, fol. 136–37.

34. 'Verordnung zur Änderung von Vorschriften über den Arbeitseinsatz und Arbeitslosenhilfe vom 1. September 1939', *RGBl.* I, 1662; 'Verordnung über Arbeitslosenhilfe vom 5. September 1939', *RGBl.* I, 1674.

35. This regulation completed a process that had begun in the mid 1930s and that linked benefits to the capacity for work. See Kahrs, 'Die ordnende Hand', 35–38.

36. See the various letters between the Reich Institution and a number of Land labour offices and labour offices, BArch, R 3901/20130–32. All companies and administrative organs important to life, the war and the military build-up had to draw up such mobilization calendars in order to prepare for potential mobilization. However, by May 1939 only around 60 per cent of companies had done so. Müller, 'Die Mobilisierung', 359.

37. Höpfner, Reich Postal Ministry, to all Reich Ministries and the Reich Chancellery, re. Urgent State Calls, 5 April 1935, BArch, R 3901/11983, n.p.

38. Reich Postal Directorate (Reichspostdirektion) Berlin to Reich Institution for Job Placement and Unemployment Insurance, 18 June 1938, BArch, R 3901/20130, fol. 168; Höpfner, Reich Postal Ministry, to all Reich Ministries and the Reich Chancellery, re. Urgent State Calls, 5 April 1935, BArch, R 3901/11983, n.p.

39. Karl Durst, Bavaria Land Labour Office, to Reich Institution for Job Placement and Unemployment Insurance, 19 March 1938, BArch, R 3901/20132, fol. 109–12. This test run took place 'in connection with the political events in Austria', that is, the so-called 'Anschluss'.

40. Note, Reich Institution for Job Placement and Unemployment Insurance, 25 November 1938, BArch, R 3901/20130, fol. 180–81.

41. See Rackow, Reich Postal Ministry, to Operations Staff General Plenipotentiary for the Economy (Führungsstab Generalbevollmächtigter für die Wirtschaft [GBW]), for the attention of Ministerial Director Sarnow, 12 October 1938, BArch, R 3901/20130, fol. 178.

42. Ernst Fraenkel, *Gesammelte Schriften*, vol. 2, 41, quoted in H. Buchstein and G. Göhler, 'Ernst Fraenkel (1898–1975)', in W. Bleek and H.J. Lietzmann (eds), *Klassiker der Politikwissenschaft. Von Aristoteles bis David Easton*, Munich: Beck, 2005, 151–64, here 156 f.; A. von Brünneck, 'Ernst Fraenkels Urdoppelstaat von 1938 und der Doppelstaat von 1941/1974', in H. Buchstein and G. Göhler (eds), *Vom Sozialismus zum Pluralismus. Beiträge und Leben Ernst Fraenkels*, Baden-Baden: Nomos: 2000, 29–42, here 30.

43. Fraenkel sought to capture this simultaneous upholding and disregarding of the legal order through the concept of the 'dual state', arguing that Nazi rule consisted of two legal spheres, each of which corresponded to a specific type of state. Within the realm of the 'normative state', the law continued to apply. In Nazi Germany, however, the persistence of the traditional legal system came under threat the moment it touched on political matters. 'In the political sector of the Third Reich there is neither objective nor subjective law, no legal guarantees, no universally valid procedural rules or provisions on jurisdiction – in short, there is no administrative law determining the obligations and rights of those involved. In this political sector, norms are absent, while [government] measures hold sway. Hence the term "prerogative state" [*Massnahmenstaat*, literally, "state of measures"].' E. Fraenkel, *Der Doppelstaat*, retranslated from the English by M. Schöps in collaboration with the author (1974), ed. A. von Brünneck, 3rd ed., Hamburg: Europäische Verlagsanstalt, 2012, 55–58, 113 f., 120, quotation 55. On the significance of legal certainty, even under Nazism, see ibid., 124, 126, 142 f., 177. On Ernst Fraenkel, see also Alexander Nützenadel's introduction to the present volume.

44. Note, Reich Ministry of Labour, Main Section V (Labour Deployment), 19 February 1939, BArch, R 3901/20130, fol. 184. This simultaneously spared the labour administration the need to pay postal charges, resolving another long-standing conflict with the Reich Postal Service.

45. *Verwaltungs-Jahrbuch*, 37.

46. Koch, Reich Ministry of Labour, re. Use of Telephones, 20 December 1939, BArch, R 3901/11983, n.p.

47. The district with the highest unemployment was that of the Rhineland Land Labour Office, with around eighteen thousand individuals registered as jobless. Rhineland Land Labour Office, re. Report on the Level of Employment for the Period 11–17 October 1939, BArch, R 3901/20246, fol. 61–63; Note, Press Conference 13 October 1939, BArch, RW

19/230; see also Recker, *Nationalsozialistische Sozialpolitik*, 63; Labour Deployment 1939, BArch, RW 19/2113, fol. 183; for general information on the absence of unemployment, see Monthly Reports on the Armaments Economy 1939, BArch, RW 19/204. On the Nazi political leaders' fears that unemployment would rise when the war began, see also Müller, 'Die Mobilisierung', 382.

48. *Verwaltungs-Jahrbuch*, esp. 37, 401, 420.

49. See note 4.

50. The rationing of scarce resources began with foreign exchange controls before being extended, notably, to steel; finally, even the distribution of manpower was organized by the state. Petzina, *Autarkiepolitik im Dritten Reich*, 18 f., 40–46; Tooze, *Wages of Destruction*, 70 f., 230–41.

51. War Economy and Armament Office of the OKW to Four-Year Plan Authority, Reich Minister of Economic Affairs (RMWi), Reich Ministry of Labour, Reich Ministry of Transport, re. Reorientation of Armament, 15 July 1940, BArch, R 3901/20246, fol. 2–4.

52. Report 'Organization of the War Economy', n.d. (probably 1943), BArch, RW 19/509.

53. Friedrich Syrup, Reich Ministry of Labour, to Land Labour Offices, re. Labour Deployment Measures to Cover the Manpower Needs of the Defence Economy, 15 September 1939, BArch, R 3901/20279, fol. 24–25; Friedrich Syrup, Reich Ministry of Labour, to Land Labour Offices, re. Implementation of the Order issued by the Chair of the Council of Ministers for the Defence of the Reich (Ministerrat für die Reichsverteidigung), Prime Minister Field Marshal Göring, 28 September 1939; here: Lack of Skilled Workers, 3 November 1939, BArch, R 3901/20279, fol. 42; Philipp Beisiegel, Reich Ministry of Labour, to Land Labour Offices, re. Evaluation of Requests for Manpower, 7 February 1942, BArch, R 3901/20289, fol. 6–7.

54. Friedrich Syrup, Reich Ministry of Labour, Main Section Va (Labour Deployment), to Land Labour Offices, re. Order issued by the Führer and Supreme Commander of the Wehrmacht, 20 August 1940, on the Implementation of the Production Programmes of the Special Level, 23 August 1940, BArch, R 3901/20246, fol. 51–52.

55. Friedrich Syrup, Reich Ministry of Labour, to Land Labour Offices, re. Use of the Compulsory Labour Decree, 24 November 1939, BArch, R 3901/20279, fol. 47.

56. This task was performed by a number of agencies. Initially, it was the GBW and the War Economy and Armament Office of the OKW that were in charge, later the Reich Ministry for Armament and Ammunition (Reichsministerium für Bewaffnung und Munition). For an overview of the various and ever-changing actors, see Müller, 'Die Mobilisierung'.

57. Tooze, *Wages of Destruction*, 341.

58. Landfried, Reich Ministry of the Economy, to the Reich Governors, Prussian Governors (Oberpräsidenten), District Presidents (Regierungspräsidenten) and Relevant Agencies, re. Reorientation of Armament, 23 July 1940, BArch, R 3901/20285, fol. 221–22.

59. Friedrich Syrup, Reich Ministry of Labour, Main Section Va (Labour Deployment), to Land Labour Offices, 23 August 1940, BArch, R 3901/20246, fol. 51–52; War Economy and Armament Office to Four-Year Plan Authority, Reich Ministry of the Economy, Reich Ministry of Labour, Reich Ministry of Transport, 15 July 1940, BArch, R 3901/20246, fol. 2–4.

60. D. Eichholtz, 'Ökonomie, Politik und Kriegführung. Wirtschaftliche Kriegsplanungen und Rüstungsorganisationen bis zum Ende der "Blitzkriegs"phase', in Eichholtz (ed.), *Krieg und Wirtschaft. Studien zur deutschen Wirtschaftsgeschichte 1939–1945*, Berlin: Metropol, 1999, 9–42, here 30.

61. Ibid., 26–29.

62. Herbst, *Der Totale Krieg*, 115 f.

63. Philipp Beisiegel, Reich Ministry of Labour, re. Meeting the Needs of the Armaments Industry; here: Managing Fluctuations in the Months of November and December 1940, Internal memorandum, 24 February 1941, BArch, R 3901/20281, fol. 45–48.

64. Nachtigall, Nordmark Land Labour Office, Reich Ministry of Labour, 17 September 1940, BArch, R 3901/20246, fol. 137. Nachtigall's letter depicts these events retrospectively.

65. Friedrich Syrup, Reich Institution, to Land Labour Offices: Equalization, 14 September 1937, BArch, R 3903/2319, n.p.

66. Brennecke, Kiel Labour Office, to Nordmark Land Labour Office, 3 September 1940, BArch, R 3901/20246, fol. 138.

67. Brennecke, Kiel Labour Office, to Nordmark Land Labour Office, re. Provision of Clockmakers for the Kiel-Wik Barrage Test Command, 3 September 1940, BArch, R 3901/20246, fol. 138; D. Marek, 'Biographien der Regierungsmitglieder (Minister und Staatsräte)', in B. Post and V. Wahl (eds), *Thüringenhandbuch. Territorium, Verfassung, Parlament, Regierung und Verwaltung in Thüringen 1920–1995*, Weimar: Böhlau, 1999, 552–648, here 633 f.

68. Central Germany Land Labour Office to Reich Ministry of Labour, re. Provision of Clockmakers for the Navy's Kiel-Wik Barrage Test Command, 28 September 1940, BArch, R 3901/20246, fol. 140.

69. Nachtigall, Nordmark Land Labour Office, to Reich Ministry of Labour, 17 September 1940, BArch, R 3901/20246, fol. 137.

70. Hubert Hildebrandt, Reich Ministry of Labour, Note re. Provision of Clockmakers for the Navy's Kiel-Wik Barrage Test Command, 4 October 1940, BArch, R 3901/20246, fol. 140.

71. Hubert Hildebrandt, Reich Ministry of Labour, to Nordmark Land Labour Office, re. Provision of Clockmakers for the Navy's Kiel-Wik Barrage Test Command, November 1942 (draft), BArch, R 3901/20246, fol. 142.

72. Schwarz, South-West Germany Land Labour Office, to Reich Ministry of Labour, re. Securing Manpower, here: Clockmakers for the Navy's Kiel-Wik Barrage Test Command, 8 October 1940, BArch, R 3901/20246, fol. 141.

73. War Economy and Armament Office to Four-Year Plan Authority, Reich Ministry of the Economy, Reich Ministry of Labour, Reich Ministry of Transport, re. Reorientation of Armament, 15 July 1940, BArch, R 3901/20246, fol. 2–4.

74. Tooze, *Wages of Destruction*, 416, 591 f.; W. Naasner, *Neue Machtzentren in der Deutschen Kriegswirtschaft, 1942–1945. Die Wirtschaftsorganisation der SS, das Amt des Generalbevollmächtigten für den Arbeitseinsatz und das Reichsministerium für Bewaffnung und Munition/ Reichsministerium für Rüstung und Kriegsproduktion im nationalsozialistischen Herrschaftssystem*, Boppard am Rhein: Boldt, 1994, 68 f., 88.

75. Herbert, *Hitler's Foreign Workers*, 74.

76. Ibid., 74, 158.

77. C. Streit, *Keine Kameraden. Die Wehrmacht und die sowjetischen Kriegsgefangenen 1941–1945*, Stuttgart: Deutsche Verlags-Anstalt, 1978, 10.

78. Herbert, *Hitler's Foreign Workers*, 149.

79. D. Rebentisch, *Führerstaat und Verwaltung im Zweiten Weltkrieg. Verfassungsentwicklung und Verwaltungspolitik 1939–1945*, Stuttgart: Steiner, 1989, 132. The appointment of Sauckel and the powers he enjoyed violated this principle in the field of labour policy.

80. See also the chapter by Ulrike Schulz in this volume.

Bibliography

Aly, G., and K.-H. Roth. *Die restlose Erfassung. Volkszählen, Identifizieren, Aussondern im Nationalsozialismus*. Frankfurt am Main: Fischer, 2000.

Ayass, W. *'Asoziale' im Nationalsozialismus*. Stuttgart: Klett-Cotta, 1995.

Brünneck, A. von. 'Ernst Fraenkels Urdoppelstaat von 1938 und der Doppelstaat von 1941/1974', in H. Buchstein and G. Göhler (eds), *Vom Sozialismus zum Pluralismus. Beiträge und Leben Ernst Fraenkels* (Baden-Baden: Nomos, 2000), 29–42.

Buchstein, H., and G. Göhler. 'Ernst Fraenkel (1898–1975)', in W. Bleek and H.J. Lietzmann (eds), *Klassiker der Politikwissenschaft. Von Aristoteles bis David Easton* (Munich: Beck, 2005), 151–64.

Eichholtz, D. *Geschichte der deutschen Kriegswirtschaft 1939–1945*, 5 vols. Munich: Saur, 2003.

Eichholtz, D. 'Ökonomie, Politik und Kriegführung. Wirtschaftliche Kriegsplanungen und Rüstungsorganisationen bis zum Ende der "Blitzkriegs"phase', in Eichholtz (ed.), *Krieg und Wirtschaft. Studien zur deutschen Wirtschaftsgeschichte 1939–1945* (Berlin: Metropol, 1999), 9–42.

Fraenkel, E. *Der Doppelstaat*, retranslated from the English by M. Schöps in collaboration with the author (1974), ed. A. von Brünneck, 3rd ed. Hamburg: Europäische Verlagsanstalt, 2012.

Fraenkel, E. *The Dual State. A Contribution to the Theory of Dictatorship*, translated from the German by E.A. Shils, in collaboration with E. Lowenstein and K. Knorr. New York: Oxford University Press, 1941. Reprinted New York: Octagon Books, 1969.

Henning, H. 'Friedrich Syrup (1881–1945)', in K. Jeserich and H. Neuhaus (eds), *Persönlichkeiten der Verwaltung. Biografien zur deutschen Verwaltungsgeschichte 1648–1945* (Stuttgart: Kohlhammer, 1991), 385–90.

Herbert, U. *Hitler's Foreign Workers. Enforced Foreign Labor in Germany under the Third Reich*, trans. W. Templer. Cambridge: Cambridge University Press, 1997.

Herbst, L. *Der Totale Krieg und die Ordnung der Wirtschaft. Die Kriegswirtschaft im Spannungsfeld von Politik, Ideologie und Propaganda 1939–1945*. Stuttgart: Deutsche Verlags-Anstalt, 1982.

Herrmann, V. *Vom Arbeitsmarkt zum Arbeitseinsatz. Zur Geschichte der Reichsanstalt für Arbeitslosenvermittlung und Arbeitslosenversicherung 1929–1939*. Frankfurt am Main: Lang, 1993.

Humann, D. *'Arbeitsschlacht'. Arbeitsbeschaffung und Propaganda in der NS-Zeit 1933–1939*. Göttingen: Wallstein, 2011.

'Jahreslagebericht 1938 des Sicherheitshauptamts', in H. Boberach (ed.), *Meldungen aus dem Reich. Die geheimen Lageberichte des Sicherheitsdienstes der SS*, vol. 2 (Munich: Deutscher Taschenbuch Verlag, 1968), 200.

Kahrs, H. 'Die ordnende Hand der Arbeitsämter. Zur deutschen Arbeitsverwaltung 1933–1939', in G. Aly and W. Gruner (eds), *Arbeitsmarkt und Sondererlass. Menschenverwertung, Rassenpolitik und Arbeitsamt* (Frankfurt am Main: Mabuse, 2009), 9–61.

Maier, D.G. *Anfänge und Brüche der Arbeitsverwaltung bis 1952. Zugleich ein kaum bekanntes Kapitel der deutsch-jüdischen Geschichte*. Brühl: Fachhochschule des Bundes für Öffentliche Verwaltung, 2004.

Maier, D.G. *Arbeitseinsatz und Deportation. Die Mitwirkung der Arbeitsverwaltung bei der nationalsozialistischen Judenverfolgung in den Jahren 1938–1945*, Berlin: Ed. Hentrich, 1994.

Maier, D.G., J. Nürnberger and S. Pabst. *Vordenker und Gestalter des Arbeitsmarktes. Elf Biografien zur Geschichte der deutschen Arbeitsverwaltung*. Mannheim: Hochschule der Bundesagentur für Arbeit, 2012.

Marek, D. 'Biographien der Regierungsmitglieder (Minister und Staatsräte)', in B. Post and V. Wahl (eds), *Thüringenhandbuch. Territorium, Verfassung, Parlament, Regierung und Verwaltung in Thüringen 1920–1995* (Weimar: Böhlau, 1999), 552–648.

Marx, H. 'The German Labour Administration in the "Protectorate Bohemia and Moravia"', in J. Rákosník and R. Šustrová (eds), *War Employment and Social Policies in the Protectorate Bohemia and Moravia* (Prague: Univerzita Karlova, 2018), 34–54.

Marx, H. *Die Verwaltung des Ausnahmezustands. Wissensgenerierung und Arbeitskräftelenkung im Nationalsozialismus.* Göttingen: Wallstein, 2019.
Milward, A.S. *The German Economy at War.* London: Athlone Press, 1965.
Müller, R.-D. 'Die Mobilisierung der deutschen Wirtschaft für Hitlers Kriegsführung', in B.R. Kroener, R.-D. Müller and H. Umbreit (eds), *Das Deutsche Reich und der Zweite Weltkrieg,* vol. 5: *Organisation und Mobilisierung des Deutschen Machtbereichs,* part-volume 1: *Kriegsverwaltung, Wirtschaft und personelle Ressourcen 1939–1941* (Stuttgart: Deutsche Verlags-Anstalt, 1988), 349–691.
Naasner, W. *Neue Machtzentren in der deutschen Kriegswirtschaft, 1942–1945. Die Wirtschaftsorganisation der SS, das Amt des Generalbevollmächtigten für den Arbeitseinsatz und das Reichsministerium für Bewaffnung und Munition/Reichsministerium für Rüstung und Kriegsproduktion im nationalsozialistischen Herrschaftssystem.* Boppard am Rhein: Boldt, 1994.
Overy, R.J. '"Blitzkriegswirtschaft"? Finanzpolitik, Lebensstandard und Arbeitseinsatz in Deutschland 1939–1942'. *Vierteljahrshefte für Zeitgeschichte* 36(3) (1988), 379–436.
Patel, K.K. *'Soldaten der Arbeit'. Arbeitsdienste in Deutschland und den USA, 1933–1945.* Göttingen: Vandenhoeck & Ruprecht, 2003.
Petzina, D. *Autarkiepolitik im Dritten Reich. Der nationalsozialistische Vierjahresplan.* Stuttgart: Deutsche Verlags-Anstalt, 1968.
Rebentisch, D. *Führerstaat und Verwaltung im Zweiten Weltkrieg. Verfassungsentwicklung und Verwaltungspolitik 1939–1945.* Stuttgart: Steiner, 1989.
Recker, M.-L. *Nationalsozialistische Sozialpolitik im Zweiten Weltkrieg.* Munich: Oldenbourg, 1985.
Scherner, J. *Die Logik der Industriepolitik im Dritten Reich.* Stuttgart: Steiner, 2008.
Schmuhl, H.-W. *Arbeitsmarktpolitik und Arbeitsverwaltung in Deutschland 1871–2002. Zwischen Fürsorge, Hoheit und Markt.* Nuremberg: Institut für Arbeitsmarkt- und Berufsforschung, 2003.
Schröder, F. *Die Reichsanstalt für Arbeitsvermittlung und Arbeitslosenversicherung. Ihr Aufbau und ihre Aufgaben.* Berlin: Zentralverband der Angestellten, [1930].
Silverman, D.P. 'Nazification of the German Bureaucracy Reconsidered: A Case Study'. *The Journal of Modern History* 60(3) (1988), 496–539.
Sommer, W. (ed.). *Die nationalsozialistische Arbeitseinsatz-Gesetzgebung.* Berlin: Elsner, 1938.
Streit, C. *Keine Kameraden. Die Wehrmacht und die sowjetischen Kriegsgefangenen 1941–1945.* Stuttgart: Deutsche Verlags-Anstalt, 1978.
Tooze, A. *The Wages of Destruction. The Making and Breaking of the Nazi Economy.* London: Penguin, 2007.
Verwaltungs-Jahrbuch für die Beamten und Angestellten der Arbeitseinsatzverwaltung 1939/40, vol. I. Berlin: Elsner, 1939.
Zschucke, M. *Das Reichsarbeitsministerium.* Berlin: Junker und Dünnhaupt, 1940.

Part III
EXPANSION, WAR AND CRIMES

Chapter 8

SOCIAL POLICY
External Propaganda and Imperial Ambitions

Kiran Klaus Patel and Sandrine Kott

In 1939, Reich Labour Minister Franz Seldte published a voluminous book entitled *Sozialpolitik im Dritten Reich* (Social Policy in the Third Reich). In this volume, he not only extolled Nazi Germany's supposed achievements, but also emphasized that 'representatives of social affairs ministries, scholars and practitioners from Europe and overseas visit us in large numbers to satisfy themselves, on the spot, as to the unique successes' of National Socialist social policy.[1] Four years earlier, as a supplement to the ministerial organ known as the *Reichsarbeitsblatt* (official gazette of the Reich Ministry of Labour), the minister had produced a markedly shorter version of the same work that was notably less triumphalist in tone. As it happens, in all probability Seldte composed neither text himself. They are likely to have been compilations of shorter texts penned by the various sections of his ministry but published under his name. In 1935, the minister merely noted that, 'when it comes to the natural international exchange of indigenous and foreign workers', the German government had 'always regarded [bilateral treaties] as the best means of guaranteeing the social protection enjoyed by every blue- and white-collar worker in Germany'. One of the text's core messages was that Germany was committed to international cooperation. In this context, among other things, the book listed treaties with Denmark, France, Poland and Czechoslovakia.[2] This was remarkable in that Germany's relationship with these neighbouring countries was fairly strained in political terms. Furthermore, far from being specific to Germany, such bilateral treaties were in fact integrated into a European network of agreements. In any case, as late as 1939, just a few months before the start of the Second World War, the minister continued to ascribe a prominent role to these bilateral accords.[3]

From 1933, the Nazi regime pursued a confrontational, radically nationalistic course on the international level with respect to a wide range of issues. It increasingly geared its social policies to preparing for and waging war. At the same time, however, it used them to showcase Germany vis-à-vis other countries, with German social policy attracting a great deal of interest internationally. Throughout the Nazi era, experts and national delegations from a wide variety of countries travelled to Germany to study the regime's policies in this field. Intensive exchanges even occurred during the war. Social policy, though, increasingly mutated from a means of showcasing the regime in the world into an instrument of domination and repression. In what follows, we flesh out these developments after providing an outline of international social policy until 1933.

During the Nazi era, the Reich Ministry of Labour drew on the international expertise it had built up over decades and carried on the German tradition of deploying social policy to stake out Germany's international profile. In this respect we find a high degree of continuity. This approach, however, was always contested within the elite of both the Nazi Party and the state. Racism and extreme nationalism explain why Adolf Hitler in particular ranged from sceptical to dismissive about all moves towards internationalization. At the same time, important competitors emerged to challenge the Reich Ministry of Labour in this field, above all the German Labour Front or DAF. But it would be wrong to assume that the ministry steadily lost influence as a result of these conflicts. The relationship between the various organizations was not always pervaded by rivalry. To a degree, their interaction took the form of a division of labour and enhanced the regime's functionality. Furthermore, the Reich Ministry of Labour remained crucially important until the end of the war, though this fact has tended to escape both researchers and the general public.

Promoting the Young Nation: International Social Policy until 1933

The International Conference on Labour Protection (Internationale Arbeiterschutzkonferenz) in Berlin, convened by Kaiser Wilhelm II in 1890, laid the foundation for internationalizing German social policy. It built upon measures introduced in the 1880s, when, under Reich Chancellor Otto von Bismarck, health insurance was made mandatory for certain groups in 1883, followed by accident insurance the next year and, finally, old-age and disability insurance in 1889. The conference not only pursued a specific social policy objective, but functioned concurrently as part of the new Kaiser's world policy (*Weltpolitik*), symbolizing the modernity and progressive character of the young German nation state.[4] The fact that Pope Leo XIII sent a greeting to the gathering in Berlin, congratulating the Kaiser for placing such 'a noble cause, deserving of such serious attention and of concern to the entire world' on the international agenda, not only illustrated that the conflict-ridden era of the 'cultural struggle' (*Kulturkampf*) between the Catholic Church and the Prussian state was over. It also demonstrated just how seriously international actors took this German initiative.[5] At the same time, this event provided politicians and experts from Germany dedicated to social policy with an opportunity to make an international name for themselves – not least in order to gain recognition, on the national level, for a still young policy field. It was above all officials at the Reich Insurance Office (Reichsversicherungsamt or RVA), the top supervisory authority with respect to social laws, who sought to glorify the accomplishments of German social policy.[6] A handbook on German labour insurance of 1893 written by an RVA official, for example, was published in an initial print run of 500,000 copies and translated into English, French, Spanish and Danish. Social policy thus functioned as a poster child and, potentially, as an export of the young nation state.[7]

Such measures were quite successful. Under the influence of the Society for Social Reform (Gesellschaft für Soziale Reform), 1901 saw the establishment, in the shape of the International Association for Labour Legislation, of a platform for social policy debate that made a particularly great impact on the international perception and prestige of German social policy. The German section made its name as the most active of the association's national members and, tellingly, German was the association's de facto working language, rather than French, which was the privileged language of international cooperation at the time.[8]

German social policy thus attracted a great deal of interest from other countries. International actors increasingly viewed German policy in this field as a model in its own right, one distinguished by mandatory insurance for certain occupational groups, the strong role of the nation state and financing through membership contributions and supplementary charges. One French expert, for example, looking back from 1937, underlined that in the three most important social policy associations founded prior to 1914, 'the representatives of German scholarship and administration [played] a leading role'.[9] During the First World War, former US President Theodore Roosevelt noted that, with respect to social policy issues, the United States had 'more to learn from Germany than from any other nation'. Precisely because of its dangerous strength, on this view, Germany represented a wake-up call for the United States, which needed to rethink its own policies.[10]

After the First World War, the Reich Ministry of Labour, founded in 1919, built on the Wilhelmine tradition. Given Germany's defeat in the war and its exclusion from many forms of international cooperation, social policy now took on signal importance as a means of gaining recognition for the vanquished country. Against this backdrop, under the Weimar Republic the Reich Ministry of Labour became a key player in the propagation of labour and social policy abroad. For example, the ministry prided itself on being solely responsible for the country's relations with the International Labour Organization, or ILO. This Geneva-based institution, like the Reich Ministry of Labour, was founded in 1919. As a subunit of the League of Nations, the ILO was tasked with facilitating agreement on international labour and social standards. The Reich Ministry of Labour's role vis-à-vis the ILO was not limited to the activities of the German delegation in Geneva. In fact, the ministry exercised an influence at the very heart of this international body. Most of the German officials working at the International Labour Office, the ILO's secretariat, were members of staff of the Reich Ministry of Labour, seconded to Geneva with its approval. They often pursued their careers in parallel in Berlin and Geneva, generating palpable synergetic effects.[11] Tellingly, moreover, between 1921 and 1934 the German branch office of the ILO was housed in the ministry's buildings. The second director of the Berlin office, social democrat Willy Donau, developed a strong relationship with a number of successive Reich labour ministers.[12] While the ILO espoused certain ideas that were not in line with German policies, the connections were close, and Germany was a social policy actor widely recognized across the globe.

It was not just via the ILO but also through direct contacts that the social policies of the Weimar Republic attracted attention in a number of other states. Building on the surge in state interventionism triggered by the First World War, social policy (which was often difficult to distinguish from labour policy) now found itself on the advance in many countries. The policies pursued by the first German democracy, which saw itself as particularly progressive in this field, thus made waves around the world, from the eight-hour day through social housing (often organized on the municipal level) to the unemployment insurance instituted in 1927.[13] Furthermore, the Weimar Republic was committed to international cooperation on the bilateral level. In the late 1920s, one social policy publication highlighted the fact that Germany 'can take credit for having been the first major country to have recognized and appreciated the importance not just of national social policy legislation, but of international social policy agreements as well'.[14]

Though the Reich Ministry of Labour played a central role in the international propagation of German social policy, even prior to 1933 it found itself in competition with other actors, such as the various social insurance institutes. The ministry was, for example, unable to prevent experts affiliated with the health insurance funds from being appointed to ILO commissions, such as hygienist Walter Pryll or Helmut Lehmann, president of the Confederation of German Health Insurance Providers (Hauptverband deutscher Krankenkassen).[15] Nonetheless, in the Weimar Republic, the ministry was Germany's leading actor on the international level. One key figure in this respect was Andreas Grieser,[16] head of the ministry's social insurance department, who was appointed as expert to the International Labour Office in 1926. The next year, Grieser was made rapporteur of the Insurance Commission at the International Labour Conference. He exercised a substantial influence on the composition of ILO Convention 24 on health insurance, which had much in common conceptually with the German Health Insurance Law (Krankenversicherungsgesetz) of 1883. Via the ILO, then, Grieser played an outstanding role in disseminating German approaches and ideas internationally.[17]

Interpretive Claims and Rivalries until 1938

In 1933, the top-level personnel at the Reich Ministry of Labour tried to build seamlessly on this tradition, aiming to ensure that social policy continued to help cement Germany's international position. The ministry's primary objective was to gain international prestige for Germany by highlighting the supposedly progressive character of its policies.

This approach was highly contested within the Nazi movement. Hitler himself showed little interest in deploying Nazi social policy as an international showpiece; he was even less interested in developing a 'brown international' in this field.[18] Hence, in significant part for racial reasons, many Nazis regarded the regime's policies as specifically German, and for Germans only. By contrast, at least during certain periods, various Nazi organizations, such as the DAF, pursued what amounted to an imperial, missionary approach, informed by the belief that the Nazi regime's social policies should be seen as a role model for other societies.

Within this spectrum of views, the Reich Ministry of Labour pursued something of a middle way. It continued to closely follow the measures introduced in other countries. As the official organ of the ministry, the *Reichsarbeitsblatt* carried regular reports on social policy elsewhere. This knowledge of policies in Italy, the United States and other countries flowed into Germany in the shape, for example, of plans to overcome mass unemployment.[19] In public statements, references to international developments played a different role. While some opted for a largely neutral tone, many included comparisons with the situation in Germany, making German policies appear in a good light.[20] The ministry also engaged in direct exchange with other countries. Seldte, for example, an admirer of Mussolini, travelled to Milan in June 1933 to take a look at fascist Italy's job creation projects.[21] Ministry officials, however, rarely adopted a missionary tone. For them, social policy was mostly a poster child that ought to be used to canvass respect for Germany internationally, but it was no template for other states.

From 1933, however, the ministry found itself facing a powerful competitor when it came to representing Germany internationally. At the very time when Seldte was travelling to Italy, the Seventeenth International Labour Conference was convened in Geneva. The ministry sent two high-ranking officials, the ministerial directors Hans Engel and Werner Mansfeld, to this gathering.[22] In Geneva, however, they were overshadowed by Robert Ley, who had also made the trip to Switzerland; Hitler had appointed him head of the German Labour Front in May 1933. Before the International Labour Conference, Ley had already staked his claim to a key role in the formulation of social policy. In Geneva, he deliberately sought to provoke and escalate conflicts. Before he had even reached the conference building, his *Sturmabteilung* (SA) escort was involved in physical altercations. At the conference itself, Ley caused an uproar. Speaking at a press conference, he declared that, with the exception of the Italians, all the delegations in attendance represented 'idiotic states' ('Idioten-Staaten').[23] Ley went out of his way to behave like a bull in a china shop – much like the German delegation to the London Economic Conference, which was held at the same time. The indignation provoked by Ley's offensive behaviour reached all the way to Mexico.[24]

By contrast, in those first months following the Nazi seizure of power, the Reich Ministry of Labour espoused a more conciliatory approach. In particular, State Secretary Johannes Krohn sought to consolidate Germany's – and thus the ministry's – position at the ILO. He was fittingly appalled by Ley's performance, which he put down to his lack of 'experience in negotiations with other countries and in other countries'.[25] This criticism, however, should not be mistaken for opposition to Nazism. What mattered to Krohn and other officials at the Reich Ministry of Labour was their ability to continue using the ILO as a conduit to propagate their own ideas – just as fascist Italy was doing with respect to its social policies. The ministry considered it particularly unfortunate that Ley had even managed to upset the Italian delegation in Geneva, and thus Germany's most important potential ally.[26] In essence, then, this was a conflict over how Nazi Germany could best promote its interests within the international sphere. For the DAF, an international organization was only acceptable if it was unambiguously dominated by Germany. The ministry, by contrast, proved more willing to compromise, and it knew how to exercise an influence upon international bodies.

In this struggle over power and policy orientation, it was Ley who initially came out on top. In October 1933, a few days after its departure from the League of Nations, Germany left the ILO as well. Since the 1920s, Hitler had been stressing that Germany must break with the 'Versailles system'. Given that the League of Nations and, in its wake, the ILO, were heavily identified with Versailles, leaving the ILO was merely consistent. The dictator's radical line thus held sway over the ministry's less confrontational approach.[27]

At first glance, then, the ministry appears to have suffered heavy defeats in the summer and autumn of 1933. Yet it would be a mistake to overstate them. At the meeting in Geneva in June, Ley had accused State Secretary Krohn and Ministerial Director Engel of torpedoing his confrontational course. According to Ley, they had gone so far as to 'enter into pacts with the state enemies of the National Socialist state'. Krohn demanded that Ley 'make amends' for this comment. After protracted discussions, which saw both camps involve the dictator personally, Ley had to make an official apology to the state secretary.[28]

More important still, the ministry continued to maintain contact with Geneva. Even once Germany had officially left the ILO, a broad range of connections endured as the ministry sought to keep abreast of international debates.[29] In 1936, some within the Nazi state even considered rejoining the ILO.[30] In the second half of the 1930s, leading officials at the Reich Ministry of Labour carried on secret negotiations with Harold Butler, director of the International Labour Office, with the last such meeting taking place in July 1938.[31]

Due to its technical expertise and long-established links with foreign actors, even after 1933 the Reich Ministry of Labour was a key player on the international stage. When it came to crucial areas of policy, the ministry's international status remained largely uncontested. One example was housing. In 1935, two international conferences were held on this topic in Europe – one in Prague in late June and the other in London towards the end of July. In both cases, the ministry provided the head of the German delegation and was represented by other experts, while the DAF played no role at all.[32]

The Labour Ministry was also in charge of the bilateral treaties on social insurance for foreign workers, of which Seldte made so much in his books.[33] Contrary to the minister's claims, however, these were not accomplishments of the Nazi regime. First, they were integrated into a large-scale European network of such agreements and, second, many of these treaties had been negotiated during the Weimar era. Some of them, however, were ratified only after 1933 – henceforth, they did not need the approval of the Reichstag, which speeded things up considerably.[34] These agreements, which were already important because they allowed foreign workers access to the social insurance systems, became steadily more significant during the last few years before the war. They formed part of the basis for the recruitment of Italians, Poles, Czechs and others, for which the German labour market had an ever more pressing need during the military build-up from 1936. At the same time, these treaties helped reduce mass unemployment in other countries. During this period, German insurance funds paid benefits, for example, even to Polish citizens. Nazi social policy, then, functioned as a lubricant for a capitalist labour market, building on an alliance of interests between German and non-German politicians, social policy experts and workers.[35] Against this backdrop, it comes as no surprise that in June 1939 the Reich Propaganda Ministry explicitly instructed the German press to hype up the renewal of the social insurance treaty with Italy.[36] This concurrently enabled the Reich Labour Ministry to highlight its leading role in this endeavour.

These bilateral treaties represented Germany's most institutionalized and impactful links with other states in the field of social policy. Ironically, however, here Nazi Germany was dependent not just on cooperation with other countries but even on the regulations of the ILO. For example, in a letter to the ILO of February 1934, Krohn gave assurances that 'there is nothing stopping Germany, at the invitation of another government, from taking part, outside of Geneva, in deliberations on the conclusion of a bilateral or multilateral international agreement, which adopts the content of a convention agreed by the International Labour Office'.[37] On the other hand, regulations negotiated with German input came to function as a kind of European blueprint. In drawing up one international convention, the ILO, which was out to achieve harmonization within the jungle of such bilateral agreements, took its lead from none other than the German-Polish treaty – regardless of the fact that by this point Germany had left the ILO. ILO Convention 48 of 1935 in turn formed the basis for a multitude of bilateral agreements in Europe – including the revised version of the German-Italian treaty of 20 July 1939.[38] Within this entire field, the position of the Reich Labour Ministry was largely uncontested in comparison with other Nazi organizations. It took its cooperation with experts from other countries very seriously. In 1936, for example, the ministry succeeded in holding an international congress of social insurance experts in Germany. Organized by the Reich Association of German Insurance Companies (Reichsverband Deutscher Versicherungsanstalten), this conference, held in Dresden in early September 1936, helped advance the coordination of national regulations across borders.[39]

Yet it would be wrong to underestimate the DAF and other actors. Significantly, in the first few years following the Nazi seizure of power, Ley abandoned his confrontational approach. He too tried to deploy social policy as an international advertisement for Nazi Germany. However, the DAF, along with other organizations, primarily became active in those fields in which the ministry had not previously played a prominent role. Despite all the conflicts, then, ultimately something of a division of labour emerged. The best example here is leisure policy (*Freizeitpolitik*), as a social policy field that was still young at the time and that was attracting a great deal of attention internationally. Ley himself had shown an interest in it prior to 1933, closely following developments in fascist Italy. The leisure organization 'Strength through Joy' (Kraft durch Freude), which he launched in November 1933 as part of the DAF, was explicitly oriented towards the fascist template. In a sleight of hand typical of Nazism, however, it was not long before Ley was promoting the DAF as a role model worthy of international emulation.[40]

In 1936, 1,500 delegates from thirty-two nations took part in the World Congress on Leisure and Recreation (Weltkongress für Freizeit und Erholung) arranged by the DAF. Hundreds of thousands of visitors from Germany and abroad attended the associated events. Nazi Germany thus laid claim to a position of global leadership in one of the most important fields of social policy debate of the 1930s. Ley went so far as to assert that Italy 'was the first to embrace our objectives'.[41] The congress, which took place a few days before the summer Olympics in Berlin, thus provided the perfect stage for the *mise en scène* of the regime's social policy. Furthermore, this gathering reflected the degree to which the DAF had become a rival to the Reich Ministry of Labour when it came to internationalization – the ministry never managed to make such a major public splash during the Nazi period. At the congress, the DAF also founded the 'Joy and Labour' International Central Office (Internationales Zentralbüro 'Freude und Arbeit'), which explicitly sought to provide an alternative to the International Labour Office in Geneva. This laid bare, once again, its status as competitor to both the ILO and the Reich Labour Ministry.[42]

The DAF also became far more important on a less visible level. Until 1933, the Reich Labour Ministry was unsurpassed in terms of its technical expertise in the field of social policy and with respect to its knowledge of relevant developments abroad. Since its establishment in 1933, however, the DAF had built up an extensive apparatus of knowledge in an attempt to become less dependent on the ministry. Crucial in this respect was the DAF's Labour Science Institute, which kept systematically abreast of, and evaluated, global developments in the domain of labour and social policy. It was not just in the field of political action, then, but also with respect to the knowledge underpinning it, that the DAF challenged the ministry's central role.[43] Again and again, in this context the DAF built on ministerial expertise. Wolfgang Pohl, leader of the Labour Science Institute from its foundation in 1935 until 1945, had a stellar career in the Reich Ministry of Labour behind him. Much the same can be said of Friedrich Sitzler,[44] who was dispatched to Geneva in March 1933 following a lengthy career at the ministry. From 1936, he too worked for the Labour Science Institute in close cooperation with Pohl.[45] On the one hand, the ministry and the DAF thus competed both for individuals and powers. On the other, we can discern synergetic effects that enhanced the regime's effectiveness.

While the DAF was the ministry's most important competitor prior to the war, it was by no means the only one. A similar role was played, for example, by the Reich Labour Service (Reichsarbeitsdienst or RAD). Until 1934, this organization, which operated at the interface of job creation, education and social policies, had been subordinate to the Reich Ministry of Labour. Reich Labour Leader (Reichsarbeitsführer) Konstantin Hierl, however, complained for so long and with such success about Seldte and other alleged enemies of the labour service concept, that Hitler detached the RAD from the ministry in July 1934 and made it formally subordinate to the Reich Ministry of the Interior. Like the DAF, the RAD attracted large numbers of visitors from abroad and promoted German social policy on the international stage, while bypassing the Reich Labour Ministry. In 1938, the head of the Department for Foreign Affairs and Enlightenment (Abteilung für auswärtige Angelegenheiten und Aufklärung) in the organization's Reich headquarters summed up the RAD's self-image as follows: 'The fact is that other countries are increasingly seeking to follow the route taken by the Reich in the shape of labour service'.[46] With no involvement from the ministry, a German model was here being proclaimed with global missionary pretentions.

While ministry officials often complained about the conflicts with the DAF and other organs of the Nazi state, as attested by the historical record, we should not overstate the dysfunctional dimension of these rivalries. To some extent, they provided further incentive for the actors involved to advocate their ideas all the more vigorously both at home and abroad. On some issues, a kind of informal division of labour even emerged on the international level. The Reich Ministry of Labour was primarily responsible for those aspects of German social policy that had existed for a long time, required a high level of technical expertise and built on long-established international relations. Examples are social insurance, housebuilding and social protection for German workers abroad or workers from other countries in Germany. From 1933, these fields were reshaped in line with Nazi ideology and oriented towards racism and war. They were no longer consonant with the social policy approach characteristic of the German Empire or the Weimar period, but still profited from its international prestige. Organizations such as the German Labour Front or the Reich Labour Service, conversely, often represented and hotly debated new social policy fields, such as leisure and recreation policy or labour service, and they proceeded with a greater sense of mission than the Reich Labour Ministry. Competition and division of labour – both characterized the relationship between the Reich Labour Ministry and other parts of the Nazi regime within this sphere of action.

Rejection, Assimilation and Fascination: Non-German Perspectives on Nazi Social Policy

But how did representatives of other countries perceive Nazi social policy, and what motivated them to study it? For Seldte the answer was simple. In the 1939 edition of *Sozialpolitik im Dritten Reich*, he not only stated that foreign actors were fascinated by the success of the Nazi measures, but added: 'The deep impression made on these experts has found expression in certain social legislation in other countries'.[47]

In reality, the reasons for the great interest in Nazi social policy, and the resulting processes of exchange, were more complex in nature. First, this interest was due to the lengthy history of social policy 'made in Germany' and the prestige it had acquired over the previous half-century. Second, the pressure arising from the global economic crisis intensified interest in the initiatives being pursued in other societies. While the world economy was coming apart at the seams and humanity gradually proceeded towards the most disastrous war in its history, experts and specialists moved closer together on the international level – mostly, it should be noted, in order to identify the best solution on the national level. Here, social policy and social engineering in the broad sense played a special role, with cross-national comparison being viewed as a fascinating means of reaching conclusions about the condition of societies and optimizing them with the aid of a socially experimental toolkit.[48] Third, policy initiatives on the right of the political spectrum had become tremendously popular. Particularly in Europe, in the mid 1930s the democratic state found itself in retreat, with most countries shifting towards authoritarian or fascist approaches. What could have made more sense than to look at the especially radical Germany, particularly because it seemed to have put the economic crisis behind it more rapidly than other countries? Time and again, fascination and analytical interest commingled with aversion. Particularly for democrats and representatives of the political left, Germany represented a textbook example of the allure of false (social policy) promises, which is precisely what made it interesting. By 1933, for example, Wilhelm Reich had already produced a study on the mass psychology of Nazism, in which, among other things, he examined the sexual economy of Reich Labour Service camps.[49] Furthermore, on the international level, to take just one example, the implications of Nazi social policy for the role of women attracted a great deal of attention, with US social reformer Alice Hamilton criticizing 'the enslavement of women'.[50]

At the same time, a number of factors militated against this exchange. Across the globe, nationalism and notions of superiority were gaining ground as nations withdrew into themselves, impeding transnational contacts and links. Particularly in public debates, every reference to measures implemented by other countries was suspected of being unpatriotic – not just in dictatorships but also in many democracies. In the era of the Great Depression, with strained public finances, exchange controls and the high costs incurred by foreign trips, the economic and logistical room for manoeuvre was highly constrained. In light of these factors, the degree of attention with which experts and politicians – and, with significantly less intensity, the majority of the population – followed Nazi social policy in many countries was all the more remarkable.

What were foreign actors particularly interested in? For the general public, it was primarily those programmes featuring strong political symbolism and linking social policy with mass mobilization that made waves. The administrative procedures and mathematical formulae involved in disability insurance remained the preserve of true experts. Attendance at a DAF conference, a visit to a RAD camp or study of a 'Strength through Joy' excursion, meanwhile, more closely reflected contemporary notions of what modern social policy ought to accomplish. It was the latter events, then, that stood at the centre of Nazi propaganda. At the same time, for visitors these tangible phenomena produced pictures that were better suited to justifying their trip to Germany, given the political and economic pressures back home.

Logically enough, the exchange with similar organizations in fascist Italy was particularly intensive, and during certain periods both regimes sought to cooperate extensively. Ultimately, however, most of these initiatives did not get very far.[51] Ideological affinity also explains the comparatively close relations with Spain under Franco. Pilar Primo de Rivera, founder of the Women's Section (Sección Femenina) of the Spanish Falange, travelled to Germany on several occasions in search of inspiration; the Spanish generals, meanwhile, showed great interest in labour service for men and women in 1939; and in 1941, the Falange's National Organization of Joy and Leisure published its own journal, which, at least on the surface, borrowed much from the periodical published by 'Strength through Joy'. The Spanish organization also cooperated closely with its German counterpart.[52] The Hamburg congress played an important role in the debate on recreation policy in Japan and in the foundation of the Japan Recreation Association (Nihon kôsei kyôkai). In very general terms, Germany was a key point of reference within the Japanese debate on leisure policy.[53] Far-right and fascist groupings in various parts of Europe also frequently referred positively to the social policies of the Nazi regime. In Sweden, for example, in 1937 the right-wing extremist National League of Sweden (Sveriges Nationella Förbund) called for the establishment of women's labour service on the German model. The driving force in this context was the most prominent representative of the country's far right, Nora Torulf, who had completed a study tour of several weeks in Germany shortly before.[54] At the same time, Nazi social policy remained embedded in cross-border circulatory flows. Nazi experts and politicians were greatly interested in the policies being pursued in other countries and kept abreast of the latest developments – not least in order to back up their claim that their own policies were vastly superior to those of other countries. There was no society that looked exclusively to Germany for inspiration. Other social policy models and practices, whether those of fascist Italy, the ILO, Western democracies or the Soviet Union, often received a great deal of attention as well.

These complex patterns of perception and interaction are also evident in the International Labour Organization. While trades union representatives working there universally condemned the destruction of the free workers' organizations in Germany and the persecution of Jewish workers,[55] representatives of employers and the state had a more ambivalent attitude. The Nazi regime's measures to combat mass unemployment were of great interest to them, not least because they tied in with debates that had been going on within the ILO since 1919.[56]

At the same time, interest and exchange were not limited to the extreme right in other societies or to the ILO. There was also a (sometimes intense) exchange with the representatives of democratic governments and experts. To an extent, this was due to the fact that Germany was a leading industrialized state, so its development was considered inherently significant. Criticism of the Nazi regime's social policies – particularly their antisemitic, racist and eugenic dimensions – was another reason why they attracted a great deal of attention. Time and again, however, references to Nazi social policies were intended to mobilize opinion within a particular country. For example, when a leading politician such as Neville Chamberlain in the United Kingdom made positive remarks about the physical fitness of German youths and the related programmes in the mid 1930s, he did so as part of his push for similar measures in his own country, though within a democratic framework.[57] In the form of the Physical Training and Recreation Act of 1937, words were soon followed by deeds. Here, as in the case of former President Theodore Roosevelt cited earlier, Germany functioned chiefly as an alarming wake-up call rather than a positive model.

A similar trend may be noted in the United States. In the late 1930s, President Franklin D. Roosevelt, a distant cousin of Theodore, personally requested a number of reports on Nazi social policy in order to learn from them. In one case, in fact, the US government emulated, in a highly selective manner, the social engineering at the heart of a programme implemented in Nazi Germany, though stripped of its ideological superstructure. The US president himself best captured the nature of this interrelationship when he noted in an internal document: 'All of this helps us in planning, even though our methods are of the democratic variety!'[58] The ethos underpinning this exchange, then, was fed by a mixture of interest and boundary maintenance.[59] This may also explain why, for example, prior to the war, German social policy had always met with tremendous scepticism in Denmark. In the late nineteenth century, this Scandinavian country was already distancing itself from its large southern neighbour. Its insistence on pursuing its own approach to constructing a welfare state in the 1930s, which deployed Germany as a negative foil, thus had a long tradition.[60]

Overall, then, what we find with respect to the Reich's relationship with societies beyond its borders during the pre-war era is a broad spectrum of motives, forms of interaction and effects. Much of the reception of German social policy remained within the realm of the merely possible, never getting beyond blueprints for the future. Nazi social policies entered into non-German debates and practices only in a very indirect form, through processes of selective assimilation and dissociation.

'Social Policy' during the War, 1938–1945

From 1938, within the international sphere, the German Reich's social policy increasingly developed from a means of self-stylization, of striking a pose of superiority, to an instrument of domination vis-à-vis third parties, above all in the annexed and occupied territories. In this respect, the occupation of Austria in March 1938, followed by the annexation of the Sudetenland in the autumn and the Protectorate of Bohemia and Moravia in March 1939, represented a more profound turning point than the beginning of the war a few months later. These territorial takeovers opened up new spheres of action for the Reich Ministry of Labour, which underlined its aspiration to lead on social policy issues internationally. As part of the Nazi war machine, its officials implemented labour and social policy measures in those areas now ruled by Germany. In 1940, in the journal *Soziale Praxis* (Social Practice), Ministerial Counsellor Friedrich Sitzler, a former ILO official, saw expanding Nazi rule as marking the beginning of a new social policy that would

> no longer take inspiration from the anaemic ideas of justice in the abstract and the affirmation of humanity, but from the natural circumstances and practical needs of the national economies involved. It will serve to advance cooperation between the European peoples, facilitating this through the rational management of manpower.[61]

The notion of superiority, which had mostly provided stimulus for the propagation of German social policy on the international level, now triggered a dual process. First, those population groups that the Nazi state wished to integrate into the Greater German Reich were to enjoy the benefits of German social policy. Here, Austria became the laboratory of social policy imperialism.[62] A special case in this regard was Alsace-Lorraine, which had been part of the German Empire until 1918. Here the goal was not to establish but to reconstruct and overhaul social policy within a Nazi framework.[63] Second, in all these areas, and in the Protectorate as well, populations were divided up according to racist criteria. Jews and others viewed as 'alien to the community' (*Gemeinschaftsfremde*) were to be refused welfare benefits. And while ethnic Germans were to be absorbed into the system of the 'Old Reich', the existing social policies in a given territory continued to apply to non-ethnic Germans.[64] This division was put into practice only to a limited extent, but it highlights the tremendous significance of racism to understanding Nazi social policy.

Furthermore, amid the administrative chaos so typical of Nazism, and depending on the territory and issue at hand, a variety of agencies were engaged in introducing and implementing social policy. In Austria, for example, the key figures were Reich Commissioner for Austria (Reichsbeauftragter für Österreich) Wilhelm Keppler and Reich Commissioner for the Reunification of Austria with the German Reich (Reichskommissar für die Wiedervereinigung Österreichs mit dem Deutschen Reich) Josef Bürckel. In Alsace, Robert Wagner who, as Gauleiter for Baden, was also head of the Civil Administration in Alsace, played a key role. On the formal level, in all these cases the Reich Labour Ministry had to hand over the reins to others. In reality, however, it provided the indispensable expertise and the staff that facilitated, on the technical level, the implementation of the various measures in cooperation with the local experts in charge of social policy. An example here was the jurist Joachim Fischer-Dieskau, an official at the Reich Labour Ministry who was dispatched to Vienna shortly after the Anschluss in order to organize housing along German lines.[65] The effort to extend the German system to other territories sometimes had paradoxical consequences. In Austria, for example, until 1938 the level of insurance for white-collar workers had been higher than in the 'Old Reich'. The Austrians' inclusion in the German system, therefore, equated to a superficially camouflaged benefits cut. Coming 'home to the Reich' ('Heim ins Reich'), then, was by no means always a profitable move.[66]

If we consider the various cases together, we find that the approaches adopted, the political and administrative practices and the precise role played by the Reich Labour Ministry in implementing labour and social policy measures varied from one area to another. Long-term continuities and the power struggles between various Nazi institutions, and between these agencies and the occupied territories' existing welfare institutions, are key to explaining a given constellation. With respect to the position of the Reich Labour Ministry, however, it would be wrong to assume that it generally declined in significance. Instead, as a result of the aggressive expansion of the area under Nazi domination, new roles accrued to the ministry beyond the old boundaries of the Reich.

This applied even more with respect to forced labour and thus to the systematic and brutal exploitation of millions of workers within those parts of Europe under Nazi occupation, in which the Reich Labour Ministry was actively involved.[67] On this level, there were institutional continuities with the work of the ministry in the pre-war period. Some of the later forced labourers had been recruited prior to 1938–1939 on the basis of those binational treaties that rendered them liable to pay social insurance contributions, something of which the ministry had always been in charge. These workers found themselves subject to ever harsher working conditions as the war progressed. The recruitment of new workers during the war, meanwhile, initially proceeded in the ways established in the interwar period before taking on more radical forms.[68]

On the international level, then, had Nazi social policy been stripped entirely of its role as showpiece? Far from it. In light of the new possibilities opened up by 'Hitler's Empire' for social policy actors,[69] concepts of superiority and utopian social plans continued to grow in importance, both vis-à-vis allied powers such as Italy, Croatia and Romania and occupied countries such as Belgium, Denmark and France. This by no means applied solely to the Reich Labour Ministry. For example, the RAD too aggressively sought to export its model of labour service to a number of other societies, including Croatia, Norway and the Netherlands. RAD experts advised collaborating elites, and similar organizations were developed in a number of states. These initially borrowed a great deal directly from the RAD model. Most of them, however, soon sank into a shadowy existence, abandoning their social policy concerns in favour of military forms of deployment.[70]

In general terms, social policy was increasingly subject to the primacy of the war, which changed its character and drew a large number of actors and institutions into this field whose responsibilities related primarily to the war economy or military matters. Often, powers over social policy now overlapped and complemented one another even more than they had done in the pre-war era. Competition and interpenetration thus continued to grow in importance.

For example, the DAF laid claim to an important role in the supervision of forced labourers within the Reich.[71] Again and again, on the ideological and propagandistic level, it extolled its social policy concepts as a model for other parts of Europe. Between 1941 and 1944, it published the *Neue Internationale Rundschau der Arbeit* (New International Labour Review), with which it sought to supplant the ILO publication *International Labour Review*, published until 1940. This aspiration found reflection not just in this periodical's name but also, for example, in the design of its cover. The DAF publication was highly ideological in character and geared towards an international readership: thus it was to appear in five languages.[72] In the circles of social policy experts in the Reich, moreover, it was in competition with the *Sozialpolitische Weltrundschau* (Socio-political World Review), published by the Reich Labour Ministry from 1940 as an essentially factual documentation of international developments inspired by the *Reichsarbeitsblatt*.[73]

During the war, however, ministerial leaders too increasingly pursued an imperialistic, missionary course. In 1938, the ministry cut its last remaining ties with the ILO; from the following year, it stepped up its efforts to develop a 'brown' international social policy under German leadership. Together with Italy and other Axis powers, the goal was to establish an alternative to the ILO, through which 'Germany could gain influence with its highly developed social policy'.[74] The DAF too was interested in this possibility and negotiated with the Italian government, but the ministry sought to keep control of this project. This was because, ultimately, 'German social policy is such an important asset in Germany's struggle for worldwide recognition and in cementing its international relations, that the maintenance of and emphasis on German pre-eminence in this field is an important and highly meaningful task'.[75] Not least because of the hegemonic pretensions of the ministry's plans and due to power struggles with the DAF, these and similar initiatives failed. But they illustrate just how much the style and content of the ministry's approach in this field had changed.[76]

The shift towards an imperialistic approach is also evident in two staffing decisions. The same Hans Engel whom, along with Krohn, Ley accused of having made pacts in Geneva with 'enemies of the state' in 1933, was appointed state secretary in the Reich Labour Ministry in March 1942. Engel had always championed efforts to stake out Nazi social policy's international profile, while also heading the group responsible for this within the ministry.[77] During the war, then, policies towards other countries were viewed as highly significant. Furthermore, in the shape of Oskar Karstedt, from 1942 at the latest a former colonial official and someone closely familiar with Africa policy headed the Working Group on International Affairs (Arbeitsgebiet Internationales), which played a significant role in the ministry.[78] Despite the fact that Karstedt was considered a moderate figure, his appointment encapsulates the new attitude that the ministry had brought to the table.

The imperial dimension of Nazi social policy had global effects during the war. Not least, it spurred the Western democracies to develop their own ideas in this field as part of their plans for the postwar period. The United States and the United Kingdom in particular emphasized the differences between their thinking and that of the Nazi regime and other societies that were referred to in the language of the day as 'totalitarian'. Thus, in the second half of the war, there was a battle, one imbued with potent political symbolism, to formulate the most persuasive social policy; this conflict mirrored the showdown between armies and ideologies. In the United Kingdom, for example, when a group of experts around William Beveridge was elaborating the reform measures later named after him, they underscored their differences from the contemporaneous ideas at large in the DAF and the Reich Ministry of Labour. Following the release of the Beveridge Report in November 1942, German experts immediately analysed the British document in detail. The Reich Labour Ministry and other institutions composed reports and counter-arguments, which were then dispatched to German embassies abroad. Often, emphasis was placed on the longer existence and alleged superiority of the German model.[79] At the same time, the ILO studied German perceptions of the British plan – observers observing the observers – which underlines the significance of international exchange processes.[80]

These international debates had interesting repercussions within Germany. In regime-internal plans developed in 1944 concerning the level of pensions, Reich Labour Minister Seldte used Beveridge's ideas as the basis for a domestic political argument. In his opinion, Germany must increase its pensions in order not to fall behind the UK.[81] He encountered massive opposition in this respect. Nonetheless, this demonstrates just how much, only a few months before the end of the war, social policy was being formulated in an international context. To give one final example: when the DAF's Labour Science Institute held an international conference on labour relations in Bad Salzbrunn in March 1944, on the topic of a 'new social order for Europe', it sought to steal a march on the ILO conference planned for the next month in Philadelphia. At the ILO meeting, meanwhile, the experts and politicians in attendance tried to formulate an explicit alternative to Nazi social policy.[82]

The Nazi regime lost this battle of ideas, programmes and concrete practices just as it succumbed to the Allies militarily. The promotional dimension of its policy and its moves towards a 'brown international' were ultimately less of a priority than tyranny, oppression and annihilation. During the war, Germany's allies increasingly perceived German social policy as repressive and sought alternatives to it. In this field, even collaborating elites mostly tried to dissociate themselves from the Nazi state.[83] They viewed the war as a window of opportunity, a chance to realize their own social policy ideas, rather than closing ranks with Germany, let alone adopting Nazi approaches. By 1945, no one believed in the 'unique' successes invoked by Seldte in 1939. Rather than functioning as a showpiece for the Reich, the policies of the Reich Ministry of Labour had primarily been dedicated to repression and violence.

Epilogue

After 1945, German social policy in both East and West retained distinctive features that drew on, and selectively perpetuated, the sociopolitical options and concepts characteristic of the period until 1945.[84] At first sight one might conclude that the international appeal of the German social policy model, acquired since the time of the Empire, had gone up in flames during the Second World War. In East Germany, social policy was framed as a socialist endeavour and did not present itself as genuinely German. As West German society constructed its self-image and as international debates played out, the strength of the national currency and economy played a far more prominent role than social policy. Tellingly, before becoming chancellor, Ludwig Erhard, symbolic representative of the West German postwar upturn, did not head the Federal Ministry of Labour but the Federal Ministry of the Economy. Furthermore, the pension reform of 1957, one of the most important changes made in the postwar era, was seen as a '"titanic" innovation' – as if no social policy of this kind had existed before in Germany.[85]

Nonetheless, it would be wrong to imagine that the thread of social policy spun since the 1880s had been broken entirely. Experts and politicians in both East and West, and abroad, viewed German social policy as highly distinct. It is telling, for example, that key German actors continued to refer to 'social policy', rather than adopting the English term 'welfare state'.[86]

In addition to this distinct, semantically fixed mentality, there were significant continuities with regard to the actors involved. While key individuals such as Hans Engel did not live beyond 1945, others were soon playing prominent roles once again. Otto Bach had helped develop the Berlin branch office of the ILO under the Weimar Republic. During the war, he headed the German Institute in Paris, giving talks that sought to demonstrate the superiority of Nazi social policy.[87] In the 1950s, he was a member of the board of the United Nations Association of Germany (Deutsche Gesellschaft für die Vereinten Nationen) and was feted for his contribution as an 'engaged European' since the 1920s.[88] Friedrich Sitzler presents us with a similar story. Upon reaching the age of seventy-five in 1956, the festschrift published in his honour brought together everyone who was anyone in the field of labour and social policy in the young West Germany. Federal Labour Minister Anton Storch, for example, praised Sitzler's 'lasting contribution to the development of the fields of social and labour law in Germany'.[89]

An interesting source of insight into contemporary thinking is provided by the findings of a study published in 1962 on German social policy in the nineteenth century as reflected in school history books with the title *Die deutsche Sozialpolitik des 19. Jahrhunderts im Spiegel der Schulgeschichtsbücher*. Its author concluded, with some surprise, that since 1945 foreign schoolbooks had dealt in great depth with the 'social question' in Germany and with the history of German social policy. By way of contrast, he stated, German books often provided no more than a brief account of other countries' social policy history. Reflecting the style of the era, he focused his praise on the absence of any 'hostile attitude' towards Germany, despite the fact that 'most of the countries that produced the texts examined here were on the side of Germany's opponents in the last war'. He concluded his reflections with the following words:

> The significantly more balanced perspective from which present-day texts discuss the various countries, and the numerous efforts by historians and teachers to achieve greater mutual understanding through debates at conferences, may give us reason to hope that certain lessons from the past have in fact been learned.[90]

German social policy, then, was still considered distinct. Having functioned as a Nazi flagship, a labour market lubricant during the Nazi state's military build-up and an instrument of exploitation from 1938, it now mutated into an expression of European rapprochement.

Kiran Klaus Patel, Dr. phil., Professor of European history at Ludwig Maximilian University Munich and a member of the Independent Commission of Historians Investigating the History of the Reich Ministry of Labour in the National Socialist Period. Publications, besides the aforementioned volume edited with Sandrine Kott, include *Project Europe: A History* (Cambridge University Press, 2020); *The New Deal: A Global History* (Princeton University Press, 2016); 'Special Section: The Dark Side of Transnationalism. Social Engineering and Nazism, 1930–40s' (edited in collaboration with Sven Reichardt), in *Journal of Contemporary History* 51(1) (2016); *Soldiers of Labor: Labor Service in Nazi Germany and New Deal America, 1933–1945* (Cambridge University Press, 2005).

Sandrine Kott, Dr. Phil., professor of modern European history at the University of Geneva, invited professor at New York University and a member of the Independent Commission of Historians Investigating the History of the Reich Ministry of Labour in the National Socialist Period. Publications include: *Nazism Across Borders: The Social Policies of the Third Reich and their Global Appeal* (edited in collaboration with Kiran Klaus Patel; Oxford University Press, 2018); *Seeking Peace in the Wake of War. Europe, 1943–1947* (edited in collaboration with Stefan-Ludwig Hoffmann, Peter Romijn and Olivier Wieviorka; Amsterdam University Press, 2015); *Sozialstaat und Gesellschaft. Das deutsche Kaiserreich in Europa* (Vandenhoeck & Ruprecht, 2014); *Globalizing Social Rights. The International Labour Organization and Beyond* (edited in collaboration with Joëlle Droux; Palgrave Macmillan, 2013).

Notes

1. F. Seldte, *Sozialpolitik im Dritten Reich, 1933–1938*, Munich: Beck, 1939, 267.
2. F. Seldte, *Sozialpolitik im Dritten Reich. Ein Bericht* (attachment to *Reichsarbeitsblatt 1935*, no. 36), Berlin: Reichsdruckerei, 1935, 4, 65.
3. Seldte, *Sozialpolitik im Dritten Reich, 1933–1938*, 267–69.
4. See M. Herren, 'La formation d'une politique du travail internationale avant la première guerre mondiale', in J. Luciani (ed.), *Histoire de l'Office du Travail. 1890–1914*, Paris: Syros-Alternatives, 1992, 409–26.
5. Internationale Arbeiterschutzkonferenz, *Die Protokolle der internationalen Arbeiterschutzkonferenz*, Leipzig: Duncker & Humblot, 1890, 37.
6. See S. Kott, *Sozialstaat und Gesellschaft. Das deutsche Kaiserreich in Europa*, trans. M. Streng, Göttingen: Vandenhoeck & Ruprecht, 2014, 160–63.
7. See G. Zacher, *Leitfaden zur Arbeiterversicherung des Deutschen Reichs*, Berlin: Asher, 1893; see also S. Kott, 'Der Sozialstaat', in E. François and H. Schulze (eds), *Deutsche Erinnerungsorte*, vol. 2, Munich: Beck, 2001, 485–502.
8. R. Gregarek, 'Le mirage de l'Europe sociale. Associations internationales de politique sociale au tournant du 20e siècle', *Vingtième Siècle* 48 (1995), 103–18.
9. M. Lazard, *L'avenir du travail, 1939–1945*, Ghent: Impr. de Laere, 1945, 6.
10. T. Roosevelt, *Fear God and Take Our Own Part*, New York: George H. Doran, 1916, v.
11. See S. Kott, 'Dynamiques de l'internationalisation. L'Allemagne et l'Organisation internationale du travail (1919–1940)', *Critique internationale* 52(3) (2011), 69–84.
12. See International Labour Organization Archives (ILOA), Geneva, CAT 7/476; on Donau, see his Geneva Personal Files, ILOA, P 2881.

13. See, for example, D.T. Rogers, *Atlantic Crossings: Social Politics in a Progressive Age*, Cambridge, MA: Belknap Press of Harvard University Press, 1998.
14. N. N., *Die deutsche Sozialpolitik in der Nachkriegszeit*, Berlin: Zentralverlag, 1928, 51.
15. See ILOA, SI 1/0/24.
16. For detailed information on Andreas Grieser, see Biographical Appendix.
17. On Grieser's role in the ILO, see ILOA, SI 1/24/8.
18. K.K. Patel, 'Welfare in the Warfare State: Nazi Social Policy on the International Stage', *Bulletin of the German Historical Institute London* 37 (2015), 3–38.
19. See, for example, 'Reichsarbeitsminister Seldte an Staatssekretär Lammers, 27.4.1933', in *Akten der Reichskanzlei. Regierung Hitler 1933–1938*, vol. 1: *Die Regierung Hitler*, part I: *1933/34*, ed. K.-H. Minuth, series editors K. Repgen and H. Booms, Boppard am Rhein: Boldt, 1983, 412–13.
20. See, for example, E. Lüders, 'Der Anteil Deutschlands an der Erfüllung sozialpolitischer Aufgaben in Afrika', *RABl.* II (1935), 101–5, 125–28; A. Geck, 'Betriebliche Sozialpolitik in England', *RABl.* II (1935), 268–71, 304–6; 'Die sozialpolitische Gesetzgebung in Kanada im Jahre 1935', *RABl.* II (1935), 419–20.
21. See 'Chefbesprechung vom 15 June 1933', in *Akten der Reichskanzlei*, 560.
22. On the delegation, see *Akten der Reichskanzlei*, 553, fn. 27.
23. Reich Ministry of Labour, translated excerpt from the *Journal des Nations*, 14 June 1933, Bundesarchiv (BArch), R 3901/20642; see also ILOA, DADG 10–14; 'Les nazis et la conférence', *Journal des Nations*, 16 June 1933; on the broader context, see D. Liebscher, *Freude und Arbeit. Zur internationalen Freizeit- und Sozialpolitik des faschistischen Italien und des NS-Regimes*, Cologne: SH-Verlag, 2009, 274–83; R. Tosstorff, *Wilhelm Leuschner gegen Robert Ley. Ablehnung der Nazi-Diktatur durch die Internationale Arbeitskonferenz 1933 in Genf*, Frankfurt am Main: VAS, 2007.
24. See Note Krohn, 17 June 1933, BArch, R 3901/20642.
25. Comment Engel on the Letter from the Supreme Leadership of the Party Organization of 9 August 1933, n.d. [1933], BArch, R 3901/0642.
26. See Liebscher, *Freude und Arbeit*, 278–83.
27. See Seldte's pointedly matter-of-fact internal commentary on the departure, in Seldte to Main Section Heads and Departmental Directors, 9 November 1933, BArch, R 3901/20796.
28. Ley to Seldte, 9 August 1933 ('Enemies of the State'); Krohn to Seldte, 11 August 1933 ('Make Amends'); on the apology, see Seldte to Krohn, 30 October 1933, all BArch, R 3901/20642.
29. See Relations with Germany, 1933–1938, ILOA, XR 24/1/4; Director's Trip to Germany, May 1935, ILOA, XT 24/1/2.
30. Report from Butler to Pône, 25 May 1936, ILOA, XH 7/24/1.
31. See BArch, R 3901/20641, esp. Note Krohn, 31 May 1937; Krohn to Mackensen, 12 May 1937, Politisches Archiv des Auswärtigen Amtes Berlin (PAAA), R 29841; German attitudes to the ILO 1939–1941, Memorandum, 23 March 1939, ILOA, Z 5/1/24. Krohn referred here to the accession of the United States to the ILO in 1934.
32. See BArch, R 3901/201011, esp. Report Büge, n.d.; BArch R 3901/201012, esp. Report Schmidt, n.d., and Reich Ministry of Labour, Main Section IV to Department I a, 12 May 1937; see also BArch, R 3901/201013, esp. Report Note Schmidt, 12 March 1935.
33. On a treaty with the Netherlands of 1937, see, for example, BArch, R 3901/20652.
34. See, for example, ILOA, SI 11/24/22 (on France), esp. ILO Branch Office Berlin to Director International Labour Office, 25 September 1933; see also ILOA, SI 11/24/50/0 (Poland); ILOA, SI 11/24/17/0 (CSSR); ILOA SI 11/24/5/0 (Austria).
35. See T.A. Glootz, *Alterssicherung im europäischen Wohlfahrtsstaat. Etappen ihrer Entwicklung im 20. Jahrhundert*, Frankfurt am Main: Campus, 2005, 101–12; on the broader context, see U. Herbert, *Geschichte der Ausländerpolitik in Deutschland. Saisonarbeiter,*

Zwangsarbeiter, Gastarbeiter, Flüchtlinge, Munich: Beck, 2001, 118–23; J. Oltmer, *Migration und Politik in der Weimarer Republik*, Göttingen: Vandenhoeck & Ruprecht, 2005, esp. 425–81; on the evolution of the German-Polish regulations in 1935, see, for example, BArch, R 152/348 and S. Stegner, *Zwischen Souveränität und Ökonomie. Zugehörigkeitskonstruktionen durch die Sozialversicherung im deutsch-polnischen Verhältnis 1918–1945*, Baden-Baden: Nomos Verlag, 2018, 199–226.

36. See *NS-Presseanweisungen der Vorkriegszeit*, vol. 7/II: 1939, ed. K. Peter, Munich: Saur, 2001, 597.

37. Statement Krohn, n.d. [1934]; Note Sitzler, 23 February 1934, both ILOA, XH 7/24/1.

38. See Glootz, *Alterssicherung*, 106–12; see also S. Sasorski, 'Die zwischenstaatlichen Zusammenhänge in der Sozialversicherung', in Reichsverband Deutscher Landesversicherungsanstalten (ed.), *Bericht über die Arbeiten des Zweiten Internationalen Kongresses der Sozialversicherungsfachleute in Dresden*, Stuttgart: Kohlhammer, 1938, 39–55; on the subsequent German-Italian negotiations, see PAAA, R 99022.

39. See Reichsverband Deutscher Landesversicherungsanstalten, *Bericht über die Arbeiten*. The first congress had taken place in Budapest in 1935.

40. See Liebscher, *Freude und Arbeit*, esp. 250–439.

41. 'Völkerfriede durch Freude', *Westdeutscher Beobachter* (morning edition), 27 July 1936, quoted in Liebscher, *Freude und Arbeit*, 482.

42. See ibid., esp. 476–85.

43. See the extensive collections of newspaper excerpts in BArch, NS 5 VI; see also K.-H. Roth, *Intelligenz und Sozialpolitik im 'Dritten Reich'. Eine methodisch-historische Studie am Beispiel des Arbeitswissenschaftlichen Instituts der Deutschen Arbeitsfront*, Munich: Saur, 1993; U. Zucht, 'Das Arbeitswissenschaftliche Institut und die Nazifizierung der Sozialwissenschaften in Europa, 1936–1944', 1999: *Zeitschrift für Sozialgeschichte des 20. und 21. Jahrhunderts* 4 (1989), 10–40.

44. For detailed information on Friedrich Sitzler, see Biographical Appendix.

45. See I. Raehlmann, *Arbeitswissenschaft im Nationalsozialismus*, Wiesbaden: Verlag für Sozialwissenschaften, 2005, 140–41; Roth, *Intelligenz und Sozialpolitik*, 216–18, esp. 223. On Sitzler, see also ILOA, P 2785.

46. H. Müller-Brandenburg, *Der Arbeitsdienst fremder Staaten*, Leipzig: Heinig, 1938, 7; for an overview of Nazi labour service, see K.K. Patel, *Soldiers of Labor: Labor Service in Nazi Germany and New Deal America, 1933–1945*, Cambridge: Cambridge University Press, 2005; on other rivalries of this kind, see Patel, 'Welfare in the Warfare State'.

47. Seldte, *Sozialpolitik im Dritten Reich, 1933–1938*, 267.

48. For more detail, see K.K. Patel and S. Reichardt, 'The Dark Sides of Transnationalism: Social Engineering and Nazism, 1930s–1940s', *Journal of Contemporary History* 51(1) (2016), 3–21.

49. See W. Reich, *Massenpsychologie des Faschismus. Zur Sexualökonomie der politischen Reaktion und zur proletarischen Sexualpolitik (1933)*, Amsterdam: de Munter, 1986, 261–63.

50. A. Hamilton, 'The Enslavement of Women', in P. van Paassen and J. Waterman Wise (eds), *Nazism: An Assault on Civilization*, New York: Smith & Haas, 1934, 76–87.

51. See Liebscher, *Freude und Arbeit*, 507–614; see also PAAA, R 29854 on bilateral contacts of this kind.

52. See A. Nuq, 'When Fascism Does Not Keep Its Promises: The Ambivalent Relations to Nazi Germany and Francoist Spain in the Field of Social Policy', in S. Kott and K.K. Patel (eds), *Nazism across Borders: The Social Policies of the Third Reich and their Global Appeal*, Oxford: Oxford University Press, 2018, 201–27; on contacts with respect to the RAD, see PAAA, Embassy Madrid/685; on the DAF contacts, see Foreign Office to DAF Central Office for International Social Policy Design (Zentralamt für internationale Sozialgestaltung), 26 March 1941, PAAA, R 99022; see also D. Brydan, 'Axis Internationalism: Spanish

Health Experts and the Nazi "New Europe", 1939–1945', *Contemporary European History* 25(2) (2016), 291–311.

53. On social policy relations with Japan, see PAAA, R 99023; for a summary, see D. Tano, '"Achse der Freizeit". Der Weltkongress für Freizeit und Erholung 1936 und Japans Blick auf die Welt', *Zeitschrift für Geschichtswissenschaft* 58(9) (2010), 709–29.

54. See N. Götz and K.K. Patel, 'Facing the Fascist Model: Discourse and Construction of Labour Services in the USA and Sweden in the 1930s and 1940s', *Journal of Contemporary History* 41(1) (2006), 57–73.

55. See International Labour Organization, *Records of Proceedings. International Labour Conference Seventeenth Session, Geneva 1933*, ed. International Labour Conference, Geneva: ILO, 1933, 422–424.

56. See International Labour Office, *Public Works Policy* (Studies and Reports by International Labour Office 19), Geneva: ILO, 1935.

57. See 'Mr. Chamberlain on Peace', *The Times*, 3 October 1936; for an overall account of this, see A.M. Lemcke, '"Proving the Superiority of Democracy". Die "National Fitness Campaign" der britischen Regierung (1937–1939) im transnationalen Zusammenhang', *Vierteljahrshefte für Zeitgeschichte* 57(4) (2009), 543–70; I. Zweiniger-Bargielowska, *Managing the Body: Beauty, Health, and Fitness in Britain, 1880–1939*, Oxford: Oxford University Press, 2010, 279–329.

58. Note Roosevelt to Wilson, 3 September 1938, National Archives and Record Administration, Washington, DC, Franklin D. Roosevelt Library, Hyde Park, NY, President's Secretary's Files, Box 32.

59. See K.K. Patel, '"All of This Helps Us in Planning". Der New Deal und die nationalsozialistische Sozialpolitik', in M. Aust and D. Schönpflug (eds), *Vom Gegner lernen. Feindschaften und Kulturtransfers im Europa des 19. und 20. Jahrhunderts*, Frankfurt am Main: Campus, 2007, 234–52; K.K. Patel, *The New Deal: A Global History*, Princeton, NJ: Princeton University Press, 2016, 85–90, 259.

60. See R. Mariager and K. Petersen, 'Danish Social Policy in the Shadow of Nazi Germany 1933–1945', in Kott and Patel, *Nazism across Borders*, 337–65.

61. F. Sitzler, 'Sozialpolitik im neuen Europa', *Soziale Praxis* 49 (1940), 481–84, here 482.

62. See U. Schulz, 'The First Takeover: The Implementation of Social Policy Measures in Austria by the Reich Labour Ministry after the Anschluss', in Kott and Patel, *Nazism across Borders*, 53–81.

63. See A. Klimo, 'An Unhappy Return: German Pension Insurance Policy in Alsace', in Kott and Patel, *Nazism across Borders*, 81–104.

64. See R. Šustrová, 'A Dilemma of Change and Co-Operation: Labour and Social Policy in Bohemia and Moravia in the 1930s and 1940s', in Kott and Patel, *Nazism across Borders*, 105–41.

65. See Schulz, 'The First Takeover'.

66. See ibid.

67. See the chapters by Elizabeth Harvey and Swantje Greve in the present book.

68. See U. Herbert, *Fremdarbeiter. Politik und Praxis des 'Ausländer-Einsatzes' in der Kriegswirtschaft des Dritten Reiches*, new ed., Berlin, 1999; U. Vergin, *Die nationalsozialistische Arbeitseinsatzverwaltung und ihre Funktionen beim Fremdarbeiter(innen)einsatz während des Zweiten Weltkriegs*, unpubl. Ph.D. dissertation, Osnabrück: University of Osnabrück, 2008.

69. On the broader context of these developments, see M. Mazower, *Hitler's Empire: Nazi Rule in Occupied Europe*, London: Allen Lane, 2008.

70. See M. Ingulstad, 'Under the Hard Law of War: Norwegian Social Reforms under German Influence', in Kott and Patel, *Nazism across Borders*, 227–59; A. Korb, 'From the Balkans to Germany and Back: The Croatian Labour Service, 1941–1945', in Kott and Patel, *Nazism across Borders*, 259–85.

71. See, for example, DAF, Central Office for International Social Policy Design to the Foreign Office, 13 February 1941, PAAA, R 99019; see also PAAA, R 99020; cf. R. Hachtmann, 'Die Deutsche Arbeitsfront im Zweiten Weltkrieg', in D. Eichholtz (ed.), *Krieg und Wirtschaft. Studien zur deutschen Wirtschaftsgeschichte 1939–1945*, Berlin: Metropol, 1999, 69–108, here 97–102.

72. *Neue Internationale Rundschau der Arbeit*, ed. on behalf of Dr Robert Ley by Zentralamt für internationale Sozialgestaltung in cooperation with the Arbeitswissenschaftliches Institut der Deutschen Arbeitsfront, Berlin: Verlag der Deutschen Arbeitsfront, 1941–1944.

73. See *Sozialpolitische Weltrundschau*, ed. Reichsarbeitsministerium, Arbeitsgebiet für internationale Sozialpolitik, Berlin: self-published, 1940/41–1944.

74. Note Krohn, 15 May 1939, BArch, R 3901/20653.

75. Reich Ministry of Labour, II b, Note for Minister plus Attachment, n.d. [1938], BArch, R 3901/20652.

76. On further negotiations during the war, see PAAA, R 99022.

77. On Engel, see BArch, R 3901/20342-20345; BArch, R 3001/55208; BArch, R 9361-I/658.

78. On Karstedt, see BArch, R 3901/104928.

79. See K. Linne, '"Die Utopie des Herren Beveridge": Zur Rezeption des Beveridge-Plans im nationalsozialistischen Deutschland', *1999: Zeitschrift für Sozialgeschichte des 20. und 21. Jahrhunderts* 4 (1993), 62–82.

80. On German perceptions, see, for example, BArch, NS 5 VI/37876; on the ILO's perception of German views, see International Labour Office, Beveridge Plan. German Views Gleaned from the Press by the International Labour Office, ILOA, SI 2/0/25/2/2.

81. See Seldte to Funk et al., 25 August 1944, BArch, R 1501/3783; for an overview, see Patel, 'Welfare in the Warfare State'.

82. See Zucht, 'Das Arbeitswissenschaftliche Institut'; on the ILO, see also International Labour Office, *Resolutions Adopted by the Twenty-Sixth Session of the International Labour Conference, Philadelphia, April–May 1944* (reprinted from the Official Bulletin, vol. XXVI), Montreal: ILO, 1944; and A. Alcock, *History of the International Labour Organisation*, London: Macmillan, 1971, 171–87.

83. See, for example, K. Bertrams and S. Rudischhauser, 'German Ambitions and Belgian Expectations: Social Insurance and Industrial Relations in Occupied Belgium 1940–1944', in Kott and Patel, *Nazism across Borders*, 389–419; Mariager and Petersen, 'Danish Social Policy'.

84. See H.G. Hockerts, 'Einführung', in Hockerts (ed.), *Drei Wege deutscher Sozialstaatlichkeit. NS-Diktatur, Bundesrepublik und DDR im Vergleich*, Munich: Oldenbourg, 1998, 7–25.

85. C. Torp, *Gerechtigkeit im Wohlfahrtsstaat. Alter und Alterssicherung in Deutschland und Grossbritannien von 1945 bis heute*, Göttingen: Vandenhoeck & Ruprecht, 2015, 399.

86. On this topic and for a general account of (dis-)continuities beyond 1945, see esp. Bundesministerium für Arbeit und Sozialordnung, and Bundesarchiv (eds), *Geschichte der Sozialpolitik in Deutschland seit 1945*, vol. 1: *Grundlagen der Sozialpolitik*, Baden-Baden: Nomos, 2001.

87. See K.-H. Roth, 'Die Sozialpolitik des "europäischen Grossraum" im Spannungsfeld von Okkupation und Kollaboration (1938–1945)', in W. Röhr (ed.), *Okkupation und Kollaboration (1938–1945). Beiträge zu Konzepten und Praxis der Kollaboration in der deutschen Okkupationspolitik*, Berlin: Hüthig, 1994, 461–565, here 465.

88. W.G. Oschilewski, 'Ein Europäer kämpft für Berlin', in B. Lampasiak and W.G. Oschilewski (eds), *Otto Bach. Ein Europäer kämpft für Berlin. Reden und Ansprachen 1947 bis 1949*, Berlin: Arani, 1969, 73.

89. A. Storch, 'Zur Frage der Schlichtung', in H.C. Paulssen et al. (eds), *Sozialpolitik, Arbeits- und Sozialrecht. Festschrift für Friedrich Sitzler zu seinem 75. Geburtstag*, Stuttgart: Forkel, 1956, 9–11, here 11.

90. J. Heinel, *Die deutsche Sozialpolitik des 19. Jahrhunderts im Spiegel der Schulgeschichtsbücher*, Braunschweig: Limbach, 1962, 94.

Bibliography

Akten der Reichskanzlei. *Regierung Hitler 1933–1938*, vol. 1: *Die Regierung Hitler*, part I: *1933/34*, ed. K.-H. Minuth, series editors K. Repgen and H. Booms. Boppard am Rhein: Boldt, 1983.

Alcock, A.E. *History of the International Labour Organisation*. London: Macmillan, 1971.

Bertrams, K., and S. Rudischhauser. 'German Ambitions and Belgian Expectations: Social Insurance and Industrial Relations in Occupied Belgium 1940–1944', in S. Kott and K.K. Patel (eds), *Nazism across Borders: The Social Policies of the Third Reich and their Global Appeal* (Oxford: Oxford University Press, 2018), 389–419.

Britz, H.-J. 'Andreas Grieser', in S. Koss and W. Löhr (eds), *Biographisches Lexikon des KV*, part 2 (Schernfeld: SH-Verlag, 1993), 38–41.

Brydan, D. 'Axis Internationalism: Spanish Health Experts and the Nazi "New Europe", 1939–1945'. *Contemporary European History* 25(2) (2016), 291–311.

Bundesministerium für Arbeit und Sozialordnung, and Bundesarchiv (eds). *Geschichte der Sozialpolitik in Deutschland seit 1945*, 11 vols. Baden-Baden: Nomos, 2001–2008.

Geck, A. 'Betriebliche Sozialpolitik in England'. *Reichsarbeitsblatt* II (1935), 268–71 and 304–6.

Glootz, T.A. *Alterssicherung im europäischen Wohlfahrtsstaat. Etappen ihrer Entwicklung im 20. Jahrhundert*. Frankfurt am Main: Campus, 2005.

Götz, N., and K.K. Patel. 'Facing the Fascist Model: Discourse and Construction of Labour Services in the USA and Sweden in the 1930s and 1940s'. *Journal of Contemporary History* 41(1) (2006), 57–73.

Gregarek, R. 'Le mirage de l'Europe sociale. Associations internationales de politique sociale au tournant du 20e siècle'. *Vingtième Siècle* 48 (1995), 103–18.

Hachtmann, R. 'Die Deutsche Arbeitsfront im Zweiten Weltkrieg', in D. Eichholtz (ed.), *Krieg und Wirtschaft. Studien zur deutschen Wirtschaftsgeschichte 1939–1945* (Berlin: Metropol, 1999), 69–108.

Hamilton, A. 'The Enslavement of Women', in P. van Paassen and J. Waterman Wise (eds), *Nazism: An Assault on Civilization* (New York: Smith & Haas, 1934), 76–87.

Heinel, J. *Die deutsche Sozialpolitik des 19. Jahrhunderts im Spiegel der Schulgeschichtsbücher*. Braunschweig: Limbach, 1962.

Herbert, U. *Fremdarbeiter. Politik und Praxis des 'Ausländer-Einsatzes' in der Kriegswirtschaft des Dritten Reiches*, new ed. Berlin, 1999.

Herbert, U. *Geschichte der Ausländerpolitik in Deutschland. Saisonarbeiter, Zwangsarbeiter, Gastarbeiter, Flüchtlinge*. Munich: Beck, 2001.

Herbert, U. *Hitler's Foreign Workers: Enforced Foreign Labor in Germany under the Third Reich*, trans. W. Templer. Cambridge: Cambridge University Press, 1997.

Herren, M. 'La formation d'une politique du travail internationale avant la première guerre mondiale', in J. Luciani (ed.), *Histoire de l'Office du Travail. 1890–1914* (Paris: Syros-Alternatives, 1992), 409–26.

Hockerts, H.G. 'Einführung', in Hockerts (ed.), *Drei Wege deutscher Sozialstaatlichkeit. NS-Diktatur, Bundesrepublik und DDR im Vergleich* (Munich: Oldenbourg, 1998), 7–25.

Horkenbach, C. (ed.). *Das Deutsche Reich von 1918 bis heute. Jahrgang 1933*. Berlin: Verlag für Presse, Wirtschaft und Politik, 1935.

Ingulstad, M. 'Under the Hard Law of War: Norwegian Social Reforms under German Influence', in S. Kott and K.K. Patel (eds), *Nazism across Borders: The Social Policies of the Third Reich and their Global Appeal* (Oxford: Oxford University Press, 2018), 227–59.

International Labour Office. *Resolutions Adopted by the Twenty-Sixth Session of the International Labour Conference, Philadelphia, April–May 1944* (reprinted from the Official Bulletin, vol. XXVI). Montreal: ILO, 1944.

International Labour Office. *Public Works Policy* (Studies and Reports by International Labour Office 19). Geneva: ILO, 1935.

International Labour Organization. *Records of Proceedings. International Labour Conference Seventeenth Session, Geneva 1933*, ed. International Labour Conference. Geneva: ILO, 1933.

Internationale Arbeiterschutzkonferenz. *Die Protokolle der internationalen Arbeiterschutzkonferenz*. Leipzig: Duncker & Humblot, 1890.

Karl, V. *Lexikon Pfälzer Persönlichkeiten*. Edenkoben: Hennig, 1995.

Klimo, A. 'An Unhappy Return: German Pension Insurance Policy in Alsace', in S. Kott and K.K. Patel (eds), *Nazism across Borders: The Social Policies of the Third Reich and their Global Appeal* (Oxford: Oxford University Press, 2018), 81–104.

Korb, A. 'From the Balkans to Germany and Back: The Croatian Labour Service, 1941–1945', in S. Kott and K.K. Patel (eds), *Nazism across Borders: The Social Policies of the Third Reich and their Global Appeal* (Oxford: Oxford University Press, 2018), 259–85.

Kott, S. 'Dynamiques de l'internationalisation. L'Allemagne et l'Organisation internationale du travail (1919–1940)'. *Critique internationale* 52(3) (2011), 69–84.

Kott, S. 'Der Sozialstaat', in E. François and H. Schulze (eds), *Deutsche Erinnerungsorte*, vol. 2 (Munich: Beck, 2001), 485–502.

Kott, S. *Sozialstaat und Gesellschaft. Das deutsche Kaiserreich in Europa*, trans. M. Streng. Göttingen: Vandenhoeck & Ruprecht, 2014.

Kott, S., and J. Droux (eds). *Globalizing Social Rights: The International Labour Organization and Beyond*. London: Palgrave Macmillan, 2013.

Kott, S., S.-L. Hoffmann, P. Romijn and O. Wieviorka (eds). *Seeking Peace in the Wake of War: Europe, 1943–1947*. Amsterdam: Amsterdam University Press, 2015.

Lazard, M. *L'avenir du travail, 1939–1945*. Ghent: Impr. de Laere, 1945.

Lemcke, A.M. '"Proving the Superiority of Democracy". Die "National Fitness Campaign" der britischen Regierung (1937–1939) im transnationalen Zusammenhang'. *Vierteljahrshefte für Zeitgeschichte* 57(4) (2009), 543–70.

Liebscher, D. *Freude und Arbeit. Zur internationalen Freizeit- und Sozialpolitik des faschistischen Italien und des NS-Regimes*. Cologne: SH-Verlag, 2009.

Linne, K. '"Die Utopie des Herren Beveridge": Zur Rezeption des Beveridge-Plans im nationalsozialistischen Deutschland'. *1999: Zeitschrift für Sozialgeschichte des 20. und 21. Jahrhunderts* 4 (1993), 62–82.

Lüders, E. 'Der Anteil Deutschlands an der Erfüllung sozialpolitischer Aufgaben in Afrika'. *Reichsarbeitsblatt* II (1935), 101–5 and 125–28.

Mariager, R., and K. Petersen. 'Danish Social Policy in the Shadow of Nazi Germany 1933–1945', in S. Kott and K.K. Patel (eds), *Nazism across Borders: The Social Policies of the Third Reich and their Global Appeal* (Oxford: Oxford University Press, 2018), 337–65.

Mazower, M. *Hitler's Empire: Nazi Rule in Occupied Europe*. London: Allen Lane, 2008.

Müller-Brandenburg, H. *Der Arbeitsdienst fremder Staaten*. Leipzig: Heinig, 1938.

Neue Internationale Rundschau der Arbeit, ed. on behalf of Dr Robert Ley by Zentralamt für internationale Sozialgestaltung in cooperation with the Arbeitswissenschaftliches Institut der Deutschen Arbeitsfront. Berlin: Verlag der Deutschen Arbeitsfront, 1941–1944.

N. N. *Die deutsche Sozialpolitik in der Nachkriegszeit*. Berlin: Zentralverlag, 1928.

NS-Presseanweisungen der Vorkriegszeit, vol. 7/II: 1939, ed. K. Peter. Munich: Saur, 2001.

Nuq, A. 'When Fascism Does Not Keep Its Promises: The Ambivalent Relations to Nazi Germany and Francoist Spain in the Field of Social Policy', in S. Kott and K.K. Patel (eds), *Nazism across Borders: The Social Policies of the Third Reich and their Global Appeal* (Oxford: Oxford University Press, 2018), 201–27.

Oltmer, J. *Migration und Politik in der Weimarer Republik*. Göttingen: Vandenhoeck & Ruprecht, 2005.

Oschilewski, W.G. 'Ein Europäer kämpft für Berlin', in B. Lampasiak and W.G. Oschilewski (eds), *Otto Bach. Ein Europäer kämpft für Berlin. Reden und Ansprachen 1947 bis 1949* (Berlin: Arani, 1969), 73.

Patel, K.K. '"All of This Helps Us in Planning". Der New Deal und die nationalsozialistische Sozialpolitik', in M. Aust and D. Schönpflug (eds), *Vom Gegner lernen. Feindschaften und Kulturtransfers im Europa des 19. und 20. Jahrhunderts* (Frankfurt am Main: Campus, 2007), 234–52.

Patel, K.K. *The New Deal: A Global History*. Princeton, NJ: Princeton University Press, 2016.

Patel, K.K. *'Soldaten der Arbeit'. Arbeitsdienste in Deutschland und den USA, 1933–1945*. Göttingen: Vandenhoeck & Ruprecht, 2003.

Patel, K.K. 'Welfare in the Warfare State: Nazi Social Policy on the International Stage'. *Bulletin of the German Historical Institute London* 37 (2015), 3–38.

Patel, K.K., and S. Reichardt. 'The Dark Sides of Transnationalism: Social Engineering and Nazism, 1930s–1940s'. *Journal of Contemporary History* 51 (2016), 3–21.

Raehlmann, I. *Arbeitswissenschaft im Nationalsozialismus*. Wiesbaden: Verlag für Sozialwissenschaften, 2005.

Reich, W. *Massenpsychologie des Faschismus. Zur Sexualökonomie der politischen Reaktion und zur proletarischen Sexualpolitik (1933)*. Amsterdam: de Munter, 1986.

Rogers, D.T. *Atlantic Crossings: Social Politics in a Progressive Age*. Cambridge, MA: Belknap Press of Harvard University Press, 1998.

Roosevelt, T. *Fear God and Take Our Own Part*. New York: George H. Doran, 1916.

Roth, K.-H. *Intelligenz und Sozialpolitik im 'Dritten Reich'. Eine methodisch-historische Studie am Beispiel des Arbeitswissenschaftlichen Instituts der Deutschen Arbeitsfront*. Munich: Saur, 1993.

Roth, K.-H. 'Die Sozialpolitik des "europäischen Grossraum" im Spannungsfeld von Okkupation und Kollaboration (1938–1945)', in W. Röhr (ed.), *Okkupation und Kollaboration (1938–1945). Beiträge zu Konzepten und Praxis der Kollaboration in der deutschen Okkupationspolitik* (Berlin: Hüthig, 1994), 461–565.

Sasorski, S. 'Die zwischenstaatlichen Zusammenhänge in der Sozialversicherung', in Reichsverband Deutscher Landesversicherungsanstalten (ed.), *Bericht über die Arbeiten des Zweiten Internationalen Kongresses der Sozialversicherungsfachleute in Dresden* (Stuttgart: Kohlhammer, 1938), 39–55.

Schmied, V.H. *Andreas Grieser (1868–1955). Das Leben und Wirken des 'Nestors' der deutschen Sozialversicherung*. Karlstadt: self-published, 1993.

Schulz, U. 'The First Takeover: The Implementation of Social Policy Measures in Austria by the Reich Labour Ministry after the Anschluss', in S. Kott and K.K. Patel (eds), *Nazism across Borders: The Social Policies of the Third Reich and their Global Appeal* (Oxford: Oxford University Press, 2018), 53–81.

Seldte, F. *Sozialpolitik im Dritten Reich, 1933–1938*. Munich: Beck, 1939.

Seldte, F. *Sozialpolitik im Dritten Reich. Ein Bericht* (attachment to *Reichsarbeitsblatt 1935*, no. 36). Berlin: Reichsdruckerei, 1935.

Sitzler, F. 'Sozialpolitik im neuen Europa'. *Soziale Praxis* 49 (1940), 481–84.

Sozialpolitische Weltrundschau, ed. Reichsarbeitsministerium, Arbeitsgebiet für internationale Sozialpolitik. Berlin: self-published, 1940/41–1944.

Stegner, S. *Zwischen Souveränität und Ökonomie. Zugehörigkeitskonstruktionen durch die Sozialversicherung im deutsch-polnischen Verhältnis 1918–1945*. Baden-Baden: Nomos Verlag, 2018.

Storch, A. 'Zur Frage der Schlichtung', in H.C. Paulssen et al. (eds), *Sozialpolitik, Arbeits- und Sozialrecht. Festschrift für Friedrich Sitzler zu seinem 75. Geburtstag* (Stuttgart: Forkel, 1956), 9–11.

Šustrová, R. 'A Dilemma of Change and Co-Operation: Labour and Social Policy in Bohemia and Moravia in the 1930s and 1940s', in S. Kott and K.K. Patel (eds), *Nazism across Borders: The Social Policies of the Third Reich and their Global Appeal* (Oxford: Oxford University Press, 2018), 105–41.

Tano, D. '"Achse der Freizeit". Der Weltkongress für Freizeit und Erholung 1936 und Japans Blick auf die Welt'. *Zeitschrift für Geschichtswissenschaft* 58(9) (2010), 709–29.

Torp, C. *Gerechtigkeit im Wohlfahrtsstaat. Alter und Alterssicherung in Deutschland und Grossbritannien von 1945 bis heute*. Göttingen: Vandenhoeck & Ruprecht, 2015.

Tosstorff, R. *Wilhelm Leuschner gegen Robert Ley. Ablehnung der Nazi-Diktatur durch die Internationale Arbeitskonferenz 1933 in Genf*. Frankfurt am Main: VAS, 2007.

Vergin, U. *Die nationalsozialistische Arbeitseinsatzverwaltung und ihre Funktionen beim Fremdarbeiter(innen)einsatz während des Zweiten Weltkriegs*, unpubl. Ph.D. dissertation. Osnabrück: University of Osnabrück, 2008.

Zacher, G. *Leitfaden zur Arbeiterversicherung des Deutschen Reichs*. Berlin: Asher, 1893.

Zucht, U. 'Das Arbeitswissenschaftliche Institut und die Nazifizierung der Sozialwissenschaften in Europa, 1936–1944'. *1999: Zeitschrift für Sozialgeschichte des 20. und 21. Jahrhunderts* 4(3) (1989), 10–40.

Zweiniger-Bargielowska, I. *Managing the Body: Beauty, Health, and Fitness in Britain, 1880–1939*. Oxford: Oxford University Press, 2010.

Chapter 9

Labour Administration and Manpower Recruitment in Occupied Europe
Belgium and the General Government

Elizabeth Harvey

The recruitment of foreign industrial workers is based on *voluntary registration*. This is self-evident in the case of friendly states. In contrast to the allegations made by the enemy press, however, it must be stressed that the same principle applies to recruitment in the occupied territories. Besides, the deployment of compulsorily recruited workers would scarcely serve the interests of German companies. Our increasingly successful placement services prove that it is possible, without the use of coercion, to recruit workers on a voluntary basis in the occupied territories as well.[1]

These lines are taken from an article published in January 1941 by Dr Walter Letsch, senior government counsellor (*Oberregierungsrat*) at the Reich Ministry of Labour, ministerial counsellor (*Ministerialrat*) from 1942 and later head of Department VI a of the Europe Office for Labour Deployment.[2] With its optimistic yet defensive tone and its peculiar logic, this quotation is a good starting point for a discussion of the labour administration and labour recruitment in the Nazi-occupied territories during the Second World War.

An extensive historiography on the wartime labour deployment of foreign workers in the German Reich has developed since the 1960s, particularly in the wake of the landmark study by Ulrich Herbert in 1985.[3] It has more recently been augmented by studies focusing on the policies and practices of the labour administration within different Nazi-occupied countries and regions. This recent work has illuminated the harnessing of labour within the occupied territories themselves as well as the dispatch of men, women and juveniles to the Reich.[4] Regional studies on Nazi occupation policy have furnished us with key information on manpower policy and the labour administration in specific areas.[5] There have also been moves towards more systematic comparison of the workings of the labour administration in various parts of occupied Europe: particularly notable among these are studies focusing on different parts of Nazi-occupied Eastern and Southeastern Europe.[6] New regional and country studies on Western, Northern and Southeastern Europe, meanwhile, have contributed to the comparison of labour administrations and manpower policy across occupied Europe as a whole.[7]

The present chapter presents two contrasting examples from Eastern and Western Europe: the General Government (as part of Nazi-occupied Poland) and occupied Belgium. As the context of this dual focus, I begin by describing the German labour administration's official view of itself during the Second World War, namely as an expert agency dedicated to 'inter-European labour exchange'.[8] I go on to outline key lines of argument from historical studies of the labour administration and 'Reich deployment', using these as the basis for a concluding comparative overview. The comparative analysis aims to shed light on how the labour administration enforced the system of forced manpower recruitment in East and West, sustaining the Nazi war economy until the end of the war.

The View from the Reich Ministry of Labour

In official publications, Reich Labour Minister Franz Seldte, State Secretary Friedrich Syrup and other ministry officials at the Berlin headquarters presented a picture of the German labour administration as an instrument of rationalization within the expanding Nazi sphere of power.[9] As an administrative apparatus, the labour administration consisted of a network of Land labour offices (Gau labour offices from 1943 onwards) and labour offices, which extended beyond the borders of the 'Old Reich' into the annexed territories.[10] The procurement of foreign civilian labourers to work in Germany was based partly on bilateral agreements between the German government and 'friendly' countries (Italy, Slovakia, Hungary, Bulgaria) and partly on the recruitment in the occupied territories carried out by the organs of labour administration that were either taken over by the occupiers or set up from scratch.[11] The official in charge of the German labour administration in the Reich was Friedrich Syrup, ex-president of the formerly independent Reich Institution for Job Placement and Unemployment Insurance and, since October 1936, head of the Working Group on Labour Deployment within Göring's Four-Year Plan apparatus. At the beginning of 1939, with the incorporation of the Reich Institution into the Reich Ministry of Labour, Syrup had become state secretary in the ministry.[12] In official self-portrayals, labour administration experts appeared as masters of improvisation, controlling the workforce in the 'European economic space', and thus overcoming the flaws of the liberal 'labour market' ('the days of a liberalistic outlook are over').[13] This standard narrative placed the recruiting of foreign workers for 'deployment' in the Reich in a two-fold context: first, the contemporary mobilization of labour reserves within Germany for the wartime economy and, second, long-term historical developments encompassing foreign 'border-crossers' and migrant labourers, including seasonal workers, in the German economy.[14] According to a 1941 article on Western Europe by Seldte, 'labour deployment', as guided by the state, was intended to overcome unemployment in all the countries involved.[15] Syrup, for his part, argued that, in the midst of war, work could even serve as a means of reconciliation: 'Nothing binds nations together more than people working collectively to reach the same goal: the welfare of Europe'.[16] At the same time, officials advocated keeping foreign workers in continual motion to avert the risks associated with long-term foreign settlement in Germany and warned against the danger of the 'unnatural mixing of European peoples and races'.[17]

The clichés of order and optimization also permeated a 1942 article by Ministerial Counsellor (*Ministerialrat*) Dr Max Timm, later head of Main Section VI (Europe Office for Labour Deployment), entitled 'The Deployment of Foreign Workers in Germany'. In his overview covering the period up to the end of 1941, he sought to justify the planned 'deployment': 'Once the war began it became even more obvious that we have to steer labour deployment systematically, while ensuring that the recruitment and placement of foreign workers is carried out uniformly, according to general principles, by the labour deployment administration'.[18] But Timm's overview of occupied and 'friendly' territories – the Reich Protectorate of Bohemia and Moravia, the General Government, Italy, Slovakia, Hungary, Croatia, Bulgaria, Serbia, the Netherlands, Belgium (with northern France), France (excluding northern France), Denmark, Norway and Spain – could not disguise the uneven patchwork of administrative forms and labour recruitment measures in the various occupied countries. Timm affirmed the principle of voluntary labour recruitment for the Reich ('The voluntary principle must be upheld', p. 9), but he also revealed the difficulties involved in 'recruitment', for example in his references to the 'need to intensify propaganda' in Serbia (p. 75) and the 'continuous process of education' required in Belgium (p. 85). His references to the 'special position of the Poles' (p. 10) and the 'special treatment of the Poles' (p. 26 f.), due to ethnopolitical and social policy factors ('volkstums- und sozialpolitische Gründe') that he left unelucidated, also laid bare the serious limitations to the principle of 'equal rights and obligations' for foreign workers in the Reich (p. 9 f.). As well as hinting at less than voluntary recruitment, Timm's text thus made clear the anything but equal basis of foreign labour recruitment from the outset and the stark discrimination against Poles that would later be replicated in the case of civilian workers from the Soviet Union.

The Labour Administration in the Occupied Territories: Questions and Comparative Perspectives

In opening up comparative perspectives on wartime labour regimes in different territories occupied by Nazi Germany, historians have suggested a number of questions and hypotheses. These can be grouped roughly around three themes, considered here in turn.

The first object of comparison comprises the objectives of manpower and labour deployment policy as a central field of occupation policy. Various factors fed into this, including the general goals of German occupation policy, namely the exploitation of the occupied territories' resources to bolster the war economy, the suppression of resistance, and the plundering, exploitation and, finally, murder of the Jews.[19] But there were also distinct goals for different countries that reflected the Nazi vision of a particular territory's place in the envisaged 'new order' in Europe.[20] This 'new order' was never elaborated in detail, but certain patterns emerged within the practice of the Nazi occupation regimes that were relevant to the policy and practice of labour administration. For example, the Nazis made a broad distinction between the 'Slavic' peoples of Eastern Europe, regarded as racially inferior and subject to potentially untrammelled 'racial restructuring' (*völkische Flurbereinigung*), and the populations of Western Europe (especially if they were considered 'Germanic'), who were to be encouraged to cooperate with the occupiers. In addition, the Nazi regime distinguished between the territories bordering on Germany in the east, south-east and west that were earmarked for annexation and Germanization in the short or long term, and those occupied areas that would retain some form of distinct statehood within a German-led Europe, with or without border changes. A third factor determining the objectives of manpower policy was the economic structure of a given occupied country. In some territories, a pre-existing industrial base was to be restored and expanded to contribute to German war production; in others, the occupiers were chiefly concerned with extracting raw materials and labour to boost production within the Greater German Reich.

Another potential factor influencing labour policy was the memory of earlier German attempts to access labour in a particular occupied country. During the First World War, foreign civilian workers as well as prisoners of war had been exploited as a resource for the German war economy.[21] Various methods of acquiring manpower, including coercive measures, were deployed by the civilian authorities (Belgian General Government and Warsaw General Government) and military administrations (the military administration in the operations and staging areas of 'Belgium and Northern France' on the one hand and 'Ober Ost' in the case of northeastern Poland, Belarus and Lithuania on the other). Complex forms of recruitment, pressure and direct coercion were pursued to acquire civilian workers for deployment locally and in the Reich in the various areas under civilian and military administration in West and East, and at various stages of the war. The most notorious measures were the deportations from Belgium to Germany in the autumn and winter of 1916–1917, which were halted in the spring of 1917, and from the areas of Belgium and northern France under military administration to the staging area and the operations zone, which continued until the end of the war.[22] The ruthless forced recruitment and deportations that took place concurrently in the Eastern European territories, albeit only within the occupied areas, aroused less indignation among contemporary observers and foreign critics.[23] For historians investigating Nazi occupation and manpower policy, the question arises as to whether the employment of forced labourers during the First World War was 'a kind of trial run for World War II',[24] with an emphasis on continuity and repetition, or whether we ought to view manpower policy in the First World War as a set of administrative experiences constituting a general context for later decision-making as opposed to a specific blueprint.[25] Given these different views, it is worth asking what parallels there might be, where differences exist, and what the German labour administrations in the various occupied territories during the Second World War learned or sought to learn from the earlier conflict.[26]

A second focus for a comparative approach to labour administrations under Nazi rule is the form of the labour administration within a particular occupied territory, whether or not it offered scope for collaboration/influence by the resident population, and the relative strength of its position within the wider occupation administration.[27] According to Florian Dierl, manpower policy in occupied Europe was 'by no means the expression of a coherent drive coordinated by the GBA [General Plenipotentiary for Labour Deployment] and the labour administration'.[28] In addition to the overarching objectives of manpower policy, then, we must also consider the labour administration as an element in a specific type of occupation regime and seek to shed light on the particular constellation of institutions and actors, conflicts and negotiation processes at the local level. Without getting too deeply into typologies of occupation administrations,[29] we might roughly differentiate between three variants. First, in the formally and de facto annexed areas, the administrative structures of the German Reich were introduced, albeit with deviations from the 'Old Reich model'. Second, different variations of occupation regimes emerged in the form of civilian administrations, for example under a Reich Commissioner or Reich Protector. The third form comprised the military governments, for example in Belgium until July 1944, in Serbia or in the occupied Soviet territories outside the civilian-administered Reich commissariats of Ukraine and Ostland. In some occupied countries (whether under civilian or military rule), indigenous administrations under German supervision were intended by the occupiers to be a sign of continuity and stability in state structures. Within such structures of collaboration and cooperation, there was varying scope for indigenous actors to influence or even object to aspects of 'labour deployment'. But there were other occupation regimes that retained an indigenous administration only at local level and merely as pawns, devoid of influence on labour recruitment policies.

A comparison needs to identify both common trends and differing developments in the practice of labour administration in occupied Europe. In some occupied territories (for example in the Reich Protectorate of Bohemia and Moravia, occupied Poland and the Western European countries), after the German invasion there was a brief or lengthy period of decline in production, shutdowns and consequent unemployment, which was conducive to the recruitment of labour for the German economy. As soon as unemployment was superseded by a labour shortage, sometimes within months, people's willingness to sign up for 'Reich deployment' declined.[30] When the labour shortage became a crisis in the winter of 1941–1942, the conflicts in the occupied territories between the labour administration, which had to fill the transports to the Reich, and other German agencies, which – depending on the local economic structure – gave priority to local production, typically worsened. In his role as general plenipotentiary for labour deployment (as of March 1942), Fritz Sauckel forced a marked increase in the recruitment of manpower for the Reich. As the extension of his apparatus in the occupied territories, from September 1942 onwards his local commissioners (*Beauftragte*), mostly specialists who already held a senior position in the relevant department of the occupation administration, received greater backing vis-à-vis other German authorities. But this did not put an end to the insoluble conflicts between different agencies over manpower. Meanwhile, the question arises as to whether the 'Sauckel system' was perceived differently by the local population depending on whether deportations to the Reich from a given area were already part and parcel of everyday life under occupation, or appeared as a new and radical stage of exploitation.

A third theme for the comparison of labour recruitment in different occupied territories encompasses the repertoire of recruitment methods and the combination of 'carrot and stick' used.[31] At first glance the same pattern was repeated, albeit at different rates, from voluntary recruitment to coercion and violence. But a simple stage-based model can be misleading.[32] The notion of such a trajectory must be tempered by a recognition of the economic plight of many who 'voluntarily' signed up.[33] Moreover, many volunteers from western countries were involuntarily detained at their workplaces in Germany after their temporary contracts expired through the mechanism of a 'compulsory labour order' (*Dienstverpflichtung*).[34] Furthermore, the idea of a trajectory from voluntary recruitment to coercion can mask contexts in which extreme coercion was applied to certain groups but where recruitment of others on a voluntary basis still continued.[35]

Another dimension of the practices of labour administrations that we might scrutinize through a comparative approach is their tendency to play different groups off against each other. Labour policy could become a means of ethnopolitical and racist differentiation and privileging, for example in mixed German-Polish East Upper Silesia, where presumed Poles were laid off in favour of Germans,[36] or in the occupied Baltic districts of the Reich Commissariat Ostland, where the Slavic inhabitants were disadvantaged due to cooperation between the German labour administration and the Baltic majority populations.[37] The differentiation between categories of workers could also serve to substitute one group for another, which was then 'freed up'. For example, foreign women were deployed as a replacement for foreign men under certain circumstances. However, on the basis of racist ideas and stereotypes, Polish and Soviet women were far more likely to be forced to work than their Western European counterparts. A gender-based privilege applied only, and only conditionally, to Western European women.[38] Processes of substitution also took place in the context of antisemitic persecution. If, from the point of view of the labour administration, replacements for Jewish workers were available among the unemployed or 'underemployed' non-Jewish population – such a scenario pertained, for example, in occupied Latvia and Belarus in the summer of 1941 after the German invasion – then non-Jews were called up to work and the Jewish workers were 'freed up', with fatal consequences for the latter.[39] Later, when the 'surplus' of workers had given way to a labour shortage, Jewish workers could stave off their annihilation if the labour administration regarded them, at least temporarily, as a substitute for non-Jewish workers.

Two Case Studies: The Labour Administration and Manpower Policy in the General Government and Belgium

In light of these considerations, in what follows I take a closer look at the labour administration and manpower policy in two contrasting areas under Nazi occupation. The first is the 'General Government for the Occupied Polish Territories', the second Belgium. According to a survey of foreign workers in the German Reich of 25 September 1941, which was based on a count by the labour offices, there were 2,140,000 foreign civilian (blue- and white-collar) workers in the Reich at the time.[40] There were also 1,367,973 prisoners of war.[41] Of the civilian workforce, almost half were Poles (1,007,561). How many of the latter came from the General Government is unknown: when it came to nationality ('former Poles'), the count did not differentiate between the General Government and the 'incorporated' western areas of Poland as regions of origin. In any event, Poles were by far the largest group by nationality, and a remarkably large minority of them were women (262,730 women compared to 744,831 men). The same count reveals that Belgians constituted the largest contingent from occupied Western Europe. At this time, the labour offices in the German Reich counted 121,501 Belgian workers, of which 106,832 were men and 14,669 women.[42] The military administration in Belgium identified significantly higher numbers of workers 'placed' in the German Reich: 206,692 as at 6 September 1941.[43] Despite the open questions regarding the figures, it is clear that at this stage the labour administration could consider the recruitment of workers from both the General Government and Belgium a success. Another piece of common ground shared between Belgium and Poland was the experience of forced labour under German occupation in the First World War and the occupiers' coercive labour recruitment. As 'experiential background' to the German labour administration in Poland from 1939 and in Belgium from 1940, two aspects of manpower policy in the occupied territories during the First World War are particularly striking. The first is how the occupiers legitimized the drive to register workers with reference to unemployment and a supposed 'aversion to work'. The second, especially from 1916, is the increased use of coercion.

The German occupiers justified the registering of civilians during the First World War in order to put them to work, a measure subject to important restrictions according to the Hague Convention,[44] in light of Germany's wartime needs. Yet in Belgium, the Warsaw General Government and the 'Ober Ost' area, which was under military administration, the occupation authorities presented such measures as a response to the unemployment and social hardship engendered by war and occupation. In the

General Governments of Belgium and Warsaw, the unemployed and 'idle' were regarded as a manoeuvrable mass that could be pushed around at will and recruited forcefully for work in Germany (or locally).[45] This logic also led to the stigmatization of broad sections of the population in the occupied West as well as in the East – Belgians, Poles, Lithuanians and especially Jews in the General Government of Warsaw and the 'Ober Ost' region – as underemployed and 'work-shy'. For them, labour deployment was also to serve as a means of discipline.[46] In addition, by shutting down industrial and craft enterprises, the occupiers helped to artificially increase unemployment, and thus intensified the economic pressure compelling the needy to sign up to work locally or in the Reich.[47]

The use of force to recruit workers during the First World War reached its peak in August 1916 after the takeover of the Supreme Army Command by Ludendorff and Hindenburg. Ludendorff pursued a strategy that, ignoring the Hague Convention, aimed at the 'total' exhaustion of human resources within the German sphere of power.[48] Here he drew on his experiences in the 'Ober Ost' region, where he had practised a policy of accelerated economic exploitation on the basis of the vigorous conscription of supposedly 'unemployed' workers for local labour deployment since September 1915.[49] Under pressure from Ludendorff, in October 1916 the two civilian administrations, first in the General Government of Warsaw and then in its Belgian counterpart, began forcibly to draft workers for labour deployment and deport them from their home areas.[50] By December 1916, about five thousand predominantly Jewish workers had been 'conscripted' from the General Government of Warsaw, some of whom were deported to the 'Ober Ost' region and organized in 'civilian worker battalions'.[51] Meanwhile, in the period from 26 October 1916 to 10 February 1917, about sixty thousand men were transported from the General Government of Belgium to Germany, where around 1,300 died as a result of the disastrous living conditions in the camps and terrible working conditions.[52] Earlier, from 8 October 1916 onwards,[53] additional contingents totalling more than sixty thousand men were deported from the militarily administered territory of Belgium and northern France to the operations and staging areas, where they were forced to work in 'civilian worker battalions'. In this case, too, more than a thousand deportees died.[54] While the workers in these 'battalions' had to perform forced labour until the war ended in the 'Ober Ost' region and in Belgium/northern France, in December 1916 and February 1917 respectively the civilian regimes of the General Government of Warsaw and the General Government of Belgium discontinued the drastic coercive measures they had introduced in October 1916. In both cases this turnaround was due to the economic ineffectiveness of the policy of coercion and the occupiers' interest in retaining at least some chance of cooperation with the population. This desire for cooperation applied not only to the Belgians, but also to the Poles, in view of the proclamation of the Polish state in November 1916. In the case of Belgium there were numerous protests, not only in the country itself, often led by the Catholic Church, but also in Germany and other countries.[55]

A look at the manpower policy of the German occupiers in Belgium and Poland in the First World War as a foil for Nazi manpower policy in these areas two decades later reveals disparate and contradictory tendencies in the various phases of war and different administrative areas.[56] On the one hand, the 'totalizing' dimension of labour policy, especially in the 'Ober Ost' region, appears as a precursor to the later racist repression of 'primitive' Slavs and 'work-shy' Jews – even though racism and antisemitism were not yet state doctrines.[57] Stereotypes of 'idlers' served to legitimize repressive measures vis-à-vis workers from Western Europe as well. On the other hand, the impact of internal pluralism in the German Empire is plainly apparent. Criticisms and doubts within the civil administrations and at the Reich level had enough weight to prompt a change of course and to stop the manhunts and deportations. Whether or not the labour administration staff moving into the same areas during the Second World War would learn lessons (and if so, which) from the contradictory developments of the First World War, and act accordingly, was another matter. But the indelible bitterness that persisted in Belgium due to these disastrous deportations was a warning for the future.[58]

Despite all the similarities and parallels between Poland and Belgium, comparison of manpower policy in the two areas during the Second World War also shows a stark contrast. Major differences in the structures of the occupation, the relationship between occupiers and occupied, and the conditions for obtaining labour are obvious. However, in view of forced recruitment in Belgium from 1942, the question arises as to whether there was convergence between the practice of labour administration in both areas in the second half of the war, or whether the fundamental contrast between Nazi occupation policy in Eastern and Western Europe persisted until the end of the war.

General Government

With the establishment of the 'General Government for the Occupied Polish Territories' under Governor General Hans Frank on 26 October 1939, the military administration in central Poland gave way to a civilian regime. In contrast to the annexed western Polish areas, which were earmarked for Germanization, the General Government was not considered part of the German Reich. Initial 'plans' for this area of twelve million inhabitants were based on a perverse and nihilistic logic which envisaged no order for the area, only disorganization and plunder.[59] The General Government was to be used as a reservoir of labour for the Reich and as a dumping-ground for 'surplus' Poles and Jews from the annexed territories. After the destruction of the Polish state and the murder of the Polish elites by the German occupiers, they regarded the population of 'rump Poland' as a mass of rightless Polish workers and of Jews who were initially to be dispossessed and enslaved.

The principle of 'disorganization' as the basis of rule in the General Government quickly proved, as even the fanatic Pole-hater Frank realized, untenable. Already by the end of 1939 some shifts in policy were evident. In the spring of 1940, Frank protested against the mass deportations of Poles and Jews from the annexed territories to the General Government; he advocated expanding rather than destroying local industrial capacity; and he even began to air the prospect of Germanizing parts of the General Government.[60] However, such partial changes made no essential difference to the oppression and the terror meted out to the native population. The occupation regime continued to expedite the deportation of Polish workers to the Reich, and to subject Jews to forced labour within the General Government, a project driven and supported by the German labour administration within the territory.

Approximately 300,000 Polish and Ukrainian prisoners of war from defeated Poland were sent to the German Reich as agricultural workers in the autumn of 1939. By this time, preparations were already underway for the recruitment of Polish civilian workers.[61] Even before the establishment of the General Government, labour offices were set up under the military administration, led by seconded Reich German specialists who were assisted by local 'ethnic German' and Polish personnel. These were among the first civilian agencies to operate in the various towns and districts.[62] By November 1939, five labour offices and twenty branch offices had commenced operations.[63] In the four original districts of the General Government – Warsaw, Cracow, Lublin and Radom – 'labour departments' were established within the district governments; after the occupation of Galicia in June–July 1941 (previously under Soviet occupation), a fifth district was established. By the summer of 1943, the number of employees in the labour administration of the General Government had grown to 4,300, including 732 Reich Germans. The Department of Labour within the Governor General's administration in Cracow (from 1941 the Main Section for Labour) was temporarily headed by former State Secretary Johannes Krohn from the Reich Ministry of Labour. After a few weeks, in November 1939, the lawyer and SS-Obersturmbannführer Dr Max Frauendorfer took over as head.⁶⁴ After Frauendorfer's departure in October 1942, Wilhelm Struve was appointed GBA commissioner and confirmed as head of the Main Section for Labour in February 1943.⁶⁵

The labour administration was part of the General Government, but retained its character as a special administration directly under the Reich Ministry of Labour.⁶⁶ As a result, there was a risk of conflict if the labour departments and labour offices received directives from Berlin that clashed with Frank's policy as governor general, or with the instructions issued by district heads (*Distriktchefs*) and county governors (*Kreishauptleute*).⁶⁷ Other agencies also had an interest in manpower policy issues. The Wehrmacht armaments inspectorates wished to secure workers for the armaments factories in the General Government.⁶⁸ The measures taken by the SS and police to pursue Germanization, settlement and anti-Jewish policies, meanwhile, also had far-reaching consequences for manpower policy, and these were sometimes contrary to the interests of the labour administration.

Fundamental to the labour administration's attempts to steer the labour market was the registering of the labour force, with the newly established labour offices creating records of the urban population and paying out unemployment benefits from September–October 1939. Beneficiaries were in turn obliged to take up work in Germany if ordered to do so. Registration was extended to the rural population from December 1939.⁶⁹ Already in the autumn of 1939, thousands of Poles were sent to the Reich as agricultural workers, having been summoned individually by name.⁷⁰ Further measures provided the labour offices with additional means of control. On the day he assumed office, 26 October 1939, Frank announced the introduction of compulsory labour for all Poles between the ages of eighteen and sixty. Labour offices were thus able to use local unemployed people for road construction, repair work and other infrastructure projects.⁷¹ At the same time, Frank imposed the obligation to perform forced labour (*Arbeitszwang*) on all Jews between the ages of fourteen and sixty. Responsibility for the organization of Jewish forced labour was assigned at this point to the SS and police rather than to the labour administration.⁷² Further steps were additionally taken to enforce 'labour deployment': workers were barred from changing jobs without permission from the labour office, while the labour card (like the labour book introduced in the Reich in 1935) was made mandatory for all non-Jewish Polish blue- and white-collar workers in the General Government.⁷³

From the point of view of the German authorities, the recruitment of agricultural workers from the supposedly inexhaustible reservoir in the General Government was the top priority from the outset. The Germans saw the agricultural sector in the territory as harbouring a surplus of unproductive labour. To quote Max Timm, a rationalizing labour policy must 'free up' for 'other tasks' a 'large number of workers currently tied up – unnecessarily from the perspective of labour deployment – in their relatives' smallholdings as they seek to secure food supplies'.[74] On 16 November 1939, Göring, as head of the Four-Year Plan, ordered the labour administration to 'conscript civilian Polish workers, in particular Polish girls, on a large scale';[75] and in January 1940 the government in Cracow set a target of one million workers to be sent to the Reich.[76] Various recruitment methods were used in parallel. In addition to the individual summons by name mentioned above, the labour offices ran advertising campaigns in rural areas featuring posters and leaflets. Initially, the tradition of seasonal work in Germany in parts of the General Government as well as economic hardship prompted some individuals to sign up for work without compulsion alongside those pressured to do so.[77] But reports home from Germany and the 'decrees on Poles' of March 1940, which prescribed the wearing of a stigmatizing 'P' badge on clothing and draconian punishments for offences both inside and outside the workplace, drastically dampened Poles' willingness to take up work in the Reich – though the German labour administration continued its efforts to attract workers on a voluntary basis until 1944.[78]

The first months of 1940 were an experimental phase for the labour administration in the General Government. A discussion in Cracow on 23 April 1940, attended by State Secretary Friedrich Syrup and State Secretary Herbert Backe of the Reich Ministry of Food and Agriculture, revealed not only Frank's demonstrative harshness towards Poles and Jews ('The Jews do not interest me at all. Whether they have anything to feed on or not is the least of my concerns'), but also the combination of zeal and uncertainty on the part of officials of the labour administration.[79] Frank emphasized 'the difficulties of recruitment and the need to use coercive methods in future'. Syrup then advocated the 'careful use of coercive measures' alongside 'an improvement in the material conditions of Polish workers in Germany and their families in the General Government'.[80] Frauendorfer followed Syrup's lead: appeals to fill recruitment quotas at the local level with the support of Polish village leaders and mayors should indeed be coupled with warnings regarding the possibility of the use of force if quotas were not met, but at the same time it was vital to 'remain in dialogue' with the people concerned: 'After all, we not only have to work with them here, but they are supposed to work in the Reich as well'.[81] For all these insights, instances of coercion and violence had already occurred in the context of recruitment. On 14 February 1940, for example, a tram in Warsaw was surrounded by police and all passengers capable of working were deported to work in the Reich.[82]

Notwithstanding uncertainties about methods, there was in 1940 consensus among the agencies of the General Government regarding the goal of manpower policy: recruitment on the largest possible scale for deployment in the Reich. Two years later, however, conflicts emerged over this objective, with some protesting against the forced removal, accelerated under Sauckel, of industrial workers, who were now needed locally due to the expansion of production within the General Government.[83] Protests came initially from Frauendorfer himself, who objected to the siphoning off of armaments workers to the Reich, but he fell into line when the Reich Labour Ministry issued a circular in April 1942.[84] The Armaments Inspectorate then protested as well.[85] In December 1942, Frank himself pointed up the contradiction between Sauckel's demands for labour and Hitler's decision to integrate the armaments industry in the General Government into the productive capacity of the Greater German Reich.[86]

The responses of the General Government's labour administration to the acute labour shortages of spring and summer 1942 are revealing in relation to the twists and turns in the 'logic of substitution' that characterized Nazi wartime labour policy. For example, from 1942 the labour administration increasingly regarded Polish women as a reserve for local industrial production, as a consequence of which the number of women as a share of Polish workers placed in industrial jobs in the General Government grew.[87] Jews of both sexes constituted another important reserve for industrial work; male Jews could also be used for construction and infrastructure projects. Responsibility for the forced labour deployment of Jews in the General Government, meanwhile, passed from the SS to the labour administration in June 1940 (and back to the SS in June 1942).[88] The labour administration regarded Jews (mostly men) as important substitutes for the Polish workers sent to the Reich: Jews were deployed in public infrastructure projects, often in dreadful conditions, but also placed in the private sector. However, the argument for the use of Jews as a labour reserve was progressively undermined from the autumn of 1941 onwards, and if they were to be deployed they were viewed merely as a stopgap measure. This was due to the Nazi leadership's fundamental decision to murder all Jews, a policy implemented in the General Government by the SS and police. For a time, at the peak of the labour crisis in the winter of 1941–1942, Heinrich Himmler and Reinhard Heydrich signalled that Jews capable of working should replace the 'missing' Soviet prisoners of war (who had died as a result of hunger and lethal conditions in the camps). The labour administration and the arms inspectorate then set about deploying Jews who were judged fit for work in armaments production. But this decision was reversed again in July 1942. In the words of Christopher Browning: 'Having planned in the spring of 1942 to replace Polish workers sent to the Reich with Jewish workers, Germans in the General Government were now being told that the Jewish workers were only temporary substitutes who were to be replaced yet again with Poles!'[89] That Polish workers were meant to replace Jews not only in the General Government, but in the Reich as well, also became apparent in the wake of the Zamość resettlement operation in the district of Lublin in the winter of 1942–1943. SS and Police Chief Odilo Globocnik in Lublin had ordered the clearing of Polish villages in the Zamość region to make way for resettled Romanian Germans from Bessarabia. The Poles, expelled from their villages, were subjected to selections. Old people and children were sent to so-called *Rentendörfer* ('reservations' for those unfit for work), where they scraped a living or died. Those branded 'undesirable' were sent to the Auschwitz or Majdanek concentration camps. Those Poles earmarked for labour deployment in the Reich arrived in Berlin towards the end of January 1943, where they replaced German Jews still employed in the armaments industry, who were now deported to Auschwitz along with their families.[90] For all the 'success' of this campaign as a boost to the labour supply for the Reich, Wilhelm Struve as Sauckel's commissioner in the General Government complained that these police actions – which had further fuelled the Polish resistance – had made it more difficult overall to 'acquire labour'.[91]

The course of the war, which constantly increased Germany's demand for labour, but simultaneously intensified resistance in the occupied territories, engendered a particularly violent dynamic when it came to forced recruitment during the final stages of the conflict. This period of recruitment for labour deployment in the General Government, as elsewhere in Nazi-dominated Europe, was characterized by repeated and ever-increasing demands for labour from Sauckel as GBA (to which Main Sections III and V of the Reich Ministry of Labour had been assigned), communicated to the various labour administrations by his commissioners in the occupied territories.[92] This led to a spiral of violence in the General Government. The authorities not only used raids and hostage-taking as recruiting methods, but 'mustered' from the spring of 1943 onwards entire cohorts of young Polish men born between 1918 and 1921.[93] The Polish resistance responded by stepping up its attacks on the labour offices. In addition to the destruction of labour records, acts of violence against staff became more and more common. In April 1943, the head of the Warsaw Labour Office was shot dead in his office in a particularly dramatic operation.[94] The tug-of-war over the workforce between arms production in the General Government and Sauckel's demands for deployment in the Reich continued. In May 1944, Frank declared that the General Government was no longer to be considered a 'reservoir of labour', and he ordered Struve to pass this message on to Berlin.[95] Nevertheless, in August 1944, the Main Section for Labour managed to chalk up one last major 'achievement', namely the deportation of some 150,000 civilians arrested after the Warsaw Uprising to perform forced labour in the Reich.[96]

Belgium

After the capitulation of Belgium in May 1940, an occupation regime was established as a military administration under General Alexander von Falkenhausen.[97] The territory under the German military administration in Brussels included not only the densely populated and highly industrialized territory of Belgium itself, with a population of 8.39 million, but also the two French *départements* of Nord and Pas de Calais, with important industrial areas and a population of 3.2 million. There is little evidence of concrete German pre-war plans for Belgium as a political entity over the long term. Insofar as Hitler had considered annexing Flanders or the whole of Belgium, such options were left out of account as immediate goals of occupation, although Germany did annex the regions of Eupen-Malmédy and Moresnet.[98] German planning for the occupation of Belgium in winter 1939/1940 focused on preparing the ground for a military administration that would – so it was anticipated – keep the lessons of the First World War in mind.[99] One lesson that might have been learned was to avoid the deportation of Belgian civilians to work in Germany, which had triggered international protest.[100] In practice, however, German occupation policy over the course of the Second World War led to the fateful repetition of such deportations, despite the assurances given to the Belgian authorities at the start of the occupation, pledges that were supposed to underpin their cooperation with the Germans.[101]

The configuration of the German occupation administration in Belgium reflected both the relatively high value ascribed especially to the Flemings within the Nazi racial hierarchy, and the Nazi regime's ambition to establish a stable foundation for economic exploitation with a minimum of German personnel. But administrative practices were also rooted in the Belgian elites' willingness to cooperate with the occupiers after the country's defeat. Important factors in the emergence of the Belgian system of supervisory administration (*Aufsichtsverwaltung*) from 1940 onwards were the king's decision to remain in the country (rather than going into exile as members of the Cabinet had done), the willingness of senior officials ('secretaries-general') to form a kind of proxy government under German occupation, and the undertaking given by Alexandre Galopin, director of the banking and industrial combine Société Générale, to cooperate with the occupiers on the economic front.[102] The readiness of the administrative elites and economic leaders to cooperate with the occupiers was impelled by a variety of motives. Some felt a collaborationist admiration for the German system, while others regarded cooperation as a lesser evil, a means of sustaining economic life and averting the danger of deportations and economic depredations.[103] Thanks to Belgian cooperation, the German occupiers could implement their policies through existing structures: the secretaries-general promulgated and legitimated the measures drawn up by Eggert Reeder, chief of the administrative staff, and the German department heads in the military administration.[104] Key positions in the Belgian administration were filled with pro-German personnel, including Victor Leemans as Secretary-General for Economic Affairs and Gerard Romsée as Secretary-General for Home Affairs.[105] On the lower levels of the administration, the German higher field commands (*Oberfeldkommandanturen*), field commands (*Feldkommandanturen*) and local commands (*Ortskommandanturen*) operated as the counterparts of the Belgian authorities.[106] Belgium remained under military administration until July 1944. After Falkenhausen's dismissal, a civilian government, the Reich Commissariat of Belgium and Northern France, was established, with Josef Grohé appointed Reich commissioner.

In the first phase of the occupation after the German invasion, when huge numbers of Belgians had fled to France, the occupiers' priority was to restart economic life, above all the industrial sectors of importance to the German war economy: mining, the metalworking industry and textiles.[107] From a Belgian point of view, too, the revival of industrial production was a top priority because it would not only enable food imports but also combat unemployment and reintegrate refugees into the labour process. Meanwhile, Belgian prisoners of war were already working in Germany. Hitler promised to expedite the release of the approximately seventy thousand Flemish-speaking prisoners of war, and after some delay they were freed over the course of 1941.[108] This pledge, however, did not apply to the French-speaking Walloons. Above and beyond prisoner-of-war labour, however, the recruitment of civilian labour for work in Germany also quickly emerged as an important goal of occupation policy.

Responsibility for manpower policy in occupied Belgium lay with Group VII (Social Affairs and Labour Deployment), part of the Economic Affairs Department of the military administration under Joseph Schultze. The German staff of Group VII, who had been seconded from the Reich, initiated the restarting and reorganization of the Belgian labour offices. The network of pre-war Belgian labour offices was in disarray after the German invasion, their staff having fled and many files having gone missing.[109] Under German occupation, by June 1940 the pre-war name of the Belgian labour administration, L'Office National du placement et du chômage/

Nationale Dienst voor Arbeidsbemiddeling en Werkloosheid, had been changed to L'Office National du placement et de contrôle/Nationale Dienst voor Arbeidsbemiddeling en Toezicht. The new name articulated the goal of controlled 'deployment' in contrast to the old model of the liberal labour market.[110] From November 1940, the Belgian system of labour offices was headed by Frits-Jan Hendriks, former chief of personnel at Philips Belgium and member of the Flemish collaborationist group Vlaams Nationaal Verbond (VNV).[111] In April 1941, the Belgian labour administration was renamed, again, as the Office National du Travail/Rijksarbeidsambt (ONT/RAA). Under Hendriks, the ONT increasingly detached itself from the Belgian Ministry of Labour and Social Welfare under Secretary-General Charles Verwilghen, though it was formally subordinate to it.[112] Hendriks instead took his lead from the instructions issued by Group VII and also fostered cooperation with the German recruitment agencies of the higher field or field commands. In this way, the ONT became in effect an executive body of the German labour administration and, from 1942, an instrument of forced recruitment for work in both Belgium and Germany.[113] The ONT offices were also involved in the forced labour deployment of Jews.

Accounts of labour recruitment in occupied Belgium describe the period until March 1942 as one of predominantly voluntary recruitment. Unemployment in Belgium rose from around 154,000 on the eve of the occupation to 500,000 in July 1940 (27 per cent of the working population). The Belgian municipalities sought to combat the rapid increase in unemployment, paid benefits to the unemployed and organized local infrastructure and repair projects, in part as job creation measures.[114] By the autumn of 1940, these policies had reduced unemployment, which had also fallen as a result of the general economic revival. The steps taken to reduce unemployment, however, also had longer-term effects, similar to those engendered by the occupiers' efforts during the First World War to 'tackle the work-shy'. Unemployment reduction measures remained in place as a form of social disciplining for 'asocials',[115] while stricter control of the unemployed was one of the mechanisms used to regulate the labour market in general, including the ONT's measures to monitor firms and 'comb out' any surplus of labour.[116]

The Reich Ministry of Labour, meanwhile, had sent recruiters to Belgium to persuade Belgians to work in Germany. In the summer of 1940, the Belgian secretaries-general agreed that recruitment for work in Germany could take place, though on a strictly voluntary basis.[117] Via the Reich Ministry of Labour and Group VII, German recruitment offices within the higher field and field commands received 'orders' submitted by German employers to the German labour offices.[118] The Belgian labour offices were co-opted into recruitment campaigns through having to display German promotional material and 'educate' the unemployed about job opportunities in Germany. Zealously collaborationist mayors also promoted work in Germany.[119] At the time, there was a genuine basis for voluntary recruitment, even if German promises regarding wages and remittances were exaggerated. Belgian workers in Germany received the same pay as their German counterparts and – in contrast to Polish workers – did not have to pay extra taxes or live under discriminatory conditions, nor were they subject to special laws. Although the recruitment campaign began at a time of high unemployment, recruitment on a voluntary basis continued even after the return to full employment.

However, one crucial element of voluntary registration was the time-limited nature of the employment contract and Belgian workers' expectation that they would be able to return home when their contracts expired. In 1942, the labour offices in Germany began to restrict this freedom and deploy the instrument of the 'compulsory labour order' (*Dienstverpflichtung*) to tie Belgians (and other Western European workers) to their jobs in Germany.[120] Those recruited freely were now working on an involuntary basis, and were forced to remain in Germany. In addition, recent studies emphasize that differing recruitment methods were used at the same time, as in the General Government. Even in the phase of predominantly voluntary recruitment, German recruitment agencies put pressure on Belgian municipalities to deprive the 'asocial' of welfare benefits and pressure them to work in Germany.[121]

In an article of March 1942, Schultze, as head of Group VII, praised his department's achievements in recruiting workers for 'Reich deployment', despite the Belgians' bitter memories of deportations during the First World War.[122] More Flemings than Walloons, according to Schultze, were prepared to go to Germany.[123] He pointed out that problems affecting the transfer of wages to Belgium had yet to be resolved. But he had no sympathy for those who breached their employment contracts: 'A strict approach will continue to be vital in responding to the relatively few breaches of contract within the Reich'.[124] Schultze also highlighted the registering of the workforce as the foundation for the methodical steering of the labour market and emphasized the disciplinary measures taken by the Belgian ONT offices. Under German supervision, these had become 'useful organs of labour deployment' and were acting on their own initiative to sanction those 'unwilling to work': 'Hard and unpleasant work, which is relatively poorly paid and far from home, serves to educate those who had got used to not working'.[125] The manpower policy of the military administration included a focus on Belgian employers. Emulating practices in Germany, male skilled workers were to be replaced, if possible, by women and unskilled workers, enabling the skilled workers to be redeployed elsewhere.

Lastly, Schultze referred to the imminent compulsory labour decree: 'This will create the opportunity to put layabouts, misplaced workers and surplus workers to profitable use in the Belgian economy. In particular, it will help tackle the overstaffed commercial and retail sector and combat the black market in particular'.[126]

The year 1942 proved a fateful turning point with respect to labour policy in occupied Belgium. In view of the labour crisis, which was already apparent at the end of 1941, Göring had instructed the 'Working Group on Labour Deployment', part of the Four-Year Plan apparatus, to increase sharply recruitment in the occupied territories for work in the Reich. The appointment of Sauckel as General Plenipotentiary for Labour Deployment on 21 March 1942 confirmed this new course. The forced recruitment of Polish workers was – as we have seen – nothing new, and from December 1941 recruitment through coercion and violence had quickly taken hold in the occupied Soviet territories as well.[127] But even in Belgium, where the fragile cooperation between the military administration and the Belgian authorities required extreme caution with regard to anything resembling forced labour, the occupiers now shifted towards coercive measures. The first step in this direction, announced by Schultze, was taken before Sauckel's appointment, namely the decree of 6 March 1942, which enabled the conscription of the inhabitants of Belgium for work within Belgium.[128] It was accompanied by measures intended to 'comb out' Belgian companies, combat the black market and the 'antisocial element', and withdraw unemployment benefit from those who refused to take up the jobs assigned to them, including positions in Germany.[129] Belgians, unsurprisingly, regarded this decree as a preliminary step towards deportations, prompting Charles Verwilghen, Secretary-General for Labour and Social Welfare, to resign in protest.[130] The second, equally predictable step followed after Hitler had conferred additional new powers on Sauckel in September 1942: Sauckel then appointed GBA commissioners in the occupied territories.[131] In this context, on 6 October 1942 the German military administration in Belgium issued a decree facilitating forced recruitment for labour deployment in the German Reich, which applied to men between the ages of eighteen and fifty and unmarried women between the ages of twenty-one and thirty-five.[132]

The year 1942 also marked a turning point in antisemitic persecution in Belgium. Forced labour had become an important dimension of the military administration's antisemitic policies since the spring. In addition to labour conscription in Belgium for non-Jewish Belgians, forced labour for Belgian Jews was imposed in March 1942, to be undertaken both within and outside Belgium. On the basis of scattered local initiatives, over the course of 1941 unemployed Belgian Jews had been sent to labour camps within Belgium to carry out land improvement projects.¹³³ These measures now gave way to a more systematic attempt to target Jews who, having had their property confiscated, were now unemployed and impoverished. Decrees of 11 March 1942 and 8 May 1942 stipulated that Jewish men between the ages of sixteen and sixty and Jewish women between the ages of sixteen and forty had to accept any job assigned to them by the Belgian labour offices.¹³⁴ Jewish forced labourers were then sent to the camps run by the Todt Organization in northern France to build the Atlantic Wall, but they were also put to work in Belgium in mines, quarries and various industrial firms.¹³⁵

The practices of the military administration and ONT offices in relation to the forced labour of Jews in Belgium were important for several reasons. First, the issue further exacerbated relations between the military administration and the secretaries-general that were already strained by the 6 March 1942 decree on labour conscription. The secretaries-general protested against any deportation of Belgians to work outside the country, and they got the German authorities to 'concede' that the decree would compel only non-Belgian Jews to perform forced labour. Of the approximately fifty thousand registered Jews in Belgium in 1941, 93 per cent were non-Belgian nationals.¹³⁶ Second, the separation of Jews from non-Jews in the context of forced labour deployment further isolated Jews in Belgium, a predicament drastically worsened by the introduction of the 'yellow star' on 27 May 1942.¹³⁷ Third, the drafting of Jews to perform forced labour revealed the varying degrees of collaboration with German recruitment agencies on the part of ONT staff – some of them supporters of the Walloon fascist movement Rex or of the VNV. In Antwerp, for example, there was a greater willingness to deport Jews to perform forced labour than in Brussels.¹³⁸ Fourth, the 2,252 Jewish men sent to the camps of the Todt Organization in northern France between June and September 1942 were not only exposed to life-threatening conditions but also found themselves in a deadly trap. In October 1942, more than a thousand Jewish forced labourers were sent back to Belgium to fill up the deportation transports to Auschwitz from the Mechelen/Malines transit camp.¹³⁹ Fifth, the transports of Jews to perform forced labour in the northern French camps served to obscure the true nature of the deportation of Jews from Belgium to Auschwitz, which began on 4 August 1942.¹⁴⁰ Adding to the confusion, transports ran in both directions on the same day. In Antwerp on 12 September 1942, for example, a contingent of Jewish forced labourers on their way to northern France had to be carefully separated from the contingent of Jews called up for deportation to the East, supposedly for 'labour deployment'.¹⁴¹

Up to the autumn of 1942 there had been varying degrees of willing and reluctant compliance – on the part of the Belgian secretaries-general, the local authorities and the ONT offices – with the implementation of German manpower policy, including recruitment for 'Reich deployment', 'combing out' company workers, sanctioning the 'asocial', and signing up Jews for forced labour. But the fragile basis for cooperation was shaken by the decree of 6 October 1942. If there had been a single principle that the secretaries-general had sought to protect, it was that no Belgians would be deported to Germany as forced labourers. Now, under pressure from Sauckel and from Schultze as his commissioner for Belgium, this principle was abandoned. Protests ensued, some of them public in nature, ranging from a strike by railway workers and a letter of protest from the king to sermons by Catholic clergy expressing opposition to the military regime.[142] The forced recruitment of women to work in Germany caused particular indignation, with the result that from March 1943 Belgian women were no longer conscripted for work in Germany, except as domestic servants and hotel personnel. Those women already transported to Germany, however, had to remain there.[143]

What was the result of using coercion as a recruitment tool? Nico Wouters and Jens Thiel point out that voluntary recruitment produced better results.[144] And compulsory recruitment can certainly be considered to have 'failed' if measured against the dizzying recruitment quotas issued by Sauckel between 1942 and 1944.[145] However, in view of the military situation, the prospect of an Allied victory and the general aversion to labour conscription, the number of Belgians recruited in the period from November 1942 to December 1943 was relatively high (91,862).[146] Various measures and methods were used to implement the decree of 6 October 1942. Company records provided the basis for the 'combing out' and 'freeing up' of younger men through the recruitment of women and older men. However, some companies resisted such measures with reference to their protected status in the programme of 'protected firms' (*Sperrbetriebe*), initiated by Armaments Minister Albert Speer as part of his campaign to expand domestic production in the occupied western territories.[147] In addition, further decrees of September 1943 and March 1944 instigated the compulsory 'mustering' of entire (male) age cohorts, first those born in 1920 and 1921, then those born in the years 1922 to 1924.[148]

However, these fruits of recruitment came at a high cost. From the military administration's point of view, the forced recruitment of workers in the final phase of the occupation created a series of insuperable problems. Production suffered when many potential draftees pre-empted their deportation by going into hiding. Meanwhile, the security situation worsened because some of those in hiding joined the Belgian resistance.[149] In a climate of growing violence, acts of revenge against collaborators and 'reprisals' against acts of resistance proliferated. The military administration's field gendarmerie supported labour recruitment through armed raids, but lacked the staff to deal with the large numbers evading the labour draft.[150] In April 1944, General von Falkenhausen's request for a further five hundred men to reinforce the field gendarmerie was declined by the Wehrmacht Supreme Command. Von Falkenhausen warned that the administration's authority was dwindling and that the 'day will come when no labour conscripts at all will turn up for transport'.[151]

Comparison and Outlook

If we compare the repertoire of methods used in the General Government and in Belgium to recruit workers and manage 'labour deployment' locally, there are certainly similarities. Despite all the differences in occupation policy and economic structure in the two areas, their German labour administrations drew on a comparable toolkit of measures. This included the establishment or reconstruction of labour offices to register the unemployed and put them to work. Other measures restricted workers' freedom to change jobs and employers' ability to hire workers. Then there was recruitment for work in Germany, involving lavish promises about salaries, workplaces and living conditions, along with the summons by name to work in Germany. Finally, entire age cohorts were 'mustered' (male cohorts only in both the General Government and Belgium). In both occupied territories, the actions of the German authorities were informed by the imperative of rationalization, which was meant to save manpower. In the General Government, family-run smallholdings were the focus of efforts to 'comb out' workers, while in Belgium it was the 'overstaffed commercial and retail sector' and the 'plethora of skilled workers' ('starke Facharbeiterdecke') in Belgian industry that were the focus of concern.[152]

One potential lesson from the experience of German manpower policy in the occupied territories during the First World War might have been that incentives had to be provided and promises kept if voluntary recruitment were to succeed.[153] However, the Reich Ministry of Labour/GBA and the German labour administration failed to learn this lesson. Instead, in both the General Government and Belgium, they relied on social hardship as their key lever. In both countries, workers were ultimately recruited for deployment in the Reich by physical force. What differed was the combination, scale, timing and intensity of the different measures, including physical force, that were applied.

Until 1942, the ratio of uncoerced, 'voluntary' registration to coercive summons, raids and 'mustering' essentially confirms the obvious and widely recognized contrast between the two territories. Despite unemployment and material hardship as well as a long tradition of seasonal work in Germany, by the spring of 1940 the German occupiers in the General Government were no longer able to meet the high recruitment quotas of Polish workers for the Reich without pressure and coercion. The discussion in Cracow in April 1940 already shows the willingness of leading figures in the labour administration in the Reich (Syrup) and in the General Government (Frauendorfer) to approve of the 'careful' use of force – even if they concurrently called for incentives and better treatment for workers. In Belgium, on the other hand, for the elites, who were generally willing to cooperate (and for whom there was no equivalent in the General Government), preventing deportations to work in the Reich was central to legitimizing their 'lesser evil' ('moindre mal') policy. Both the military administration and Schultze as head of Group VII (Social Affairs and Labour Deployment) were well aware of the memory of the Belgian deportations during the First World War. Nevertheless, with few scruples, the authorities took a coercive approach to the recording and disciplining of the 'asocial' even before 1942. Here the prejudices of the German labour administration and those of the collaborationist mayors and the Belgian ONT offices seem to have converged.

Further parallels and differences emerge if we consider German policies on female workers and Jewish workers. From the beginning, Polish women as well as men were made to work in the Reich, no doubt partly because of the tradition of Polish women working in German agriculture, but also because of a racist view of Eastern European women. When it came to 'inferior races', as the underlying logic would have it, gender could be ignored. Nevertheless, the 'mustering' of age cohorts in the General Government from 1943 onwards applied only to young men. In Belgium, perhaps surprisingly, women were subject to forced recruitment from October 1942. This was, however, restricted to unmarried women and a particular age range, signalling a certain 'sensitivity to gender' or a desire to avoid enflaming public opinion in Belgium. This also explains the rescinding, with some exceptions, of compulsory labour conscription for women in March 1943.

Any comparison of Jewish workers in the General Government and in Belgium must keep in mind the large difference in the absolute numbers of Jews in the two areas. Nevertheless, there are parallels. Both in the General Government (from the outset) and in Belgium (systematically from 1942, limited to non-Belgian Jews) Jews were subjected to forced labour, which served to boost 'labour deployment' but was also a tool of humiliation and stigmatization. For Jews (mostly but not exclusively men) employed in this way, forced labour merely put off the day when they would be deported to their deaths: despite the labour shortages in both areas, from 1942 onwards work provided no guarantee of survival.

Finally, one must consider the effect of the 'Sauckel System' in both occupied territories from 1942. The sharp increase in recruitment quotas for workers from Poland, after Sauckel's appointment in the spring of 1942, merely confirmed the existence of a system already based on coercion – even though some recruitment on a voluntary basis continued. These heightened demands, however, greatly exacerbated the conflict over the deployment of workers locally in the armaments industry in the General Government, as advocated by the Armaments Inspectorate and, in some instances, by the labour administration in the General Government. In Belgium, although the obligation to work within the country was introduced before Sauckel's appointment, the decree of 6 October 1942, which introduced compulsory recruitment for Reich deployment, was clearly down to Sauckel and to Schultze as Sauckel's commissioner for Belgium. This undermined the basis for cooperation between the military administration and the secretaries-general, though willing collaborators in the ONT offices functioned until the end of the occupation as the executive arm of the German administration.

In the summer of 1944, Sauckel was convinced that the authorities in Western Europe were failing to approach the acquisition of manpower with 'the necessary rigour'. He wondered whether the full repertoire of repression and violence that had been established in Eastern and Southeastern Europe should now be unleashed in the West as well: large-scale manhunts, including the forcing of entire segments of the population and refugees into labour deployment in the context of military withdrawal.[154] But it seems that even Sauckel hesitated to put such ideas into practice. Thus, on the eve of the liberation of France and Belgium, he reaffirmed 'the racially structured gradient from West to East' that was such a striking feature of manpower policy until the end of the Second World War.[155]

Elizabeth Harvey, Professor of History at the University of Nottingham, UK, and member of the Independent Commission of Historians Investigating the History of the Reich Ministry of Labour in the National Socialist Period. Publications include *Private Life and Privacy in Nazi Germany* (Cambridge University Press, 2019), co-edited with Johannes Hürter, Maiken Umbach and Andreas Wirsching; *Hitler – New Research* (*German Yearbook of Contemporary History*, vol. 3) (De Gruyter, 2018), co-edited with Johannes Hürter; and *Women and the Nazi East. Agents and Witnesses of Germanization* (Yale University Press, 2003).

Notes

I would like to thank Karl Christian Führer, Tim Kirk, Karsten Linne and Jens Thiel for their advice and suggestions on the present chapter.

1. Senior Government Counsellor Dr Walter Letsch, 'Der Einsatz gewerblicher ausländischer Arbeitskräfte in Deutschland', *RABl.* V (1941), 42–45, here 44 (original emphasis).

2. *Handbuch für die Dienststellen des Generalbevollmächtigten für den Arbeitseinsatz und die interessierten Reichsstellen im Grossdeutschen Reich und in den besetzten Gebieten*, vol. 1: *Vollmachten, Verlautbarungen, Verordnungen, Organisation des GBA*, ed. F. Didier, Berlin: Rotadruck W. Meyer KG, 1944, 271. Department VI a was responsible for the 'regulation of labour deployment in Eastern Europe' and 'labour deployment in trade and industry'.

3. E. Seeber, *Zwangsarbeiter in der faschistischen Kriegswirtschaft. Die Deportation und Ausbeutung polnischer Bürger unter besonderer Berücksichtigung der Lage der Arbeiter aus dem sogenannten Generalgouvernement*, Berlin: Deutscher Verlag der Wissenschaften, 1964; E.L. Homze, *Foreign Labor in Nazi Germany*, Princeton, NJ: Princeton University Press, 1967; U. Herbert, *Fremdarbeiter. Politik und Praxis des 'Ausländer-Einsatzes' in der Kriegswirtschaft des Dritten Reiches*, Berlin and Bonn: Dietz, 1985; English-language edition, U. Herbert, *Hitler's Foreign Workers. Enforced Foreign Labor in Germany under the Third Reich*, trans. W. Templer, Cambridge: Cambridge University Press, 1997.

4. M. Spoerer, *Zwangsarbeit unter dem Hakenkreuz. Ausländische Zivilarbeiter, Kriegsgefangene und Häftlinge im Deutschen Reich und im besetzten Europa 1939–1945*, Stuttgart: Deutsche Verlags-Anstalt, 2001, 304–19; D. Pohl and T. Sebta (eds), *Zwangsarbeit in Hitlers Europa. Besatzung, Arbeit, Folgen*, Berlin: Metropol, 2013, 457–71, also provide comprehensive references.

5. C. Gerlach, *Kalkulierte Morde. Die deutsche Wirtschafts- und Vernichtungspolitik in Weissrussland 1941–1944*, Hamburg: Hamburger Edition, 1999; D. Pohl, *Die Herrschaft der Wehrmacht. Deutsche Militärbesatzung und einheimische Bevölkerung in der Sowjetunion 1941–1944*, Munich: Oldenbourg, 2008; C. Dieckmann, *Deutsche Besatzungspolitik in Litauen 1941–1944*, 2 vols, Göttingen: Wallstein, 2012.

6. K. Linne and F. Dierl (eds), *Arbeitskräfte als Kriegsbeute. Der Fall Ost- und Südosteuropa 1939–1945*, Berlin: Metropol, 2011; F. Dierl, Z. Janjetović and K. Linne, *Pflicht, Zwang und Gewalt. Arbeitsverwaltungen und Arbeitskräftepolitik im deutsch besetzten Polen und Serbien 1939–1944*, Essen: Klartext, 2013.

7. New research and comparative perspectives on labour administration and manpower policy in Nazi-occupied Europe were the topic of a conference organized by the project supported by the Federal Ministry of Labour and Social Affairs on the history of the Reich Ministry of Labour in the Nazi period, Berlin, 3–5 December 2015, 'Regimenting Unfree Labour in Europe during the Second World War'; see conference Working Papers online at https://www.historikerkommission-reichsarbeitsministerium.de/Publikationen/Working-Papers (accessed 11 December 2019).

8. Dr Friedrich Syrup, 'Intereuropäischer Arbeiteraustausch', *RABl.* V (1941), 335.

9. Franz Seldte, 'Der Arbeitseinsatz in Frankreich, in den Niederlanden und in Belgien', *RABl.* V (1941), 413–17; F. Syrup, 'Probleme des Arbeitseinsatzes im europäischen Grossraum', *Der Vierjahresplan* 5(1–3) (1941), 20–21; F. Syrup, *Arbeitseinsatz im Krieg und Frieden*, Essen: Essener Verlagsanstalt, 1942; P. Beisiegel, 'Der Arbeitseinsatz in Europa', in Verein Berliner Kaufleute und Industrieller und Wirtschafts-Hochschule Berlin (eds), *Europäische Wirtschaftsgemeinschaft*, 2nd ed., Berlin: Haude [and] Spener, 1943, 117–39.

10. K. Linne, 'Von der Arbeitsvermittlung zum Arbeitseinsatz. Zum Wandel der Arbeitsverwaltung 1933–1945', in M. Buggeln and M. Wildt (eds), *Arbeit im Nationalsozialismus*, Munich: De Gruyter Oldenbourg, 2014, 53–70.

11. Letsch, 'Der Einsatz'.

12. D.G. Maier, 'Friedrich Syrup (1881–1945). Von der Gewerbeaufsicht an die Spitze

der Arbeitsverwaltung', in D.G. Maier, J. Nürnberger and S. Pabst, *Vordenker und Gestalter des Arbeitsmarktes. Elf Biografien zur Geschichte der deutschen Arbeitsverwaltung*, Mannheim: Hochschule der Bundesagentur für Arbeit, 2012, 115–40.

13. W. Stothfang, *Der Arbeitseinsatz im Kriege*, Berlin: Junker und Dünnhaupt, 1940, 5.
14. Ibid., 27–29.
15. Seldte, 'Der Arbeitseinsatz in Frankreich', 417.
16. Syrup, 'Probleme des Arbeitseinsatzes', 21; see also Letsch, 'Der Einsatz', 45; also quoted in Herbert, *Hitler's Foreign Workers*, 107; Beisiegel, 'Der Arbeitseinsatz in Europa', 139.
17. Syrup, 'Probleme des Arbeitseinsatzes', 20–21; Letsch, 'Der Einsatz', 45.
18. M. Timm, *Der Einsatz ausländischer Arbeitskräfte in Deutschland*, Berlin: n.p., 1942 [special issue of *Reichsarbeitsblatt*], 5.
19. W. Röhr, 'System oder organisiertes Chaos? Fragen einer Typologie der deutschen Okkupationsregime im Zweiten Weltkrieg', in R. Bohn (ed.), *Die deutsche Herrschaft in den 'germanischen' Ländern 1940–1945*, Stuttgart: Steiner, 1997, 11–45.
20. H. Umbreit, 'Auf dem Weg zur Kontinentalherrschaft', in B.R. Kroener, R.-D. Müller and H. Umbreit, *Das Deutsche Reich und der Zweite Weltkrieg*, vol. 5: *Organisation und Mobilisierung des Deutschen Machtbereichs*, part-volume 1: *Kriegsverwaltung, Wirtschaft und personelle Ressourcen 1939–1941*, Stuttgart: Deutsche Verlags-Anstalt, 2009, 3–348, here 3–135.
21. U. Herbert, 'Zwangsarbeit als Lernprozess. Zur Beschäftigung ausländischer Arbeiter in der westdeutschen Industrie im Ersten Weltkrieg', *Archiv für Sozialgeschichte* 24 (1984), 285–304; F. Lemmes, '"Ausländereinsatz" und Zwangsarbeit im Ersten und Zweiten Weltkrieg: Neuere Forschung und Ansätze', *Archiv für Sozialgeschichte* 50 (2010), 395–444; J. Thiel, 'Menschenbassin Belgien'. *Anwerbung, Deportation und Zwangsarbeit im Ersten Weltkrieg*, Essen: Klartext, 2007, 319–36; C. Westerhoff, *Zwangsarbeit im Ersten Weltkrieg. Deutsche Arbeitskräftepolitik im besetzten Polen und Litauen 1914–1918*, Paderborn: Schöningh, 2012, 311–46.
22. Thiel, 'Menschenbassin Belgien'.
23. Ibid., 10; Westerhoff, *Zwangsarbeit*, 224–45.
24. Herbert, *Hitler's Foreign Workers*, 26.
25. Westerhoff, *Zwangsarbeit*, 329.
26. Thiel, 'Menschenbassin Belgien', 321–22; K.C. Priemel, 'Lernversagen: Der Erste Weltkrieg und die nationalsozialistische Wirtschaftspolitik', in G. Krumeich (ed.), *Nationalsozialismus und Erster Weltkrieg*, Essen: Klartext, 2010, 299–322; J. Oltmer, 'Erzwungene Migration: "Fremdarbeit" in zwei Weltkriegen', in Krumeich, *Nationalsozialismus und Erster Weltkrieg*, 347–62.
27. F. Dierl, 'Arbeitsverwaltungen und Arbeitskräftepolitik im besetzten Polen und Serbien. Ein Vergleich', in Dierl, Janjetović and Linne, *Pflicht, Zwang und Gewalt*, 443–63.
28. Ibid., 443.
29. Umbreit, 'Auf dem Weg', 95–102; Röhr, 'System oder organisiertes Chaos'.
30. On the general trends, see Spoerer, *Zwangsarbeit unter dem Hakenkreuz*, 37–88.
31. Dierl, 'Arbeitsverwaltungen', 444 f.
32. Herbert, *Hitler's Foreign Workers*, 80.
33. K. Linne, '"Sklavenjagden" im Arbeiterreservoir – das Beispiel Generalgouvernement', in Dierl, Janjetović and Linne, *Pflicht, Zwang und Gewalt*, 171–316, here 205 f.
34. Herbert, *Hitler's Foreign Workers*, 194.
35. Dierl, 'Arbeitsverwaltungen', 459.
36. V.M. Stefanski, 'Nationalsozialistische Volkstums- und Arbeitseinsatzpolitik im Regierungsbezirk Kattowitz 1939–1945', *Geschichte und Gesellschaft* 31(1) (2005), 38–67.
37. T. Plath, *Zwischen Schonung und Menschenjagden. Die Arbeitseinsatzpolitik in den baltischen Generalbezirken des Reichskommissariats Ostland 1941–1944*, Essen: Klartext, 2012, 215–20.

38. Herbert, *Hitler's Foreign Workers*, 297.
39. Plath, *Zwischen Schonung und Menschenjagden*, 233 f.; Gerlach, *Kalkulierte Morde*, 453 f., 578 f.
40. 'Die ausländischen Arbeiter und Angestellten im Deutschen Reich nach der Staatsangehörigkeit und nach Berufsabteilungen am 25. September 1941', *Der Arbeitseinsatz im Deutschen Reich* 21, 5 November 1941, 19–23; 'Die Ergebnisse der Erhebung über die ausländischen Arbeiter und Angestellten vom 25. September 1941', *Der Arbeitseinsatz im Deutschen Reich* 22, 20 November 1941, 14–17. These figures for 'German Reich territory' did not include those for the annexed Polish areas.
41. 'Die Entwicklung des Arbeitseinsatzes im Deutschen Reich 1940/41', *Der Arbeitseinsatz im Deutschen Reich* 21, 5 November 1941, 3.
42. 'Die ausländischen Arbeiter und Angestellten im Deutschen Reich nach der Staatsangehörigkeit und nach Berufsabteilungen am 25. September 1941', *Der Arbeitseinsatz im Deutschen Reich* 21, 5 November 1941, 21.
43. Mathias G. Haupt identifies two reasons for the higher figures calculated by the German military administration. First, he states, these figures included the placement of non-Belgian residents of Belgium in the Reich, which the labour offices in Germany counted on the basis of citizenship rather than area of origin. Second, 'placements' may have been counted twice, when returnees from 'deployment' in Germany were placed there again. M.G. Haupt, *Der 'Arbeitseinsatz' der belgischen Bevölkerung während des Zweiten Weltkrieges*, Ph.D. dissertation, Bonn: University of Bonn, 1970, 82–85.
44. Thiel, 'Menschenbassin Belgien', 26.
45. Ibid., 64–73; Westerhoff, *Zwangsarbeit*, 99 f.
46. Thiel, 'Menschenbassin Belgien', 53, 73–79, 89–102; Westerhoff, *Zwangsarbeit*, 100–103, 149–53.
47. Westerhoff, *Zwangsarbeit*, 66; Thiel, 'Menschenbassin Belgien', 241.
48. Thiel, 'Menschenbassin Belgien', 103–9.
49. Westerhoff, *Zwangsarbeit*, 80–85, 143–77, 189 f.
50. Ibid., 198–209; Thiel, 'Menschenbassin Belgien', 136–47.
51. Westerhoff, *Zwangsarbeit*, 202–9.
52. Thiel, 'Menschenbassin Belgien', 148–56.
53. Ibid., 127 f.
54. Ibid., 128 f.
55. Ibid., 156–62, 176–237; Westerhoff, *Zwangsarbeit*, 241–43.
56. Westerhoff, *Zwangsarbeit*, 328 f.; Thiel, 'Menschenbassin Belgien', 319–29.
57. Westerhoff, *Zwangsarbeit*, 328.
58. Thiel, 'Menschenbassin Belgien', 163–99.
59. Umbreit, 'Auf dem Weg', 40–45.
60. Ibid., 45; G. Eisenblätter, *Grundlinien der Politik des Reichs gegenüber dem Generalgouvernement, 1939–1943*, Ph.D. dissertation, Frankfurt am Main: University of Frankfurt, 1969, 152; Linne, '"Sklavenjagden"', 172; K.M. Pospieszalski, *Hitlerowskie 'Prawo' Okupacyjne w Polsce. Częsć II. Generalna Gubernia*, Poznań: Instytut Zachodni, 1958, 618.
61. Spoerer, *Zwangsarbeit unter dem Hakenkreuz*, 45.
62. Linne, '"Sklavenjagden"', 181–84; R. Seidel, *Deutsche Besatzungspolitik in Polen. Der Distrikt Radom 1939–1945*, Paderborn: Schöningh, 2006, 27 f., 38.
63. Linne, '"Sklavenjagden"', 181.
64. On Frauendorfer, see ibid., 201–5; T. Schlemmer, 'Grenzen der Integration. Die CSU und der Umgang mit der nationalsozialistischen Vergangenheit – der Fall Dr. Max Frauendorfer', *Vierteljahrshefte für Zeitgeschichte* 48(4) (2000), 675–742.
65. Linne, '"Sklavenjagden"', 187, 197 f.
66. Seidel, *Deutsche Besatzungspolitik*, 41 f.
67. Linne, '"Sklavenjagden"', 184–90.

68. Seidel, *Deutsche Besatzungspolitik*, 85 f.
69. Ibid., 100–102.
70. Linne, '"Sklavenjagden"', 182 f.
71. Seidel, *Deutsche Besatzungspolitik*, 102; Linne, '"Sklavenjagden"', 261. From 1941, the district heads in Warsaw and Lublin extended 'the obligation to work' for Polish males to those between the ages of fourteen and eighteen.
72. Seidel, *Deutsche Besatzungspolitik*, 260.
73. Ibid., 103.
74. Timm, *Der Einsatz ausländischer Arbeitskräfte*, 50; see also Linne, '"Sklavenjagden"', 227.
75. Quoted in Herbert, *Hitler's Foreign Workers*, 63.
76. 'Abteilungsleitersitzung vom 19.1.1940', in H. Frank, *Das Diensttagebuch des deutschen Generalgouverneurs in Polen. 1939–1945*, ed. W. Präg and W. Jacobmeyer, Stuttgart: Deutsche Verlags-Anstalt, 1975, 97.
77. Herbert, *Hitler's Foreign Workers*, 79–85.
78. Linne, '"Sklavenjagden"', 205–7. On the 'decrees on Poles', see Herbert, *Hitler's Foreign Workers*, 69–79; Spoerer, *Zwangsarbeit unter dem Hakenkreuz*, 93.
79. 'Arbeitssitzung anlässlich der Anwesenheit des Staatssekretärs Backe, 23.4.1940', in Frank, *Diensttagebuch*, 186–89, quotation 186.
80. Ibid., 188; Maier, 'Friedrich Syrup', 138.
81. 'Arbeitssitzung anlässlich der Anwesenheit des Staatssekretärs Backe, 23.4.1940', in Frank, *Diensttagebuch*, 186–89, here 188 f.; Linne, '"Sklavenjagden"', 215 f.
82. Linne, '"Sklavenjagden"', 208.
83. Ibid., 258; Seidel, *Deutsche Besatzungspolitik*, 110, 148.
84. Linne, '"Sklavenjagden"', 267.
85. Ibid., 268.
86. 'Hauptabteilungsleitersitzung, 8.12.1942', in Frank, *Diensttagebuch*, 585; Linne, '"Sklavenjagden"', 268.
87. Seidel, *Deutsche Besatzungspolitik*, 111.
88. W. Gruner, 'The Labor Office versus the SS – Forced Labor in the General Government, 1939–1944', in W. Gruner, *Jewish Forced Labor under the Nazis: Economic Needs and Racial Aims, 1938–1944*, trans. K.M. Dell'Orto, Cambridge: Cambridge University Press, 2006, 230–75; Linne, '"Sklavenjagden"', 274–94. See also the chapter by Michael Wildt in this volume.
89. C. Browning, *Nazi Policy, Jewish Workers, German Killers*, Cambridge: Cambridge University Press, 2000, 78.
90. This series of 'displacements' is described in Linne, '"Sklavenjagden"', 175–78.
91. 'Polizeibesprechung, 25.1.1943', in Frank, *Diensttagebuch*, 598–612, here 611.
92. On Sauckel as GBA and the Reich Ministry of Labour, see the chapter by Swantje Greve in this volume.
93. Linne, '"Sklavenjagden"', 232 f., 239.
94. Ibid., 306.
95. Frank, *Diensttagebuch*, 846 (10 May 1944).
96. Linne, '"Sklavenjagden"', 246 f.
97. Umbreit, 'Auf dem Weg', 54–69; W. Warmbrunn, *The German Occupation of Belgium 1940–1944*, New York: Lang, 1993, 70 f.
98. Umbreit, 'Auf dem Weg', 54–56; Warmbrunn, *German Occupation*, 66–70.
99. Umbreit, 'Auf dem Weg', 56.
100. Jens Thiel and Nico Wouters, 'Paper on the Belgian Case', unpublished talk given at the conference 'Regimenting Unfree Labour', 3–5 December 2015 in Berlin, 2; Spoerer, *Zwangsarbeit unter dem Hakenkreuz*, 60.
101. Thiel and Wouters, 'Paper on the Belgian Case', 2.

102. Umbreit, 'Auf dem Weg', 67; Warmbrunn, *German Occupation*, 49–52.

103. S.M. Harrison, 'Belgian Labour in Nazi Germany: A Social History', Ph.D. dissertation, Edinburgh: University of Edinburgh, 2012, 34.

104. Haupt, *Der 'Arbeitseinsatz'*, 22–32. On Eggert Reeder, see W. Seibel, 'Polykratische Integration: Nationalsozialistische Spitzenbeamte als Netzwerker in der deutschen Besatzungsverwaltung in Belgien 1940–1944', in S. Reichardt and W. Seibel (eds), *Der prekäre Staat. Herrschen und Verwalten im Nationalsozialismus*, Frankfurt am Main: Campus, 2011, 241–73.

105. Warmbrunn, *German Occupation*, 105 f.

106. Haupt, *Der 'Arbeitseinsatz'*, 26–32.

107. Warmbrunn, *German Occupation*, 46 f.

108. F. Hartmannsgruber, 'Einleitung', in *Akten der Reichskanzlei. Regierung Hitler 1933–1945*, vol. 7: *1940*, ed. F. Hartmannsgruber, series editors H.G. Hockerts and M. Hollmann, Munich: De Gruyter Oldenbourg, 2015, XIX–LVI, here LIV; Syrup, *Arbeitseinsatz im Krieg und Frieden*, 14.

109. Timm, *Der Einsatz ausländischer Arbeitskräfte*, 82.

110. N. Wouters, *Oorlogsburgemeesters 40/44: Lokaal bestuur en collaboratie in België*, Tielt: Lannoo, 2004, 265.

111. Warmbrunn, *German Occupation*, 226.

112. Haupt, *Der 'Arbeitseinsatz'*, 64–67; N. Wouters, *Mayoral Collaboration Under Nazi Occupation in Belgium, the Netherlands and France, 1938–46*, London: Palgrave Macmillan, 2016, 58.

113. Thiel and Wouters, 'Paper on the Belgian Case', 5.

114. Haupt, *Der 'Arbeitseinsatz'*, 55; Wouters, *Oorlogsburgemeesters*, 265; Thiel and Wouters, 'Paper on the Belgian Case', 7.

115. Haupt, *Der 'Arbeitseinsatz'*, 60.

116. Thiel and Wouters, 'Paper on the Belgian Case', 7.

117. Warmbrunn, *German Occupation*, 227; Harrison, 'Belgian Labour', 37.

118. Haupt, *Der 'Arbeitseinsatz'*, 78.

119. Wouters, *Oorlogsburgemeesters*, 266.

120. Herbert, *Hitler's Foreign Workers*, 194; Spoerer, *Zwangsarbeit unter dem Hakenkreuz*, 97.

121. Wouters, *Oorlogsburgemeesters*, 266; Thiel and Wouters, 'Paper on the Belgian Case', 7.

122. Schultze, Oberkriegsverwaltungsrat, 'Der Arbeitseinsatz in Belgien', *Der Vierjahresplan* 6(3) (1942), 135–37, here 136.

123. Ibid.

124. Ibid., 137.

125. Ibid.

126. Ibid.

127. See the chapter by Swantje Greve in this volume.

128. Originally, Belgians were also to be sent to work in the Nord-Pas-de-Calais region; this plan was dropped after protests.

129. Warmbrunn, *German Occupation*, 229 f.

130. Thiel and Wouters, 'Paper on the Belgian Case', 6.

131. Haupt, *Der 'Arbeitseinsatz'*, 108 f.; Homze, *Foreign Labor*, 141.

132. Haupt, *Der 'Arbeitseinsatz'*, 107–16.

133. F. Seberechts, 'Spoliation et travail obligatoire', in R. van Doorslaer et al. (eds), *La Belgique docile: Les autorités belges et la persécution des Juifs en Belgique pendant la Seconde Guerre mondiale*, Brussels: CEGESOMA, 2007, 416–50.

134. Ibid., 430 f.

135. S. Vandepontseele, 'Le travail obligatoire des Juifs en Belgique et dans le nord de la

France', in J.-P. Schreiber and R. van Doorslaer (eds), *Les curateurs du ghetto. L'Association des Juifs en Belgique sous l'occupation Nazie*, Brussels: Labor, 2004, 189–231, here 197–205.

136. Seberechts, 'Spoliation et travail obligatoire', 427; 'Einleitung', in *Die Verfolgung und Ermordung der europäischen Juden durch das nationalsozialistische Deutschland 1933–1945*, ed. on behalf of Bundesarchiv, Institut für Zeitgeschichte and Lehrstuhl für Neuere und Neueste Geschichte an der Albert-Ludwigs-Universität Freiburg by S. Heim et al., vol. 12: *West- und Nordeuropa Juni 1942–1945*, ed. K. Happe, B. Lambauer and C. Maier-Wolthusen, Munich: Oldenbourg, 2015, 13–84, here 45.

137. Ibid., 46.

138. Ibid., 47.

139. A. Godfroid, 'À qui profite l'exploitation des travailleurs forcés juifs de belgique dans le Nord de la France?', *Cahiers d'histoire du temps présent* 10 (2002), 107–27, here 112. Different sources provide differing estimates of the number of Jewish forced labourers returned to Malines/Mechelen from northern France in October 1942; ibid., 112; M. Steinberg, 'The Judenpolitik in Belgium within the West European Context: Comparative Observations', in D. Michman (ed.), *Belgium and the Holocaust. Jews, Belgians, Germans*, Jerusalem: Yad Vashem, 2000, 199–221, here 215; I. Meinen, 'Die Deportation der Juden aus Belgien und das Devisenschutzkommando', in J. Hürter and J. Zarusky (eds), *Besatzung, Kollaboration, Holocaust. Neue Studien zur Verfolgung und Ermordung der europäischen Juden*, Munich: Oldenbourg, 2008, 45–79, here 54.

140. Godfroid, 'À qui profite', 113; Seberechts, 'Spoliation et travail obligatoire', 450; Vandepontseele, 'Le travail obligatoire', 231.

141. 'Einleitung', in *Verfolgung und Ermordung der europäischen Juden*, vol. 12, 49.

142. Haupt, *Der 'Arbeitseinsatz'*, 108–14.

143. Minutes of meeting of Secretaries-General, 12 March 1943. CEGESOMA archive, Brussels. AA MIC 44, film no. 2.

144. Thiel and Wouters, 'Paper on the Belgian Case', 4.

145. Harrison, 'Belgian Labour', 76.

146. Herbert, *Hitler's Foreign Workers*, 194, 275. These figures come from the Reich Ministry of Labour, not from the military administration in Belgium.

147. Harrison, 'Belgian Labour', 59–61.

148. Haupt, *Der 'Arbeitseinsatz'*, 126–36.

149. Warmbrunn, *German Occupation*, 58 f., 237 f.; Harrison, 'Belgian Labour', 71.

150. B.R. Kroener, '"Menschenbewirtschaftung", Bevölkerungsverteilung und personelle Rüstung in der zweiten Kriegshälfte (1942–1944)', in B.R. Kroener, R.-D. Müller and H. Umbreit, *Das Deutsche Reich und der Zweite Weltkrieg*, vol. 5: *Organisation und Mobilisierung des deutschen Machtbereichs*, part-volume 2: *Kriegsverwaltung, Wirtschaft und personelle Ressourcen 1942–1944/45*, Stuttgart: Deutsche Verlags-Anstalt, 1999, 777–1002, here 898.

151. Ibid., 897 f.

152. Schultze, 'Der Arbeitseinsatz in Belgien', 137.

153. Westerhoff, *Zwangsarbeit*, 325.

154. Kroener, '"Menschenbewirtschaftung"', 911–14.

155. Herbert, *Hitler's Foreign Workers*, 287.

Bibliography

Akten der Reichskanzlei. Regierung Hitler 1933–1945, vol. 7: *1940*, ed. F. Hartmannsgruber, series editors H. G. Hockerts and M. Hollmann. Munich: De Gruyter Oldenbourg, 2015.

Beisiegel, P. 'Der Arbeitseinsatz in Europa', in Verein Berliner Kaufleute und Industrieller und Wirtschafts-Hochschule Berlin (eds), *Europäische Wirtschaftsgemeinschaft*, 2nd ed. (Berlin: Haude [and] Spener, 1943), 117–39.

Browning, C. *Nazi Policy, Jewish Workers, German Killers*. Cambridge: Cambridge University Press, 2000.
Dieckmann, C. *Deutsche Besatzungspolitik in Litauen 1941–1944*, 2 vols. Göttingen: Wallstein, 2012.
Dierl, F. 'Arbeitsverwaltungen und Arbeitskräftepolitik im besetzten Polen und Serbien. Ein Vergleich', in F. Dierl, Z. Janjetović and K. Linne, *Pflicht, Zwang und Gewalt. Arbeitsverwaltungen und Arbeitskräftepolitik im deutsch besetzten Polen und Serbien 1939–1944* (Essen: Klartext, 2013), 443–64.
Dierl, F., Z. Janjetović and K. Linne. *Pflicht, Zwang und Gewalt. Arbeitsverwaltungen und Arbeitskräftepolitik im deutsch besetzten Polen und Serbien 1939–1944*. Essen: Klartext, 2013.
Eisenblätter, G. *Grundlinien der Politik des Reichs gegenüber dem Generalgouvernement, 1939–1943*, Ph.D. dissertation. Frankfurt am Main: University of Frankfurt, 1969.
Frank, H. *Das Diensttagebuch des deutschen Generalgouverneurs in Polen. 1939–1945*, ed. W. Präg and W. Jacobmeyer. Stuttgart: Deutsche Verlags-Anstalt, 1975.
Gerlach, C. *Kalkulierte Morde. Die deutsche Wirtschafts- und Vernichtungspolitik in Weissrussland 1941–1944*. Hamburg: Hamburger Edition, 1999.
Godfroid, A. 'À qui profite l'exploitation des travailleurs forcés juifs de belgique dans le Nord de la France?' *Cahiers d'histoire du temps présent* 10 (2002), 107–27.
Gruner, W. 'The Labor Office versus the SS – Forced Labor in the General Government, 1939–1944', in W. Gruner, *Jewish Forced Labor under the Nazis: Economic Needs and Racial Aims, 1938–1944*, trans. K.M. Dell'Orto (Cambridge: Cambridge University Press, 2006), 230–75.
Handbuch für die Dienststellen des Generalbevollmächtigten für den Arbeitseinsatz und die interessierten Reichsstellen im Grossdeutschen Reich und in den besetzten Gebieten, vol. 1: *Vollmachten, Verlautbarungen, Verordnungen, Organisation des GBA*, ed. F. Didier. Berlin: Rotadruck W. Meyer KG, 1944.
Harrison, S.M. 'Belgian Labour in Nazi Germany: A Social History', Ph.D. dissertation. Edinburgh: University of Edinburgh, 2012.
Haupt, M.G. *Der 'Arbeitseinsatz' der belgischen Bevölkerung während des Zweiten Weltkrieges*, Ph.D. dissertation. Bonn: University of Bonn, 1970.
Herbert, U. *Fremdarbeiter. Politik und Praxis des 'Ausländer-Einsatzes' in der Kriegswirtschaft des Dritten Reiches*. Berlin and Bonn: Dietz, 1985.
Herbert, U. *Hitler's Foreign Workers. Enforced Foreign Labor in Germany under the Third Reich*, trans. W. Templer. Cambridge: Cambridge University Press, 1997.
Herbert, U. 'Zwangsarbeit als Lernprozess. Zur Beschäftigung ausländischer Arbeiter in der westdeutschen Industrie im Ersten Weltkrieg'. *Archiv für Sozialgeschichte* 24 (1984), 285–304.
Homze, E.L. *Foreign Labor in Nazi Germany*. Princeton, NJ: Princeton University Press, 1967.
Kroener, B.R. '"Menschenbewirtschaftung", Bevölkerungsverteilung und personelle Rüstung in der zweiten Kriegshälfte (1942–1944)', in B.R. Kroener, R-D. Müller and H. Umbreit, *Das Deutsche Reich und der Zweite Weltkrieg*, vol. 5: *Organisation und Mobilisierung des deutschen Machtbereichs*, part-volume 2: *Kriegsverwaltung, Wirtschaft und personelle Ressourcen 1942–1944/45* (Stuttgart: Deutsche Verlags-Anstalt, 1999), 777–1002.
Lemmes, F. '"Ausländereinsatz" und Zwangsarbeit im Ersten und Zweiten Weltkrieg: Neuere Forschung und Ansätze'. *Archiv für Sozialgeschichte* 50 (2010), 395–444.
Linne, K. '"Sklavenjagden" im Arbeiterreservoir – das Beispiel Generalgouvernement', in F. Dierl, Z. Janjetović and K. Linne, *Pflicht, Zwang und Gewalt. Arbeitsverwaltungen und Arbeitskräftepolitik im deutsch besetzten Polen und Serbien 1939–1944* (Essen: Klartext, 2013), 171–316.

Linne, K. 'Von der Arbeitsvermittlung zum Arbeitseinsatz. Zum Wandel der Arbeitsverwaltung 1933–1945', in M. Buggeln and M. Wildt (eds), *Arbeit im Nationalsozialismus* (Munich: De Gruyter Oldenbourg, 2014), 53–73.

Linne, K., and F. Dierl (eds). *Arbeitskräfte als Kriegsbeute. Der Fall Ost- und Südosteuropa 1939–1945*. Berlin: Metropol, 2011.

Maier, D.G. 'Friedrich Syrup (1881–1945). Von der Gewerbeaufsicht an die Spitze der Arbeitsverwaltung', in D.G. Maier, J. Nürnberger and S. Pabst, *Vordenker und Gestalter des Arbeitsmarktes. Elf Biografien zur Geschichte der deutschen Arbeitsverwaltung* (Mannheim: Hochschule der Bundesagentur für Arbeit, 2012), 115–40.

Meinen, I. 'Die Deportation der Juden aus Belgien und das Devisenschutzkommando', in J. Hürter and J. Zarusky (eds), *Besatzung, Kollaboration, Holocaust. Neue Studien zur Verfolgung und Ermordung der europäischen Juden* (Munich: Oldenbourg, 2008), 45–79.

Oltmer, J. 'Erzwungene Migration: "Fremdarbeit" in zwei Weltkriegen', in G. Krumeich (ed.), *Nationalsozialismus und Erster Weltkrieg* (Essen: Klartext, 2010), 347–62.

Plath, T. *Zwischen Schonung und Menschenjagden. Die Arbeitseinsatzpolitik in den baltischen Generalbezirken des Reichskommissariats Ostland 1941–1944*. Essen: Klartext, 2012.

Pohl, D. *Die Herrschaft der Wehrmacht. Deutsche Militärbesatzung und einheimische Bevölkerung in der Sowjetunion 1941–1944*. Munich: Oldenbourg, 2008.

Pohl, D., and T. Sebta (eds). *Zwangsarbeit in Hitlers Europa. Besatzung, Arbeit, Folgen*. Berlin: Metropol, 2013.

Pospieszalski, K.M. *Hitlerowskie 'Prawo' Okupacyjne w Polsce. Część II. Generalna Gubernia*. Poznań: Instytut Zachodni, 1958.

Priemel, K.C. 'Lernversagen: Der Erste Weltkrieg und die nationalsozialistische Wirtschaftspolitik', in G. Krumeich (ed.), *Nationalsozialismus und Erster Weltkrieg* (Essen: Klartext, 2010), 299–322.

Röhr, W. 'System oder organisiertes Chaos? Fragen einer Typologie der deutschen Okkupationsregime im Zweiten Weltkrieg', in R. Bohn (ed.), *Die deutsche Herrschaft in den 'germanischen' Ländern 1940–1945* (Stuttgart: Steiner, 1997), 11–45.

Schlemmer, T. 'Grenzen der Integration. Die CSU und der Umgang mit der nationalsozialistischen Vergangenheit – der Fall Dr. Max Frauendorfer'. *Vierteljahrshefte für Zeitgeschichte* 48(4) (2000), 675–742.

Schultze, Oberkriegsverwaltungsrat. 'Der Arbeitseinsatz in Belgien'. *Der Vierjahresplan* 6(3) (1942), 135–37.

Seberechts, F. 'Spoliation et travail obligatoire', in R. van Doorslaer et al. (eds), *La Belgique docile: Les autorités belges et la persécution des Juifs en Belgique pendant la Seconde Guerre mondiale* (Brussels: CEGESOMA, 2007), 416–50.

Seeber, E. *Zwangsarbeiter in der faschistischen Kriegswirtschaft. Die Deportation und Ausbeutung polnischer Bürger unter besonderer Berücksichtigung der Lage der Arbeiter aus dem sogenannten Generalgouvernement*. Berlin: Deutscher Verlag der Wissenschaften, 1964.

Seibel, W. 'Polykratische Integration: Nationalsozialistische Spitzenbeamte als Netzwerker in der deutschen Besatzungsverwaltung in Belgien 1940–1944', in S. Reichardt and W. Seibel (eds), *Der prekäre Staat. Herrschen und Verwalten im Nationalsozialismus* (Frankfurt am Main: Campus, 2011), 241–73.

Seidel, R. *Deutsche Besatzungspolitik in Polen. Der Distrikt Radom 1939–1945*. Paderborn: Schöningh, 2006.

Seldte, F. 'Der Arbeitseinsatz in Frankreich, in den Niederlanden und in Belgien'. *Reichsarbeitsblatt* V (1941), 413–17.

Spoerer, M. *Zwangsarbeit unter dem Hakenkreuz. Ausländische Zivilarbeiter, Kriegsgefangene und Häftlinge im Deutschen Reich und im besetzten Europa 1939–1945*. Stuttgart: Deutsche Verlags-Anstalt, 2001.

Stefanski, V.M. 'Nationalsozialistische Volkstums- und Arbeitseinsatzpolitik im Regierungsbezirk Kattowitz 1939–1945'. *Geschichte und Gesellschaft* 31(1) (2005), 38–67.

Steinberg, M. 'The Judenpolitik in Belgium within the West European Context: Comparative Observations', in D. Michman (ed.), *Belgium and the Holocaust. Jews, Belgians, Germans* (Jerusalem: Yad Vashem, 2000), 199–221.

Stothfang, W. *Der Arbeitseinsatz im Kriege*. Berlin: Junker und Dünnhaupt, 1940.

Syrup, F. *Arbeitseinsatz im Krieg und Frieden*. Essen: Essener Verlagsanstalt, 1942.

Syrup, F. 'Probleme des Arbeitseinsatzes im europäischen Grossraum'. *Der Vierjahresplan* 5(1–3) (1941), 20–21.

Thiel, J. *'Menschenbassin Belgien'. Anwerbung, Deportation und Zwangsarbeit im Ersten Weltkrieg*. Essen: Klartext, 2007.

Timm, M. *Der Einsatz ausländischer Arbeitskräfte in Deutschland*. Berlin: n.p., 1942 [special issue of *Reichsarbeitsblatt*].

Umbreit, H. 'Auf dem Weg zur Kontinentalherrschaft', in B.R. Kroener, R.-D. Müller and H. Umbreit, *Das Deutsche Reich und der Zweite Weltkrieg*, vol. 5: *Organisation und Mobilisierung des Deutschen Machtbereichs*, part-volume 1: *Kriegsverwaltung, Wirtschaft und personelle Ressourcen 1939–1941* (Stuttgart: Deutsche Verlags-Anstalt, 2009), 3–348.

Vandepontseele, S. 'Le travail obligatoire des Juifs en Belgique et dans le nord de la France', in J.-P. Schreiber and R. van Doorslaer (eds), *Les curateurs du ghetto. L'Association des Juifs en Belgique sous l'occupation Nazie* (Brussels: Labor, 2004), 189–231.

Die Verfolgung und Ermordung der europäischen Juden durch das nationalsozialistische Deutschland 1933–1945, ed. on behalf of Bundesarchiv, Institut für Zeitgeschichte and Lehrstuhl für Neuere und Neueste Geschichte an der Albert-Ludwigs-Universität Freiburg by S. Heim et al., vol. 12: *West- und Nordeuropa Juni 1942–1945*, ed. K. Happe, B. Lambauer and C. Maier-Wolthusen. Munich: Oldenbourg, 2015.

Warmbrunn, W. *The German Occupation of Belgium 1940–1944*. New York: Lang, 1993.

Westerhoff, C. *Zwangsarbeit im Ersten Weltkrieg. Deutsche Arbeitskräftepolitik im besetzten Polen und Litauen 1914–1918*. Paderborn: Schöningh, 2012.

Wouters, N. *Mayoral Collaboration under Nazi Occupation in Belgium, the Netherlands and France, 1938–46*. London: Palgrave Macmillan, 2016.

Wouters, N. *Oorlogsburgemeesters 40/44: Lokaal bestuur en collaboratie in België*. Tielt: Lannoo, 2004.

Chapter 10

The General Plenipotentiary for Labour Deployment and the Reich Ministry of Labour

Swantje Greve

I don't mind telling you: if it has proved possible, right up to the present day, to make sufficient manpower available to the German economy at all times, then this is due to the establishment of the German Ministry of Labour in general and the work of its men. . . . Let me be explicit. The credit belongs not to me but to this apparatus.[1]

These are the words with which Fritz Sauckel,[2] the general plenipotentiary for labour deployment (Generalbevollmächtigter für den Arbeitseinsatz or GBA) expressed his appreciation for the work of the Reich Ministry of Labour in a speech before representatives of the press in December 1943. Above all, he highlighted the work of the ministry's main sections III (Labour Law and Wages Policy) and V (Labour Deployment) and their subordinate agencies, these parts of the ministry having been placed at Sauckel's disposal upon his appointment as GBA.[3] In the same speech, he stated: 'Because we had such an outstanding labour administration available to us, we could begin our work immediately, with the greatest vigour and intensity, when the institution of a General Plenipotentiary for Labour Deployment was created'.[4]

Adolf Hitler appointed Thuringian Gauleiter and Reich Governor Fritz Sauckel as general plenipotentiary for labour deployment by decree on 21 March 1942.[5] This entailed a redistribution of authority over labour policy: the GBA was to be the central agency steering manpower policy throughout the territory under German control. Many of the areas of responsibility now handed to the GBA had already lain within the bailiwick of the two main sections of the Reich Ministry of Labour mentioned above.[6] However, given his comprehensive powers and their extension to the entire area under German rule, including the occupied territories, the tasks entrusted to the GBA through the decree of March 1942 went far beyond the jurisdiction of the Reich Ministry of Labour.

Up to the end of the war, the GBA was responsible for the recruitment of millions of foreign civilian workers and their deportation to Germany.[7] By exploiting forced labourers from all over Europe, during the Second World War the Germans were able to sustain the war economy, despite the ceaseless conscription of German workers into the Wehrmacht. In autumn 1944 alone, 7.6 million foreign labourers were working in Germany, equating to around 20 per cent of all workers in the Reich. This included 5.7 million civilian workers and about 1.9 million prisoners of war.[8]

As 'the GBA', to this day Fritz Sauckel does much to shape the view of this office within scholarly discourse. The very term 'general plenipotentiary' suggests that the GBA was an individual, and this is one reason why developments in labour deployment tend to be projected onto Sauckel. This frequently goes hand in hand with the interpretation that his appointment signalled a major rupture in manpower policies and a loss of authority on the part of the Reich Ministry of Labour. In this chapter, I aim to supplant this one-dimensional perspective with a more nuanced account of the organizational structure of the office of GBA and its modus operandi. The quote from Sauckel with which this chapter begins indicates the fundamental importance to his work as GBA of the two main sections of the Labour Ministry placed at his disposal. Hitherto historians have paid little attention to these main sections, the GBA task force established by Sauckel or his representatives in the occupied territories.[9] How did this agency, responsible for the recruitment and deportation of millions of workers into the Reich over the course of the Second World War, function? In what follows, I seek to answer this question through an in-depth analysis of the GBA as an organization.[10] Taking the example of occupied Ukraine, from which around 1.7 million people were deported into the Reich between 1941 and 1944 alone, I then describe the organization's practical activities in the occupied territories.[11]

The Organizational Structure of the GBA

Nazi leaders had been discussing the establishment of a new agency to amalgamate all powers over labour policy since October 1941. Key participants in this debate were Hans Heinrich Lammers, head of the Reich

Chancellery, Martin Bormann, head of the Party Chancellery, Robert Ley,[12] head of the German Labour Front, and Wilhelm Keitel, head of the Wehrmacht Supreme Command. This debate was closely bound up with the growing shortage of labour within the German war economy, particularly the armaments and food production sectors, a deficit triggered by Germany's war against the Soviet Union. In autumn 1941, it became clear that the war, launched in June, would not be brought to an end within just a few months as originally envisaged, but would instead take the form of a lengthy war of attrition. In light of the altered military situation on the German-Soviet front, there was no longer any prospect of disbanding large portions of the Wehrmacht, as planned just a few weeks before, a step that would have eased the strained labour market substantially. As the Wehrmacht continued to call up workers, the labour shortage developed into a core problem for the German war economy.[13]

In light of these issues, in autumn 1941 the Nazi leadership around Hitler made a fundamental decision that brought about a step-change in labour policy. Soviet prisoners of war and civilian workers were now to be deployed on a large scale within the boundaries of the Reich. On 7 November 1941, Reich Marshal Hermann Göring, who was in charge of the Four-Year Plan, announced this decision to representatives of the economy, Wehrmacht, state and Nazi Party. The Working Group on Labour Deployment (Geschäftsgruppe Arbeitseinsatz), part of the Four-Year Plan Authority and led by officials of the Reich Ministry of Labour, was to be chiefly responsible for implementing this new approach.[14]

This decision having been made, the Nazi leaders continued to debate the establishment of a coordinating agency. While the Reich Labour Ministry and the Working Group on Labour Deployment possessed the expertise required to carry out these complex tasks, what was lacking was a single individual in charge of manpower policy at the highest level, one who could reconcile the various interests involved, if need be in the face of resistance from specific actors. For in addition to the Reich Labour Ministry and the Working Group, a broad range of other agencies and offices, sometimes with opposing objectives, were involved in labour policy. These included the Reich Ministry of the Economy (Reichswirtschaftsministerium), the Reich Ministry for Armament and Ammunition (Reichsministerium für Bewaffnung und Munition), the War Economy and Armament Office (Wehrwirtschafts- und Rüstungsamt) within the Wehrmacht Supreme Command, the German Labour Front, as well as numerous business groups and Reich associations.[15]

As GBA, Fritz Sauckel was to play this coordinating role and steer labour policy as a whole.[16] His appointment by Adolf Hitler himself was crucial to legitimizing his office, enabling him to evoke Hitler's backing as he went about his tasks. The Working Group on Labour Deployment within the Four-Year Plan Authority was disbanded and its responsibilities transferred to the GBA, who was formally directly subordinate to the commissioner for the Four-Year Plan, Hermann Göring.[17] To enable him to carry out his tasks effectively, Göring endowed the GBA with the authority to issue instructions to the supreme Reich authorities, the Nazi Party offices, the Reich protector, the governor general, the military commanders and the heads of the civil administration. Furthermore, Göring decreed that, as GBA, Sauckel could claim the authority of the Reich labour minister.[18] The GBA, then, was endowed with a wealth of powers and rights to issue instructions, giving him an extraordinarily strong position within the matrix of Nazi power.

So far, historians have generally taken the view that, in light of the appointment of the GBA, the Reich Ministry of Labour was the big loser, ceding key powers over labour deployment to the new authority and degenerating into a 'rump ministry'.[19] Is this assumption tenable when we consider that main sections III and V, which were placed at the disposal of the GBA, remained within the ministry's organizational structure until 1945? Did the GBA really gut the Reich Labour Ministry when it came to labour policy?[20]

In January 1942, the Reich Labour Ministry consisted of five main sections, all of which came under the authority of Reich Labour Minister Franz Seldte. In addition, the Berlin ministry included an extensive and many-branched apparatus of subordinate agencies.[21] In terms of staffing policy and budget law, the main sections for Labour Law and Wages Policy (III) and Labour Deployment (V), along with their personnel, which were placed at the disposal of the GBA in March 1942, were not hived off from the Reich Labour Ministry but remained a component of it in organizational terms. At a meeting with Seldte in April 1942, Sauckel denied any ambitions to hold ministerial office.[22] Yet in reality key powers over labour policy were successively transformed: instead of the Reich labour minister, it was now the GBA who enjoyed the authority to instruct the staff of two main sections. Initially, however, these powers related solely to technical matters; the GBA was unable to unilaterally instigate measures relating to staff or organization within the main sections placed at his disposal or their subordinate agencies. Immediately after Sauckel's appointment by Hitler, however, Reich Labour Minister Seldte was instructed to cooperate with the GBA, to which he readily assented. Should complications arise, Sauckel's powers were to be extended.[23]

Along with their new head, the two main sections also got a new label. They were now to be known as 'The Commissioner for the Four-Year Plan – The General Plenipotentiary for Labour Deployment'.[24] Beyond this, for the staff of the two main sections, initially very little changed in terms of their daily working practices. They continued to deal with and administer labour deployment, labour law and wages policy. To help him successfully carry out the task with which he had been entrusted, namely the consistent and coherent management of manpower within the territory under German rule, the GBA could now make targeted use of their wide-ranging practical experience and expertise.[25]

Supplementing the two main departments, Sauckel established a small task force initially made up of fifteen individuals. This was to be in charge of his Berlin office and of communication with the various Reich ministries, Nazi organizations, economic and military agencies, which were all involved in labour policy in the broadest sense. Examples include the German Labour Front and the Party Chancellery. In the programme he set out on 20 April 1942, Sauckel underlined that he aimed, 'with the smallest possible circle of close colleagues of his choosing, to draw exclusively on the existing Party, state and economic institutions and, through the goodwill and cooperation of everyone involved, ensure that his policies are implemented as rapidly and successfully as possible'.[26] The task force, therefore, functioned as the coordinating hub between the numerous actors involved in labour policy. A carefully calibrated exchange between the various parties was facilitated, in particular, by the newly established forum of staff meetings, at which all members of staff, as well as various department heads at the Reich Ministry of Labour, came together under Sauckel's chairmanship.

Sauckel manned his task force almost exclusively with individuals he knew from his activities as Gauleiter and Reich governor in Thuringia. Of the fifteen initial members of the task force, twelve were from Thuringia. Some were members of the Thuringian Gau clique, a group within the Thuringian Gau apparatus, which had grown up around Gauleiter Sauckel in the 1930s and steered regional policy efficiently in line with his demands.[27] This Gau clique included a number of experienced administrative experts and specialists in regional policy, such as Walter Escher, Gau Office head and member of staff at the Thuringia Governor's Office, and Rudolf Peuckert,[28] another Gau Office head and leading representative of the Thuringian farmers, whom Sauckel appointed to his GBA staff.[29] In addition to various members of the Thuringian Gau machinery, Sauckel also appointed a number of long-standing confidants from the business world to his new task force, including Carl Goetz, chairman of the board at the Dresdner Bank, and Karl Beckurts, director of the Gustloff Werke in Weimar. The members of the task force held their new posts concurrently with their existing ones, enabling them to further expand the multifarious networks of relations that they mostly already enjoyed within state, party and economy.[30] This accumulation of offices gave them access to information and resources from different spheres of society that they could use to expedite their own activities – including their work at the GBA, which thus fused the interests of the political and economic spheres. Via the GBA task force, these resources also benefited main sections III and V of the Reich Labour Ministry.[31]

Examination of the GBA as an organization reveals that Sauckel did not create a new agency to carry out the task with which he had been entrusted. Instead he made use of the existing main sections of the Reich Labour Ministry and merely formed a small task force to function as a coordinating office and smooth cooperation with the ministry. To manage this cooperation, within his task force Sauckel appointed specific representatives to take charge of direct communication with main sections III and V and with Main Section I, which was responsible for administrative and staffing issues.[32] In addition to these liaison officers within the GBA staff, the heads of main sections III and V and of some of the departments within them also played an important role in coordinating tasks and managing the interaction between the GBA staff and the ministry. One example was Dr Max Timm, who rose to the position of head of Main Section VI (Europe Office for Labour Deployment) under Sauckel, and ministerial counsellors Dr Hubert Hildebrandt and Dr Walter Letsch,[33] the two department heads (*Abteilungsdirigenten*) for labour deployment in Western and Eastern Europe respectively.

Both the GBA staff and the main sections of the Labour Ministry benefited from this cooperation. The task force staff brought with them their many-faceted relational networks and used them to pursue the GBA's labour policy objectives, which were of course also the objectives of the Reich Labour Ministry. Combined with the expertise of ministry staff, this gave rise to complex synergetic effects. For the office of the GBA, Sauckel had thus created an efficient, mutually complimentary apparatus, which achieved its efficacy through the specific constellation it embodied – the combination of traditional administration and personalized, network-based political leadership, which attained an institutionalized frame in the shape of the task force.[34] Sauckel himself took charge of communication at the highest level on behalf of the ministry and thus enjoyed de facto minister-like responsibilities. Whenever complications arose in the course of the two main sections' everyday administrative activities with respect to cooperation with other agencies, Sauckel turned to the top-level decision-makers in order to ensure decisions consonant with the GBA's – and thus the Reich Labour Ministry's – plans. For example, in March 1943 he wrote to Reichsführer SS Heinrich Himmler in an attempt to ensure the support of the SS and police forces, of which Himmler was in charge, for labour recruitment in the occupied Soviet territories.[35]

The Europe Office for Labour Deployment

For Reich Labour Minister Franz Seldte, Sauckel's appointment as GBA brought in its wake a severe loss of power within his own institution. In March 1942, Seldte lost the power of instruction with respect to key competencies of the ministry relating to labour and wages policy. His influence was curtailed even further thereafter. Towards the end of 1942, the GBA planned an initial organizational restructuring of Main Section V, which was responsible for labour deployment. The plan was to create, out of parts of this main section, the Europe Office for Labour Deployment as the new Main Section VI of the Labour Ministry. Seldte, however, was not prepared to keep his head down and simply implement Sauckel's proposals to restructure the organization and staff of the main sections, though he had pledged to give the GBA his full support in March 1942. In December of that year, conflict flared up between Seldte and Sauckel over the organizational details of this process, with Sauckel ultimately forcing his plan through unilaterally.[36] As a result of the labour minister's resistance in this matter, the GBA's powers were subsequently extended. On 4 March 1943, Hitler issued an implementing decree stating that the GBA now also enjoyed authority over staffing decisions relating to the main sections of the ministry under his authority. Henceforth, he would be permitted to take organizational steps independently in their subordinate agencies as well. This gave him access to the relevant parts of Main Section I.[37] This new curtailment of the power of the Reich labour minister with respect to staffing and administrative issues in his own ministry was a bitter defeat, involving as it did the most fundamental decision-making powers of his post. Sauckel could now undertake personnel-related and organizational changes in main sections III and V and in the newly established Main Section VI at his own discretion, without first seeking Seldte's approval.

The organizational restructuring of Main Section V in the spring of 1943 and the formation of Main Section VI (Europe Office for Labour Deployment), headed by Section Head Max Timm, highlights the increasing importance to the war economy of the labour deployment of foreign workers in Germany.[38] Consonant with this, as well as being organized on the basis of economic and business sectors, the Europe Office was also structured in line with geography. Certain departments were thus given responsibility for labour deployment in specific regions of the territory under Nazi rule as well as in allied or neutral states, with further subdivisions within departments. For example, Department VI a under Ministerial Counsellor Dr Letsch, was responsible for labour deployment in Eastern Europe, that is, in the occupied Soviet territories, the General Government and the Protectorate of Bohemia and Moravia. Department VI b under Ministerial Counsellor Dr Hildebrandt dealt with Western Europe. In accordance with the schedule of responsibilities, therefore, it was responsible for the Netherlands, Belgium, France, Spain and Portugal. Overall, the central planning and administrative work of the ministry with respect to labour deployment throughout Nazi-occupied Europe converged within the newly formed Europe Office. For example, the Main Section's fields of activity included the planning of so-called rationalization and efficiency enhancement measures, statistical tasks and the recruitment of foreign labourers. The officials working in these fields also accompanied the GBA as experts on his trips to France or Ukraine to take part in negotiations and meetings.[39]

German Manpower Policy in Occupied Ukraine

Within the Nazi regime, the GBA's success was chiefly defined in terms of whether he managed to make available the labourers, and especially skilled workers, requested by the German war economy via the Central Planning agency.[40] The GBA was responsible for mobilizing German manpower but also for the increasingly important recruitment of foreign labourers, which de facto became the GBA's focus. Here, occupied Ukraine, which became the main area for the recruitment of forced labourers in Europe in 1942, thus took on particular relevance to the GBA. In addition, as the largest and economically most important occupied Soviet republic, Ukraine played a special role in Nazi plans. It thus forms the focus of the following analysis.[41]

Within occupied Ukraine, the Germans established a civilian and military administrative zone. By examining the two forms of administration, which existed in parallel, we can tease out the specific features of Reich Labour Ministry and GBA policy under military and civilian rule. When it comes to labour policy, it is crucial to examine both spheres together, given the close links that existed between them, both in terms of policy content and staff, as manifest especially in the GBA commissioner (GBA-Beauftragter) and the distribution of responsibilities within the Reich Labour Ministry.[42] The recruitment of workers in occupied Ukraine began before the appointment of the GBA. By December 1941, the Reich Labour Ministry and the Working Group on Labour Deployment had already laid down organizational structures on which the GBA could build from March 1942. He did not, therefore, create a new administrative structure. In fact, we can discern a high degree of organizational and personnel-related continuity in this regard. As the war wore on, intensifying the needs of the German war economy, the recruitment of labour in occupied Ukraine took on increasingly radical forms. On the local level, this engendered a sphere of violence that fundamentally shaped the everyday lives of the indigenous population. This potential for violence of German rule in occupied territories is particularly apparent in the case of Ukraine.

On 22 June 1941, Germany launched its invasion of the Soviet Union. The Wehrmacht's initially rapid advance meant that by November 1941 the territory of Ukraine almost in its entirety was under German occupation, including Kiev, the capital. The German military administration that was initially set up gradually transferred authority over the occupied territory to the civil administration. In the regions of western and central Ukraine, the civilian-run Reich Commissariat of Ukraine, under Reich Commissioner Erich Koch, was formed on 1 September 1941 and over the following months its jurisdiction expanded eastwards, step by step, in parallel with the German army's advance. It reached its greatest territorial extent in September 1942, before the Germans' final retreat began in 1943. The Wehrmacht's rear area, which adjoined the Reich Commissariat of Ukraine in the east, remained under German military administration throughout the occupation.[43]

Trends in labour policy and the development of labour recruitment in Ukraine were closely bound up with the various other aspects of occupation policy, so we must examine them in this light.[44] There was, for example, an interplay between labour policy and economic policy, food policy, campaigns against partisans, and the overall military situation. Within the policies pursued by the German occupiers in Ukraine, right from the start the economic exploitation of agriculturally productive regions as well as industrial towns and mining areas played a key role.[45] The provisioning of German troops with Ukrainian produce and the removal of raw materials and foodstuffs to Reich territory led to local food shortages. The occupiers enforced an active 'starvation policy' at the expense of the local population, a policy initially directed chiefly at urban residents but later at all those not in work. In the winter of 1941–1942, thousands died as a consequence of the catastrophic food shortages induced by the Germans, particularly the urban population, with at least twelve thousand people dying in Kharkov alone. The occupiers had consciously factored their deaths into their plans.[46]

Another significant element in the German occupiers' economic policy was the exploitation of the local population's labour, which became ever more important as the war dragged on. German officials of the labour administration moved in immediately after the occupation of Ukrainian territory and began to establish their organizational structures, that is, labour offices (*Arbeitsämter*), initially called labour agencies (*Arbeitsbehörden*). The labour offices were thus among the first German authorities to be established. During the entire period of German occupation, in other words until the retreat of 1943–1944, the occupiers exploited the labour of the Ukrainian population to advance their own objectives. It was the deployment of the indigenous population locally that initially stood centre stage. They were put to work provisioning troops, reconstructing transport routes, clearing towns and villages, rebuilding those industries of importance to the war and vital to survival, and in agriculture.[47] The newly established labour offices were responsible for the local placement of workers in this context.

Right from the outset, when it came to the administration of labour, the Germans used coercive measures and restricted individuals' scope for decision-making. By 1941, they had, for example, already introduced compulsory labour service for the indigenous population in the civilian-administered area.[48] The first basic prerequisite for the activities of the German labour administration, and later for the work of the Reich recruitment commissions (Reichswerbekommissionen) as well, was the registration of the population, a task the newly established labour administration began as early as 1941. This was also a precondition for enforcing compulsory labour service. By registering the population, the labour administration sought to record the unemployed, while simultaneously gaining an overview of the general population's age structure, ethnic composition and sex ratio as well as information on skilled workers. With this knowledge, the occupiers gained control over the people's labour, having stripped them of the ability to make their own decisions about their employment. The entire process of registration proceeded sluggishly, because in many places the local population refused to register as ordered. In a number of districts, the occupiers thus implemented another coercive measure: they linked the issuance of ration cards with registration at a labour agency.[49] In place of passports, the authorities introduced labour cards or labour passes, on the back of which the issuance of ration cards could be recorded.[50]

In addition to the labour offices, within the occupation administration the Germans established a multi-level labour administration, whose actors differed depending on whether they were operating under military or civil administration (see Figure 10.1). The Economic Staff East (Wirtschaftsstab Ost) was largely responsible for the economic exploitation of eastern Ukraine, which was under military administration. In organizational terms, this was the executive organ of the Economic Command Staff East (Wirtschaftsführungsstab Ost), which had been established by the Commissioner for the Four-Year Plan before the start of the war against the Soviet Union. Subordinate to the Economic Staff East were the economic inspectorates, which were in turn in charge of the economic commandos. It was the Economic Inspectorate South that was chiefly active in

Ukraine.[51] Both in the Economic Staff East as well as in the economic inspectorates and commandos, a Senior Group (Chefgruppe) or Group for Labour (Gruppe für Arbeit) was established, which was responsible for all labour policy issues in the territory of which it was in charge. The labour offices coordinated their activities with the groups for labour within the economic commandos.

Within the civilian-administered areas of the Reich Commissariat of Ukraine, the occupation administration had a different structure. The Reich Commissariat of Ukraine, which was subordinate to the Reich Ministry for the Occupied Eastern Territories under Alfred Rosenberg, was divided into general districts (Generalbezirke) and district areas (Kreisgebiete).[52] Here, offices headed by general and area commissioners respectively were established. In the Ministry for the Occupied Eastern Territories, the Reich Commissariat of Ukraine and the offices of the general and area commissioners, meanwhile, main sections and departments dedicated to labour policy were set up. The labour offices were located in the territories under the authority of the area commissioners, which took charge of them when the area concerned was transferred from military to civilian control.

The offices of the area commissioners and the economic commandos represented the lowest level of the German occupation administration. Supplementing them, the Germans also established an indigenous administration, though it had no decision-making powers of its own and was

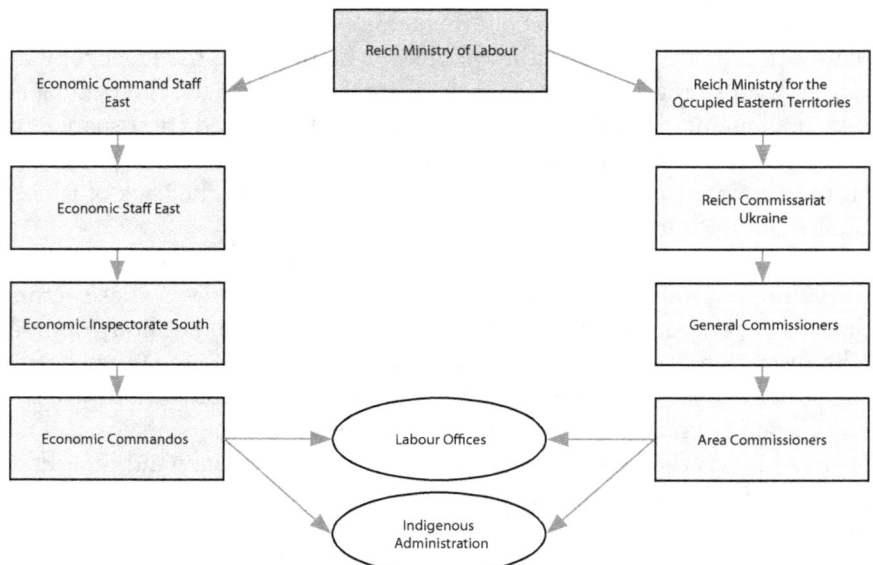

Figure 10.1. Organizational and communicative structure of the occupation regime in Ukrainian territory under military and civilian administration, autumn 1941

strictly bound by the regulations and guidelines laid down by the occupiers. These local administrations, headed by raion heads, mayors and village elders, were of crucial importance to the occupiers. In the absence of the knowledge and insight of the local staff they employed, it would have been impossible to administer the extensive Ukrainian territories. One of the main problems for the Germans was the language barrier, along with their lack of knowledge about the indigenous population and its way of life. Furthermore, in staffing terms they were dependent on the local population, as there were not enough German personnel available to administer the Ukrainian territory. Even the labour offices, then, were largely staffed by local workers, with Germans holding the senior posts.[53]

The labour administration as established within the occupation regime had no direct links with the German Labour Ministry. The Reich did not envisage giving its ministries direct authority over the various parts of the civilian and military administration in Ukraine. The Reich Ministry for the Occupied Eastern Territories, meanwhile, occupied a special position as a kind of territorial ministry, one that represented the highest authority within the civilian administration.[54] Via this ministry, all submissions from Reich agencies were to be passed to the Reich Commissioner for Ukraine, who would then transmit them to the general and area commissioners. Within the military administration, the official channels of communication flowed from the Reich ministries via the Economic Command Staff East to the Economic Staff East and from there to the economic inspectorates, which in turn informed the economic commandos. This official chain of command also applied to submissions from the Reich Ministry of Labour and, from March 1942, to the GBA. In practice, however, there were ways of evading these official channels. For example, Department Head Letsch of Main Section VI at the Reich Labour Ministry, or Sauckel himself, could directly contact the subordinate agencies within the occupation administration of Ukraine, informing their superior offices either not at all or on a 'for information only' basis. This led to complaints on a number of occasions from Reich Minister Rosenberg, who felt that his ministry was being bypassed.[55] The heads of the departments and groups for labour within the occupation administration played an important role when it came to circumventing the official channels. They recruited their staff from the Reich German labour administration – both from the Berlin headquarters, in other words the Reich Ministry of Labour, and from its subordinate authorities. On matters of policy substance, there was close cooperation between the Berlin headquarters and these employees, which facilitated the unproblematic curtailment of the official chain of command. One of those engaged in this process was the head of the Senior Group for Labour within the Economic Staff East, Head of Wartime Administration

(*Kriegsverwaltungschef*) Günther Rachner, a section head at the Reich Ministry of Labour who had been posted to the Economic Staff East.[56]

Recruiting Manpower for the Reich

The Nazi regime's decision, in the autumn of 1941, to deploy Soviet civilian workers and prisoners of war on a large scale within the Reich changed the situation in Ukrainian territory fundamentally over the following months. The agencies operating in Ukraine now had to make available a large number of workers, who had previously been deployed locally, to work in the Reich. The shortage of skilled workers rapidly became evident and by the summer of 1942 at the latest conflict flared, as the goals of the local agencies clashed with the manpower requirements of the Reich.[57] When it came to places of deployment, human considerations very rarely played a role in the actions of the German occupiers, who took virtually no account of those affected by recruitment.

In an attempt to expedite the recruitment of workers for Germany, in late 1941 the Reich Labour Ministry established so-called Reich recruitment commissions and sent them into the occupied Soviet territories. The recruitment commissions were de facto responsible for providing the labour contingents demanded by Berlin, and they were supposed to carry out their work in collaboration with the labour agencies, which were in charge of labour procurement on the local level. In parallel to the recruitment of civilian workers, the Reich recruitment commissions were also tasked with scouring the prisoner-of-war camps for skilled workers who could work in Germany.[58]

A list drawn up in the Reich Labour Ministry reveals that in December 1941 ten Reich recruitment commissions were dispatched to the Reich Commissariat of Ukraine.[59] This document detailed the composition of these commissions and identified the 'recruitment districts' entrusted to them. Each commission apparently consisted of between three and five members and was accompanied by an officer of the Wehrmacht Supreme Command, who was to liaise with military offices and ensure smooth cooperation.[60] The other members were staff of the labour offices and Land labour offices, in other words from the Reich German labour administration. Each of the Land labour offices in Reich territory was responsible for putting together a commission, to be headed by an 'experienced civil servant' – it was mostly government counsellors or other senior civil servants who were selected in these cases.[61] The Reich recruitment commissions were named either after their head or after the Land labour office that provided their staff. For example, the Reich Recruitment Commission

Graf Spreti consisted of Government Counsellor Graf von Spreti and a white-collar worker named Hermann, both seconded from the Freising Labour Office (Bavaria Land Labour Office District). These two men were accompanied by Captain Binder of the Wehrmacht Supreme Command.[62] On 13 December 1941, following an introductory meeting at the Reich Labour Ministry in Berlin, the members of the ten Reich recruitment commissions, including the Commission Graf Spreti, set off for the Ukrainian 'recruitment district' allocated to them.

By early December 1941 it had been decreed that the labour offices in Ukraine should prepare for the arrival of the Reich recruitment commissions and furnish them with local knowledge of the economic situation and labour deployment.[63] In organizational terms, the Reich recruitment commissions were affiliated with the area commissioners or the economic commandos. While they had been dispatched by the Reich Labour Ministry or the Working Group on Labour Deployment within the Four-Year Plan Authority and were technically subordinate to them, they were to be integrated into the official communicative structures within occupied Ukraine. With respect to the civilian-administered area, this meant, for example, that the submissions and directives of Main Section V, or later the Europe Office, had to pass through the prescribed channels, via the Ministry for the Occupied Eastern Territories, the Reich Commissariat of Ukraine, then the general commissioners and area commissioners, before being passed on to the recruitment commissions.

When the Reich recruitment commissions were established, the initial plan was for them to return to Reich territory after completing their task. It soon emerged, however, that their assignment would require a longer stint in occupied Ukrainian territory. This was to be no one-off recruitment campaign. One significant hallmark of the commissions was their mobility, an indispensable attribute given the vast size of the Ukrainian territory and the 'recruitment districts' allocated to them. This was one of the main reasons why their complement of staff was to remain extremely limited and why they were not permitted to develop a large administrative apparatus of their own. This was true especially of the commissions deployed in rural areas. In contrast to their urban counterparts, these were not tied to a particular location. Instead, they travelled through the 'recruitment districts' allocated to them from one village to the next in an attempt to mobilize local residents to work in Germany. They made use of specially produced promotional materials in the form of posters and leaflets, which set out the supposed benefits of employment in the Reich and were intended to prompt individuals to sign up on a 'voluntary' basis. Work in the Reich was presented as an opportunity to develop new skills. The prospect of a good income and a return home in the foreseeable future provided further incentives. Furthermore, the authorities pledged to facilitate the transfer home of a portion of workers' wages in order to provide for family members left behind.[64]

Initially, these methods of 'enticement' seemed to work, and in a number of areas locals showed an interest in a job in Germany. In addition to German propaganda, a number of other factors played a role here.[65] For example, during the first few months of the occupation, in many places the local population had a positive attitude towards the Germans, whom they welcomed as liberators from the repressive Stalinist regime. They hoped for an improvement in living conditions in Ukraine. Nationalist circles, meanwhile, particularly members of the Organization of Ukrainian Nationalists, hoped for the chance to create a Ukrainian nation state.[66] Further, the 'recruitment' of workers for jobs within Reich territory, which began in January 1942, appeared to offer a route out of a hopeless situation, particularly for urban residents hit hard by the occupiers' 'starvation policy'. Large numbers of individuals in cities such as Kharkov, one of the places worst affected by that policy, thus enrolled to work in Germany, far from their homes.[67]

It seems highly dubious to refer to locals' initial enrolment for work in Germany as 'voluntary'. The urban population, plagued by starvation, was willing to take up such work in large part because of the disastrous living conditions deliberately created by the Germans. Furthermore, German propaganda deceived the local people and made promises that were generally not kept. If not before, then as soon as people were confronted with the living and working conditions that actually pertained within the Reich, they perceived the discrepancy between the illusory world paraded by the Germans and reality.[68] Isolated from the rest of the population, accommodated in camps surrounded by barbed wire, they were de facto treated like Soviet prisoners of war.[69] Through correspondence with family members back home and through the reports provided by the first of those to return from Reich territory, most of whom were ill or unable to work, the conditions under which Soviet labourers had to live and work in the Reich soon became known in Ukraine. The people's willingness to sign up for work in Germany rapidly diminished.

Rather than 'enticement', the occupiers soon deployed coercive methods in order to recruit the requisite manpower for the Reich. If an insufficient number of people registered 'voluntarily' with the Reich recruitment commissions, the indigenous administration was forced to fulfil quotas by a specific deadline. This measure was based on the apportionment procedure already established by early 1942. The Reich Labour Ministry or the GBA passed on the total recruitment quota to the relevant offices within the occupation administration, which then divided it between the various districts within Ukraine. Every urban district or village had to provide a specified contingent of workers. When registering the population, the labour administration had built up a picture of the local demographic structure, knowledge that played a key role here.[70]

From the perspective of the German agencies, then, the recruitment of workers in Ukraine became increasingly problematic, while the demand for labour in the German war economy constantly increased, particularly in the armaments sector and, in spring 1942, agriculture as well. In this context, in March 1942, before the appointment of the GBA, the transports carrying Soviet labourers gained a new importance for the head of the Transportation System within the Wehrmacht Supreme Command. On his list of priorities, they were second only to troop transports and thus took precedence over the economic transports, carrying, for example, raw materials or grain from Ukraine to the Reich.[71] This underlines the tremendous dependency of the German war economy on foreign labourers. By early March 1942, meanwhile, the Commissioner for the Four-Year Plan had ordered the provision of additional staff for the Reich recruitment commissions in an attempt to satisfy the growing demand for manpower and provide more labourers for the transports. The demand for labour in the Reich was to take priority over local needs within Ukraine.[72]

The GBA's Labour Policy in Occupied Ukraine

On 21 March 1942, the appointment of the GBA instigated a shift in authority, at the highest level, with respect to labour policy and thus also in terms of the recruitment of manpower. When it came to manpower policy in Ukraine, before March was over the GBA had ordered an increase in the 'recruitment quotas' as one of his first official acts. The Reich recruitment commissions were to triple their 'recruitment figures'.[73] The commissions now answered to the GBA, who made the new chain of command unambiguously clear by renaming them the 'recruitment commissions of the general plenipotentiary for labour deployment'. He also strengthened the commissions, a step announced by the commissioner for the Four-Year Plan in early March, and doubled their staff. The GBA undertook no other technical or organizational changes within the apparatus of recruitment in Ukraine now under his authority. The administrative structures were to remain more or less the same.

The raising of the recruitment quotas, announced by Sauckel in late March, increased the pressure on the recruitment commissions significantly. The contingents he demanded were communicated via official channels down to the local level in Ukraine – with every office making the one below it within the chain of command responsible for fulfilling the quotas. Ultimately, this put tremendous pressure on the members of the recruitment commissions and of the indigenous administrations, which represented the lowest links in the chain of command. Immediately after his appointment as GBA, Sauckel had instructed the agencies in Ukraine 'to exhaust completely every means of supplying the Reich with civilian workers from the occupied Eastern territories as rapidly as possible and on the largest possible scale'.[74] At the same time, official communications repeatedly stated that recruitment was to take place on a 'voluntary basis'. 'Should the requisite voluntary registrations fail to meet our target, in reality it will of course be necessary to take drastic measures in accordance with the law of war.'[75] Just what these measures ought to look like in the detail was generally not specified in official instructions and was left to the interpretation of the offices involved. This fostered the use of coercion and force at the local level: the recruitment commissions could justify virtually any method with reference to their imprecise instructions.

The 1.6 million workers demanded by the GBA in March 1942 to work in the Reich were made available by the end of July 1942, of whom more than 1.3 million were from the occupied Soviet territories alone. Yet it was not long before the GBA announced the next quotas.[76] Until the Germans' withdrawal from the occupied Ukrainian territories, he continually demanded more workers. The recruitment commissions were instructed to muster more residents to work in Germany in a number of cities, towns and villages that had already been subject to recruitment. The locals, however, did everything they could to evade the recruitment campaigns and the deportation to Germany they entailed. An increasing number of forged medical certificates were produced to prove an inability to work; doctors were bribed, and some individuals resorted to injuring themselves.[77]

By November 1942, the Office of the General Commissioner for Volhynia and Podolia was already reporting that 'when it comes to recruitment in Volhynia, the same picture always pertains: by the time the recruitment commission appears, the residents have fled, because there are not enough policemen to occupy the individual villages ambush-style'.[78] Due to their meagre staff, the recruitment commissions were quite unable to carry out their tasks on their own, making them highly dependent on the cooperation of the indigenous administration. In the context of the recruitment of workers for Germany, close cooperation developed between the commissions and the local city and raion administrations. This cooperation extended down to the level of individual caretakers, who, for example, provided lists of residents of particular buildings, facilitating comprehensive control that encompassed the individual citizens of cities, towns and villages.[79] The local auxiliary police, the so-called protection squads (*Schutzmannschaften*), which acted on the occupiers' behalf, were also involved in the recruitment process, compelling individuals who put up resistance to report to recruitment points and carrying out house searches and raids.[80]

In the spring of 1943, the German agencies in occupied Ukraine introduced a new method of labour recruitment, the so-called 'age group campaigns', which aimed to subject entire age groups to compulsory labour service in Germany. While the GBA issued an official decree on the rounding up of those born between 1925 and 1927 in July 1943, the German agencies had already been doing this since the spring in a number of regions under both civilian and military administration.[81] Through these campaigns, which saw continued cooperation between the recruitment commissions and the indigenous administration and police, the occupiers stepped up the pressure on the population. They resembled a military draft. Every man and woman resident in a particular village or urban district had to appear before the recruitment commission at a specified time in order to be examined and potentially selected for labour in Germany. Because locals of particular age cohorts were instructed to 'sign up' in advance, it was easier for them to evade these measures and flee into the woods before the recruitment commissions arrived. The commissions responded by having the police arrest members of these individuals' families until they showed up.[82]

The 'age-group campaigns' and the radicalization of recruitment set in motion a coercive dynamic, which made the everyday lives of the Ukrainian population increasingly impossible. One of the consequences was the strengthening of the partisan movement, which acted to oppose the occupiers and the indigenous administration that served them.[83] Particularly during the German forces' retrograde movements in response to the Soviet offensive between January and March 1943, and then from autumn 1943 onwards, the partisans gained considerable support. Those who fled into the forests from their villages to evade the recruitment commissions often joined the partisans. As a result of the partisan groups' increasing activity, particularly in the Wehrmacht's rear area, the military authorities repeatedly expressed opposition to the recruitment of labour for the Reich and imposed so-called 'recruitment bans' in their areas, fearful that security was at risk.[84]

The GBA Commissioners

In the autumn of 1942, the GBA's authority in the occupied territories and thus also in occupied Ukraine received a substantial boost. Through the implementing decree of 30 September 1942, Hitler authorized Sauckel to take all steps necessary to ensure the 'orderly deployment of labour for the German war economy' throughout the territory under German control.[85] To this end, the GBA could now appoint commissioners, directly answerable to him, to be assigned to the agencies of the civilian and military administration. These commissioners were authorized to issue instructions to the departments responsible for labour policy. The commissioners thus extended the GBA's reach directly into the occupation administrations.

The selection of the commissioners in the various occupied territories adhered to no uniform schema. In some cases, individuals already working in the occupation administrations were appointed, mostly from the sphere of labour policy, while in other cases external individuals were integrated into the occupation administrations. For the Reich Commissariat of Ukraine and for the area under the jurisdiction of the economic inspectorates serving the Don-Donets and Caucasus regions, which were active in the areas of eastern Ukraine under military administration, Sauckel appointed provincial agricultural leader Rudolf Peuckert from Thuringia as his commissioner. Senior Government Counsellor Meincke from the Reich Ministry of Labour was made Peuckert's deputy, chiefly to help him complete his work relating to the Don-Donets Economic Inspectorate.[86] In the shape of Peuckert, Sauckel had selected a colleague from the Thuringian Gau administration with whom he had enjoyed a long collaboration, marked by a high degree of trust, a man he had also appointed to his GBA staff as Commissioner for Agriculture and the Wartime Provision of Food. On the basis of his experience as provincial farmers' leader in Thuringia and head of the Nazi Party Office for Agricultural Policy (Amt für Agrarpolitik) and in light of his activities as a member of the Personal Staff of the Reich Farmers' Leader, Peuckert was a proven agriculture expert – a major advantage given the dominance of agriculture in the Ukrainian economy.[87]

The decree of 30 September 1942 officially authorized the GBA, within the framework of his remit, to issue instructions to the departments and groups responsible for labour and wages policy within Ukraine's civilian and military administration (see Figure 10.2). Particularly in light of increasing tensions over the sites of labour deployment, that is, locally in occupied Ukraine or in Reich territory, and given the growing number of 'recruitment bans' imposed by the army groups, the GBA's direct conduit into the occupation administration played a key role in his ability to get things done. His commissioners, working on site in the occupied territory, could keep him informed of developments more rapidly and more directly, enabling him to intervene if necessary. Over the next few months, Peuckert further strengthened his position within occupied Ukraine. In spring 1943, complementing his other posts, he took charge of the Main Section for Labour Policy and Social Administration within the Ministry for the Occupied Eastern Territories and the Senior Group for Labour within the Economic Staff East. One year later, he was appointed GBA commissioner for the occupied Eastern territories in their entirety.[88]

Sauckel made his commissioners responsible for the fulfilment of the quotas.[89] The recruitment commissions, renamed the 'GBA labour deployment units' (Arbeitseinsatzstäbe des GBA) in October 1942 on Sauckel's instructions, were subject to the technical directives of the GBA commissioner and his deputy. This did not change the units' organizational position. But in the shape of the GBA commissioners they now had specialist interlocutors within the occupation administration on site, enabling a more direct and targeted flow of communication than had been possible via Main Section VI of the Reich Labour Ministry or the GBA headquarters in Berlin. As a result of their activities in Ukraine, Peuckert and Meincke had a detailed knowledge of local labour policy developments and could therefore tailor their directives to the labour deployment units in a more targeted way, coordinating them with the local agencies.

Within the occupation administration, the commissioners functioned as the GBA's liaison officers, informing him of current trends and problems in labour policy and representing his interests in negotiations and meetings. Regular exchanges took place within the framework of so-called roadmap meetings with Ministerial Counsellor Walter Letsch from Main Section VI of the Reich Ministry of Labour and through direct reports delivered to Sauckel in person. For example, in his activity report to Sauckel of March 1943, GBA Commissioner Peuckert reported on an agreement reached with Reich Commissioner Erich Koch and the responsible Senior SS and Police Chief Hans-Adolf Prützmann, concerning, among other things, planned cooperation within the framework of a 'Campaign against Banditry'.[90] This campaign, to be carried out in April 1943, was to clear large areas in the north of the Reich Commissariat of Ukraine, apprehending the entire fit-for-work population to perform labour in the Reich. A large number of labour deployment units were to take part in this campaign. For them, cooperation with SS and police forces provided a welcome new means of obtaining labourers for transportation into the Reich. Peuckert requested permission from the GBA to deport entire extended families to Germany to work in agriculture within the context of this campaign. Previously, 'family deployment' of this kind was subject to a range of restrictions.

This activity report sheds light on the structures of communication, which changed as a result of the appointment of the GBA commissioner. Evidently, Peuckert took charge of the meetings with Reich Commissioner Koch on Sauckel's behalf, vigorously advocating the position set out by the GBA in Berlin. At the same time, he informed Sauckel of the progress of the negotiations and obtained from him the requisite permission to make fundamental changes in approach, in this case with respect to the 'evacuation' of entire extended families to Germany. Peuckert also passed on Sauckel's guidelines and demands to all the actors involved in

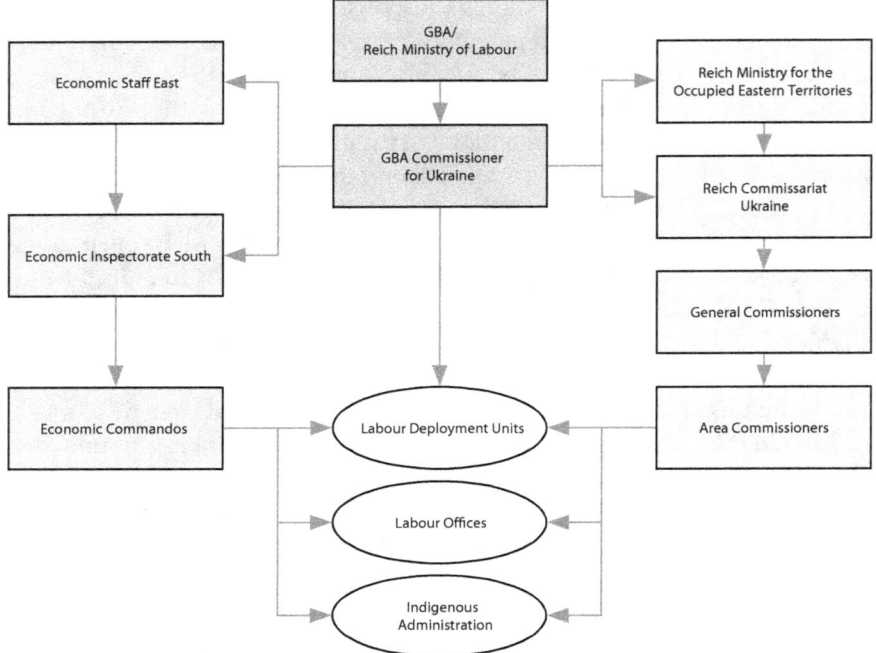

Figure 10.2. Changed communicative structures of the occupation regime in Ukrainian territory under military and civilian administration, spring 1943

the Ukrainian occupation administration, mostly at meetings. In addition to the heads of the labour deployment units, he informed the departmental heads responsible for labour issues within the civilian and military administration as well as other functionaries, such as the inspector in charge of the Economic Inspectorate South. As GBA commissioner, then, Peuckert occupied a crucial point of intersection between the office of the GBA in Berlin and the actors involved in labour policy in Ukraine. Sauckel, meanwhile, thanks to his loyal commissioner, could rest assured that his interests were being promoted in Ukraine, without always having to be present in person himself. The GBA commissioners in Ukraine, then, were closely involved in implementing the manpower policy decreed by the GBA.

Conclusion

Sauckel's appointment as GBA in March 1942 restructured the chain of command in relation to labour policy. As close examination of the organizational structure of the office of the GBA and its modus operandi reveals, however, this did not lead to a major rupture in German manpower policies. Instead, we can discern fundamental organizational and staffing continuities beyond the caesura of March 1942. This refutes the idea that the Reich Ministry of Labour was hollowed out and degenerated into a 'rump ministry' following the appointment of the GBA. These continuities also reveal that the GBA, particularly when it came to the recruitment of labour in the occupied territories, could fall back on structures already established by the Reich Labour Ministry before his appointment.

In March 1942, as GBA, Sauckel, along with his task force, took on the task of steering and coordinating key areas of the Reich Labour Ministry's work, while essentially allowing the ministry to go on as before, and relying on its administrative structures to carry out his assignment. The GBA and the ministry cooperated efficiently. Only after several months did Sauckel make changes by restructuring the main sections of the Labour Ministry and appointing GBA commissioners in the occupied territories. In this way, he sought to optimize the administrative apparatus under his authority to effectively pursue his objectives and strengthen his position, particularly with respect to the occupied areas of such crucial importance to him. The organizational modifications he made did not signal a loss of power for the Reich Labour Ministry. Quite the opposite: they resulted in more effective working and communicative structures, ensuring that the ministry packed a greater political punch. The cooperation between the ministry's main sections and the staff of the GBA and GBA commissioners was frictionless, as far as was possible under wartime conditions.

As this chapter has laid bare, the Reich Labour Ministry's administrative practices, encompassing an extreme demand for manpower that came under the remit of the GBA from March 1942, extended deep into the lives of the Ukrainian population. These administrative practices became part and parcel of Nazi occupation policy, which was geared towards exploiting the local population. The targets of the GBA and the Reich Labour Ministry, as set in Berlin, flowed down through the various administrative offices to the local administration. Due to the excessive recruitment quotas and under the influence of the war, their instructions led to a fateful case of cooperation between German agencies, the indigenous administration and the police. The administrative work set in motion in Berlin, then, ultimately engendered a spiral of violence, shattering the hopes of the Ukrainian people for a normal life.

Swantje Greve, Ph.D., study of history and cultural anthropology at the University of Göttingen; trainee and member of staff at the Topography of Terror Documentation Centre (Stiftung Topographie des Terrors) in Berlin (2010–2014); doctoral student at Humboldt University of Berlin (2014–2018) and contributor (thanks to a scholarship) to the project being pursued by the Independent Commission of Historians Investigating the History of the Reich Ministry of Labour in the National Socialist Period, with a study of the General Plenipotentiary for Labour Deployment. Curator of the exhibition 'The Reich Ministry of Labour 1933–1945: Civil Servants of the Nazi State' at the Topography of Terror. Publications: *Das 'System Sauckel'. Der Generalbevollmächtigte für den Arbeitseinsatz und die Arbeitskräftepolitik in der besetzten Ukraine 1942–1945* (Wallstein, 2019); *Werner Finck und die 'Katakombe'. Ein Kabarettist im Visier der Gestapo* (Hentrich und Hentrich, 2015).

Notes

1. Sauckel's Speech at the Fourth Reich Press Conference in Weimar, in the Kreishaus-Saale, 5 December 1943, Thüringisches Hauptstaatsarchiv Weimar (ThHStAW), Der Reichsstatthalter in Thüringen, no. 190, fol. 162–91, here fol. 165.

2. For detailed information on Fritz Sauckel, see Biographical Appendix.

3. On the subordinate agencies of the two main sections, in other words the labour offices, Land labour offices and Reich labour trustees, see the chapters by Henry Marx and Sören Eden in this volume.

4. Sauckel's Speech at the Fourth Reich Press Conference in Weimar, in the Kreishaus-Saale, 5 December 1943, ThHStAW, Der Reichsstatthalter in Thüringen, no. 190, fol. 162–91, here fol. 165 f.

5. See 'Erlass des Führers über einen Generalbevollmächtigten für den Arbeitseinsatz vom 21.3.1942', RGBl. I 1942, 179. Also in *Handbuch für die Dienststellen des Generalbevollmächtigten für den Arbeitseinsatz und die interessierten Reichsstellen im Grossdeutschen Reich und in den besetzten Gebieten*, vol. 1: *Vollmachten, Verlautbarungen, Verordnungen, Organisation des GBA*, ed. F. Didier, Berlin: Rotadruck W. Meyer KG, 1944, 21.

6. See the Schedule of Responsibilities of Main Sections I–V of the Reich Ministry of Labour, 1 January 1942, Bundesarchiv (BArch) R 3901/20039, fol. 2–19.

7. At the Nuremberg trial of the major war criminals of 1945–1946, Sauckel was sentenced to death by the Allied judges due to his responsibility for the recruitment of forced labourers, and executed in October 1946. See the chapter by Kim Christian Priemel in this volume.

8. See U. Herbert, *Geschichte Deutschlands im 20. Jahrhundert*, Munich: Beck, 2014, 490.

9. On the GBA as an organization, see W. Naasner, *Neue Machtzentren in der deutschen Kriegswirtschaft, 1942–1945*, Boppard am Rhein: Boldt, 1994, 48–51.

10. In what follows, GBA sometimes refers to the person of Fritz Sauckel and at other times to the agency of the GBA as a whole. The reader will generally be able to tell which from the context. The nature of the term, however, makes a degree of ambiguity unavoidable.

11. On the figures, which relate to civilian labourers, see M. Spoerer, *Zwangsarbeit unter dem Hakenkreuz. Ausländische Zivilarbeiter, Kriegsgefangene und Häftlinge im Deutschen Reich und im besetzten Europa 1939–1945*, Stuttgart: Deutsche Verlags-Anstalt, 2001, 80.

12. Robert Ley himself aspired to this position. On the German Labour Front, see the chapter by Rüdiger Hachtmann in this volume.

13. See D. Eichholtz, 'Die Vorgeschichte des "Generalbevollmächtigten für den Arbeitseinsatz"', *Jahrbuch für Geschichte* 9 (1973), 339–83, here 347–54; U. Herbert, *Hitler's Foreign Workers. Enforced Foreign Labor in Germany under the Third Reich*, trans. W. Templer, new ed., Cambridge: Cambridge University Press, 1997, 143–53; Hans Heinrich Lammers,

Reich Chancellery, to Martin Bormann, Party Chancellery, re. Labour Deployment of Foreign Workers, 31 October 1941, Archive of the United States Holocaust Memorial Museum (USHMM), ITS Digital Archive, 2.2.0.1/82388233–235.

14. See Eichholtz, 'Vorgeschichte', 346–48.

15. For more information on the background to the GBA, see Herbert, *Hitler's Foreign Workers*, 143–61; Naasner, *Neue Machtzentren*, 30–35; D. Eichholtz, *Geschichte der deutschen Kriegswirtschaft 1939–1945*, vol. 2, Munich: Saur, 2003, 74–79, 190–202; Eichholtz, 'Vorgeschichte'.

16. No comprehensive scholarly biography of Fritz Sauckel has been published to date. Relevant publications include S. Rassloff, *Fritz Sauckel. Hitlers 'Muster-Gauleiter' und 'Sklavenhalter'*, Erfurt: Landeszentrale für politische Bildung Thüringen, 2008; S. Lehnstaedt and K. Lehnstaedt, 'Fritz Sauckels Nürnberger Aufzeichnungen. Erinnerungen aus seiner Haft während des Kriegsverbrecherprozesses', *Vierteljahrshefte für Zeitgeschichte* 57(1) (2009), 117–50; M. Weissbecker, 'Fritz Sauckel. "Wir werden die letzten Schlacken unserer Humanitätsduselei ablegen...", in K. Pätzold and M. Weissbecker (eds), *Stufen zum Galgen. Lebenswege vor den Nürnberger Urteilen*, Leipzig: Militzke, 1999, 297–331. On the gap in the research, see M. Fleischhauer, *Der NS-Gau Thüringen 1939–1945. Eine Struktur- und Funktionsgeschichte*, Cologne: Böhlau, 2010, 34 f.

17. See Göring's 'Anordnung zur Durchführung des Erlasses des Führers über einen GBA vom 27.3.1942', *RGBl.* I 1942, 180. Also in *Handbuch für die Dienststellen*, 22.

18. See Göring's 'Verordnung über die Rechtsetzung durch den GBA vom 25.5.1942', *RGBl.* I 1942, 347. Also included in the *Handbuch für die Dienststellen*, 25.

19. See, for example, Herbert, *Hitler's Foreign Workers*, 163; Naasner, *Neue Machtzentren*, 38 f.

20. See S. Reichardt and W. Seibel, 'Radikalität und Stabilität: Herrschen und Verwalten im Nationalsozialismus', in S. Reichardt and W. Seibel (eds), *Der prekäre Staat. Herrschen und Verwalten im Nationalsozialismus*, Frankfurt am Main: Campus, 2011, 7–27, here 13.

21. See the Schedule of Responsibilities of Main Sections I–V of the Reich Ministry of Labour, 1 January 1942, BArch, R 3901/20039, fol. 2–19.

22. See '"Antrittsbesprechung" Sauckel mit Seldte', 15 April 1942, doc. 318-EC, in *Der Prozess gegen die Hauptkriegsverbrecher vor dem Internationalen Militärgerichtshof. Nürnberg, 14. November 1945–1. Oktober 1946*, vol. 36, Nuremberg: Internationaler Militärgerichtshof Nürnberg, 1949, 310–16. The series as a whole comprises forty-two volumes (Nuremberg, 1947–1949); abbreviated as *IMT* in what follows. See also Naasner, *Neue Machtzentren*, 39.

23. The instruction to Seldte appears to have been initiated by Speer; see Letter from Speer, re. Powers of the GBA, 23 March 1942, reprinted in Eichholtz, 'Vorgeschichte', 382 f.; see also ibid., 369. Also Hans Heinrich Lammers to Fritz Sauckel, re. Appointment as GBA, 23 March 1942, ThHStAW, Der Reichsstatthalter in Thüringen, no. 491, fol. 11.

24. See Fritz Sauckel to Land Labour Offices, re. Appointment of a GBA, 24 April 1942, BArch, R 43 II/652, fol. 218–20. The missives dispatched by the two main sections, however, continued to feature the abbreviation for the main section of the Reich Labour Ministry concerned below this designation.

25. See E.L. Homze, *Foreign Labor in Nazi Germany*, Princeton, NJ: Princeton University Press, 1967, 104.

26. GBA Programme of 20 April 1942, see *Handbuch für die Dienststellen*, 29.

27. See Fleischhauer, *Der NS-Gau Thüringen*, 80. On the concept of the Gau clique, see P. Hüttenberger, *Die Gauleiter. Studie zum Wandel des Machtgefüges in der NSDAP*, Stuttgart: Deutsche Verlags-Anstalt, 1969, 56 f. See also Nolzen's critique of Hüttenberger's concept of the Gau clique: A. Nolzen, 'Die Gaue als Verwaltungseinheiten der NSDAP. Entwicklungen und Tendenzen in der NS-Zeit', in J. John, H. Möller and T. Schaarschmidt (eds), *Die NS-Gaue. Regionale Mittelinstanzen im zentralistischen 'Führerstaat'*, Munich: Oldenbourg, 2007, 199–217.

28. For detailed information on Rudolf Peuckert, see Biographical Appendix.
29. See Fleischhauer, *Der NS-Gau Thüringen*, 80, 96–98.
30. Ibid., 100 f.
31. The web of relationships around Sauckel as Gauleiter and GBA is the focus of my dissertation. I scrutinize this relational matrix encompassing Sauckel, his close confidants and his staff with the help of network analysis in an attempt to determine how Sauckel managed to get things done in his role as GBA. My study spotlights not so much the actors involved and their attributes as the relationships between them. See S. Greve, *Das 'System Sauckel'. Der Generalbevollmächtigte für den Arbeitseinsatz und die Arbeitskräftepolitik in der besetzten Ukraine 1942–1945*, Wallstein: Göttingen, 2019.
32. See *Mitteilungen des Beauftragten für den Vierjahresplan – Der GBA* (1942), no. 1, 11 f.
33. For detailed information on Walter Letsch, see Biographical Appendix.
34. See also studies of the special representatives (*Sonderbeauftragte*), whom Sven Reichardt and Wolfgang Seibel describe as 'interface managers'; see Reichardt and Seibel, 'Radikalität und Stabilität', 13; R. Hachtmann and W. Süss (eds), *Hitlers Kommissare: Sondergewalten in der nationalsozialistischen Diktatur*, Göttingen: Wallstein, 2006.
35. See Fritz Sauckel to Heinrich Himmler, re. Cooperation with the SS Agencies, March 1943, Institut für Zeitgeschichte (IfZ), RFSS, MA 464, Folder 244.
36. On this conflict, see BArch, R 3901/20029, esp. fol. 99–106.
37. See *Handbuch für die Dienststellen*, 24.
38. See Schedule of Responsibilities of Main Section VI of the Reich Ministry of Labour, 1 March 1943, BArch, R 3901/20039, fol. 20, 38–48. The newly established Main Section VI consisted mainly of Department V a, previously integrated into Main Section V. See also Naasner, *Neue Machtzentren*, 48 f.; *Handbuch für die Dienststellen*, 271–76.
39. See, for example, Report by Gauleiter Sauckel on his Visit to Soviet Ukraine in his Capacity as GBA, 26–31 May 1942, BArch, R 3901/20029, fol. 25–30.
40. On the complex relations between the GBA, Reich Minister Speer and the Central Planning, in which the quotas were drawn up, see, for example, A. Tooze, *The Wages of Destruction. The Making and Breaking of the Nazi Economy*, New York: Penguin, 2006, 559–66; Eichholtz, *Kriegswirtschaft*, 79–83; Homze, *Foreign Labor*, 92–94, 121.
41. See T. Penter, 'Arbeiten für den Feind in der Heimat. Der Arbeitseinsatz in der besetzten Ukraine 1941–1944', *Jahrbuch für Wirtschaftsgeschichte* 1 (2004), 65–94, here 65 f.; H. Baum, '"Für die Stadt Kiew wird eine 'Fangaktion' vorbereitet . . .". Akteure und Praxis der Zwangsarbeiterrekrutierungen in der Ukraine während des Zweiten Weltkriegs', in K. Linne and F. Dierl (eds.), *Arbeitskräfte als Kriegsbeute. Der Fall Ost- und Südosteuropa 1939–1945*, Berlin: Metropol, 2011, 270–302, here 273, 298.
42. See M. Dubyk, 'Arbeitseinsatz und Lebensbedingungen im Reichskommissariat Ukraine und im ukrainischen Gebiet unter Militärverwaltung (1941–1944)', in D. Pohl and T. Sebta (eds), *Zwangsarbeit in Hitlers Europa: Besatzung, Arbeit, Folgen*, Berlin: Metropol, 2013, 195–213, here 197 f.
43. On the occupation of Ukrainian territory and the establishment of the civilian administration, see K. Berkhoff, *Harvest of Despair. Life and Death in Ukraine under Nazi Rule*, Cambridge, MA: Belknap Press of Harvard University Press, 2004, 11–13, 36 f. See also Second Decree of the Führer on the Implementation of the Civilian Administration in the Newly Occupied Eastern Territories, 20 August 1941, IfZ, Documentary Evidence of the Nuremberg War Crimes Trials, NG-953.
44. On the German labour administration in occupied Ukraine, see especially M. Eikel, 'Arbeitseinsatz in der besetzten Sowjetunion 1941–1944. Das Reichskommissariat Ukraine als Fallbeispiel', in B. Quinkert and J. Morré (eds), *Deutsche Besatzung in der Sowjetunion 1941–1944. Vernichtungskrieg – Reaktionen – Erinnerung*, Paderborn: Schöningh, 2014, 175–95; M. Eikel, '"Weil die Menschen fehlen". Die deutschen Zwangsarbeiterrekrutierungen und -deportationen in den besetzten Gebieten der Ukraine 1941–1944', *Zeitschrift für*

Geschichtswissenschaft 53(5) (2005), 405–33; T. Penter, *Kohle für Stalin und Hitler. Arbeiten und Leben im Donbass 1929–1953*, Essen: Klartext, 2010, 197–230; Baum, '"Für die Stadt Kiew"'; Berkhoff, *Harvest of Despair*, 253–74. A comprehensive account of German manpower policy in occupied Ukraine with special reference to the activities of the GBA and his representatives as well as the recruitment commissions is part of my dissertation.

45. For general information on this, see K.C. Priemel, 'Occupying Ukraine. Great Expectations, Failed Opportunities, and the Spoils of War, 1941–1943', *Central European History* 48(1) (2015), 31–52; on the Donbass region, see Penter, *Kohle*.

46. For a general account of the occupiers' 'starvation policy', see D. Pohl, *Die Herrschaft der Wehrmacht. Deutsche Militärbesatzung und einheimische Bevölkerung in der Sowjetunion 1941–1944*, Munich: Oldenbourg, 2008, 63–66, 183–200; Penter, *Kohle*, 185–95.

47. See Economic Command Staff East, Guidelines on Steering the Economy (Green Folder), Part 1: Tasks and Organization of the Economy, July 1941, BArch, R 26 VI/33a, esp. 16–18.

48. See *Amtliche Mitteilungen* no. 3, First Decree on Implementation, 1 November 1941, Central State Archive of the Supreme State Organs and Administrations of Ukraine (CDAVO), 3206-2-193, fol. 8 f.; Decree issued by the Reich Ministry for the Occupied Eastern Territories on the Introduction of Compulsory Labour Service in the Occupied Eastern Territories, 19 December 1941, in *Verordnungsblatt des Reichskommissars für die Ukraine*, 1942. See the discussion of the dating of the introduction of compulsory labour service in Eikel, 'Arbeitseinsatz', 188.

49. See, for example, General Commissioner Kiev to Commissioner for the City of Kiev, re. Labour Book, 9 January 1942, CDAVO, 3206-2-185, fol. 1; Introduction of a Labour Card in the General Commissariat of Kiev, 13 February 1942, USHMM, RG-31.059M, Reel 55. The issuance of ration cards was linked with registration at the labour authorities on subsequent occasions as well; see, for example, Activities of the Kharkov Labour Agency for the Period 16 September–15 October 1942, State Archive of Kharkov Oblast (DAKhO), 3080-1-37, fol. 20–23.

50. See the collection of labour passes from 1943, DAKhO, 3200-1-1.

51. See Göring, Letter re. Establishment of the Economic Command Staff and the Economic Staff East, 30 July 1941, BArch, R 6/291, fol. 29 f. Over the course of the military advance, the Economic Inspectorate South was subdivided on several occasions and renamed, resulting in the economic inspectorates A and B, Don-Donets and Caucasus. On the establishment of the economic administration in the areas under military administration, see R.-D. Müller (ed.), *Die deutsche Wirtschaftspolitik in den besetzten sowjetischen Gebieten 1941–1943. Der Abschlussbericht des Wirtschaftsstabes Ost und Aufzeichnungen eines Angehörigen des Wirtschaftskommandos Kiew*, Boppard am Rhein: Boldt, 1991.

52. On the Reich Commissariat of Ukraine, see Berkhoff, *Harvest of Despair*; on the establishment of the labour administration within the occupation regime, see also Eikel, '"Weil die Menschen fehlen"', 406.

53. On the motives underlying the cooperation of the indigenous administration, see M. Eikel, 'Arbeitsteilung und Verbrechen. Die ukrainische Lokalverwaltung unter deutscher Besatzung 1941–1944', in T.C. Richter (ed.), *Krieg und Verbrechen. Situation und Intention. Fallbeispiele*, Munich: Meidenbauer, 2006, 135–46, here 143–45; M. Eikel and V. Sivaieva, 'City Mayors, Raion Chiefs and Village Elders in Ukraine 1941–44: How Local Administrators Cooperated with the German Occupation Authorities', *Contemporary European History* 23(3) (2014), 405–28, here 424–26. For a general account of the indigenous administration, see W. Lower, *Nazi Empire-Building and the Holocaust in Ukraine*, Chapel Hill, NC: University of North Carolina Press, 2005, 50 f.

54. See Wuttke, 'Der deutsche Verwaltungsaufbau in der Ukraine', in *Deutsche Verwaltung. Organ der Verwaltungsrechtswahrer des NS.-Rechtswahrerbundes*, 10 June 1942, Sammlung der Bundesagentur für Arbeit zur Entwicklung der Arbeitsverwaltung in Deutschland

(SEAD-BA), Historische Sammlung Maier, Folder 164; see also A. Zellhuber, 'Unsere Verwaltung treibt einer Katastrophe zu . . .'. Das Reichsministerium für die besetzten Ostgebiete und die deutsche Besatzungsherrschaft in der Sowjetunion 1941–1945, Munich: Vögel, 2006, 8, 105 f., 264 f.

55. No serious conflicts ensued, however. Zellhuber, 'Unsere Verwaltung', 294.

56. See, for example, Günther Rachner, Economic Staff East, to Friedrich Syrup, Reich Ministry of Labour, re. Reports Produced by the Group for Labour of the Economic Staff, 22 September 1941, IfZ, Reich Ministry of Labour, MA 219, fol. 321–46. See also Zellhuber, 'Unsere Verwaltung', 123.

57. See Baum, '"Für die Stadt Kiew"', 297.

58. See Günther Rachner, Economic Staff East, to Economic Inspectorates, re. Labour Deployment of Soviet Russian Labourers in the Reich, 4 December 1941, USHMM, ITS Digital Archive, 2.2.0.1/82385355-360.

59. See Ernst Meincke, Reich Ministry of Labour: Labour Deployment of Soviet Russians, here: Allocation of the Recruitment Districts in the New Eastern Territories to the Land Labour Offices in the Reich, 10 December 1941, Staatsarchiv (StA) Munich, Arbeitsämter, no. 762.

60. See also Economic Staff East to Friedrich Syrup, Reich Ministry of Labour, Biweekly Report, 1–15 December 1941, 15 January 1942, BArch, R 3901/20137.

61. See Günther Rachner, Economic Staff East, to Economic Inspectorates, re. Labour Deployment of Soviet Russian Labourers in the Reich, 4 December 1941, USHMM, ITS Digital Archive, 2.2.0.1/82385355-360.

62. My dissertation includes a detailed account of the activities of the Recruitment Commission Spreti in the recruitment of manpower in occupied Ukraine.

63. See Economic Staff East to Friedrich Syrup, Reich Ministry of Labour, Biweekly Report, 1–15 December 1941, 15 January 1942, BArch, R 3901/20137.

64. In 1942 the occupiers also introduced a monthly benefit payment for the family members of labourers deported to Germany, but the beneficiaries sometimes had difficulty obtaining it. See, for example, the Applications for Benefit and Tally Sheet, DAKhO, 3067-1-30.

65. On what follows, see Berkhoff, *Harvest of Despair*, 255 f.; Spoerer, *Zwangsarbeit*, 71.

66. On the ambitions of the Ukrainian nationalists, see, for example, Lower, *Nazi Empire-Building*, 38 f., 46; Berkhoff, *Harvest of Despair*, 51. A critical view of the Organization of Ukrainian Nationalists is provided by G. Rossoliński-Liebe, *Stepan Bandera. The Life and Afterlife of a Ukrainian Nationalist. Fascism, Genocide, and Cult*, Stuttgart: Ibidem, 2014.

67. On Kharkov, see Penter, *Kohle*, 188; Biweekly Report of the Economic Staff East, 15–31 December 1941, 26 January 1942, BArch, R 3901/20137.

68. See Berkhoff, *Harvest of Despair*, 256–58.

69. See Herbert, *Hitler's Foreign Workers*, 152.

70. On the apportionment procedure, see, for example, Baum, '"Für die Stadt Kiew"', 289 f.

71. See Dr Philipp Beisiegel to Neumann, Four-Year Plan Authority, re. Deployment of Soviet Russians, 23 March 1942, SEAD-BA, Historische Sammlung Maier, Folder 64.

72. See Alfred Meyer, Reich Ministry for the Occupied Eastern Territories, to Reich Commissioners, re. Recruitment of Civilian Labourers from the Occupied Eastern Territories, 6 March 1942, StA Munich, Arbeitsämter, no. 758.

73. On this and what follows, see the various letters in doc. 382-USSR, in *IMT*, vol. 39, 493–97. See also Eichholtz, *Kriegswirtschaft*, 205.

74. Letter from Sauckel re. 'Deployment of Russians', 31 March 1942, doc. 382-USSR, in *IMT*, vol. 39, 494–96.

75. Recruitment of Eastern Workers, Meeting at the Reich Ministry for the Occupied Eastern Territories on 14 October 1942, BArch, R 58/225, fol. 209 f.; see also 'Russische Zivilarbeiter für das Reichsgebiet', *Zentralblatt des Reichskommissars für die Ukraine*, no. 21, 26 September 1942.
76. On the figures, see Sauckel's Report to Hitler, re. Labour Deployment, 27 July 1942, doc. 1296-PS, in *IMT*, vol. 27, 115.
77. See Berkhoff, *Harvest of Despair*, 268–71.
78. Status Report by the General Commissioner for Volhynia and Podolia, 1 November 1942, BArch, R 6/687, fol. 65–68.
79. On the indigenous administration's entanglement in the occupiers' policies, see Eikel and Sivaieva, 'City Mayors'; Lower, *Nazi Empire-Building*, 105 f.
80. See, for example, Report by the Commander of the Sipo and SD, 15 September 1942, CDAVO, 3676-4-474, fol. 163–302. On the indigenous auxiliary police, see Berkhoff, *Harvest of Despair*, 42; Eikel, '"Weil die Menschen fehlen"', 430; Eikel, 'Arbeitsteilung', 139.
81. See Reich Ministry for the Occupied Eastern Territories to Reich Commissariat of Ukraine, re. Age-Group-Based Roundup for the Reich, 3 September 1943, BArch, R 6/73, fol. 102.
82. See, for example, Letter to BdS Ukraine re. Recruitment of Manpower from the East, 25 May 1942, National Archives and Records Administration (NARA), T 175, Roll 250; Commander of the Sipo/SD Kiev, Status Report May 1942, 2 June 1942, CDAVO, 3676-4-475, fol. 173–97; Groh to District Farmers' Representative Jarun, re. Transfer of Workers to the Reich, 16 March 1943, USHMM, RG-31.096M, Reel 6, Folder 6, 117.
83. On the activities of the partisans in the area under the control of the General Commissariat of Shitomir, see Lower, *Nazi Empire-Building*, 181–87.
84. On the discussion of 'recruitment bans', see, for example, the entries of 24 and 28 July 1942 in *Kriegstagebuch Wirtschaftsstab Ost*, vol. 1, 1 July–30 September 1942, BArch, RW 31/20; Economic Staff East, Note on the Top-Level Meeting on 23 July 1942, 26 July 1942, BArch, RW 31/21. See also Baum, '"Für die Stadt Kiew"', 297 f.
85. See 'Erlass des Führers zur Durchführung des Erlasses über einen Generalbevollmächtigten für den Arbeitseinsatz vom 30.9.1942', reprinted in M. Moll (ed.), *'Führer-Erlasse' 1939–1945. Edition sämtlicher überlieferter, nicht im Reichsgesetzblatt abgedruckter, von Hitler während des Zweiten Weltkrieges schriftlich erteilter Direktiven aus den Bereichen Staat, Partei, Wirtschaft, Besatzungspolitik und Militärverwaltung*, Stuttgart, 1997, 284 f. Also in *Handbuch für die Dienststellen*, 23.
86. On the appointment of the commissioners, see Max Timm to Walter Escher, List of the Commissioners of the GBA, 1942, ThHStAW, Der Reichsstatthalter in Thüringen, no. 491, fol. 27–29; Fritz Sauckel, GBA, to Otto Stapf, Economic Staff East, re. Appointment of Commissioner Meincke, 14 October 1942, BArch, RW 31/24.
87. On Peuckert's various offices and posts, see D. Marek, 'Bibliographien der Regierungsmitglieder (Minister und Staatsräte)', in B. Post and V. Wahl (eds), *Thüringen-Handbuch. Territorium, Verfassung, Parlament, Regierung und Verwaltung in Thüringen 1920 bis 1995*, Weimar: Böhlau, 1999, 552–648, here 617.
88. See Meeting between Rosenberg, Sauckel, Meyer and Peuckert, 21 January 1943, BArch, R 6/46, fol. 9–11; Fritz Sauckel, GBA, to Alfred Rosenberg, Reich Ministry for the Occupied Eastern Territories, re. Appointment of a Commissioner for the Occupied Eastern Territories, 27 January 1944, BArch, R 6/291, fol. 51, 55 f. See also C. Gerlach, *Kalkulierte Morde. Die deutsche Wirtschafts- und Vernichtungspolitik in Weissrussland 1941–1944*, Hamburg: Hamburger Edition, 1999, 464.
89. See Instructions to the Commissioners of the GBA in the Occupied Territories and Implementing Regulations on Directive no. 10 of the GBA re. Deployment of Workers

from the Occupied Territories, 29 October 1942, BArch, R 3901/20289, fol. 108–14. See also Fritz Sauckel, GBA, re. Commissioners of the GBA, 25 October 1942, ThHStAW, Der Reichsstatthalter in Thüringen, no. 491, fol. 20 f.

90. See Peuckert's Activity Report, 13 March 1943, BArch, R 3901/20274, fol. 52 f. This campaign occurred in the context of the operations carried out from 1943 by SS and police forces as well as Wehrmacht units in collaboration with the labour deployment units, which increasingly fused the struggle against the partisans with the recruitment of forced labourers for Germany; see, for example, Pohl, *Herrschaft*, 291–97, 316.

Bibliography

Baum, H. '"Für die Stadt Kiew wird eine 'Fangaktion' vorbereitet . . .". Akteure und Praxis der Zwangsarbeiterrekrutierungen in der Ukraine während des Zweiten Weltkriegs', in K. Linne and F. Dierl (eds), *Arbeitskräfte als Kriegsbeute. Der Fall Ost- und Südosteuropa 1939–1945* (Berlin: Metropol, 2011), 270–302.

Berkhoff, K.C. *Harvest of Despair. Life and Death in Ukraine under Nazi Rule*. Cambridge, MA: Belknap Press of Harvard University Press, 2004.

Dubyk, M. 'Arbeitseinsatz und Lebensbedingungen im Reichskommissariat Ukraine und im ukrainischen Gebiet unter Militärverwaltung (1941–1944)', in D. Pohl and T. Sebta (eds), *Zwangsarbeit in Hitlers Europa: Besatzung, Arbeit, Folgen* (Berlin: Metropol, 2013), 195–213.

Eichholtz, D. *Geschichte der deutschen Kriegswirtschaft 1939–1945*, 5 vols. Munich: Saur, 2003.

Eichholtz, D. 'Die Vorgeschichte des "Generalbevollmächtigten für den Arbeitseinsatz"'. *Jahrbuch für Geschichte* 9 (1973), 339–83.

Eikel, M. 'Arbeitseinsatz in der besetzten Sowjetunion 1941–1944. Das Reichskommissariat Ukraine als Fallbeispiel', in B. Quinkert and J. Morré (eds), *Deutsche Besatzung in der Sowjetunion 1941–1944. Vernichtungskrieg – Reaktionen – Erinnerung* (Paderborn: Schöningh, 2014), 175–95.

Eikel, M. 'Arbeitsteilung und Verbrechen. Die ukrainische Lokalverwaltung unter deutscher Besatzung 1941–1944', in T.C. Richter (ed.), *Krieg und Verbrechen. Situation und Intention. Fallbeispiele* (Munich: Meidenbauer, 2006), 135–46.

Eikel, M. '"Weil die Menschen fehlen". Die deutschen Zwangsarbeiterrekrutierungen und -deportationen in den besetzten Gebieten der Ukraine 1941–1944'. *Zeitschrift für Geschichtswissenschaft* 53(5) (2005), 405–33.

Eikel, M., and V. Sivaieva. 'City Mayors, Raion Chiefs and Village Elders in Ukraine 1941–44: How Local Administrators Cooperated with the German Occupation Authorities'. *Contemporary European History* 23(3) (2014), 405–28.

Fleischhauer, M. *Der NS-Gau Thüringen 1939–1945. Eine Struktur- und Funktionsgeschichte*. Cologne: Böhlau, 2010.

Gerlach, C. *Kalkulierte Morde. Die deutsche Wirtschafts- und Vernichtungspolitik in Weissrussland 1941–1944*. Hamburg: Hamburger Edition, 1999.

Greve, S. *Das 'System Sauckel'. Der Generalbevollmächtigte für den Arbeitseinsatz und die Arbeitskräftepolitik in der besetzten Ukraine 1942–1945*. Wallstein: Göttingen, 2019.

Hachtmann, R. 'Sauckel, Fritz', in H.G. Hockerts (ed.), *Neue Deutsche Biographie*, vol. 22: Rohmer–Schinkel (Berlin: Duncker & Humblot, 2005), 448–49.

Hachtmann, R., and W. Süss (eds). *Hitlers Kommissare: Sondergewalten in der nationalsozialistischen Diktatur*. Göttingen: Wallstein, 2006.

Handbuch für die Dienststellen des Generalbevollmächtigten für den Arbeitseinsatz und die interessierten Reichsstellen im Grossdeutschen Reich und in den besetzten Gebieten, vol. 1:

Vollmachten, Verlautbarungen, Verordnungen, Organisation des GBA, ed. F. Didier. Berlin: Rotadruck W. Meyer KG, 1944.

Herbert, U. *Geschichte Deutschlands im 20. Jahrhundert*. Munich: Beck, 2014.

Herbert, U. *Hitler's Foreign Workers. Enforced Foreign Labor in Germany under the Third Reich*, trans. W. Templer, new ed. Cambridge: Cambridge University Press, 1997.

Homze, E.L. *Foreign Labor in Nazi Germany*. Princeton, NJ: Princeton University Press, 1967.

Hüttenberger, P. *Die Gauleiter. Studie zum Wandel des Machtgefüges in der NSDAP*. Stuttgart: Deutsche Verlags-Anstalt, 1969.

Lehnstaedt, S., and K. Lehnstaedt. 'Fritz Sauckels Nürnberger Aufzeichnungen. Erinnerungen aus seiner Haft während des Kriegsverbrecherprozesses'. *Vierteljahrshefte für Zeitgeschichte* 57(1) (2009), 117–50.

Lower, W. *Nazi Empire-Building and the Holocaust in Ukraine*. Chapel Hill, NC: University of North Carolina Press, 2005.

Marek, D. 'Bibliographien der Regierungsmitglieder (Minister und Staatsräte)', in B. Post and V. Wahl (eds), *Thüringen-Handbuch. Territorium, Verfassung, Parlament, Regierung und Verwaltung in Thüringen 1920 bis 1995* (Weimar: Böhlau, 1999), 552–648.

Moll, M. (ed.), *'Führer-Erlasse' 1939–1945. Edition sämtlicher überlieferter, nicht im Reichsgesetzblatt abgedruckter, von Hitler während des Zweiten Weltkrieges schriftlich erteilter Direktiven aus den Bereichen Staat, Partei, Wirtschaft, Besatzungspolitik und Militärverwaltung*. Stuttgart, 1997.

Müller, R.-D. (ed.). *Die deutsche Wirtschaftspolitik in den besetzten sowjetischen Gebieten 1941–1943. Der Abschlussbericht des Wirtschaftsstabes Ost und Aufzeichnungen eines Angehörigen des Wirtschaftskommandos Kiew*. Boppard am Rhein: Boldt, 1991.

Naasner, W. *Neue Machtzentren in der deutschen Kriegswirtschaft, 1942–1945*. Boppard am Rhein: Boldt, 1994.

Nolzen, A. 'Die Gaue als Verwaltungseinheiten der NSDAP. Entwicklungen und Tendenzen in der NS-Zeit', in J. John, H. Möller and T. Schaarschmidt (eds), *Die NS-Gaue. Regionale Mittelinstanzen im zentralistischen 'Führerstaat'* (Munich: Oldenbourg, 2007), 199–217.

Penter, T. 'Arbeiten für den Feind in der Heimat. Der Arbeitseinsatz in der besetzten Ukraine 1941–1944'. *Jahrbuch für Wirtschaftsgeschichte* 1 (2004), 65–94.

Penter, T. *Kohle für Stalin und Hitler. Arbeiten und Leben im Donbass 1929–1953*. Essen: Klartext, 2010.

Pohl, D. *Die Herrschaft der Wehrmacht. Deutsche Militärbesatzung und einheimische Bevölkerung in der Sowjetunion 1941–1944*. Munich: Oldenbourg, 2008.

Priemel, K.C. 'Occupying Ukraine. Great Expectations, Failed Opportunities, and the Spoils of War, 1941–1943'. *Central European History* 48(1) (2015), 31–52.

Der Prozess gegen die Hauptkriegsverbrecher vor dem Internationalen Militärgerichtshof. Nürnberg, 14. November 1945–1. Oktober 1946, 42 vols. Nuremberg: Internationaler Militärgerichtshof Nürnberg, 1947–1949.

Rassloff, S. *Fritz Sauckel. Hitlers 'Muster-Gauleiter' und 'Sklavenhalter'*. Erfurt: Landeszentrale für politische Bildung Thüringen, 2008.

Reichardt, S., and W. Seibel. 'Radikalität und Stabilität: Herrschen und Verwalten im Nationalsozialismus', in S. Reichardt and W. Seibel (eds), *Der prekäre Staat. Herrschen und Verwalten im Nationalsozialismus* (Frankfurt am Main: Campus, 2011), 7–27.

Rossoliński-Liebe, G. *Stepan Bandera. The Life and Afterlife of a Ukrainian Nationalist. Fascism, Genocide, and Cult*. Stuttgart: Ibidem, 2014.

Spoerer, M. *Zwangsarbeit unter dem Hakenkreuz. Ausländische Zivilarbeiter, Kriegsgefangene und Häftlinge im Deutschen Reich und im besetzten Europa 1939–1945*. Stuttgart: Deutsche Verlags-Anstalt, 2001.

Tooze, J.A. *The Wages of Destruction. The Making and Breaking of the Nazi Economy*. New York: Penguin, 2006.

Weissbecker, M. 'Fritz Sauckel. "Wir werden die letzten Schlacken unserer Humanitätsduselei ablegen...''', in K. Pätzold and M. Weissbecker (eds), *Stufen zum Galgen. Lebenswege vor den Nürnberger Urteilen* (Leipzig: Militzke, 1999), 297–331.

Zellhuber, A. *'Unsere Verwaltung treibt einer Katastrophe zu...'. Das Reichsministerium für die besetzten Ostgebiete und die deutsche Besatzungsherrschaft in der Sowjetunion 1941–1945.* Munich: Vögel, 2006.

Chapter 11

HOLOCAUST AND LABOUR ADMINISTRATION
Jewish Labour Deployment in the Ghettos of the Occupied Eastern Territories

Michael Wildt

This chapter shows that the German labour administration was involved in the persecution and murder of the European Jewry. Labour administration staff did not participate in the shootings of Jews in front of their own mass graves, but they made a crucial contribution to deciding which individuals were killed and which were not. 'Fitness for work' was the key criterion that determined whether men and women in the ghettos continued to perform forced labour or were murdered as 'deadweight unfit for work'. Until 1943, it was the labour administration that made decisions on labour deployment in the occupied territories, including that of Jewish workers in the ghettos, though always under the conditions particular to a given occupation administration. In this chapter, then, I present three examples from the occupied territories in eastern Europe: the Litzmannstadt (as Łódź was called under German occupation) Ghetto in the Warthegau of annexed Western Poland, which was to be 'Germanized' by settlers and become part of the German Reich; the so-called General Government, in other words the rump Polish state, which had its own German occupation regime; and the Kaunas Ghetto, as an example of the occupied Soviet territories.

In all three territories, it was the German labour offices, which were established along with the occupation administration, that made decisions on the forced labour deployment of Jews, and they played a decisive role in selecting individuals as 'fit for work' or 'unfit for work'. What varied, however, was the role of the Reich Ministry of Labour. In annexed Western Poland, which was incorporated into the German Reich, the ministry retained authority over the labour offices, whereas in the General Government and in the occupied Soviet territories the labour administrations were part of the German occupation authorities. There, too, the labour offices were established and led by German officials posted from the Reich. In the occupied territories, then, officials whose knowledge and experience had been gleaned within the administrative context of the German Reich were responsible for the organization of the labour administration in a material, though not in a direct administrative sense.

The examples discussed in this chapter reveal that, in terms of how these officials conducted themselves, a number of options were open to them on the ground. Their facilitation of the murderous regime of selection and their assiduous efforts to distinguish the 'unfit for work' from the 'fit for work' were by no means inevitable. While many officials carried out such selection with willingness and dedication, and thus condemned thousands of people to death, others sought to put as many Jews as possible on labour deployment in an attempt to save their lives. It was always specific individuals in specific places who not only carried out orders, adhered to administrative regulations and were required to obey, but who made decisions on who lived or died.

Reichsgau Wartheland

When the German Wehrmacht attacked Poland on 1 September 1939, it made a reality of the war for 'living space' (*Lebensraum*), which Adolf Hitler had been striving to obtain since the Nazis took power. As Hitler had made unmistakably clear to his inner circle of military and political leaders in November 1937, the objective of German policy was to 'secure and preserve the masses [and facilitate their] proliferation'. It was vital to 'gain a larger living space', which must be found not in distant colonies but in Europe itself. History, Hitler averred, had shown that every instance of the 'expansion of space' could only take place through the 'breaking of resistance and at great risk'. 'The German question can only be resolved by force.'[1]

The invasion of Poland, which had become possible following the pact with the Soviet Union of 23 August 1939, was planned from the outset as a 'battle of folkdom (*Volkstum*)'. On 20 September, Hitler set out to his supreme army commanders his plans for 'large-scale resettlement', which encompassed both the displacement of Poles and Jews from the western Polish territories and the ghettoization of Jews. The civil administration, SS and police would be responsible for this 'reallocation of land' (*Flurberei-*

nigung) to *völkisch* ends.² The next day, Reinhard Heydrich held an important meeting in Berlin with the heads of the Secret State Police Office and the leaders of the SS taskforces in Poland. He informed them that the plan for occupied Poland was to turn the western provinces into German Gaus and to establish a 'Gau with a foreign-language population, with Cracow as its capital', the later so-called General Government. Heinrich Himmler was to be appointed Settlement Commissioner for the East (*Siedlungskommissar für den Osten*). 'The deportation of Jews to the foreign-language Gau', Heydrich went on, had been 'approved by the Führer'. The Polish intelligentsia must be 'disposed of', while the 'primitive Poles are to be integrated into the labour process as itinerant labourers and will gradually be transferred from the German Gaus to the foreign-language Gau'.³ The Jews in the western Polish territories were to be penned up in ghettos in order to 'improve our capacity to control them and evacuate them later on'. Heydrich summed up his orders in four key points: '1. Jews into the cities as quickly as possible, 2. Jews out of the Reich to Poland, 3. The remaining 30,000 Gypsies to Poland as well, 4. Systematic dispatch of the Jews from the German territories by goods trains'.⁴ What is striking about this directive is that the measures to be taken against the Polish Jews were linked with the planned deportation of German Jews, which did not commence until the autumn of 1941, and with the deportation of Roma and Sinti from Germany to Poland, which began in the spring of 1940. At this early stage, then, the persecution of the Jews in Poland was already being conceived within a larger framework. The conquest of 'living space' in the East was to go hand in hand with the 'cleansing' of the Jewish population of the 'Old Reich'.

From the beginning of the invasion, Polish Jews were hounded, mistreated, physically attacked and harassed. Jewish businesses and homes were plundered, synagogues and houses of prayer were burnt to the ground, and Jews were arrested or forced to perform labour of all kinds. Many Jews hardly dared leave their homes, fearing they might be scooped off the street as the authorities carried out raids for manpower.⁵ Businesses, warehouses, bank deposits and other assets were confiscated, stripping Jews of the economic basis for survival.⁶

Through the formation of ghettos, the German occupation administrations organized their persecutory policies more systematically, but no less brutally. Initially, the concentration of the Jewish population in a small number of urban ghettos was conceived as a transitional measure. The plan was to subsequently deport them to the General Government, thus rendering the annexed western Polish territories 'clear of Jews' (*judenrein*). The newly vacated homes were mostly made available to ethnic German newcomers from the Baltic region. Further, through 'resettlement', the

German occupiers sought to facilitate the theft of all Jewish assets, including jewellery and money, before their owners were deported. Another significant justification for isolating the Jewish population was the antisemitic fantasy that 'dirty Jews' were carriers of illnesses and epidemics. Of course, because Jews were penned up in cramped quarters under catastrophically unhygienic conditions and were vastly undersupplied with foodstuffs, as a result of ghettoization the risk of typhus, Fleckfieber (typhus exanthimaticus) and other illnesses did in fact increase.[7] In the largest ghetto in the newly established Reich Gau of Wartheland, in Litzmannstadt, just under 164,000 people were forced to live within an area of around 3 km².[8]

The authorities' plan was to use stolen Jewish assets to maintain the ghettos until the deportations began. Yet it proved difficult to implement this programme of displacement. In particular, the General Government's occupation administration baulked at absorbing hundreds of thousands of people, whom the German officials viewed as an immense burden. Governor General Hans Frank finally managed to have the deportations stopped in March 1940.[9] This transformed the ghettos in the annexed western Polish territories from short-term improvisations into long-term settlements. As a result, those within the occupation administration calling for Jews in the ghettos to be put to work in order to finance their new 'home' began to win converts. In the occupied Polish territories, Jewish forced labour now became part of the practice of persecution, emulating the approach taken in the German Reich, Austria and occupied Czechoslovakia since 1938.[10] The president of the Reich Institution for Job Placement and Unemployment Insurance issued the crucial edict on the forced labour of Jews within the German Reich on 20 December 1938. Among other things, it stated:

> The state has no interest in leaving fit-for-work unemployed Jews' manpower unused, and, as the case may be, supporting them out of the public purse despite the absence of any contribution in return. The goal must be to step up the employment of all jobless and fit-for-work Jews and, as far as possible, to combine this with the freeing up of German workers for urgent tasks of importance to government policy. Deployment will take place in firms and operating divisions, on building sites, in land improvement schemes, etc., separate from the followers [Gefolgschaft].[11]

The forced labour deployment of Jews in occupied Poland, then, was no novelty for the German occupation authorities.

Even the Jewish autonomous administrations in the ghettos expedited labour deployment, as it held out the prospect of saving people from deportation and could help provision Jews in the ghettos with vital foodstuffs. In April 1940, Chaim Rumkowski, president of the Jewish Council in the Litzmannstadt Ghetto, made the concrete proposal to the German city commissioner to establish production facilities in the ghetto and employ the available skilled Jewish workers.[12] The head of the German ghetto administration, 38-year-old coffee trader Hans Biebow from Bremen,[13] backed this plan. In a letter to the police president of Litzmannstadt of August 1940, he underlined

> that I have two main objectives, first, to extract value from the ghetto in order to ensure that the Jews are fed for as long as possible without the need for recourse to Reich funds and, second, I am doing my utmost to harness manpower, most of which lies fallow, to the maximum extent possible.[14]

In the administration of the Reich Governor (*Reichsstatthalter*) for the Warthegau, Arthur Greiser, Biebow worked closely with the head of Department V a ('Labour'), Ernst Kendzia. The latter had joined the Nazi Party in 1931 and the SS in 1933, had attained the senior rank of SS-Obersturmbannführer, and had been head of the Labour Office in Danzig. In Litzmannstadt, he now functioned as both Reich labour trustee and as head of the Land Labour Office. Reich Labour Minister Franz Seldte claimed authority over the labour administration, but was unable to impose his will on the powerful Greiser. Kendzia, meanwhile, emphasized to the Reich Ministry of Labour that, as a result of his good relations with Greiser, he had managed to maintain the independence of Department V a to a certain degree, despite the fact that its incorporation into the Reich governor's authority impeded its work.[15]

As the war dragged on, and as Polish labourers were deported to Germany, the labour deployment of Jews became more important in the eyes of the German occupation authorities, though in fact they were keen to be rid of them as quickly as possible. In the words of the district vice president of Litzmannstadt, Walter Moser, the ghetto was

> a highly undesirable institution, yet a necessary evil. The Jews, the vast majority of whom live useless lives at the expense of the German people, must be fed; it goes without saying that they cannot be approached as average consumers within the framework of food production and distribution.[16]

By the summer of 1940, the Wehrmacht had already given the ghetto administration its first assignments, and these were soon expanded into a larger programme mainly involving textile production, in other words the making of uniforms. In 1941, almost all ghetto firms worked for the Wehrmacht but also for private companies such as the Josef Neckermann fashion house and department store in Berlin. It was tremendously difficult to get hold of raw materials, yet the Jewish Council managed to secure jobs and thus the possibility of survival for a growing number of people.

In March 1941 there were around twenty-two thousand individuals employed in the ghetto, a figure that had increased to thirty-five thousand by September 1941 and to seventy-five thousand by August 1942.[17]

But skilled Jewish workers were also deployed beyond Litzmannstadt. For example, approximately 1,400 Jewish tailors from the ghetto worked in Pabianice, and around 5,600 in Brzeziny. Michael Alberti underlines that in these smaller cities, the scale of Jewish forced labour deployment is comparable with the situation in the Litzmannstadt Ghetto.[18] In east Upper Silesia, the Breslau police president Albrecht Schmelt established a system of camps for Jewish forced labourers, who were deployed to build the motorway between Breslau and Cracow and in armaments firms. In the autumn of 1941, around seventeen thousand Jewish men and women worked within this system, known as the 'Schmelt Organization'.[19]

Furthermore, as Kendzia announced at a meeting in Litzmannstadt on 12 November 1940, unskilled Jewish workers were to be deployed in infrastructure projects in the Warthegau and in the area bordering the 'Old Reich', such as the planned Reich motorway from Frankfurt an der Oder to Posen.[20] Reich Governor Greiser even offered the Reich Ministry of Labour 42,187 Jewish males and 30,936 females for labour deployment in the 'Old Reich'. The ministry then contacted the Land labour offices in Germany instructing them to find jobs for Jewish workers, setting great store by the deployment of Jewish work gangs in isolation from other workers and accommodated in separate camps.[21] This deployment, however, was scuppered by a veto from Hitler, who decided that none of the Jews from the General Government and the Warthegau would be deployed in the Reich.[22]

Kendzia thus focused his efforts on forced labour deployment in the Warthegau and instructed the labour offices to register all Jews capable of working, divided by gender.[23] The labour offices coordinated the deployment of Jewish forced labourers among themselves, moving people from one site to another depending on demand. The city and district administrations had to submit applications for labour deployment to the labour offices.[24] The state administration at the municipal or regional level, or the German Labour Front, were then responsible for the forced labour camps. Jewish forced labourers were deployed in the broadest range of infrastructural projects, in land improvement and road building, agriculture and factories. Alberti estimates that between 1939 and 1944, thirty to forty thousand Jews were transported to at least 232 forced labour camps, of which 187 were in the Warthegau, and 45 on the territory of the 'Old Reich'. In the Gau capital of Posen alone, officially declared 'free of Jews' since 1939, there were around fifteen thousand Jewish forced labourers in 1941.[25]

As the supply situation in the forced labour camps was extraordinarily bad and the severe lack of hygiene caused illnesses, mortality in the camps was extremely high, as a result of which we lack reliable figures. The forced labourers had to work ten or more hours a day, often seven days a week, with one day off a month; the journey to their places of work itself typically required several hours on foot. The forced labourers had little means to shield themselves from rain, snow and cold. The supply of foodstuffs was wholly inadequate. For example, the women in the 'Fort Radziwill' women's labour camp in Posen received just eight hundred calories' worth of food a day, prompting them to scour the roadside for herbs, roots and rotting vegetable waste on the way to and from work. Severe cases of diarrhoea resulted. The camp heads, mostly SS men, older ethnic Germans but also Poles, were not subject to supervision, and some of them presided over a sadistic regime of violence. Severe punishments were an everyday occurrence. Anyone attempting to flee was publicly hanged. The Gestapo even set up a central execution facility in Posen's sports stadium to serve the Jewish forced labour camps in the city.[26] Labour office staff also participated in abuses. For example, the head of the Labour Office in Bełchatów, in the district of Łask, had the wives and daughters of Jews who had fled labour deployment detained in an attempt to force them to turn themselves in. When the men did not show up, the head of the Labour Office had most of the women stripped naked and flogged, punishment he himself helped mete out.[27]

The situation was much the same in the large ghetto in Litzmannstadt. Due to malnourishment, lack of medical care, exhaustion, illnesses such as dysentery and Fleckfieber, as well as the guards' brutal violence, by the end of 1941 more than ten thousand individuals had already died in the ghetto.[28] Ghetto administrator Biebow certainly tried to increase the supply of food in order to achieve his objective of making the ghetto self-financing and productive. But the other German occupation authorities had little interest in this and were more worried about the possibility of illnesses spreading from the ghetto to the rest of the city. Furthermore, transportation was constantly impeded by the war. Promised deliveries often failed to materialize. Hunger, meanwhile, was a dreadful torment for the ghetto inhabitants. Even for those who had work, the minimal wages were not even enough to pay for food rations, let alone to buy foodstuffs on the black market.[29]

Hence, from the perspective of Nazi antisemites, it was a small step to contemplate the decimation of these 'surplus' mouths to feed as a means of enhancing the supply of food to those 'fit for work'.[30] Summing up a number of meetings on the 'resolution of the Jewish question' within the Reich Governor's authority, on 16 July 1941 Rolf-Heinz Höppner, in charge of the SD Head Office Posen, wrote to Eichmann that in the coming winter there was a risk that 'it will not be possible to feed all the Jews. Serious consideration should thus be given to the question of whether it is not the most humane solution to dispose of the Jews, in as much as they are not fit for work, through some sort of fast-acting means'.[31] Officials within the German occupation administration increasingly distinguished between Jews who were 'fit' and 'unfit' for work, with key figures pushing for a rapid 'resolution of the Jewish question'.[32] Kendzia too declared that with the help of the Gestapo, the ghetto administration could deport Jews permanently unable to work 'from the ghetto in one way or another'.[33]

As a result of Hitler's decision, in mid September 1941, to deport the German, Austrian and Czech Jews before the end of the war against the Soviet Union, the situation in Litzmannstadt grew worse. On 18 September, Himmler informed Arthur Greiser that the 'Führer wishes' the 'Old Reich and the Protectorate to be emptied and freed of Jews from west to east as soon as possible'. If possible before the end of 1941, the Jews of the 'Old Reich' and the Protectorate were to be temporarily deported to the Litzmannstadt Ghetto, before 'sending them further east' in the spring of 1942.[34] Greiser put Government Director Dr Herbert Mehlhorn in charge of all issues 'connected with the accommodation and labour deployment of Jews and gypsies in the Reichsgau Wartheland', making Ernst Kendzia his deputy.[35]

A total of just under twenty thousand Jews and a further five thousand Sinti and Roma from Burgenland and Styria were deported to Litzmannstadt. By early December 1941, the ghetto was home to more than 163,000 people.[36] Plans to carry out the mass murder of ghetto inhabitants 'unfit for work' were now firmed up. Greiser agreed with Himmler that around 100,000 Jews in the Warthegau would be killed, the total number of Jews there having been estimated at 247,500, of which just over 105,000 were classified as 'fit for work'.[37] At a meeting at the Reich Ministry of Labour in late November 1941, Kendzia declared that by the end of March 1942, 'apart from those fit for work, all of the Jews [would be] deported', a typical euphemism for murder in Nazi correspondence at the time.[38]

As a killing site, an uninhabited manor house had been identified in the small town of Kulmhof (Chełmno), about 55 km from Litzmannstadt, which lay on a railway line. There the 'Lange Special Commando' (Sonderkommando Lange) installed gas vans and began to murder the first Jews from the vicinity of Kulmhof in early December 1941.[39] On 16 January 1942, the first trains departed from Litzmannstadt. By the end of May, around ninety-seven thousand people had been killed in these vans.[40]

Initially, the 'Resettlement Commission' (Aussiedlungskommission), which Rumkowski had tasked with selecting deportees, had focused on criminals, critics of the Jewish Council's measures, and the families of those deployed as forced labourers outside the ghetto. Later, those receiving welfare benefits were included, precisely those 'unproductive elements' the German occupation administration was so keen to be rid of.[41] In late August 1942, the Reich Security Main Office decreed that all children below the age of ten, all of those above the age of sixty-five, all sick individuals and those without work were to be deported to the Kulmhof death camp.[42] Close to sixteen thousand individuals were deported, including 5,860 children. This left just under ninety thousand people of 'working' age living in the Litzmannstadt Ghetto. It resembled nothing more than a vast forced labour factory.[43]

General Government

From 26 October 1939, Jews were subject to forced labour in the General Government, as central Poland had been renamed, an area about which Goebbels noted in his diary that everyone wished to dump 'their refuse' there: 'Jews, the sick, idlers, etc',[44] but at the same time, at Hitler's behest, it was to be a 'vast reservoir of manpower'. All male Jews between the ages of fourteen and sixty were subject to compulsory labour service.[45] As in the annexed western Polish territories, in the General Government too the Jewish population had been corralled into ghettos, the largest being in Warsaw and Cracow. In order to evade arbitrary arrests and raids and to gain a chance of acquiring food through paid labour, many ghetto residents were eager to work. In a number of ghettos, the Jewish councils formed so-called work battalions, for which many individuals voluntarily signed up, offering these to the German authorities for labour deployment.[46] The Jewish workers' meagre wages had to be provided by the Jewish councils themselves, but their financial resources were exhausted over the course of 1940.[47]

Yet the demand for manpower within the General Government grew exponentially over time. From autumn 1939, the Germans moved Polish workers to the Reich on a massive scale for labour deployment – initially on a voluntary basis but increasingly on a coercive one. Skilled Jewish workers had to do the jobs they had left behind.[48] To organize this complex shift, in early July 1940, as decreed by General Governor Hans Frank, the German labour administration in the General Government was endowed with sole responsibility for the deployment of Jewish forced labourers, the police and SS having initially been in charge of this.[49]

Officials from the Reich Ministry of Labour had also made the trip to Poland as part of General Governor Frank's administrative staff. For a brief period, former State Secretary Johannes Krohn led the 'Main Section for Labour' (Hauptabteilung Arbeit) in the General Government in Cracow, succeeded in November 1939 by Dr Max Frauendorfer.[50] Each of the four districts of Cracow, Lublin, Radom and Warsaw were divided into five labour office districts. The district subdivisions (*Kreishauptmannschaften* and *Stadthauptmannschaften*), as the lowest German administrative levels in occupied Poland, each received a labour office, while larger cities such as Warsaw also saw the establishment of branch offices. In late 1940, the administrative apparatus dealing with labour deployment had just under 2,800 members of staff, including 478 Reich Germans and 325 ethnic Germans. As late as 1944, more than 1,100 Reich and ethnic German employees still worked in the labour offices, along with more than twice as many Polish staff members, though they were restricted to menial tasks.[51]

The labour offices saw their main task as meeting the German occupation economy's need for manpower as well as they could and thus exploiting both Polish and Jewish labourers to the maximum extent possible. However, they were interested in maintaining rather than annihilating these workers and would, therefore, not hesitate to intervene if Jewish workers were suffering a lack of provisions. 'The purpose of the labour deployment of Jews', as stated in a circular sent by the General Government's Labour Department to all labour offices on 5 July 1940, was 'to help remedy the lack of manpower in the General Government'.[52] In line with this, on the basis of the decree of 26 October 1939, Jews could be deployed in both remunerated positions and to perform forced labour without compensation – a crucial distinction when it came to the later debate on ghetto pensions.[53] Jews' employment relationships, then, could take various forms, from violent deportations to labour camps through work in ghetto workshops to paid employment in firms, some of which even paid social insurance contributions or distributed food as a benefit in kind.

Firms and governmental authorities registered their manpower requirements with the labour offices, which instructed the various Jewish councils to make available the desired quantity of workers. To this end, the labour offices established branches in certain ghettos, also called 'Jewish deployment offices' (*Judeneinsatzstellen*). In a postwar interview, German official Heinz Weber stated:

> Around August or September 1941, I arrived at the Lemberg Labour Office from the Reichhof Labour Office, to which I had been posted by the Karlsruhe Labour Office. I was assigned the task of placing Jews in employment by Government Director Dr Nitsche, the head of the Lemberg Labour Office. Until that point, Jewish labour deployment had been the responsibility of the Jewish Council of the City of Lemberg. As instructed, I believe it was in a former school at 1 Missionarsplatz, I set up a Jewish job placement office. This office

was established precisely in line with the German model, that is, the placement officers were Jewish men or women who had been recommended by the Jewish Council. The work was informed by German principles of job placement. I was the head of this Lemberg branch office as the only Reich German'.[54]

Through the work of these branch offices, the number of Jewish workers placed in employment grew rapidly.

Jews were not only deployed at nearby sites, but were also taken to other districts where they had to live in forced labour camps.[55] These camps were by no means always fenced-in barracks. Jewish workers were also accommodated in former synagogues, schools or factory buildings. Guarding practices, which were the responsibility of the employers, also took a variety of forms. Only in a minority of cases did SS units guard the labour camps.[56] Initially, firms and public authorities received Jewish workers free of charge and had only to provide them with provisions and, if necessary, accommodation. Both provisioning and the conditions in the camps, then, depended on the particular employers involved, who exercised this responsibility in quite different ways. While reports attest that some German firms provided their Jewish workers with adequate meals, in the forced labour camps for land improvement in the district of Lublin, for example, under the notorious SS and police chief Odilo Globocnik, conditions were disastrous. Around ten thousand individuals, not just from the district of Lublin but also from those of Radom and Warsaw, were accommodated there in thirty-four camps. The conditions were so miserable and the mortality rates so high that the labour offices from the other districts ceased to send Jewish workers to Lublin in the autumn of 1941. This had much to do with the dramatic growth in demand for Jewish workers in their own districts since the beginning of the war against the Soviet Union, due to the increased number of Polish workers being dispatched to Germany.[57]

In Cracow, the seat of the General Government's occupation administration, a Jewish Council headed by the teacher Marek Bieberstein had already been established on German orders just a few days after the invasion in early September 1939.[58] As in the other Polish cities, Jews there had to surrender money and valuables. From 1 December 1939, meanwhile, Jews in the General Government had to wear a white armband bearing a blue Star of David. Bieberstein too sought to organize a regulated form of labour deployment in order to bring the arbitrary raids to an end. In November 1939, he established a Jewish Labour Office, recorded men and women fit for work in a card index and facilitated the employment of Jewish workers.[59]

Governor General Hans Frank, however, wanted to rapidly reduce the number of Jews in 'his' seat of government. Of the around sixty-five thousand Jews in Cracow, a maximum of ten thousand urgently needed 'working Jews' (*Arbeitsjuden*) were to remain. On 18 May 1940, German City Captain (*Stadthauptmann*) Carl Schmid ordered the resettlement of Cracow's Jews in other cities. This expulsion, however, proceeded at a sluggish pace, and by the end of November 1940, around sixty thousand Jews still lived in Cracow. The governor of the District of Cracow, Otto Wächter, responded by putting a new person in charge of the 'Resettlement Campaign' (*Aussiedlungsaktion*). In December, around twenty thousand Jews then had to leave Cracow. In early March 1941, the German occupation administration ordered the establishment of a 'Jewish residential district' for the remaining Jews in order to round them up and control them, while also being in a better position to systematically exploit them as forced labourers.[60]

The Cracow Ghetto also had a branch office of the German Labour Office ('Labour Office Department for Jewish Deployment'). After demanding a certain number of Jewish workers from the Jewish Council's Labour Office Department, it distributed them to various workplaces. The Council's Labour Department maintained a card index of those 'fit-for-work' ghetto residents who had not yet been issued with an employment certificate. The index included details of professional qualifications, enabling individuals to be allocated in a targeted way. To this end, they had to report to the Jewish Labour Office in the morning with their identity cards.[61] In addition to the workshops established in the ghetto, Jews were also deployed outside it in firms located in Cracow, including Oskar Schindler's enamel factory.[62]

For many of Cracow's Jews, it was very difficult to find stable employment, as their professional skills were scarcely in demand. The factories and workshops were not looking for teachers, lawyers, writers or journalists. What they wanted were artisans and individuals capable of performing heavy physical labour. Yet people desperately needed a job if they were to provide themselves with the most basic of necessities. The result, as ghetto survivor Anna Lermer put it in her postwar account, was a 'frantic race to the Labour Office'.[63]

By July 1940, the labour administration had already begun to demand that firms pay their Jewish workers wages, which were around 20 per cent lower than those of Polish workers.[64] The background to this step was certainly not altruism or concern for Jewish workers, but rather the sober insight that the Jewish autonomous administration in the ghettos was not in a position to feed the ghetto residents itself, while the allocation of foodstuffs was to occur only in exchange for payment. The Jewish workers, therefore, were to receive a wage in order to pay for their own provisions and those of their families. According to Frauendorfer, the payment of wages was necessary 'in order to maintain Jews' fitness for work, ensure families' subsistence and avoid illnesses and epidemics'.[65] Social insurance contributions were even deducted from Jewish workers' wages, but in no way did they benefit from this, as the social security benefits offices in the General Government simply held onto these contributions to cover benefits claims from non-Jewish employees.[66]

Most firms, however, if they complied with the ordinance in the first place, avoided paying their Jewish workers in cash and instead offset their wages against in-house meals or other food provisions. But bread and other foodstuffs were in fact greatly valued by the Jews concerned. In the Warsaw ghetto in March 1942, more than 420,000 people received just 2 kg of bread per person per month. Meanwhile, the twenty-five thousand workers in the armaments firms and other important businesses, as well as employees of the Jewish Council, got twice as much, and the two thousand members of the Jewish security service no less than 10 kg per person.[67] Furthermore, public agencies and firms could pay the money owed to Jewish workers to the various Jewish councils to fund the social welfare and provisioning of ghetto residents. Some Jewish councils paid at least part of this directly to Jewish workers, while others held onto these payments in full to cover their communities' provisioning costs and alleviate the worst hardship in the ghettos.

The systematic annihilation of the Polish Jews began in March 1942. Between 16 March and 20 April, the ghetto in Lublin was cleared almost entirely, with around thirty thousand individuals being deported to the Belzec death camp, where they were murdered in the gas chambers.[68] Around fifteen thousand Jews defined as 'unfit for work' from Lemberg, which had been seized in 1941, were also taken to Belzec and killed there. In annexed Upper Silesia too, the ghettos were cleared, and the residents transported to Auschwitz and killed. In June 1942, senior SS and police chief in the General Government, Friedrich Wilhelm Krüger, was given authority over all 'Jewish affairs'. On 19 July 1942, Himmler gave the order to kill all the Polish Jews by the end of the year. Three days later, on 22 July, the deportations began from the Warsaw ghetto to the Treblinka death camp, where more than 250,000 people were murdered by September.[69]

As authority over 'Jewish affairs' passed to the SS, it also took charge of the forced labour system for Jews. On 25 June, the labour administration informed the labour offices in the General Government that in future Jewish workers could be placed in employment only in consultation with the SS. One month later, Krüger explained to the armaments inspectorates that all agreements reached with respect to the deployment of Jewish workers were no longer valid, and that now the SS would regulate the forced labour deployment of Jews, who would be interned in special SS camps.[70] Himmler agreed to leave irreplaceable Jewish workers in the General Government in view of the severe shortage of manpower.[71] But in a letter to Globocnik and Krüger, he made it clear that this was only a temporary concession. Jewish workers must be removed from firms and interned in bespoke, self-contained concentration camp firms within the General Government.

> It will then be our aim to replace these Jewish workers with Poles and to amalgamate the large number of these Jewish concentration camp firms into a small number of large-scale Jewish concentration camp firms, as far as possible in the east of the General Government. However, in accordance with the Führer's wishes, the Jews are eventually to vanish from there as well.[72]

The authority over Jewish forced labourers was no longer held by the German labour administration but by the SS, which now adopted a policy of murdering the Jews throughout the territory under German control. Until that point, however, the labour offices had undoubtedly participated in the Holocaust. Whether a Jew was deported or not depended on the labour pass, which demonstrated that its holder was performing labour 'of importance to defence'. On 25 March 1942, the city captain of Lemberg thus instructed all firms and public agencies employing Jewish workers to provide the Labour Office with 'lists of all skilled Jewish workers who do not currently seem expendable'. The Labour Office then decided, together 'with other interested agencies', who was to be considered a 'working Jew' and distributed armbands and passes accordingly – a direct decision over life and death.[73]

Before the clearing of the ghetto in Lublin began in March 1942, SS and police chief Globocnik agreed with the Labour Office that work in progress should not be interrupted. The 'working Jews' received an identity card, stamped both by the Labour Office and the SS. Of the approximately forty thousand Jews in the Lublin Ghetto, thirty-eight thousand were deported to their deaths over the next few weeks. Only around eight hundred skilled workers and their families remained.[74] In the District of Galicia, employees of the labour administrations took part in the SS's 'meetings on deployment' and contributed to decisions on which workers should be excepted from the deportations.[75] During a 1966 hearing, Hans Hantelmann, former member of staff at the Labour Office in Jasło, stated that 'at the time there were discussions about . . . what was being done with the Jews, that is, what the purpose of evacuating them was. Generally, what people said was that the Jews would be gassed or shot. This was talked about quite openly among my group of colleagues'.[76]

There were, however, other cases, such as that of Adalbert Szepessy, then head of the labour branch office in the Cracow Ghetto, who was arrested in June 1942 for his 'pro-Jewish attitude' (*Judenfreundlichkeit*). Senior SS and Police Chief Krüger alleged that he had 'issued Jews with passes enabling them to continue to avoid expulsion from Cracow by referring to their services'. Szepessy, a Viennese of Hungarian origin, had in fact attempted to help people in the ghetto, as ghetto survivor Anna Schermer reported after the war: 'Especially later, when the deportations had begun, [Szepessy] gave out fictional work assignments and changed the occupations on identity cards. He really wanted to save people'.[77] Though Governor General Hans Frank ordered Szepessy's release, he had already been sent to the Sachsenhausen concentration camp on Himmler's orders, from which he was finally released in November 1942.[78]

The Occupied Soviet Territories

Right from the outset, a different situation pertained in the occupied Soviet territories, reflecting the Nazi regime's planned war of annihilation against the Soviet population. Almost two million Soviet prisoners of war died of hunger, exhaustion and illness in the camps run by the Wehrmacht. Because German soldiers were supposed to feed themselves from Soviet resources, the Nazi leaders factored millions of deaths by famine into their plans. During the first few months of the war, the task forces of the Security Police and the SD, together with units of the Order Police and the Waffen-SS, murdered hundreds of thousands of Jews, Roma and Sinti, as well as the sick and disabled. Within the framework of Nazi logic, these killings were necessary to dispose of 'excess eaters' and establish 'security' in the difficult-to-control rural areas. In the ghettos of the larger towns, meanwhile, the lives of the Jews penned up there and classified as fit for work were initially spared.[79]

Lithuania was still home to more than two hundred thousand Jews when the Wehrmacht invaded. By December 1941, around 80 per cent of them had been murdered. Smaller ghettos established at the beginning of the occupation were rapidly cleared. It was essentially the larger ghettos in Wilna (Vilnius), Kaunas (Kovno) and Šiauliai (Shavli) that now remained.[80] Kaunas was the largest city in Lithuania at the time, and from 1920 until the arrival of the Red Army in June 1940 it was the capital of the independent Republic of Lithuania. The German invasion on 24 June 1941 resulted in terrible anti-Jewish pogroms, which claimed the lives of around three thousand people.[81] The first wave of murders then resulted in the deaths of roughly six thousand Jews, and another approximately twelve thousand in September and October, now including women and children. In August 1941, around 29,000 people had still been living in the Kaunas Ghetto, but by November the figure was just 17,400, made up of 9,900 women and 7,500 men.[82]

In his memorandum of 29 April 1941, the future Reich minister for the occupied Eastern territories, Alfred Rosenberg, had planned the criminal exploitation of indigenous workers, which affected around twenty-four million individuals.[83] Within the racist hierarchy of the German occupation authorities, Jewish workers, along with Soviet prisoners of war, were at the very bottom. Nonetheless, they were vital to the war economy in the occupied territories. In the occupied Soviet Union, the Reich Ministry of Labour was not in charge of labour deployment, with power instead in the hands of the Senior Group for Labour (Chefgruppe Arbeit) in the Economic Staff East (Wirtschaftsstab Ost) under Section Head Dr Günther Rachner, though his background was in the Reich Ministry of Labour. Authority was shared with the Reich Ministry for the Occupied Eastern Territories (Reichsministerium für die besetzten Ostgebiete), whose Department of Labour and Social Affairs (Abteilung Arbeit und Soziales) was also headed by Rachner. From March 1942, a new institution was then developed in the shape of the General Plenipotentiary for Labour Deployment.[84]

In Lithuania, the Wehrmacht's Economic Commando (Wirtschaftskommando) put Martin Peschel in charge of what had been the Lithuanian Labour Ministry in July 1941. German personnel from the East Prussian Land Labour Office and the Reich Labour Ministry followed. In the spring of 1942, Günther Dammer, just twenty-nine years old at the time and a member of the Nazi Party since 1931, took over from Peschel as head of the Department of Labour Policy and Social Administration (Abteilung Arbeitspolitik und Sozialverwaltung) in the General Commissariat of Lithuania.[85] In Kaunas, until the end of February 1942, the Jewish labour administration in the ghetto received its assignments from the German Labour Office, headed by SA-Hauptsturmführer Fritz Jordan. The German Labour Office determined the demand for civilian workers, while the Wehrmacht's Armaments Commando (Rüstungskommando) did the same for the needs of the military, with both of them addressing their demands to the Labour Department of the Jewish ghetto administration.[86] From February 1942, a branch office of the German Labour Office was established within the ghetto. This was headed by SA-Obersturmführer Gustav Hörmann, who worked together closely with the Jewish Labour Office under Dr Isaac Rabinovič.[87]

As a result of the decree issued by the Reich minister for the occupied Eastern territories of 16 August 1941, in the Reich Commissariat Ostland, of which Lithuania formed part under German occupation, as throughout occupied Soviet territory, Jews were required to perform forced labour or could be deployed by firms and public authorities. Their meagre remuneration was divided between the occupation administration and the various

Jewish councils, which had to provide for those living in the ghettos.⁸⁸ Given the wave of murders, surviving Jews had a great interest in evading the firing squad (for the time being) through their labour. As elsewhere, in the remaining ghettos in the occupied Soviet territories, the Jewish councils' approach is captured in the phrase 'work saves our lives'. In the summer of 1941, the German occupation administration, like the Wehrmacht offices, still assumed that the remaining Jewish workers would soon be killed. Yet the failed 'blitzkrieg' against the Red Army, which saw the Wehrmacht defeated just outside Moscow in December 1941, finally made it clear that the war would continue for some time, making manpower a crucial resource. In early December 1941, therefore, the Reich commissioner for Ostland, Hinrich Lohse, ordered the killing of the Jews to be discontinued. At this point, around 17,500 Jews still lived in the Kaunas Ghetto.⁸⁹ After the mass killings, the ghetto now provided some protection, albeit of a minimal nature. But how would Jews even begin to organize their everyday lives? They lived under constant pressure, due to periodic selection, which meant death for the 'unfit for work', hunger, cold, illness and forced labour. The will to survive became the most precious commodity. 'A sho gelebt ist oych gelebt' ('An hour lived is still lived'), as Shmuel Gringauz, who survived the Kaunas Ghetto, expressed the maxim to which ghetto inhabitants adhered.⁹⁰ Jews in the occupied Soviet territories were well aware that only the Germans' defeat could save them. They thus hoped for a Red Army victory and did their best to hold out and persevere, and play for time.⁹¹

A 'Jewish Labour Deployment Office for the Ghetto Community of Vilijampole' (Jüdische Arbeitseinsatzstelle Ghetto-Gemeinde Vilijampole) had existed since August 1941 and kept a register of all Jewish workers. It issued Jews with employment documents, so-called 'Jordan certificates' and later labour cards, which could provide protection from future selection.⁹² In three major campaigns extending from the end of September to the end of October, the SS and the police selected those in the ghetto who lacked an employment document and again murdered more than ten thousand individuals – a 'thinning' (*Ausforstung*), to quote the term used by H. Schmitz, head of the Gestapo at the Commander of the Security Police and SD Lithuania, at a postwar hearing.⁹³ In February 1942, the SS and police were evidently planning another 'clean-up operation' in the ghetto, which was intended to leave around three to four thousand Jewish artisans working while murdering the so-called 'intelligentsia'. On the orders of the police, Hörmann had to draw up a list detailing Jews according to occupational group and gender, as well as a list of all academics, and single Jewish women who were elderly or who had not been assigned to forced labour, a total of two to three thousand people. Hörmann, however, along with his Jewish colleagues, falsified the list, which contained only artisans, semiskilled workers and auxiliary workers. The Gestapo's 'Jew officer' (*Judensachbearbeiter*) in Kaunas, Ernst Stütz, was suspicious of the data, but the planned 'clean-up operation' did not take place.[94]

Initially, Jews were deployed in workplaces throughout the city. The Jewish Council of Elders, however, proposed the establishment of workshops within the ghetto itself, and this was in fact decreed by the German city commissioner in early December. Before long, a variety of operations were established. There was a turner's workshop and a laundry. In 1942, a furniture factory was established on the periphery of the ghetto. The number of workers thus increased. In early April 1942, there were around four hundred Jewish workers, a figure that had increased to 9,705 by April 1943, consisting of 4,765 men and 4,940 women. At this point in time, 15,888 people lived in the ghetto, including 3,611 under the age of sixteen (a strict ban on pregnancy came into force in the summer of 1942, and in the September of that year the Jewish Council of Elders was compelled to announce that every pregnant woman would be shot dead).[95] Almost 80 per cent of adult ghetto inhabitants were thus subject to labour deployment. In June 1942, ghetto passes were introduced, and the Jewish autonomous administration compiled a comprehensive card index detailing all residents of the ghetto. As in the General Government, the Wehrmacht offices had to pay Jewish workers a wage, which was to equate to approximately 80 per cent of the standard wage. It was, however, the German occupation administration that received almost all this money. As a result, substantial sums flowed into the city coffers on a monthly basis, while the provisioning of the ghetto remained wholly inadequate.[96]

In April 1943, just under 6,000 Jews worked outside the ghetto, and about 3,700 within it. One important place of work was the airfield in Kaunas. The authorities had already demanded that around a thousand Jewish workers be dispatched there in September 1941. Two months later, a daily total of around two thousand Jews were deployed there, a figure that briefly climbed to 2,500 in June 1942. The airport was 15 km from the ghetto, that is, Jews had to make a daily trip of 30 km there and back. This was heavy work, so the number of those signing up on a voluntary basis was not always sufficient. Nonetheless, the Council of Elders pushed for the authorities' demands to be met in full: the ghetto's survival was closely bound up with the forced labour performed at the airfield. There were many forced labour camps in the vicinity of Kaunas, of which the camp in Palemonas, where around a hundred Jewish workers had to cut peat under terrible conditions, was the most notorious.[97]

Certain businesses in Kaunas, such as the construction firm Grün und Bilfinger, also had a bad reputation because employees, in this case an engineer by the name of Bolt, harassed the Jews working there. Hörmann expressed concern about the inadequate meals provided by Grün und Bilfinger, prompting Bolt to chide him, asking why on earth an SA-Obersturmführer was intervening on behalf of Jews.[98] A memorandum, sent by the German Labour Office to the Area Commissioner (*Gebietskommissar*) of October 1942, stated that Hörmann had pushed for better meals at Grün und Bilfinger, as a result of which he had suffered instances of 'personal unpleasantness'.[99] Because the occupation administration, the Wehrmacht and German firms were ever more dependent on Jewish workers, the German police often carried out house searches in the ghetto in an attempt to discover Jews who had evaded mandatory labour service, a crime that carried the death penalty.[100]

In 1943, the SS succeeded in taking charge of the ghettos and labour camps in the occupied Soviet territories as well. After the uprising in the Warsaw Ghetto in April–May 1943, having consulted Hitler on 21 June 1943, Himmler ordered the 'assembling in concentration camps of all Jews still present in ghettos on the territory of Ostland'.[101] The ghettos in Vilnius and other locations were dismantled and Kaunas became the central concentration camp in Lithuania. Of the 23,980 Jews still working in Lithuania at the end of August 1943, just 9,065 were still alive one month later. All the rest had been deported to Estonia by the SS and murdered.[102]

In Kaunas in late July, Hörmann informed the president of the Jewish Council of Elders, Dr Elkhanan Elkes, of the plan for the SS to take control of the ghetto and of the firing squads that would surely follow, enabling the latter to help as many Jews as possible to flee or go into hiding. It was not until October that the SS gained full control, with SS-Obersturmbannführer Wilhelm Göcke taking charge of what was now the Kaunas concentration camp. Before the end of that month, the SS had carried out major manhunts within the ghetto, resulting in the capture of around 2,700 Jews, of whom 2,000 were transported to Estonia to perform forced labour in oil shale mining, while the rest were deported to Auschwitz. In March 1944, the SS sought out children and elderly people in the ghetto. According to survivors' accounts, this raid was 'the most terrible thing we had to live through in the ghetto'. Around a thousand children under the age of twelve and three hundred individuals above the age of fifty-five were rounded up and killed. In July 1943, in light of the approach of the Red Army, the SS and police cleared the ghetto. Around three thousand Jews were deported west by train. The houses in the ghetto were burnt down, suffocating or burning to death a likely total of around two thousand individuals hiding in them. Just 265 survivors were liberated by the Red Army on 1 August 1944.[103]

Conclusion

The German labour administration in the occupied territories of Eastern Europe, as I have demonstrated here through the examples of the Warthegau, the General Government and Lithuania, was integrated into the occupation administration in a wide variety of ways. In the Reich Gau of Wartheland, which was part of the German Reich and was earmarked for 'Germanization', the Reich Ministry of Labour pressed to be granted authority over the labour administration as in the rest of the Reich, and vied for power with Reich Governor Arthur Greiser, though ultimately in vain. In central Poland, meanwhile, the labour administration was subordinate to the administrative apparatus under Governor General Hans Frank. Finally, in the occupied territories, the Reich Ministry for the Occupied Eastern Territories under Arthur Rosenberg or, in some cases, the various regional Reich commissioners, held authority over the labour administration.

Nonetheless, close personal ties existed between the German Reich and the labour administrations in the occupied territories. By November 1939, former state secretary in the Reich Ministry of Labour Dr Johannes Krohn had established the 'Main Section for Labour' within the General Government. Just under 30 per cent of those employed within the General Government's labour administration, meanwhile, were German, and naturally they held the leading positions. Of these, well over half had come from the Reich, such as the aforementioned Heinz Weber, who had originally worked in the Karlsruhe Labour Office before being posted first to the Reichhof Labour Office and then, in 1941, being dispatched to occupied Lemberg, where he headed the German Job Placement Office in the Jewish ghetto. In the occupied Soviet territories, a section head from the Reich Ministry of Labour, Dr Günther Rachner, was in charge of the Senior Group for Labour within the Economic Staff East and concurrently led the Department for Labour and Social Affairs within the Reich Ministry for the Occupied Eastern Territories. In Lithuania, many labour administration officials came from the labour offices in East Prussia. While these civil servants were not subject to the authority of the Reich Ministry of Labour, in staffing terms there were close links with the Reich German labour administration, which underpinned the continuity of administrative experience and bureaucratic practices.

Though the leaders and staff of the labour offices were not directly involved in the firing squads, the resulting mass graves or the death camps, they participated in the Holocaust nonetheless. They recorded and registered those living in the Jewish ghettos and determined which of them were 'fit for work', as well as those who were not, effectively condemning the latter to death. Due to the tremendous demand for manpower, from late 1941 the SS and police were provisionally forced to ensure that their murderous campaigns did not impede the deployment of Jewish forced labourers in the occupied territories. The selections undertaken by the labour offices provided the basis on which the murderers determined who in the ghettos was to be seized and killed. That the staff of the labour administration were aware of the fate that awaited those 'selected' is only too evident from the aforementioned eyewitness testimony of Hans Hantelmann, an employee of the Labour Office in Jasło.

Yet there was some room for manoeuvre, some potential for individuals to opt not to participate in these mass crimes. Adalbert Szepessy, head of the Labour Office division in the Cracow Ghetto until June 1942, issued passes and altered occupations on identity cards in order to save Jews from looming deportation. SA-Obersturmführer Gustav Hörmann, head of the Labour Office division in the Kaunas Ghetto, took steps to improve the provisioning of Jewish forced labourers and falsified lists in an attempt to pull the wool over the eyes of the SS and avert a killing spree in the ghetto. Others, meanwhile, actively supported the policy of annihilation. The labour administration's role as a key player in the organization of Jewish forced labour came to an end when the SS took charge of the ghettos in 1943.

Until this juncture, in structural and administrative terms the staff of the labour administration in the occupied territories were involved in the murderous selection of Jews in the ghettos. But there was no inevitability about their participation. It was clearly possible to refuse to take part. It was a personal decision whether to become an accomplice or do everything possible to save human lives.

Epilogue: Ghetto Pensions

The history of the restitution of stolen assets and of material compensation for injustices suffered under the Nazi regime is, according to Constantin Goschler, 'a core element in the post-history of the Third Reich, a post-history always closely intertwined with the postwar German present'.[104] The London Agreement on German External Debts of 1953 stipulated that claims by foreign states against which Nazi Germany had waged war or that had been occupied by it were to be put on ice until such time as the issue of reparations was finally settled. This gave West Germany – East Germany ruled out all reparation payments on principle – the legal option of rejecting all claims for compensation for foreign victims of Nazi persecution until the 2+4 negotiations on German reunification of 1990–1991 put the issue of reparations back on the agenda. The Federal Indemnification Law (Bundesentschädigungsgesetz) of 1956, which chiefly provided compensation for those who had been held in concentration camps, applied in principle only to Germans.

However, in parallel with the negotiations in London, Germany had concluded an agreement with Israel on a lump-sum compensation payment and over the next few years it took the same approach with Western European countries, and after 1989 with Eastern European states as well. With reference to the London agreement, however, forced labourers were explicitly excepted from the resulting payments. It was only in the late 1990s, when major German companies were confronted with group actions, that new life was breathed into this debate. As a result, in the year 2000 a foundation was established into which German businesses, together with the German government, paid around 10 billion Deutschmarks to make one-off payments to former forced labourers.

In the course of these debates, key German actors began to discuss whether those who had performed labour as ghetto residents were entitled to a pension. In 1997, with reference to a case in the Litzmannstadt Ghetto, the Federal Social Court ruled that, within the framework of the social insurance system, in principle employment in a ghetto could give rise to the same entitlements as any other form of work.[105] The Federal Social Court called for appropriate legislation, and in 2002 the Bundestag passed the Law Regarding the Conditions for Making Pensions Payable on the Basis of Employment in a Ghetto (Gesetz zur Zahlbarmachung von Renten aus Beschäftigungen in einem Ghetto, or ZRBG), which facilitated the payment of pensions to other countries if individuals could credibly claim to have been 'employed voluntarily in a ghetto in return for payment' (ZRBG § 1).[106] The two key criteria, 'voluntarily' and 'payment', were necessary, first, in order to distinguish pension claims from compensation payments made in accordance with the Federal Indemnification Law and from payments for forced labour made by the Foundation Remembrance, Responsibility and Future (Stiftung Erinnerung, Verantwortung, Zukunft, or EVZ). Second, the ZRBG finally put Jewish workers on the same footing as non-Jewish ones: as a rule, the firms in which Jewish ghetto residents were employed had deducted social insurance contributions from their pay, yet Jewish employees gained no benefit from this after the war.

When it came to its practical implementation, however, the ZRBG demonstrated serious shortcomings, because pension insurance providers and social courts knew nothing about the actual conditions in the ghettos and made decisions on the basis of unrealistic criteria. For example, applicants had to indicate in a questionnaire whether their employment relationship had come about 'voluntarily', 'through an intermediate agency' or 'through allocation'. If an individual ticked all three options, which tallied with the everyday reality in the ghettos, this generally resulted in the rejection of their application because the 'voluntary nature' of the employment relationship was not clearly established.[107]

Of approximately seventy thousand applications submitted by 2006, sixty-one thousand were rejected and five thousand accepted, a rate of just 8 per cent.[108] Rejected applicants' complaints before the social courts initially did nothing to change things because many judges, ignorant of the actual conditions in the ghetto, could only discern coercion rather than 'voluntary' labour. Recognition of the complexity of the situation emerged only gradually. Jews had of course been penned up in the ghettos by force, while hunger and the fear of looming deportation drove them to seek work. As Uri Chanoch, survivor of the Kaunas Ghetto, underlined at a hearing of the Committee for Labour and Social Affairs (Ausschuss für Arbeit und Soziales) of the German Bundestag on 10 December 2012:

> My father went to work and had a labour card. My mother also had a labour card and my sister Miriam. I had no labour card because I was too young. But I could work. . . . I signed up at the German Labour Office as a courier. A job as courier was a good one to have, I must admit. But then I understood: those who did not work would be killed. There was no forced labour in that situation. Everyone wanted to work.[109]

The criticisms emanating from Israel of the rulings of German social courts had also become impossible to ignore, prompting the German government to commit to remedying the situation.[110] In 2009, the Federal Social Court ruled that the relevant practices must be amended and declared that the 'voluntary nature' of such labour must be considered the norm, because the ghetto residents had an interest in working. In case of remuneration, the court stated, low wages and benefits in kind, which the pension insurers and social courts had not accepted as 'payment', must also be recognized.[111] In accordance with these rulings, pension insurers and social courts modified their decision-making practices, though with respect to the so-called 'rectification' (*Heilung*) of already binding judgements, in other words in dealing with the sixty-one thousand rejections, they recognized a retroactive effect of just four years, that is, stipulated that pension payments would be backdated to 2005 rather than 1997 as originally envisaged.

The Bundestag too began to reconsider the situation, having originally assumed that, subsequent to the passing of the ZRBG in 2002, the Federal Ministry of Labour, the pension insurance institutes and the social courts would find appropriate ways of implementing the new law. In May 2014, during a plenary debate in the Bundestag, CDU pensions expert and Bundestag deputy Peter Weiss spoke in clear terms: 'It was not the intention of German parliamentarians in 2002 to pass a law that resulted in 90 per cent of those affected receiving no payment at all because most of the applications were rejected by the authorities'.[112] In short order, the Federal Ministry for Labour and Social Affairs under Andrea Nahles drew up an amended version of the ZRBG. Passed unanimously by the Bundestag in June 2014 and coming into force on 1 August the same year, this facilitated the payment of pensions with retroactive effect from 1997.[113]

Michael Wildt, Dr. phil., Professor of twentieth-century German history at Humboldt University of Berlin, with a focus on Nazism, and member of the Independent Commission of Historians Investigating the History of the Reich Ministry of Labour in the National Socialist Period. Publications include: *Revolutions and Counter-Revolutions. 1917 and Its Aftermath from a Global Perspective* (Campus, 2017; co-edited with Stefan Rinke); *Arbeit im Nationalsozialismus* (De Gruyter Oldenbourg, 2014; co-edited with Marc Buggeln); *Hitler's Volksgemeinschaft and the Dynamics of Racial Exclusion. Violence against Jews in Provincial Germany, 1919–1939* (Berghahn Books, 2012; translated by Bernard Heise).

Notes

1. 'Niederschrift über die Besprechung in der Reichskanzlei, 5 November 1937 (Hossbach-Protokoll)', in *Trial of the Major War Criminals before the International Military Tribunal, Nuremberg 14 November 1945–1 October 1946*, vol. 25, Nuremberg: n.p., 1947, 402–13. On 'living space', see U. Jureit, *Das Ordnen von Räumen. Territorium und Lebensraum im 19. und 20. Jahrhundert*, Hamburg: Hamburger Edition, 2012.

2. Generaloberst Halder, *Kriegstagebuch. Tägliche Aufzeichnungen des Chefs des Generalstabes des Heeres, 1939–1942*, ed. H.-A. Jacobsen in collaboration with A. Philippi, vol. 1, Stuttgart: Kohlhammer, 1962–1964, 82.

3. Minutes of the Meeting of 21 September 1939, Bundesarchiv (BArch), R 58/825, fol. 26–30; see also Heydrich's Express Letter to the Task Force Leaders in Poland, 21 September 1939, reprinted in *Die Verfolgung und Ermordung der europäischen Juden durch das nationalsozialistische Deutschland 1933–1945*, ed. on behalf of Bundesarchiv, Institut für Zeitgeschichte and Lehrstuhl für Neuere und Neueste Geschichte an der Albert-Ludwigs-Universität Freiburg by S. Heim et al., vol. 4: *Polen, September 1939–Juli 1941*, ed. K.-P. Friedrich in collaboration with A. Löw, Munich: Oldenbourg, 2011, 88–92 (Doc. 12).

4. Minutes of the meeting of 21 September 1939, BArch, R 58/825, fol. 26–30.

5. A. Löw, *Juden im Getto Litzmannstadt. Lebensbedingungen, Selbstwahrnehmungen, Verhalten*, Göttingen: Wallstein, 2006, 69–81; M. Alberti, *Die Verfolgung und Vernichtung der Juden im Reichsgau Wartheland 1939–1945*, Wiesbaden: Harrassowitz, 2006, 41 f.

6. Alberti, *Verfolgung*, 105.

7. See C. Browning, 'Nazi Ghettoization Policy in Poland 1939–1941', in C. Browning, *The Path to Genocide. Essays on Launching the Final Solution*, Cambridge: Cambridge University Press, 1992, 28–56; and C. Dieckmann and B. Quinkert (eds), *Im Ghetto 1939–1945. Neue Forschungen zu Alltag und Umfeld*, Göttingen: Wallstein, 2009; D. Pohl, 'Ghettos',

in W. Benz and B. Distel (eds), *Der Ort des Terrors. Geschichte der nationalsozialistischen Konzentrationslager*, vol. 9: *Arbeitserziehungslager, Ghettos, Jugendschutzlager, Polizeihaftlager, Sonderlager, Zigeunerlager, Zwangsarbeiterlager*, Munich: Beck, 2009, 161–91.

8. Alberti, *Die Verfolgung*, 161. While the territory of the ghetto comprised a total of approximately 4.5 square kilometres, 1.5 square kilometres was undeveloped waste ground. On the Litzmannstadt Ghetto, see also the detailed exhibition volume '*Unser einziger Weg ist Arbeit*'. *Das Getto in Łódź 1940–1944, eine Ausstellung des Jüdischen Museums Frankfurt am Main*, 30. März bis 10. Juni 1990, ed. H. Loewy and G. Schoenberner, Frankfurt am Main: Löcker, 1990.

9. P. Longerich, *Politik der Vernichtung. Eine Gesamtdarstellung der nationalsozialistischen Judenverfolgung*, Munich: Piper, 1998, 268 f.

10. See D. Maier, *Arbeitseinsatz und Deportation. Die Mitwirkung der Arbeitsverwaltung bei der nationalsozialistischen Judenverfolgung in den Jahren 1938–1945*, Berlin: Hentrich, 1994; W. Gruner, *Der Geschlossene Arbeitseinsatz deutscher Juden. Zur Zwangsarbeit als Element der Verfolgung 1938–1943*, Berlin: Metropol, 1997.

11. Quoted in Maier, *Arbeitseinsatz und Deportation*, 29.

12. Löw, *Juden im Getto Litzmannstadt*, 116 f.; Alberti, *Die Verfolgung*, 229.

13. On Biebow, see Alberti, *Die Verfolgung*, 172–76; P. Klein, *Die 'Ghettoverwaltung Litzmannstadt' 1940 bis 1944. Eine Dienststelle im Spannungsfeld von Kommunalbürokratie und staatlicher Verfolgungspolitik*, Hamburg: Hamburger Edition, 2009, 86–88.

14. Quoted in Alberti, *Die Verfolgung*, 233.

15. K. Linne, 'Die deutsche Arbeitsverwaltung zwischen "Volkstumspolitik" und Arbeiterrekrutierung – das Beispiel Warthegau', in F. Dierl, Z. Janjetović and K. Linne, *Pflicht, Zwang und Gewalt. Arbeitsverwaltungen und Arbeitskräftepolitik im deutsch besetzten Polen und Serbien 1939–1944*, Essen: Klartext, 2013, 47–170, here 63–75, 83–87. On the labour trustees, see the chapter by Sören Eden in this volume.

16. Memorandum of 25 October 1940 on a Meeting at the District Council (Regierungspräsidium) on the Previous Day, quoted in Alberti, *Die Verfolgung*, 254; on the wholly inadequate food supply in the ghetto and on protests against Rumkowski, see Löw, *Juden im Getto Litzmannstadt*, 124–41.

17. Alberti, *Die Verfolgung*, 235, 266, 269.

18. Ibid., 280, 282.

19. A. Konieczny, 'Die Zwangsarbeit der Juden in Schlesien im Rahmen der "Organisation Schmelt"', in G. Aly et al., *Sozialpolitik und Judenvernichtung. Gibt es eine Ökonomie der Endlösung?* Berlin: Rotbuch, 1987, 91–110; S. Steinbacher, '*Musterstadt*' *Auschwitz. Germanisierungspolitik und Judenmord in Ostoberschlesien*, Munich: K.G. Saur, 2000, 138–53; W. Gruner, *Jewish Forced Labor under the Nazis. Economic Needs and Racial Aims, 1938–1944*, trans. K.M. Dell'Orto, Cambridge: Cambridge University Press, 2006, 196–229.

20. Linne, 'Die deutsche Arbeitsverwaltung', 151; Klein, *Die 'Ghettoverwaltung Litzmannstadt'*, 224–28.

21. Express Letter from the Reich Labour Minister to the Presidents of the Land Labour Offices, 14 March 1941, BArch, R 3901/20193, fol. 99, quoted in Linne, 'Die deutsche Arbeitsverwaltung', 152; see W. Gruner, 'Juden bauen die "Strassen des Führers". Zwangsarbeit und Zwangsarbeitslager für nichtdeutsche Juden im Altreich 1940 bis 1943/44', *Zeitschrift für Geschichtswissenschaft* 44(9) (1996), 789–808.

22. See Maier, *Arbeitseinsatz und Deportation*, 89–95; Circular issued by the Reich Ministry of Labour, Section V a, to the Presidents of the Land Labour Offices, 7 April 1941, BArch, R 3901/20193, fol. 97, quoted in Linne, 'Die deutsche Arbeitsverwaltung', 152.

23. Alberti, *Die Verfolgung*, 285.

24. Klein, *Die 'Ghettoverwaltung Litzmannstadt'*, 296–317.

25. Alberti, *Die Verfolgung*, 288; Anna Ziółkowska provides a figure of 173 forced labour camps in the Reich Gau of Wartheland; A. Ziółkowska, 'Zwangsarbeitslager für Juden im

Reichsgau Wartheland', in J.A. Młynarczyk and J. Böhler (eds), *Der Judenmord in den eingegliederten polnischen Gebieten 1939–1945*, Osnabrück: Fibre, 2010, 179–202, here 180.

26. Alberti, *Die Verfolgung*, 323.
27. Linne, 'Die deutsche Arbeitsverwaltung', 155.
28. Alberti, *Die Verfolgung*, 301.
29. Löw, *Juden im Getto Litzmannstadt*, 155–91.
30. On the clash within the German occupation administration between, as Christopher Browning has called them, 'productionists' and 'attritionists', see C. Browning, 'Jewish Workers in Poland: Self-Maintenance, Exploitation, Destruction', in C. Browning, *Nazi Policy, Jewish Workers, German Killers*, Cambridge: Cambridge University Press, 2000, 58–88, here 66–69; and Browning, 'Nazi Ghettoization Policy'.
31. Note Höppner with Covering Letter to Eichmann, 16 July 1941, reprinted in P. Longerich, *Die Ermordung der europäischen Juden. Eine umfassende Dokumentation des Holocaust 1941–1945*, Munich: Piper, 1989, 74 f.; see Klein, *Die 'Ghettoverwaltung Litzmannstadt'*, 336–52.
32. For a detailed account, see Alberti, *Die Verfolgung*, 339–72; J.A. Młynarczyk, 'Mordinitiativen von unten. Die Rolle Arthur Greisers und Odilo Globocniks im Entscheidungsprozess zum Judenmord', in Młynarczyk and Böhler, *Der Judenmord*, 27–56.
33. See Klein, *Die 'Ghettoverwaltung Litzmannstadt'*, 321–23.
34. Himmler to Greiser, 18 September 1941, BArch, NS 19/2655, fol. 3, reprinted as a facsimile in P. Witte, 'Zwei Entscheidungen in der "Endlösung der Judenfrage": Deportationen nach Lodz und Vernichtung in Chelmno', in M. Kárný, R. Kemper and M. Kárná (eds), *Theresienstädter Studien und Dokumente 1995*, Prague: Academia, 1995, 38–68, here 50. However, Greiser and the district president of Litzmannstadt, Friedrich Uebelhoer, opposed the figure announced by Himmler of sixty thousand people and managed to ensure that for the time being 'just' twenty thousand Jews were deported to the Litzmannstadt Ghetto (Alberti, *Die Verfolgung*, 387–95).
35. Klein, *Die 'Ghettoverwaltung Litzmannstadt'*, 356 f.
36. Alberti, *Die Verfolgung*, 397 f.; Löw, *Juden im Getto Litzmannstadt*, 224–33.
37. Alberti, *Die Verfolgung*, 417.
38. Note on a Departmental Meeting at the Reich Ministry of Labour on 28 November 1941, quoted in Alberti, *Die Verfolgung*, 418.
39. For a detailed account, see ibid., 421–33.
40. Ibid., 444.
41. Löw, *Juden im Getto Litzmannstadt*, 266 f.; Alberti, *Die Verfolgung*, 420 f.
42. Löw, *Juden im Getto Litzmannstadt*, 292; Alberti, *Die Verfolgung*, 447.
43. For a detailed account, see Löw, *Juden im Getto Litzmannstadt*, 292–308.
44. *Die Tagebücher von Joseph Goebbels. Sämtliche Fragmente*, Part I: *Aufzeichnungen 1924–1941*, vol. 4: *1.1.1940–8.9.1941*, ed. E. Fröhlich, Munich: Saur, 1987, 387 (entry of 5 November 1940). Goebbels also wrote: 'And Frank is reluctant. Not without some justification. He wants to make a model country out of Poland. That's going too far. He cannot and shall not do so. For us, as the Führer has decided, Poland is to be a great reservoir of labour. . . . And at some point in the future we will deport the Jews from this territory as well'.
45. Decree on the Introduction of Compulsory Labour for the Jewish Population of the General Government (Verordnung über die Einführung des Arbeitszwangs für die jüdische Bevölkerung des Generalgouvernements), 26 October 1939, reprinted in *Verfolgung und Ermordung der europäischen Juden*, vol. 4, 115 (Doc. 27); and 2nd Implementing Provision issued by the Senior SS and Police Chief, 12 December 1939, reprinted in ibid., 177–79 (Doc. 58); see S. Lehnstaedt, 'Die deutsche Arbeitsverwaltung im Generalgouvernement und die Juden', *Vierteljahrshefte für Zeitgeschichte* 60(3) (2012), 409–40, here 415 f.

46. Ibid., 417 f.; K. Linne, '"Sklavenjagden" im Arbeiterreservoir – das Beispiel Generalgouvernement', in Dierl, Janjetovič and Linne, *Pflicht, Zwang und Gewalt*, 171–316, here 275.

47. Lehnstaedt, 'Die deutsche Arbeitsverwaltung', 427 f.

48. From 26 October 1939, Poles between the ages of eighteen and sixty were also subject to compulsory labour, that is, every Pole had to do the job allocated to them by the Labour Office without the possibility of termination. Anyone refusing to do so faced severe punishment; ibid., 414.

49. Ibid., 415; Linne, '"Sklavenjagden"', 277.

50. On Frauendorfer, see T. Schlemmer, 'Grenzen der Integration. Die CSU und der Umgang mit der nationalsozialistischen Vergangenheit – der Fall Dr. Max Frauendorfer', *Vierteljahrshefte für Zeitgeschichte* 48(4) (2000), 675–742.

51. D.G. Maier, *Anfänge und Brüche der Arbeitsverwaltung bis 1952. Zugleich ein kaum bekanntes Kapitel der deutsch-jüdischen Geschichte*, Brühl: Fachhochschule des Bundes für Öffentliche Verwaltung, 2004, 114 f.; Lehnstaedt, 'Die deutsche Arbeitsverwaltung', 413 f.

52. Quoted in *Faschismus – Getto – Massenmord. Dokumentation über Ausrottung und Widerstand der Juden in Polen während des zweiten Weltkrieges*, ed. Jüdisches Historisches Institut Warschau, Frankfurt am Main: Röderberg, 1962, 210–12.

53. Ibid.; Linne, '"Sklavenjagden"', 277. On the issue of ghetto pensions, see the epilogue at the end of this chapter.

54. Examination of the Witness Heinz Weber, 14 October 1960, BArch, B 162/2137, fol. 640, quoted in Linne, '"Sklavenjagden"', 284.

55. See the examples in M. Wenzel, 'Die Arbeitslager für Juden im Distrikt Krakau des Generalgouvernement 1940–1941', in D. Pohl and T. Sebta (eds), *Zwangsarbeit in Hitlers Europa. Besatzung, Arbeit, Folgen*, Berlin: Metropol, 2013, 173–94, here 184–86.

56. Ibid., 187, 193.

57. D. Pohl, *Von der 'Judenpolitik' zum Judenmord. Der Distrikt Lublin des Generalgouvernements 1939–1944*, Frankfurt am Main: Lang, 1993, 79–85; B. Musial, *Deutsche Zivilverwaltung und Judenverfolgung im Generalgouvernement. Eine Fallstudie zum Distrikt Lublin 1939–1944*, Wiesbaden: Harrassowitz, 1999, 164–70; Browning, 'Jewish Workers', 63 f.; Lehnstaedt, 'Die deutsche Arbeitsverwaltung', 419 f.; Linne, '"Sklavenjagden"', 279–83.

58. A. Löw and M. Roth, *Juden in Krakau unter deutscher Besatzung 1939–1945*, Göttingen: Wallstein, 2012, 13 f.

59. Ibid., 27–32.

60. Ibid., 33–45, 52 f.

61. A. Löw, 'Arbeit in den Ghettos: Rettung oder temporärer Vernichtungsaufschub?', in M. Buggeln and M. Wildt (eds), *Arbeit im Nationalsozialismus*, Munich: De Gruyter Oldenbourg, 2014, 293–308, here 297.

62. Löw and Roth, *Juden in Krakau*, 76 f.

63. Quoted in Löw, 'Arbeit in den Ghettos', 298.

64. Lehnstaedt, 'Die deutsche Arbeitsverwaltung', 428. Frauendorfer's circular of 5 July 1940 is reprinted in part in *Faschismus – Getto – Massenmord*, 210–12.

65. Minutes of the Meeting on the Deployment of Jews, 6 August 1940, quoted in Lehnstaedt, 'Die deutsche Arbeitsverwaltung', 428; see Browning, 'Jewish Workers', 62.

66. Lehnstaedt, 'Die deutsche Arbeitsverwaltung', 434–36.

67. Ibid., 433.

68. Longerich, *Politik der Vernichtung*, 504; for a detailed account, see Musial, *Deutsche Zivilverwaltung*, 193–254.

69. Longerich, *Politik der Vernichtung*, 505–8.

70. Ibid., 510; Linne, '"Sklavenjagden"', 290 f.

71. Longerich, *Politik der Vernichtung*, 510; Browning, 'Jewish Workers', 78–80.

72. Himmler to Pohl, Krüger, Globocnik, Reich Security Main Office and Wolff, 2 October 1942, reprinted as a facsimile in H. Grabitz and W. Scheffler, *Letzte Spuren. Ghetto Warschau, SS-Arbeitslager Trawniki, Aktion Erntefest. Fotos und Dokumente über Opfer des Endlösungswahns im Spiegel der historischen Ereignisse*, Berlin: Edition Hentrich, 1988, 179.

73. G. Aly and S. Heim, *Vordenker der Vernichtung. Auschwitz und die deutschen Pläne für eine neue europäische Ordnung*, Hamburg: Hoffmann und Campe, 1991, 451.

74. Linne, '"Sklavenjagden"', 287.

75. Report by the Lublin Labour Office for the Month of March 1942, 7 April 1942, quoted in Musial, *Deutsche Zivilverwaltung*, 231.

76. Questioning of the Witness Hans Hantelmann, 9 February 1966, quoted in Linne, '"Sklavenjagden"', 289.

77. Quoted in Löw and Roth, *Juden in Krakau*, 77.

78. Maier, *Anfänge und Brüche*, 60 f.; Löw and Roth, *Juden in Krakau*, 77.

79. See Hamburger Institut für Sozialforschung (ed.), *Verbrechen der Wehrmacht. Dimensionen des Vernichtungskrieges 1941–1944*, Hamburg: Hamburger Edition, 2004.

80. R. Leiserowitz, 'Litauen. Arbeit und Arbeitssituation in den Ghettos', in J. Hensel and S. Lehnstaedt (eds), *Arbeit in den nationalsozialistischen Ghettos*, Osnabrück: Fibre, 2013, 209–31, here 211 f.

81. C. Dieckmann, *Deutsche Besatzungspolitik in Litauen 1941–1944*, 2 vols, Göttingen: Wallstein, 2012, vol. 1, 315.

82. Ibid., vol. 2, 1056.

83. 'Denkschrift Rosenberg, 29.4.1941', in *Trial of the Major War Criminals before the International Military Tribunal, Nuremberg 14 November 1945–1 October 1946*, vol. 26, Nuremberg: n.p., 1947, 560–66.

84. Dieckmann, *Deutsche Besatzungspolitik*, vol. 1, 658; T. Plath, *Zwischen Schonung und Menschenjagden. Die Arbeitseinsatzpolitik in den baltischen Generalbezirken des Reichskommissariats Ostland 1941–1944*, Essen: Klartext, 2012, 50–54. On the General Plenipotentiary for Labour Deployment, see the chapter by Swantje Greve in this volume.

85. Dieckmann, *Deutsche Besatzungspolitik*, vol. 1, 660.

86. Ibid., vol. 2, 1074.

87. J. Tauber, *Arbeit als Hoffnung. Jüdische Ghettos in Litauen 1941–1944*, Berlin: de Gruyter Oldenbourg, 2015, 138; C. Dieckmann, 'Das Ghetto und das Konzentrationslager in Kaunas 1941–1944', in U. Herbert, K. Orth and C. Dieckmann (eds), *Die nationalsozialistischen Konzentrationslager. Entwicklung und Struktur*, 2 vols, Frankfurt am Main: Suhrkamp, 2002, vol. 1, 439–71, here 447.

88. Tauber, *Arbeit als Hoffnung*, 114–19; Plath, *Zwischen Schonung und Menschenjagden*, 402–8; Dieckmann, *Deutsche Besatzungspolitik*, vol. 1, 664 f.

89. Dieckmann, *Deutsche Besatzungspolitik*, vol. 2, 1010; Leiserowitz, 'Litauen', 216.

90. Quoted in Dieckmann, *Deutsche Besatzungspolitik*, vol. 2, 1050.

91. Ibid., 1053.

92. Tauber, *Arbeit als Hoffnung*, 129; Leiserowitz, 'Litauen', 221; Dieckmann, *Deutsche Besatzungspolitik*, vol. 2, 1072–75.

93. Dieckmann, 'Das Ghetto', 446–48.

94. Ibid., 448 f.

95. Dieckmann, *Deutsche Besatzungspolitik*, vol. 2, 1098 f.

96. Leiserowitz, 'Litauen', 221 f.; Dieckmann, *Deutsche Besatzungspolitik*, vol. 2, 1078–81; for detailed information on remuneration, see Tauber, *Arbeit als Hoffnung*, 226–48.

97. Dieckmann, *Deutsche Besatzungspolitik*, vol. 2, 1082–91; Tauber, *Arbeit als Hoffnung*, 190–95.

98. Interrogation of Hörmann, 3 November 1960, quoted in Tauber, *Arbeit als Hoffnung*, 189.

99. Ibid., 246, fn. 953.

100. Dieckmann, *Deutsche Besatzungspolitik*, vol. 2, 1074.
101. Order issued by Himmler, 21 June 1943, reprinted in Longerich, *Politik der Vernichtung*, 148 f.; see Dieckmann, *Deutsche Besatzungspolitik*, vol. 2, 1248 f.; Tauber, *Arbeit als Hoffnung*, 345 f.
102. Dieckmann, *Deutsche Besatzungspolitik*, vol. 2, 1290.
103. Ibid., 1289–301; Tauber, *Arbeit als Hoffnung*, 367–69.
104. C. Goschler, 'Wiedergutmachungspolitik – Schulden, Schuld und Entschädigung', in P. Reichel, H. Schmid and P. Steinbach (eds), *Der Nationalsozialismus – Die zweite Geschichte. Überwindung – Deutung – Erinnerung*, Munich: Beck, 2009, 62–84, here 62. See C. Goschler, *Schuld und Schulden. Die Politik der Wiedergutmachung für NS-Verfolgte seit 1945*, 2nd ed., Göttingen: Wallstein, 2008.
105. Judgement of 18 June 1997, Bundessozialgericht, B 5 Rj 66/95 B, reprinted in S. Lehnstaedt, *Geschichte und Gesetzesauslegung. Kontinuität und Wandel des bundesdeutschen Wiedergutmachungsdiskurses am Beispiel der Ghettorenten*, Osnabrück: Fibre, 2011, 114–22; cf. J.-R. von Renesse, 'Wiedergutmachung fünf vor zwölf. Das "Gesetz zur Zahlbarmachung von Renten aus Beschäftigungen in einem Ghetto"', in J. Zarusky (ed.), *Ghettorenten. Entschädigungspolitik, Rechtsprechung und historische Forschung*, Munich: Oldenbourg, 2010, 13–37; S. Lehnstaedt, 'Wiedergutmachung im 21. Jahrhundert. Das Arbeitsministerium und die Ghettorenten', in *Vierteljahrshefte für Zeitgeschichte* 61(3) (2013), 363–90. My thanks go to Annette Schicke, Federal Ministry for Labour and Social Affairs, for valuable pointers.
106. *Bundesgesetzblatt (BGBl)*. I 2002, 2074; see Lehnstaedt, 'Wiedergutmachung', 369–73.
107. Lehnstaedt, 'Wiedergutmachung', 376.
108. Ibid., 365; a detailed overview can be found in ibid., 380.
109. Minutes of the Public Hearing of the Committee for Labour and Social Affairs of the German Bundestag, 10 December 2012, Minutes 17/118, 1856, Federal Ministry for Labour and Social Affairs. Chanoch also mentioned Gustav Hörmann, whom he referred to as a 'good man' who did not hit or scold (ibid.); see also K. Platt, *Bezweifelte Erinnerung, verweigerte Glaubwürdigkeit. Überlebende des Holocaust in den Ghettorenten-Verfahren*, Paderborn: Fink, 2012.
110. Lehnstaedt, 'Wiedergutmachung', 379.
111. Ibid., 366 f.
112. Quoted in S. Lehnstaedt, 'Der Deutungsstreit um die "Ghettorenten". Anmerkungen zur Diskurspraxis des Landessozialgerichts Nordrhein-Westfalen', *Vierteljahrshefte für Zeitgeschichte* 63(1) (2015), 109–18, here 116.
113. 'Erstes Gesetz zur Änderung des Gesetzes zur Zahlbarmachung von Renten aus Beschäftigungen in einem Ghetto vom 15.7.2014', BGBl. I 2014, 952–53.

Bibliography

Alberti, M. *Die Verfolgung und Vernichtung der Juden im Reichsgau Wartheland 1939–1945*. Wiesbaden: Harrassowitz, 2006.
Aly, G., and S. Heim. *Vordenker der Vernichtung. Auschwitz und die deutschen Pläne für eine neue europäische Ordnung*. Hamburg: Hoffmann und Campe, 1991.
Browning, C. 'Jewish Workers in Poland: Self-Maintenance, Exploitation, Destruction', in C. Browning, *Nazi Policy, Jewish Workers, German Killers* (Cambridge: Cambridge University Press, 2000), 58–88.
Browning, C. 'Nazi Ghettoization Policy in Poland 1939–1941', in C. Browning, *The Path to Genocide. Essays on Launching the Final Solution* (Cambridge: Cambridge University Press, 1992), 28–56.

Dieckmann, C. *Deutsche Besatzungspolitik in Litauen 1941–1944*, 2 vols. Göttingen: Wallstein, 2012.
Dieckmann, C. 'Das Ghetto und das Konzentrationslager in Kaunas 1941-1944', in U. Herbert, K. Orth and C. Dieckmann (eds), *Die nationalsozialistischen Konzentrationslager. Entwicklung und Struktur*, vol. 1 (Frankfurt am Main: Suhrkamp, 2002), 439–71.
Dieckmann, C., and B. Quinkert (eds). *Im Ghetto 1939–1945. Neue Forschungen zu Alltag und Umfeld*. Göttingen: Wallstein, 2009.
Faschismus – Getto – Massenmord. Dokumentation über Ausrottung und Widerstand der Juden in Polen während des zweiten Weltkrieges, ed. Jüdisches Historisches Institut Warschau. Frankfurt am Main: Röderberg, 1962.
Generaloberst Halder. Kriegstagebuch. Tägliche Aufzeichnungen des Chefs des Generalstabes des Heeres, 1939–1942, ed. H.-A. Jacobsen in collaboration with A. Philippi, 3 vols. Stuttgart: Kohlhammer, 1962–1964.
Goschler, C. *Schuld und Schulden. Die Politik der Wiedergutmachung für NS-Verfolgte seit 1945*, 2nd ed. Göttingen: Wallstein, 2008.
Goschler, C. 'Wiedergutmachungspolitik – Schulden, Schuld und Entschädigung', in P. Reichel, H. Schmid and P. Steinbach (eds), *Der Nationalsozialismus – Die zweite Geschichte. Überwindung – Deutung – Erinnerung* (Munich: Beck, 2009), 62–84.
Grabitz, H., and W. Scheffler. *Letzte Spuren. Ghetto Warschau, SS-Arbeitslager Trawniki, Aktion Erntefest. Fotos und Dokumente über Opfer des Endlösungswahns im Spiegel der historischen Ereignisse*. Berlin: Edition Hentrich, 1988.
Gruner, W. *Der Geschlossene Arbeitseinsatz deutscher Juden. Zur Zwangsarbeit als Element der Verfolgung 1938–1943*. Berlin: Metropol, 1997.
Gruner, W. *Jewish Forced Labor under the Nazis. Economic Needs and Racial Aims, 1938–1944*, trans. K.M. Dell'Orto. Cambridge: Cambridge University Press, 2006.
Gruner, W. 'Juden bauen die "Strassen des Führers". Zwangsarbeit und Zwangsarbeitslager für nichtdeutsche Juden im Altreich 1940 bis 1943/44'. *Zeitschrift für Geschichtswissenschaft* 44(9) (1996), 789–808.
Hamburger Institut für Sozialforschung (ed.). *Verbrechen der Wehrmacht. Dimensionen des Vernichtungskrieges 1941–1944*. Hamburg: Hamburger Edition, 2004.
Jureit, U. *Das Ordnen von Räumen. Territorium und Lebensraum im 19. und 20. Jahrhundert*. Hamburg: Hamburger Edition, 2012.
Klein, P. *Die 'Ghettoverwaltung Litzmannstadt' 1940 bis 1944. Eine Dienststelle im Spannungsfeld von Kommunalbürokratie und staatlicher Verfolgungspolitik*. Hamburg: Hamburger Edition, 2009.
Konieczny, A. 'Die Zwangsarbeit der Juden in Schlesien im Rahmen der "Organisation Schmelt"', in G. Aly et al., *Sozialpolitik und Judenvernichtung. Gibt es eine Ökonomie der Endlösung?* (Berlin: Rotbuch, 1987), 91–110.
Lehnstaedt, S. 'Die deutsche Arbeitsverwaltung im Generalgouvernement und die Juden'. *Vierteljahrshefte für Zeitgeschichte* 60(3) (2012), 409–40.
Lehnstaedt, S. 'Der Deutungsstreit um die "Ghettorenten". Anmerkungen zur Diskurspraxis des Landessozialgerichts Nordrhein-Westfalen'. *Vierteljahrshefte für Zeitgeschichte* 63(1) (2015), 109–18.
Lehnstaedt, S. *Geschichte und Gesetzesauslegung. Kontinuität und Wandel des bundesdeutschen Wiedergutmachungsdiskurses am Beispiel der Ghettorenten*. Osnabrück: Fibre, 2011.
Lehnstaedt, S. 'Wiedergutmachung im 21. Jahrhundert. Das Arbeitsministerium und die Ghettorenten'. *Vierteljahrshefte für Zeitgeschichte* 61(3) (2013), 363–90.
Leiserowitz R. 'Litauen. Arbeit und Arbeitssituation in den Ghettos', in J. Hensel and S. Lehnstaedt (eds), *Arbeit in den nationalsozialistischen Ghettos* (Osnabrück: Fibre, 2013), 209–31.

Linne, K. 'Die deutsche Arbeitsverwaltung zwischen "Volkstumspolitik" und Arbeiterrekrutierung – das Beispiel Warthegau', in F. Dierl, Z. Janjetovič and K. Linne, *Pflicht, Zwang und Gewalt. Arbeitsverwaltungen und Arbeitskräftepolitik im deutsch besetzten Polen und Serbien 1939–1944* (Essen: Klartext, 2013), 47–170.

Linne, K. '"Sklavenjagden" im Arbeiterreservoir – das Beispiel Generalgouvernement', in F. Dierl, Z. Janjetovič and K. Linne, *Pflicht, Zwang und Gewalt. Arbeitsverwaltungen und Arbeitskräftepolitik im deutsch besetzten Polen und Serbien 1939–1944* (Essen: Klartext, 2013), 171–316.

Longerich, P. *Die Ermordung der europäischen Juden. Eine umfassende Dokumentation des Holocaust 1941–1945.* Munich: Piper, 1989.

Longerich, P. *Politik der Vernichtung. Eine Gesamtdarstellung der nationalsozialistischen Judenverfolgung.* Munich: Piper, 1998.

Löw, A. 'Arbeit in den Ghettos: Rettung oder temporärer Vernichtungsaufschub?', in M. Buggeln and M. Wildt (eds), *Arbeit im Nationalsozialismus* (Munich: De Gruyter Oldenbourg, 2014), 293–308.

Löw, A. *Juden im Getto Litzmannstadt. Lebensbedingungen, Selbstwahrnehmungen, Verhalten.* Göttingen: Wallstein, 2006.

Löw, A., and M. Roth. *Juden in Krakau unter deutscher Besatzung 1939–1945.* Göttingen: Wallstein, 2012.

Maier, D. *Arbeitseinsatz und Deportation. Die Mitwirkung der Arbeitsverwaltung bei der nationalsozialistischen Judenverfolgung in den Jahren 1938–1945.* Berlin: Hentrich, 1994.

Maier, D.G. *Anfänge und Brüche der Arbeitsverwaltung bis 1952. Zugleich ein kaum bekanntes Kapitel der deutsch-jüdischen Geschichte.* Brühl: Fachhochschule des Bundes für Öffentliche Verwaltung, 2004.

Młynarczyk, J.A. 'Mordinitiativen von unten. Die Rolle Arthur Greisers und Odilo Globocniks im Entscheidungsprozess zum Judenmord', in J.A. Młynarczyk and J. Böhler (eds), *Der Judenmord in den eingegliederten polnischen Gebieten 1939–1945* (Osnabrück: Fibre, 2010), 27–56.

Musial, B. *Deutsche Zivilverwaltung und Judenverfolgung im Generalgouvernement. Eine Fallstudie zum Distrikt Lublin 1939–1944.* Wiesbaden: Harrassowitz, 1999.

Plath, T. *Zwischen Schonung und Menschenjagden. Die Arbeitseinsatzpolitik in den baltischen Generalbezirken des Reichskommissariats Ostland 1941–1944.* Essen: Klartext, 2012.

Platt, K. *Bezweifelte Erinnerung, verweigerte Glaubwürdigkeit. Überlebende des Holocaust in den Ghettorenten-Verfahren.* Paderborn: Fink, 2012.

Pohl, D. 'Ghettos', in W. Benz and B. Distel (eds), *Der Ort des Terrors. Geschichte der nationalsozialistischen Konzentrationslager*, vol. 9: *Arbeitserziehungslager, Ghettos, Jugendschutzlager, Polizeihaftlager, Sonderlager, Zigeunerlager, Zwangsarbeiterlager* (Munich: Beck, 2009), 161–91.

Pohl, D. *Von der 'Judenpolitik' zum Judenmord. Der Distrikt Lublin des Generalgouvernements 1939–1944.* Frankfurt am Main: Lang, 1993.

Renesse, J.-R. v. 'Wiedergutmachung fünf vor zwölf. Das "Gesetz zur Zahlbarmachung von Renten aus Beschäftigungen in einem Ghetto"', in J. Zarusky (ed.), *Ghettorenten. Entschädigungspolitik, Rechtsprechung und historische Forschung* (Munich: Oldenbourg, 2010), 13–37.

Schlemmer, T. 'Grenzen der Integration. Die CSU und der Umgang mit der nationalsozialistischen Vergangenheit – der Fall Dr. Max Frauendorfer'. *Vierteljahrshefte für Zeitgeschichte* 48(4) (2000), 675–742.

Steinbacher, S. *'Musterstadt' Auschwitz. Germanisierungspolitik und Judenmord in Ostoberschlesien.* Munich: K.G. Saur, 2000.

Die Tagebücher von Joseph Goebbels. Sämtliche Fragmente, part 1: *Aufzeichnungen 1924–1941*, ed. E. Fröhlich. Munich: Saur, 1987.

Tauber, J. *Arbeit als Hoffnung. Jüdische Ghettos in Litauen 1941–1944*. Berlin: de Gruyter Oldenbourg, 2015.

Trial of the Major War Criminals before the International Military Tribunal, Nuremberg 14 November 1945–1 October 1946, 42 vols. Nuremberg: International Military Tribunal Nuremberg, 1947–1949.

'*Unser einziger Weg ist Arbeit*'. *Das Getto in Łódź 1940–1944, eine Ausstellung des Jüdischen Museums Frankfurt am Main, 30. März bis 10. Juni 1990*, ed. H. Loewy and G. Schoenberner. Frankfurt am Main: Löcker, 1990.

Die Verfolgung und Ermordung der europäischen Juden durch das nationalsozialistische Deutschland 1933–1945, ed. on behalf of Bundesarchiv, Institut für Zeitgeschichte and Lehrstuhl für Neuere und Neueste Geschichte an der Albert-Ludwigs-Universität Freiburg by S. Heim et al., vol. 4: *Polen, September 1939–Juli 1941*, ed. K.-P. Friedrich in collaboration with A. Löw. Munich: Oldenbourg, 2011.

Wenzel, M. 'Die Arbeitslager für Juden im Distrikt Krakau des Generalgouvernement 1940–1941', in D. Pohl and T. Sebta (eds), *Zwangsarbeit in Hitlers Europa. Besatzung, Arbeit, Folgen* (Berlin: Metropol, 2013), 173–94.

Witte, P. 'Zwei Entscheidungen in der "Endlösung der Judenfrage": Deportationen nach Lodz und Vernichtung in Chelmno', in M. Kárný, R. Kemper and M. Kárná, (eds), *Theresienstädter Studien und Dokumente 1995* (Prague: Academia, 1995), 38–68.

Ziółkowska, A. 'Zwangsarbeitslager für Juden im Reichsgau Wartheland', in J.A. Młynarczyk and J. Böhler (eds), *Der Judenmord in den eingegliederten polnischen Gebieten 1939–1945* (Osnabrück: Fibre, 2010), 179–202.

PART IV

THE MINISTRY AFTER 1945

Chapter 12

A VANISHING ACT
The Reich Ministry of Labour and the Nuremberg Trials, 1945–1949

Kim Christian Priemel

Two years after the end of the Second World War, in May 1947, the ministerial counsellor sat down at the table in his prison cell, directly adjacent to the Nuremberg Palace of Justice, and began to write. Walter Letsch, born in 1895, a Ph.D. economist, had worked in the German labour administration for many years, and had most recently been responsible for the recruitment and allocation of Eastern European workers. He wanted to compile an activity report, a genre that, with its peculiar fusion of apologetics and expertise, was just what he needed. Entitled 'The Reich Ministry of Labour, the General Plenipotentiary for Labour Deployment, and the Deployment of Foreigners during the Second World War' (*Das Reichsarbeitsministerium und der Generalbevollmächtigte für den Arbeitseinsatz beim Ausländereinsatz im Zweiten Weltkrieg*), his report sought to meet at least two objectives at the same time. It aimed both to provide the American prosecutors with the insights they had requested into the labyrinthine German administrative system and to downplay Letsch's own role in the forced labour deployment of millions of people during the Second World War. To this end, the ministerial counsellor ranged far back in time, making historical connections with the traditional labour migration into Germany since the nineteenth century, before going on to bring order to the 'Third Reich's' administrative structures in a detailed and expert account. Department by department, he went through the entire ministry, briefly describing the senior staff, including General Plenipotentiary for Labour Deployment (GBA) Fritz Sauckel. In particular, Letsch underlined the increased pressure on the labour administration, even before the war had begun, to meet the demands of the Greater German war economy, emanating from the private sector as well as the constantly expanding apparatus of the Reich Ministry for Armaments and War Production. The report painted the ministry as having been pushed and pulled, and ground down, by its more powerful rival institutions as it strove to maintain orderly administrative processes.[1]

Letsch was not the only official at the former Reich Ministry of Labour to put pen to paper in 1947 in an attempt to explain the policies of his institutional home and to explain himself. In September 1947, his colleague Walter Stothfang, born in 1902, another Ph.D. economist and until recently ministerial counsellor at the Reich Ministry of Labour, as well as personal adviser to Sauckel, wrote a detailed memorandum for the Nuremberg prosecutors. Here he portrayed the recruitment of foreign workers for the German war economy in great detail, neatly broken down according to time period, country, occupational status and responsibilities. Stothfang's report was noticeably similar to Letsch's. Here too, the Reich Ministry of Labour, particularly those of its departments assigned to the GBA, appeared as a voice of reason vis-à-vis the radical demands of the SS and the Nazi Party as well as employers' self-interest.[2]

By this point, Letsch and Stothfang had had the time and opportunity to consider strategies of self-justification. As high-ranking ministerial officials as well as Nazi Party members, in May 1945 they were subject to automatic arrest. Following stopovers in a number of internment camps, they were finally imprisoned in Nuremberg. There they met not only their old bosses, namely Sauckel and Reich Labour Minister Franz Seldte, but also a number of colleagues, including Hubert Hildebrandt,[3] Letsch's equivalent for Western Europe, and their superior, the head of Main Section VI (Labour Deployment), Max Timm.[4] In the shape of Wilhelm Kimmich[5] (Main Section III: Labour Law, Wages and Social Policy) and Wilhelm Börger (Main Section I: Budget), two more main section heads had also been summoned. Between the late summer of 1946 and the spring of 1947, then, a small but illustrious group of former ministry officials came together in Nuremberg. Their fate, for the time being, was clear neither to them nor their interrogators. For several months, it was by no means a foregone conclusion whether they had been detained as witnesses or as potential defendants. Timm, Hildebrandt and Stothfang, for example, had been brought to the International Military Tribunal (IMT) in 1946 in order to testify on behalf of Sauckel.[6] The tendency for witnesses before the four-power tribunal to turn rapidly into defendants in subsequent trials before the Nuernberg Military Tribunals (NMT), however, can hardly have escaped the notice of the half-dozen Reich Labour Ministry officials. In the first three

NMT trials, Reich Commissioner for Military and Civilian Health Services Karl Brandt, along with state secretaries Erhard Milch and Franz Schlegelberger, had already found themselves in the dock.[7]

Hence, for more than a year, between autumn 1946 and autumn 1947, Letsch, Stothfang and their colleagues found themselves in a state of constant uncertainty, in Nuremberg limbo, so to speak. It was only with the beginning of the so-called Wilhelmstrasse trial, the last to be concerned with the ministerial administration of the 'Third Reich', with the filing of the indictment taking place in November 1947, that the former labour administrators could breathe a sigh of relief. However, if they had followed the American prosecutors' previous questioning strategies attentively, they might already have concluded that the Labour Ministry group would be seeing the inside of the courtroom solely from the witness box. These career civil servants themselves made a tangible contribution to this outcome by giving the prosecutors what they wanted, namely information on forced labour deployment and the agencies involved. They withheld almost as much, however, namely all those facts that risked incriminating them. The image of the Reich Ministry of Labour as a conservatively led but weak authority is in large part down to these strategies of interrogation and response.

Labour Policy on Trial

The plan to pursue retribution for the Axis Powers' war crimes by legal means had crystallized during the second half of the war, but the final decision to do so was made at a late stage. Since the Moscow Declaration of 1943, the Big Three's declaration of intent to this effect had been on record. Behind the scenes, it was above all the US and Soviet lawyers who paved the way for a juridical approach to the punishment of German war criminals. In the summer of 1945, the Allied delegations – now four in number, since France had been incorporated into the ranks of the victorious powers – came together in London to elaborate the legal and organizational prerequisites for an international series of criminal trials. Through the London Agreement and the Charter of 8 August 1945, the International Military Tribunal was established. The rapidly promulgated Allied Control Council Law No. 10, of 20 December 1945, which was similar in substance but differed in certain key paragraphs, was to serve as the legal foundation for the later trials.[8]

That forced labour would play a key role in the proceedings before the IMT had become apparent in advance. Certainly, the early reports on war crimes had focused chiefly on the classic atrocities, such as mass shootings and the crimes committed in the German concentration camps (with the murder of the European Jewry quickly coming to the fore). Among the leading jurists, however, there was little doubt that the forced labour programme was also justiciable under international criminal law.[9] The relevance of the forced labour complex was plainly apparent in view of the millions of individuals affected, a picture that soon emerged thanks to studies such as the one produced by the International Labour Organization and read by the Nuremberg prosecutors.[10] Certain premises dear to the Allies as well as the governments of formerly occupied countries also played a role. States in both Western and Eastern Europe were unwilling to see the deportation of their citizens go unpunished, not least because prosecution was bound up with hopes of reparation payments.[11] Last but not least, forced labour offered the advantage of extending the spotlight to non-Jewish groups of victims – a prospect that allayed the concerns of the British and Americans and satisfied the Soviet delegation, which tended to incorporate the Jews into broad categories such as 'victims of fascism'.[12]

The sheer number of victims already made it seem obvious that slave labour, as the forced labour programme was soon officially being called, must be presented as a key offence. The concept also suited those lawyers arguing that it was vital to lay down a foundation of materially substantiated and legally uncontested charges in order to offset the more innovative and thus more risky allegations such as conspiracy and crimes against peace. An associate of the American chief prosecutor, Robert H. Jackson, advised that overwhelming evidentiary material was necessary so that 'neither the public of today nor the historian of tomorrow will say that the defendants were not guilty or not proven guilty'.[13] Forced labour promised to provide just such material, and in ample quantities.

At the same time, the focus on labour policy measures forged valuable links between different issues. For example, the German Labour Front had not only been responsible for failing to provide for the needs of foreign workers (*Fremdarbeiter*, in racially loaded Nazi parlance) during the war, but it had also – in the prosecutors' reading, which was informed by a literal conspiracy theory – played a crucial role in the establishment of the Nazi dictatorship as well as helping prepare for war. The dissolution of the trades unions, their expropriation and replacement by the DAF[14] figured in a narrative that interpreted the exclusion of domestic political opponents as the first step towards international aggression. Likewise, the DAF, alongside Joseph Goebbels' apparatus, Baldur von Schirach's Hitler Youth and Julius Streicher's inflammatory weekly newspaper *Der Stürmer*, appeared as a significant actor in the psychological and propagandistic mobilization of the German people for war in the 1930s. In the words of the lawyer responsible for this issue in Jackson's team, Drexel Sprecher, the DAF had served to 'impose their ideology on the masses, to frustrate potential resistance, and to insure [sic] effective control of the productive labor capacity of Germany'.[15]

Sprecher, a young lawyer keen to play his part in what was likely to be the biggest criminal trial of the twentieth century, often got carried away by his enthusiasm and overestimated the credibility of the evidence. Nonetheless, he was by no means alone in believing that the prosecution could effectively portray the war of aggression that Jackson had placed at the heart of the US strategy only by showing that it entailed a substantial economic aspect. One influential adviser to Jackson, Charles Horsky, held very similar views. But he warned that economic factors were tremendously complex and difficult to integrate straightforwardly into the prosecution narrative. Nonetheless, he asserted, the case for the prosecution must aim to demonstrate the complicity of those governmental representatives whose involvement was not obvious at first sight, 'such as Schacht (Finance), von Krosick [sic] (Finance), Seldte (Labor), Funk (Reichsbank). . . . It should not be complex, however; all it needs do is to demonstrate that which is probably obvious – that war requires that the economic life of the state be mobilized; that it was done; who did it; and, in general, how'.[16]

Who, then, ought to stand trial for economic offences and in particular for the organization of forced labour? Selecting the defendants was one of the notorious weaknesses in the process of preparing for trial, because in London – due to divergences of principle and differing interpretations of legal theory – the Allies had agreed on a rather incoherent approach, putting their faith in the idea that certain prominent individuals were 'obvious' candidates.[17] With respect to the 'Economic Case', Jackson had assigned his colleague Francis Shea to identify possible candidates. The ten names on the resulting list included widely if not universally acceptable figures like Hjalmar Schacht and Walter Funk, both Reichsbank presidents and economy ministers, along with Armaments Minister Albert Speer and GBA Fritz Sauckel. More surprising and by no means uncontroversial – with criticism coming chiefly from the British, who were sceptical about prosecuting industrialists but also Schacht – was the listing of Gustav Krupp von Bohlen und Halbach. He was to be charged both with paving the way for war by producing arms and with deploying tens of thousands of forced labourers. Conversely, the Allies unanimously agreed to include Robert Ley. As head of the DAF, vociferous propagandist and prominent supporter of Hitler, he virtually thrust himself forward as a candidate. In fact, Ley had appeared on the lists of possible defendants circulating since 1944, as had Sauckel, whose image as the 'slave driver' of the 'Third Reich' appears to have been cemented long before the trials began.[18]

The same did not go for Franz Seldte. Certainly, as a member of the Cabinet, the Reich labour minister also appeared on a variety of shortlists, though not on the decisive ones.[19] His name cropped up neither on the more restrictive British rosters nor among the ten 'economic defendants' identified in Shea's memorandum. Even the more detailed lists drawn up in the summer of 1945 by, among others, Franz Neumann and Carl Schorske, to which numerous figures from the private sector and the civil service had been added, failed to include Seldte. His name was apparently not even mentioned at the London conference,[20] and the first interrogation transcripts categorized the minister as a mere also-ran. Seldte, to quote Albert Speer, had 'no authority as labour minister and shunned his work'.[21] Little surprise, then, given mundane limitations such as the length of the dock (which could hold no more than twenty-four individuals), that Seldte simply fell through the cracks. In the shape of Sauckel and Speer (along with Göring, Keitel and a number of others), political decisions and the organization of forced labour were already covered sufficiently; when it came to the practice of forced labour, Ley and above all Krupp stood *pars pro toto*. There was no room left for figures such as Seldte, and the same applied to Reich Finance Minister Lutz Graf Schwerin von Krosigk and Reich Transport Minister Julius Dorpmüller, all three of them identified by a well-informed (and much-read) observer such as Sebastian Haffner as loyal partners of the Nazi leadership but not members of its inner circle.[22]

Forced Labour Policy before the International Military Tribunal

Whether or not the plan to deal with the forced labour complex by prosecuting the quartet of Sauckel, Speer, Ley and Krupp was a good one, it was certainly ill-starred. Ley hanged himself in his cell before the first day of the trial, having already clearly gone 'nuts' in the preceding weeks, as one prosecutor crudely put it.[23] Things went no better in the case of Gustav Krupp, whose lawyer successfully argued that his client was unfit to stand trial, much to the chagrin of Jackson, who thus lost the only industrialist among the accused and whose request for Krupp to be replaced by his son Alfried was indignantly rejected by the judges.[24] With respect to forced labour, the now truncated charge focused chiefly on the two remaining men whose periods in office largely coincided with the quantitative and qualitative escalation of the 'deployment of foreign workers' and the use of coercion, as the final remnants of workers' freedom had been swept away – a shift noted by Sauckel's lawyer Robert Servatius.[25]

The presentation of the forced labour charges before the IMT was mainly the responsibility of the French and Soviet delegations. Consonant with the division of labour among the Allies, they dedicated themselves to crimes against humanity and war crimes in Western and Eastern Europe respectively. For the French team, the Service du Travail Obligatoire (Compulsory Labour Service) played a central role, around 650,000 French citizens having been conveyed into the German Reich and put to work – mostly against their will – through this scheme. Furthermore, for a lengthy period, French prisoners of war had made up one of the largest groups of foreign workers, before either being given civilian status or, through a kind of exchange, repatriated in return for civilians brought to Germany.[26] The largest single group of forced labourers, however, had come from the occupied Soviet Union. German civilian and military authorities had brought more than 4.7 million individuals (including just under two million prisoners of war), in the vast majority of cases against their will, into the Reich and other occupied territories. There they had literally performed frontline service, working, for example, for the Todt Organization, often under dreadful living and working conditions, with terrible consequences for their health, including high mortality rates, particularly among members of the Red Army.[27]

As a result, this topic figured prominently on the Soviet agenda, not least because forced labour could be presented as part of the Nazi regime's racist policy of establishing a 'new order'. This was consonant with parts of the American case. Influenced by Raphaël Lemkin's broad concept of genocide, slave labour was interpreted as both end and means of the Nazi war of aggression and the regime's efforts to achieve hegemony in Europe. 'The use of vast numbers of foreign workers, most of whom were impressed as slaves', to quote the prosecuting lawyers, 'was planned before Germany went to war and was an integral part of the conspiracy for waging aggressive war'. On this view, the goal had been 'the strengthening of the Nazi war machine by supplying the manpower required for German war production' and 'the depopulation and impoverishment of the rest of Europe, the destruction of people deemed inferior by the Nazis and the permanent weakening of potential enemies'. Forced labour thus appeared as an integral component of the Nazi war of aggression and 'racial war'.[28] While the US prosecution team submitted the entire ILO study as evidence and provided a broad outline of German plans, the Soviet delegation shed light on the practice of forced labour. In great detail it sought to demonstrate deliberate underprovision, abuse and their deadly consequences, aiming to dispel any doubts as to the fundamental differences from classic labour migration.[29]

Given the dimensions of the crimes involved, many of the prosecutors regarded the convictions of Sauckel and Speer as certain, and death sentences as virtually inevitable. As the trial progressed, however, the two defendants' paths diverged rapidly and fundamentally. Even before the filing of the indictment, both had understood that their best prospect of survival lay in imputing to the other the lion's share of responsibility for the radicalized forced labour policy during the second half of the war. In interviews during his brief period of detention in Flensburg, Speer had already given the distinct impression that a possible war crimes trial would inevitably have to include Sauckel. At pains to distinguish his own activities (in terms of both habitus and content), first as an architect and artist from a bourgeois background, then as organizer and technocrat, from the doings of the Nazi Party's petit bourgeois upper echelons, it was above all Sauckel whom Speer successfully depicted as his negative analogue. The GBA had had a rather rudimentary education, came across as unsophisticated, and made it rather easy for Speer: he still sported his Hitler moustache and was handicapped by his former title of Gauleiter, a category of official generally held to have been an ardent Nazi as well as brutal and corrupt. He was thus the ideal foil for Speer as he sought to show himself in a more favourable light, while simultaneously foisting the main burden of responsibility for forced labour deployment onto his former colleague.[30]

In several debriefings and in memoranda composed in the summer of 1945 for the Allied interrogators, Speer – displaying the superficial contrition that would come to be typical of his defence strategy – blamed himself for Sauckel's appointment. After all, he himself had proposed Sauckel's appointment in order to place German labour deployment policy in firmer hands than those of Seldte. But after a promising start, Speer contended, Sauckel had proved 'disloyal and unreliable', and in fact 'often truly spiteful', doing everything he could to thwart Speer's objective of the more rational use of manpower resources. Sauckel had, Speer claimed, consistently refused to submit to the authority of Speer's Armaments Ministry and the Central Planning organization, an interministerial steering body and the clearinghouse that calculated and allocated economic resources during the second half of the war. Speer's only concession was to acknowledge Sauckel's efforts to improve the treatment of foreign workers, though not without pointing out that the expansion of forced recruitment had itself undermined these efforts.[31]

Whatever his intellectual limitations, the threat represented by Speer's adroit performance and eloquent self-historicization did not escape Sauckel's notice. Speer, a former confidant of Hitler, was attempting 'to play the great innocent with respect to Fremdarbeiter', Sauckel informed Servatius. He sent the latter a series of notes in which he consistently emphasized that, in his role as GBA, he had been subordinate to Speer and had always complied with his – increasingly prodigious – demands. It was, he stated, simply untrue that Speer had not been informed of the magnitude and circumstances of forced labour deployment.³² Servatius and his colleague, Hans Flächsner, who was representing Speer, tried to avoid a direct confrontation in court, which could only damage both defendants.³³ But this did not solve Sauckel's fundamental dilemma: the textbook Nazi came off poorly in direct comparison with the former armaments minister, who was generally perceived as the only thoughtful and, at least in the view of some, remorseful defendant.

Sauckel's attempts to make a candid and cooperative impression on the Allied officers and jurists who repeatedly interrogated him in 1945 and 1946 came off as pitiful. His demeanour at hearings – in September 1945, before the filing of the indictment, he was interrogated on a daily basis – and the tone of his written testimony were obsequious, while his factual testimony sought to make a virtue of his lack of sophistication. Sauckel portrayed himself as a simple man. Endowed with negligible social and cultural capital, he had always been concerned for the well-being of the working population – regardless of nationality or background – and had never failed to do his patriotic duty. In retrospect, he could not rule out having made mistakes. Like many others, he had been taken in by Nazi propaganda (rather than having spread it himself, as the prosecution claimed). Given the regime's crimes, which had now come to light and were news to him, he sincerely regretted having been fooled in this way, a sentiment he sought to convey time and again. 'I regret from the bottom of my heart', he insisted, 'having become and having been a Nazi'.³⁴

Sauckel presented himself unambiguously as impelled by external pressures. There was nothing he could have done to evade Hitler's or Speer's demands, even when he had considered them wrong or counterproductive. He claimed to have urged the regime to fall back on women workers, but he had been rebuffed by Speer (who, at around the same time, was putting forward the same argument to his interrogators, but with the roles reversed). 'Those were fearful days for me', the Gauleiter and general plenipotentiary assured his interrogator, highlighting that Speer had enjoyed the support not just of Hitler but of Goebbels and Himmler as well.³⁵ Whether with respect to the actions of the security police or increasing food rations, then, most of his efforts to maintain voluntary recruitment and better the lot of 'foreign workers' had been opposed by rival or superior offices.³⁶ At the end of the day, Sauckel contended, his situation was captured perfectly by a dictum that had done the rounds during the war: 'The devil takes the hindmost, and that's Sauckel'.³⁷

The hearings, however, did not go as Sauckel had hoped. Initially, Major John J. Monigan, who carried out all the interrogations in September and October 1945, had allowed the prisoner to speak freely – rather as in an undirected biographical interview – but the dialogue increasingly turned into an interrogation. Monigan confronted Sauckel with statements and documents, some of which glaringly contradicted the GBA's assertions. Particularly when the hearing touched on the murder of the European Jewry and evidence came to light that incriminated Sauckel, he responded with outright panic. He was clearly well aware that any proximity to the Holocaust or the system of concentration camps would take him one step closer to the gallows. His response, that it was a mystery to him how his signature had got onto pertinent documents, was scarcely apt to exonerate a functionary who had held so many important offices.[38] Sauckel's inability to prepare himself for such accusations or react with a modicum of spontaneity was also to prove detrimental to his cause during his trial. Under cross-examination by the French and Soviet prosecutors, Sauckel lurched from one disaster to the next, stammering and entangling himself in contradictions. Finally, in a fine demonstration of a piercing interrogation, the American judge stripped him of the last shreds of credibility. When Sauckel left the witness stand, few observers were in any doubt about his likely fate.[39]

Whatever hopes remained to the GBA and his lawyer, they inevitably centred on his former colleague Speer, because Sauckel had sought refuge in an interesting argument. On a number of occasions in the course of his interrogations, the GBA – though his office had been the prototype of the plenipotentiary so widespread in the 'Third Reich'[40] – explained that he had by no means shut out the Reich Ministry of Labour. In fact, he asserted, he had cooperated very closely with its officials. Unlike Speer, who had been dissatisfied with the ponderous processes of the ministerial bureaucracy, he had been impressed by the members of staff placed under his authority and had rarely clashed with them:

> He [Speer] had expected me to have nothing to do with the Labour Ministry and to work with him alone. I couldn't do that out of conviction, because I found a number of highly qualified officials in the Labour Ministry who were not out-of-touch office workers; in fact, some of the most capable were from the business world. I shared my thoughts with these people, and we established that we had the same view of things and as a result I worked together a great deal with these gentlemen.[41]

For Timm, Hildebrandt and Stothfang, called to the witness stand by Servatius in late May and early June 1946, this line of defence forced them to perform a balancing act. On the one hand, the priority was to confirm Sauckel's argument that the office of the GBA – in which, after all, they themselves had worked – had pursued a sensible and constructive policy of voluntary labour recruitment and of partnership with the collaboration governments, but had constantly been overruled by other agencies. On the other hand, it was vital to draw a line between the personnel taken over from the Reich Ministry of Labour and Sauckel's own inner circle. Timm thus characterized the GBA as a strongman who was supposed to bring order to the chaos of the German labour administration – 'a very energetic, hard-working man, who was inclined to get excited at times, even angry no doubt, and who demanded much of his co-workers, but also made great demands on himself' – and had counted on the long-time associates he had brought with him from the Thuringian Gau administration. On the other hand, he and his colleagues confirmed that they were subordinate to Speer's armaments administration and highlighted the enduring conflicts with the SS and DAF when it came to the treatment and provisioning of 'foreign workers'.[42]

It was plainly apparent from the statements of the three ministerial officials – Servatius had submitted a request to interrogate other members of staff from the Reich Labour Ministry and the GBA, but due to redundancy he had had to accept the removal of several names from his list of witnesses[43] – that they were less interested in exonerating their former superior than in making their own involvement in the forced labour programme appear as harmless as possible, if not benign. The information they provided thus did little to help Servatius as he sought to save his client from a death sentence. When the eight Allied judges convened in the late summer of 1946 to discuss judgements and sentences, they regarded the GBA as a straightforward case. Along with Hans Frank, Wilhelm Frick, Hermann Göring, Alfred Jodl, Ernst Kaltenbrunner, Wilhelm Keitel, Alfred Rosenberg, Arthur Seyss-Inquart and Julius Streicher, they unanimously sentenced him to death. Speer, meanwhile, despite being comparably implicated, evaded the gallows, receiving a twenty-year prison sentence, much to the chagrin of some of the prosecutors, who considered the armaments minister no less guilty than the plenipotentiary.[44] While Sauckel's punishment was carried out two weeks after the end of the proceedings, Speer remained in the Nuremberg prison as a witness in other trials. The same went for Sauckel's former subordinates, who were detained in the Nuremberg witnesses' wing for many more months.

From the Dock to the Witness Stand: The Investigations for the Nuernberg Military Tribunals

It was clear from late 1945 that the proceedings before the Four-Power Tribunal would not spell the end of the legal reckoning with the Nazi state. In parallel to the Nuremberg trials, the Allied powers had initiated investigations and commenced initial proceedings against alleged war criminals in their zones of occupation, mostly applying their respective national military laws.⁴⁵ The number of cases tried in Nuremberg in accordance with Control Council Law No. 10, meanwhile, was far smaller, and only these – twelve trials under the aegis of the Americans and one carried out by the French – built directly on the IMT.⁴⁶ In the case of the Nuernberg Military Tribunals, this was plainly apparent, given that they were held at the Palace of Justice and some of the personnel were identical. Certainly, most of the American prosecutors and all the judges returned home in 1946, but a small core group around Jackson's staff members Telford Taylor and Drexel Sprecher remained. Also significant was the continuity among the counsels for the defence – more than two-thirds of them accepted briefs at the NMT – and among defendants and witnesses.⁴⁷

The prosecution's plans initially focused on the economic field, since here the absence of Ley and Krupp had torn major holes in the case before the IMT. Taylor, moreover, had already warned in 1945 of the need to consider a greater number of (private sector) economic actors. A number of other candidates had positively thrust themselves forward in their witness statements. Emil Puhl, Reichsbank vice-president and member of its board of directors, had implicated his boss Walter Funk and himself in the robbing of concentration camp victims. Erhard Milch, a functionary with a wide-ranging remit, appeared to be partly responsible for the military build-up, forced labour, and experiments on human beings. In the late summer and autumn of 1946, out of the legal lacunae, open questions and those cases left unresolved at the IMT – including that of the Wehrmacht generals – Taylor and his staff put together an initial programme envisaging four categories of trials. These were focused on the (private) economy, the military, the SS and the ministerial administration. Which specific cases ought to be brought to trial, however, was far less clear. Particularly with respect to the ministries, the first priority was to sift the available source materials and establish what the strongest charges might be. For several months it remained an open question whether complexes of crimes – such as those against prisoners of war or forced labour⁴⁸ – or individual groups of perpetrators ought to structure the series of trials. In the autumn, Sprecher thus opted to initiate proceedings on forced labour. This case, he underlined, should be pursued separately from the trials of industrialists. It could document 'far more bestiality than even Case 1 [the doctors' trial]' and it would put, among others, Timm, Kimmich and Hildebrandt in the dock.⁴⁹ It was clear, however, that even a detailed programme of twenty or more trials, which is what Taylor originally had in mind, could not encompass all the ministries and supreme Reich authorities.⁵⁰

Over the summer of 1946, in the Office of the Chief of Council for War Crimes (OCCWC), Taylor's staff began to trawl through the vast quantity of material that had been amassed in the various collecting points.

Many but by no means all files had ended up in Allied hands after the war. Some were kept under lock and key by the Soviet authorities while others' whereabouts were simply unknown due to the war's chaotic denouement. One of the first questions put to Franz Seldte in the autumn of 1946, therefore, was where the records of the Reich Ministry of Labour might be – information that the former minister, as so often, was unable to provide.[51] Nonetheless, this question was an indication that Seldte – who had not even been questioned as a witness before the International Military Tribunal – and thus the complex consisting of the Reich Ministry of Labour and the GBA, had now made it onto the American agenda. In September, the Berlin branch of Taylor's team set about sifting through the files of the Berlin-based authorities amassed at Tempelhof Airport, in search of relevant documents, particularly those relating to the Reich ministries. Yet on the list of those agencies about which the first dossiers were compiled – on the Foreign Office, Occupied Eastern Territories, Education, Finances, Interior Affairs, Justice, Propaganda, Armaments, Four-Year Plan and Economy – the Labour Ministry was conspicuous only by its absence.[52] This was due to the still missing files: at the same time, in Nuremberg interrogations began of those officials from the authority who had already been summoned to the IMT proceedings, while other members of ministry staff and those employed by the GBA had also been subpoenaed to give evidence. Seldte himself now became the object of the investigations, though the prosecutors were clearly in little doubt that he had played an essentially marginal role in formulating the ministry's policies. But Taylor's colleagues were taking their lead from a theoretical handout, circulating within the OCCWC, that privileged an 'institutional approach'. This prioritized the thorough investigation of organizations as such and only then envisaged attempts to determine the responsibilities of individual members of staff. According to this approach,

> the agency [was] subject to prosecution, thus including several defendants who may easily be joined, rather than simply attacking the one who happened to hold the highest post when the war ended, and who is no more criminal than his predecessors in office or those who formulated the details. Criminality may depend not upon the individual's conduct, but upon his position in the agency whose role in world affairs was criminal, and the picture of the agency may have more significance than an attack primarily aimed against the individual.[53]

Within such a procedural approach Seldte was guaranteed a place in the dock, and the American interrogators did their best to pin down the former minister. The interrogations carried out in 1946, however, did little to further this end. First, Seldte pointed out that his remit had constantly been curtailed by Sauckel, Speer and Ley, and that his ministry had not been responsible for the policy of forced labour so central to the prosecution case. Second, he proved remarkably ignorant about what was going on not just in the Nazi state but in his own ministry. Seldte, given to frequent bouts of blabbering, served up one bromide after the other. He could recall neither names nor circumstances, and he conveyed the impression of having spent twelve years in his office reading the newspaper – if that. He praised his state secretaries, who had done a wonderful job ('Syrup is the best in the business for labour issues and [Hans] Engel is the best social policy expert')[54] and portrayed himself as a mild-mannered leader from a bourgeois background, a man with a business education who had certainly been 'very national[ist] . . . but tolerant'. This attitude had not made things easy for him and he had been isolated within the regime. 'You have to bear in mind', he explained to his interrogator, that 'I always had to struggle. I hadn't a friend in the world. . . . I was shackled. I was spied on and kept under close watch'.[55]

Such responses, unsurprisingly, left his questioners 'less than satisfied', not least because they caught Seldte out more than once in inconsistencies and found documents demonstrating his involvement in the deployment of forced labour prior to March 1942, the date of Sauckel's appointment.[56] Yet even after viewing such documents, Seldte claimed to remember nothing, contending that his state secretaries had likely signed on his behalf. Moreover, he testified that he had had virtually no contact with leading business representatives – 'perhaps not much, because otherwise I would be able to remember. The president of the Shopkeepers' Association (Kleinhändlerverband) often came to see me and I also remember the Allotment Holders' Association (Kleingärtnerverband)'.[57]

Such statements left the American investigators nonplussed. Yet they found themselves facing the problem that multiple witnesses – whether intentionally or not – confirmed Seldte's self-portrait. One leading figure in the steel industry, for example, responded curtly to the question of whether he had ever visited the minister: 'Me? Not once! He wasn't important enough'.[58] Seldte's own colleagues described him as a blend of incompetent and lazy, but also portrayed him as a marginal figure within the regime and ultimately harmless. 'On a personal level, he was not a malicious man', Letsch recalled, adding that 'he was good-natured. He was a decent character'.[59] Kimmich stated that his boss had been 'extraordinarily weak in party political terms' and had been 'outdone by every Gauleiter'.[60] Schacht confirmed that Johannes Krohn had been the 'real manager within the Reich Ministry of Labour' and had effectively led the institution, together with Syrup. Even Constantin Hierl, Seldte's old rival for authority over the Reich Labour Service and not necessarily well-disposed to the minister, had little to say of a negative nature. He was unable even to describe

Seldte as a convinced Nazi or antisemite, a point on which he was backed up by a number of officials from the ministry.[61]

While lies may well have been told and many statements were no doubt intended to exonerate the witness involved as much as Seldte, the prosecutors rapidly concluded that the minister was not the most important person within the Reich Ministry of Labour and that there was no getting away from the significance of Sauckel's enthronement as GBA. In 1947, an internal memorandum concluded that 'Seldte cannot be held responsible for the deportation of foreign laborers, organized by Sauckel in 1943'.[62] This did not, however, lead to Seldte's removal from the group of possible defendants. His name still showed up on a list in mid March 1947,[63] and the interrogations of his staff now focused discernibly on holding him liable in his role as head of the ministry. Even if he had contributed very little to the ministry's work, so the argument went, as the man at the top he had nonetheless been responsible for everything his leading staff had set in motion. Letsch's objection that this was a 'highly juridical' consideration – raising the question of what, precisely, the ministerial counsellor thought he was doing in Nuremberg – was expressed in much the same way by his colleagues. The bottom line, however, was that no one disputed Seldte's fundamental responsibility.[64]

And yet the next, drastically trimmed list of charges, of May 1947, did not mention the labour minister – Seldte died in prison in April. This heightened the dilemma facing Taylor's team, given that two out of three state secretaries (Syrup and Engel) had already died. Krohn, meanwhile, had left the ministry in autumn 1941, so he had played no role during the peak period of the recruitment and deployment of forced labourers. Separate proceedings against staff members of the Reich Ministry of Labour and the GBA, however, were unlikely in the absence of a reasonably prominent figurehead. What remained was the possibility of integrating the group of officials around Max Timm into a larger case against members of the ministerial bureaucracy, a prospect that began to emerge in mid 1947. Under pressure from Washington to bring the longer than expected proceedings to an end, Taylor was forced to reduce his ambitious programme, which led him to weld together a diverse range of originally separate cases. Incorporating officials from the Reich Ministry of Labour was rather difficult in the absence of a good figurehead. But it was far from impossible, particularly given that the charges relating to forced labour had, from the perspective of the OCCWC, fared well in the courtroom so far, usually resulting in prison terms of several years. The ministerial officials thus continued to proceed defensively under interrogation, even when it had long since become evident that they were no longer at risk.[65]

Timm, Hildebrandt and Kimmich had already delineated the main elements of their arguments during the IMT, while their colleagues Stothfang and Letsch, and, with some caveats, Börger, largely adopted the same narrative (as the man in charge of the budget, Börger had been less directly involved in the recruitment of forced labourers, but he was regarded as one of the Nazi Party's champions in the ministry and thus felt a greater need to justify himself).[66] What crystallized during the interrogations carried out between autumn 1946 and summer 1947 was a dual strategy of distancing – internally from Sauckel and his Thuringian staffers and externally from those offices that had pushed for the expansion and radicalization of forced labour deployment, in other words the private sector and the armaments ministry's administration. This amounted to a tightrope walk. The civil servants sought to distance themselves from Sauckel and insisted on their identity as members of the Reich Ministry of Labour, even when they had been assigned to the GBA. At the same time, it was crucial not to show the GBA – in terms of both its personnel and overall apparatus – in too bad a light, because their subordination under Sauckel was beyond dispute.

The staff of the Reich Ministry of Labour pursued this dual imperative with great consistency. What helped the officials here was the fact that – again with the exception of Börger – they shared many biographical similarities. Born between 1888 and 1903, they had studied economics or law, often earning Ph.D.s, had pursued careers in the Reich Institution for Job Placement and Unemployment Insurance since the 1920s, and had subsequently transferred to the ministry.[67] Still, such parallels did not mean that there were no conflicts of interest. Particularly when the goal was to maintain distance from the practice of forced labour, and thus from specific cases in which businesses had requested and deployed unfree workers, every one of the ministerial counsellors, permanent secretaries and section heads was visibly eager to emphasize that they had not been responsible and to point the investigators towards their colleagues or the conveniently deceased Syrup. This game of pass-the-parcel did not, of course, escape the attention of the exasperated American investigators, who pressed the officials to answer their questions: 'If we ask Timm, he states that the people went to Letsch, and if we ask him, he tells us that he sent them to you [Hildebrandt]. Now we at least want to hear about the people who came to you'.[68]

But if the prosecution hoped that the potential defendants would incriminate one another, they were to be disappointed. In fact, the civil servants spoke largely with one voice, underlining that the ministry's sections assigned to Sauckel had maintained traditional ministerial routines, and insisted on the 'sensible' standards they had applied in managing labour migration and labour deployment. Time and again, in terms of both content and language, the officials described their activities as a matter of orderly administration, tried-and-tested routines and legalistic procedure. In contrast to Sauckel, who had had 'no idea about administrative matters' and had viewed 'labour deployment as essentially no more than getting hold of people', according to Hildebrandt the experts at the ministry had seen their task 'primarily [as involving] making adjustments to the domestic market, as a regulatory task'. Their goal had always been to obtain the available manpower – not least that of women not in gainful employment – by redeploying it between different economic sectors, 'balancing companies" demands, and 'steering fluctuations'. 'After all', Hildebrandt explained, 'foreigners could never replace the workers we obtained by inducing movement in the domestic market'. Hildebrandt evidently tried to conceal the coercive elements in the deployment of foreign workers behind seemingly technical language. Instead of referring to Sauckel's policies as involuntary or forcible, he spoke euphemistically of *Anreicherungspolitik*, a neologism that implied enhancement and growth. He asserted that the dividing line between the GBA and the Reich Ministry of Labour did not boil down to coercion versus freedom of decision, but instead reflected the contrast between foreigners' labour and national labour.[69] Hildebrandt and his colleagues unanimously underlined 'the entirely voluntary basis' of labour deployment before 1942. When this was difficult to maintain argumentatively, particularly in the case of the deployment of prisoners of war, they blamed the military authorities.[70]

When it came to the treatment of 'foreign workers', the civil servants, echoing the executed GBA, claimed always to have done their best to ensure an adequate supply of foodstuffs, clothing and other provisions. When such was lacking, they blamed the SS, DAF or employers, though mostly without mentioning specific names or details. In particular, they repeatedly sought refuge in legislation. Blithely brushing aside paper's well-known inability to blush, the quintet deduced from the wording of decrees that these had ensured the equal treatment of foreign labour and particularly 'eastern workers' (*Ostarbeiter*). When asked whether he had really had the impression that 'eastern workers' had been treated like all others, Letsch responded in formalistic terms:

> In the spring of 1945, full equality of 'eastern workers' was legally mandated in a decree. . . . In our institution the eastern worker was treated just like any other worker. The Reich labour minister constantly sought to improve things with the objective of striving for equality. The resistance came from the Reichsführer SS.

Letsch was unwilling to accept that deportees from Eastern Europe had died in large numbers on the transports or in the labour camps, other than in 'rare cases'. And whenever officials had learned of shortcomings, he claimed, they had of course immediately sought to rectify the situation.[71]

In their accounts and in the face of long-established facts, Letsch and his colleagues often referred to the fundamentally good conditions that typified the deployment of foreign workers (*Fremdarbeitereinsatz*). Problems thrown up by the war, Kimmich conceded, had of course strained the system – 'the apparatus could not absorb these quantities. It was simply overcrowded'. But he had 'discerned very little sign of ill intent as such, let alone laxity'. Moreover, on many occasions he had 'come across camps in which the people were quite content and happy to be there'.[72] Letsch also recalled firms 'where everything was arranged quite impeccably' and regretted the fact that in retrospect people tended to focus 'very strongly [on the] negative aspect'. His claim that sickness levels among 'eastern workers' had been only half as high as among Germans prompted his irritated interrogator to respond that on paper this looked 'very nice, but the reality was quite different'.[73]

In many respects, the arguments put forward by the officials were similar to those made by Sauckel before and during his trial before the International Military Tribunal. In fact, his former subordinates expressed surprisingly little criticism of the GBA. Kimmich attested that he had been a 'fundamentally decent man', who (not unlike Seldte) had simply not been up to his task: 'He was harsher in word than deed. Of course he puffed himself up' and had been plagued by an inferiority complex vis-à-vis his academically educated colleagues.[74] Nonetheless, the officials who had been on loan to the GBA from the Reich Ministry of Labour insisted that they had at no point been involved in Sauckel's decision-making. According to Timm, Sauckel had discussed all the crucial matters solely with his confidants from 'Thuringia House', that is, his Gau administration. He had merely informed Timm and the other officials of the outcomes of these deliberations and issued them with instructions.[75]

Hence, when the quintet described a graduated hierarchy of responsibility to their Nuremberg interrogators, they portrayed Sauckel as far more directly involved in the truly criminal decisions and actions than they had been. Yet they carefully avoided casting him as the lynchpin. Instead, they ascribed responsibility to two key actors, namely the DAF and the firms (especially the respective works leaders), for specific failures relating to accommodation, provisioning and treatment in the workplace. Furthermore, they stated, either directly or via their representative organizations, companies had forcefully pressed the regime to expand the recruitment of foreigners. Unlike the Reich Ministry of Labour, meanwhile, these companies had showed a clear preference for non-voluntary workers from the East. More than a few employers, according to Kimmich, had preferred 'eastern workers', because these had been considered 'more docile and more content'. Unlike the demanding Dutch and Norwegians, people from the occupied East 'did what they were told and put up no resistance. . . . . The eastern workers were simply brought up differently'.[76] Yet the ministerial officials almost entirely refrained from identifying specific firms, let alone managers. Only reluctantly did they concede names, in cases where these had cropped up in the files anyway or if the investigators were particularly forceful in demanding them. In the majority of cases they feigned ignorance or claimed not to remember. The only actor they identified frequently and readily was IG Farbenindustrie, about which the OCCWC was already well-informed. Its representative at the Four-Year Plan Authority, namely the General Plenipotentiary for Special Issues in Chemical Production (Generalbevollmächtigter für Sonderfragen der chemischen Erzeugung) Carl Krauch, had repeatedly encroached on the ministry's powers and made 'extremely radical' demands.[77]

Companies, the officials claimed, had increasingly bypassed both the ministry and the GBA in putting forward their demands, because they had been dissatisfied with the labour administration's supposedly 'steady approach'. The major industrial firms had found their key interlocutors elsewhere, chiefly in Speer's constantly expanding armaments administration.[78] Here the defence narrative had discerned another target on which it could foist responsibility. Once again in accordance with Sauckel's earlier testimony, officials emphasized his subordination to Speer's authority and lamented the armaments authorities' constant intervention in matters of labour policy. The pressure on his ministry, according to Timm, had increased continuously since 1941 and 'always via the Armaments Ministry, because of course it was there that the powerful men were to be found. This was already the case before [Fritz] Todt. These men enjoyed easier access to Hitler', and none of them put it more successfully to use than Speer.[79] In addition to the armaments minister, another figure increasingly came to the fore, namely Erhard Milch. Responding to the prosecutors, who were on the lookout for incriminating statements in 'Case 2' against Milch in late 1946 and early 1947, the ministerial officials picked up the ball and ran with it. They pointed to Central Planning, a steering body that had dominated the allocation of economic resources in the final years of the war. The officials asserted that all decisions had been made by the 'triumvirate' of Speer, Milch and Paul Körner (Four-Year Plan), while the labour administration had been merely responsible for their 'technical implementation'. How many workers had come and where they had gone, they asserted, had been decided entirely outside the apparatus of both the Labour Ministry and the GBA.[80]

Epilogue

In their statements on rival agencies, namely Albert Speer's apparatus, but also the offices of Erhard Milch and Paul Körner, and in their take on major industrial complexes such as the Reichswerke 'Hermann Göring', the leading staff of the Reich Ministry of Labour gathered in Nuremberg proved to be profound sources, insiders who were quite willing to provide information. The differences in their testimony had to do chiefly with the precision with which they spoke. They personally implicated the already convicted Speer, Field Marshal Erhard Milch, who was a lost cause, and Reichswerke CEO Paul Pleiger, a man disavowed on all sides. They portrayed the private firms, by contrast, as an amorphous mass rather than as identifiable and prosecutable actors. In their court appearances, the officials – perhaps mindful of their uncertain professional prospects – continued to give little away.[81] Nonetheless, they could not always paper over irreconcilable interpretations, particularly in cases where employers sought to highlight their supposed struggle 'against Sauckel's methods' in an attempt to exonerate themselves, which was hardly in the interest of the former GBA staff.[82]

This clash of interests suited the prosecutors down to the ground. In the second half of 1947, it became clear that the status of Hildebrandt, Kimmich, Letsch, Stothfang and Timm had altered. From potential defendants, they now mutated into expert witnesses. Again and again, the prosecution drew on their insights to prepare for the trial of industrialists from the private and state sectors, but also members of the Wehrmacht and SS, the latter with respect to the deployment of prisoners of war. The interrogations thus went on until the spring of 1948 in an attempt to tap the ministerial officials' inside knowledge.[83] By this point, it had long been clear that none of the members of staff from the Reich Ministry of Labour and the GBA was going to face charges. In mid November 1947, the OCCWC lawyers had filed the indictment in Case 11, the penultimate trial before the Nuernberg Military Tribunals. This entailed an eclectic mix of staff members from various ministries, businesses, the Reichsbank and SS agencies, which explains the Wilhelmstrasse case's derisive epithet of 'the omnibus trial'. But while the indictment charged a whole number of men with involvement in forced labour deployment, including Körner and Pleiger, there was no mention of the officials at the Reich Ministry of Labour. Timm and his colleagues could finally heave a sigh of relief, given that the parallel case 12 exclusively charged Wehrmacht personnel. The officials appeared to have permanently evaded the ordeal of a criminal trial.

If it had been down to Telford Taylor, though, the half-dozen officials would have faced a sequel to their detention at Nuremberg. Having had to abandon some of the trials planned in the original outline, in 1948 Taylor established a new department, the so-called Special Projects Division. This was tasked with collecting incriminating evidence relating to cases that could not be brought before Allied courts. The rapidly growing list included numerous ministerial representatives from the Four-Year Plan Office, the Ministry for the Occupied Eastern Territories and the Foreign Office. There was also a plan to institute proceedings against those members of the labour and armaments ministries who had been instrumental in organizing the forced labour programme. Here the Special Projects Division identified Gustav Schlotterer, Walther Schieber and Karl-Otto Saur and, quite emphatically, Ernst Letsch, Hubert Hildebrandt and Max Timm.[84]

When the Nuremberg trials were over, Taylor's team handed the incriminating documents to the justice ministries of the West German states, in the hope that they would initiate investigations and ultimately hold criminal proceedings. In the vast majority of cases, these hopes were to be disappointed. The political climate of the first postwar decade was not conducive to any efforts to initiate a West German epilogue to the tremendously unpopular Nuremberg trials, to which the Federal Republic's politicians as well as the daily and weekly press were equally hostile. Even when the establishment, in 1958, of the Central Office of the Land Judicial Authorities for the Investigation of National Socialist Crimes in Ludwigsburg injected new dynamism into the prosecution of Nazi-era perpetrators in West Germany, the labour administration of the 'Third Reich' played no appreciable role. No more than a handful of investigations was ever carried out, and these related exclusively to members of agencies in occupied Poland and the Soviet territories. Not a single trial resulted.[85] In the Soviet occupation zone, and in the courts of the German Democratic Republic, a handful of local protagonists had to stand trial, the most prominent example being Ernst Kendzia, head of the Gau Labour Office in Posen. In the course of the Waldheim trials – which fell drastically short of the rule of law – Kendzia was condemned to death in 1950 and executed the same year.[86]

For the group of Reich Labour Ministry officials who had been detained in Nuremberg, this meant they could return to their middle-class lives – though not in every case to the labour administration.[87] Evidently, they were not only at peace with their own past, but felt a sense of satisfaction at what they had achieved in their careers. During the Nuremberg hearings, however defensive the witnesses may have been, again and again a certain pride shone through, for example when Stothfang testified that:

> Through the presence of a constantly expanded and improved labour deployment administration, and through the introduction of the labour book, along with the associated labour book card index kept by the labour offices, Germany had provided itself with a powerful instrument for regulating labour deploy-

ment in peacetime. Furthermore, based on the negative experiences of the First World War, now the state also had an instrument for managing labour deployment in the event of military conflict.[88]

Here Stothfang was on the same page as his former boss, who had congratulated himself in Nuremberg on having made a signal contribution to the advancement of German social policy. According to Franz Seldte, he had always been an exponent of balancing different social interests. He had, he asserted, succeeded in pacifying industrial relations, placing them on stable and well-balanced foundations. Not least, he had provided a template for the British welfare state. Summing things up with a self-assurance unperturbed by factual knowledge, Seldte claimed that its founding father, William Beveridge, had 'taken a good deal from our plan'. This was something of which Seldte was determined to be proud.[89]

Kim Christian Priemel, Dr. phil., Professor of Contemporary European History, University of Oslo; academic advisor to the project being undertaken by the Independent Commission of Historians Investigating the History of the Reich Ministry of Labour in the National Socialist Period. Publications include: *The Betrayal. The Nuremberg Trials and German Divergence* (Oxford University Press, 2016); with Stefanie Middendorf: 'Jenseits des Primats. Kontinuitäten der nationalsozialistischen Finanz- und Wirtschaftspolitik', in B. Kundrus and S. Steinbacher (eds), *Kontinuitäten und Diskontinuitäten. Der Nationalsozialismus in der Geschichte des 20. Jahrhunderts* (Wallstein, 2013, 94–120); *Flick. Eine Konzerngeschichte vom Kaiserreich bis zur Bundesrepublik* (Wallstein, 2007).

Notes

1. 'The Reich Ministry of Labour and the General Plenipotentiary for Labour Deployment in Relation to the Deployment of Foreigners during the Second World War', 14 May 1947, Staatsarchiv Nürnberg (StA N), Rep. 502, KVA, Interrogations, L-40.

2. [Stothfang], Untitled Memorandum, 7 September 1947, StA N, Rep. 502, KVA, Interrogations, S-318.

3. For detailed information on Hubert Hildebrandt, see Biographical Appendix.

4. For detailed information on Max Timm, see Biographical Appendix.

5. For detailed information on Wilhelm Kimmich, see Biographical Appendix.

6. 'Zeugenbefragungen 31.5.1946 und 1.6.1946', in *Trial of the Major War Criminals before the International Military Tribunal, Nuremberg 14 November 1945–1 October 1946*, vol. 15, Nürnberg 1948, 207–47. This edition comprises 42 vols, Nuremberg 1947–1949; abbreviated as IMT in what follows.

7. See the contributions in K.C. Priemel and A. Stiller (eds), *NMT. Die Nürnberger Militärtribunale zwischen Geschichte, Gerechtigkeit und Rechtschöpfung*, Hamburg: Hamburger Edition, 2014.

8. B. Smith, *The Road to Nuremberg*, New York: Basic Books, 1981; A.J. Kochavi, *Prelude to Nuremberg. Allied War Crimes Policy and the Question of Punishment*, Chapel Hill: University of North Carolina Press, 1998; K.C. Priemel, *The Betrayal. The Nuremberg Trials and German Divergence*, Oxford: Oxford University Press, 2016.

9. See, for example, R. Lemkin, *Axis Rule in Occupied Europe. Laws of Occupation. Analysis of Government. Proposals for Redress*, Washington, DC: Carnegie Endowment for International Peace, 1944, 67–78; see Priemel, *The Betrayal*, 63, 115 f.

10. International Labor Office (ed.), *The Exploitation of Foreign Labor by Germany*, Montreal: International Labor Office, 1945; Memorandum to Mr. Allan Evans, 7 July 1945, University of Wyoming, Murray C. Bernays Papers, Box 2, F. Preparation of Evidence 3; Inter-Office Memorandum, 5 June 1946, National Archives and Records Administration (NARA), Washington, DC, RG 238, Entry 202, Box 2, F. Various Correspondences from May 1946.

11. See, for example, French thinking as embodied in Evaluation des dommages subis par la France du fait de la guerre et de l'occupation ennemie (1939/1945), undated, Archives Nationales (AN), BB 35, 79, F. 4, and in the two folders AN, BB 35, 81, F. 9.8 and 9.9 ('Main d'œuvre française I + II').

12. See D. Bloxham, *Genocide on Trial. War Criminals and the Formation of Holocaust, History and Memory*, Oxford: Oxford University Press, 2001, 57–70.

13. Memorandum for Justice Jackson, 15 July 1945, Library of Congress (LoC), Robert H. Jackson Papers, Box 96, F. Preliminary Drafts.

14. See the chapters by Sören Eden and Rüdiger Hachtmann in this volume.

15. Destruction of the Free Trade Unions and the Acquisition of Control over the Productive Labor Capacity of Germany, n.d., John F. Kennedy Presidential Library (JFKL), Drexel A. Sprecher Papers, Box 53, F. Trade Unions-Trial Briefs; see also Preliminary Trial Brief on the Development of the Case on Offenses Involved in the Breakdown of the Trade Unions and the Representation of Labor, 15 September 1945, ibid.: 'The suppression of unions in Germany is one of the "crimes against peace". Removing the possibility of any open independent action or resistance by organizations of workers in Germany was an important part of the total liquidation of the opposition to Nazism within Germany. It was an integral part of the preparation for waging war within Germany. It was an integral part of the preparation for waging aggressive war. … the continued suppression of the trade unions in the occupied countries was an important phase of exploiting foreign labor in the waging of war itself. The maltreatment and murder of union leaders and the confiscation of trade union property was a violation of the laws or customs of war, and hence one of the "war crimes"'.

16. Memorandum for Justice Jackson, 4 August 1945, LoC, Robert H. Jackson Papers, Box 104, F. Horsky memo.

17. Priemel, *The Betrayal*, 80–84.

18. IMT, vol. 19, 415–17.

19. Clyde to Dean, 6 June 1945, Columbia Law School (CLS), Telford Taylor Papers (TTP), 20-1-1-4; Lists of 23 June 1945, CLS, TTP, 20-1-1-4; Preliminary List of War Criminals, 30 June 1945, NARA, RG 226, Entry 146, Box 39, F. Valentin; Memorandum, German Arch-Criminals, n.d., Harvard Law Library, Belle Mayer Zeck Papers, Box 4, F. 33; The Street-Wheeler List of Individuals with Biographical Notes, 26 July 1945, CLS, TTP, LC4.1, F. Declaration.

20. Memorandum by the Secretary of State for Foreign Affairs, 16 June 1944, National Library of Wales, Frederick Elwyn Jones Papers, C1; Memorandum to All Members of the Staff, 26 June 1945, NARA, RG 238, Entry 52E, Box 10, F. 312.2; List of Major War Criminals as released 29 August 1945, Thomas J. Dodd Research Center (TDRC), Thomas Dodd Papers, Box 322, F. 8211.

21. On the Background to the GBA, 24 August 1945, Bundesarchiv (BArch), N 1340/466.
22. S. Haffner, *Germany. Jekyll and Hyde*, New York: Dutton, 1941, 114 f. Dorpmüller had in any case died in July 1945. But his state secretary, Albert Ganzenmüller, also initially evaded criminal prosecution until investigations began in the 1960s.
23. Fite to her Parents, 28 October 1945, Harry S. Truman Presidential Library, Katherine Fite Papers, Box 1, F. Nuremberg letters, 1945.
24. See Bloxham, *Genocide on Trial*, 28–32; Priemel, *The Betrayal*, 152 f.
25. Version C. Evidentiary Brief (Documents) for the Accused Fritz Sauckel, 1 April 1946, BArch, AllProz 3/201.
26. See P. Arnaud, 'Die französische Zwangsarbeit im Reichseinsatz', Working Paper Series A, No. 11, 2015. Retrieved 26 September from https://www.historikerkommission-reichsarbeitsministerium.de/sites/default/files/inline-files/Working%20Paper%20UHK%20A11_Arnaud_0.pdf.
27. For more on this, see M. Buggeln, 'Unfreie Arbeit im Nationalsozialismus. Begrifflichkeiten und Vergleichsaspekte zu den Arbeitsbedingungen im Deutschen Reich und in den besetzten Gebieten', in M. Buggeln and M. Wildt (eds), *Arbeit im Nationalsozialismus*, Munich: De Gruyter Oldenbourg, 2014, 231–52.
28. The Slave Labor Program, the Illegal Use of Prisoners of War, and the Special Responsibility of Defendants Sauckel and Speer, therefor [sic], n.d., TDRC, Thomas Dodd Papers, Box 288, F. 7347.
29. IMT, vol. 3, 402–93; IMT, vol. 7, 370–402, 470 f.; IMT, vol. 10, 434–38; see also TDRC, Thomas Dodd Papers, Box 282, F. 7360.
30. M. Kitchen, *Albert Speer. Hitler's Architect*, New Haven, CT: Yale University Press, 2015, 285–303; Priemel, *The Betrayal*, 138–41.
31. Interrogation Albert Speer, 4 July 1945, BArch, N 1340/466; and On the Background to the GBA, 24 August 1945, BArch, N 1340/466.
32. Sauckel Affidavit, 29 June 1946, BArch, AllProz 3/203; quote: Handwritten Note Sauckel, n.d., BArch, AllProz 3/201.
33. IMT, vol. 14, 617; IMT, vol. 15, 54; IMT, vol. 16, 438, 447, 465 f., 478–80; Motion of Evidence, 25 February 1946, TDRC, Thomas Dodd Papers, Box 315, F. 8046; Flächsner to IMT, 28 March 1946, TDRC, Thomas Dodd Papers, Box 315, F. 8046.
34. Testimony of Fritz Sauckel, 11 September 1946 [1945], 20 September 1945 and 25 September 1945, and quote, Sauckel to Interrogator [Monigan], 14 October 1945, NARA, M 1270, Roll 18.
35. Testimony of Fritz Sauckel, 15 September 1945 and 13 October 1945, NARA, M 1270, Roll 18; Interrogation Albert Speer, 4 July 1945, BArch, N 1340/466.
36. Testimony of Fritz Sauckel, 28 September 1945 and 8 October 1945, NARA, M 1270, Roll 18.
37. Testimony of Ernst Friedrich Christoph Sauckel, 13 September 1945, NARA, M 1270, Roll 18.
38. Testimony of Fritz Sauckel, 11 October 1945, NARA, M 1270, Roll 18.
39. IMT, vol. 15, 106–8, 125–268, 186–207. An audio version of Sauckel's interrogation is available, which conveys the disastrous impression he made in court: *Die NS-Führung im Verhör. Original-Tondokumente der Nürnberger Prozesse*, documented by U. Lampen, introduction by P. Steinbach, 8 CDs, Berlin: Audio-Verlag, 2006, CD 7.
40. See R. Hachtmann and W. Süss (eds), *Hitlers Kommissare: Sondergewalten in der nationalsozialistischen Diktatur*, Göttingen: Wallstein, 2006.
41. Interrogations Fritz Sauckel, 15 September 1945 and 21 September 1945, NARA, M 1270, Roll 18; quote, Interrogation Fritz Sauckel, 6 September 1946, NARA, M 1019, Roll 61.

42. IMT, vol. 15, 208–10, 216, 218 f., 222–24, 237 f., 243–45, quote, 208.

43. The defence's requests to question Seldte and Rudolf Peuckert (who committed suicide in prison in Dachau) were rejected as cumulative; it proved impossible to locate other members of the Reich Labour Ministry staff. See IMT, vol. 8, 579–84; BArch, AllProz 3/215 and 223.

44. Priemel, *The Betrayal*, 145 f.

45. See the overviews in N. Frei (ed.), *Transnationale Vergangenheitspolitik. Der Umgang mit deutschen Kriegsverbrechern in Europa nach dem Zweiten Weltkrieg*, Göttingen: Wallstein, 2006.

46. The British Manstein trial in Hamburg adhered to the Nuremberg model with respect to content, but was based on a Royal Warrant of 1945. Conversely, the Soviet occupation authorities drew on the Control Council law when it came to the cases tried in their zone, but deviated from it substantially both in terms of content and by failing to comply with the rule of law.

47. See Priemel, *The Betrayal*, 158–61.

48. Inter-Office Memorandum, Subject: Slave Labor, 14 October 1946, Columbia University, Rare Books and Manuscripts Library, Norbert Barr Papers, Box 3, F. Memoranda 1946.

49. Inter-Office Memorandum, 30 November 1946, JFKL, Drexel A. Sprecher Papers, Box 51, F. Trial Preparation.

50. On the early plans, see K.J. Heller, *The Nuremberg Military Tribunals and the Origins of International Criminal Law*, Oxford: Oxford University Press, 2011, 43, 83.

51. Interrogation Franz Seldte, 11 October 1946, NARA, M 1019, Roll 68.

52. Work Progress of the Berlin Branch, OCCWC to Taylor, 21 September 1946, NARA, RG 238, Entry 202, Box 2, F. Various Correspondences August 1946–January 1947.

53. Ibid.; see also Intra-Office Memorandum, 2 October 1946, NARA, RG 238, Entry 202, Box 2, F. Various Correspondences August 1946–January 1947.

54. Interrogation Franz Seldte, 1 November 1946, NARA, MF 1019, Roll 68.

55. Interrogations Franz Seldte, 29 October 1946 and 23 October 1946, NARA, MF 1019, Roll 68.

56. Interrogation Franz Seldte, 23 October 1946, NARA, MF 1019, Roll 68 (quote).

57. Ibid.

58. Interrogation Friedrich Flick, 3 December 1946, StA N, Rep. 502, KVA, Interrogations, F-47.

59. Interrogation Walter Letsch, 27 January 1947, NARA, M 1019, Roll 41.

60. Interrogation Wilhelm Kimmich, 7 November 1946, StA N, Rep. 502, KVA, Interrogations, K-60.

61. Affidavit [Schacht], September 1946, StA N, Rep. 502, KVA, Interrogations, S-203; Interrogation Constantin Hierl, 19 February 1947, StA N, Rep. 502, KVA, Interrogations, H-130.

62. Ministries Division Research Section, n.d. [1947/48], StA N, Rep. 502, KVA, Interrogations, S-203.

63. Heller, *The Nuremberg Military Tribunals*, 70.

64. Interrogation Max Timm, 10 October 1946, NARA, M 1019, Roll 73; Interrogation Wilhelm Kimmich, 18 November 1946, StA N, Rep. 502, KVA, Interrogations, K-60; Interrogations Hubert Hildebrandt, 11 October 1946 and 31 October 1946, NARA, M 1019, Roll 27; quote: Interrogation Walter Letsch, 27 January 1947, NARA, M 1019, Roll 41.

65. Attorney's Request for Interrogation, 25 February 1947, StA N, Rep. 502, KVA, Interrogations, L-40. This found expression, for example, in a prosecuting counsel's remark that he was not concerned with Letsch's 'old affair', but solely with obtaining information about IG Farben; Interrogation Walter Letsch, 23 May 1947, NARA, M 1019, Roll 41.

66. Interrogation Wilhelm Börger, 30 April 1947, StA N, Rep. 502, KVA, Interrogations, B-115. Seldte referred to Börger as 'too radical for me'; Interrogation Franz Seldte, 31 October 1946, NARA, M 1019, Roll 68.

67. Kimmich (b. 1888) was older than his colleagues from Main Section VI, who were born between 1895 and 1902; after 1933, Timm (b. 1898) had advanced rapidly through multiple career stages, outstripping the somewhat older Letsch and Hildebrandt. Stothfang was the youngest of the Nuremberg group.

68. Interrogation Max Timm, 3 October 1946, NARA, M 1019, Roll 73; Interrogation Hubert Hildebrandt, 22 January 1948, NARA, M 1019, Roll 27; quote: Interrogation Hubert Hildebrandt, 10 January 1947, NARA, M 1019, Roll 27.

69. Interrogation Hubert Hildebrandt, 10 October 1946, NARA, M 1019, Roll 27; for similar remarks, see Interrogation Max Timm, 10 October 1946, NARA, M 1019, Roll 73. On the reorganization of the ministry in 1942, see the chapters by Swantje Greve and Ulrike Schulz in this volume.

70. Interrogation Hubert Hildebrandt, 10 October 1946, NARA, M 1019, Roll 27; Interrogation Walter Letsch, 24 January 1947, and Interrogation Summary No. 1129, Walter Letsch, 27 January 1947, NARA, M 1019, Roll 41; quote: [Stothfang], Untitled Memorandum, 7 September 1947, StA N, Rep. 502, KVA, Interrogations, S-318.

71. Interrogation Walter Letsch, 27 January 1947, NARA, M 1019, Roll 41; [Stothfang], Untitled Memorandum, 7 September 1947, StA N, Rep. 502, KVA, Interrogations, S-318.

72. Interrogation Wilhelm Kimmich, 8 November 1946, StA N, Rep. 502, KV-Interrogations, K-60.

73. Interrogation Walter Letsch, 11 March 1947, NARA, M 1019, Roll 41.

74. Interrogation Wilhelm Kimmich, 8 November 1946, StA N, Rep. 502, KVA, Interrogations, K-60.

75. Interrogation Max Timm, 10 October 1946, and Interrogation Summary No. 268, Max Timm, 19 October 1946, NARA, M 1019, Roll 73. Letsch made the same claim in: *Das Reichsarbeitsministerium und der Generalbevollmächtigte für den Arbeitseinsatz beim Ausländereinsatz im Zweiten Weltkrieg*, 14 May 1947, StA N, Rep. 502, KVA, Interrogations, L-40.

76. Interrogation Wilhelm Kimmich, 7 November 1946, StA N, Rep. 502, KV-Anlage, Interrogations, K-60; see also Hubert Hildebrandt, Sworn Statement, n.d., StA N, Rep. 502, KVA, H-132.

77. Quote: Hubert Hildebrandt, Sworn Statement, n.d., StA N, Rep. 502, KVA, H-132; Walter Letsch, Sworn Statement, 21 March 1947, StA N, Rep. 502, KVA, Interrogations, L-40; Interrogation Walter Letsch, 3 November 1947, NARA, M 1019, Roll 41; Interrogations Hubert Hildebrandt, 10 October 1946, 10 January 1947 and 22 January 1947, NARA, M 1019, Roll 27.

78. Quote: Interrogation Hubert Hildebrandt, 15 April 1947, StA N, Rep. 502, KVA, Interrogations, H-132; Interrogation Hubert Hildebrandt, 10 October 1946, NARA, M 1019, Roll 27.

79. Quote: Interrogation Max Timm, 3 October 1946, NARA, M 1019, Roll 73; [Stothfang], Untitled Memorandum, 7 September 1947, StA N, Rep. 502, KVA, Interrogations, S-318; Interrogation Hubert Hildebrandt, 10 October 1946, NARA, M 1019, Roll 27; Interrogation Walter Letsch, 4 February 1947, NARA, M 1019, Roll 41.

80. Hildebrandt to Myers, 1 January 1947, StA N, Rep. 502, KVA, Interrogations, H-132; Interrogation Summary No. 77; Interrogation Max Timm, 4 September 1946, NARA, M 1019, Roll 73; quote: [Letsch], *Das Reichsarbeitsministerium und der Generalbevollmächtigte für den Arbeitseinsatz beim Ausländereinsatz im Zweiten Weltkrieg*, 14 May 1947, StA N, Rep. 502, KVA, Interrogations, L-40. Sauckel had made similar remarks during nu-

merous interrogations, carried out between the end of his trial and his sentencing; see, for example, Interrogations Fritz Sauckel, 6 September 1946 and 11 September 1946, NARA, M 1019, Roll 61.

81. See the appearances of Kimmich, Stothfang and Letsch in Case 5: StA N, Rep. 501, KV-Prozesse, Fall 5, 2586-2699, 5822-5938, 7774-7835. Nonetheless, these statements, particularly that of Kimmich, were a thorn in the side of the accused industrialists, as evident in the retrospective diatribe penned by one indicted manager: Military Tribunal Case V. Nuremberg 1947, n. d., Landesarchiv Nordrhein-Westfalen – Abteilung Rheinland – RWB 27820/46, fol. 44.

82. Information provided by Steinbrinck, Thoughts on Defence PP, 17 March 1948, BArch, AllProz 3/93.

83. See, for example, the Interrogations of Max Timm for OCCWC's Economics, Ministries, SS and Military Divisions on 15 June, 19 June, 22 July, 6 August, 8 September, 15 September, 19 September and 23 September 1947 as well as 27 January, 4 February and 16 February 1948, NARA, M 1019, Roll 74.

84. Memorandum Herman Lang, 9 January 1948, Towson University, Paul Gantt Papers, Box 32, F. 6.

85. See the investigation files in BArch, B 162/7683, 20847, 27146 and 27227. A number of former Reich Labour Service staff were also investigated.

86. See, for example, C.F. Rüter and L. Demps (eds), *DDR-Justiz und NS-Verbrechen. Sammlung ostdeutscher Strafurteile wegen nationalsozialistischer Tötungsverbrechen*, vol. 12, Amsterdam: Amsterdam University Press, 2002–2010, 445–64. On Kendzia, see M. Alberti, *Die Verfolgung und Vernichtung der Juden im Reichsgau Wartheland 1939–1945*, Wiesbaden: Harrassowitz, 2006, 60, 252, 377; B. Withöft, *Die Todesurteile der Waldheimer Prozesse*, Ph.D. dissertation, Vienna: University of Vienna, 2008, 21, 90–93.

87. Timm continued his career in Schleswig-Holstein; on Stothfang's transfer to the Federal Institution for Job Placement and Unemployment Insurance, see the chapter by Martin Münzel in this volume; see also K.-D. Godau-Schüttke, *Die Heyde/Sawade-Affäre. Wie Juristen und Mediziner den NS-Euthanasieprofessor Heyde nach 1945 deckten und straflos blieben*, 3rd ed., Baden-Baden: Nomos, 2010, 126 f.

88. [Stothfang], Untitled Memorandum, 7 September 1947, StA N, Rep. 502, KVA, Interrogations, S-318. Stothfang had made very similar statements during the war; see K. Linne, 'Von der Arbeitsvermittlung zum Arbeitseinsatz. Zum Wandel der Arbeitsverwaltung 1933–1945', in Buggeln and Wildt, *Arbeit im Nationalsozialismus*, 53–73, here 63.

89. Interrogation Franz Seldte, 23 October 1946, NARA, M 1019, Roll 68.

Bibliography

Alberti, M. *Die Verfolgung und Vernichtung der Juden im Reichsgau Wartheland 1939–1945*. Wiesbaden: Harrassowitz, 2006.

Arnaud, P. 'Die französische Zwangsarbeit im Reichseinsatz', *Working Paper Series A*, No. 11, 2015. Retrieved 26 September from https://www.historikerkommission-reichsarbeitsministerium.de/sites/default/files/inline-files/Working%20Paper%20UHK%20A11_Arnaud_0.pdf.

Bloxham, D. *Genocide on Trial. War Criminals and the Formation of Holocaust, History and Memory*. Oxford: Oxford University Press, 2001.

Buggeln, M. 'Unfreie Arbeit im Nationalsozialismus. Begrifflichkeiten und Vergleichsaspekte zu den Arbeitsbedingungen im Deutschen Reich und in den besetzten Gebieten', in M. Buggeln and M. Wildt (eds), *Arbeit im Nationalsozialismus* (Munich: De Gruyter Oldenbourg, 2014), 231–52.

Das deutsche Führerlexikon. Berlin: Stollberg, 1934.
Frei, N. (ed.). *Transnationale Vergangenheitspolitik. Der Umgang mit deutschen Kriegsverbrechern in Europa nach dem Zweiten Weltkrieg*. Göttingen: Wallstein, 2006.
Godau-Schüttke, K.-D. *Die Heyde/Sawade-Affäre. Wie Juristen und Mediziner den NS-Euthanasieprofessor Heyde nach 1945 deckten und straflos blieben*, 3rd ed. Baden-Baden: Nomos, 2010.
Hachtmann, R., and W. Süss (eds). *Hitlers Kommissare: Sondergewalten in der nationalsozialistischen Diktatur*. Göttingen: Wallstein, 2006.
Haffner, S. *Germany. Jekyll and Hyde*. New York: Dutton, 1941.
Heller, K.J. *The Nuremberg Military Tribunals and the Origins of International Criminal Law*. Oxford: Oxford University Press, 2011.
Horkenbach, C. (ed.). *Das Deutsche Reich von 1918 bis heute. Jahrgang 1933*. Berlin: Verlag für Presse, Wirtschaft und Politik, 1935.
International Labor Office (ed.). *The Exploitation of Foreign Labor by Germany*. Montreal: International Labor Office, 1945.
Kitchen, M. *Albert Speer. Hitler's Architect*. New Haven, CT: Yale University Press, 2015.
Kochavi, A.J. *Prelude to Nuremberg. Allied War Crimes Policy and the Question of Punishment*. Chapel Hill: University of North Carolina Press, 1998.
Lemkin, R. *Axis Rule in Occupied Europe. Laws of Occupation. Analysis of Government. Proposals for Redress*. Washington, DC: Carnegie Endowment for International Peace, 1944.
Linne, K. 'Von der Arbeitsvermittlung zum Arbeitseinsatz. Zum Wandel der Arbeitsverwaltung 1933–1945', in M. Buggeln and M. Wildt (eds), *Arbeit im Nationalsozialismus* (Munich: De Gruyter Oldenbourg, 2014), 53–73.
Die NS-Führung im Verhör. Original-Tondokumente der Nürnberger Prozesse, documented by U. Lampen, introduced by P. Steinbach, 8 CDs. Berlin: Audio-Verlag, 2006.
Priemel, K.C. *The Betrayal. The Nuremberg Trials and German Divergence*. Oxford: Oxford University Press, 2016.
Priemel, K.C., and A. Stiller (eds). *NMT. Die Nürnberger Militärtribunale zwischen Geschichte, Gerechtigkeit und Rechtschöpfung*. Hamburg: Hamburger Edition, 2014.
Rüter, C.F., and L. Demps (eds). *DDR-Justiz und NS-Verbrechen. Sammlung ostdeutscher Strafurteile wegen nationalsozialistischer Tötungsverbrechen*, 14 vols. Munich: Saur, and Amsterdam: Amsterdam University Press, 2002–2010.
Smith, B. *The Road to Nuremberg*. New York: Basic Books, 1981.
Trial of the Major War Criminals before the International Military Tribunal, Nuremberg 14 November 1945–1 October 1946, 42 vols. Nuremberg: International Military Tribunal Nuremberg, 1947–1949.
Withöft, B. *Die Todesurteile der Waldheimer Prozesse*, Ph.D. dissertation. Vienna: University of Vienna, 2008.

Chapter 13

NEW BEGINNING AND CONTINUITIES
The Top Personnel of the Central German Labour Authorities, 1945–1960

Martin Münzel

On 12 July 1950, the young German Bundestag was the scene of a heated debate on the civil service, the principles underpinning it, and the restaffing of the West German authorities. SPD deputy Adolf Arndt warned that 'a tacit coalition of former [Nazi] party comrades [is making a push] to seize power over personnel policy once again', and referred in particular to the Federal Ministry of Labour (Bundesministerium für Arbeit, or BMA), established a few months earlier. According to Arndt, it had

> surely escaped the notice of Federal Minister [Anton] Storch[1] that due to their feelings of resentment, a group of former party comrades is resolutely determined not to accept a single unencumbered [*unbelastet*] individual, let alone one of the persecuted, into their circle. . . . They always trot out the same old pretext that there aren't any, and if on occasion an unencumbered (female) adviser does come to light, it takes repeated representations to the minister in person and his state secretary [to get anywhere] because otherwise the application or file is nowhere to be found. By no means does this apply only to Social Democrats. Even when it comes to members . . . of the FDP . . . and CDU, there is virtually no chance of promotion if an individual is unencumbered.[2]

Arndt was publicly casting suspicion on an authority whose significance to the development of postwar West German society, given its broad spectrum of governmental tasks, can scarcely be overstated. The responsibilities of the Bonn ministry with the largest budget encompassed, for example, labour market policy, labour law, occupational safety, wages and collective bargaining, social insurance, provision for war victims and international social policy, as well as the supervision of numerous subordinate agencies. But while the Federal Labour Ministry's role in the design of labour and social policy has been subject to intensive research,[3] its staffing structures have largely been ignored from a historical perspective. Overall, for more than half a century, astonishingly little attention has been paid to the staffing composition of the West German ministries. As historians have investigated German governmental authorities over the last few years, however, they have made up a good deal of lost time.[4] Nonetheless, with respect to the Federal Ministry of Labour, we are still in the dark about the repercussions of the years 1945 and 1949 on the composition of its staff. Can we discern caesuras and continuities when it comes to personnel? Did a particularly large number of former Nazi Party members gain posts and influence within the BMA, as asserted by Adolf Arndt?

Along with a brief overview of basic institutional structures, in what follows, on the basis of extensive analysis of the sources, I seek to shed light on these questions by providing the first systematic examination of the senior personnel of the Federal Ministry of Labour and its predecessors. By linking empirical surveys and case studies, I scrutinize the top personnel between 1945 and 1960 and thus during the first decade of West German labour and social policy, a period when the Federal Labour Ministry initiated groundbreaking reforms. I take account of both sociostructural features and the Nazi past of leading ministerial officials. When it comes to the analysis of staffing continuities and discontinuities, hitherto researchers have neglected the relevant agencies in the Allied occupation zones, which functioned as important 'hinges' between 1945 and 1949 – as the former 'proconsuls' of the Reich ministry and as predecessors of its Federal counterpart. Within the framework deployed here, I can address only peripherally the direction and content of labour and social policy, and possible continuities with the pre-1945 period. The same applies to the ministry's organizational history as such.

On the other hand, I consider the central labour authorities in East Germany, and thus a topic to which recent studies of the ministry have paid little attention. For the time being, the sources do not permit as deep an analysis as is possible for West Germany, but complimentary consideration of the Soviet occupation zone and the GDR can extend our perspective, alerting us to contrary developments as well as possible parallels. I focus on the period up to the dissolution of the Ministry of Labour and Vocational Training in 1958. During this era, the East German authorities comprehensively eliminated former Nazi Party members from the civil service, while the growing dominance of the SED and its cadre policy influenced the recruitment of personnel, trends that amount to a markedly different set of historical conditions than in West Germany.[5]

Institutional Continuities in West Germany, 1946–1960

The end of the war in Europe on 8 May 1945 signalled the final fall of the Reich Labour Ministry, symbolized by the heavily damaged ministerial building on Berlin's Saarlandstrasse. In all the Western occupation zones, it was initially the individual Länder that carried on the tasks previously performed by the ministry. Only in the British zone did a central, supreme labour authority soon emerge. In organizational and staffing terms, this developed into the 'nucleus' of the Federal Ministry of Labour, which began its work in October 1949.

In the American occupation zone, responsibility for labour policy remained in the hands of the Land ministries, while the military government merely retained a veto. From October 1945, however, it was the Council of Länder (Länderrat) that functioned as coordinating body with legislative competence, its Department for Social Policy, Welfare Provision and Refugee Issues (Abteilung für Sozialpolitik, Wohlfahrtspflege und Flüchtlingswesen) headed by Ludwig Preller. Preller had worked from 1926 to 1933 as government counsellor in the Reich Labour Ministry and in the Saxony Ministry of Labour and Welfare. A federal setup also prevailed within the French occupation zone, though it was tightly controlled by the Allies. Between 1945 and 1947, the Central Office for Economic and Social Organization (Zentralstelle für wirtschaftliche und soziale Organisation) and later the Central Office for Economy and Labour (Zentralamt für Wirtschaft und Arbeit) functioned as largely ineffective advisory organs.[6]

In the British occupation zone, meanwhile, the Länder played a merely secondary role. Here the key administrative agencies were ten central offices established from the summer of 1945 onwards, which were structurally oriented towards the earlier Reich ministries. With ever-increasing authority to issue instructions and their heads' substantial powers, they themselves resembled ministries, though without the democratic legitimation.[7] The Central Office for Labour (Zentralamt für Arbeit, or ZfA) was based on the Advisory Office for Labour, Settlement and Housing (Beratungsstelle für Arbeit, Siedlungs- und Wohnungswesen), which had been established in March 1946 at the behest of the Control Council Committee (Kontrollratskommission). At least in light of its location in Bad Oeynhausen in eastern Westphalia and, from July 1946, at the Spiegelberg barracks in nearby Lemgo, the Advisory Office seemed like a clear break with the institutional apparatus located in the Reich capital of Berlin. Beset by constant conflicts over centralization and devolution of power to the local level, in early August 1946 the Advisory Office underwent expansion, becoming the Main Office for Labour Administration (Hauptamt

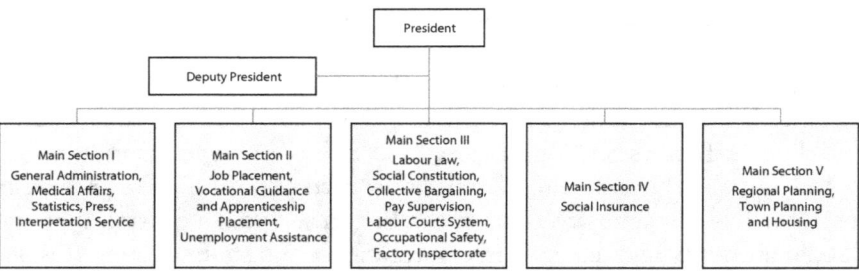

Figure 13.1. Structure of the Central Office for Labour, 1947

für Arbeitsverwaltung) in the British zone; from November 1946, it traded under the name of the Central Office for Labour (Zentralamt für Arbeit).

Despite the fresh start, the structure of the Central Office, with its five main sections, clearly borrowed from the 'classic' structure of the Reich Ministry of Labour as it had existed until the late 1930s.

The ZfA was charged with supporting the military government and, in consultation with the Manpower Division of the British Control Commission, with helping draw up laws and decrees and coordinating their implementation in the Länder. It also issued its own instructions. The appointment, promotion, transfer and dismissal of senior civil servants required the approval of the Central Office, which monitored budgets, inspected business operations and collated statistics on the labour market and employees.

The formation of the United Economic Area, the so-called 'Bizone', as a result of the fusion of the US and British occupation zones on 10 June 1947, went hand in hand with the establishment of five shared special administrations, supplemented by a bespoke Personnel Office. Due both to the Allies' tactical considerations and a number of Länder ministers' reservations about the ZfA, it was not until 13 September 1948 that these bodies were supplemented by the Administration for Labour of the United Economic Area (Verwaltung für Arbeit des Vereinigten Wirtschaftsgebiets, or VfA) in Frankfurt am Main.[8] The latter absorbed the ZfA, which was finally disbanded on 1 April 1949. While this extended the body's reach in a spatial sense, the structure of its divisions remained largely unchanged. One exception was the former Main Section V of the ZfA, which remained in Lemgo as the independent 'Zonal Advisory Office for Housing and Settlement and Urban and Rural Planning' ('Zonale Beratungsstelle für Wohnungs- und Siedlungswesen, Stadt- und Landplanung').

In the course of discussions on the number and profile of the future Federal ministries, the key actors all agreed on the need for a labour ministry, in contrast to the situation in 1919.[9] What was controversial, however, was the question of whether this ministry should be solely devoted to labour issues or whether other powers over social affairs and welfare ought to be

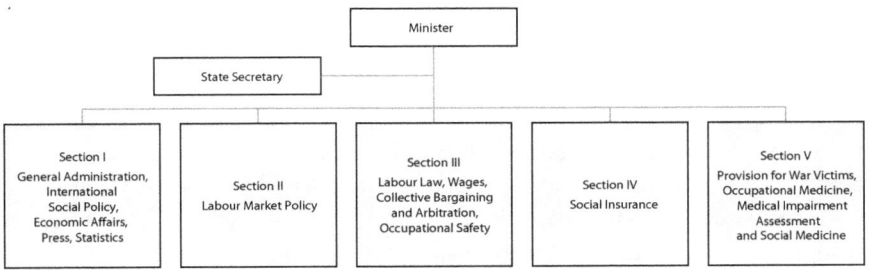

Figure 13.2. Structure of the Federal Ministry of Labour, 1955

integrated into it. The first variant won out, making the Federal Ministry of Labour a direct extension of the VfA. Initially housed, with a small staff, in a former police training college and then in the Troilo barracks in Bonn, the ministry was subdivided into the sections of General Administration (Allgemeine Verwaltung), Labour Market Policy (Arbeitsmarktpolitik), Labour Law (Arbeitsrecht) and Social Insurance (Sozialversicherung), as well as eleven subdivisions; the number of departments increased from sixty-one to sixty-nine between November 1950 and November 1960. Responsibility for welfare and health was transferred to the departments of the Federal Ministry of the Interior (Bundesministerium des Innern), while a separate ministry was established for displaced persons' affairs. The hiving off of the Department for Town Planning and Housing (Städtebau- und Wohnungswesen), which had already been initiated, represented a sharp break with the traditions of the Ministry of Labour. In view of the tremendous challenges arising from wartime destruction and the need for proportionality among the governing coalition parties of the CDU, CSU and FDP, the government decided to establish a Federal Ministry of Housing (Bundesministerium für Wohnungsbau).[10]

With the transfer of occupational and social medicine from Section I, and of provision for war victims from Section IV, to the newly established Section V, on 1 January 1955 the BMA underwent a modification of its basic structure, which then remained largely unchanged for almost fifteen years. In 1957, the authority was renamed the Federal Ministry of Labour and Social Order (Bundesministerium für Arbeit und Sozialordnung).

A Fresh Start on Staffing in the British Occupation Zone and the Bizone, 1945–1949

The direct link with traditional organizational structures evident within the labour authorities was not immediately replicated in the development of its staff. In fact, the end of the war had profound consequences for the leading staff of the former Reich Labour Ministry. Labour Minister Franz Seldte was arrested by the Allies and died in detention in April 1947 in Fürth. State Secretary Friedrich Syrup, previously the long-standing president of the Reich Institution for Job Placement and Unemployment Insurance, was arrested in June 1945 and died a few weeks later in the Soviet camp of Oranienburg-Sachsenhausen. Ministerial Counsellor Oskar Karstedt also died there in October 1945, having been, among other things, a key specialist in international social policy at the Reich Labour Ministry since 1919. State Secretary Hans Engel also died in Soviet internment, probably also in 1945.[11]

The year 1945 also represented a profound turning point for around three-quarters of the officials from the upper reaches of the ministerial hierarchy. They were never again to find their feet professionally in any of the central German labour or housing authorities. Even among the government counsellors and senior government counsellors, who were only forty-five years old on average, less than a third returned. Many of those who were unable to retire are likely to have shifted permanently into the private sector. Others managed to find positions in the extensive network of subordinate agencies, such as the labour offices, the Federal Institute for Labour (Bundesanstalt für Arbeit), the social insurance institutes or the labour and social courts. Finally, the labour and social administrations of the federal Länder also offered potential occupational boltholes.

Of the Jewish members of staff expelled from the Reich Ministry of Labour after 1933, Ministerial Counsellor Dorothea Hirschfeld was the only one to resume her professional career. Responsible for the field of welfare provision under the Weimar Republic, she had survived the Theresienstadt Ghetto and in 1945, at the age of sixty-eight, had made herself available to the Main Administration for Healthcare (Hauptverwaltung für das Gesundheitswesen) in the Soviet occupation zone (SBZ) as an adviser. Ministerial Director Oscar Weigert, an influential expert on labour law and long-standing section head in the Reich Ministry of Labour, had been forced into retirement on 1 April 1933. Now in the United States, he contacted the Federal Labour Ministry to present his claim to compensation and a retirement pension. The correspondence with Weigert, who had been working since 1938 as an academic and member of staff of the US Department of Labor in Washington DC, following stints as adviser to that institution and to the Turkish Ministry of the Economy, was conciliatory in tone, though there was no substantial exchange on policy issues.[12]

For those members of ministerial staff dismissed from the civil service after the war and subject to automatic arrest as senior personnel, a period of uncertainty and a struggle to maintain a middle-class existence began. On the subjective level, many of them were shocked by their loss of status, the 'repression' they suffered and by the looming prospect of sanctions and 'atonement measures' – experiences that were, of course, not remotely comparable with the loss of rights and persecution suffered by Jewish officials within the Nazi state.[13] Former State Secretary Johannes Krohn, for example, penned a powerful account of his impressions of his just under one year of internment in Bayreuth Prison and in the Bavarian camp of Moosburg in 1945–1946. He related his experience of undernourishment, depression and utter despair, which sometimes prompted him to long for death.[14] From the perspective of those affected, the professional rupture alone could engender a sense of insecurity, leaving them shaken and fearful for the future, with possible long-term effects that are hard to assess. Sometimes for years, many later officials of the Federal Labour Ministry had little choice but to find employment in law practices, tax consultancies and insurance firms, craft businesses and breweries, and even as assistant carpenters and forestry or sawmill workers.

At the same time, immediately after Germany's capitulation, the Western Allies set about utilizing the specialist knowledge of the German administrative elite. More than 1,200 former members of ministerial staff, including fourteen top officials of the former Labour Ministry, were taken to the Ministerial Collecting Center in Hessisch Lichtenau, south-east of Kassel. On the premises of a former ammunition factory, the internees were tasked with sifting through and sorting 1,250 tonnes of files, and with drawing up hundreds of memoranda and reports, while also being questioned by occupation officers and deployed as special advisers. This collective stint in the camp is likely to have helped forge networks that would play a key role in future.[15]

In the British zone, the occupiers initially proceeded with a large staff of their own administrative officials, before falling back on expert personnel of the former Reich administration to staff the zonal agencies, which they did with far less inhibition than their US counterparts.[16] The composition of the Central Office for Labour, however, at least when it came to its leading personnel, clearly signalled a fresh start, featuring individuals of impeccable political standing who also had relevant experience.

The decision to appoint Julius Scheuble[17] president was reinforced by the arrival of Vice-President Walter Auerbach at the ZfA in October 1946.[18] After gaining his Ph.D., from 1930 to 1933 Auerbach was a member of the executive board of an employees' association. As a Jewish emigrant, he then joined the International Transport Workers' Federation, initially in Amsterdam and, when the war broke out, in London, where he also campaigned for the political and social reform of Germany after the war. The leadership of the ZfA thus lay in the hands of two men with a trades union background. It was also balanced in the sense that Scheuble's roots lay in the Christian trades union movement and he became a member of the CDU, while Auerbach had been involved in the socialist trades union movement and had been a member of the SPD since 1926.

When it came to the other personnel responsible for a territory of more than twenty-two million inhabitants, at a ZfA press conference in the summer of 1946, Scheuble pointed out that to make up for the dismissed former Nazi Party members, 80 per cent of posts had had to be filled with new people, who would require some time to learn the ropes.[19] In light of the severe lack of staff and of skilled specialists, the Central Office was in fact a heterogeneous microcosm (see Figure 13.3).[20] Less than a quarter of the section and department heads had previously worked at the Reich Ministry of Labour (Reichsarbeitsministerium, or RAM), and a somewhat larger proportion in its subordinate agencies. Almost 45 per cent of them, meanwhile, were temporary newcomers from other fields, local experts and other employees from a variety of backgrounds, such as associations and professional bodies. This group included architects and businessmen as well as the former staff of establishments such as the Berlin Institute for Economic Research (Berliner Institut für Wirtschaftsforschung). With the exception of Section Head Rudolf Petz from Graz, who had worked at the Reich Ministry of the Interior from 1938, there were no former officials from other Reich ministries. Overall, then, we find marked differences from the traditional recruitment and composition of Reich Labour Ministry staff.[21] At forty-nine, staff members' average age was fairly low, while 65 per cent of them had obtained a doctorate.

The staffing tableau encompassed the 65-year-old former mayor of Ratibor (Racibórz) and department head in Section I, Adolf Kaschny, along with architect and building researcher Hans Steckeweh as head of Sec-

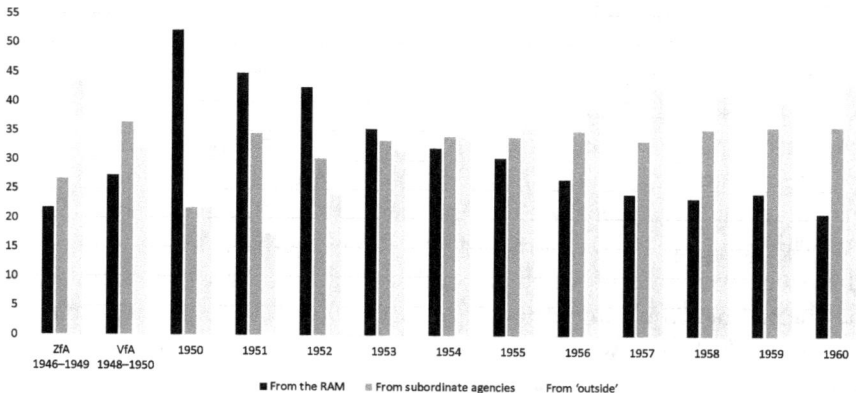

Figure 13.3. Institutional background of senior personnel at the Central Office for Labour, the Administration for Labour and the Federal Ministry of Labour, 1946–1960 (in per cent)

tion V, that is, the later Zonal Advisory Office in Lemgo. Like Steckeweh's predecessor Philipp Rappaport, a number of department heads worked for the ZfA in addition to their employment elsewhere. Rappaport had been dismissed as director of the Ruhrkohlenbezirk Settlement Association (Siedlungsverband Ruhrkohlenbezirk) in Essen in 1933, and was reappointed to the post in 1945. At the ZfA, however, his dual role led to tensions, prompting him to submit his resignation in June 1947.[22] Similarly, the director-general of the Westfälische Heimstätte GmbH in Münster, Heinrich Vormbrock, worked as an adviser on the organization and financing of housing; likewise, the return of other members of staff to their original professional fields made the difficult staffing situation worse.

From autumn 1948, the incorporation of the Central Office for Labour into the Administration for Labour in Frankfurt am Main went hand in hand with the large-scale integration of its staff into that institution. Just under 70 per cent of the department heads had previously been employed at the ZfA, and only a few members of staff transferred from the Council of Länder in the US zone to the bizonal administration.[23] At the same time, however, former officials of the Reich Ministry of Labour and its subordinate agencies began to gain posts in greater numbers (see Figure 13.3), a tendency reinforced by the general political shift away from proportionality between SPD and CDU/CSU, as the latter sought to assert its dominance.[24] The 'collective efforts, made over months, to at least keep the Administration for Labour out of the party-political conflict, and to emulate the all-party union by establishing an Administration for Labour that genuinely stood apart from the political parties' had failed, as Walter Auerbach resignedly stated. He declined to accept a VfA post that he regarded as 'devoid of all influence' and 'toothless'.[25] Julius Scheuble, as a representative of the left wing of the CDU, a man about whom the southern German Länder in particular had considerable reservations, also lost influence. On 10 September 1948, as deputy to Anton Storch, he was merely appointed vice-president of the Administration for Labour. Contrary to his firm expectations, and to the great chagrin of the Christian trades unionists, he was not made state secretary in the new Federal Ministry of Labour. At the insistence of the coalition partners of the FDP and DP, he was instead appointed to a far less significant post as head of Section II.[26]

Reconstruction in the Federal Ministry of Labour, 1949–1960

By the time the Federal Republic of Germany was founded in 1949, it was plainly apparent that the authorities were increasingly drawing on officials from the Nazi era. A small group of ex-officials from the Reich Ministry of the Interior, reflecting, not least, the wishes of Konrad Adenauer, drew up staff lists, with the objective of appointing representatives of the old civil service to posts in the upper echelons of the Bonn ministries and other key positions. They were also keen to push back against the social democratic influences that had supposedly been cemented with the help of the Bizone Personnel Office. As a result, in August 1950, almost 43 per cent of all section heads came from the former Reich ministries, while half were members of the CDU/CSU; somewhat more than 9 per cent were members of the SPD.[27]

Within the central labour authorities as well, the rapid enlargement of the corpus of personnel was intertwined with a dramatic reconstruction of staffing structures. Overall, the number of civil servants, white-collar and blue-collar workers grew rapidly until 1952, and more slowly over the next few years. In its December 1950 issue alone, the *Bundesarbeitsblatt* (Federal Labour Gazette) reported ninety-eight staffing changes, encompassing promotions, civil service appointments and the absorption of new employees from other agencies (see Figure 13.4).[28]

The employment relationships that had pertained at the ministry's predecessor agency, in other words the VfA, were to a large degree perpetuated, and the number of top officials who had been employed at the Reich Ministry of Labour increased over the course of 1950 to 52.2 per cent (see Figure 13.3). To a significant degree, however, this was a merely temporary effect. Given an average age of fifty-nine, which was about four years older than that of the top staff in the Reich Ministry of Labour at the end of the war, in 1950 almost a third and in 1951 a quarter of these officials had been born before 1890. Hence, in the summer of 1953, in the shape of ministerial counsellors Heinrich Goldschmidt and Michael-Josef Bauer, as well as Section Head Kurt Classen, three leading officials had already

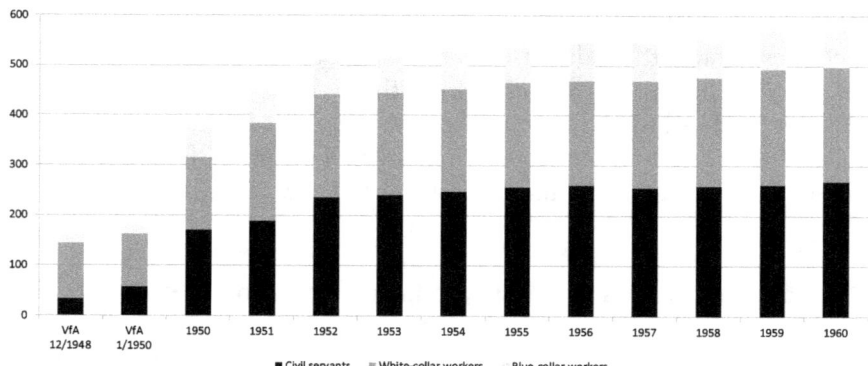

Figure 13.4. Number of civil servants, white-collar workers and blue-collar workers at the Administration for Labour and Federal Ministry of Labour, 1948–1960

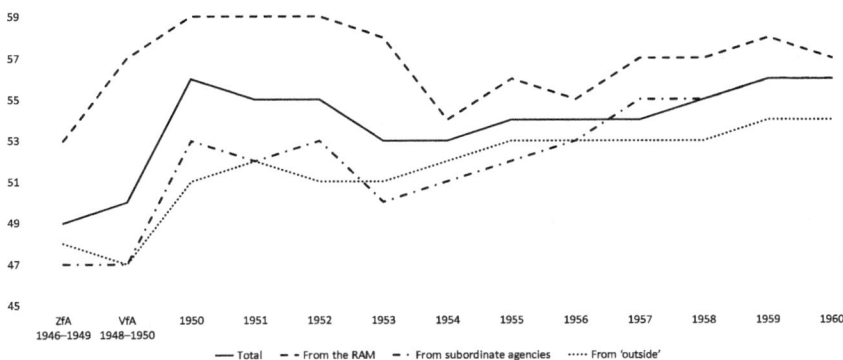

Figure 13.5. Average age of senior personnel at the Central Office for Labour, the Administration for Labour and the Federal Ministry of Labour, 1946–1960 (in per cent)

departed at the same time, all of whom had previously worked at the Reich Ministry of Labour since 1919–1921. Overall, between 1950 and 1960, the degree of continuity of staff vis-à-vis the old Reich authority stood at 27.4 per cent, about the same as at the Federal Ministry of Economic Affairs (Bundesministerium für Wirtschaft, or BMWi). Of ninety-eight members of staff in the upper echelons of the Foreign Ministry, by contrast, between 1949 and 1955 almost two-thirds came from the old Foreign Office.[29] Until 1960, the share of staff members from the former subordinate agencies of the Reich Ministry of Labour remained relatively constant, at a little over one-third. This suggests that it was business as usual in West Germany, with up-and-coming young workers transferring to the 'mother institution' over the course of their professional career.

As far as religious affiliation is concerned, the senior levels of the BMA were no fundamental exception to the prevalent overrepresentation of Protestants within the ministries (see Figure 13.6). Official surveys of re-

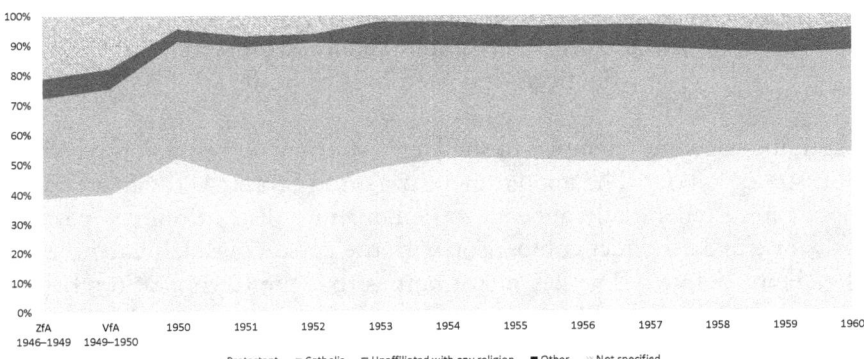

Figure 13.6. Religious affiliation of senior personnel at the Central Office for Labour, the Administration for Labour and the Federal Ministry of Labour, 1946–1960 (in per cent)

ligious adherents, however, revealed that the share of Catholic staff members at the BMA, at 40 per cent in 1950 and 38.3 per cent in 1960, lay significantly above the average figure for the ministries as a whole (26 per cent in 1950 and 26.9 per cent in 1960); for a brief period in 1952, Catholics even held the majority of posts at the top of the Federal Ministry of Labour.[30] The equivalent group of officials at the Reich Ministry of Labour had been comprised on average of around three-quarters Protestants, so it is reasonable to think in terms of a shift in staff members' religious affiliation after 1949. A key factor here was geographical origin. Around one-fifth of leading BMA staff members came from the largely Catholic former Rhine Province, and, in the early years of the ministry, several of them hailed from Bavaria and Baden. It was not until 1953 that a greater number of officials born in the (largely Protestant) Berlin-Brandenburg region than in other Federal authorities were promoted to senior positions.[31]

Finally, when it came to educational qualifications, the BMA again stood foursquare in the tradition of the Reich Ministry of Labour. As in other ministries, the most striking hallmark here was the classic jurists' monopoly, but in fields such as insurance, occupational safety and medicine, the institution relied on a broad-based cadre of specialists. Over the medium term, economists, engineers and natural scientists, who had already been present in the ZfA and VfA in fairly large numbers, became more important. Among members of the upper-level civil service as well, in comparison with the other Federal ministries, the BMA featured by far the largest share of 'outsiders' not educated in law, at 29 per cent (1958).[32] At the same time, there was a decline in the number of staff members without a university degree among senior personnel. The fact that 56.3 per cent of them held a Ph.D. (1950–1960) attests to the high educational level overall.

Insights into Personnel: Federal Ministers, Sections and Members of Staff

Let us look at some examples to shed light on the senior staff at the Federal Ministry of Labour. The appointment of Anton Storch as the first Federal labour minister initially appears to demonstrate discontinuity – particularly if we make a direct comparison with the person of Reich Labour Minister Franz Seldte.[33] The key factor here is that the Catholic Storch (and his successor Theodor Blank, already favoured to take over by Adenauer in 1949), born in Fulda in 1892, was a prominent trades unionist. Certainly, his curriculum vitae tallied with the demands of the CDU/CSU, and of Konrad Adenauer himself, for a figure with close ties to the working class and the trades unions. Yet even his appointment as director of the VfA, on 20 August 1948, occurred in the face of resistance. It was ultimately Storch's nomination for the ministerial post that imperilled the formation of the first Bonn coalition in September 1949 – in light of the profound reservations and resistance of business and other interest groups, the FDP and DP, and even from the ranks of the CDU/CSU.[34]

Storch remained a controversial figure during his time in office. For some, this may have been reinforced by the fact that, even as head of the ministry, he still came across as a 'man fresh from the carpenter's bench', one who made his way through the capital on a bicycle.[35] But above all, many doubted that he was effectively steering the Labour Ministry to pursue the government's goals, and he faced increasing public criticism regarding his lack of initiative when it came to social policy reforms. The first and most severe attacks, however, came in response to his willingness to consider a system of universal insurance.

The background here was the fact that, seen in the round, Section IV (Social Insurance) formed the nucleus of the young ministry. For many political actors, meanwhile, the battle, fought with missionary zeal, against universal insurance and to maintain the independence of the various branches of the insurance system (and a plurality of insurance companies) became a key part of their identity. This was reinforced by the fact that the advocates of the 'classic' social insurance system saw it as a realm largely untouched by Nazi influences.[36] Given these premises, Storch's call for the amalgamation of all insurance companies and the establishment of unified Land-level insurance institutes made him seem like a 'socialist in disguise' to some. Those holding this view wanted him stripped of the power to shape the social insurance system, even if this meant establishing a separate social affairs ministry.[37]

Ultimately, Storch was widely accepted as Federal labour minister because Maximilian Sauerborn[38] was made his deputy, an 'experienced state secretary' who had already been put forward as a rival candidate to Storch when the latter was selected as director of the VfA. In 1949, Sauerborn had even been brought into play as a possible minister. As a member of staff at the Social Insurance Department of the Reich Ministry of Labour since July 1923, he was one of the large number of West German state secretaries of the first generation who had had an administrative career or gained experience in a Reich ministry. He was regarded as a guardian par excellence of the traditional system of social insurance, a man who had helped fend off the Nazi leaders' attempts to misuse it. As early as 1946, Sauerborn had been recruited as an expert consultant in the US zone, and it was for good reason that the BMA deferred his retirement, originally earmarked for 1954, three times until 1957.[39]

Also caught up in the wake of the controversies over social insurance was mathematician Wilhelm Dobbernack. While he had been employed at the Reich Ministry of Labour since 1927, as head of Main Section IV of the ZfA he sympathized with efforts to reform social insurance law and favoured close ties to the trades unions.[40] Dobbernack complained that he had been subjected to 'many tactless and snide remarks', and in autumn 1952 he took up a post at the International Labour Organization in Geneva, having been prevented from becoming head of Section IV of the BMA. With much bitterness, he referred to a 'petit bourgeois, in some cases downright reactionary politics in my policy field, one centred on an unimaginative process of restoration' and a 'staffing policy that threatened to starve me of air, one that puts the screws on staff, at least those of my ilk, and holds us down'.[41]

Instead, in 1949, Josef Eckert, a close friend of Sauerborn, became head of the Social Insurance Section. He had worked as a department head in the Reich Ministry of Labour since 1920 and defended the classic system of social insurance with journalistic zeal.[42] With his 'extreme immobility',[43] however, until his retirement at the end of 1954, Eckert obstructed urgent programmatic reform initiatives. It was not until the establishment of the 'General Secretariat for Social Reform' ('Generalsekretariat für die Sozialreform') that the government managed to achieve a breakthrough. This entailed setting a fundamentally new course for social policy, centred on the pension reform of 1957, a move that did much to stabilize postwar West German society. Nonetheless, once again a former social insurance adviser of the Reich Labour Ministry was put at the top of the General Secretariat, namely Kurt Jantz, born in 1908. Under his leadership, officials born between 1901 and 1928 came together in the secretariat, including a new generation of pro-reform academics. According to Hans Günter Hockerts, this turned the General Secretariat into a model 'for the expeditious regeneration of the ministerial civil service in the Adenauer era'. In his eyes, it also made the secretariat the basis for the continuity of senior officials at the BMA, right into the 1980s.[44]

The highest-ranking surviving representative of the old Reich Labour Ministry, Johannes Krohn (Jantz had been his personal adviser for a time), also rose to become a key figure once again from the late 1940s onwards.[45] 'Thirteen years ago, I became state secretary', he noted in February 1946; 'Just think of everything that has happened since'.[46] As the president of the Civil Servants' Protection League (Beamtenschutzbund), founded in Bavaria in 1948, Krohn advanced to become a standard-bearer of the opposition to reform plans that threatened to shake the very foundations of the German civil service. Not only did large sections of the general population feel resentment towards civil servants, but the Allies were also planning to pull the rug from under the traditions of the civil service by creating a Personnel Office answerable to no one, breaking the jurists' monopoly and opening up the civil service career to white-collar workers and other applicants. The successful lobbying carried out by Krohn and others not only led to the abandonment of such plans. It also ensured, on the basis of Article 131 of the Basic Law (Grundgesetz; the German constitution), the return to the civil service of 'ousted officials' who had lost their jobs as displaced persons after 1945 or had been dismissed as a consequence of Allied denazification measures. From the early 1950s until 1961, the various branches of the administrative system had to fill 20 per cent of their established posts with '131ers' (named for Article 131), of whom at least 430,000 managed to return to public service.[47] The 'dire state of affairs', featuring a 'great deal of misery, distress and bitterness', which Krohn had assailed in June 1949, had thus been averted. 'Germany can no longer afford to forgo the manpower of tried-and-tested and loyal officials, who have dedicated their lives to the general public.'[48]

Of at least equal importance was Krohn's role as the great white hope who would 'save' social insurance as it had existed hitherto. He was giving talks on this subject before his internment was even over, and after being released he composed numerous memoranda, expert reports and essays. Krohn pursued his cause with tremendous energy, through tireless correspondence, and at personal meetings, for example with high-ranking representatives of the occupation zones and trades unions, but also with Julius Scheuble and Wilhelm Dobbernack in Lemgo; he was also invited to speak at associations and insurance companies. 'Like you, I believe it is worthwhile to keep on trying everything possible to avert disaster from befalling our tried-and-tested system of social insurance', as Krohn underlined in April 1947 to former SPD Labour Minister Rudolf Wissell, whose support for Krohn's cause lent it a considerable degree of prestige. 'Why on earth should everything always be changed from top to bottom! With all these reforms we never get around to doing any real work. But I hope reason might still prevail in the end.'[49] While there was no longer any prospect of Krohn returning to a ministerial post, he made up for this through his impact at association level well into his later years. In June 1953, he was elected president of the Cologne-based Society for Insurance Science and Organization (Gesellschaft für Versicherungswissenschaft und -gestaltung e. V.), founded in May 1947. Krohn headed this body for six years, one of the most influential umbrella organizations representing insurance firms on both the national and European levels. The society advocated on behalf of a variety of interest groups, against the background of the German insurance companies' close links with the political sphere.[50]

In contrast to the field of social insurance and the self-image of its representatives, labour law was viewed as having been severely undermined by Nazi influences. And it was Wilhelm Herschel,[51] head of Section III of the BMA (Labour Law, Wages, Collective Wage Agreements and Arbitration, Occupational Safety), who represented the most exceptional case of a BMA section head from 'outside'. With considerable reluctance, this professor of labour law, who had absolutely no ministerial experience, had taken over as head of Main Section III of the ZfA in October 1946, and he went on to hold this position in both the VfA and the BMA, until his retirement in 1960. His exceptional position took on great importance because, beyond his leadership of the section, few tasks were ever passed on to the Minister's Office.[52]

Unlike Herschel, however, his successor Günther Schelp had worked at the Reich Ministry of Labour since 1934, and had made himself available as a consultant to the legal department of the Nazi Party's Foreign Organization (Auslandsorganisation).[53] In addition, Subdivision III a (Labour Law), which he headed, became a gathering point for former staff members of the Reich trustee administration created in 1933; in 1960, they made up half of the eight department heads.[54] The melange of continuities and discontinuities with respect to staff became more complicated: in the shape of Franz Ringer and Karl Fitting, two of the politically or 'racially' persecuted held posts there. And it was none other than Fitting, forced to abandon his study of law in 1933, who made a signal contribution to drawing up the Coal and Steel Co-Determination Law (Montanmitbestimmungsgesetz, 1951) and the Works Constitution Law (Betriebsverfassungsgesetz, 1952), two early milestones in the West German push to consolidate workers' rights of participation.

Finally, if we turn to the role of women employees, we find that the upper echelons of the central West German labour authorities remained male domains. In the shape of Marie Schulte Langforth and Maria Tritz, by 1960 just two women had managed to obtain senior posts at the Federal Ministry of Labour.[55] Schulte Langforth, with her Ph.D. in law, worked from 1929 until 1945 for the Frankfurt-based lobbying organization known as the Archive of German Occupational Guardians (Archiv deutscher Berufsvormünder; now the German Institute for Youth Human Services and Family Law [Deutsches Institut für Jugendhilfe und Familienrecht]), and after the war at the East German health administration. From there she transferred to Section III of the BMA. In Maria Tritz, in 1950 the ministry gained a department head who had previously worked in the Rhineland labour administration, for the Reich Commissioner for the Occupied Dutch Territories (Reichskommissar für die besetzten niederländischen Gebiete) in the Hague in 1940–1941 and at the North Rhine-Westphalia Land

Labour Office in 1945 as a specialist in women's labour deployment. In 1950, then, they became the first female department heads in the history of the Federal Ministry of Labour, with responsibility for the protection of women, children and young people (Schulte Langforth) and the gainful employment of women (Tritz). The appointment of Marie-Elisabeth Wendland in 1956 was a special case: she was the daughter, born in 1914, of Johannes Krohn. She gained a Ph.D. in 1941 on 'the state and social insurance in Great Britain and Germany', and between 1947 and 1949 she also worked in the field of social insurance at the ZfA. Having launched a new career in 1956, Wendland worked in Section IV, eventually becoming head of the department in charge of accident insurance in 1966, and she was appointed ministerial counsellor in 1967, just as her father had been forty-four years earlier.[56]

Denazification and Defensive Moves under the Western Allies, 1945–1949

One important aspect bound up with the question of continuities of personnel beyond 1945, an issue that requires analysis in its own right, are those 'encumbrances' or 'burdens' (*Belastungen*) resulting from biographical links extending back into the Nazi era, and the West German government's approach to them. Initially, the starting point here was the process of so-called denazification. While this ultimately led to the de facto rehabilitation of 90 per cent of all those registered, from 1945 the former staff members of the Reich ministries and applicants for posts in the newly established agencies were subject to comprehensive investigation, with an uncertain outcome. At the Central Office for Labour, as elsewhere, this was a complex and time-consuming affair, and those seeking employment there had to complete the denazification process and obtain classification in Category V ('exonerated'; '*Entlastet*').[57]

Even those classified as 'followers' ('*Mitläufer*', Category IV) had good prospects. In a new appointment procedure, they could highlight their allegedly apolitical if not anti-Nazi stance, with reference to matching eye-witness statements. For example, Ministerial Counsellor Fritz Paetzold, who had been working at the ZfA since 1947, managed to persuade the investigating committee that he had joined the Nazi Party in 1940 'only under extreme pressure from the then head of personnel [at the Reich Ministry of Labour], who was known to be a brutal party functionary', namely Wilhelm Börger. Paetzold's long-standing boss, Prof. Otto Martineck, also attributed to him a 'highly ethical view of his profession as physician, [he is] always ready to help in the manner of a good doctor'.[58]

Given the uncertainty that prevailed during the first few years after the war, the intensive efforts made by former high officials of the Reich Ministry of Labour, in the context of denazification, to procure a 'clearance certificate' (*Entlastungszeugnis*), reactivated and consolidated collegial networks of solidarity. Johannes Krohn, for example, was able to build on the issuance of a large number of *Persilscheine* ('denazification certificates'), in which, among others, Rudolf Wissell, Maximilian Sauerborn and Dorothea Hirschfeld attested to his impeccable if not resistant attitude during the years of the dictatorship. In June 1946, Krohn then informed former section head at the Reich Ministry of Labour, Alexander Wende, that he was 'proud that my former colleagues have shown me such loyalty, and their recognition of the manner in which I discharged my office is tremendously gratifying'.[59]

Josef Eckert went further still in a justificatory text that first appeared in 1947. There he linked the defence of the personnel policy pursued by the Reich Labour Ministry and the attitude of civil servants after 1933 with a word of warning: Germany must not 'come apart at the seams because it is split between [Nazi] party comrades and non-party comrades'. The only individuals who ought to be punished were those who had 'behaved like "political pigs" or committed crimes'; a 'process of purification' should be applied only to those who had been 'genuine "Nazi officials"'.[60]

Fundamentally, Eckert's line of argument differed little from that of Julius Scheuble, who argued against 'a schematic form of denazification operating in light of external characteristics' in February 1946, against the background of staffing shortages but also in light of his self-image as an administrative official. Particularly in the labour administration, he asserted, there had been virtually no senior officials

> who were not members of the party. This regrettable truth is down to the fact that the labour authorities were misused by the Nazis as special instruments for pursuing their policies. Unrelenting pressure was brought to bear in order to prompt officials to join the party. The German civil servant had meagre political skills. Trained to be obedient, after 1933, unfortunately, he carried out his Nazi superiors' instructions all too willingly. If we do not hold it against the soldier that he had to carry out orders to fire his weapon and destroy, why should the civil servant be made to pay for administering, in response to official instructions, that which the soldiers conquered by force of arms'.

Scheuble warned that 'large numbers of people are succumbing to political radicalism, and thus being lost to the peaceful development of a new state'. As a pragmatic solution, he proposed that those who had joined the Nazi Party between 1933 and 1937 could be employed as white-collar workers reporting to politically unencumbered senior civil servants or white-collar staff.[61]

As far as formal Nazi 'encumbrance' was concerned, at least half of all section and department heads at the ZfA had never joined the Nazi party, a proportion that was generally even higher at the VfA, while former party members made up around a third (see Figure 13.7). Evidently, under the circumstances a certain number of potential staff members initially refrained from applying for jobs, even though denazification was pursued pragmatically in the British zone and allowed for exceptions for those regarded as indispensable to keeping the economy and administrative system going.

That specific cases nonetheless entailed the potential for conflict was evident, among other things, in the recruitment of former head of the Reich Association of German Non-Profit Housing (Reichsverband des deutschen gemeinnützigen Wohnungswesens), Julius Brecht, whose Nazi Party past made it impossible to appoint him deputy head of Main Section V. Julius Scheuble also struggled to retain Jakob Käfferbitz, who had joined the Nazi Party in May 1933; as head of Main Section I b of the ZfA, he was earmarked for demotion from senior government counsellor to government inspector. The idea of appointing Käfferbitz personnel officer in the Administration for Labour subsequently came to nothing. He had little choice but to take up a post in the Budget Department and wait until 1 February 1950, when he was appointed subdivision head at the Federal Ministry of Labour.[62]

Nazi 'Encumbrances' in the Federal Ministry of Labour, 1949–1960

From 1949, the Federal Ministry of Labour too helped expedite the 'silent, gradual, insidious, inexorable return of yesterday's men', to quote from the trenchant reckoning penned in 1954 by journalist and political scientist Eugen Kogon, who assailed this process as the fate of West Germany and as the victory of the '131ers' over the '45ers'.[63] What is more, the BMA led from the front in employing 'ousted officials' in accordance with Article 131 of the Basic Law. By 1 July 1951, a third of its permanent civil service posts were already occupied by such officials, well above the overall ministerial share of 23.7 per cent; by 30 September 1953, 39.1 per cent (compared with a ministerial figure of 23.3 per cent) of its posts were occupied by '131ers'.[64]

By late September 1949, Walter Auerbach was expressing alarm at the likelihood that 'even the "Brown Guard" will be appointed as officials in the Federal Ministry of Labour to come. It may be necessary to bring this to the attention of the Bundestag deputies'.[65] As it turned out, Auerbach's fears were justified. By 1953, the number of top officials in the newly established authority who had been members of the Nazi Party already outweighed the number of non-party members. This had increased to two-thirds by 1955 and 70.1 per cent by 1960 (see Figure 13.7). By the start of the 1960s, only nineteen out of sixty-seven civil servants had never been members of the Nazi Party, while during the 1950–1960 period as a whole, around 60 per cent of top civil servants in the Federal Ministry of Labour had been members. From a horizontal perspective, we can discern significant differences. In 1960, three out of the five section heads had been in the Nazi Party, while by 1950 this already applied to half of those one level down, namely the subdivision heads, reaching a peak in 1956 at 92.3 per cent. From a vertical vantage point, in 1960 all the leading personnel in Section V (Provision for War Victims, Social and Occupational Medicine) had been in the Nazi Party; with the exception of the section head, this was true also of Section I (General Administration).

Factoring in the date when officials became members of the party might lead us to expect that the advance of younger officials, who had not joined until 1937, played a role here, the German Civil Service Law of 1 July 1937 having granted the party greater involvement in appointments and promotions. Yet the BMA increasingly employed the very officials who had already been members of the Nazi Party in 1933.[66] In 1953, they abruptly increased in number to one-third (ten individuals) of top officials; by 1960, this had risen to just under 43 per cent (twenty individuals). Many of them had also held posts within the party, while in 1960 a third of all top officials had been involved in the SA as well (see Figures 13.7 and 13.8). Officials of the former Reich Labour Ministry were particularly significant here, whereas far fewer staff members of an 'external' background, who had not even worked at the ministry's subordinate agencies, had been in the Nazi Party or SA. The heterogeneous composition of the latter group is a serious impediment to systematic comparison. But if we attempt to explain these trends by singling out the six top officials at the ministry in 1960 who had previously worked at the Reich Ministry of Labour and had already been members of the Nazi Party in 1933, we can discern a highly homogeneous group. Almost all of them were born between 1902 and 1908, and in 1933 they were studying law or were about to enter a career in the labour administration. We can thus assume that career considerations at least helped influence their decision to join the party. All of them then took up posts in the Reich Ministry of Labour in 1938–1939. When appointed to the BMA, they had reached an age by 1954 at which personal experience and future potential for the ministry were optimally combined. Before 1937–1938, it would be inaccurate to suggest that the top officials in the Reich Ministry of Labour had been completely 'Nazified'. This is evident in the fact that among those BMA officials born before 1900, the proportion of Nazi Party members was far smaller, and they joined the party notably later.

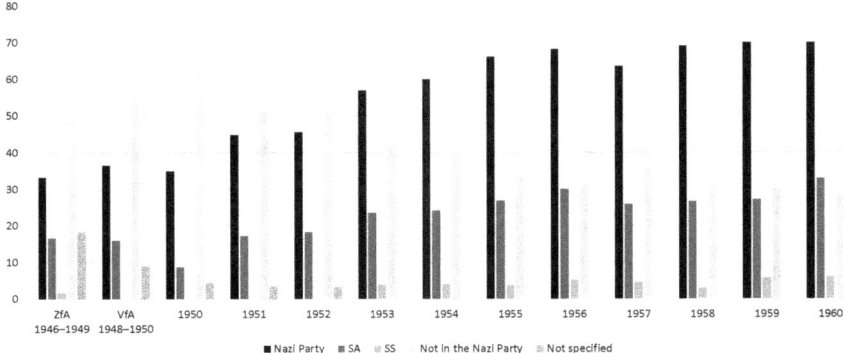

Figure 13.7. Former Nazi Party, SA and SS members as a share of senior personnel at the Central Office for Labour, the Administration for Labour and the Federal Ministry of Labour, 1946–1960 (in per cent)

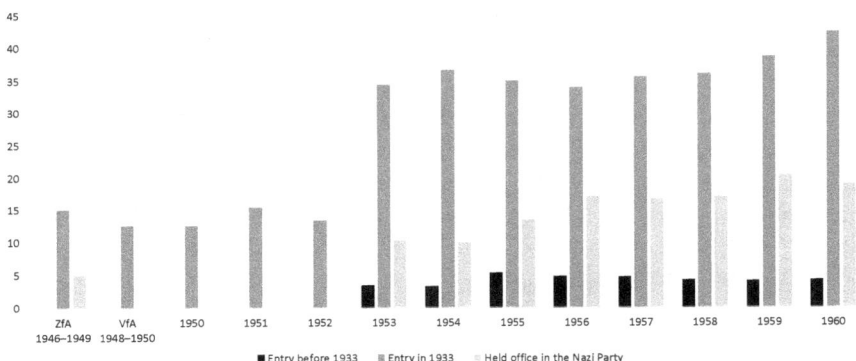

Figure 13.8. Date of entry into and post held in the Nazi Party among senior personnel at the Central Office for Labour, the Administration for Labour and the Federal Ministry of Labour, 1946–1960 (in per cent)

It would make sense to compare these figures with the situation in other Federal authorities. But this is problematic as the relevant surveys generally referred to differently structured samples of people and divergent time frames. We can draw at least general parallels with the Federal Ministry of the Interior (Bundesinnenministerium), in which the share of former Nazi Party members among leading officials was 61 per cent in September 1953 and 66 per cent in 1961.[67] In the Federal Ministry of Justice (Bundesjustizministerium), meanwhile, the figure among employees at the department head level and above was particularly high in 1957, at 76 per cent, though it fell back to 55 per cent by 1963. In the Federal Foreign Office, on the other hand, only just over one-third of senior staff were in this category at the beginning of 1952.[68] In terms of its staffing structure, the Federal Ministry of Labour can be clearly distinguished from organizations established after 1945, such as the Federal Office for the Protection of the Constitution (Bundesamt für Verfassungsschutz), the Federal Criminal Police Office (Bundeskriminalamt) and the Federal Intelligence Service (Bundesnachrichtendienst). A considerable number of their staff were former members of the Gestapo, SS or Reich Security Main Office, while even some of their heads were seriously 'encumbered'.[69]

Beyond the empirical findings, on the basis of the available sources it is very hard to determine to what extent, when it came to the possible impact on the Federal Ministry of Labour's public image, its personnel policy was down to indifference or strategy, or whether the Nazi past of individuals was consciously disregarded. We may assume, however, that its approach to recruitment did not remain unaffected by public controversies of the kind inspired, for example, by the reconstruction of the Federal Foreign Office.[70] The attacks emanating from the GDR must have caused disquiet, particularly the 'blood-soaked judges' (*Blutrichter*) campaign launched in the mid 1950s and the *Braunbuch* ('Brown Book'), published for the first time in 1965. Among other things, on the basis of generally correct information, this volume denounced the Nazi past of numerous ministerial officials.[71] One of those to get a mention here was State Secretary Wilhelm Claussen.[72] In November 1957, he succeeded Hans Busch, who had briefly held the post. Furthermore, Claussen was targeted by 'inflammatory pamphlets from the Soviet zone' and was one of fifteen state secretaries assailed for their 'heavily encumbered Nazi past'. Specifically, he was denounced for having allegedly organized a system of slave labour in Serbia during the war.[73] The State Security of the GDR (Staatssicherheitsdienst der DDR or Stasi) too targeted leading officials at the BMA, such as Kurt Jantz, who was accused of having 'implemented and expounded the fascist social legislation' and thus of indirect involvement in the Nazi War of plunder and conquest.[74]

In any case, the personnel recruitment of the BMA tended to be associated with the rapid resumption of individuals' careers within the civil service, even in the case of those officials, such as Walter Stets, who had been demoted due to past Nazi Party membership. Recommended by Julius Scheuble, among others, as a 'first-rate talent of ministerial calibre', when he was finally appointed in March 1954 this expert in vocational counselling was promoted to the position of ministerial counsellor he had held before.[75] However, towards the end of 1950, some members of the government expressed reservations about the plan to appoint Hans Schraft, head of the Department for Accident Insurance, as ministerial counsellor.[76] Despite having been a member of the Nazi Party and the SA, Schraft had risen through the ministerial ranks, attaining the position of senior government counsellor just the previous year, which now caught the attention of the Federal Ministry of the Interior and Federal Finance Ministry. Yet his supporters could point to comparable instances of promotion, and both State Secretary Sauerborn and the head of Section I, Joseph Schneider, intervened, emphasizing Schraft's knowledge and experience and the BMA's 'official interests'. The Labour Ministry got its way. On 1 February 1951, Schraft was made ministerial counsellor, and in July 1954 took up an appointment as a judge at the Federal Social Court in Kassel.

At the same time, Josef Siemer, head of the Department of Labour Market Policy, sought to defend himself against his classification as an 'old fighter' (*Alter Kämpfer*).[77] As one of two top officials at the BMA, Siemer had joined the Nazi Party prior to 1933 and explosive documents from 1936 had now turned up that further underscored his enthusiasm for the Nazis at the time. The opaque circumstances of the alleged interruption to Siemer's party membership and contradictory information concerning this supposed event led to a prolonged exchange of letters. This culminated in an assessment by the relevant department head, Jakob Käfferbitz, who concluded that after 1945 Siemer had shown himself to be a dependable democrat and had 'otherwise proved himself both personally and professionally in every respect'.[78] The Federal Interior Ministry raised no further objections, and in April 1952 Siemer was promoted to the position of senior government counsellor, and then ministerial counsellor three years later.

If we take past membership of, or candidacy for, the SS as evidence of a Nazi encumbrance, what we find is that this evidently applied to just a few individuals in the BMA until 1960. One of these was Alfred Theile, whose background lay in the Reich Insurance Office and who had been posted to the BMA since July 1952 as head of Division (Unterabteilung) IV a. Despite having joined the SS Cavalry Corps (Reiter-SS) twenty years earlier, Theile was not only appointed ministerial counsellor in early 1953 but, two years into his retirement, was brought back as research associate (*wissenschaftlicher Mitarbeiter*) in Section IV. Another case was that of Hans Reichel, who gained a post at the BMA's Department of Labour Law on 1 May 1954, despite his past as candidate for the SS.[79] The limits to tacit toleration, however, were reached in the special case of Ministerial Counsellor M.[80]

The lawyer M., who had worked as a senior civil servant in various district administrative offices in the Protectorate of Bohemia and Moravia before 1945, was employed by the Federal Ministry of Labour in the early 1950s, despite a lack of experience in the field of labour and social administration, and was assigned to the Section for Social Insurance at the personal request of Section Head Josef Eckert. Before the year was over, M. was promoted to the post of senior government counsellor. Before long, he was appointed government director (*Regierungsdirektor*), and subsequently ministerial counsellor, a role in which he functioned as a department head.

Fourteen years after the end of the war, however, M.'s rapid advance up the ministerial ladder stalled. In the course of a review in May 1959, it happened to come to light that M. had joined the Nazi Party in April 1931, six years earlier than he had stated, and that he had worked as a training manager. M. had kept quiet about his membership of the SA between 1930 and 1933 and of the SS from 1933, while also providing false information about his exam results. After both the BMA and the Federal Ministry of the Interior, which had also been consulted, expressed reservations about dismissing M., a formal disciplinary procedure was initiated, culminating in a ruling by a Federal Disciplinary Chamber (Bundesdisziplinarkammer), which concluded that M. had 'proved to be the prototype of a thoroughly opportunistic beneficiary of the demand generated by the development of the Federal authorities in Bonn'.[81] As a result of an appeal judgement by the Federal Disciplinary Court (Bundesdisziplinarhof) two years later, M.'s swingeing downgrading to senior government counsellor was reduced to demotion to the post of government director.

In the case of M., the BMA strikingly demonstrated its willingness to finally set aside the personal Nazi pasts of its staff members. The ministry considered the 'punitive intent' of the judgement to have been fulfilled by 1969, believing that 'the time has come to draw a clear line under what happened', after which it again promoted M. to the post of ministerial counsellor.[82] Furthermore, it had already granted none other than M. responsibility for the legal provisions on compensation for Nazi injustice within the social insurance system.

The Case of Walter Stothfang

The biography of Ministerial Counsellor Walter Stothfang is a striking reflection of the potential and limits of the authorities' efforts to achieve continuity of personnel. In the early history of the West German labour administration, Stothfang's biography featured an inherent potential for conflict.[83] Born in Burgsteinfurt in Westphalia in 1902 and a Ph.D. economist, he took up the post of personal adviser to Reich Institution president Friedrich Syrup on 1 April 1935. He continued as adviser to Syrup when the latter was appointed state secretary in the Reich Ministry of Labour in 1939. On 19 April 1943, Stothfang, who had joined the Nazi Party on 1 May 1933 and had become a supporting member of the SS the year after, was assigned, in the same role, to General Plenipotentiary for Labour Deployment (GBA) Fritz Sauckel. At 'Thuringia House', Sauckel's

Berlin headquarters, Stothfang was in charge of office administration; he was present at staff meetings and took part in trips of inspection, featuring visits to the various Gauleiters.[84] In addition, a range of publications attest to Stothfang's intensive engagement with the challenges thrown up, from his perspective, by labour deployment in Germany: 'particularly during the war', he stated, the 'orderly regulation [of this field is among] the most important tasks of the state leadership'.[85]

Released after the war from the Neumünster Internment Camp and the Ministerial Collecting Center, where he had produced numerous written reports as an adviser, for a time Stothfang worked as a farmhand. In February 1948, he was entrusted with various tasks central to the planning and implementation of job placement and manpower management in Main Section II of the Central Office for Labour. In autumn 1946, Stothfang had already sought out Julius Scheuble, his former superior at the Rhineland Land Labour Office, to request that he be assigned to a new position within the German labour administration. In so doing, he linked his specialist skills and his conscientiousness as an official in much the same way as he did a few months later during his denazification process. Despite intervention by the interior minister of North Rhine-Westphalia, this concluded in March 1948 with Stothfang's final classification as 'follower' (*Mitläufer*).[86]

The simultaneous perception of Stothfang as a person of integrity and an established expert, but also as an adviser to Sauckel who had held a key position within the Nazi state, was reflected in his conspicuously frequent stints as a witness at the Nuremberg trials.[87] But this dichotomy also found expression in the ZfA, when Stothfang's appointment triggered a major confrontation with Vice-President Walter Auerbach. The latter had no personal aversion to Stothfang, but warned that there was likely to be sharp criticism within the German public sphere and in the formerly occupied countries, and that there was also a risk that the Allies would lose trust in the Central Office. On the day of Stothfang's appointment, Auerbach, 'in a highly agitated state', then informed Scheuble that he would like to be released from his duties at once. For him, Stothfang was a 'symbol of Sauckel's methods', one that might 'inspire the idea that the Central Office for Labour identifies with the power politics of the Third Reich when it comes to the management of manpower'. Shortly afterwards, Auerbach confirmed that while Stothfang's professional qualifications were beyond reproach, 'through his close collaboration with Sauckel, [he had] become a symbol of a system that trampled on human rights and international law'; should there be changes in the senior staff dealing with manpower management, Auerbach claimed, Stothfang might very quickly be appointed to a key position once again.[88]

In other quarters, too, the 'utmost displeasure' was soon being expressed regarding Stothfang's employment at the ZfA. Even the former main section head at the Reich Ministry of Labour, Werner Mansfeld, was astonished that 'very wrongly . . . no particular significance [seems] to be attached to [Stothfang's] collaboration with Sauckel'. 'Personally, after such collaboration, I consider it quite appropriate to air the prospect of a judicial process, and I believe the decision that has been taken with regard to St[othfang], as much as I value him personally and objectively, was a mistake.'[89] However, the controversial department head's situation changed only when the issue of his transfer to the Administration for Labour came up in November 1948. As one prominent example among others, his case now inspired critical reportage and public scrutiny of the personnel policy of Director Anton Storch. In a general sense, it threatened to bring the criteria used to select officials in the British zone into disrepute. Before the plenary assembly of the Economic Council of the United Economic Area (Wirtschaftsrat des Vereinigten Wirtschaftsgebietes), Storch had to defend himself against persistent accusations; he lambasted the press for 'poisoning wells' and took up the cudgels on Stothfang's behalf, but ultimately decided not to turn his posting from the ZfA to the VfA into a permanent appointment. At the same time, he gave Stothfang hope that 'when it comes to employment in the future ministries, different political viewpoints will pertain than in the past'.[90]

After a period as a freelance writer and at an auditing firm, an opportunity opened up for Walter Stothfang to return to the Labour Administration, in line with Anton Storch's aforementioned remark of August 1949. This was a position at the Federal Institution for Job Placement and Unemployment Insurance (Bundesanstalt für Arbeitsvermittlung und Arbeitslosenversicherung), established on 1 May 1952. On 1 October 1953, Stothfang was employed as head of the 'Labour Market Policy' Subdivision of the Nuremberg-based agency, which was subject to the BMA's legal supervision. He rose to become director and finally chief administrative director and, on 1 March 1957, took over as acting head of Section 1. Once again, however, Stothfang's previous role at the GBA proved a barrier, as members of the board of the Federal Institution raised concerns about his possible appointment as section head, fearing that his past 'might lead to political complications during negotiations with foreign states'.[91]

Finally, just under eighteen months later, in September 1959, it was Federal Labour Minister Theodor Blank who concluded that the time had come to stop worrying about Stothfang's past, and he transferred him to the Federal Labour Ministry as ministerial counsellor and head of Subdivision II a, which oversaw the Federal Institution.[92] Stothfang, however, was still the target of attacks, which shows that his specific formal encumbrance made it impossible to keep attention focused solely on his acknowledged expertise.⁹³

Institutional and Personnel Structures in the Soviet Occupation Zone, 1945–1949

In order to contrast, at least partially, the development of the institutional and staffing structures of the central labour authorities in both German states, it is vital to supplement our investigation, so far focused on West Germany, with an account of East Germany. Given the sources, this will be necessarily brief. The first striking feature is fundamental parallels in the administrative structure. On the orders of the Soviet Military Administration in Germany (Sowjetische Militäradministration in Deutschland, or SMAD), issued on 17 July 1945, eleven central administrations, each headed by a president, were established. Beyond their initial function as providers of technical advice, these increasingly gained governmental powers of their own and enjoyed rights of instruction vis-à-vis the Länder. It was the Central Administration for Labour and Social Welfare (Zentralverwaltung für Arbeit und Sozialfürsorge, or ZVAS) that functioned as de facto labour ministry. It took up its work on 15 August 1945, its founding statute initially establishing sections dedicated to labour and wages; social welfare; labour deployment and censuses; and labour for the masses, as well as a legal section. On 14 June 1946, it was renamed the German Administration for Labour and Social Welfare (Deutsche Verwaltung für Arbeit und Sozialfürsorge, or DVAS). In the course of an intensified process of centralization, on 12 February 1948 the agency was incorporated into the German Economic Commission (Deutsche Wirtschaftskommission, or DWK), along with most of the other central administrations of the SBZ, as the Main Administration for Labour and Social Welfare (Hauptverwaltung für Arbeit und Sozialfürsorge, or HVAS).⁹⁴

Initially, beyond its coordinating function, the labour administration made only a negligible impact. Conflicts smouldered with the Länder (dissolved in July 1952), which felt that their powers were being curtailed. Increasingly, however, the ZVAS, DVAS and HVAS were endowed with authority and legislative powers, and they featured a growing number of subordinate agencies. The character and designation of the various divisions underwent a range of modifications at relatively short intervals. Regardless of this, the labour administrations, which were also assigned responsibility for education and retraining, occupational safety, housing and settlement, social insurance and statistics, largely corresponded to the traditional labour ministry.⁹⁵

When it came to personnel, the growth in the number of employees – around 80 staff members at the ZVAS in August and 113 in December 1945, compared with 142 employees of the DVAS on 12 August 1947 – could not obscure the fact that the central labour authorities suffered from an acute lack of staff, which made itself felt particularly in the field of social insurance.[96] More than in the Western occupation zones, particularly the British, it was denazification that was partly responsible for this, being carried out significantly more consistently and more radically. Rather than just a 'purge' of personnel, this amounted to a change of system.[97] With the removal of all former Nazi Party members from the civil service and many professional posts, more than half a million East Germans lost their jobs. Even at the cost of administrative inefficiency, the administrative system in particular was regarded as a key target for denazification. After the dissolution of the denazification commissions in 1948, however, exceptions for skilled workers facilitated the reappointment of former Nazi Party members to the administrative service, as long as they had not been active members. Furthermore, the elimination of the civil service system ushered in a change of system, one that broke with the traditions of the labour and social administration.

While we are not yet in a position to precisely quantify the staffing structures of the central East German labour authorities, or to make confident statements about recruiting processes, examination of leaders and department heads shows just how seriously, on this level at least, denazification was taken.[98] In the shape of its first president, Gustav Gundelach, the ZVAS/DVAS was one of the few central administrations headed by a KPD member upon its establishment. Gundelach had already been active in Communist circles under the Weimar Republic, and he returned from Moscow to Germany in 1945 as part of the group around Walter Ulbricht. Due to his 'previous experiences working in firms and for the trades unions', Gundelach brought with him 'certain prerequisites for playing this role', but ultimately it was his political background that predestined him – proposed to the Soviet occupiers by Ulbricht and Wilhelm Pieck – to head the labour administration.[99] After taking up a post in Hamburg and then being elected as a deputy to the first German Bundestag, in April 1946 Gundelach succeeded Gustav Brack, a Social Democrat who had been active as a trades unionist and suffered persecution in the Nazi era. Vice-President Max Herm was a former KPD Reichstag deputy, while Jenny Matern, born in 1904, had also become involved in the Communist Party early on; she had first emigrated to Prague in 1934 and then to the USSR. Trained there as an official, in 1946 Matern returned to Germany, where she became vice-president and main section head in the labour administration and worked as state secretary in the Ministry of Healthcare (Ministerium für Gesundheitswesen) from 1950 to 1959.[100]

The case of Helmut Lehmann was rather different. As first vice-president of the ZVAS between August 1945 and April 1946, it was chiefly on the basis of his expertise that he became the real head of the institution. During the Nazi era, as an SPD member and resistance fighter, Lehmann had been repeatedly detained, but at the same time, as long-standing managing director of the Confederation of German Health Insurance Providers (Hauptverband deutscher Krankenkassen),[101] he had the professional expertise that allowed him, after the war, not only to rise rapidly to the status of the SED's undisputed social policy expert, but also to organize the East German social insurance system largely as he saw fit. These plans, already initiated by the summer of 1945, were geared towards the idea of one central and universal system of insurance. The ground having been laid at Land level, in January 1947 this system was introduced throughout the Soviet occupation zone. The Soviet allies allowed the German institutions fairly broad room for manoeuvre here. As the 'founding father of universal insurance', Lehmann, with the support of a small, informal, Berlin-based network of social policy actors, was thus in charge of a project of constitutive social significance, one antipodally at variance with the objectives advocated so vociferously in the Western occupation zones and, during the founding phase of the Federal Labour Ministry, by former and up-and-coming representatives of the labour administration.

In contrast to Lehmann's case, when it came to the general recruitment of personnel, at least in the early days, professional experience mostly seems to have enjoyed far less priority than in the Central Office for Economy and Labour or the Administration for Labour of the United Economic Area. Members of staff with a university degree, let alone a Ph.D., were also significantly fewer in number, and there was no jurists' monopoly. One of the exceptions was Ernst Holstein, head of the DVAS's Section for Occupational Safety and Accident Prevention (Abteilung Arbeitsschutz und Unfallverhütung), an occupational physician holding a postdoctoral degree who had worked as a state works doctor (*Gewerbearzt*) from 1928 to 1945. In the shape of Hans Thalmann, on 1 January 1947, the DVAS gained a Ph.D. economist and later professor of social policy and labour economics, as a department head, while from January 1946 until November 1947 the legal department of the ZVAS/DVAS was led by lawyer Rolf Helm.[102] Among the main administrations of the German Economic Commission, at the HVAS in particular the number of those who had occupied key positions in former Reich agencies was particularly low.[103] However, in light of the average age of about fifty, the group of just under fifty staff members considered here, most of them department heads, did not differ significantly from the age structures of those employed in the comparable agencies in the Western occupation zones.

Increasingly, it was not just the selection of 'unencumbered' staff members with antifascist biographies that came to the fore. The upper echelons of the ZVAS/DVAS were ever more saturated with SED members. While the three vice-president posts were initially occupied by members of the SPD (Helmut Lehmann), KPD (Max Herm) and CDU (Albert Voss), parity was abandoned when Lehmann was replaced by Jenny Matern in April 1946. Meanwhile, when Christian trades unionist Voss died in November 1947, he was succeeded by Willy Donau.[104]

Herm, Matern and Donau, the latter having headed the Berlin branch of the International Labour Organization from 1925 to 1933 and then, until 1939, worked at the ILO in Geneva,[105] became SED members when the party was formed from the fusion of the SPD and KPD in April 1946. They remained in leading positions in the HVAS. Of the 102 white-collar employees at the ZVAS on 1 May 1946, more than three-quarters were already members of the state party, while of the block parties, just under 10.8 per cent were members of the CDU and 1 per cent held membership of the Liberal Democratic Party (Liberal-Demokratische Partei, or LDP); around 12 per cent of staff members did not belong to any political party. Of those employed at the DVAS, between April and December 1947 the share of SED members increased from 67.1 per cent to 70.5 per cent. Consonant with this, the share of members of the other parties fell from 17.1 per cent to 12.9 per cent.[106]

It is reasonable to assume that conflicts flared up as policies, including personnel policy, were put into practice. One indication of this is the dismissal of former company lawyer, legal adviser and foreign exchange adviser Franz Hirschfeld, who had headed the ZVAS's legal office since September 1945. He was soon accused of having 'spread distrust of the leadership of the Central Administration in a highly irresponsible manner', in the absence of reasons or evidence, and of having imputed to it 'capitalist, Nazi methods'.[107]

The Labour Administration in the German Democratic Republic, 1949–1958

In 1949, like the Federal Republic, the GDR built on the institutional structures of the occupation period. The state founded on 7 October 1949 largely took over the existing main administrations of the DWK. However, the new Ministry of Labour and Healthcare not only absorbed the HVAS but also the Main Administration for Healthcare (Hauptverwaltung Gesundheitswesen). The ministry was initially subdivided into the four main sections of Labour, Social Welfare, Healthcare and Mother and Child.[108]

While responsibility for housing still lay with the Labour Ministry (though the field was greatly influenced by the municipal authorities), as in West Germany a separate authority dedicated to housing and town planning was established in the shape of the Ministry of Construction (Ministerium für Aufbau). This was based on the Main Administration for the Building Industry (Hauptverwaltung Bauwirtschaft), whose establishment within the DWK in May 1949 had been spurred by planning and coordination problems within the construction industry; it brought together the competencies of several main administrations.

During the brief history of the Labour Ministry in East Berlin, its sections were restructured, a complex if not impenetrable process, and its remit was repeatedly altered. This included the hiving off, once again, of healthcare in November 1950, which was passed to a bespoke ministry. In 1952, the authority now going by the name of the Ministry of Labour was subdivided into the two main sections of Labour and Occupational Safety, which were supplemented by five separate departments, plus the General Administration (Allgemeine Verwaltung) and the Main Division for Training (Hauptreferat Schulung).[109] Another key turning point came in November 1954, with the amalgamation of the ministry with what had been the independent State Secretariat for Vocational Training (Staatssekretariat für Berufsausbildung). The resulting Ministry of Labour and Vocational Training (Ministerium für Arbeit und Berufsausbildung) was dissolved along with other GDR ministries in July 1958. Vocational education was assigned to the Ministry of National Education (Ministerium für Volksbildung), while the other divisions were integrated into the newly established Committee for Labour and Wages (Komitee für Arbeit und Löhne). After itself being restructured on a number of occasions, this was in turn integrated into the remit of the State Planning Commission (Staatliche Plankommission), which claimed ever more administrative competencies within the context of centralized state planning. In contrast to the situation in the western part of Germany, then, the tradition of an independent central labour ministry established in 1919 came to an end, to be revived only in 1989 with the establishment of the Ministry of Labour and Wages (Ministerium für Arbeit und Löhne).

In the first few years after the founding of the GDR, the staffing levels of the Labour Ministry grew only slowly, such that its broad spectrum of responsibilities always risked overwhelming its staff. Once healthcare had been cleaved off, in November 1950 the number of personnel stood at 204, with the Section for Planning and Statistics along with the Section for Ad-

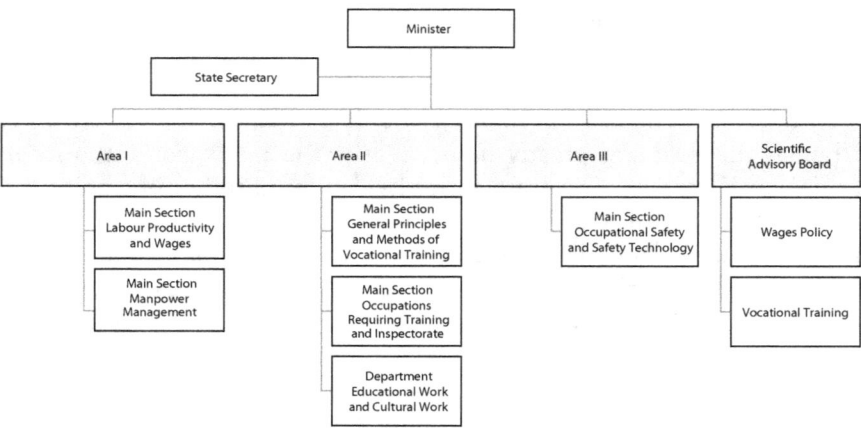

Figure 13.9. Structure of the Ministry of Labour and Vocational Training, spring 1956

ministration having the largest number of staff.[110] In 1949, the composition of the senior positions deviated in a number of respects from general patterns of recruitment. First, the heads of the main sections for Labour and Social Welfare, and Health, were not integrated into the ministry. Second, in the shape of Luitpold Steidle, a minister was appointed who was not a member of the SED but in fact a senior representative of the CDU, one who evidently tried to mitigate the influence of the state party. Further, Steidle's background as a landowner and farmer in the 1920s was atypical of his post and not obviously a source of the relevant specialist knowledge. He had also joined the Nazi Party on 1 May 1933 (from which he was excluded in 1934), though he kept his party membership secret from the authorities.[111]

Steidle held the post for just a short time, becoming head of the Section for Healthcare in 1950, which was turned into a ministry in its own right. His replacement as labour minister was Roman Chwalek, who remained in office until 1953, a man whose curriculum vitae fit better with the prevailing political ideal. Born in 1898, Chwalek had trained as a machine fitter, and he represented the KPD in the Reichstag between 1930 and 1933. During the Nazi dictatorship, he spent several years in prison for illegal political activity and 'making preparations to commit high treason' (*Vorbereitung zum Hochverrat*).[112] A new shakeup in 1953 saw Chwalek switch to the Ministry of Railways (Ministerium für Eisenbahnwesen) and the appointment of SED member Friedrich Macher as minister, a former telegraph construction worker and just thirty-one years of age.[113]

The biographies of State Secretary Paul Peschke (1949–1950) and his successor Friedel Malter[114] (1950–1956) provide another indication that it was one's background and an anti-Nazi past, rather than a career in an administrative authority, that weighed heaviest. While machine fitter and toolmaker Peschke had returned to Berlin in 1946 after emigrating to Sweden, Malter, who had been elected to the Prussian Landtag as deputy for the KPD in 1932, had spent several years in prisons and concentration camps under Nazi rule.[115] The State Secretariat for Vocational Training, which existed from November 1950 until its amalgamation with the Ministry of Labour in November 1954, was headed by Rudolf Wiessner, a trained precision engineer who was just twenty-three years old upon his appointment. As the *Neues Deutschland* newspaper declared, 'for the first time in the history of Germany . . . youths are being entrusted to lead state secretariats and ministries'.[116]

A concurrent and increasingly important development was that now, in order to manage the ministries, key decisions on personnel were made by the Politbüro or the Secretariat of the Central Committee of the SED. In the Ministry of Labour too, those appointed as heads of the main sections, and to some extent the departments as well, were selected on the basis of a cadre policy, as the political centre moved to control the education, selection and assignments of senior staff in particular.[117]

Evidently, the dearth of specialist knowledge and administrative experience resulting from this personnel policy was not without effect on the quality of the top administrative staff, and the ministry was blamed for a number of mistakes.[118] A cry for help from State Secretary Paul Peschke in April 1950 casts light on the situation in the authority. 'In light of the current staffing of its various departments', the Ministry of Labour and Healthcare was 'in no position to carry out the tasks assigned to it with respect to the implementation of economic plans and the tasks of government'. Minister Steidle too was 'almost entirely' incapable of carrying out 'practical work within our ministry'. As Peschke reported, due to the lack of 'leaders reasonably equal to their responsibilities professionally and politically', certain members of staff were nearing a state of physical collapse. In the Main Section for Healthcare in particular, its head Karl Linser had allowed a state of 'complete chaos' to arise, while 'our academics' lacked 'entirely the organizational abilities to organize the implementation even of good plans'.[119]

This was largely because, in stark contrast to the West German Labour Ministry, virtually none of the departmental heads of the Reich Labour Ministry made it into its East German counterpart. Among the short-term exceptions were Ernst Knoll and Fritz Foerster. Knoll, a brother-in-law of Johannes Krohn employed at the Reich Labour Ministry since 1924, was first temporarily laid off on 1 September 1939 as ministerial director and main section head, before being transferred to the Court of Appeal (Kammergericht) in Berlin on 1 November 1940. In 1945 he was appointed head of the 'Division for Settlement and Housing' (Abschnitt Siedlungs- und Wohnungsbetreuung) within the ZVAS's Department of Social Welfare. At around the same time, Ministerial Counsellor Foerster, Knoll's former colleague at the ministry, was working as an adviser on support for the disabled (*Invalidenbetreuung*) in the ZVAS. It is no coincidence that neither had been members of the Nazi Party. In fact, in 1939 Knoll had been hounded out of office, evidently due to conflicts with the party.[120] Beyond this, however, there is no evidence at all of the kind of continuities that began to emerge in the labour authorities of the British occupation zone as early as 1946.[121]

There was no professional future in the labour administration on offer to the most prominent representative of the old Reich Ministry of Labour to come to the attention of the East German authorities. The lawyer Werner Mansfeld had advanced to become head of Main Section III in May 1933. After the wartime relocation and ultimate liquidation of the Salzdetfurth potash mining and processing firm, of whose executive board he had been a member since October 1943, Mansfeld had settled in Halle an der Saale. Since 1947, the East German authorities had been considering investigating him. He faced the prospect of imprisonment and a conviction for war crimes, and although initially his 'in every respect . . . good conscience' prompted him to stay in East Germany, he moved to West Berlin in 1949. 'The constant uncertainty', Mansfeld stated in May 1948, had been 'quite detrimental to my mental constitution. I would be pleased if I were able to sleep peacefully again'.[122]

Conclusion

We cannot understand the history of the leading staff at the central German labour authorities between 1945 and 1960 through simplistic concepts of continuity and discontinuity. This is partly because developments in west and east diverged after the caesura of 1945. Above all, with respect to West Germany's early days, however, we also find that processes of personnel reconstruction were bound up with generational ruptures. Key moments that set the course for staffing policy, meanwhile, were always partly influenced by departmental traditions and self-images. And while department heads who had worked in the Nazi-specific Reich trustee administration could generally continue their careers without much trouble, previous links to the general plenipotentiary for labour deployment, as apparent in the case of Walter Stothfang, revealed the 'limits to integration'.[123]

In terms of its extent, the return of expert staff from the Nazi era to leading positions in the Federal Labour Ministry was in line with the general trends within the young West German administrative apparatus. But the reappointment of large numbers of officials from the old Reich Ministry of Labour and its subordinate agencies becomes especially apparent when we consider that, on a smaller scale, alternative approaches to the recruitment of staff had begun to emerge during the occupation years. One of the most striking results of the present study is that from the mid 1950s onwards, the Federal Ministry of Labour, at least its upper echelons, was one of the Federal ministries employing the highest proportion of former Nazi Party members – a finding whose applicability to the mid-level and junior staff, the broad field of the subordinate agencies, and to external experts and advisory bodies, is yet to be established. This institution became a professional home for many individuals who had quickly made their peace with Nazism, had joined the Nazi Party and SA as early as 1933, whether in order to advance their careers or out of conviction, or who had gone further and become the regime's henchmen. This requires emphasis even if we opt for a concept of 'encumbrance' that goes beyond the formal party membership foregrounded here to take in specific patterns of thinking and acting. What kind of attitudes and beliefs did officials articulate after 1933? What was their individual potential to exercise an influence within their post? And what degree of complicity, if not personal guilt and perpetration, might we attribute to them?[124]

Of course, past membership of the Nazi Party and preceding careers under Nazi rule permit no simplistic conclusions about the content of ministerial policies or about the labour and social policy initiatives launched by the ministry from 1949. As with many representatives of the administrative system and civil service, under the banner of anti-communism, as a viable integrative ideology, and in light of the opportunity to achieve material security and career advancement, many members of staff at the Federal Ministry of Labour are likely to have at least put up with, if not fully accepted, the rules of the democratic game.[125]

Regardless of this, however, the Federal Ministry of Labour's sheer willingness to recruit officials with backgrounds in the Nazi Party and SA, and its silence about this practice, casts a shadow over the institution's early history. The negligible degree of critical reflection and circumspection evident in its appointment practices seems all the more noteworthy given that the labour ministers at the time were Anton Storch and Theodor Blank, who were themselves among the victims of the Nazi dictatorship. In addition to many ministerial officials' self-image as unpolitical administrative experts, it was apparently effective interest networks that made themselves felt here, as brought to the attention of the Bundestag by Adolf Arndt as early as 1950.

It must be recognized that, right from the start, the constraints and limited room for manoeuvre afflicting the Central Office for Labour were the result of permanent shortages of trained personnel. While the West German tendency to draw on long-serving specialist workers undoubtedly helped ensure administrative efficiency and performance, in the Soviet Occupation Zone and the GDR too, functioning labour authorities developed, despite the fact that the authorities seriously pursued a fresh start when it came to the recruitment of personnel, at least when it came to the top positions. Future research might delve more deeply into the East German authorities' attempts to compensate for the lack of specialist knowledge and formal qualifications traditionally required and the consequences of these efforts. Another imperative is to determine whether, and if so to what extent, the composition of staff at the junior levels showed less discontinuity. At the very least, the East German institutions did not have to face the accusations repeatedly levelled at West Germany, namely that the restorative personnel structures and the 'encumbrance' of the administrative apparatus had proved a considerable burden on postwar society, one associated with a loss of moral credibility.

Martin Münzel, Ph.D., research associate (2014–2018) on the project being undertaken by the Independent Commission of Historians Investigating the History of the Reich Ministry of Labour in the National Socialist Period and, since 2008, responsible editor of the journal *Archiv und Wirtschaft*, and since 2020, also managing director of an archives association. Publications include *Building for the Future: Siemensstadt* (Siemens Historical Institute, 2019); 'Tempelhof–Manhattan und zurück. Ullstein und der Einfluss der Emigration', in D. Oels and U. Schneider (eds), *'Der ganze Verlag ist einfach eine Bonbonniere'. Ullstein in der ersten Hälfte des 20. Jahrhunderts* (de Gruyter, 2015), 388–406; *Die jüdischen Mitglieder der deutschen Wirtschaftselite 1927–1955. Verdrängung – Emigration – Rückkehr* (Schöningh, 2006).

Notes

1. For detailed information on Anton Storch, see Biographical Appendix.
2. German Bundestag, Stenographic Report, 73rd Session, 12 July 1950, Minutes of Plenary Session 01/73, 2631 f.
3. See esp. the eleven-volume descriptive and documentary series published by the Federal Ministry of Labour and Social Order (Bundesministerium für Arbeit und Sozialordnung) and the Federal Archive (Bundesarchiv) between 2001 and 2008, *Geschichte der Sozialpolitik in Deutschland seit 1945*, Baden-Baden: Nomos.
4. For the most recent overview, see C. Mentel and N. Weise, *Die zentralen deutschen Behörden und der Nationalsozialismus. Stand und Perspektiven der Forschung*, Munich: Institut für Zeitgeschichte München, and Potsdam: Zentrum für Zeithistorische Forschung, 2016.

5. For their support as I wrote this chapter, important pointers and criticisms, I would like to thank my colleagues in the research group on the history of the Reich Ministry of Labour, including the student assistants.

6. See, for example, U. Wengst, *Staatsaufbau und Regierungspraxis 1948–1953. Zur Geschichte der Verfassungsorgane der Bundesrepublik Deutschland*, Düsseldorf: Droste, 1984, 20–23; W. Vogel, *Westdeutschland 1945–1950. Der Aufbau von Verfassungs- und Verwaltungseinrichtungen über den Ländern der drei westlichen Besatzungszonen*, part 3: *Einzelne Verwaltungszweige: Finanzen; Post und Verkehr; Arbeit und Soziales; Flüchtlinge, Suchdienst und Kriegsgefangene; Justiz; Inneres*, Boppard am Rhein: Boldt, 1983, 390–92.

7. See, for example, I. Girndt, *Zentralismus in der britischen Zone. Entwicklungen und Bestrebungen beim Wiederaufbau der staatlichen Verwaltungsorganisation auf der Ebene oberhalb der Länder 1945–1948*, Ph.D. dissertation, Bonn: University of Bonn, 1971, 92–123; T. Pünder, *Das bizonale Interregnum. Die Geschichte des Vereinigten Wirtschaftsgebiets 1946–1949*, Cologne: Grote, 1966, 43–46. On the structure and responsibilities of the Central Office for Labour as described in what follows, see 'Das Zentralamt für Arbeit in der Britischen Zone. Bericht über die Tätigkeit von Juli 1946 bis Juli 1948', *Arbeitsblatt für die britische Zone* 2(78/8) (1948) (special supplement); 'Aufgaben des Zentralamts für Arbeit in der britischen Zone', *Arbeitsblatt für die britische Zone* 1(12) (1947), 427–29; Activity Report Julius Scheuble, 16 June 1947, Bundesarchiv (BArch), Z 40/319; U. Wengst, 'Sozialpolitische Denk- und Handlungsfelder', in U. Wengst (ed.), *Geschichte der Sozialpolitik in Deutschland seit 1945*, vol. 2/1: *1945–1949. Die Zeit der Besatzungszonen. Sozialpolitik zwischen Kriegsende und der Gründung zweier deutscher Staaten. Darstellung*, Baden-Baden: Nomos, 2001, 77–149, here 143–45; Vogel, *Westdeutschland*, part 3, 392, 422–31.

8. On the VfA, see Vogel, *Westdeutschland*, part 3, 393–401, 444–54; K. Oppler, 'Die Zuständigkeit des Vereinigten Wirtschaftsgebietes auf dem Gebiete der Arbeit', *Recht der Arbeit* 1 (1948), 18–20.

9. On the genesis and structure of the BMA, see F.P. Kahlenberg and D. Hoffmann, 'Sozialpolitik als Aufgabe zentraler Verwaltungen in Deutschland', in Bundesministerium für Arbeit und Sozialordnung and Bundesarchiv (eds), *Geschichte der Sozialpolitik in Deutschland seit 1945*, vol. 1: *Grundlagen der Sozialpolitik*, Baden-Baden: Nomos, 2001, 103–82, here 116–19; H.G. Hockerts, *Sozialpolitische Entscheidungen im Nachkriegsdeutschland. Alliierte und deutsche Sozialversicherungspolitik 1945 bis 1957*, Stuttgart: Klett-Cotta, 1980, 110–18; M. Sauerborn, 'Das Bundesministerium für Arbeit', *BABl.* 1(1) (1950), 4–6; Bundesarchiv and Institut für Zeitgeschichte (eds), *Akten zur Vorgeschichte der Bundesrepublik Deutschland 1945–1949*, vol. 5: *Januar–September 1949*, Munich: Oldenbourg, 1976 and 1981, 665 f., 733–38, 818–24; The Activities of the Federal Ministry of Labour, 1949–1952, BArch, B 106/4102.

10. For a detailed account, see G. Schulz, *Wiederaufbau in Deutschland. Die Wohnungsbaupolitik in den Westzonen und der Bundesrepublik von 1945 bis 1957*, Düsseldorf: Droste, 1994, 175–202; Wengst, *Staatsaufbau*, 171 f. See also the chapter by Karl Christian Führer in this volume.

11. Evidently, Hans Engel was initially interned in the Weesow and Sachsenhausen camps, but after his transfer to the special camp in Landsberg an der Warthe in July 1945 his trail is lost. D.G. Maier, 'Friedrich Syrup (1881–1945). Von der Gewerbeaufsicht an die Spitze der Arbeitsverwaltung', in D.G. Maier, J. Nürnberger and S. Pabst, *Vordenker und Gestalter des Arbeitsmarktes. Elf Biografien zur Geschichte der deutschen Arbeitsverwaltung*, Mannheim: Hochschule der Bundesagentur für Arbeit, 2012, 115–40, here 140; information generously provided by Annette Karstedt-Meierrieks, Werner Peycke, Dr Enrico Heitzer and Holm Kirsten.

12. Verein Aktives Museum e. V. (ed.), *Vor die Tür gesetzt. Im Nationalsozialismus verfolgte Berliner Stadtverordnete und Magistratsmitglieder 1933–1945*, Berlin: self-published, 2006, 229 f.; E. Lembeck, *Die Partizipation von Frauen an der öffentlichen Verwaltung in der*

Weimarer Republik 1918–1933, Ph.D. dissertation, Hanover: University of Hanover, 1991, 198–210; Correspondence between Oscar Weigert and the BMA on compensation, BArch, B 149/7444.

13. For a general account, see K. Jarausch, *Die Umkehr. Deutsche Wandlungen 1945–1995*, Bonn: Bundeszentrale für politische Bildung, 2004, 66–70; U. Herbert, *Best. Biographische Studien über Radikalismus, Weltanschauung und Vernunft, 1903–1989*, Bonn: Dietz, 1996, 434 f.; on the legal position of dismissed civil servants, see W. Langhorst, *Beamtentum und Artikel 131 des Grundgesetzes. Eine Untersuchung über Bedeutung und Auswirkung der Gesetzgebung zum Artikel 131 des Grundgesetzes unter Einbeziehung der Position der SPD zum Berufsbeamtentum*, Frankfurt am Main: Lang, 1994, 21–30.

14. Diary-like Notes by Krohn during his Internment in Bayreuth Prison and the Moosburg Camp, 1945–1946, BArch, NL 430/3; Curriculum Vitae Krohn, 4 January 1947, BArch, NL 430/5.

15. In light of the planned establishment of a German central administration, the Ministerial Collecting Center was relocated to Berlin-Tempelhof in late January 1946, but it played an ever more negligible role there. L.K. Born, 'The Ministerial Collecting Center Near Kassel, Germany', *The American Archivist* 13 (1950), 237–58; W. Vogel, *Westdeutschland 1945–1950. Der Aufbau von Verfassungs- und Verwaltungseinrichtungen über den Ländern der drei westlichen Besatzungszonen*, part 2: *Einzelne Verwaltungszweige: Wirtschaft, Marshallplan, Statistik*, Boppard am Rhein: Boldt, 1964, 11 f.

16. Wengst, *Staatsaufbau*, 23.

17. For detailed information on Julius Scheuble, see Biographical Appendix.

18. On Auerbach's biography, see E. Babendreyer, *Walter Auerbach. Sozialpolitik aus dem Exil*, Ph.D. dissertation, Duisburg and Essen: University Duisburg-Essen, 2007, esp. 242–50, 257–59; Curriculum Vitae Auerbach, 11 June 1947, BArch, Z 40/319.

19. 'Mit warmem Herzen', *Der Spiegel*, 6 July 1947, 6.

20. I have included a total of 141 individuals working in the upper echelons of the labour administration in compiling the following statistical analyses. For the ZfA and VfA I took account of all identifiable staff members with the rank of adviser (*Referent*) or above (60 and 44 individuals respectively), while for the BMA I considered all officials with the rank of government director or above (96 individuals), so the figures for the occupation period and for the Federal Republic are not fully comparable. The sources are incomplete: I was unable to find a large portion of the personal files of the BMA, despite intensive efforts. Our current state of knowledge leaves open the possibility that the ministry may have destroyed them. In Holding B 149 (Federal Ministry of Labour and Social Order) of the Bundesarchiv Koblenz, moreover, a number of crucial files on the founding era of the Federal Labour Ministry are missing. A partial holding of personal files is currently stored at the Federal Ministry of Economic Affairs and Energy (Bundesministerium für Wirtschaft und Energie) in Berlin; their transfer to the Bundesarchiv is planned. Other important holdings, at the Bundesarchiv Berlin-Lichterfelde, include R 3901 (personal files), R 601/464–66, 2091–110 and the files of the former Berlin Document Center; Z 40, Z 11, B 126/16930-17061, PERS 101 and the organizational plans and schedules of responsibility of the BMA, 1949–1960, at the Bundesarchiv Koblenz; and denazification and personal files (NW-Bestände) at the Landesarchiv (LArch) NRW, Abt. Rheinland, in Duisburg; see also organizational plans and schedules of responsibility of the BMA at the Bundesarchiv Berlin-Lichterfelde and the folder 'Organisationspläne des Bundesministeriums für Arbeit/Bundesministeriums für Arbeit und Sozialordnung 1953–1998' at the Federal Ministry of Labour and Social Affairs in Berlin as well as the staffing-related announcements in *Dienstliche Mitteilungen über die vorläufige Regelung des Geschäftsbetriebes der Verwaltung für Arbeit bzw. des Bundesministeriums für Arbeit (und Sozialordnung)*, 1948–1960 and in *Arbeitsblatt für die britische Zone/Arbeitsblatt/BABl.*, 1947–1960.

21. See the chapter by Ulrike Schulz in this volume.

22. BArch, Z 40/312.
23. In addition to long-standing ministerial counsellor at the Reich Ministry of Labour Heinrich Goldschmidt, this group included former president of the Land labour offices of Bavaria and East Prussia, Anton Kerschensteiner, who was one of the few agency heads to have refrained from joining the Nazi Party after 1933 and who did what he could to protect his colleagues in Munich. I thank Henry Marx for this information.
24. Hockerts, *Sozialpolitische Entscheidungen*, 109.
25. Auerbach to Anton Storch, August 1948, Archiv der sozialen Demokratie (AdsD), Papers Walter Auerbach, Folder 198; and Auerbach on 17 October 1948, quoted in Babendreyer, *Walter Auerbach*, 258.
26. Vogel, *Westdeutschland*, part 3, 394; Wengst, *Staatsaufbau*, 164 f.; H.G. Hockerts, 'Anton Storch (1892–1975)', in J. Aretz, R. Morsey and A. Rauscher (eds), *Zeitgeschichte in Lebensbildern*, vol. 4: *Aus dem deutschen Katholizismus des 19. und 20. Jahrhunderts*, Mainz: Matthias-Grünewald-Verlag, 1980, 250–66, here 258 f.; Comments/Recommendations by Hermann Pünder to Various Ministries (carbon copy, undated [October 1949?]), BArch, Z 11/104, fol. 33–36.
27. Wengst, *Staatsaufbau*, 89–96; R. Morsey, 'Personal- und Beamtenpolitik im Übergang von der Bizonen- zur Bundesverwaltung (1947–1950). Kontinuität oder Neubeginn?', in R. Morsey (ed.), *Verwaltungsgeschichte. Aufgaben, Zielsetzungen, Beispiele. Vorträge und Diskussionsbeiträge der verwaltungsgeschichtlichen Arbeitstagung 1976 der Hochschule für Verwaltungswissenschaften Speyer*, Berlin: Duncker & Humblot, 1972, 191–243; Langhorst, *Beamtentum*, 153–83.
28. BABl. 1(12) (1950), 438–39. Staff figures for 1948–1960 from *Wirtschaft und Statistik* NF 1(10) (1950), January 1950, 722; Overview of the Number of Staff in the Agencies of the Bizone, 20 January 1950, BArch, B 106/45734; *Bundeshaushaltspläne für die Haushaltsjahre 1950–1960*, Berlin and Bonn: n.p., 1950–1960.
29. The information on the BMWi refers to 204 senior civil servants with prominent roles between 1949 and 1963; as for the Federal Foreign Office, it should be remembered that it had no subordinate agencies. See B. Löffler, *Soziale Marktwirtschaft und administrative Praxis. Das Bundeswirtschaftsministerium unter Ludwig Erhard*, Stuttgart: Steiner, 2002, 166; E. Conze et al. (eds), *Das Amt und die Vergangenheit. Deutsche Diplomaten im Dritten Reich und in der Bundesrepublik*, Munich: Blessing, 2010, 493 f.
30. While Protestants soon dominated at close to 60 per cent, the question of the religious composition of the BMA was something of a hot potato, as press reports had triggered disquiet over the supposedly pro-Catholic hiring practices of Federal authorities, which was claimed to extend even to office porters and cleaning ladies. W. Zapf, 'Die Verwalter der Macht. Materialien zum Sozialprofil der höheren Beamtenschaft', in W. Zapf (ed.), *Beiträge zur Analyse der deutschen Oberschicht*, 2nd ed., Munich: Piper, 1965, 77–94, here 84; Wengst, *Staatsaufbau*, 181 f.; see the correspondence and documents relating to the recording of religious affiliation by the Federal Ministry of the Interior in BArch, B 102/16737, 32215. According to Zapf, in 1950 the large number of Catholic trades unionists was reflected in the BMA; Dieter Marschall, who entered the Federal Ministry of Labour in 1970, recalled that many of the up-and-coming staff members in the ministry at the time had belonged to Catholic student associations. Spoken communication from retired Ministerial Counsellor Dr Dieter Marschall to the present author, 18 February 2016.
31. On the distribution of places of birth among civil servants and white-collar workers at the supreme Federal authorities in April 1950, see Löffler, *Soziale Marktwirtschaft*, 157, table 2.
32. Zapf, 'Verwalter der Macht', 90 f.; 'Soziale Struktur der Angehörigen des höheren Dienstes in den Ministerien', *Monatsschrift der Vereinigung deutscher Auslandsbeamten* 25 (1962), 357 f.
33. On Storch as an individual, see esp. Hockerts, 'Anton Storch'; see also A. Storch, 'Lebenserinnerungen. Erfahrungen und Erlebnisse', in Deutscher Bundestag (ed.), *Abge-

ordnete des Deutschen Bundestages. Aufzeichnungen und Erinnerungen, vol. 2: Curt Becker, Franz Marx, Ernst Paul, Hans Schütz, Elisabeth Schwarzhaupt, J. Hermann Siemer, Anton Storch, Boppard am Rhein: Boldt, 1983, 313–44.

34. See Hockerts, Sozialpolitische Entscheidungen, 112–18; Hockerts, 'Anton Storch', 257–59; Auftakt zur Ära Adenauer. Koalitionsverhandlungen und Regierungsbildung 1949, ed. U. Wengst, series ed. Kommission für Geschichte des Parlamentarismus und der Politischen Parteien, Düsseldorf: Droste, 1985, doc. 17a, 28, 37, 58, 83, 86, 87.

35. Hockerts, 'Anton Storch', 250 (quotation); W. Henkels, 99 Bonner Köpfe, Düsseldorf: Econ, 1963, 299.

36. For more detail, see Hockerts, Sozialpolitische Entscheidungen, esp. 47–50, 114–17. I am unable to delve into the historical substance of contemporary claims here. For a telling account, see H. Köhrer, 'Die Geschichte der Gesellschaft für Versicherungswissenschaft und -gestaltung e.V. (GVG)', in M. Jung, H. Köhrer and V. Leienbach, Im Dienste freiheitlicher Sozialpolitik. 40 Jahre Gesellschaft für Versicherungswissenschaft und -gestaltung (GVG), Bergisch Gladbach: Vollmer, 1987, 18–72, esp. 20; on social insurance under Nazism, see the chapter by Alexander Klimo in this volume.

37. A. Storch, 'Was erwarten die Arbeitnehmer von der Neuordnung der deutschen Sozialversicherung?', Arbeitsblatt für die britische Zone 1(4) (1947), 139–41; Hockerts, Sozialpolitische Entscheidungen, 112 f.

38. For detailed information on Maximilian Sauerborn, see Biographical Appendix.

39. Hockerts, 'Anton Storch', 258 f.; H.G. Hockerts, 'Die sozialstaatlichen Grundentscheidungen in der frühen Bundesrepublik', in P. Masuch et al. (eds), Grundlagen und Herausforderungen des Sozialstaats. Denkschrift 60 Jahre Bundessozialgericht. Eigenheiten und Zukunft von Sozialpolitik und Sozialrecht, vol. 1, Berlin: Schmidt, 2014, 139–59, quotation 147 (from a confidential note from Robert Pferdmenges to Konrad Adenauer, 31 August 1949); Bundesarchiv and Institut für Zeitgeschichte (eds), Akten zur Vorgeschichte der Bundesrepublik Deutschland 1945–1949, vol. 1: September 1945–Dezember 1946, Munich: Oldenbourg, 1976 and 1981, 773; Personal Files Sauerborn, BMWi, BArch, R 3001/73522.

40. Personal files Dobbernack, BArch, R 3901/102369; Curriculum Vitae Dobbernack, 11 June 1947, BArch, Z 40/319; Hockerts, Sozialpolitische Entscheidungen, 24, 114. See, for example, Johannes Krohn to Rudolf Wissell, 30 October 1947, and Wissell to Krohn, September (?) 1949, BArch, NL 430/6.

41. Dobbernack to Walter Auerbach, 14 February 1950 and 8 August 1952, AdsD, Papers Walter Auerbach, Folders 34 and 193.

42. J. Eckert, Schuldig oder entlastet? 2nd ed., Munich, now Schliersee: Rechts- und Wirtschaftsverlag Gruber, 1948, 196–202.

43. Hockerts, 'Anton Storch', 264.

44. On the General Secretariat, see Hockerts, Sozialpolitische Entscheidungen, 117 f., quotation 118; on the significance of social policy as generator of consensus and framework of integration within the early West Germany, see ibid., 435; E. Wolfrum, Die geglückte Demokratie. Geschichte der Bundesrepublik Deutschland von ihren Anfängen bis zur Gegenwart, Bonn: Bundeszentrale für politische Bildung, 2007, 88–95.

45. On Krohn's role before 1945, see the chapter by Ulrike Schulz in this volume; Curricula Vitae Krohn among other things in BArch, NL 430/5.

46. Diary entry Johannes Krohn, 24 February 1946, BArch, NL 430/3, 42.

47. For more detail, see U. Wengst, Beamtentum zwischen Reform und Tradition. Beamtengesetzgebung in der Gründungsphase der Bundesrepublik Deutschland 1948–1953, Düsseldorf: Droste, 1988; Langhorst, Beamtentum, esp. 183–95; N. Frei, Vergangenheitspolitik. Die Anfänge der Bundesrepublik und die NS-Vergangenheit, Munich: Beck, 2012, 69–100.

48. Krohn to Hermann Pünder, 27 June 1949, BArch, Z 11/247.

49. Krohn to Wissell, 16 April 1947, BArch, NL 430/6.

50. On the organization's self-portrayal, which tells us much about the perspective of those opposed to a system of universal insurance, see Köhrer, 'Die Geschichte'. My thanks to Heike Wieters for some illuminating remarks in this regard.

51. For detailed information on Wilhelm Herschel, see Biographical Appendix.

52. Personal Files Herschel, BMWi; Curriculum Vitae Herschel, 9 June 1947, BArch, Z 40/319; Hockerts, 'Anton Storch', 262.

53. See Reich Labour Minister's Proposal to Appoint Schelp Government Counsellor, 24 September 1938, BArch, R 601/2104.

54. Ulrich Witting (Berlin 1936–1945), Hans Joachim Reichel (various economic fields 1935–1945), Werner Libbert (Berlin-Brandenburg 1937–1945), Karl Andres (Mitteldeutschland [roughly present-day Saxony, Saxony-Anhalt and Thuringia] 1934–1945). Further examples include the head of Subdivision III b (Occupational Safety and Factory Inspectorate) Hans Stephany; Walter Hennig, who worked in the Subdivision for Provision for War Victims; and Walter Kobe, adviser to the Working Group on 'Special Problems of Social Order'. On the Reich labour trustees, see the chapter by Sören Eden in this volume.

55. If we include the ZfA and VfA, the circle of women expands to encompass economist Hildegard Wicht, who was transferred from the VfA to a white-collar post at the Federal Ministry of Labour in light of her professional experience in the labour administration, her abilities as a statistician and her background in the management of personnel; the statistician Margarete Lichey, who gained a Ph.D. in 1927 on 'Socialism and Women's Labour', had been a long-term member of staff at the Berlin Institute for Economic Research (Berliner Institut für Wirtschaftsforschung) and, following stints at the ZfA, VfA and BMA, was posted to the Federal Institute for Labour in 1952, as was the lawyer Maria Lohmann, who had held white-collar posts in the labour deployment administration in Bregenz, Linz and Vienna between 1938 and 1941; finally, graduate engineer Margarete Raffloer worked as an adviser in Department V of the ZfA until 1948.

56. On Schulte Langforth, Tritz and Wendland, see the Review of Proposed Appointments at the Federal Ministry of Finance, BArch, B 126/17039, 17047, 17055; and on Schulte Langforth's resignation as chief adviser at the Ministry of Labour and Healthcare of the GDR, see the list of 5 December 1949, BArch, DQ 2/1344, fol. 38.

57. See the correspondence and lists on a number of denazification processes at the ZfA in BArch, Z 40/313, 6; on the screening practices within the VfA, see, for example, BArch, Z 11/548.

58. Paetzold to the Screening Panel in Kiel (enclosure), 20 February 1948, and testimonial for Paetzold by Martineck, 14 November 1947 (copy), LArch NRW, NW 1072-LB, 842. Even the cases of Heinrich Pelzer and Hans Linthe, who were placed in Category III ('less encumbered' [Minderbelastet]), proved essentially unproblematic. After being reclassified into Category V, they were appointed as BMA department heads in 1952 and 1955 respectively.

59. Krohn to Section Head Dr A. Wende, 20 June 1946, BArch, NL 430/5 (which also contains numerous clearance certificates).

60. Eckert, Schuldig, foreword 4, 76 f., 100.

61. Julius Scheuble to Headquarters of the Military Government for the North Rhine Province, 19 February 1946, BArch, Z 40/312.

62. Note Wilhelm Melohn, 2 July 1947, Certificate Scheuble for Käfferbitz, 10 May 1947, Scheuble to the Labour Minister of the Land of North Rhine-Westphalia, 19 May 1947, all BArch, Z 40/312; Memo Government Counsellor Oel on the meeting of 8 September 1949, 9 September 1949, BArch, Z 11/548.

63. E. Kogon, 'Beinahe mit dem Rücken an der Wand', *Frankfurter Hefte* 9(9) (1954), 641–45, quotation 641.

64. Figures in Langhorst, *Beamtentum*, 186–95.

65. Auerbach to State Minister Halbfell, Land Government of North Rhine-Westphalia, 30 September 1949, AdsD, Papers Walter Auerbach, 9/1/126.

66. At the ZfA and VfA three advisers were employed who had already joined the Nazi Party by 1933: Jakob Käfferbitz, Fritz Molle and Walter Stothfang.

67. Frank Bösch and Andreas Wirsching, *Abschlussbericht der Vorstudie zum Thema 'Die Nachkriegsgeschichte des Bundesministeriums des Innern (BMI) und des Ministeriums des Innern der DDR (MdI) hinsichtlich möglicher personeller und sachlicher Kontinuitäten zur Zeit des Nationalsozialismus 2015'*, Ms., as at 29 October 2015, 31, 33, http://www.ifz-muenchen.de/fileadmin/user_upload/Neuigkeiten%202015/BMI_Abschlussbericht%20der%20Vorstudie.pdf (accessed 7 September 2016).

68. M. Görtemaker and C. Safferling, *Die Akte Rosenburg. Das Bundesministerium der Justiz und die NS-Zeit*, Munich: Beck, 2016, 260–64; Conze et al., *Das Amt*, 493 f.

69. C. Goschler and M. Wala, *'Keine neue Gestapo'. Das Bundesamt für Verfassungsschutz und die NS-Vergangenheit*, Reinbek bei Hamburg: Rowohlt, 2015; I. Baumann et al., *Schatten der Vergangenheit. Das BKA und seine Gründungsgeneration in der frühen Bundesrepublik*, Cologne: Luchterhand, 2011; C. Rass, *Das Sozialprofil des Bundesnachrichtendienstes. Von den Anfängen bis 1968*, Berlin: Ch. Links, 2016, esp. 170–85, 223–31.

70. A series of articles published in the *Frankfurter Rundschau* in early September 1951 on the staffing policies of the Foreign Office prompted the appointment of a committee of enquiry and a Bundestag debate in October 1952, with the latter discussing the 'abuses at the Foreign Office'. Conze et al., *Das Amt*, 471–87; German Bundestag, Stenographic Report, 234. Meeting, 22 October 1952, Minutes of the Plenary Session 01/234, 10720-10750.

71. M. von Miquel, *Ahnden oder amnestieren? Westdeutsche Justiz und Vergangenheitspolitik in den sechziger Jahren*, Göttingen: Wallstein, 2004; N. Podewin (ed.), *Braunbuch. Kriegs- und Naziverbrecher in der Bundesrepublik und in Berlin (West)*, reprint, Berlin: Edition Ost, 2002. Among the jurists identified in the course of the 'Blood-Soaked Judges' campaign was Joseph Schneider (adviser on social insurance in the Protectorate of Bohemia and Moravia 1939–1942, head of the Section on Social Insurance at the Ministry of Economy and Labour [Ministerium für Wirtschaft und Arbeit] in Prague until 1945, head of Section I of the BMA from November 1950, first president of the Federal Social Court in 1954) and Alois Lentz (judge at the Special Court within the Land Court Berlin 1944–1945, VfA 1948–1950, department head at the BMA 1950–1953). Lentz's successor at the BMA, Wilhelm Ansorge, had been working at the Reich Ministry of Justice since 1940, where in 1943 Ministerial Director Günther Vollmer, among other things, confirmed that Ansorge had contributed to 'matters of life and death' and that he was 'politically . . . reliable'. Report by Ministerial Director Dr Vollmer at the Reich Ministry of Justice, 9 August 1943, LArch NRW, NW Pe/3946.

72. For detailed information on Wilhelm Claussen, see Biographical Appendix.

73. BArch, N 1299/3; here too the quotation: Hans Globke to Claussen, 17 April 1963. On Claussen, see Personal Files Claussen, BMWi; Foreword to finding aid on the holding BArch, N 1299 – Claussen, Wilhelm.

74. Federal Plenipotentiary for the Documents of the State Security of the Former GDR (Bundesbeauftragte[r] für die Unterlagen des Staatssicherheitsdienstes der ehemaligen DDR or BStU), MfS HA IX/11 PA, 20, fol. 16.

75. Personal Files Stets, BMWi; here too the quotation: head of Section II (Rudolf Petz) to the head of Section I (Joseph Schneider), 2 February 1953.

76. On what follows, see Review of Proposed Appointments at the Federal Ministry of Finance, BArch, B 126/17038.

77. On what follows, see Personal Files Siemer, BMWi; Review of Proposed Appointments at the Federal Ministry of Finance, BArch, B 126/17029; Correspondence Siemer with the Nazi Party, BArch, VBS 1/1110055607.

78. The Federal Minister for Labour, Department Head Käfferbitz, to the Federal Minister of the Interior, 7 December 1951 (draft), Personal Files Siemer, BMWi.

79. On Theile and Reichel, see the Review of Proposed Appointments at the Federal Ministry of Finance, BArch, B 126/17045, 17021; Nazi Party Questionnaires, 1 July 1939, BArch, R 9361-I/3624; *Dienstliche Mitteilungen BMA* 12/1959, 11 September 1959. On Walter Stothfang, see "The Case of Walter Stothfang" within this chapter.

80. On what follows, see esp. Personal Files M., BMWi.

81. Quoted in the judgement on appeal of the Federal Disciplinary Court 1962, Personal Files M., BMWi.

82. Federal Minister for Labour and Social Order, Central Section, 25 July 1969, and Head of Section IV and General Secretary for Social Reform, Jantz, to the Head of the Central Section, 2 June 1969/4 May 1971, Personal Files M., BMWi.

83. On what follows, see Documents and Curricula Vitae Private Archive Stothfang (PAS); Personal Files Stothfang, BArch, R 3901/109969; File on the Transfer of Stothfang to the BMA in 1959, BArch, B 126/17044; Nazi Party Questionnaire, 29 June 1939, BArch, R 9361-I/3520; Denazification Files, LArch NRW, NW 1067/2973 and NW 1037-AV/45. My thanks go to Ms. Gisela Stothfang and Mr Jan Stothfang (Nuremberg) for making available various private documents, and to Ms. Yasuna Hashimoto (Tokyo) for valuable information.

84. According to Stothfang during his interrogation at Nuremberg on 1 June 1946, in *Der Prozess gegen die Hauptkriegsverbrecher vor dem Internationalen Militärgerichtshof. Nürnberg, 14. November 1945–1. Oktober 1946*, vol. 15: *Verhandlungsniederschriften 29. Mai 1946-10. Juni 1946*, Munich and Zurich: n.p., 1984 (reprint of the 1948 Nuremberg edition), 266–74. See also Stothfang to Gerhard Erdmann, 8 December 1957, and Stothfang to Direktor Gassmann [Walter Gassmann], Bundestag Deputy, 12 February 1958, PAS.

85. See, for example, W. Stothfang, *Der Arbeitseinsatz im Kriege*, Berlin: Junker und Dünnhaupt, 1940; W. Stothfang, '5 Jahre Arbeitseinsatz im Kriege', *RABl.* V (1944), 264–67, quotation 264; see also Attachment 9 to Curriculum Vitae Stothfang, 8 August 1947, LArch NRW, NW 1067/2973; Press Articles in BArch, R 8034-III/450, fol. 138–46.

86. Stothfang to Scheuble, 17 September 1946, 26 September 1946, BArch, Z 40/312; Curriculum Vitae Stothfang, 8 August 1947, LArch NRW, NW 1067/2973; Stothfang to Gerhard Erdmann, 8 December 1957, PAS; the Interior Minister of the Land of North Rhine-Westphalia to the Special Representative for Denazification (Sonderbeauftragter für die Entnazifizierung), Land Court President Dr Kremer, 27 February 1948, LArch NRW, NW 1037-AV/45.

87. See the chapter by Kim Christian Priemel in this volume.

88. Auerbach to Scheuble, 31 January 1948, Note Scheuble, 4 February 1948, Auerbach to Mr Karl (?), 7 February 1948, all BArch, Z 40/312. Auerbach initially remained in office and became state secretary in the Lower Saxony Ministry of Labour and Social Affairs in November 1948.

89. Record of the Meeting of the Advisory Committee at the Hamburg Land Labour Office on 27 May 1948, BArch, Z 40/312; Mansfeld to Lawyer and Notary Dr O. Kunze, Halle, 30 May 1948, BArch, DC 1/115.

90. Institut für Zeitgeschichte and Deutscher Bundestag (eds), *Wörtliche Berichte und Drucksachen des Wirtschaftsrates des Vereinigten Wirtschaftsgebietes 1947–1949*, vol. 3: 23.–40. *Vollversammlung*. Munich: Oldenbourg, 1977, 1128; quotation: Storch to Stothfang, 23 August 1949, PAS.

91. Stothfang to Direktor Gassmann [Walter Gassmann], Bundestag Deputy, 12 February 1958, PAS.

92. The Federal Minister for Labour and Social Order, signed Blank, to the State Secretary of the Federal Chancellery, 16 September 1959, BArch, B 126/17044.

93. Before his early death in late 1961, Stothfang once again became the target of public debates when the main SED organ *Neues Deutschland* picked up on a report in the Deutscher Gewerkschaftsbund weekly *Welt der Arbeit* and drew parallels between Stothfang's position at the GBA and his involvement in the formulation of a draft of an emergency service law, a precursor of the later emergency laws. 'NS-Spezialist für Zwangsarbeit entwarf Notdienstgesetz', *Welt der Arbeit*, 10 June 1960; 'Urnazi macht in Bonn Gesetze. Sauckels rechte Hand – Autor der Notdienstpflicht', *Neues Deutschland*, 10 June 1960, 2 (plus several follow-up articles); Blueprints and Correspondence relating to the Planned Emergency Service Law, BArch, B 106/28223-28224.

94. Kahlenberg and Hoffmann, 'Sozialpolitik', 108–10; B. Niedbalski, 'Deutsche Zentralverwaltungen und Deutsche Wirtschaftskommission (DWK). Ansätze zur zentralen Wirtschaftsplanung in der SBZ 1945–1948', *Vierteljahrshefte für Zeitgeschichte* 33(3) (1985), 456–77; W. Zank, *Wirtschaft und Arbeit in Ostdeutschland 1945–1949. Probleme des Wiederaufbaus in der Sowjetischen Besatzungszone Deutschlands*, Munich: Oldenbourg, 1987, 86–96; D. Hoffmann, *Sozialpolitische Neuordnung in der SBZ/DDR. Der Umbau der Sozialversicherung 1945–1956*, Munich: Oldenbourg, 1996, 23–28; M. Boldorf, *Sozialfürsorge in der SBZ/DDR 1945–1953. Ursachen, Ausmass und Bewältigung der Nachkriegsarmut*, Stuttgart: Steiner, 1998; 128 f.; 'Einleitung', in *Bundesarchiv. Online-Findbuch, Ministerium für Arbeit und Berufsausbildung, DQ 2, 1948–1955*, ed. C. Fengler, Koblenz, 2005, http://startext.net-build.de:8080/barch/MidosaSEARCH/DQ2-28582/index.htm (accessed 7 September 2016); Data on the Departmental Structure of the ZVAS and DVAS in BArch, DQ 2/588.

95. Decree of 22 September 1946, quoted in Boldorf, *Sozialfürsorge*, 134 f.

96. Manuscript Gustav Gundelach on his Curriculum Vitae, Stiftung Archiv der Parteien und Massenorganisationen der DDR im Bundesarchiv (SAPMO-BArch), NY 4066/3, fol. 278; Breakdown of the Staff of the ZVAS on 13 December 1945, BArch, DQ 2/588, fol. 18–24; List of White-Collar Employees of the DVAS on 12 August 1947, BArch, DQ 2/1300; Kahlenberg and Hoffmann, 'Sozialpolitik', 176.

97. For an overall view, see H.A. Welsh, '"Antifaschistisch-demokratische Umwälzung" und politische Säuberung in der sowjetischen Besatzungszone Deutschlands', in K.-D. Henke and H. Woller (eds), *Politische Säuberung in Europa. Die Abrechnung mit Faschismus und Kollaboration nach dem Zweiten Weltkrieg*, Munich: Deutscher Taschenbuch-Verlag, 1991, 84–107; on denazification within the social insurance administration, see Hoffmann, *Sozialpolitische Neuordnung*, 99–104.

98. It was not yet possible to make use of more comprehensive documents on the staffing of the central East German labour authorities for the present chapter. However, on the basis, among other things, of staffing lists in BArch, DQ 1/1344 and BArch, DQ 2/588, 1272, 1300 and a number of cadre files, I have so far been able to consider sixty-five members of staff for the period 1945–1958 from advisers upwards. For biographical information, see www.bundesstiftung-aufarbeitung.de/wer-war-wer-in-der-ddr-%2363%3b-1424.html (accessed 8 October 2016); G. Baumgartner and D. Hebig (eds), *Biographisches Handbuch der SBZ/DDR*, Munich: Saur, 1996; M. Broszat and H. Weber (eds), *SBZ-Handbuch. Staatliche Verwaltungen, Parteien, gesellschaftliche Organisationen und ihre Führungskräfte in der Sowjetischen Besatzungszone Deutschlands 1945–1949*, 2nd ed., Munich: Oldenbourg, 1993; see also D. Hoffmann, 'Netzwerke und Sonderinstanzen. Die Marginalisierung der Länder bei der Vereinheitlichung der Sozialversicherung in der SBZ (1945–1949)', in A. Schuhmann (ed.), *Vernetzte Improvisationen. Gesellschaftliche Subsysteme in Ostmitteleuropa und in der DDR*, Cologne: Böhlau, 2008, 43–56, here 44–47; Zank, *Wirtschaft*, 92 f.; E.W. Gniffke, *Jahre mit Ulbricht*, Cologne: Verlag Wissenschaft und Politik, 1966, 338 f.

99. Manuscript Gustav Gundelach on his Curriculum Vitae, SAPMO-BArch, NY 4066/3, fol. 277–79, quotation fol. 277. Gundelach's personal adviser was the later DVAS section head Jakob Schlör, whom Gundelach knew as they had worked together on the central committee of the KPD's 'Red Aid' organization.

100. Here and in what follows, see Gniffke, *Jahre mit Ulbricht*, 338 f., 97 f.; Hoffmann, 'Netzwerke', 44–46.

101. Lehmann's colleagues there, who had been dismissed like him in 1933, were Karl Litke, a trained lithographer and former Reichstag deputy, who headed the ZVAS administrative department as ministerial director in 1945–1946, and Fritz Bohlmann, who held leading positions in the East German labour and welfare administration between 1945 and 1950. See Curricula Vitae and Questionnaires on Litke and Bohlmann, SAPMO-BArch, NY 4073/1 and DY 34/28122.

102. See, for example, Curricula Vitae and Staff Questionnaires Ernst Holstein and Hans Thalmann, SAPMO-BArch, DR 3-B/15340 and DR 3-B/15209 respectively; R. Helm, *Anwalt des Volkes. Erinnerungen*, Berlin: Dietz, 1978, 146–58.

103. J. Kuhlemann, *Braune Kader. Ehemalige Nationalsozialisten in der Deutschen Wirtschaftskommission und der DDR-Regierung (1948–1957)*, Ph.D. dissertation, Jena: University of Jena, 2005, online edition 2012, 136, fn. 621.

104. Voss, whose background lay in the trades union and cooperative movement, had also been dismissed in 1933 and he had links with the German resistance. J. Kaiser, 'Albert Voss †', *Neue Zeit*, 11 November 1947, 1 f.; 'Vizepräsident Albert Voss †', *Arbeit und Sozialfürsorge* 2(21/22) (1947), 469.

105. Curriculum Vitae and Staff Questionnaire Willy Donau, SAPMO-BArch, DY 34/28189; on Donau, see also the chapter by Kiran Klaus Patel and Sandrine Kott in this volume.

106. Breakdown of the Party Political Composition of White-Collar Workers at the ZVAS on 1 May 1946, BArch, DQ 2/588, fol. 9; Overview of the Number and Trades Union and Party Affiliation of DVAS White-Collar Employees April–December 1947, BArch, DQ 2/1300.

107. Note Gundelach (?), 14 December 1945, BArch, DQ 2/588, fol. 17. Hirschfeld took up the post of in-house lawyer at the Berlin-Schöneberg District Office in 1946 and became a member of the Berlin House of Representatives (Abgeordnetenhaus) in 1951.

108. Here and in what follows, see Hoffmann, *Sozialpolitische Neuordnung*, 171–75; Kahlenberg and Hoffmann, 'Sozialpolitik', 169–73; J. Rowell, 'Wohnungspolitik', in D. Hoffmann and M. Schwartz (eds, on behalf of the Institut für Zeitgeschichte München-Berlin), *Geschichte der Sozialpolitik in Deutschland seit 1945*, vol. 8: *1949–1961. Deutsche Demokratische Republik. Im Zeichen des Aufbaus des Sozialismus*, Baden-Baden: Nomos, 2004, 699–726, here esp. 707–10. On the departmental structure in November 1949, see BArch, DQ 1/1344, fol. 2–29.

109. Kahlenberg and Hoffmann, 'Sozialpolitik', 169.

110. Hoffmann, *Sozialpolitische Neuordnung*, 172; Overview of Established Posts of 13 November 1950, BArch, DQ 2/1404; see also the lists in BArch, DQ 2/1272 and BArch, DQ 1/1344.

111. Kuhlemann, *Braune Kader*, 167 f., 213, 240 f., 261 f.

112. L. Dollmann, 'Chwalek, Roman (1898–1974)', in S. Mielke (ed.), *Gewerkschafter in den Konzentrationslagern Oranienburg und Sachsenhausen. Biographisches Handbuch*, vol. 1, Berlin: Edition Hentrich, 2002, 44–55.

113. 'Fritz Macher zum Minister für Arbeit berufen', *Neues Deutschland*, 10 December 1953, 1.

114. For detailed information on Frieda (known as Friedel) Malter, see Biographical Appendix.

115. K. Barnstedt and K. Scheel, 'Apelt, Frieda (Friedel Malter) (1902–2001). Vom Webstuhl ins Ministerium. Oder: "Wenn die Partei ruft, geht man."', in S. Mielke (ed.), *Gewerkschafterinnen im NS-Staat. Verfolgung, Widerstand, Emigration*, Essen: Klartext, 2008, 60–71.

116. 'Freie Deutsche Jugend verkörpert die grosse Zukunft unseres Volkes', *Neues Deutschland*, 9 March 1951, 4; see also 'Zwei junge Minister – eine Sensation?', *Neues Deutschland*, 20 September 1958, 14.

117. C. Boyer, 'Kaderpolitik und zentrale Planbürokratie in der SBZ/DDR (1945–1961)', in S. Hornbostel (ed.), *Sozialistische Eliten. Horizontale und vertikale Differenzierungsmuster in der DDR*, Opladen: Leske + Budrich, 1999, 11–30; Kahlenberg and Hoffmann, 'Sozialpolitik', 177 f.

118. P.J. Lapp, *Der Ministerrat der DDR. Aufgaben, Arbeitsweise und Struktur der anderen deutschen Regierung*, Opladen: Westdeutscher Verlag, 1982, 225.

119. Peschke to SED Party Executive, Department of Labour and Social Welfare, for the Attention of Max Herm, 27 April 1950, SAPMO-BArch, DY 30/IV 2/2.027/2.

120. Note and Document on Knoll's Placing on Non-Active Service, 14 [?] July and 1 August 1939, BArch, R 43 II/1138b, fol. 34 f.; Breakdown of Staff at the ZVAS on 13 December 1945, BArch, DQ 2/588, fol. 21; Statement Foerster, 1 February 1946, BArch, NL 430/5; see also my earlier remarks on Dorothea Hirschfeld.

121. The highest-ranking individual to leave East Germany and take up a post in the West German Labour Ministry was former CDU minister for labour and social affairs in Brandenburg, Fritz Schwob. In February 1950, Schwob fled to West Berlin, after which the BMA put him in charge of its Berlin office, appointing him ministerial counsellor in 1952. Personal Files Schwob, BArch, PERS 101/43030; Proposed Appointment of Schwob as Ministerial Counsellor and Note, 6 November and 4 December 1952, BArch, B 126/17041.

122. Mansfeld to Lawyer and Notary Dr O. Kunze, Halle, 30 May 1948, BArch, DC 1/115. In February 1949, Mansfeld settled in the western part of Berlin, where he had to submit to a process of denazification prior to his death in February 1952, during which he had to explain and justify his role in the Reich Ministry of Labour and in the deployment of forced labourers. See Mansfeld's Correspondence, Records, Documents and Detailed Curricula Vitae in the Context of his Defence and of the Denazification Process in BArch, DP 1/20617, LArch Berlin, B-Rep. 031-01-02, 2198, BStU, MfS BV Halle/Ast 7473.

123. To quote the title of an article referring to the case of the former head of the Main Section for Labour in the General Government in Cracow, Max Frauendorfer: T. Schlemmer, 'Grenzen der Integration. Die CSU und der Umgang mit der nationalsozialistischen Vergangenheit – der Fall Dr. Max Frauendorfer', *Vierteljahrshefte für Zeitgeschichte* 48(4) (2000), 675–742.

124. On this discussion, see, for example, Bösch and Wirsching, *Abschlussbericht*, 7 f.; Langhorst, *Beamtentum*, 182 f.

125. See Wolfrum, *Die geglückte Demokratie*, 58.

Bibliography

Auftakt zur Ära Adenauer. Koalitionsverhandlungen und Regierungsbildung 1949, ed. U. Wengst, series ed. Kommission für Geschichte des Parlamentarismus und der Politischen Parteien. Düsseldorf: Droste, 1985.

Babendreyer, E. *Walter Auerbach. Sozialpolitik aus dem Exil*, Ph.D. dissertation. Duisburg and Essen: University Duisburg-Essen, 2007. Retrieved 6 September 2018 from https://duepublico.uni-duisburg-essen.de/servlets/DocumentServlet?id=15811.

Barnstedt, K., and K. Scheel. 'Apelt, Frieda (Friedel Malter) (1902–2001). Vom Webstuhl ins Ministerium. Oder: "Wenn die Partei ruft, geht man."', in S. Mielke (ed.), *Gewerkschafterinnen im NS-Staat. Verfolgung, Widerstand, Emigration* (Essen: Klartext, 2008), 60–71.

Baumann, I., et al. *Schatten der Vergangenheit. Das BKA und seine Gründungsgeneration in der frühen Bundesrepublik*. Cologne: Luchterhand, 2011.

Baumgartner, G., and D. Hebig (eds). *Biographisches Handbuch der SBZ/DDR*. Munich: Saur, 1996.

Boldorf, M. *Sozialfürsorge in der SBZ/DDR 1945–1953. Ursachen, Ausmass und Bewältigung der Nachkriegsarmut*. Stuttgart: Steiner, 1998.

Born, L.K. 'The Ministerial Collecting Center Near Kassel, Germany'. *The American Archivist* 13 (1950), 237–58.

Boyer, C. 'Kaderpolitik und zentrale Planbürokratie in der SBZ/DDR (1945–1961)', in S. Hornbostel (ed.), *Sozialistische Eliten. Horizontale und vertikale Differenzierungsmuster in der DDR* (Opladen: Leske + Budrich, 1999), 11–30.

Broszat, M., and H. Weber (eds). *SBZ-Handbuch. Staatliche Verwaltungen, Parteien, gesellschaftliche Organisationen und ihre Führungskräfte in der Sowjetischen Besatzungszone Deutschlands 1945–1949*, 2nd ed. Munich: Oldenbourg, 1993.

Bundesarchiv and Institut für Zeitgeschichte (eds). *Akten zur Vorgeschichte der Bundesrepublik Deutschland 1945–1949*, vol. 1: *September 1945–Dezember 1946* and vol. 5: *Januar–September 1949*. Munich: Oldenbourg, 1976 and 1981.

Bundesministerium für Arbeit und Sozialordnung and Bundesarchiv (eds). *Geschichte der Sozialpolitik in Deutschland seit 1945*, 11 vols. Baden-Baden: Nomos 2001–2008.

Conze, E., et al. (eds). *Das Amt und die Vergangenheit. Deutsche Diplomaten im Dritten Reich und in der Bundesrepublik*. Munich: Blessing, 2010.

Dollmann, L. 'Chwalek, Roman (1898–1974)', in S. Mielke (ed.), *Gewerkschafter in den Konzentrationslagern Oranienburg und Sachsenhausen. Biographisches Handbuch*, vol. 1 (Berlin: Edition Hentrich, 2002), 44–55.

Eckert, J. *Schuldig oder entlastet?* 2nd ed. Munich, now Schliersee: Rechts- und Wirtschaftsverlag Gruber, 1948.

Frei, N. *Vergangenheitspolitik. Die Anfänge der Bundesrepublik und die NS-Vergangenheit*. Munich: Beck, 2012.

Girndt, I. *Zentralismus in der britischen Zone. Entwicklungen und Bestrebungen beim Wiederaufbau der staatlichen Verwaltungsorganisation auf der Ebene oberhalb der Länder 1945–1948*, Ph.D. dissertation. Bonn: University of Bonn, 1971.

Gniffke, E.W. *Jahre mit Ulbricht*. Cologne: Verlag Wissenschaft und Politik, 1966.

Görtemaker, M., and C. Safferling. *Die Akte Rosenburg. Das Bundesministerium der Justiz und die NS-Zeit*. Munich: Beck, 2016.

Goschler, C., and M. Wala. *'Keine neue Gestapo'. Das Bundesamt für Verfassungsschutz und die NS-Vergangenheit*. Reinbek bei Hamburg: Rowohlt, 2015.

Helm, R. *Anwalt des Volkes. Erinnerungen*. Berlin: Dietz, 1978.

Henkels, W. *99 Bonner Köpfe*. Düsseldorf: Econ, 1963.

Herbert, U. *Best. Biographische Studien über Radikalismus, Weltanschauung und Vernunft, 1903–1989*. Bonn: Dietz, 1996.

Hockerts, H.G. 'Anton Storch (1892–1975)', in J. Aretz, R. Morsey and A. Rauscher (eds), *Zeitgeschichte in Lebensbildern*, vol. 4: *Aus dem deutschen Katholizismus des 19. und 20. Jahrhunderts* (Mainz: Matthias-Grünewald-Verlag, 1980), 250–66.

Hockerts, H.G. *Sozialpolitische Entscheidungen im Nachkriegsdeutschland. Alliierte und deutsche Sozialversicherungspolitik 1945 bis 1957*. Stuttgart: Klett-Cotta, 1980.

Hockerts, H.G. 'Die sozialstaatlichen Grundentscheidungen in der frühen Bundesrepublik', in P. Masuch et al. (eds), *Grundlagen und Herausforderungen des Sozialstaats. Denkschrift 60 Jahre Bundessozialgericht. Eigenheiten und Zukunft von Sozialpolitik und Sozialrecht*, vol. 1 (Berlin: Schmidt, 2014), 139–59.

Hoffmann, D. 'Netzwerke und Sonderinstanzen. Die Marginalisierung der Länder bei der Vereinheitlichung der Sozialversicherung in der SBZ (1945–1949)', in A. Schuhmann (ed.), *Vernetzte Improvisationen. Gesellschaftliche Subsysteme in Ostmitteleuropa und in der DDR* (Cologne: Böhlau, 2008), 43–56.

Hoffmann, D. *Sozialpolitische Neuordnung in der SBZ/DDR. Der Umbau der Sozialversicherung 1945–1956*. Munich: Oldenbourg, 1996.

Institut für Zeitgeschichte and Deutscher Bundestag (eds). *Wörtliche Berichte und Drucksachen des Wirtschaftsrates des Vereinigten Wirtschaftsgebietes 1947–1949*, vol. 3: *23.–40. Vollversammlung*. Munich: Oldenbourg, 1977.

Jarausch, K. *Die Umkehr. Deutsche Wandlungen 1945–1995*. Bonn: Bundeszentrale für politische Bildung, 2004.

Kahlenberg, F.P., and D. Hoffmann. 'Sozialpolitik als Aufgabe zentraler Verwaltungen in Deutschland', in Bundesministerium für Arbeit und Sozialordnung and Bundesarchiv (eds), *Geschichte der Sozialpolitik in Deutschland seit 1945*, vol. 1: *Grundlagen der Sozialpolitik* (Baden-Baden: Nomos, 2001), 103–82.

Kaiser, J. 'Albert Voss †'. *Neue Zeit*, 11 November 1947, 1.

Kogon, E. 'Beinahe mit dem Rücken an der Wand'. *Frankfurter Hefte* 9(9) (1954), 641–45.

Köhrer, H. 'Die Geschichte der Gesellschaft für Versicherungswissenschaft und -gestaltung e. V. (GVG)', in M. Jung, H. Köhrer and V. Leienbach, *Im Dienste freiheitlicher Sozialpolitik. 40 Jahre Gesellschaft für Versicherungswissenschaft und -gestaltung (GVG)* (Bergisch Gladbach: Vollmer, 1987), 18–72.

Kuhlemann, J. *Braune Kader. Ehemalige Nationalsozialisten in der Deutschen Wirtschaftskommission und der DDR-Regierung (1948–1957)*, Ph.D. dissertation. Jena: University of Jena, 2005.

Langhorst, W. *Beamtentum und Artikel 131 des Grundgesetzes. Eine Untersuchung über Bedeutung und Auswirkung der Gesetzgebung zum Artikel 131 des Grundgesetzes unter Einbeziehung der Position der SPD zum Berufsbeamtentum*. Frankfurt am Main: Lang, 1994.

Lapp, P.J. *Der Ministerrat der DDR. Aufgaben, Arbeitsweise und Struktur der anderen deutschen Regierung*. Opladen: Westdeutscher Verlag, 1982.

Leibfried, S., and F. Tennstedt. *Berufsverbote und Sozialpolitik 1933. Die Auswirkungen der nationalsozialistischen Machtergreifung auf die Krankenkassenverwaltung und die Kassenärzte. Analyse, Materialien zu Angriff und Selbsthilfe, Erinnerungen*. Bremen: University of Bremen, Presse- und Informationsamt, 1980.

Lembeck, E. *Die Partizipation von Frauen an der öffentlichen Verwaltung in der Weimarer Republik 1918–1933*, Ph.D. dissertation. Hanover: University of Hanover, 1991.

Löffler, B. *Soziale Marktwirtschaft und administrative Praxis. Das Bundeswirtschaftsministerium unter Ludwig Erhard*. Stuttgart: Steiner, 2002.

Maier, D.G. 'Friedrich Syrup (1881–1945). Von der Gewerbeaufsicht an die Spitze der Arbeitsverwaltung', in D.G. Maier, J. Nürnberger and S. Pabst, *Vordenker und Gestalter des Arbeitsmarktes. Elf Biografien zur Geschichte der deutschen Arbeitsverwaltung* (Mannheim: Hochschule der Bundesagentur für Arbeit, 2012), 115–40.

Mentel, C., and N. Weise. *Die zentralen deutschen Behörden und der Nationalsozialismus. Stand und Perspektiven der Forschung*. Munich: Institut für Zeitgeschichte München, and Potsdam: Zentrum für Zeithistorische Forschung, 2016.

Miquel, M. von. *Ahnden oder amnestieren? Westdeutsche Justiz und Vergangenheitspolitik in den sechziger Jahren*. Göttingen: Wallstein, 2004.

Morsey, R. 'Personal- und Beamtenpolitik im Übergang von der Bizonen- zur Bundesverwaltung (1947–1950). Kontinuität oder Neubeginn?', in R. Morsey (ed.), *Verwaltungsgeschichte. Aufgaben, Zielsetzungen, Beispiele. Vorträge und Diskussionsbeiträge der verwaltungsgeschichtlichen Arbeitstagung 1976 der Hochschule für Verwaltungswissenschaften Speyer* (Berlin: Duncker & Humblot, 1972), 191–243.

Niedbalski, B. 'Deutsche Zentralverwaltungen und Deutsche Wirtschaftskommission (DWK). Ansätze zur zentralen Wirtschaftsplanung in der SBZ 1945–1948'. *Vierteljahrshefte für Zeitgeschichte* 33(3) (1985), 456–77.

Oppler, K. 'Die Zuständigkeit des Vereinigten Wirtschaftsgebietes auf dem Gebiete der Arbeit', *Recht der Arbeit* 1 (1948), 18–20.

Podewin, N. (ed.). *Braunbuch. Kriegs- und Naziverbrecher in der Bundesrepublik und in Berlin (West)*, reprint. Berlin: Edition Ost, 2002.

Der Prozess gegen die Hauptkriegsverbrecher vor dem Internationalen Militärgerichtshof. Nürnberg, 14. November 1945–1. Oktober 1946, 42 vols. Munich and Zurich: n.p., 1984 (reprint of the 1948 Nuremberg edition).
Pünder, T. *Das bizonale Interregnum. Die Geschichte des Vereinigten Wirtschaftsgebiets 1946–1949*. Cologne: Grote, 1966.
Rass, C. *Das Sozialprofil des Bundesnachrichtendienstes. Von den Anfängen bis 1968*. Berlin: Ch. Links, 2016.
Rowell, J. 'Wohnungspolitik', in D. Hoffmann and M. Schwartz (eds on behalf of Institut für Zeitgeschichte München-Berlin), *Geschichte der Sozialpolitik in Deutschland seit 1945*, vol. 8: *1949–1961. Deutsche Demokratische Republik. Im Zeichen des Aufbaus des Sozialismus* (Baden-Baden: Nomos, 2004), 699–726.
Sauerborn, M. 'Das Bundesministerium für Arbeit'. *Bundesarbeitsblatt* 1(1) (1950), 4–6.
Schlemmer, T. 'Grenzen der Integration. Die CSU und der Umgang mit der nationalsozialistischen Vergangenheit – der Fall Dr. Max Frauendorfer'. *Vierteljahrshefte für Zeitgeschichte* 48(4) (2000), 675–742.
Schmuhl, H.-W. *Arbeitsmarktpolitik und Arbeitsverwaltung in Deutschland 1871–2002. Zwischen Fürsorge, Hoheit und Markt*. Nuremberg: Institut für Arbeitsmarkt- und Berufsforschung, 2003.
Schulz, G. *Wiederaufbau in Deutschland. Die Wohnungsbaupolitik in den Westzonen und der Bundesrepublik von 1945 bis 1957*. Düsseldorf: Droste, 1994.
Storch, A. 'Der erste Präsident der Bundesanstalt für Arbeitsvermittlung und Arbeitslosenversicherung Dr. h. c. Julius Scheuble trat in den Ruhestand'. *Bundesarbeitsblatt* 7(13) (1957), 437.
Storch, A. 'Lebenserinnerungen. Erfahrungen und Erlebnisse', in Deutscher Bundestag (ed.), *Abgeordnete des Deutschen Bundestages. Aufzeichnungen und Erinnerungen*, vol. 2: *Curt Becker, Franz Marx, Ernst Paul, Hans Schütz, Elisabeth Schwarzhaupt, J. Hermann Siemer, Anton Storch* (Boppard am Rhein: Boldt, 1983), 313–44.
Storch, A. 'Was erwarten die Arbeitnehmer von der Neuordnung der deutschen Sozialversicherung?' *Arbeitsblatt für die britische Zone* 1(4) (1947), 139–41.
Stothfang, W. '5 Jahre Arbeitseinsatz im Kriege'. *Reichsarbeitsblatt* V (1944), 264–67.
Stothfang, W. *Der Arbeitseinsatz im Kriege*. Berlin: Junker und Dünnhaupt, 1940.
Stump, W. 'Anton Storch (1892–1975)'. *Vierteljahresschrift für Sozialrecht* 4 (1976), 129–39.
Verein Aktives Museum e. V. (ed.). *Vor die Tür gesetzt. Im Nationalsozialismus verfolgte Berliner Stadtverordnete und Magistratsmitglieder 1933–1945*. Berlin: self-published, 2006.
Vogel, W. *Westdeutschland 1945–1950. Der Aufbau von Verfassungs- und Verwaltungseinrichtungen über den Ländern der drei westlichen Besatzungszonen*, part 2: *Einzelne Verwaltungszweige: Wirtschaft, Marshallplan, Statistik*. Boppard am Rhein: Boldt, 1964.
Vogel, W. *Westdeutschland 1945–1950. Der Aufbau von Verfassungs- und Verwaltungseinrichtungen über den Ländern der drei westlichen Besatzungszonen*, part 3: *Einzelne Verwaltungszweige: Finanzen; Post und Verkehr; Arbeit und Soziales; Flüchtlinge, Suchdienst und Kriegsgefangene; Justiz; Inneres*. Boppard am Rhein: Boldt, 1983.
Welsh, H.A. '"Antifaschistisch-demokratische Umwälzung" und politische Säuberung in der sowjetischen Besatzungszone Deutschlands', in K.-D. Henke and H. Woller (eds), *Politische Säuberung in Europa. Die Abrechnung mit Faschismus und Kollaboration nach dem Zweiten Weltkrieg* (Munich: Deutscher Taschenbuch-Verlag, 1991), 84–107.
Wengst, U. *Beamtentum zwischen Reform und Tradition. Beamtengesetzgebung in der Gründungsphase der Bundesrepublik Deutschland 1948–1953*. Düsseldorf: Droste, 1988.
Wengst, U. 'Sozialpolitische Denk- und Handlungsfelder', in U. Wengst (ed.), *Geschichte der Sozialpolitik in Deutschland seit 1945*, vol. 2/1: *1945–1949. Die Zeit der Besatzungszonen. Sozialpolitik zwischen Kriegsende und der Gründung zweier deutscher Staaten. Darstellung* (Baden-Baden: Nomos, 2001), 77–149.

Wengst, U. *Staatsaufbau und Regierungspraxis 1948–1953. Zur Geschichte der Verfassungsorgane der Bundesrepublik Deutschland.* Düsseldorf: Droste, 1984.
Wolfrum, E. *Die geglückte Demokratie. Geschichte der Bundesrepublik Deutschland von ihren Anfängen bis zur Gegenwart.* Bonn: Bundeszentrale für politische Bildung, 2007.
Zank, W. *Wirtschaft und Arbeit in Ostdeutschland 1945–1949. Probleme des Wiederaufbaus in der Sowjetischen Besatzungszone Deutschlands.* Munich: Oldenbourg, 1987.
Zapf, W. 'Die Verwalter der Macht. Materialien zum Sozialprofil der höheren Beamtenschaft', in W. Zapf (ed.), *Beiträge zur Analyse der deutschen Oberschicht*, 2nd ed. (Munich: Piper, 1965), 77–94.

Appendix I

DESIGNATIONS OF OFFICE (IN ORDER OF SENIORITY)

State secretary	Staatssekretär
Ministerial director	Ministerialdirektor
Section head	Ministerialdirigent
Ministerial counsellor	Ministerialrat
Government director	Regierungsdirektor
Senior government counsellor	Oberregierungsrat
Government counsellor	Regierungsrat

Appendix II

BIOGRAPHIES

Walter Bogs (b. 3 April 1899 in Bromberg, d. 22 October 1991) served in the First World War before studying law in Marburg and Berlin. He gained a Ph.D. in Marburg in 1922. After working for the General German Trades Union Confederation (Allgemeiner Deutscher Gewerkschaftsbund, or ADGB), he served as a judge at the Berlin Labour Court (Arbeitsgericht) from 1928 to 1933, but was already partly responsible for social insurance as a result of an outside appointment at the Reich Insurance Office. He worked at the Reich Ministry of Labour from 1939, where he headed Section II b (International Affairs). There he dealt with, among other things, social insurance in the occupied territories and special regulations on foreign workers within the Reich. In 1944, he returned to the Reich Insurance Office as president of the Senate (*Senatspräsident*). After the Second World War, he initially worked as a lecturer in social insurance and labour law at the University of Göttingen and then as a judge at the District and Land Court in Göttingen from 1946 to 1949. He continued his academic career as full professor at the College of Labour, Politics and Economics (Hochschule für Arbeit, Politik und Wirtschaft) in Wilhelmshaven, serving as rector in 1951 and 1952. From 1954 to 1967, he worked as president of the Senate at the Federal Social Court (Bundessozialgericht) in Kassel. In addition, from 1958 to 1978, he was a member of the West German government's Social Security Advisory Council (Sozialbeirat).[1]

Wilhelm Börger (b. 14 February 1896 in Kray [Essen], d. 29 June 1962 in Heidelberg) completed an apprenticeship as a locksmith before seeing active service in the navy during the First World War between 1915 and 1918. He then worked as a locksmith and electrician and became the business secretary (*Betriebssekretär*) of the city of Neuss. Having begun to involve himself in party politics in 1922 as a member of the *Völkisch* Freedom Movement (Völkische Freiheitsbewegung) and after failing to gain a seat in the Reichstag in 1924, he joined the Nazi Party in 1929, becoming Reich speaker (*Reichsredner*) and local group leader (*Ortsgruppenleiter*) at the same time. Over the next few years, Börger not only occupied a number of other party offices but, from 1933, was also a member of the Reichstag; he was later appointed to the Prussian State Council (Staatsrat). In 1933 he was appointed labour trustee for the Rhineland and joined the SS in 1935, where he had risen to the rank of SS brigade leader (*SS-Brigadeführer*) by 1939. In 1938 Börger was made ministerial director at the Reich Ministry of Labour, where he was responsible for the administration of the ministry and its subordinate bodies as head of Main Section I until 1945. After the war, Börger was incarcerated and then worked as a sales representative following his release in 1948.[2]

Heinrich Brauns (b. 3 January 1868 in Cologne, d. 19 October 1939 in Lindenberg) studied theology and philosophy in Bonn and Cologne before working, from 1890 onwards, as a Catholic chaplain in parishes in Krefeld and Essen-Borbeck. In 1900 he took up a post at the headquarters of the People's Association for Catholic Germany and studied political economy (*Nationalökonomie*) and constitutional law in Bonn and Freiburg, where he obtained a doctorate in 1905. As a deputy for the Centre Party, in 1919 he participated in the Constituent National Assembly in Weimar, chairing the Committee for National Economy (Ausschuss für Volkswirtschaft). In June 1920, Brauns was appointed Reich minister of labour, a post he held until 1928. During his tenure he exercised considerable influence on state social and labour policy in the Weimar Republic. Following his period in office he became the director general of the People's Association for Catholic Germany, remained a member of the Reichstag until 1933 and continued to work in the field of social and labour policy, for example as president of the German delegations to the international labour conferences from 1928 to 1931 and as chair of the so-called Brauns Commission, which was tasked with investigating the world economic crisis of 1931. Following the Nazi seizure of power, Brauns retired from politics and was repeatedly subject to repressive measures.[3]

After obtaining his Ph.D. in law, **Kurt Classen** (b. 28 February 1888, d. 1962) worked from 1920 to 1945 in the main departments for Collective Bargaining Law and Labour Law of the Reich Ministry of Labour, ultimately as ministerial counsellor. He missed out on promotion to department head in 1942 due to his failure to join the Nazi Party. In 1933 he joined the SA Reserve and in 1934 became a contributing member (*förderndes Mitglied*) of the National Socialist Air Corps (Nationalsozialistischer Fliegerkorps). Classified as 'unencumbered' or 'free of guilt' (Category V; *unbelastet*) in the denazification process, after the war he worked at the Central Office for Labour (Zentralamt für Arbeit), the Administration for Labour of the United Economic Area (Verwaltung für Arbeit des Vereinigten Wirtschaftsgebiets) and the Federal Ministry of Labour. Among other things, he was involved in the statutory regulation of industrial relations. In 1953, he received the Grand Cross of the Order of Merit (Grosses Verdienstkreuz) for his work. He retired from his civil service post as department head the same year.[4]

Wilhelm Claussen (b. 5 August 1901 in Husum, d. 4 August 1980 in Niederaula) studied philosophy in Munich and Erlangen and gained his Ph.D. in 1924. After teaching for just under three years at the Protestant Social School (Evangelisch-Soziale Schule) run by the Christian trades unions in Berlin-Spandau, he took up a post as adviser at the Berlin branch of the International Labour Office. Following its disbandment in 1934, he was the ILO's correspondent for Germany. In 1937, Claussen obtained a post in the economic policy division of IG Farben, before being drafted into the Wehrmacht in 1939. After being seriously wounded, in 1942 he went to Serbia to serve as a clerk under the general plenipotentiary for the economy (Generalbevollmächtigter für die Wirtschaft). After the war, Claussen held senior positions at the Maritime Office (Seeschifffahrtsamt) in Hamburg and at the seamen's accident prevention and insurance associations, before taking up a post in the Section for Maritime Transport (Abteilung Seeverkehr) at the Federal Ministry of Transport (Bundesverkehrsministerium) in 1951. He was appointed ministerial director in 1953 and became head of the ministry's Central Section (Zentralabteilung). From 1957 until 1965, Claussen was state secretary at the Federal Ministry of Labour and, finally, held the post of general plenipotentiary for economic policy issues in the insurance industry (Generalbevollmächtigter für wirtschaftspolitische Fragen in der Versicherungswirtschaft).[5]

Hans Engel (b. 17 November 1887 in Magdeburg, d. presumably in 1945, in Landsberg an der Warthe [Gorzów Wielkopolski]) gained his doctorate in December 1910 after studying law and political science in Berlin, Freiburg and Marburg. During the First World War, Engel was initially a member of the Magdeburg 66th Infantry Regiment. Following a serious injury, he served in the Luftwaffe on the Western Front until the end of the war. Until August 1920, he then worked for the Prussian-Hessian State Railway (Preussisch-Hessische Staatsbahn) as government assessor (*Regierungsassessor*), before transferring to the Reich Ministry of Food and Agriculture. In February 1933, he switched to the Reich Ministry of Labour as ministerial director, where he headed Main Section II (Social Insurance) until the beginning of the Second World War. He joined the Nazi Party in 1936. In 1940 and 1941, he was adjutant to Friedrich Christiansen, *Fliegergeneral* (general of the aviators) and Wehrmacht commander in the Netherlands. Following his return to the ministry, in March 1942 he was appointed state secretary and head of the 'International Social Policy' Working Group (Arbeitsgruppe 'Internationale Sozialpolitik'). He died, most likely in 1945, in the Soviet Special Camp No. 4 in Landsberg an der Warthe.[6]

Joachim Fischer-Dieskau (until 1934 Joachim Fischer) (b. 27 November 1896 in Berlin, d. 20 July 1977 in Bad Godesberg) studied law in Berlin, Königsberg and Marburg, and was awarded a doctorate in law on 6 March 1925 at the University of Marburg for a study of 'The Repercussions of Collective Wage Agreements'. After a period of probation in the Reich Ministry of the Economy, from 1 April 1927 Fischer-Dieskau worked in the Reich Ministry of Labour, where he rose to the position of section head (*Ministerialdirigent*) in the (Main) Section for Housing, Settlement and Town Planning ([Haupt-]Abteilung für Wohnungs-, Siedlungswesen und Städtebau). From August 1930 until July 1931, he worked as social affairs attaché to the German embassies in Vienna, Budapest and Belgrade, before being delegated to the Reich housing commissioner in 1941. He joined the Nazi Party on 1 May 1937. After a period of employment in the private sector and at the supreme building authority within the Bavarian State Ministry of the Interior, in October 1949 Fischer-Dieskau took over as head of Section I (Housing and Settlement, Housing Industry) of the newly established Federal Ministry of Housing (Bundesministerium für Wohnungsbau) in Bonn. On 1 April 1957, he went into temporary retirement, later joining the board of directors of the Deutsche Bau- und Bodenbank, whose supervisory board he had been a member of since 1951. He retired in 1964.[7]

Hermann Geib (b. 22 June 1872 in Bergzabern, d. 23 September 1939 in Berlin) studied law and national economy in Munich and Erlangen. After working in the Bavarian State Ministry of the Interior and the Bavarian Ministry of Education and Cultural Affairs, in 1903 he became mayor (*Bürgermeister*) of Regensburg, then senior mayor (*Oberbürgermeister*) in 1907. After resigning in 1910 for health reasons, he devoted himself to studies in natural science until 1914. Having worked on a voluntary basis at the Department for Disabled Ex-Servicemen (Abteilung für Kriegsbeschädigte) of the German Red Cross, he was chief executive of the Reich Committee on Support for Disabled Ex-Servicemen (Reichsausschuss der Kriegsbeschädigtenfürsorge) between 1915 and 1919. Geib was involved in the foundation of the Reich Labour Office in 1918 and was appointed permanent secretary. Beginning in February 1919, he headed the Department for Social Welfare for Disabled Ex-Servicemen and their Surviving Dependents (Abteilung für Soziale Kriegsbeschädigten- und Kriegshinterbliebenenfürsorge) in the Reich Ministry of Labour, before being appointed undersecretary (*Unterstaatssekretär*) in July and finally state secretary (*Staatssekretär*) the next year. In 1932, after twelve years in office, Geib, who was never affiliated with any political party, left the Reich Ministry of Labour and worked until the end of his life as chair of a supervisory board in the ceramics industry.[8]

Andreas Grieser (b. 31 March 1868 in Bliesdalheim, d. 18 October 1955 in Munich) broke off a theology degree to study law and national economy in Munich. He was subsequently appointed district court judge (*Amtsrichter*), public prosecutor and municipal counsellor (*Stadtrat*) in Munich with responsibility for social welfare. In 1918, Grieser was elected the first mayor of the city of Würzburg, before becoming ministerial director at the Reich Ministry of Labour in 1921. From 1932 he held the post of state secretary. Grieser played a key role in consolidating German social policy during the world economic crisis. His work as an expert at the International Labour Organization furnished him with an excellent international reputation, while also enabling him to further disseminate the German model of social insurance. In 1933, under pressure from the new labour minister Franz Seldte, Grieser tendered his resignation and retreated to his home region of Saarland, where he largely withdrew from public life. He was never to join the Nazi Party. In 1947, at the age of seventy-nine, Grieser was made state secretary in the Bavarian Ministry of State, becoming one of the leading protagonists pushing for the preservation of the traditional German form of social insurance and resisting Allied efforts to initiate reform.[9]

Wilhelm Herschel (b. 17 October 1895 in Bonn, d. 7 January 1986 in Bad Honnef), after studying law, political science and philosophy in Bonn, worked for the League of Christian Trades Unions of Germany (Gesamtverband der christlichen Gewerkschaften Deutschlands) and, from 1925, at the State School of Economy and Administration Düsseldorf (Staatliche Fachschule für Wirtschaft und Verwaltung Düsseldorf). From 1931, he was a professor at the state-run Vocational Education Institute (Berufspädagogisches Institut) in Cologne (and from 1940 in Frankfurt am Main). From 1944 to 1946, he held a professorship in labour law at the University of Halle. On 23 October 1946, Herschel, who had never been a member of the Nazi Party, was appointed head of Main Section III (Labour Law) at the Central Office for Labour in the British occupation zone. In September

1948, he continued in the same role at the Administration for Labour in the 'Bizone'. With the establishment of the Federal Ministry of Labour, he was appointed to the post of permanent secretary and headed Section III (Labour Law, Wages, Collective Wage Agreements and Arbitration, Occupational Safety) until his retirement in 1960.[10]

Hubert Hildebrandt (b. 10 September 1897 in Sabinengrund [Radosławice] in Lower Silesia, District of Freystadt) attended a vocational high school (*Mittelschule*) and then studied at a teachers' training college. At the age of seventeen he joined the armed forces and served in the First World War until 1918. After the war, Hildebrandt completed his teacher training, going on to study psychology and political science (*Staatswissenschaften*) from 1919 to 1923 in Berlin. After gaining his doctorate in 1923, he worked as a factory school teacher for the firm of Borsig, before taking up a position in 1928 at the Reich Institution for Job Placement and Unemployment Insurance, initially as deputy head of the Bochum Labour Office and later as head of the labour offices in Hagen (1930) and Frankfurt an der Oder (1932). In 1936, he gained civil servant status as government counsellor; in 1938, he was promoted to the post of senior government counsellor and transferred to the headquarters of the Reich Institution, where he was responsible for job placement, vocational guidance and arranging apprenticeships. When the Reich Institution was incorporated into the Reich Ministry of Labour in 1939, he was assigned to Main Section V (Job Placement and Labour Administration). There, among other things, he procured manpower for the iron and metal industry as well as the textiles and chemicals sectors. When his section was placed under the authority of the GBA, Hildebrandt, a ministerial counsellor since 1941, was appointed head of Main Section VI b ('Labour Deployment' in Western Europe). He joined the Nazi Party in May 1933 and the SA-Reserve in November of the same year. He was also a member of the National Socialist League of German Legal Professionals (Nationalsozialistischer Rechtswahrerbund), the Air Raid Protection League (Luftschutzbund) and the Civil Servants' League (Beamtenbund). Hildebrandt was awarded the Cross of Merit and the Knight's Cross.[11]

Dorothea Hirschfeld (b. 26 February 1877 in Berlin, d. 12 June 1966 in West Berlin), having pursued her further education independently, in 1904 took up a post at the Central Office for Poor Relief and Charity (Zentralstelle *or* Deutscher Verein für Armenpflege und Wohltätigkeit) in Berlin, rising to the position of managing director in 1911. She was also active in the field of social welfare, was one of the founders of the Workers' Welfare Association (Arbeiterwohlfahrt) and was a counsellor for the SPD in Berlin from 1919 to 1920. In May 1919 she was appointed department head in charge of welfare for the surviving dependants of servicemen at the Reich Ministry of Labour and had already risen to the rank of ministerial counsellor by 1920. Transferred to the Reich labour administration in 1924, Hirschfeld was made head of the newly established Reich Institution for Job Placement and Unemployment Insurance in 1927 before returning to the post of department head at the Reich Ministry of Labour in 1929. As an adherent of the Jewish faith, the 'Civil Service Law' forced her into retirement in April 1933. She survived the Theresienstadt Ghetto, to which she had been deported in 1942, and worked in the Soviet Occupation Zone as department head in the Main Administration for Healthcare (Hauptverwaltung für Gesundheitswesen) between 1945 and 1948.[12]

Theodor Hupfauer (b. 17 July 1906 in Dellmensingen, d. 31 August 1993 in Munich) studied law and political science in Würzburg and Lausanne from 1926 to 1931 and gained his doctorate in 1932. In 1920–1921 Hupfauer became involved in the German National Youth League (Deutschnationaler Jugendbund). He joined the Nazi Party for the first time in late 1922 and again in early October 1930, while also taking up membership of the SS in 1931. Hupfauer gained professional experience as a junior lawyer at the District Court, Labour Court and Regional Court of Würzburg and with the Munich Political Police. From 1933 until early 1936 he headed the 'DAF Training' Main Bureau of the Nazi Party Reich Training Office (Reichsschulungsamt). Hupfauer was also in charge of the Office for Corporate Organization (Amt für Ständischen Aufbau) at the Nazi Party Reich Organizational Leadership from July 1933 to 1934–1935, then headed the DAF's 'Social Self-Responsibility' agency from 1936 to 1944; in addition, he was the executive director of the Reich Chamber of Labour (Reichsarbeitskammer). In 1936 Ley also appointed him commissioner for the overall execution of the (annual) Companies' Performance Battle. In 1938, moreover, Hupfauer functioned as DAF representative in the Office of the Reich Commissioner for the Reunification of Austria with the Reich (Reichskommissar für die Wiedervereinigung Österreichs mit dem Reich), and from 1938 to 1939 in the Office of the Reich Commissioner for the Sudeten German Region (Reichskommissar für das sudetendeutsche Gebiet). In 1943 he switched to the Ministry for Armaments and War Production under Speer, where he worked until 1945 as office group head (*Amtsgruppenchef*) and general consultant (*Generalreferent*) for statistics, and, from late 1944 until 1945, as head of the Central Office of this ministry as well as head of the 'Rhine and Ruhr' Task Force (Einsatzstab 'Rhein und Ruhr'). From spring 1946 until autumn 1949 Hupfauer was detained in Günzburg and in the Nuremberg prison. He was a witness at a total of four

Nuremberg trials. Initially categorized as a 'follower' (*Mitläufer*) during a denazification trial, Hupfauer himself requested that this be changed to 'activist' (*Aktivist*) during appeal proceedings before the Bielefeld court in 1947. From the 1950s until his retirement, he was manager of the Turkish branch of a Munich firm.[13]

Oskar Karstedt (b. 10 March 1884 in Lübeck, d. October 1945 in the Soviet Special Camp of Sachsenhausen), after obtaining his high school leaver's certificate (*Abitur*) and completing his military service, studied geography, ethnology (*Völkerkunde*) and colonial science (*Kolonialwissenschaften*) in Leipzig and Berlin from 1902, obtaining a doctorate in 1905. In 1906 he was employed as a colonial official in the Administrative Service (Verwaltungsdienst) of German East Africa before giving up his post in 1913 for health reasons and initially retiring. After pursuing voluntary activities in the field of aid for war victims, in 1918 he returned to public service, working as an adviser to the Reich Committee on Support for Disabled Ex-Servicemen before transferring to the Reich Ministry of Labour as government counsellor in 1919. Following his promotion to the position of ministerial counsellor in 1920, he was put in charge of a number of departments concerned with social policy and literature, and after 1933 he was made head of the temporary institution known as the Special Office (Sonderreferat) for 'Complaints by Non-Aryan Physicians'. In 1941 he was put in charge of International Affairs (*Arbeitsgebiet Internationales*). He did not join the Nazi Party. Beginning in 1912, Karstedt published a large number of texts on colonial policy.[14]

Wilhelm Kimmich (b. 25 June 1888 in Kleinsachsenheim) initially attended a primary school teachers' training college before passing the school leaver's exam at the Oberrealschule (a secondary school emphasizing maths and science). After studying German language and literature, national economics and law, he went on to obtain a Ph.D. During the First World War, Kimmich was responsible for refugees at the Württemberg Labour Ministry, where he continued to work after the war, now in the field of welfare for the war-disabled. In the 1920s, he began a successful career as an industrial relations arbitrator, becoming chair of the Arbitration Committee for Württemberg, Baden and Hohenzollern in 1928. His remit was later expanded to include Hesse and Lower Saxony. Kimmich remained in office after 1933, but now his title was changed to that of labour trustee. He portrayed himself as the only 'expert among the labour trustees' and as a 'black sheep' at the Reich Ministry of Labour, to which Franz Seldte appointed him in 1939. There Kimmich was put in charge of Main Section III b (Labour Law and Social Policy), reporting to Permanent Secretary

Werner Mansfeld. Following a brief interlude in Stuttgart, supposedly the result of a conflict with the DAF, Kimmich returned to the Reich Ministry of Labour in 1942, where he succeeded Mansfeld, becoming permanent secretary and head of Main Section III (Labour Law and Wages Policy) until the end of the war. Kimmich joined the Nazi Party in May 1933 and was, among other things, a member of the National Socialist Association of German Legal Professionals and the National Socialist People's Welfare (Nationalsozialistische Volkswohlfahrt).[15]

Johannes Krohn (b. 4 July 1884 in Stettin, d. 11 July 1974 in Bad Neuenahr-Ahrweiler), a doctor of law, participated in the First World War and took up a post at the RVA in 1919 before switching to the Reich Ministry of Labour as government counsellor in 1920. There he was made senior government counsellor in 1921 and was then promoted to the post of ministerial counsellor in 1923. In 1928 he was put in charge of the Department of Social Insurance and Public Welfare (Abteilung Sozialversicherung und Wohlfahrtspflege) and in 1932 became permanent secretary and head of the Main Section for Social Insurance and Social Welfare (Hauptabteilung für Sozialversicherung und soziale Fürsorge). Krohn was appointed state secretary in February 1933 but had to leave this post in 1939 due to a conflict with the DAF. He joined the Nazi Party in 1938. He then headed a department in the labour administration of the General Government for two months before a period of active wartime service. In November 1941 Krohn was appointed state commissioner for the processing of enemy assets (Staatskommissar für die Behandlung feindlichen Vermögens) in the Reich Ministry of Justice. After the war he was interned for just under a year and then campaigned for the retention of the civil service and the traditional system of social insurance. Between 1953 and 1959, Krohn headed the Association for Social Security Policy and Research (Gesellschaft für Versicherungswissenschaft und -gestaltung e. V.) and the Federal Committee of Physicians and Health Insurers (Bundesausschuss der Ärzte und Krankenkassen) between 1955 and 1968.[16]

Walter Letsch (b. 26 January 1895 in Schweidnitz, d. 1965), after completing his *Abitur* and serving as a war volunteer and reserve lieutenant (1914–1919), studied law, political science and economics in Breslau from 1919. He gained a Ph.D. (Dr. rer. pol.) in 1922. From 1928, Letsch worked in the labour administration, initially as president and director of the Waldenburg Labour Office (Silesia) and then as department head at the Silesia Land Labour Office. He was appointed to the civil service in 1933 and promoted to the post of senior government counsellor in 1936. The same year, he also took up a post at the headquarters of the Reich

Appendix II

Institution for Job Placement and Unemployment Insurance. Following its integration, as Main Section V, into the Reich Ministry of Labour, he was employed by that institution in 1939. This meant that Letsch worked for the GBA from March 1942. When Department V a was turned into Main Section VI in 1943, Letsch, now promoted to the post of ministerial counsellor, was made head of Department VI a and thus responsible for labour deployment in Eastern Europe and in trade and industry. Letsch joined the Nazi Party and SA in 1933. Arrested by the Allies after the war, he testified as a witness at the Nuremberg trials.[17]

Robert Ley (b. 15 February 1890 in Niederbreidenbach, near Gummersbach, d. 25 October 1945 in Nuremberg [suicide]) studied food chemistry in Jena, Bonn and Münster between 1910 and 1914 and obtained his doctorate in 1920. In 1914 he volunteered to fight in the First World War and was taken prisoner of war by the French in 1917 (until 1920); he struggled with the consequences of a serious war injury for the rest of his life. From 1921 to 1927 he worked as a chemical scientist for Bayer then IG Farben. In March 1925 he joined the Nazi Party and was appointed Gauleiter of Rhineland-South (Rheinland-Süd) the same year (a post he held until 1931). Ley was elected to the Prussian Landtag in 1928, and also to the Reichstag in 1930. In early December 1932 he succeeded Gregor Strasser as staff leader (*Stabsleiter*) of the Nazi Party and by the end of the Nazi dictatorship – as Nazi Party Reich organizational leader from November 1934 – he had risen to become the leading rival of 'Deputy Führer' Rudolf Hess. In the spring of 1933 Ley played a major role in the destruction of the trades unions. Hitler appointed him head of the DAF, by far the largest mass Nazi organization, at its founding congress on 10 May 1933. Among the most important of his numerous offices was that of Reich commissioner for social housing from 15 November 1940 and, beginning in October 1942, that of Reich housing commissioner. This close confidant of Hitler and fanatical antisemite was charged at the Nuremberg trials of major war criminals but committed suicide before his trial began.[18]

Frieda (known as Friedel) Malter/Apelt (b. Raddünz, mar. Franz, b. 1 November 1902 in Breslau [Wrocław], d. 15 December 2001 in Berlin) initially worked as a domestic servant and weaver before serving in the Silesia Provincial Diet (Provinziallandtag) from 1926 to 1933. She was active in the Communist Party of Germany (KPD) from 1927 onwards and was elected to the Prussian Landtag in 1932. Convicted of illegal activities the following year, she was held in various prisons until 1938 and then worked, among other things, as an office clerk. After being detained again in 1944, she survived the concentration camps of Ravensbrück and Sachsenhausen. In late 1945, she took up a post as head of the Department for Women's Issues of the Central Committee of the KPD in Berlin, and among other things served as deputy in the People's Council (Volksrat) and People's Parliament (Volkskammer). Over the subsequent decades, she held senior positions at the Free Federation of German Trades Unions (Freier Deutscher Gewerkschaftsbund, or FDGB) and from 1959 to 1990 chaired the GDR Committee for Human Rights (DDR-Komitee für Menschenrechte). From 1950 until 1956, Frieda Malter served as state secretary and deputy minister at the Ministry of Labour (and Vocational Education).[19]

Werner Mansfeld (b. 12 December 1893 in Uchte, Kreis Stolzenau, d. 10 February 1953 in Berlin) studied law and served as a volunteer in the First World War before joining the 'Stahlhelm' paramilitary organization for eleven years, among other things as local group leader in Essen. After gaining his doctorate and working as a trainee judge (*Gerichtsassesor*), from 1924 he worked in the legal and social policy departments of the Mine Owners' Association; he was also a member of its executive board. He was concurrently a member of the executive committee of the Ruhr Miners' Insurance Association (Ruhrknappschaft), various divisions of the Reich Insurance Office and a number of organs of the Reich Institution for Job Placement and Unemployment Insurance. In 1926, he joined the Legal Committee of the Reich Association of German Industry (Reichsverband der Deutschen Industrie) and labour and social policy committees of the Association of German Employers' Organizations (Vereinigung der Deutschen Arbeitgeberverbände). He completed his postdoctoral thesis in 1930. Mansfeld joined the Nazi Party shortly before taking charge of Main Section III (Labour Law and Wages Policy) in the Reich Ministry of Labour in May 1933, as ministerial director. In addition, from 1936, together with Friedrich Syrup he headed the Office of Labour Deployment (Geschäftsstelle Arbeitseinsatz) of the Four-Year Plan Authority. As predecessor to the general plenipotentiary for labour deployment, in January and February 1942 he briefly held authority over this field. After his replacement, he retired from political life as a member of the executive board of Salzdetfurth AG.[20]

Rudolf Peuckert (b. 18 August 1908 in Wiebelsdorf, d. 3 October 1946 in Dachau [suicide]) gained experience in agriculture while still a youth, through attendance at an agricultural college and working on his father's estate. Peuckert joined the Nazi Party in 1926 and again in 1928. Within the party, he began his career with a focus on agricultural policy. He became head of the peasant youth organization (*bäuerliche Landjugend*) within the

Hitler Youth, adviser on agriculture to the Nazi Party Gauleitung and also rose to become a provincial farmers' leader. He assumed various roles in the Nazi Party's (Reich) Office for Agricultural Policy and the Office of the Reich Farmers' Leader. He was appointed to the GBA staff as commissioner for agriculture and wartime food production in 1942 and was also made GBA commissioner for the territories of the Reich Commissariat of Ukraine and the Don-Donets and Caucasus economic inspectorates. In 1943, his remit was extended to the territory under the control of the Economic Staff East and the Reich Ministry for the Occupied Eastern Territories, and to the occupied Eastern territories in their entirety in 1944. Following his arrest by members of the US Armed Forces in May 1945, he committed suicide at the Dachau internment camp in October 1946.[21]

Wolfgang Pohl (b. 24 April 1897 in Breslau, d. 1962 in Berlin) studied at the Friedrich Wilhelm University (Friedrich-Wilhelms-Universität) and the Berlin School of Commerce (Handelshochschule Berlin) from 1917 until 1921, obtaining his doctorate in 1922. From autumn 1921 to mid 1922 he worked as senior manager in the Social Policy Department of the firm AEG. Over the next five years he gained experience in journalism as editor of the *Deutsche Allgemeine Zeitung*; via this prestigious daily newspaper he also gained access to the elite economic networks of the German Reich. It thus came as little surprise when, in the summer of 1927, he was appointed press officer at the Reich Ministry of the Economy (Social Policy Section [Abteilung Sozialpolitik]), a post he held until June 1933. Pohl joined the Nazi Party in early May 1933. Henceforth he took on senior roles both in the DAF and in the Reich ministries of Labour and Economy. From mid 1934 until mid 1935, as ministerial counsellor or section head, he was in charge of Section IIIb of the Labour Ministry; he was then ministerial director in the Reich Ministry of the Economy from 1935 to early 1938. A member of Robert Ley's entourage, Pohl, who made a major contribution to the AOG, was soon playing a number of important roles, from November 1933 onwards as head of the Nazi Party's 'Department for Social Issues' (Abteilung für Sozialfragen). Of all the roles he played, the most important was his work at the DAF's Labour Science Institute, which he headed from 1935 until the end of the Nazi state. Already arrested in the Soviet occupation zone in May 1945, on the basis of Control Council Law No. 10 he was initially sentenced to twenty-five years in prison by a Soviet military tribunal in October 1945; he was sent to Waldheim Prison. In 1950 the Chemnitz District Court reduced his sentence to twenty years in prison; in early 1953 it was further reduced to ten years. Around the beginning of 1956 Pohl was discharged and allowed to move to West Berlin.[22]

Fritz Sauckel (b. 27 October 1894 in Hassfurt, d. 16 October 1946 in Nuremberg), having obtained his secondary school leaving certificate (*mittlere Reife*) and trained as a sailor, spent the 1914–1919 period as a civilian internee in France. Following his release, he worked as a labourer in Schweinfurt, began an apprenticeship as a metalworker and, from 1921, attended the technical college in Ilmenau, which he left without a qualification in 1924. Sauckel joined the German Nationalist Protection and Defiance Federation in 1919 and the Nazi Party in 1923 and again in 1925. He began his career within the party in 1925 as Gau secretary (*Gaugeschäftsführer*) before becoming a Gauleiter in Thuringia in 1927. In addition, from 1922 and then 1925 Sauckel was a member of the SA and of the SS from 1934. When the Nazis took power, Hitler appointed him Reich governor in Thuringia in 1933, then Reich defence commissioner when the war began in 1939. Hitler appointed him the general plenipotentiary for labour deployment on 21 March 1942. This made Sauckel one of the leading Nazi functionaries and responsible for the recruitment of millions of forced labourers in the occupied territories until 1945. He was arrested by members of the US forces in Upper Bavaria in April 1945. Sauckel was tried before the International Military Tribunal as a major war criminal. He was sentenced to death and executed in October 1946.[23]

Maximilian Sauerborn (b. 28 August 1889 in Montabaur, d. 17 May 1963 in Bonn), after studying law and serving in the First World War, worked from 1920 in the judicial service in Düsseldorf and Frankfurt am Main. He was a department head in the Reich Ministry of Labour from July 1923 until 1945. Appointed ministerial counsellor in 1931, he served continuously in (Main) Section II, where he was in charge of health insurance; a few years before the end of the war he became section head. Following his internment and a period working as a freelancer, Sauerborn, who had never been a member of the Nazi Party, joined the staff of the Bavarian State Ministry of Labour and Social Welfare (Staatsministerium für Arbeit und soziale Fürsorge) in December 1947. He served as president of the Bavarian Insurance Office (Bayerisches Versicherungsamt) for a few months in 1949. From 28 October 1949 to 28 February 1957, Sauerborn was the first state secretary in the Federal Ministry of Labour and from 1954 to 1958 he was also a member of the Governing Body of the International Labour Organization.[24]

Julius Scheuble (b. 23 May 1890 in Lienheim [Baden], d. 22 December 1964 in Freiburg im Breisgau) worked as a carpenter and for the Central Association of Christian Woodworkers (Zentralverband christlicher Holzarbeiter) before becoming director of the Insurance Office of the City of

Cologne in 1928 and president of the Rhineland Land Labour Office in Cologne on 15 August 1930. Dismissed by the Nazis, from 1933 he was initially unemployed for a number of years before taking up a job at an insurance company in 1937. In 1945, Scheuble was made head of the Cologne Labour Office and the North Rhine Province Land Labour Office, before being appointed president of the Central Office for Labour in the British occupation zone on 23 July 1946. At the successor body in the 'Bizone', the Administration for Labour, Scheuble was appointed vice-president on 10 September 1948. With the foundation of the Federal Republic, in January 1950 he was made head of Section II in the Federal Ministry of Labour and was put in charge of the newly established Federal Institute for Labour in Nuremberg as its first president, a post he held from 1 May 1952 until 31 July 1957.[25]

Rudolf Schmeer (b. 16 March 1905 in Saarbrücken, d. 11 September 1966 in Erlangen) began an apprenticeship as an electrician in 1919, which he completed by passing the state master workman exam in 1923. Schmeer became active in far-right organizations in the early 1920s, among other things joining the illegal Roßbach Association ('Arbeitsgemeinschaft' Roßbach) in 1922–1923, successor organization to the Roßbach Free Corps (Freikorps Roßbach); the association collectively joined the Nazi Party in 1923. Having first joined the party in April 1923, he took up membership again in September 1925 and joined the SA the same year. From 1926 to 1931, as a close confidante of Ley he occupied important posts in the Nazi Party Gau of Cologne-Aachen, among other things as Nazi Party head for the administrative district of Aachen from 1926 to 1931, and was subsequently deputy Nazi Party Gauleiter of the Gau of Cologne-Aachen until August 1932. From September 1930 he was a Nazi Party deputy in the Reichstag. As nominal deputy to Ley, from 1933 until mid 1936 Schmeer was responsible for organizing the Nazi Party Reich congresses. He then headed the DAF Central Office for the 'Four-Year Plan' until late 1938. During that year he was also appointed Reich commissioner for small businesses (Reichskommissar für den gewerblichen Mittelstand), a role of which he appears to have made very little. From the end of 1938 until autumn 1942 he was ministerial director in Main Section III (Economic Organization, 'Jewish Affairs') of the Reich Ministry of the Economy, but concurrently continued to play a leading role in the DAF and in the Nazi Party Reich Organization Leadership. In 1941 he also headed the 'Aufbaustab Moskau'. In October 1942 Schmeer switched to the Ministry for Armaments and War Production (with responsibility for 'special assignments'). In addition, he was put in charge of the Central Agency for Reporting (Zentralstelle für Berichtswesen) within the Construction Office (Amt Bau) of the Todt Organization (Organisation Todt). In July 1944 he took up a post as permanent deputy to Reich housing Commissioner Ley. Schmeer came through the denazification process essentially unscathed; from 1945 until his death he worked as a merchant in Frauenaurach (District of Erlangen).[26]

Franz Seldte (b. 29 June 1882 in Magdeburg, d. 1 April 1947 in Fürth) completed a commercial apprenticeship then studied chemistry in Braunschweig. After a year of military service as a one-year volunteer in Magdeburg, he took over his father's chemical products factory in 1908. After volunteering to fight in the First World War he eventually attained the rank of captain, losing his left arm in battle in 1916. In November 1918 he co-founded the *völkisch*, right-wing conservative Steel Helmets paramilitary organization, which he headed until its dissolution in 1935. Seldte was politically active in the Weimar Republic, as a member of the German People's Party (Deutsche Volkspartei, or DVP) between 1918 and 1927, and then in the DNVP and in shifting alliances with other national conservative, *völkisch* and finally Nazi forces. Seldte, who joined the Nazi Party in April 1933, was appointed Reich minister of labour in January 1933 and retained this post until 1945. He concurrently held the office of Reich commissioner for voluntary labour service (Reichskommissar für den Freiwilligen Arbeitsdienst) between March 1933 and July 1934. He was arrested by the American army at the end of the war and interrogated. Seldte died in an American military hospital in Fürth before, potentially, facing charges in Nuremberg.[27]

Friedrich Sitzler (b. 10 December 1881 in Tauberbischofsheim, d. 22 January 1975 in Stuttgart) studied law and economics in Strasbourg, Berlin, Heidelberg and Freiburg, gaining his first degree in 1905 and doctorate in 1909. He worked at the Baden administrative service before taking up a position as temporary assistant at the Reich Insurance Office from March 1910. He was then made a permanent member of that institution as government counsellor in September 1915. In December 1916, he took up a temporary post at the Reich Office of the Interior, switching, when the latter institution was subdivided, to the Reich Economic Office, before finally being appointed to the Reich Ministry of Labour upon its establishment. He was made ministerial counsellor there in October 1919. At the ministry, he was section head from 1920 and was finally put in charge of Main Section III (responsible for labour law, occupational safety and wages policy) from 1924 until 1933. In 1933, he was appointed head of department at the International Labour Organization, resigning after the German Reich departed from the League of Nations. Sitzler worked as an arbitrator, helping resolve a multitude of wage disputes, and was head of the social affairs division at Wilhelm Bleyle KG from 1942 to 1945. Between 1913 and 1956 he published numerous essays and books on labour law and was editor of the journal *Neue Zeitschrift für Arbeitsrecht* between 1921 and 1933. In the journal *Soziale Praxis*, which he edited from 1936 to 1942, Sitzler backed Nazi social policy, sometimes explicitly. From 1947, he was honorary professor at the University of Heidelberg and lectured in labour law at the Mannheim College of Economics (Wirtschaftshochschule Mannheim).[28]

Anton Storch (b. 1 April 1892 in Fulda, d. 26 November 1975 in Fulda), after serving his apprenticeship as a carpenter and working as a journeyman carpenter, pursued a career within the Central Association of Christian Woodworkers. He joined the Centre Party in 1919. In 1931, Storch became president of the Confederation of Christian Trades Unions (Dachverband der Christlichen Gewerkschaften) for the Province of Hanover. After his dismissal in 1933, he worked as an insurance salesman and was subjected to a compulsory labour order in the Hanover Fire Protection Police (Feuerschutzpolizei) in 1939. In 1946, Storch became head of the social policy division of the Trades Union Federation (Gewerkschaftsbund) in the British occupation zone and from 1947 was a member of the Economic Council of the United Economic Area ('Bizone'). On 20 August 1948, he became director of the Administration for Labour in the United Economic Area. Storch was a member of the West German government as the first federal minister for labour, from 20 September 1949 to 29 October 1957. He was a deputy in the German Bundestag (for the CDU) from 1949 to 1965 and a member of the European Parliament from 1958 to 1965.[29]

Friedrich Syrup (b. 9 October 1881 in Lüchow, d. 31 August 1945 in the Soviet Special Camp at Sachsenhausen) studied engineering before being appointed to a post at the Prussian Working Conditions Inspectorate in 1905. At the end of the First World War, he was posted to the Demobilization Office (Demobilmachungsamt). He was appointed president of the newly established Reich Office for Job Placement (Reichsamt für Arbeitsvermittlung) in 1920, which laid the foundation for the Reich Institution for Job Placement and Unemployment Insurance, established in 1927, of which he became president. Appointed Reich labour minister for a few weeks in 1932, from 1933 he once again headed the Reich Institution until its incorporation into the Reich Ministry of Labour in 1939. There he was made second state secretary. He joined the Nazi Party only in 1937 after a lot of badgering. From 1941, his health deteriorated rapidly, so he could perform his duties only sporadically. After the war, Syrup was interned in the Soviet Special Camp No. 7 at Sachsenhausen, where he died shortly afterwards.[30]

Max Timm (b. 19 March 1898 in Lunden) served in the First World War and was held as a prisoner of war. In 1920 he began to study economics in Cologne, gaining a Ph.D. in Göttingen in 1923. In 1928, after several years in the private sector, he took over as head of the Heide Labour Office in Holstein. In April 1933, he replaced Senior Government Counsellor Albert Gutmann, who had been dismissed as a consequence of the 'Civil Service Law', at the Reich Institution for Job Placement and Unemployment Insurance. In May 1933, Timm joined the Nazi Party. He made a rapid ascent through the ranks of the Reich Institution and was appointed section head. Under the General Plenipotentiary for Labour Deployment, he became head of Main Section VI (Europe Office for Labour Deployment [Europaamt für den Arbeitseinsatz]) and was responsible for the recruitment of forced labourers. From 1941, his health deteriorated, forcing him to take lengthy periods off work towards the end of the war. After the war, Timm attained the post of *Regierungsdirektor* (a senior government official) in the Schleswig-Holstein civil service.[31]

Oscar Weigert (b. 12 August 1886 in Berlin, d. 6 January 1968 in Chevy Chase, USA) studied law in Berlin, Freiburg and Kiel and then worked in the Prussian justice system from 1909 to 1917 and in the provincial administration of Posen from 1917 to 1919. The same year he took up a post in the Reich Ministry of Labour as ministerial counsellor. As head of department he was initially responsible for the labour market and later for social policy as well. In the wake of the 'Civil Service Law', Weigert, who had attained the rank of ministerial director, had to leave the ministry in March 1933. He then emigrated first to the United States to work for the Department of Labor in Philadelphia, before making his way to Turkey in 1935, where he was employed at the Ministry of the Economy as an adviser until 1938. He then returned to the United States, where he initially taught as a visiting lecturer and then, from 1940, as a professor at the American University in Washington DC. Beginning in May 1946, Weigert also worked as a senior official at the Department of Labor and from 1952 as head of the Division of Foreign Labor Conditions at the Bureau of Labor Statistics.[32]

Notes

1. H.F. Zacher, 'Walter Bogs – 90 Jahre alt', *Zeitschrift für ausländisches und internationales Arbeits- und Sozialrecht* 3 (1989), 69–72.
2. Papers Wilhelm Börger, Bundesarchiv (BArch), N 2032; Files Wilhelm Börger, BArch, R 3901/11931–11939; Personnel files Wilhelm Börger, BArch, R 3901/20336.
3. Personnel files Heinrich Brauns, BArch, R 3901/10094; H. Grebing, 'Brauns, Heinrich', in *Neue Deutsche Biographie*, vol. 2, Berlin: Duncker & Humblot, 1955, 334; H. Mockenhaupt, 'Heinrich Brauns (1868–1939)', in R. Morsey (ed.), *Zeitgeschichte*

in Lebensbildern. Aus dem deutschen Katholizismus des 20. Jahrhunderts, Mainz: Matthias-Grünewald-Verlag, 1973, 148–59.

4. Personnel files Kurt Classen, BArch, R 3001/53521; 'Personalnachrichten', *Dienstliche Mitteilungen Bundesministerium für Arbeit* 36 (1953), 30 March 1953, 585; 'Ministerialdirigent a. D. Dr. Kurt Classen', *Sozialer Fortschritt* 10 (1961), 188.

5. Papers Wilhelm Claussen, BArch, NL 1299; Personnel files Wilhelm Claussen, Federal Ministry of Economy and Energy (Bundesministerium für Wirtschaft und Energie), Berlin.

6. C. Horkenbach (ed.), *Das Deutsche Reich von 1918 bis heute. Jahrgang 1933*, Berlin: Verlag für Presse, Wirtschaft und Politik, 1935, 935; Information provided by Dr Enrico Heitzer (Gedenkstätte und Museum Sachsenhausen) and Holm Kirsten (Stiftung Gedenkstätten Buchenwald und Mittelbau-Dora).

7. H.A.L. Degener (ed.), *Degeners Wer ist's?*, 10th ed., Berlin: Degener, 1935, 413; W. Habel (ed.), *Wer ist wer? Das deutsche Who's who*, 12th ed. of *Degeners Wer ist's?*, Berlin: Arani, 1955, 280; G. Schulz, *Wiederaufbau in Deutschland. Die Wohnungsbaupolitik in den Westzonen und der Bundesrepublik von 1945 bis 1957*, Düsseldorf: Droste, 1994, 192–94; 'Biographie Fischer-Dieskau, Joachim', in 'Die Kabinettsprotokolle der Bundesregierung' online, retrieved 22 September 2016 from www.bundesarchiv.de/cocoon/barch/0/z/z1960a/kap1_6/para2_38.html; Appointment Processes in the Presidential Chancellery (Präsidialkanzlei) and the Federal Ministry of Finance (Bundesministerium der Finanzen), BArch, R 601/18429 and B 126/16957; Personnel files Joachim Fischer-Dieskau, Reich Ministry of Justice, BArch, R 3001/55851.

8. Papers Hermann Geib, BArch, N 2091; *Reichshandbuch der deutschen Gesellschaft*, vol. I, A–K, Berlin: Deutscher Wirtschaftsverlag, 1930, 527.

9. Personnel files Andreas Grieser, BArch, R 3901/100289; H.-J. Britz, 'Andreas Grieser', in S. Koss and W. Löhr (eds), *Biographisches Lexikon des KV*, part 2, Schernfeld: SH-Verlag, 1993, 38–41; V.H. Schmied, *Andreas Grieser (1868–1955). Das Leben und Wirken des 'Nestors' der deutschen Sozialversicherung*, Karlstadt: self-published, 1993; V. Karl, *Lexikon Pfälzer Persönlichkeiten*, Edenkoben: Hennig, 1995, 208 f.

10. Personnel files Wilhelm Herschel, BMWi; Curriculum Vitae Herschel, 9 June 1947, BArch, Z 40/319; 'Biogramm Wilhelm Herschel', retrieved 7 September 2016 from www.catalogus-professorum-halensis.de/herschelwilhelm.html.

11. Proposed Appointments 1936 and 1938, BArch, R 601/466 and R 601/2103.

12. Personnel files Dorothea Hirschfeld, BArch, R 3901/100393; E. Lembeck, *Die Partizipation von Frauen an der öffentlichen Verwaltung in der Weimarer Republik 1918–1933*, Ph.D. dissertation, Hanover: University of Hanover, 1991, 198–210; C. Fischer-Defoy (ed.), *Vor die Tür gesetzt. Im Nationalsozialismus verfolgte Berliner Stadtverordnete und Magistratsmitglieder 1933–1945*, Berlin: self-published, 2006, 229 f.

13. Archiv der Stiftung für Sozialgeschichte des 20. Jahrhunderts, Bremen, DAF holdings, 6.2 Biographies, File Hi-Kosiol; Personnel files Theodor Hupfauer, BArch, ZA I/7117, A.11, and BDC 00183; *Dienstaltersliste der Schutzstaffel der NSDAP (SS), as at 1 Dec. 1938 and 15 June 1939*, reprint, Osnabrück: Biblio, 1996, 76 f.; D. Eichholtz, *Geschichte der deutschen Kriegswirtschaft*, vol. 3: *1943–1945*, Berlin: Akademie, 1996, 67; *Wer leitet? Die Männer der Wirtschaft und der einschlägigen Verwaltung 1940*, Berlin: Hoppenstedt & Co, 1940, 385.

14. Personnel files Franz Oskar Karstedt, BArch, R 3901/104928; F. Goldschmidt, *Meine Arbeit bei der Vertretung der Interessen der jüdischen Ärzte in Deutschland seit dem Juli 1933*, Bremen: Universität Bremen, 1979.

15. *Das Deutsche Führerlexikon 1934/35*, Berlin: Stollberg, 1934, 229; C. Horkenbach, *Das Deutsche Reich von 1918 bis heute. Jahresband 1932*, Berlin: Verlag für Presse, Wirtschaft und Politik, 1933, 534.

16. Papers Johannes Krohn, BArch, NL 430; Personnel files Johannes Krohn in the Reich Ministry of Justice, BArch, R 3001/64860; W. Rohrbeck and M. Sauerborn (eds), *Bei-*

träge zur Sozialversicherung. Festgabe für Johannes Krohn zum 70. Geburtstag, Berlin: Duncker & Humblot, 1954; D. O'Byrne, 'Career Civil Servants during the Third Reich. The Case of Dr. Johannes Krohn', unpublished manuscript, 2016; F. Tennstedt, 'Krohn, Johannes', in Neue Deutsche Biographie, vol. 13, Berlin: Duncker & Humblot, 1982, 69.

17. Personnel files Walter Letsch, BArch, R 3901/106064; Handbuch für die Dienststellen des Generalbevollmächtigten für den Arbeitseinsatz und die interessierten Reichsstellen im Grossdeutschen Reich und in den besetzten Gebieten, vol. 1: Vollmachten, Verlautbarungen, Verordnungen, Organisation des GBA, ed. F. Didier, Berlin: Rotadruck W. Meyer KG, 1944, 271 f.

18. J. Lilla, Statisten in Uniform. Die Mitglieder des Reichstages 1933–1945. Ein biographisches Handbuch, Düsseldorf: Droste, 2004, 636–38; R.M. Smelser, Robert Ley. Hitler's Labor Front Leader, Oxford: Berg, 1989.

19. K. Barnstedt and K. Scheel, 'Apelt, Frieda (Friedel Malter) (1902–2001). Vom Webstuhl ins Ministerium. Oder: "Wenn die Partei ruft, geht man."', in S. Mielke (ed.), Gewerkschafterinnen im NS-Staat. Verfolgung, Widerstand, Emigration, Essen: Klartext, 2008, 60–71.

20. Personnel files Werner Mansfeld, BArch, R 3901/20400-20402; Personnel files Werner Mansfeld, BArch, R 3001/67542; S. Felz, Recht zwischen Wissenschaft und Politik. Die Rechts- und Staatswissenschaftliche Fakultät der Universität Münster 1902 bis 1952, Münster: Aschendorff, 2016, 507.

21. D. Marek, 'Bibliographien der Regierungsmitglieder (Minister und Staatsräte)', in B. Post and V. Wahl (eds), Thüringen-Handbuch. Territorium, Verfassung, Parlament, Regierung und Verwaltung in Thüringen 1920 bis 1995, Weimar: Verlag Hermann Böhlaus Nachfolger, 1999, 552–648, here 617; Handbuch für die Dienststellen, ed. F. Didier, 23, 25 f.

22. K.-H. Roth, Intelligenz und Sozialpolitik im 'Dritten Reich'. Eine methodisch-historische Studie am Beispiel des Arbeitswissenschaftlichen Instituts der Deutschen Arbeitsfront, Munich: Saur, 1993, esp. 216–18; Wer leitet? Die Männer der Wirtschaft und der einschlägigen Verwaltung 1940, 671, and 1941–42, 751; Personnel files Wolfgang Pohl, BArch, BDC 08237.

23. Marek, 'Bibliographien der Regierungsmitglieder', 552–648, here 624 f.; R. Hachtmann, 'Sauckel, Fritz', in Neue Deutsche Biographie, vol. 22, Berlin: Duncker & Humblot, 2005, 448–49; S. Raßloff, Fritz Sauckel. Hitlers 'Muster-Gauleiter' und 'Sklavenhalter', Erfurt: Landeszentrale für politische Bildung Thüringen, 2008.

24. Personnel files Maximilian Sauerborn, BMWi; 'Staatssekretär Dr. h. c. Maximilian Sauerborn im Ruhestand', BABl. 7(7) (1957), 297–99; Entry 'Sauerborn, Maximilian' in Munzinger Online/Personen – Internationales Biographisches Archiv, retrieved 7 September 2016 from www.munzinger.de/document/00000003024.

25. Curriculum Vitae Scheuble, 16 June 1947, BArch, Z 40/319; H.-W. Schmuhl, Arbeitsmarktpolitik und Arbeitsverwaltung in Deutschland 1871–2002. Zwischen Fürsorge, Hoheit und Markt, Nuremberg: Institut für Arbeitsmarkt- und Berufsforschung, 2003, 362 f.; A. Storch, 'Der erste Präsident der Bundesanstalt für Arbeitsvermittlung und Arbeitslosenversicherung Dr. h. c. Julius Scheuble trat in den Ruhestand', BABl. 7(13) (1957), 437.

26. Das Deutsche Führerlexikon 1934/35, 1934, 419; Lilla, Statisten in Uniform, 961 f.; Wer ist's? Zeitgenossenlexikon, comp. and ed. H.A.L. Degener, 10th ed., Berlin: Herrmann Degener, 1935, 1397; Wer leitet? Die Männer der Wirtschaft und der einschlägigen Verwaltung 1940, 778, and 1941–42, Berlin 1942, 872; Personnel files Rudolf Schmeer, BArch, BDC P 0098 and NS 5 I/340.

27. V. Berghahn, Der Stahlhelm. Bund der Frontsoldaten 1918–1935, Düsseldorf: Droste, 1966; C. Copes, '. . . one of the less harmful personalities of Hitler's government'. Der ehemalige NS-Reichsarbeitsminister Franz Seldte in seiner Darstellung und in der Fremdwahrnehmung der Alliierten anhand der Akten der Nürnberger Prozesse 1945–1946, Master's dissertation, Berlin: Humboldt-Universität zu Berlin, 2017; R. Hachtmann, 'Seldte, Franz', in Neue Deutsche Biographie, vol. 24, Berlin: Duncker & Humblot, 2010, 215–16.

28. Papers Friedrich Sitzler, BArch, N 1687; Horkenbach, *Das Deutsche Reich von 1918 bis heute. Jahrgang 1933*, 511; 'Zum 70. Geburtstag von Ministerialdirektor a. D. Prof. Dr. Sitzler', *BABl.* 2(11) (1951), 555.

29. H.G. Hockerts, 'Anton Storch (1892–1975)', in J. Aretz, R. Morsey and A. Rauscher (eds), *Zeitgeschichte in Lebensbildern*, vol. 4: *Aus dem deutschen Katholizismus des 19. und 20. Jahrhunderts*, Mainz: Matthias-Grünewald-Verlag, 1980, 250–66; A. Storch, 'Lebenserinnerungen. Erfahrungen und Erlebnisse', in Deutscher Bundestag (ed.), *Abgeordnete des Deutschen Bundestages. Aufzeichnungen und Erinnerungen*, vol. 2: *Curt Becker, Franz Marx, Ernst Paul, Hans Schütz, Elisabeth Schwarzhaupt, J. Hermann Siemer, Anton Storch*, Boppard am Rhein: Boldt, 1983, 313–44; W. Stump, 'Anton Storch (1892–1975)', *Vierteljahresschrift für Sozialrecht* 4 (1976), 129–39.

30. D.G. Maier, J. Nürnberger and S. Pabst, *Vordenker des Arbeitsmarktes. Elf Biografien zur Geschichte der deutschen Arbeitsverwaltung*, Mannheim: Hochschule der Bundesagentur für Arbeit, 2012, 115–40; H. Henning, 'Friedrich Syrup (1881–1945)', in K.G.A. Jeserich and H. Neuhaus (eds), *Persönlichkeiten der Verwaltung. Biographien zur deutschen Verwaltungsgeschichte 1648–1945*, Stuttgart: Kohlhammer, 1991, 385–90.

31. Personnel files Max Timm, BArch, R 3901/20456; K.-D. Godau-Schüttke, *Die Heyde/Sawade-Affäre. Wie Juristen und Mediziner den NS-Euthanasieprofessor Heyde nach 1945 deckten und straflos blieben*, Baden-Baden: Nomos, 2010, 126 f.

32. Proposals from the Area of Operations of the BMA. Weh-Wei, no. 7444, BArch, B 149/7444; W. Röder and H. Strauss (eds), *Biographisches Handbuch der deutschsprachigen Emigration nach 1933*, vol. 1, Munich: Saur, 1980, 803.

Index

In this index the following abbreviations are used for the different governmental forms of Germany:

GE – German Empire
WR – Weimar Republic
NG – Nazi Germany
WG – West Germany
EG – East Germany

*Page numbers in **bold** refer to figures.*

accommodation
  of BMA, 429
  of RML (WR), 30, 250, 427
acts. *See* laws/acts/codes/decrees
Adenauer, Konrad, 434, 436
administration
  of Länder/municipalities, 37–38
  Weberian visions on, 23–25, 85
  See also labour administrations; occupation administrations; public aid administration (NG); public aid administration (WR)
Administration for Labour of the United Economic Area (Verwaltung für Arbeit des Vereinigten Wirtschaftsgebiets; VfA)
  absorbing ZfA, 428, 433
  and former personnel of RML (NG), 433
  personnel of. *See* personnel of VfA
  personnel structure at, **432**, 434, **434**, **435**, 436
administrative academies, 100–103, 105
administrative practice
  at DAF, 130
  at public aid administration (NG), 99
  at public aid administration (WR), 84
  at RML (NG), 130
Advisory Office for Labour, Settlement and Housing (Beratungsstelle für Arbeit, Siedlungs- und Wohnungswesen), 427
age group campaigns, 348

age structures
  of personnel at BMA, **435**
  of personnel at DAF, 131, 135
  of personnel at RML (NG), 131, 135
  of personnel at RML (WR), 32, **33**
  of personnel at VfA/ZfA, **435**
  of personnel at ZVAS/DVAS, 453–54
agricultural workers
  employment contracts, breaches of, 218–19
  labour market situation of, 212
  prisoners of war as, 308, 309
  recruitment in General Government, 309–10
  shortage of, 242
airfields, 380
Alberti, Michael, 368
Alsace-Lorraine, 190, 283
Alsatian workers, 190
American occupational zone, 427, 428
annihilation of Jews
  in General Government, 375, 376
  in Lithuania, 377, 379, 381
  in Poland, 370–71, 375, 376
annihilation of Roma/Sinti, 377
Anschluss. *See* Austria
antisemitic policies
  and civil servants, 45–46, 58–59, 94
  against Jewish insurees, 195–201, 202
  against Jewish physicians/dentists, 161
  See also under annihilation; deportation; forced labour deployment; ghettoization; racist policies
Antwerp, 318
AOG (Law on the Organization of National Labour)
  consequences of, 127–28
  and DAF, 117–18
  objectives of, 54, 215
  passing of, 55, 211
  reform of, 224
  reinterpretations of, 220–21, 222–23, 225

Arbeitsbuch (labour books), 57, 219, 223, 242–43, 417
Arbeitseinsatz. *See* labour deployment
armaments industry, 251, 252–53
Arndt, Adolf, 425, 459
Aryan/non-Aryan descent, 48, 58, 94, 96, 125, 160, 161
Association of German Pension Insurance Institutes (Verband Deutscher Rentenversicherungsträger), 193
Auerbach, Walter, 431–32, 433, 443, 449
Auschwitz, 312, 318, 375, 381
Austria
  administration of, 63
  annexation of, 62–63
  deportation of Jews in, 370
  German cooperation with, 39
  social policies (NG) in, 283–84
Austrian Jews, 370

Bach, Otto, 288
Backe, Herbert, 310
Baden Land Insurance Company, 181, 190, 195–96
barrage command, 254–56
Basic Law (Grundgesetz), 439, 443
Bauer, Gustav, 27, 30
Bauer, Michael-Josef, 434
Bauernschaften (farmers' associations), 218–19
Das Beamtenjahrbuch (Offical's Yearbook), 82
Beckurts, Karl, 336
Belgian Jews
  deportation of, 318
  forced labour deployment of, 317–18, 321–22
Belgian prisoners of war, 314
Belgian workers
  and breaches of employment contracts, 316
  and compulsory labour order, 316
  female, 319, 321
  forced labour deployment of, 305, 317, 319–20, 321
  going into hiding, 319–20
  recruitment methods for, 315–16
Belgium
  industrial production of, 314
  Jews from. *See* Belgian Jews
  labour administration in, 314–22
  labour deployment in, 302, 305–7, 315–22
  labour offices in, 314–15, 316
  occupation administration in, 64, 313–14
  prisoners of war from. *See* Belgian prisoners of war
  voluntary labour recruitment in, 315–16
  workers from. *See* Belgian workers
Belzec, 375
Betriebsführer (works leaders), 124, 209, 211, 218, 414
Betriebsgemeinschaft (Works Community), 209, 211, 215
Beveridge, William, 286, 418

Beveridge Report, 286, 418
Bieberstein, Marek, 373
Biebow, Hans, 367, 369
bilateral treaties, 199–200, 269–70, 275–76
Binder, Captain, 345
Bizone (United Economic Area), 428, 430–33
Blank, Theodor, 436, 450, 459
blue-collar workers
  growth in, 434, **434**
  pension insurance for, 28, 165, 186, 187, 193
  promotional opportunities of, 91
  at RML (WR), 34
  welfare provisions for, 27
Bogs, Walter, 199, 200, 476
Börger, Wilhelm, 47, 398, 412, 441, 476–77
Bormann, Martin, 334
Brack, Gustav, 452
Brandt, Karl, 399
Brandt, Willy, 172
Braunbuch (Brown Book), 446
Brauns, Heinrich, 31–32, 42, 153, 477
Brecht, Julius, 443
British occupational zone, 427–28
Broszat, Martin, 49, 133
Brown Book (*Braunbuch*), 446
Browning, Christopher, 311–12
Brüning, Heinrich, 152, 155, 156
Budget Office (Haushaltsabteilung), 40
budgets
  of public aid administration (WR), 85
  of Reich Institution for Job Placement and Unemployment Insurance (WR), 41
  of RML (WR), 40–41
  See also funding
Bundesrepublik Deutschland. *See* West Germany
Bürckel, Josef, 62–63, 121, 283
Bürgerliches Gesetzbuch (Civil Code), 220
Busch, Hans, 446
Butler, Harold, 275

Campaign against Banditry, 351
Catholic Centre Party, 123, 152–53
Central Administration and Reich Public Aid (Section of RML [WR]; Zentrale Verwaltung und Reichsversorgung), 30
Central Administration for Labour and Social Welfare (Zentralverwaltung für Arbeit und Sozialfürsorge; ZVAS)
  establishment of, 451
  personnel of. *See* personnel of ZVAS
  personnel structure of, 452–53
Central Office for Labour (Zentralamt für Arbeit; ZfA)
  establishment of, 427–28
  integration into VfA, 428, 433
  organizational structure of, **428**
  personnel of. *See* personnel of ZfA
  personnel structure at, 432–33, **432**, **435**
  responsibilities of, 428
Chamberlain, Neville, 281–82

– 497 –

Index

Chanoch, Uri, 385
Chełmno (Kulmhof), 370–71
Chwalek, Roman, 456
citizenship, loss of, 197–200
Civil Code (*Bürgerliches Gesetzbuch*), 220
civil servants (NG)
   dismissals of, 44–45, 94, 161
   entry requirements for, 98–99
   at Ministerial Collecting Center, 431
   Nazi Party membership of, 45, 46–47, **46, 47,** 58, 96–97, 98, 105–6
   preparatory service of, 98
   recruitment of, 96–97
   and Reich Institution's personnel, 244–45
   training of, 96
civil servants (WG), 439
civil servants (WR), 85
   entry requirements for, 89–90
   mid-level. *See* mid-level civil servants
   and Nazi policies, 94
   pay grades, **87,** 88, **88**
   at RML, **37**
   senior. *See* senior civil servants
   threats against, 92
   workload of, 91–92
civil service (NG), 95
civil service (WG), 438–39
civil service (WR), 86–87, 91, 100
Classen, Kurt, 216, 434, 477–78
Claussen, Wilhelm, 446, 478
clock makers, 254–56
Code of Civil Procedure (*Zivilprozessordnung*), 220–21
codes. *See* laws/acts/codes/decrees
commissarial system, 60–61
Committee for Labour and Wages (Komitee für Arbeit und Löhne), 455
communications
   with labour administrations, 343
   with occupation administrations, **342,** 345, 351
   by telephone, 39–40, 247–48
   within RML (WR), 39–40
Communist Party of Germany (Kommunistische Partei Deutschlands; KPD), 94, 161, 452
compulsory labour orders (*Dienstverpflichtung*), 57, 243, 254, 316
Compulsory Labour Service (Service du Travail Obligatoire), 403
Council of Länder (Länderrat), 427
Cracow, 308, 310, 372, 373–74
Cracow Ghetto, 374, 376–77, 383
Czech Jews, 370

Daeschner, Leon, 220
DAF (German Labour Front; Deutsche Arbeitsfront)
   administrative practice at, 130
   and AOG, 117–18
   establishment of, 115
   expansion of, 121
   international propagation of social policies by, 277, 285
   leadership of, 131, 133
   legal advisory services of, 127–28
   media presence of, 116–17
   and military build-up, 118–19
   organizational structure of, 118–21, 135
   personnel of. *See* personnel of DAF
   power of, 53–54, 116–17, 119
   power of, loss of, 122
   responsibilities of, 115–16, 135. *See also under* housing
   and revoking of pensions, 191
   and RML, cooperation with, 132–34
   and RML, rivalries with, 114–15, 129–31, 136, 161–62, 168–72, 274–75, 277–78
   role in establishing Nazi rule, 400–401
   and Working Conditions Inspectorate, 128–29
   See also Labour Science Institute
Dammer, Günther, 378
Danner, Julius, 181, 182
DDR (Deutsche Demokratische Republik). *See* East Germany
Decree on the Curtailment of Changes of Job (*Verordnung zur Beschränkung des Arbeitsplatzwechsels*), 227
Decree on Wage-Setting (*Verordnung über die Lohngestaltung*), 224, 225–26
decrees. *See* laws/acts/codes/decrees
denazification, 439, 441–43, 452
Denmark, 282
deportation
   of Austrian Jews, 370
   of Belgian Jews, 318
   of Czech Jews, 370
   of German Jews, 195–96, 198, 312, 365, 370
   of Polish Jews, 365–66
   of Roma/Sinti, 365, 370
Dersch, Hermann, 217
detonators, 254
Deutsche Arbeitsfront. *See* DAF
Deutsche Demokratische Republik (DDR). *See* East Germany
der Deutsche Gruss (Hitler salute), 57
Die deutsche Sozialpolitik des 19. Jahrhunderts im Spiegel der Schulgeschichtsbücher (Heinel), 288
Development Law (*Aufbaugesetz*), 55–56, 184, 186–87
Dienstverpflichtung (compulsory labour order), 57, 243, 254, 316
Dierl, Florian, 302
diplomas, 100, 102
disable people. *See* public aid recipients
discrimination. *See* antisemitic policies; racist policies
dismissals
   of German Jews, 161

– 498 –

at Reich Institution for Job Placement and Unemployment Insurance (NG), 45, 241
at RML (NG), 44–45, 94, 161, 430–31
at ZVAS, 454
Dobbernack, Wilhelm, 438, 439
Donau, Willy, 272, 454
Dorpmüller, Julius, 402
Double Earner Campaign (*DoppelverdienerKampagne*), 45, 123
Durst, Karl, 155, 158, 247

East Germany
 administration of, 451
 labour administration of, 454–58, 460
 Nazi trials in, 417
 social policies of, 287–88
 See also under specific governmental bodies
Eckert, Josef, 438, 442, 447
economic crisis (1929), 40, 150, 280
Eden, Sören, 230–31
educational qualifications
 of mid-level civil servants (WR), 82–83
 of personnel at BMA, 436
 of personnel at RML (WR), 32, **33**, 100–101
 of personnel at ZVAS/DVAS, 453
Eichmann, Adolf, 370
Eisenach Labour Office, 254–55
Elkes, Elkhanan, 381
employees. *See* workers
employment contracts, breaches of, 208, 210, 228–30
 before 1933, 209–10
 in agriculture, 218–19
 of Belgian workers, 316
 consequences of, 213
 criminalization of, 210, 219–28
 and labour relations, 215
 and labour trustees, 215–16, 218, 219–23, 224–28
 in Nazi period, 210–11
 as negotiating tool, 211
 and RML (NG), 220–24, 225–28
 stigmatization of, 213
 as symbol of dissatisfaction, 212
Enabling Law (Ermächtigungsgesetz), 50
Engel, Hans
 appointment of, 45, 285–86
 biography of, 478–79
 and DAF, 275
 death of, 430
 on Jewish insurees, 196
 on labour books, 219
 at Labour Conference, 274
 on labour trustees, 221
 and pension insurance, 185–86
Erhard, Ludwig, 287
Escher, Walter, 336
ethnic Germans, 283, 372
Europe Office for Labour Deployment (Section of RML [NG]), 338–39

Eviction Protection Law (Kündigungsschutzgesetz), 151

Falkenhausen, Alexander von, 313, 320
family deployment, 351
farmers' associations (*Bauernschaften*), 218–19
Feder, Gottfried, 157–58, 161, 164, 170
Federal Indemnification Law (Bundesentschädigungsgesetz), 383–84
Federal Ministry for Labour and Social Affairs, 386
Federal Ministry of Housing (Bundesministerium für Wohnungsbau), 429
Federal Ministry of Justice (Bundesjustizministerium), 445
Federal Ministry of Labour (Bundesministerium für Arbeit; BMA), 458–59
 accommodation of, 429
 as extension of VfA, 429
 and former personnel of RML (NG), 434–35
 organizational structure of, 429, **429**
 personnel structure at, 425–26, **432**, **434**, 435–36, **435**
 responsibilities of, 425–26
Federal Ministry of the Interior (Bundesministerium des Innern), 429, 445
Federal Republic of Germany (FRG). *See* West Germany
Fiehler, Karl, 160
financing
 of housing, 126, 149, 150–51, 153–54, 155, 164–66, 169
 of Länder/municipalities, 150–51
 See also budgets
First World War, 302, 305–7
Fischer-Dieskau, Joachim, 171, 283, 479
Fitting, Karl, 440
Flächsner, Hans, 405
Foerster, Fritz, 457–58
food supplies, 340, 346, 366, 369, 374, 375
forced labour camps, 368–69, 373, 380
forced labour deployment. *See* labour deployment/forced labour deployment
Foundation Remembrance, Responsibility and Future (Stiftung Erinnerung, Verantwortung, Zukunft; EVZ), 384
Four-Year Plan, 59–61, 119, 125, 223, 224
Four-Year Plan Authority (Vierjahresplanbehörde), 223, 224, 242, **243**, 245, 248, 415. *See also* Working Group on Labour Deployment
Fraenkel, Ernst, 42, 210, 248–49
France
 bilateral treaty with NG, 200
 German forced labour deployment in, 306, 403
 See also French occupational zone; French prisoners of war; Northern France
Frank, Hans
 appointment of, 307

Index

and forced labour deployment, 309, 310, 311, 312, 371
and mass deportations, 308, 366
and Polish Jews, 373–74
power of, 382
sentence of, 407
and Szepessy, 377
Frauendorfer, Max, 308–9, 310, 311, 321, 372, 374–75
Freizeitpolitik (leisure policy), 277, 281
French occupational zone, 427
French prisoners of war, 257, 403
French workers, 302, 403
Frick, Wilhelm, 52, 407
Frontgemeinschaft, 115
Führer, Karl Christian, 173
funding. *See* financing
Funk, Walter, 401, 408

Galopin, Alexandre, 313
Gauwaltungen, 119, 192
GBA (General Plenipotentiary for Labour Deployment; Generalbevollmächtigter für den Arbeitseinsatz)
  commissioners of, 349–52, 353
  labour deployment units of, 351, 352
  labour policy in Ukraine of, 347–49
  and Letsch, 337, 338, 397
  organizational structure of, 333–34, 337, 352–53
  responsibilities of, 332–33, 334
  and RML (NG), 61–62, 335, 337–38, 353, 406–7
  Sauckel as. *See* Sauckel, Fritz
  task force of, 336–37, 353
GBA commissioners, 349–52, 353
GBA labour deployment units (Arbeitseinsatzstäbe des GBA), 351, 352. *See also* Reich recruitment commissions
GDR (German Democratic Republic). *See* East Germany
Gebrüder Junghans, 256
Geib, Hermann, 31–32, 42, 479–80
General Government for the Occupied Polish Territories (Generalgouvernement für die besetzten polnischen Gebiete), 307–8, 365
  annihilation of Jews in, 375, 376
  Jewish councils in, 371, 372–73, 374–75
  labour administration in, 308–13, 320–22, 363–64, 371–77, 382–83
  labour deployment in 1916–17, 305–7
  labour deployment in 1940–44, 309–13, 320–22
  labour deployment of Jews in, 306, 311–12, 321–22, 371–73, 374–76
  labour offices in, 308, 309
General Plenipotentiary for Labour Deployment. *See* GBA

Generalbevollmächtigter für den Arbeitseinsatz. *See* GBA
genocide, concept of, 403
geographical origin, of personnel at BMA, 436
German Administration for Labour and Social Welfare (Deutsche Verwaltung für Arbeit und Sozialfürsorge; DVAS)
  founding of, 451
  leaders of departments at, 452–53
  personnel of. *See* personnel of DVAS
German constitution, 439, 443
German Democratic Republic (GDR). *See* East Germany
German Economic Commission (Deutsche Wirtschaftskommission; DWK), 451, 453
German Empire
  labour deployment of, 302, 305–7
  social policies of, 270–71
German Health Insurance Law (Krankenversicherungsgesetz), 273
German Jews
  deportation of, 195–96, 198, 312, 365, 370
  dismissals of, 161
  loss of citizenship of, 197–200
  pension insurance of, 195–201, 202
German Labour Front. *See* DAF
Gestapo, 369, 370, 446
Gewerbeordnung (Industrial Code), 220
ghetto pensions, 384–86
ghettoization
  of Lithuanian Jews, 377
  of Polish Jews, 366, 371, 374
ghettos, 371, 377, 383. *See also* Cracow Ghetto; ghetto pensions; Kovno/Kaunas Ghetto; Łódz/Litzmannstadt Ghetto; Lublin Ghetto; Warsaw Ghetto
Gisbertz, Wilhelm, 159
Globocnik, Odilo, 312, 373, 376
Göcke, Wilhelm, 381
Goetz, Carl, 336
Goldschmidt, Heinrich, 48, 434–35
Göring, Hermann
  and Decree on Wage-Setting, 224
  and Four-Year Plan, 59–60, 242, 245, 310
  and GBA, 335
  and labour deployment, 334, 347
  sentence of, 407
  and Settlement Programme, 125
  and Working Group on Labour Deployment, 310
  mention of, 43, 248
Great Depression (1929), 40, 150, 280
Great War, 302, 305–7
Greiser, Arthur, 367, 368, 370, 382
Greve, Swantje, 353–54
Grieser, Andreas, 43, 44, 273, 480
Gringauz, Shmuel, 379
Grohé, Josef, 314
Grün und Bilfinger, 380–81

Gundelach, Gustav, 452
'Gypsies'. *See* Roma and Sinti

Haffner, Sebastian, 402
Hague Convention, 305, 306
Hamilton, Alice, 280
Hantelmann, Hans, 376, 383
Hartrodt, Georg, 35, **36**
Harvey, Elizabeth, 322
health insurance, 187–88, 270, 273
Heilmann, Georg, 159
Helm, Rolf, 453
Hendriks, Frits-Jan, 315
Herbert, Ulrich, 67, 298
Herm, Max, 452, 454
Herrmann, Volker, 244
Herschel, Wilhelm, 440, 480–81
Heydrich, Reinhard, 311, 365
Hierl, Konstantin, 278, 410
Hildebrandt, Hubert
   biography of, 481
   and GBA, 337, 339
   imprisonment of, 398
   at Nuremburg trials, 406, 408, 412–13, 416, 417
Himmler, Heinrich, 311, 365, 370, 375–76, 377, 381
Hindenburg, Paul von, 43, 50, 115, 306
Hirschfeld, Dorothea, 430, 442, 481–82
Hirschfeld, Franz, 454
Hirtsiefer, Heinrich, 152
Hitler, Adolf
   access to, 51–52, 120
   and annihilation of Jews, 381
   appointment of Seldte, 43
   and Belgium, 313, 314
   and deportations, 370
   and drafting of laws, 50–51
   and forced labour deployment, 368, 371
   and housing policies, 147–48, 160
   and *Lebensraum*, 364
   and Ley, 113, 170
   pledge of personal fealty to, 49
   and Sauckel, 317, 332, 334, 338, 349
   on workers' revolution, 215
Hitler salute (*der Deutsche Gruss*), 57
Hitler Youth (Hitlerjugend), 97
Hockerts, Hans Günter, 438
Holocaust. *See* antisemitic policies; ghettos; Jewish councils; Jews
Holstein, Ernst, 453
Höppner, Rolf-Heinz, 369
Hörmann, Gustav, 378, 379, 381, 383
Horsky, Charles, 401
housing
   boom in, 162–63
   and DAF, 124–26, 147, 160, 162, 168–71
   financing of, 126, 149, 150–51, 153–54, 155, 164–66, 169
   and Länder/municipalities, 28, 149–50, 152, 153, 155
   and Ministry of Housing (WG), 172
   in NG, 147–48, 157, 158–62, 163–69
   private initiatives in, 148, 165–66, 167, 172
   and racist policies, 125, 160
   restrictions on, 153
   and RLO (WR), 28
   and RME (NG), 157
   and RML (NG), 147–48, 157, 158–60, 163–69
   and RML (WR), 149–56
   selection for, 125, 160–61
   shortage in, 163
   state controlled, 151–53, 155, 156, 166–68, 171
   for unemployed, 154–55, 160
   in Weimar Republic, 28, 149–56
   in West Germany, 172–73
   See also housing subsidies
Housing and Settlement (Section of RML [NG]; Wohnungs- und Siedlungswesen), 147–48, 162
   re-establishment of, 157
Housing and Settlement (Section of RML [WR]; Wohnungs- und Siedlungswesen), 29, 30
   organisational structure of, 35, **36**
housing subsidies, 126, 148, 150, 151, 158, 166, 171
Hugenberg, Alfred, 44
Hungary, 200, 299
Hupfauer, Theodor, 133, 134, 482–83

IG Farbenindustrie, 415
Imperial Council (Reichsrat), 51
Industrial Code (*Gewerbeordnung*), 220
insurees, Jewish, 195–201, 202
International Association for Labour Legislation, 271
International Conference on Labour Protection (Internationale Arbeiterschutzkonferenz; 1890), 270–71
International Labour Office, 272
International Labour Organization (ILO), 272, 274–75, 276, 281, 285
International Labour Review (of ILO), 285
International Military Tribunal (IMT), 398, 399–400
   forced labour charges before, 402–3
   identification of candidates for, 401–2
   Sauckel during, 405–6
   sentences at, 407
Israel, 384, 385
Italy
   bilateral treaty with NG, 200, 276
   social policies in, 274, 277, 280

Jackson, Robert H., 400
Jantz, Kurt, 438, 446
Japan, 281

Jewish councils
  in General Government, 371, 372–73, 374–75
  in Lithuania, 378–79, 380, 381
  at Łódź/Litzmannstadt ghetto, 366–67, 370–71
Jewish Labour Offices, 373, 374, 378
Jews. *See* Belgian Jews; Czech Jews; German Jews; insurees, Jewish; Latvian Jews; Lithuanian Jews; Polish Jews
Job Placement and Administration (Section of RLM (WR); Arbeitsvermittlung und -verwaltung), 30
Jodl, Alfred, 407
Jordan, Fritz, 378
Jordan certificates, 379
'Joy and Labour' International Central Office (Internationales Zentralbüro 'Freude und Arbeit'), 277
Judenfreundlichkeit (pro-Jewish attitude), 376–77

Käfferbitz, Jakob, 443, 447
Kalckbrenner, Otto, 223
Kaltenbrunner, Ernst, 407
Karstedt, Oskar, 48, 68, 286, 430, 483
Kaschny, Adolf, 432
Kaunus. *See* Kovno/Kaunus; Kovno/Kaunus Ghetto
Keitel, Wilhelm, 334, 407
Kendzia, Ernst, 367, 368, 370, 417
Keppler, Wilhelm, 283
Kiehl, Walter, 113
Kiel, 254–56
Kimmich, Wilhelm, 398, 412, 414–15, 416, 483–84
Kleinsiedlungen, 154–55, 157, 159–60
Klimo, Alexander, 202
Knoll, Ernst, 159, 161, 163, 457–58
Koch, Erich, 340, 351
Kogon, Eugen, 443
Körner, Paul, 415, 416
Kott, Sandrine, 288–89
Kovno/Kaunus, 380–81
Kovno/Kaunus Ghetto, 377, 383
  annihilation of Jews in, 377, 381
  conditions in, 379
  forced labour deployment of Jews in, 379–80
Kraft durch Freude (Strength through Joy), 277
Krauch, Carl, 415
Krohn, Johannes
  and AOG, 118
  on bilateral treaties, 276
  biography of, 114, 484
  career after the war, 439
  career at RML, 44
  and civil service reform, 438–39
  and DAF, 119, 275
  and DAF leadership, 133
  and denazification, 442
  on experiences in captivity, 431
  and ILO, 274
  on labour trustees, 214
  Nazi party membership of, 47
  and occupied territories, 308, 372, 382
  on pension insurance, 56
  and personnel appointments, 47
  and Schmeer, 113
  and social insurance, 182, 439
  mention of, 158
Krüger, Friedrich Wilhelm, 375, 376–77
Krupp von Bohlen und Halbach, Gustav, 401, 402
Kulmhof (Chełmno), 370–71

labour
  concept of, 183–84, 209
  See also employment contracts, breaches of; Law on the Organization of National Labour
labour administrations, 258–59, 298–99
  agencies involved in, 334
  in Belgium, 314–22
  communications with, 343
  in East Germany, 454–58, 460
  and Four-Year Plan Authority, **243**, 245, 248
  in General Government, 308–13, 320–22, 363–64, 371–77, 382–83
  during Great War, 302
  in Lithuania, 363, 377–83
  and occupation policies, 301
  and occupation regimes, 302–3
  organizational structure of, 240–41, **243**, 299
  in Poland. *See* General Government for the Occupied Polish Territories; Wartheland
  in Soviet occupational zone, 451–54
  in Ukraine, 340–41, 343–49
  in Wartheland, 363–71, 382
  in West Germany, 458–59
  See also Four-Year Plan Authority; labour deployment/forced labour deployment; labour offices; Reich Institution for Job Placement and Unemployment Insurance; Reich Labour Ministry
labour books (*Arbeitsbuch*), 57, 219, 223, 242–43, 417
labour cards/passes, 309, 341, 379
Labour Deployment (Section of RML [NG]), 332, 335, 338
labour deployment/forced labour deployment, 56, 61, 284, 300–301, 304
  of Belgian Jews, 317–18, 321–22
  of Belgian workers, 305, 317, 319–20, 321
  in Belgium, 302, 305–7, 315–22
  and compensation payments, 384
  during First World War, 302, 305–7
  in France, 306
  of French workers, 302, 403
  in General Government, 305–7, 309–13, 320–22. *See also* manpower management
  during Great War, 302, 305–7
  justiciability of, 400–401
  of Lithuanian Jews, 378–81
  in Nazi Germany, 305

at Nuremburg trails (IMT), 402–7
at Nuremburg trials (NMT), 407–17
and pension insurance, 182–95
of Polish Jews, 306, 311–12, 321–22, 366–68, 371–73, 374–76
of Polish workers, 310, 311–13, 317, 321, 367, 371
recruitment methods of, 304, 305–6
RML's role in, 251–56
and social insurance system, 276
of Soviet workers, 334, 403
of Ukrainian workers, 341, 346–48
and War Law, 190–95
of women, 304, 319–20, 321
Labour Front. *See* DAF
Labour Law and Wages Policy (Section of RML [NG]; Arbeitsrecht und Lohnpolitik), 216, 222, 242, 332, 335. *See also* Reich Labour Trustees
Labour Law and Wages Policy (Section of RML [WR]; Arbeitsrecht und Lohnpolitik), 30, 45
labour laws. *See* employment contracts, breaches of; *under specific laws*
labour ministers
Bauer, Gustav, 27, 30
Brauns, Heinrich, 31–32, 42, 477
Schäffer, Hugo, 43
Schlicke, Alexander, 30–31
Seldte, Franz. *See* Seldte, Franz
Stegerwald, Adam, 42, 152, 153
Syrup, Friedrich. *See* Syrup, Friedrich
Wissell, Rudolf, 42, 439, 442
labour offices (*Arbeitsämter*)
in Belgium, 314–15, 316
in General Government, 308, 309
importance of, 241
and Jewish forced labour, 369
in Poland, 363–64, 372, 375
responsibilities of, 239, 251, 252, 253
in Ukraine, 340–41, 344–45
labour policies
in American occupational zone, 427
in British occupational zone, 427–28
in French occupational zone, 427
of Nazi regime, 54–55, 56–57, 347–49
in Soviet occupational zone, 426
Labour Science Institute (Arbeitswissenschaftliches Institut; AWI), 54, 126, 169, 277, 286
labour shortages, 184, 242, 254–56, 303, 334
labour trustees. *See* Reich Labour Trustees
labour unions. *See* trade unions
Lammers, Hans Heinrich, 51, 101, 102, 333–34
Land Insurance Company of the Sudetenland, 189
Land Labour Offices, 240, 247, 251–52, 254–56, 344–45
Länder/municipalities
administration of, 37–38

financing methods of, 150–51
and housing, 28, 149–50, 152, 153, 155
political importance of, 51
power of, 150
landlords, 155
Latvian Jews, 304
Law for the Restoration of the Professional Civil Service (Gesetz zur Wiederherstellung des Berufsbeamtentums or Berufsbeamtengesetz), 44–45, 58, 88, 94
Law on the Organization of National Labour. *See* AOG
Law on the Provision of Public Aid to Fighters for the National Uprising (Gesetz über die Versorgung der Kämpfer für die nationale Erhebung), 97, 98
Law Regarding the Conditions for Making Pensions Payable on the Basis of Employment in a Ghetto (Gesetz zur Zahlbarmachung von Renten aus Beschäftigungen in einem Ghetto; ZRBG), 384–86
Law to Secure the Unity of Party and State (Gesetz zur Sicherung der Einheit von Staat und Partei), 50, 52
laws/acts/codes/decrees
Basic Law, 439, 443
Civil Code, 220
Code of Civil Procedure, 220–21
concurrence of, 227
Decree on the Curtailment of Changes of Job, 227
Decree on Wage-Setting, 224, 225–26
Development Law, 55–56, 184, 186–87
Enabling Law, 50
Eviction Protection Law, 151
Federal Indemnification Law, 383–84
German Health Insurance Law, 273
Industrial Code, 220
Law for the Restoration of the Professional Civil Service, 44–45, 58, 88, 94
Law on the Organization of National Labour. *See* AOG
Law on the Provision of Public Aid to Fighters for the National Uprising, 97, 98
Law Regarding the Conditions for Making Pensions Payable on the Basis of Employment in a Ghetto, 384–86
Law to Secure the Unity of Party and State, 50, 52
Maternity Protection Law, 124
Ordinance to Combat Breaches of Employment Contract, Labour Piracy and Demands for Disproportionate Remuneration in the Private Sector, 228
Penal Code, 221
procedure for drafting (NG), 50–51
Rehabilitation Law, 55–56, 184–85
Reich Citizen Law, 197–99
Reich Rent Law, 151, 155–56, 168

Reich Social Insurance Code, 196, 198, 199
Reich War Victims Compensation Law, 90, 97
Salary Law, 88
6th Emergency Decree, 41–42
Trustee Act, 54, 213–14
War Law, 190–95
Wehrmacht Public Aid Law, 90
Works Councils Act, 28
LDP (Liberal-Demokratische Partei), 454
League of Nations, 272, 275
Leemans, Victor, 314
legal advisory services (Rechtsberatung), 127–28
Lehfeld, Bernhard, 48
Lehmann, Helmut, 273, 453, 454
Leistungsgemeinschaft, 115, 116, 118
leisure policy (*Freizeitpolitik*), 277, 281
Lemkin, Raphaël, 403
Leo XII, Pope, 271
Leopold III, King of Belgium, 313
Lermer, Anna, 374
Letsch, Walter
  biography of, 484–85
  and communicative structures, 343
  on foreign workers, 298
  and GBA, 337, 338, 397
  imprisonment of, 398
  at NMT, 412, 413–14, 416, 417
  publications of, 397–98
  on Seldte, 410
Ley, Robert
  access to Hitler of, 119
  and AOG, 54–55, 117–18, 211
  biography of, 485
  as candidate for IMT, 401
  confidants of, 113–14
  on housing, 147–48, 168, 171
  as housing commissioner, 60–61, 122, 125–26, 170
  and Hupfauer, 134
  at Labour Conference, 274
  leisure policy of, 277
  power of, 53–54, 60–61, 68, 121
  replacement of, 120–21
  speeches of, 116
  suicide of, 402
  Waldbröl clique of, 133
Liberal Democratic Party (Liberal-Demokratische Partei; LDP), 454
Lithuania
  Jewish councils in, 378–79, 380, 381
  Jews in. *See* Kovno/Kaunus Ghetto; Lithuanian Jews
  labour administration in, 363, 377–83
Lithuanian Jews
  annihilation of, 377, 379, 381
  forced labour deployment of, 378–81
  ghettoization of, 377
  See also Kovno/Kaunus Ghetto
Litzmannstadt. *See* Łódź/Litzmannstadt Ghetto

living space (*Lebensraum*), 364
Łódź/Litzmannstadt Ghetto, 363, 366
  annihilation of Jews from, 370–71
  conditions in, 369
  Jewish council at, 366–67, 370–71
  Jews employed in, 366–68
Lohse, Hinrich, 379
London Agreement on German External Debts, 383
Lublin Ghetto, 375, 376
Lücke, Paul, 172
Ludendorff, Erich Friedrich Wilhelm, 306
Ludowici, Wilhelm, 161

M., lawyer, 447–48
Main Administration for Healthcare (Hauptverwaltung für das Gesundheitswesen), 430
Main Administration for Labour and Social Welfare (Hauptverwaltung für Arbeit und Sozialfürsorge; HVAS), 451
Main Office for Labour Administration (Hauptamt für Arbeitsverwaltung), 427–28
Main Section II (RML). *See* Social Insurance in All Fields
Main Section III (RML). *See* Labour Law and Wages Policy; Reich Labour Trustees
Main Section IV (RML). *See* Housing and Settlement
Main Section V (RML). *See* Labour Deployment; Reich Institution for Job Placement and Unemployment Insurance
Main Section VI (RML). *See* Europe Office for Labour Deployment
Majdanek, 312
Malter/Apelt, Frieda (Friedel), 456–57, 485–86
manpower management. *See* labour deployment
Mansfeld, Werner
  and AOG, 54–55, 118
  biography of, 486
  and breaches of employment contracts, 223, 226, 227
  career at RML, 45, 216
  on DAF, 128
  and DAF leadership, 133
  investigations of, 458
  at Labour Conference, 274
  on Stothfang, 450
  mention of, 242
Marrenbach, Otto, 114, 127, 128, 133
Martineck, Otto, 441
Marx, Henry, 259
Matern, Jenny, 452–53, 454
Maternity Protection Law (Mutterschutzgesetz), 124
Medical Review Committee (Vertrauensärztlicher Dienst), 187–88
Mehlhorn, Herbert, 370
Meincke, Ernst, 350, 351

mid-level civil servants (NG)
  chance of role of, 95
  and military build-up, 103–4, 105
  and Nazi Party membership, 105–6
  promotional opportunities of, 101–2
  training of, 105
  workload of, 103
mid-level civil servants (WR), 85–86
  educational background of, 82–83, 100–101
  entry requirements for, 89
  examinations of, 90, 93–94
  interaction with claimants, 92–93
  oaths of loyalty, 86
  pay grades of, 93
  permanent posts for, 91
  preparatory service of, 89–90
  with public aid certificates, 90–91
  at RML, 34
  vs. senior civil servants, 86–87, 100
  training of, 91, 92, 104–5
Milch, Erhard, 399, 408, 415, 416
Military Economy Department (Wehrwirtschaftsstab), 251, 253
Ministerial Collecting Center (Hessisch Lichtenau), 431
ministers
  access to Hitler of, 51–52
  of labour. *See* labour ministers
  oaths of office of, 49
  responsibilities of, 49
  See also under specific ministers
ministries
  and commissarial system, 60–61
  loss of power of, 61–64
  under Nazi state system, 50–54
  See also under specific ministries
Ministry of Construction (Ministerium für Aufbau), 455
Ministry of Housing (WG; Ministerium für Wohnungsbau), 171
Ministry of Labour and Healthcare (EG), 454–55
Ministry of Labour and Vocational Training (Ministerium für Arbeit und Berufsausbildung), 426, 455, **456**
Ministry of Labour and Wages (Ministerium für Arbeit und Löhne), 455
Ministry of Labour (East Berlin), 455
Ministry of National Education (Ministerium für Volksbildung), 455
mobilization, 239, 245–46
Monigan, John J., 405
Moser, Walter, 367
motorways, 368
Münz, Ludwig, 156–57
Münzel, Martin, 460

Nahles, Andrea, 386
National Assembly (Weimar Republic), 24, 27, 29

National League of Sweden (Sveriges Nationella Förbund), 281
Naumann, Werner, 128
Nazi Germany
  bilateral treaties of, 199–200, 269–70, 275–76
  and ILO, 274–75, 276
  labour deployment by. *See* labour deployment
  legal certainty in, 248–49
  military build-up of, 59–61, 103, 119–20, 242
  occupation administrations of. *See* occupation administrations
  occupied territories of. *See* Nazi occupied territories
  policies of. *See* Nazi policies
  public building projects in, 167
  seizure of power by, 43, 95–96, 156–57
  state system of, 50–54, 60
  See also Nazi Party; Volksgemeinschaft; *under specific governmental bodies*
Nazi occupied territories
  administration of. *See* occupation administrations
  resistance in, 312–13, 319–20
  social policies implemented in, 282–83
  See also under specific territories
Nazi Party
  agencies of, 52–53
  membership of. *See* Nazi Party membership
  Party Chancellery of, 46, 52
Nazi Party membership
  of BMA personnel, 443–44, **445**, 446–47, 448, 459
  of Bundesministerium personnel, 445
  of civil servants in East Germany, 452
  and DAF personnel, 119
  and public aid, 97
  and RML (NG) personnel, 45, 46–47, **46**, **47**, 58, 96–97, 98, 105–6
  of VfA personnel, 443, **445**
  of ZfA personnel, 443, **445**
Nazi policies
  antisemitic. *See* antisemitic policies
  on housing, 147–48, 157, 158–62, 163–69
  on labour deployment. *See* labour deployment
  on occupation, 301, 307, 313, 314, 320, 340–41, 353
  on pension insurance. *See* pension insurance
  and personnel at RML, 58–59, 67–69
  prevention of deviations from, 58
  racist. *See* racist policies
  social. *See* social policies
  for starvation, 340, 346, 369
Nazi state system, 50–54, 60
Neue Internationale Rundschau der Arbeit (New International Labour Review), 285
Neues Deutschland, 457
Neumann, Franz, 402
Nitsche, Dr., 372
Northern France, 306, 313–14, 318

November Revolution (1918), 27
Nuernberg Military Tribunals (NMT), 398–99, 407–8
  prosecution's plan at, 408–9
  RML personnel at, 409–17
Nuremberg Trials. *See* International Military Tribunal; Nuernberg Military Tribunals

oaths of loyalty, 86
oaths of office, 49
occupation administrations, 63–64, 302–3
  in Austria, 63
  in Belgium, 64, 313–14
  communicative structure of, 342, 351–52, **352**
  and GBA commissioners, 351
  in Northern France, 313–14
  of Ukraine, 340, 341–43, **342**
  See also Nazi occupied territories
occupation policies, 301, 307, 313, 314, 320, 340–41, 353
Offical's Yearbook (*Das Beamtenjahrbuch*), 82
Office National du Travail/Rijksarbeidsambt (ONT/ RAA), 315
Office of the Chief of Council for War Crimes (OCCWC), 408
old-age pensioners, reintegration into labour process, 190, 191–94. *See also* pension insurance
Ordinance to Combat Breaches of Employment Contract, Labour Piracy and Demands for Disproportionate Remuneration in the Private Sector (Anordnung gegen Arbeitsvertragsbruch und Abwerbung sowie das Fordern unverhältnismässig hoher Arbeitsentgelte in der privaten Wirtschaft), 228
Organization of Ukrainian Nationalists, 346
organizational structure
  of BMA, 429, **429**
  of Central Office for Labour, **428**
  of DAF, 118–21, 135
  of European Office for Labour Deployment, 338–39
  of GBA, 333–34, 337, 352–53
  of labour administrations, 240–41, **243**, 299
  of Ministry of Labour and Healthcare, 455
  of Ministry of Labour (East Berlin), 455
  of occupation administration in Ukraine, 341–43, **342**
  of public aid administration, 83–84
  of Reich Institution for Job Placement (NG), 244–45
  of Reich Institution for Job Placement (WR), 240–41
  of RML (WR), 29–30, 34–38, **35**, **36**

Paetzold, Fritz, 441
Papen, Franz von, 43
Patel, Kiran Klaus, 289
pay grades, of personnel at RML (WR), **87**, 88, 93

Peckert, Heinrich, 254, 255
Penal Code (*Strafgesetzbuch*), 221
pension insurance, 201–2
  assessment practices for, 182, 184–85, 187–88
  and Development Law, 56, 186–87
  disputes about, 181, 182, 185
  establishment of, 270
  of German Jews, 195–201, 202
  and ghetto pensions, 384–86
  and labour deployment, 182–95
  reform of (WG), 287
  and Rehabilitation Law, 56, 184–85
  reinterpretation of function of, 182, 190–91
  revoking of, 181, 184, 189, 190, 191–94
  and right to review, 189
  and RML (NG), 184–87, 190–95
  and War Law, 190–95
pension insurance institutes
  assessment practices of, 187–88
  and labour deployment, 189–90
  pension withdrawal by, 191–93
  supervision of, 186–87
people's homes (*Volkswohnungen*), 164–65
personnel
  at BMA. *See* personnel at BMA
  at DAF. *See* personnel at DAF
  at DVAS. *See* personnel of DVAS
  of labour administrations, 363–65, 369, 372, 382–83
  of labour trustees, 214
  of Ministry of Labour (EG), 455–57
  of Reich Institution for Job Placement and Unemployment Insurance (NG), 244–45
  at RML (NG). *See* personnel at RML (NG)
  at RML (WR). *See* personnel at RML (WR)
  of ZVAS. *See* personnel at ZVAS
  See also blue-collar workers; civil servants (NG); civil servants (WR); white-collar workers
personnel at BMA
  age structure of, **435**
  continuities/discontinuities of, 436–40
  educational qualifications of, 436
  geographical origin of, 436
  Nazi Party membership of, 443–44, **445**, 446–47, 448, 459
  religious affiliation of, 435–36, **435**
  SA membership of, 444, **445**, 448, 459
  SS membership of, **445**, 447–48
  women among, 440–41
personnel at DAF
  age structures of, 131, 135
  educational qualifications of, 119
  entry requirements for, 119
  and Nazi Party membership, 119
  women among, 123–24
personnel at DVAS
  age structure of, 453–54
  denazification of, 452
  educational qualifications of, 453

political affiliation of, 454
recruitment of, 453
personnel at RML (NG), 67
   age structure of, 131, 135
   appointment of, 45
   civil servants at. *See* civil servant (NG);
      mid-level civil servants (NG); senior civil
      servants (RML; NG)
   conduct of, 67–69
   denazification of, 441–42
   dismissals of, 44–45, 94, 161
   dismissals of, after capitulation, 430–31
   and GBA, 335–36
   and Hitler salute, 57
   Jewish members of, 45, 430
   at Ministerial Collecting Center, 431
   and Nazi Party membership, 45, 46–47, **46,
      47**, 58, 96–97, 98, 105–6
   and Nazi policies, 58–59, 67–69
   at Nuremberg trials, 409–17
   training of, 96, 105
   women among, 44–45
   See also labour ministers
personnel at RML (WR), 67
   age structure of, 32, **33**
   civil servants among, **86–87, 100**. *See also*
      civil servants (WR); mid-level civil
      servants (WR); senior civil servants
      (RML; WR)
   educational qualifications of, 32, **33**, 82–83,
      100–101
   pay grades of, **87**, 88, 93
   political affiliation, 34
   religious affiliation, 32, **33**
   training of, 39, 91, 92, 104–5
   women among, 32
   working at ILO, 272
   workload of, 40
   See also labour ministers
personnel at VfA
   Nazi Party membership of, 443, **445**
   religious affiliation of, **435**
   SA membership of, **445**
   SS membership of, **445**
personnel at ZfA
   age structure of, **435**
   Nazi Party membership of, 443, **445**
   recruitment of, 431–32
   religious affiliation of, **435**
   SA membership of, **445**
   SS membership of, **445**
Personnel Department (Personalabteilung), 46
personnel of ZVAS
   age structure of, 453–54
   denazification of, 452
   dismissals of, 454
   educational qualifications, 453
   leaders of departments at, 452–53
   political affiliation of, 454
   recruitment of, 453

personnel structure
   at BMA, 425–26, **432, 434**, 435–36, **435**
   at civil service (WR), 86–87, 91, 100
   at RLM (WR), 29, 31–35, **33, 37**
   at VfA, **432, 434, 434, 435**, 436
   at ZfA, 432–33, **432, 435**
   of ZVAS, 452–53
Peschel, Martin, 378
Peschke, Paul, 456–57
Petz, Rudolf, 432
Peuckert, Rudolf, 336, 350, 351–52, 486–87
Pieck, Wilhelm, 452
Pleiger, Paul, 416
Pohl, Wolfgang, 117, 133, 278, 487
Poland
   bilateral treaty with NG, 276
   invasion of, 364
   Jews in. *See* Cracow Ghetto; Łódź/
      Litzmannstadt Ghetto; Lublin Ghetto;
      Polish Jews
   labour administrations in, 363–64, 372, 375,
      376
   resettlements in, 312, 364, 365–66
   workers in. *See* Polish workers
Polish Jews
   annihilation of, 370–71, 375, 376
   deportation of, 365–66
   expulsion from Cracow, 374
   forced labour deployment of, 306, 311–12,
      321–22, 366–68, 371–73, 374–76
   ghettoization of, 366, 371, 374
   in labour camps, 368–69, 373
   payment of wages to, 374–75
   treatment of, 365, 369, 374–75
   See also Cracow Ghetto; Łódź/Litzmannstadt
      Ghetto; Lublin Ghetto
Polish prisoners of war, 257
Polish workers
   female, 310, 311, 321
   forced labour deployment of, 310, 311–13,
      317, 321, 367, 371
   in NG, 305
   recruitment methods of, 310, 312
Politburo (Secretariat of the Central Committee
   of the SED), 457
political affiliation
   of personnel at Ministry of Labour (EG), 456
   of personnel at RML (NG), 45
   of personnel at RML (WR), 34
   of personnel at ZVAS/DVAS, 454
   See also Nazi Party membership
pregnancies, 380
Preller, Ludwig, 427
Priemel, Kim Christian, 418
Primo de Rivera, Pilar, 280
prisoners of war
   as agricultural workers, 308, 309
   from Belgium, 314
   from France, 257, 403
   from Poland, 257

from Soviet Union, 257, 308, 309, 311, 334, 377, 378
pro-Jewish attitude (Judenfreundlichkeit), 376–77
Proksch, Alfred, 62–63
promotional opportunities
  of blue-collars workers, 91
  of mid-level civil servants (NR), 101–2
  of white-collar workers (WR), 91
propaganda, international
  of social policies (GE), 270–71
  of social policies (NG), 269–70, 273–78
  of social policies (WR), 272–73
Protectorate of Bohemia and Moravia (Reichsprotektorat Böhmen und Mähren), 64, 283, 370
Prussian Domestic Administration (Innenverwaltung), 26–27
Prüssian State Ministry (Staatsministerium), 51
Prützmann, Hans-Adolf, 351
Pryll, Walter, 273
public aid administration (NG), 98, 99
public aid administration (WR)
  administrative practice at, 84
  budget of, 85
  closure of offices of, 93
  laws underpinning work of, 93
  mid-level civil servants at. *See* mid-level civil servants (WR)
  organizational structure of, 83–84
  responsibilities of, 84, 92–93
  workload at, 91–92, 93
public aid certificates, 90–91
public aid recipients
  benefits enjoyed by, 29, 84, 92
  and housing, 125
  and Nazi ideology, 95, 98
  and public aid certificates, 90
  as responsibility of RLO (WR), 29
  restructuring of categories of, 98
public buildings, 167
public prosecutors, 226–27
Puhl, Emil, 408

Rabinovič, Isaac, 378
Rachner, Günther, 344, 382
racist policies
  and housing, 125, 160
  against Poles, 310
  See also antisemitic policies; Aryan/non-Aryan descent
Rappaport, Philipp, 433
recreation policies, 277, 281
recruitment for labour deployment, 304, 305–6
  in Belgium, 315–16
  in First World War, 305–6
  in General Government, 310, 312
  in Ukraine, 339–40, 344–49, 353
recruitment of personnel
  at BMA, 459

  at DVAS/ZVAS, 453
  at Ministry of Labour (EG), 457
  at RML (NG), 96–97
  at ZfA, 431–32
Reeder, Eggert, 314
reform
  of AOG, 224
  of civil service (WG), 438–39
  of pension insurance, 287
Rehabilitation Law (Sanierungsgesetz), 55–56, 184–85
Reich, Wilhelm, 280
Reich Association of German Insurance Companies (Reichsverband Deutscher Versicherungsanstalten), 276
Reich Association of Land Insurance Companies (Reichsverband Deutscher Landesversicherungsanstalten), 191
Reich Chancellery (Reichskanzlei)
  and appointment of personnel at RML, 47
  and drafting of laws, 50–51
  loss of power of, 60
Reich Citizen Law (Reichsbürgergesetz), 197–99
Reich Commissariat of Ukraine, 340, 342, 344, 345, 350, 351
Reich Economic Office (Reichswirtschaftsamt), 26–27, 28
Reich equalization, 254–56
Reich Food Corporation, 218–19, 251
Reich Fund for Labour Deployment (Reichsstock für den Arbeitseinsatz), 250
Reich guarantees, 165–66
Reich Institution for Job Placement and Unemployment Insurance (NG)
  dismissals at, 45, 241
  and forced labour of Jews, 366
  importance of, 241–42
  incorporation in Four-Year Plan Authority, 245
  incorporation in RML, 239–40, 244–45, 249
  and Nazi policies, 56
  organizational structure of, 244–45
  personnel of, 244–45
  power of, 242–43
  preparations for war by, 245–47, 249
  and Reich Postal Service, 247–48
  responsibilities of, 250–51
  See also employment contracts, breaches of
Reich Institution for Job Placement and Unemployment Insurance (WR)
  branches coordinated by, 35, **36**
  budget of, 41
  foundation of, 240
  organizational structure of, 240–41
Reich Insurance Company for White-Collar Workers (Reichsversicherungsanstalt für Angestellte)
  branches coordinated by, 35, **36**
  and Jewish insurees, 196, 197, 198–99, 200
  and War Law, 193–94

Index

Reich Insurance Company (Reichsversicherungsanstalt), 27, 41
Reich Insurance Office (Reichsversicherungsamt; RVA)
  and disability pensions, 181
  international propagation of social policies by, 271
  and labour deployment, 189–92
  responsibilities of, 186
  and right to review, 189
  and RML (NG), 186
  supervisory powers of, 186–87
  on War Law, 194
Reich Labour Office (WR), 26–29. *See also* Reich Ministry of Labour (WR; RLM)
Reich Labour Service (Reichsarbeitsdienst; RAD), 278, 284
Reich Labour Trustees (section of RML [NG]; Reichstreuhänder der Arbeit), 213–14
  and breaches of employment contracts, 208, 215–16, 218, 219–23, 224–28
  and labour relations, 214–15
  power of, 217–18, 224
  and public prosecutors, 226–27
  and RML (NG), 216–18
  scope of action of, 224
  supervision of, 216–17
  See also Labour Law and Wages Policy
Reich Ministry for the Occupied Eastern Territories (Reichsministerium für die besetzten Ostgebiete), 342, 343, 378, 382
Reich Ministry of Economy (NG), 59–60, 157
Reich Ministry of Food and Agriculture (NG), 219, 221, 251
Reich Ministry of Justice, 226–27
Reich Ministry of Labour (NG; RML)
  administrative practice at, 130
  and bilateral treaties, 269–70, 275–76
  and breaches of employment contracts, 220–24, 225–28
  and DAF, cooperation with, 132–34
  and DAF, rivalries with, 114–15, 129–31, 136, 161–62, 168–72, 274–75, 277–78
  and employment of women, 124
  Europe Office for Labour Deployment. *See* Europe Office for Labour Deployment
  fall of, 427
  and GBA, 61–62, 335, 337–38, 353, 406–7
  and housing, 147–48, 157, 158–60, 163–69
  and ILO, 274, 275, 285
  image of, 60, 399
  international propagation of social policies by, 273–76, 282–84, 285–86
  and Jewish insurees, 195–201, 202
  and labour administrations, 343
  Labour Deployment Section. *See* Labour Deployment
  and labour trustees, 216–18
  leadership of, 131. *See also* senior civil servants (NG)
  Letsch on, 397–98
  and military build-up, 59–61
  and Nazi policies, 54–58, 67–70
  and occupied territories, 62–64, 282–84, 363–64
  and pension insurance, 184–87, 190–95
  personnel at. *See* personnel at RML (NG)
  power of, 130
  power of, loss of, 61–64, 338
  and RAD, 278
  recruitment commissions of, 344–46, 347–48, 351
  and Reich Institution's incorporation, 239–40, 244–45, 249
  responsibilities of, 56–57, 64–65. *See also* forced labour deployment; housing; labour deployment; pension insurance
  subordinate realm of. *See under specific bodies*
  supervisory powers of, 186–87, 216–17
Reich Ministry of Labour (WR; RML), 66
  accommodation of, 30, 250, 427
  budget of, 40–41
  cooperation with other organizations, 38
  diplomatic links of, 38–39
  founding of, 272
  and ILO, 272
  internal communication at, 39–40
  international propagation of social policies by, 272–73
  organizational structure of, 29–30, 34–38, **36**
  personnel at. *See* personnel at RML (WR)
  personnel structure at, 29, 31–35, **33**, **37**
  policymaking powers of, 41–42
  power of, 149
  responsibilities of, 30, 41. *See also* housing
  standardization of, 39
  subordinate realm of, 35, **36**, 37–38, 67
  See also under specific bodies
Reich Ministry of the Interior (NG), 97
Reich Ministry of the Interior (WR), 26–27, 30
Reich Postal Authority (Reichspost), 246–48, 249
Reich Propaganda Ministry, 276
Reich Provisioning Court (Reichsversorgungsgericht), 35
Reich Public Aid (Reichsversorgung), 29–30, **36**, 84–85, 93
Reich recruitment commissions, 344–46, 347–48, 351. *See also* GBA labour deployment units
Reich Rent Law (Reichsmietengesetz), 126, 155–56, 168
Reich Social Insurance Code (Reichsversicherungsordnung), 196, 198, 199
Reich Statistical Office (Statistisches Reichsamt), 38
Reich War Victims Compensation Law (Reichsversorgungsgesetz), 90, 97
Reichel, Hans, 447
Reichsarbeitsblatt, 156, 158, 161, 183, 186, 269, 273, 285

– 509 –

Index

Das Reichsarbeitsministerium und der Generalbevollmächtigte für den Ausländereinsatz im Zweiten Weltkrieg (Letsch), 397–98
Reichsgau Wartheland, 363–71, 382. *See also* Łódź/Litzmannstadt Ghetto
religious affiliation
   of personnel at BMA, 435–36, **435**
   of personnel at RML (WR), 32, **33**
   of personnel at VfA/ZfA, **435**
rent control, 172
rents, 151–52
resettlements, 312, 364, 365–66
resistance, in Nazi occupied territories, 312–13, 319–20
Rettig, Hermann, 46–47
Rheumatism Research Institute (Rheumaforschungsinstitut), 38
Ringer, Franz, 440
road building, 368
Roma and Sinti, 365, 370, 377
Romsée, Gerard, 314
Roosevelt, Franklin D., 282
Roosevelt, Theodore, 271
Rosenberg, Alfred, 39–40, 342, 343, 378, 407
Ruhla, 254
Ruhrkohlenbezirk Settlement Association (Siedlungsverband Ruhrkohlenbezirk), 433
Rumkowski, Chaim, 366, 370–71
Rutschke, Wilfriede, 208, 209, 210, 228

SA (Sturmabteilung)
   membership of BMA personnel of, 444, **445**, 448, 459
   membership of VfA/ZfA personnel of, **445**
Saemisch, Friedrich, 184
Salary Law (Besoldungsgesetz), 88
Sauckel, Fritz
   appointment as GBA of, 60, 240, 257, 317, 332–33, 334–35
   appointment of Peuckert by, 350
   biography of, 488
   and communicative structures, 343, 351
   identification as candidate for IMT, 401
   during IMT, 405–6
   Kimmich on, 414
   and labour deployment, 303, 311, 317, 322, 332, 347–48
   Letsch on, 397
   power of, 61–62, 68, 121, 335, 337, 338
   sentence of, 407
   on Speer, 404
   Speer on, 403–4
   task force of, 336–37, 353
   mention of, 448
Sauerborn, Maximilian, 437, 442, 447, 488
Saur, Karl-Otto, 417
Schacht, Hjalmar, 160, 401
Schäffer, Hugo, 43
Scheel, Walter, 172
Schelp, Günther, 440
Schermer, Anna, 377
Scheuble, Julius, 431–32, 433, 439, 442, 446, 488–89
Schieber, Walther, 417
Schindler, Oscar, 374
Schlegelberger, Franz, 399
Schleicher, Kurt von, 155
Schlicke, Alexander, 30–31
Schlotterer, Gustav, 417
Schmeer, Rudolf, 113–14, 117, 133, 489–90
Schmelt, Albrecht, 368
Schmelt Organization, 368
Schmid, Carl, 374
Schmuhl, Hans-Walter, 244
Schneider, Jospeh, 447
schoolbooks, 288
Schorske, Carl, 402
Schraft, Hans, 446–47
Schreiber, Hans, 220, 222–23
Schroeder, Max, 97
Schulte Langforth, Marie, 440–41
Schultze, Joseph, 314, 316–17
Schulz, Ulrike, 70
Schutzstaffel (SS). *See* SS
Schwerin von Krosigk, Lutz Graf, 402
SED (Sozialistische Einheitspartei Deutschlands), 426, 454, 457
Selbstverwaltung (self-administration), 122, 184, 186–87, 241, 244
Seldte, Franz, 67
   access to Hitler of, 52
   appointment of, 43
   on bilateral treaties, 269
   biography of, 490
   death of, 411, 430
   exoneration of, 43–44
   and GBA, 335
   on housing, 148, 161, 163
   image of, 60, 66, 410–11
   imprisonment of, 398
   journey to Italy, 274
   on labour deployment, 300
   leadership style of, 47–48, 49
   Letsch on, 410
   and Nuremburg trials, 402, 409–10
   on pensions, 286
   position within Nazi state, 65–66
   power of, 121
   power of, loss of, 338
   pride of achievements of, 418
   publications of, 269, 279
   recruitment policy of, 99
   responsibilities of, 411
self-administration (*Selbstverwaltung*), 122, 184, 186–87, 241, 244
senior civil servants (RML; NG), 46–47, **46**, **47**, 131
senior civil servants (RML; WR), 32, **33**, 86–87, 100

Servatius, Robert, 402, 404, 406, 407
Service du Travail Obligatoire (Compulsory Labour Service), 403
Settlement Programme, 125
Seventeenth International Labour Conference, 274
Seyss-Inquart, Arthur, 407
Shea, Francis, 401
Siemer, Josef, 447
Simon, Heinrich, 114, 133
Sinti and Roma, 365, 370, 377
Sinzheimer, Hugo, 42
Sitzler, Friedrich, 278, 283, 288, 490–91
6th Emergency Decree (Notverordnung), 41–42
slave labour. *See* labour deployment/forced labour deployment
small suburban housing estates (*vorstädtische Kleinsiedlungen*), 154–55, 157, 159–60, 163–64
Social Democratic Party of Germany (Sozialdemokratische Partei Deutschlands; SPD), 25, 32, 161
Social Honours Court, 220–21, 223
social housing. *See* housing
Social Insurance in All Fields (Section of RML [NG]; Sozialversicherung in allen Bereichen), 182, 186, 187
Social Insurance in All Fields (Section of RML [WR]; Sozialversicherung in allen Bereichen), 30
social insurance system, 28, 122, 182–83, 186–87, 276, 437
social policies
  in East Germany, 287–88
  in German Empire, 270–71
  in Italy, 274, 277, 280
  in Nazi Germany. *See* social policies (NG)
  in Weimar Republic, 272–73
  in West Germany, 287–88
social policies (NG), 269
  imperialistic approach to, 285–86
  and international developments, 273–74
  international interest in, 279–82
  international propagation of, 269–70, 273–79, 282–87
  racism in, 283
  role of women in, 280
  during war, 282–87
Society for Insurance Science and Organization (Gesellschaft für Versicherungswissenschaft und -gestaltung e. V.), 439
Society for Social Reform (Gesellschaft für Soziale Reform), 271
Soviet Military Administration in Germany (Sowjetische Militäradministration in Deutschland; SMAD), 451
Soviet occupational zone, 426, 430, 451–54
Soviet prisoners of war, 257, 308, 309, 311, 334, 377, 378
Soviet Union
  NG's war against, 334, 340, 349, 379

  occupational zone of, 426, 430
  occupied territories of, 363–83. *See also* Lithuania; Ukraine
  prisoners of war from. *See* prisoners of war
  workers from. *See* Soviet workers
Soviet workers
  forced labour deployment of, 334, 403
  See also Ukrainian workers
Soziale Praxis (Social Practice), 283
Sozialpolitik im Dritten Reich (Seldte), 269, 279
Sozialpolitische Weltrundschau (Socio-political World Review), 285
Spain, 280–81
Special Projects Division, 417
Speer, Albert
  and Nuremburg trials, 401
  and protected firms, 319
  responsibilities of, 415
  on RML (NG), 60, 66
  on Sauckel, 403–4
  Sauckel on, 404
  on Seldte, 402
  sentence of, 407
  mention of, 416
Sprecher, Drexel, 400–401, 408
Spreti, Graf von, 345
SS (Schutzstaffel)
  and annihilation of Jews, 312, 376, 379, 381
  and Jewish forced labour deployment, 309, 311, 373, 375–76, 383
  membership of, 445
  membership of BMA personnel of, **445**, 447–48
  membership of VfA personnel of, **445**
  membership of ZfA personnel of, **445**
  taking charge of labourcamps/ghettos, 381
staff. *See* personnel
starvation policies, 340, 346, 369
State Planning Commission (Staatliche Plankommission), 455
State Security of the GDR (Staatssicherheitsdienst der DDR; Stasi), 446
Steckeweh, Hans, 432–33
Stegerwald, Adam, 42, 152, 153
Steidle, Luitpold, 456
Stets, Walter, 446
Stinnes-Legien Agreement (Stinnes-Legien-Abkommen), 27
Storch, Anton
  appointment of, 436–37
  biography of, 491
  as controversial figure, 437
  personnel policy of, 450
  on Sitzler, 288
  mention of, 433, 459
Stothfang, Walter
  appointment at ZfA of, 449
  biography of, 448–51
  denazification of, 449

imprisonment of, 398
during IMT, 406
at NMT, 412, 416, 417–18
responsibilities of, 449
mention of, 458
Streicher, Julius, 407
Strength through Joy (Kraft durch Freude), 277
Struve, Wilhelm, 309, 312
Stuckrad, Ernst von, 165
Sturmabteilung (SA). *See* SA
Stütz, Ernst, 379
supervision
of labour trustees, 216–17
of pension insurance institutes, 186–87
Supreme Command (Oberkommando der Wehrmacht; OKW), 194
Sweden, 281
Syrup, Friedrich
appointment of, 299–300
biography of, 491
on chaos in labour market, 249
death of, 430
on labour deployment, 300, 310
as labour minister, 43
Nazi party membership of, 47
renumeration of, 245
mention of, 242, 448
Szepessy, Adalbert, 376–77, 383

task force (of GBA), 336–37, 353
Taylor, Telford, 408, 416–17
telephone systems, 39–40, 247–48
tenant protection, 28, 151, 152, 155–56
Thalmann, Hans, 453
'The Reich Ministry of Labour, the General Plenipotentiary for Labour Deployment, and the Deployment of Foreigners during the Second World War' (*Das Reichsarbeitsministerium und der Generalbevollmächtigte für den Arbeitseinsatz beim Ausländereinsatz im Zweiten Weltkrieg*; Letsch), 397–98
Theile, Alfred, 447
Thiel, Jens, 319
Thiel, Reinhold, 254–55
Thomas, Albert, 31
Thuringian Gau apparatus, 336
Timm, Max
biography of, 492
and GBA, 337
imprisonment of, 398
on labour deployment, 300–301
on labour policy, 310
and Nuremburg trials, 406–7, 412, 414, 415, 416, 417
Todt, Fritz, 257, 415
Todt Organization, 318, 403
Torulf, Nora, 281
trades unions, 25, 27, 32, 153
and DAF, 115–16, 117, 129

demobilization campaigns of, 123
dissolution of, 54–55, 211, 217, 400
housing associations of, 125–26
training
of civil servants (NG), 96
of mid-level civil servants (NG), 105
of mid-level civil servants (WR), 91, 92, 104–5
of personnel of RML (WR), 39
Traulsen, Bernhard, 102
Treblinka, 375
Tritz, Maria, 440–41
Trustee Act (Treuhändergesetz), 54, 213–14. *See also* Reich Labour Trustees

Ukraine
Campaign against Banditry in, 351
food shortages in, 340, 346
GBA's labour policy in, 347–49
labour administration in, 340–41, 343–49
labour offices in, 340–41, 344–45
occupation administration of, 340, 341–43, **342**
occupation policies in, 340–41
positive attitude towards Germans in, 346
recruitment commissions in, 344–46, 347–48
recruitment of labour in, 339–40, 344–49, 353
workers in. *See* Ukrainian workers
Ukrainian workers
and age group campaigns, 348
forced labour deployment of, 341, 346–48
transportation of, 347
'voluntary' deployment of, 346
Ulbricht, Walter, 452
unemployment
cause by economic crisis of 1929, 40–41
elimination of, 241
and housing, 154–55, 160
unemployment insurance, 250
United Economic Area (Bizone), 428, 430–33
United Kingdom, 281–82, 286, 427–28
United States, 271, 282, 427, 428
Unity Party of Germany (Sozialistische Einheitspartei Deutschlands; SED), 426, 454, 457
universal insurance sytem, 437, 453

Verwilghen, Charles, 317
Vilijampole. *See* Kovno/Kaunus Ghetto
Volksgemeinschaft
and DAF, 115–16, 118, 126, 127–28, 131, 134, 135
and disable persons, 98–99
establishment of, 209
membership of, 183
obligation to, 184
propagation of, 53, 56, 96
See also Works Community
Völtzer, Friedrich, 215
Vormbrock, Heinrich, 433
Voss, Albert, 454

Wächter, Otto, 374
wages, 215–16, 218
Wagner, Robert, 283
Waldbröl clique, 133
Waldheim trials, 417
War Economy and Armament Office (Wehrwirtschafts- und Rüstungsamt), 251, 253
War Law, 190–95
war production, 251, 252–53
war veterans. *See* public aid recipients
Warsaw Ghetto, 375
  uprising in, 313, 381
Wartheland, 363–71, 382. *See also* Łódź/Litzmannstadt Ghetto
Weber, Alfred, 23, 24
Weber, Heinz, 372, 382
Weber, Max, 23–25, 69, 85
Wehrmacht
  and arms production, 251, 253
  demobilization of, 256
  in Lithuania, 377–78
  and mobilization, 239, 245–46, 258, 334
  Supreme Command of, 194, 251, 347
  in Ukraine, 340
  See also armaments industry
Wehrmacht Public Aid Law (Wehrmachtsversorgungsgesetz), 90
Wehrmacht Supreme Command (Oberkommando der Wehrmacht; OKW), 194, 251, 347
Weigert, Oscar, 45, 430, 492
Weimar National Assembly (Nationalversammlung), 24, 27, 29
Weimar Republic
  bilateral treaties of, 275–76
  economic crisis (1939) in, 40, 150
  housing in, 28, 149–56
  and ILO, 272
  National Assembly of, 24, 27, 29
  social policies of, 272–73
  See also under specific governmental bodies
Weiss, Peter, 385
Wende, Alexander, 219, 442
Wendland, Marie-Elisabeth, 441
West Germany
  compensation payments made by, 383–84
  housing in, 172–73
  labour administration in, 458–59
  Nazi investigations in, 417
  social policies of, 287–88
  See also under specific governmental bodies
white-collar workers
  growth in, 434
  pay grades, **87**
  pension insurance for, 28, 193
  promotional opportunities of, 91
  at RML, 30
  welfare provisions for, 27
  See also blue-collar workers

White-Collar Workers' Insurance (Angestelltenversicherung), 26–27
white-collar workers (WR). *See* white-collar workers
Wiesel, Karl Heinrich, 222
Wiessner, Rudolf, 457
Wildt, Michael, 386
Wilhelm II, German Emperor, 270–71
Wissell, Rudolf, 42, 439, 442
Wölz, Otto, 150
women
  at BMA, 440–41
  at DAF, 123–24
  deployment of, 310, 311, 321
  employment of, 124, 128, 257
  forced labour deployment of, 304, 319–20, 321
  labour camps for, 369
  at RML (NG), 44–45
  at RML (WR), 32
  in social policies (NG), 280
workers
  in agriculture. *See* agricultural workers
  from Alsace. *See* Alsatian workers
  from Belgium. *See* Belgian workers
  disempowerment of, 211, 214
  from Poland. *See* Polish workers
  shortage of. *See* labour shortages
  from Soviet Union. *See* Soviet workers
  strikes by, 215
  from Ukraine. *See* Ukrainian workers
  See also blue-collar workers; labour deployment; white-collar workers
Workers' Insurance (Arbeiterversicherung), 29
Workers' Issues (Arbeiterfragen), 29
Working Conditions Inspectorate (Gewerbeaufsicht), 128–29
Working Group on Labour Deployment (Geschäftsgruppe Arbeitseinsatz), 317, 334, 335. *See also* Four-Year Plan Authority
workload
  of civil servants (WR), 91–92
  of mid-level civil servants (NG), 103
  of personnel at RML (WR), 40
  at public aid administration (WR), 91–92, 93
Works Community (Betriebsgemeinschaft), 209, 211, 215
Works Councils Act (Betriebsrätegesetz), 28
works leaders (Betriebsführer), 124, 209, 211, 218, 414
World Congress on Leisure and Recreation (Weltkongress für Freizeit und Erholung), 277
World War I, 302, 305–7
Wouters, Nico, 319

Zamość resettlement, 312
Zschucke, Martin, 245

www.ingramcontent.com/pod-product-compliance
Lightning Source LLC
Chambersburg PA
CBHW072042110526
44590CB00018B/3008